lonely planet

Rajasthan

Sarina Singh
Michelle Coxall

LONELY PLANET PUBLICATIONS
Melbourne • Oakland • London • Paris

RAJASTHAN

ELEVATION

1000 m
500 m
200 m
100 m
0

0   60   120 km

Multan

Ganganagar

Indus River

Sutlej River

Anupgarh

BIKANER
Ancient fort; Karni Mata
Temple at nearby Deshnok
with its hordes of holy rats

PAKISTAN

BIKANER

OSIYAN
Exquisitely sculpted
ancient temples

DESERT

Gajner
Wildlife
Sanctuary

Bikaner

THAR

15

Kolayat

Deshnok

Sukkur

Indus

Indira Gandhi Canal

Nokha

Ramgarh

JAISALMER

Phalodi

Khichan

Nagaur

15

Ramdevra

Sam

Jaisalmer

Pokaran

Osiyan

Khuri

JODHPUR

JAISALMER
Enchanting fort and
havelis (mansions);
desert camel safaris

Jodhpur

Saraswati

Bilara

Dhawa
Doli
Wildlife
Sanctuary

Sardar
Samand

BARMER

Barmer

Balotra

Rohet

Pali

Hyderabad

15

Luni River

14

PALI

Jalor

ARAVALLI

JODHPUR
The 'Blue City' with
its mighty fort; safaris
to outlying villages

JALOR

SIROHI

Sirohi
Guru
Shikhar
(1721 m)

RAJSAMAND

Nathdwara

Nagda

Udaipur

8

Mt Abu

Abu Road

MEWAR

HILLS

RANN OF KUTCH

Palanpur

Dungarpur

Radhanpur

15

UDAIPUR
Romantic island palaces
on Lake Pichola and
the grand City Palace

Mahesana

Himatnagar

GUJARAT

8A

8A

Gandhidham

Gandhinagar

Ahmedabad

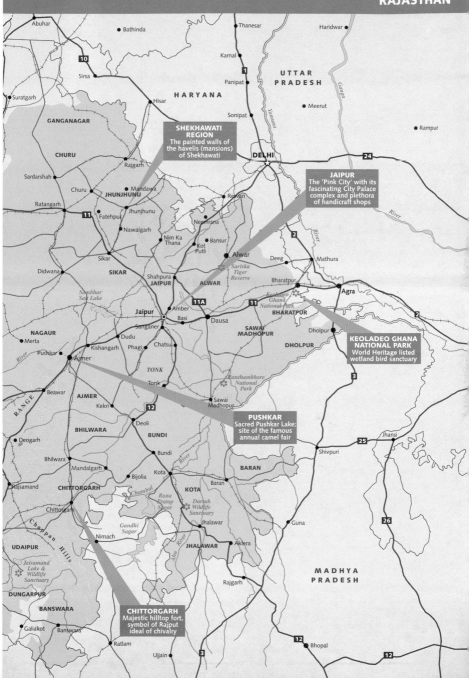

Rajasthan
2nd edition – October 1999
First published – January 1997

Published by
Lonely Planet Publications Pty Ltd A.C.N. 005 607 983
192 Burwood Rd, Hawthorn, Victoria 3122, Australia

Lonely Planet Offices
Australia PO Box 617, Hawthorn, Victoria 3122
USA 150 Linden St, Oakland, CA 94607
UK 10a Spring Place, London NW5 3BH
France 1 rue du Dahomey, 75011 Paris

Photographs
Many of the images in this guide are available for licensing from
Lonely Planet Images.
email: lpi@lonelyplanet.com.au

Front cover photograph
Village girl, Rajasthan (John Hay)

ISBN 0 86442 743 3

Printed by Craft Print Pte Ltd
Printed in Singapore

Although the authors and Lonely Planet try to make the information as accurate as possible, we accept no responsibility for any loss, injury or inconvenience sustained by anyone using this book.

Contents – Text

THE AUTHORS   5

THIS BOOK   7

FOREWORD   8

INTRODUCTION   11

FACTS ABOUT RAJASTHAN   13

History 13   Sanctuaries 29   Music 38
Geography & Geology 17   Government & Politics 32   Architecture 47
Climate 19   Economy 33   Society & Conduct 54
Ecology & Environment 20   Population & People 35   Religion 61
Flora & Fauna 22   Education 35
National Parks &   Arts 36

FACTS FOR THE VISITOR   66

Highlights 66   Newspapers & Magazines 84   Dangers & Annoyances 100
Suggested Itineraries 67   Video Systems 85   Legal Matters 102
Planning 68   Photography & Video 85   Business Hours 102
Responsible Tourism 70   Time 86   Public Holidays & Special
Tourist Offices 70   Electricity 86   Events 102
Visas & Documents 71   Weights & Measures 86   Activities 103
Embassies & Consulates 73   Laundry 86   Courses 107
Customs 75   Toilets 86   Volunteer Work 107
Money 75   Health 87   Accommodation 109
Post & Communications 79   Women Travellers 98   Drinks 111
Internet Resources 81   Gay & Lesbian Travellers 99   Entertainment 115
Books 81   Disabled Travellers 99   Spectator Sports 115
Films 84   Senior Travellers 100   Shopping 116
CD-ROMs 84   Travel with Children 100

GETTING THERE & AWAY   119

India 119   Organised Tours 127   Train 129
Air 119   Rajasthan 128   Car & Motorcycle 129
Land 125   Air 128
Sea 127   Bus 129

GETTING AROUND   131

Air 131   Car 135   Hitching 138
Bus 131   Motorcycle 137   Local Transport 138
Train 132   Bicycle 137   Organised Tours 140

JAIPUR   142

Festivals & Ceremonies (colour)   Jal Mahal 171   Ramgarh 172
Around Jaipur 169   Sanganer & Bagru 171   Abhaneri 173
Amber 169   Samode 172   Balaji 173
Jaigarh 171   Bairat 172   Karauli 173

EASTERN RAJASTHAN 174

History 174
Bharatpur & Keoladeo
Ghana National Park 177
Deeg 184
Alwar 185

Sariska Tiger Reserve &
National Park 189
Ajmer 190
Pushkar 197
Tonk 203

Sawai Madhopur & Ran-
thambhore National Park ..204
Dholpur 210

SOUTHERN RAJASTHAN 211

History 213
Bundi 215
Kota 220
Around Kota 223

Jhalawar 224
Chittorgarh (Chittor) 226
Udaipur 230
North of Udaipur 247

South of Udaipur 251
Mt Abu 253
Abu Road 262

NORTHERN RAJASTHAN (SHEKHAWATI) 263

History 263
The Havelis 265
Responsible Tourism 266
Nawalgarh 268
Parsurampura 272
Dundlod 273

Mukundgarh 274
Jhunjhunu 274
Baggar 278
Bissau 278
Mahansar 279
Ramgarh 280

Fatehpur 281
Mandawa 283
Lakshmangarh 285
Churu 287

WESTERN RAJASTHAN 288

History 288
Jodhpur 290
Nagaur 303

Jodhpur to Jaisalmer
(Northen Route) 304
Jaisalmer 308

Traditional Dress (colour)
Barmer 326
Bikaner 327

AGRA 338

Around Agra 346

Places to Stay 343

Getting There & Away 345

DELHI 348

Information 349
Old Delhi 352

New Delhi 354
Places to Stay 355

Getting There & Away 359

MUMBAI (BOMBAY) 366

Around Mumbai 379

Places to Stay 372

Getting There & Away 376

LANGUAGE 381

Hindi 381

GLOSSARY 383

ACKNOWLEDGMENTS 389

INDEX 396

Text 396

Boxed Text 399

MAP LEGEND back page

METRIC CONVERSION inside back cover

Contents – Maps

INTRODUCTION

Rajasthan 11

JAIPUR

Jaipur 146   Around Jaipur 170

EASTERN RAJASTHAN

Eastern Rajasthan 175   Ajmer 191   Sawai Madhopur &
Bharatpur 178   Pushkar 198   Ranthambhore 205
Alwar 186

SOUTHERN RAJASTHAN

Southern Rajasthan 212   Chittorgarh 227   Mt Abu 254
Bundi 216   Udaipur 232   Central Mt. Abu 256
Kota 221   Around Udaipur 247

NORTHERN RAJASTHAN (SHEKHAWATI)

NorthernRajasthan   Nawalgarh 269   Fatehpur 282
(Shekhawati) 264   Jhunjhunu 275   Mandawa 284

WESTERN RAJASTHAN

Western Rajasthan 289   Jaisalmer 310   Bikaner 328
Jodhpur 291   Jaisalmer Fort 312
Meherangarh 293   Camel Safari Routes 317

AGRA

Agra 339   Agra Fort 341   Taj Ganj 343

DELHI

Delhi 350   New Delhi 356   Paharganj 362
Old Delhi 353   Connaught Place 360

MUMBAI

Mumbai 368   Fort Area 371   Colaba 373

MAPS

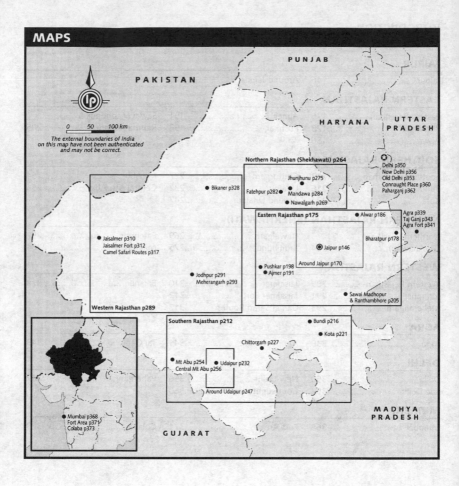

PAKISTAN

PUNJAB

HARYANA

UTTAR
PRADESH

0   50   100 km

*The external boundaries of India
on this map have not been authenticated
and may not be correct.*

Northern Rajasthan (Shekhawati) p264

Jhunjhunu p275

Fatehpur p282   Mandawa p284
Nawalgarh p269

● Bikaner p328

Delhi p350
New Delhi p356
Old Delhi p353
Connaught Place p360
Paharganj p362

Eastern Rajasthan p175

● Alwar p186

Agra p339
Taj Ganj p343
Agra Fort p341

Bharatpur p178

● Jaipur p146

● Jaisalmer p310
Jaisalmer Fort p312
Camel Safari Routes p317

Around Jaipur p170

● Pushkar p198
● Ajmer p191

● Jodhpur p291
Meherangarh p293

● Sawai Madhopur
& Ranthambhore p205

Western Rajasthan p289

Southern Rajasthan p212

● Bundi p216
● Kota p221

Chittorgarh p227

● Mt Abu p254   ● Udaipur p232
Central Mt Abu p256

Around Udaipur p247

● Mumbai p368
Fort Area p371
Colaba p373

MADHYA
PRADESH

GUJARAT

The Authors

Sarina Singh
A passionate traveller ever since she can remember, Sarina took the plunge and bought a one-way ticket to India after completing a business degree in Melbourne, Australia. After recovering from malaria, she did a corporate traineeship with Sheraton Hotels then worked as a freelance journalist and foreign correspondent. Writing mainly about India, assignments also took her to East Africa, Nepal, the Middle East and Pakistan where she interviewed a notorious Mujahideen warlord at his clandestine headquarters near the Afghanistan border. After 3½ years in India, Sarina returned to Australia, pursued post-graduate journalism qualifications and wrote two television documentary scripts. She later wrote a book about a prominent polo player. Other Lonely Planet books Sarina has worked on include *Africa*, *India*, *Mauritius, Réunion & Seychelles*, *Sacred India* and the *Out to Eat* restaurant guides to Melbourne and Sydney.

Michelle Coxall
Michelle trained as an editor with Lonely Planet before leaving to work with the Tibetan community in Dharamsala in northern India. She stayed on to update the Gujarat chapter of LP's *India* guide and later co-authored Lonely Planet's *Indian Himalaya* and *Rajasthan*.

FROM THE AUTHOR

Sarina Singh Destiny has taken me to Rajasthan time and time again, making this compelling state my second home over the years. Personal thanks to Amit Jhaveri and his family in Mumbai; Arvind Singh Mewar in Udaipur; and Sanjay Singh Badnor and his parents, Raghuraj and Lucky, in Ajmer – for all so warmly welcoming me into their homes. And to Jitendra Singh Rathore in Udaipur for his perpetual assistance. I'd also like to express my gratitude to the late Dr G.K Bhatt, ayurvedic doctor and philosopher extraordinaire – Udaipur will never be the same without you.

I'm deeply grateful to the countless people who have so generously offered their knowledge and help. In Jaipur, special thanks to Digvijay Singh Patan and his family for looking after me so well; to Pushpendra 'Bunty' Singh for making sure I got a look inside the Raj Mandir cinema; and to Sangeeta Singh for helping me locate the animal hospital. In Jodhpur, thanks to the inimitable Dalvir Singh for keeping me incognito; to Rattan Singh for helping me test out lassis and spices; and to Raju Singh for his offerings of cold beer and cool conversation after exhausting research trips. Special credit also to Laxmi Kant Jangid in Jhunjhunu for his comprehensive insights on Shekhawati; to Thakur Digvijay Singh of Dhamotar for sharing his jungle retreat; to M.K Harshvardhan Singh for showing me around downtown Dungarpur; to Mukesh Mehta for his enthusiastic help in Bundi; to Mr and Mrs Vishwa Vijay Singh in Udaipur for making New Year's Eve an unexpected blast; to the effervescent Himmat Singh in Pushkar; and to R.S Shekhawat at the Bikaner tourist office.

A personal vote of admiration to Priyadarshini Singh in Jodhpur – for having the intrepidity to be a spirited individual in a Rajput society which has certain hypocritical undertones towards women.

Thanks for valuable feedback from the following travellers I met on the way: Paul Robinson (USA), Amber Ellington (UK), John and Amanda Black (USA), Jean-Marc Duvergé (France), Ellen Banks (Australia), Adam McIntyre (Australia), Evelyn Mayers (Germany), Alice Maguire (New Zealand) and Christophe Dubois (Switzerland). Many thanks also to the hundreds of travellers who wrote into Lonely Planet – I read each and every letter.

In Melbourne, I'm thankful to my parents and Gaurav Singh Rathore for assisting me with proofreading; and to fellow connoisseur of fine wine, Robyn Anderson, for helping me escape to that whimsical cottage by the beach. At Lonely Planet a big thank you to Jocelyn Harewood for being a terrific editor and to the supportive Sharan Kaur, Brett Moore, Joyce Connolly and Geoff Stringer.

This book is for Amit, Swati and Parth Jhaveri – for always being there.

This Book

The first edition of this book was written by Michelle Coxall and Sarina Singh. The second edition was updated by Sarina Singh. Material from the Rajasthan, Agra, Mumbai and Delhi chapters of Lonely Planet's India guide were also used. These were first updated by David Collins, Mark Honan and Richard Plunkett.

From the Publisher

This book was produced at Lonely Planet's Melbourne office. Jocelyn Harewood (editor) and Brett Moore (designer) coordinated, advised by Sharan Kaur, Verity Campbell, Adriana Mammarella and Vince Patton. Assistance was given by editors Shelley Muir, Joyce Connolly and Michelle Coxall and cartographers Katie Butterworth, Anna Judd, Maree Styles, Rod Zandbergs and Sonya Brooke.

The language section was prepared by Quentin Frayne. Matt King advised on illustrations and Tim Uden on layout. New illustrations were drawn by Sarah Jolly.

The climate charts were drawn by Paul Piaia and Maria Vallianos designed the cover.

Foreword

ABOUT LONELY PLANET GUIDEBOOKS

The story begins with a classic travel adventure: Tony and Maureen Wheeler's 1972 journey across Europe and Asia to Australia. Useful information about the overland trail did not exist at that time, so Tony and Maureen published the first Lonely Planet guidebook to meet a growing need.

From a kitchen table, then from a tiny office in Melbourne (Australia), Lonely Planet has become the largest independent travel publisher in the world, an international company with offices in Melbourne, Oakland (USA), London (UK) and Paris (France).

Today Lonely Planet guidebooks cover the globe. There is an ever-growing list of books and there's information in a variety of forms and media. Some things haven't changed. The main aim is still to help make it possible for adventurous travellers to get out there – to explore and better understand the world.

At Lonely Planet we believe travellers can make a positive contribution to the countries they visit – if they respect their host communities and spend their money wisely. Since 1986 a percentage of the income from each book has been donated to aid projects and human rights campaigns.

Updates Lonely Planet thoroughly updates each guidebook as often as possible. This usually means there are around two years between editions, although for more unusual or more stable destinations the gap can be longer. Check the imprint page (following the colour map at the beginning of the book) for publication dates.

Between editions up-to-date information is available in two free newsletters – the paper *Planet Talk* and email *Comet* (to subscribe, contact any Lonely Planet office) – and on our Web site at www.lonelyplanet.com. The *Upgrades* section of the Web site covers a number of important and volatile destinations and is regularly updated by Lonely Planet authors. *Scoop* covers news and current affairs relevant to travellers. And, lastly, the *Thorn Tree* bulletin board and *Postcards* section of the site carry unverified, but fascinating, reports from travellers.

Correspondence The process of creating new editions begins with the letters, postcards and emails received from travellers. This correspondence often includes suggestions, criticisms and comments about the current editions. Interesting excerpts are immediately passed on via newsletters and the Web site, and everything goes to our authors to be verified when they're researching on the road. We're keen to get more feedback from organisations or individuals who represent communities visited by travellers.

> Lonely Planet gathers information for everyone who's curious about the planet – and especially for those who explore it first-hand. Through guidebooks, phrasebooks, activity guides, maps, literature, newsletters, image library, TV series and Web site we act as an information exchange for a worldwide community of travellers.

Research Authors aim to gather sufficient practical information to enable travellers to make informed choices and to make the mechanics of a journey run smoothly. They also research historical and cultural background to help enrich the travel experience and allow travellers to understand and respond appropriately to cultural and environmental issues.

Authors don't stay in every hotel because that would mean spending a couple of months in each medium-sized city and, no, they don't eat at every restaurant because that would mean stretching belts beyond capacity. They do visit hotels and restaurants to check standards and prices, but feedback based on readers' direct experiences can be very helpful.

Many of our authors work undercover, others aren't so secretive. None of them accept freebies in exchange for positive write-ups. And none of our guidebooks contain any advertising.

Production Authors submit their raw manuscripts and maps to offices in Australia, USA, UK or France. Editors and cartographers – all experienced travellers themselves – then begin the process of assembling the pieces. When the book finally hits the shops, some things are already out of date, we start getting feedback from readers and the process begins again ...

WARNING & REQUEST

Things change – prices go up, schedules change, good places go bad and bad places go bankrupt – nothing stays the same. So, if you find things better or worse, recently opened or long since closed, please tell us and help make the next edition even more accurate and useful. We genuinely value all the feedback we receive. Julie Young coordinates a well travelled team that reads and acknowledges every letter, postcard and email and ensures that every morsel of information finds its way to the appropriate authors, editors and cartographers for verification.

Everyone who writes to us will find their name in the next edition of the appropriate guidebook. They will also receive the latest issue of *Planet Talk*, our quarterly printed newsletter, or *Comet*, our monthly email newsletter. Subscriptions to both newsletters are free. The very best contributions will be rewarded with a free guidebook.

Excerpts from your correspondence may appear in new editions of Lonely Planet guidebooks, the Lonely Planet Web site, *Planet Talk* or *Comet*, so please let us know if you *don't* want your letter published or your name acknowledged.

Send all correspondence to the Lonely Planet office closest to you:

Australia: PO Box 617, Hawthorn, Victoria 3122
USA: 150 Linden St, Oakland, CA 94607
UK: 10A Spring Place, London NW5 3BH
France: 1 rue du Dahomey, 75011 Paris

Or email us at: talk2us@lonelyplanet.com.au

For news, views and updates see our Web site: www.lonelyplanet.com

HOW TO USE A LONELY PLANET GUIDEBOOK

The best way to use a Lonely Planet guidebook is any way you choose. At Lonely Planet we believe the most memorable travel experiences are often those that are unexpected, and the finest discoveries are those you make yourself. Guidebooks are not intended to be used as if they provide a detailed set of infallible instructions!

Contents All Lonely Planet guidebooks follow roughly the same format. The Facts about the Destination chapters or sections give background information ranging from history to weather. Facts for the Visitor gives practical information on issues like visas and health. Getting There & Away gives a brief starting point for researching travel to and from the destination. Getting Around gives an overview of the transport options when you arrive.

The peculiar demands of each destination determine how subsequent chapters are broken up, but some things remain constant. We always start with background, then proceed to sights, places to stay, places to eat, entertainment, getting there and away, and getting around information – in that order.

Heading Hierarchy Lonely Planet headings are used in a strict hierarchical structure that can be visualised as a set of Russian dolls. Each heading (and its following text) is encompassed by any preceding heading that is higher on the hierarchical ladder.

Entry Points We do not assume guidebooks will be read from beginning to end, but that people will dip into them. The traditional entry points are the list of contents and the index. In addition, however, some books have a complete list of maps and an index map illustrating map coverage.

There may also be a colour map that shows highlights. These highlights are dealt with in greater detail in the Facts for the Visitor chapter, along with planning questions and suggested itineraries. Each chapter covering a geographical region usually begins with a locator map and another list of highlights. Once you find something of interest in a list of highlights, turn to the index.

Maps Maps play a crucial role in Lonely Planet guidebooks and include a huge amount of information. A legend is printed on the back page. We seek to have complete consistency between maps and text, and to have every important place in the text captured on a map. Map key numbers usually start in the top left corner.

Although inclusion in a guidebook usually implies a recommendation we cannot list every good place. Exclusion does not necessarily imply criticism. In fact there are a number of reasons why we might exclude a place – sometimes it is simply inappropriate to encourage an influx of travellers.

Introduction

The colourful and exotic state of Rajasthan, the Land of the Kings, encapsulates the essence of India. This is the home of the Rajputs, a group of warrior clans who variously claim descent from the sun, the moon and the flames of a sacrificial fire, and who controlled this part of India for over 1000 years. The Rajputs' highly evolved code of chivalry and honour is akin to that of the medieval European knights. They were fiercely independent and renowned for their valour and pride, preferring, when defeat was imminent in battle, to die an honourable death rather than to treat with the enemy. For the Rajput women, this translated into occasions of grim mass self-destruction known

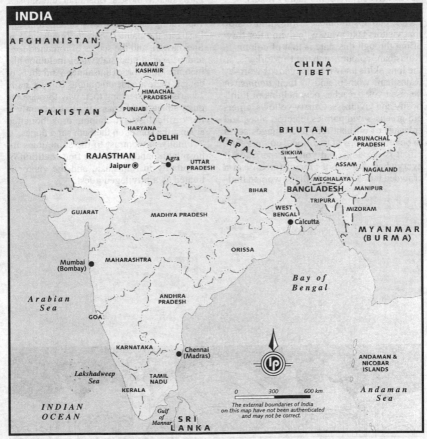

INDIA

as *jauhar*, in which they hurled themselves onto massive funeral pyres rather than face dishonour at the hands of the enemy.

Fiercely defending their territories to the death, the Rajputs entrenched themselves in this harsh desert land, building enormous forts such as those at Chittorgarh, Jodhpur and Jaisalmer, which still stand today.

Rajasthan is also replete with stunning palaces, containing exquisite furnishings, mirrored halls, airy galleries and beautiful gardens. Once exclusively the homes of the erstwhile kings of India, today many of these have been converted into luxury hotels.

Although Rajasthan is full of visual spectacles, perhaps the most lasting impression that visitors take away with them after travelling through this state is that of colour. In Rajasthan, colour – apparent in turbans, in the long skirts known as *ghagharas* worn by Rajasthani women, and in their *odhnis*, or headscarves – reaches new heights of luminosity and vividness. Canary yellows, emerald greens, vivid purples, electric blues and splashes of brilliant reds and oranges seem to be reinventions of traditional colours. The effect is dazzling, and you'll experience it everywhere – a sea of vibrant turbans on a crowded bus; a group of village women huddled around a stall in a busy bazaar; or even in the middle of the desert, as a lone, iridescent pink turbaned villager leads his sleepy-eyed camel home across the parched plains. In a land characterised by desert wastelands and sandy monotone landscapes, the Rajasthanis have created beauty amid this starkness, introducing a myriad of colours which challenge the bleached, arid terrain.

Rajasthan is one of the most popular tourist destinations in India, but this vast state can easily accommodate its visitors – there's simply so much to see, from picturesque national parks such as those at Bharatpur and Sariska, thriving cities such as Jaipur and Jodhpur, the captivating lakeside towns of Udaipur and Pushkar, the painted *havelis* (mansions) of Shekhawati, and the scores of romantic forts and palaces dotted statewide, including the incomparable fort of Jaisalmer. And then, of course, there are the ubiquitous camels, gaily caparisoned, threading their way through the dusty streets and bazaars, waiting patiently at the traffic lights in Jaipur, or silhouetted against the sunset on the Sam sand dunes.

Finally, in contrast to the sometimes inhospitable land, there is a fine tradition of hospitality in Rajasthan, and the visitor is treated as a privileged guest.

Facts about Rajasthan

HISTORY
Early History

The north-western region of India, which incorporates Rajasthan, remained for the most part independent from the great empires consolidating their hold on the subcontinent in early history. Buddhism failed to make substantial inroads here; the Mauryan empire (321-184 BC), whose most renowned emperor, Ashoka, converted to Buddhism in 262 BC, had minimal impact in Rajasthan. However, there are Buddhist caves and *stupas* (Buddhist shrines) at Jhalawar, in southern Rajasthan.

Ancient Hindu scriptural epics make reference to sites in present-day Rajasthan. The holy pilgrimage site of Pushkar is mentioned in both the *Mahabharata* and *Ramayana*.

Emergence of the Rajputs

The fall of the Gupta Empire, which held dominance in northern India for nearly 300 years until the early 5th century, was followed by a period of instability as various local chieftains sought to gain supremacy. Powers rose and fell in northern India. Stability was only restored with the emergence of the Gurjara Pratiharas, the earliest of the Rajput (from 'Rajputra', or Sons of Princes) dynasties which were later to hold the balance of power throughout Rajasthan.

The emergence of the Rajput warrior clans in the 6th and 7th centuries played the greatest role in the history of Rajasthan. From these clans came the name Rajputana, as the princely states were known during the Muslim invasion of India. The Rajputs fled aggressors in their homelands in Punjab, Gujarat and Uttar Pradesh, to settle in the area, subjugating the indigenous tribes, the Bhils and Mers. There is evidence to suggest that some of the Rajput clans can trace their emergence to the arrival of foreign invaders such as the White Huns, who may have been assimilated here, and other invaders and settlers from central Asia.

Whatever their actual origins, the Rajputs have evolved a complex mythological genealogy. This ancestry can be divided into two main branches: the Suryavansa, or Race of the Sun (Solar Race), which claims direct descent from Rama; and the Induvansa, or Race of the Moon (Lunar Race), which claims descent from Krishna. Later a third branch was added, the Agnikula, or 'Fire Born'. These people claim they were manifested from the flames of a sacrificial fire on Mt Abu. From these three principal races emerged the 36 Rajput clans.

As they were predominantly of lower castes, the Rajputs should not have aspired to warrior status – an occupation reserved for those in the upper echelons of the caste hierarchy. Their (albeit contrived) celestial origins, however, enabled them to claim descent from the Kshatriya, or martial caste, which in the caste hierarchy falls only just below that of the Brahmins.

The Rajput clans gave rise to dynasties such as the Chauhans, Sisodias, Kachhwahas and Rathores. Chauhans of the Agnikula Race emerged in the 12th century and were renowned for their valour. Their territories included the Sapadalaksha kingdom, which encompassed a vast area including present-day Jaipur, Ranthambhore, part of Mewar, the western portion of Bundi district, Ajmer, Kishangarh and even, at one time, Delhi. Branches of the Chauhans also ruled territories known as Ananta (in present-day Shekhawati) and Saptasatabhumi.

The Sisodias of the Suryavansa Race, originally from Gujarat, migrated to Rajasthan in the mid-7th century and reigned over Mewar, which encompassed Udaipur and Chittorgarh.

The Kachhwahas, originally from Gwalior in Madhya Pradesh, travelled west in the 12th century. They built the massive fort at Amber, and later shifted the capital to Jaipur. Like the Sisodias, they belonged to the Suryavansa Race.

Also belonging to the Suryavansa Race, the Rathores (earlier known as Rastrakutas) travelled from Kanauj, in Uttar Pradesh. Initially they settled in Pali, south of present-day Jodhpur, but later moved to Mandore in 1381 and ruled over Marwar (Jodhpur). Later they started building the stunning Meherangarh (fort) at Jodhpur.

The Bhattis, who belong to the Induvansa Race, driven from their homeland in the Punjab by the Turks, installed themselves at Jaisalmer in 1156. They remained more or less entrenched in their desert kingdom until they were integrated into the state of Rajasthan following Independence.

The Warrior Legacy

The first external threat to the dominance of the Rajputs was that posed by the Arabs who took over Sind in 713. The Gurjara Pratiharas' response was largely defensive. The Arabs were repulsed by them led by their king, Nagabhata I, founder of the Pratihara empire. The Arabs also tested their strength against the Rastrakutas. Unfortunately, when not pitting their wits against the Arabs, the Pratiharas and Rastrakutas were busy fighting each other.

By the third decade of the 8th century, a new threat was emerging – the Turks, who had occupied Ghazni in Afghanistan.

Around 1001 AD, Mahmud of Ghazni's army descended upon India, destroying infidel temples and carrying off everything of value that could be moved. The Rajputs were not immune from these incursions; a confederation of Rajput rulers assembled a vast army and marched northwards to meet the advancing Turks. Unfortunately, however, it was a case of too little, too late, and they were decisively and crushingly vanquished. The Pratiharas, then centred at Kanauj, fled the city before the Turks arrived, and in their absence the temples of Kanauj, as with so many others in northern India, were sacked and desecrated.

Towards the end of the 12th century, Mohammed of Ghori invaded India to take up where Mahmud of Ghazni had left off. He met with a collection of princely states which failed to mount a united front. Although initially repulsed, Ghori later triumphed, and Delhi and Ajmer were lost to the Muslims. Ajmer remained a Muslim stronghold over the centuries, apart from a brief period when it was retaken by the Rathores. Today it is an important Muslim place of pilgrimage.

The Rajputs vs the Sultans of Delhi

Mohammed of Ghori was killed in 1206, and his successor, Qutb-ud-din, became the first of the sultans of Delhi. Within 20 years, the Muslims had brought the whole of the Ganges basin under their control.

In 1297, Ala-ud-din Khilji pushed the Muslim borders south into Gujarat. He mounted a protracted siege of the massive fort at Ranthambhore, ruled at the time by the Rajput chief Hammir Deva. Hammir was reported as dead (although it's unknown if he did actually die in the siege) and upon hearing of their chief's demise, the womenfolk of the fort collectively threw themselves on a pyre, thus performing the first instance of *jauhar*, or collective sacrifice, in the history of the Rajputs. In 1303 Alu-ud-din went on to sack the fort at Chittorgarh, held by the Sisodia clan. According to tradition, he had heard of the great beauty of Padmini, the consort of the Sisodian chief, and resolved to carry her off with him. Like Ranthambhore before it, Chittorgarh fell to the Muslim leader.

The Rajputs vs the Mughals

The Delhi sultanate weakened at the start of the 16th century, and the Rajputs took advantage of this to restore and expand their territories. The kingdom of Mewar, ruled by the Sisodias under the leadership of Rana Sangram Singh, gained pre-eminence among the Rajput states. Under this leader, Mewar pushed its boundaries far beyond its original territory, posing a formidable threat to the new Mughal empire which was emerging under the leadership of Babur (reigned 1527-30).

Babur, a descendent of both Timur and Genghis Khan, marched into Punjab from his capital at Kabul in Afghanistan in 1525 and defeated the sultan of Delhi at Panipat. He then focused his attention on the Rajput princely states, many of whom, anticipating his designs, had banded together to form a united front under Rana Sangram Singh.

Unfortunately, the Rajputs were defeated by Babur. They sustained great losses, with many Rajput chiefs falling in the fray, including Rana Sangram Singh himself, who reputedly had 80 wounds on his body suffered during this and previous campaigns.

The defeat shook the foundations of the princely states. Mewar's confidence was shattered by the death of its illustrious leader, and its territories contracted following subsequent attacks by the sultan of Gujarat.

Now Marwar, under its ruler Maldeo, emerged as the strongest of the Rajput states, and it recorded a victory against the claimant to the Mughal throne, Sher Shah. However, none of the Rajputs was able to withstand the formidable threat posed by the most renowned of the Mughal emperors, Akbar (reigned 1556-1605).

Recognising that the Rajputs could not be conquered by mere force alone, Akbar contracted a marriage alliance with a princess of the important Kachhwaha clan who held Amber (and later founded Jaipur). The Kachhwahas, unlike their Rajput brethren, aligned themselves with the powerful Mughals, and even sent troops to aid them in times of battle.

Akbar also used conventional methods to assert his dominance over the Rajputs, wresting Ajmer from the Rathores of Marwar which had been briefly restored to them under Maldeo. All the important Rajput states eventually acknowledged Mughal sovereignty and became vassal states, except Mewar, which fiercely clung to its independence, refusing to pay homage to the infidels.

An uneasy truce was thus maintained between the Rajputs and the Mughal emperors, until the reign of Aurangzeb, the last great Mughal emperor, when relations were characterised by mutual hostility.

Aurangzeb devoted his resources to extending the empire's boundaries. Punitive

Sons of the Sun

Legend has it that the Rajput royal houses are descendants of the heavens, hailing from the moon and the flames of a sacrificial fire. The maharana of Udaipur (Mewar), king of all Rajput kings, is from the illustrious Sisodia clan, which traces its origin to the sun.

Most royal families of India have their own coat of arms, symbolic of their family's history. The focus of the Udaipur coat of arms is a blazing sun, since their ancestors were born of the sun. There are two figures flanked on either side of the sun: one is a Rajput warrior holding a shield (which signifies the upholding of Mewar) and the other is a Bhil tribal archer.

The Bhil tribals were renowned for their skilled archery and the maharanas of Udaipur relied on them to protect the kingdom. In the past, at the coronation of a maharana, a Bhil chieftain would cut his thumb and place a blood *tika* (a mark devout Hindus put on their forehead) on the maharana before leading him to the *gaddi* (throne of a prince).

Mewar Coat of Arms:
'The Almighty protects those who stand steadfast in upholding righteousness'.

taxes which he levied on his subjects to pay for his military exploits and his religious zealotry eventually secured his downfall.

The Rajputs were united in their opposition to Aurangzeb; the Rathores and Sisodias raised arms against him. It didn't take long for revolts by his enemies to break out on all sides and, with his death in 1707, the Mughal empire's fortunes rapidly declined.

The Rajputs vs the Marathas

Following the death of Aurangzeb and the dissolution of the Mughal empire came the Marathas. They first rose to prominence with Shivaji who, between 1646 and 1680, performed feats of arms and heroism across central India. The Maratha empire continued under the Peshwas, hereditary government ministers who became the real rulers. They gradually took over more and more of the weakening Mughal empire's powers, first by supplying troops and then by actually taking control of Mughal land.

The Marathas conducted numerous raids on the Rajputs, and the latter, too busy fighting among themselves, laid themselves open, resulting in numerous defeats in battle, the loss of territories and the inevitable decline of the Rajput states.

The Emergence of the British

In the early 19th century, the East India Company, a London trading company which had a monopoly on trade in India, was taken over by the British government, and India was effectively under British control.

Meanwhile, the Marathas continued to mount raids on the Rajputs. Initially the British adopted a policy of neutrality towards the feuding parties. However, they eventually stepped into the fray, negotiating treaties with the leaders of the main Rajput states. British protection was offered in return for Rajput support.

Weakened by habitual fighting between themselves and their skirmishes with the Marathas, one by one the princely states forfeited their independence in exchange for this protection. British residents were gradually installed in the princely states. The British ultimately eliminated the Maratha threat, but by this stage the Rajputs were effectively reduced to puppet leaders and lackeys of the British.

While the Rajput leaders enjoyed the status and prestige of their positions, discontent was manifesting itself among their subjects, which broke out in rebellion in 1857. This was a precursor to widespread opposition to British rule throughout India. It was Mohandas Gandhi, later to be known as Mahatma Gandhi, who galvanised the peasants and villagers into the nonviolent resistance which was to spearhead the nationalist movement.

Road to Independence

By the time WWII had ended, Indian independence was inevitable. The war dealt a deathblow to the myth of European superiority, and Britain no longer had the power nor the desire to maintain a vast empire. Within India, however, a major problem had developed: the large Muslim minority had realised that an independent India would also be a Hindu-dominated India.

The country was divided along religious lines, with the Muslim League, led by Muhammad Ali Jinnah, speaking for the Muslims, and the Congress Party led by Jawaharlal Nehru, representing the Hindu population.

Gandhi was absolutely opposed to severing the Muslim dominated regions from the prospective new nation. However, Jinnah was intransigent: 'I will have India divided, or India destroyed,' was his uncompromising demand. The new viceroy, Louis Mountbatten, made a last-ditch attempt to convince the rival factions that a united India was a more sensible proposition, but the reluctant decision was made to divide the country. Independence was finally instituted on 15 August 1947, with the concomitant partitioning of the nascent country. The result was a Hindu-dominated India and a Muslim-dominated West and East Pakistan.

Emergence of the State of Rajasthan

It took time for the boundaries of the proposed new state of Rajasthan to be defined.

In 1948, it comprised the south and south-eastern states of Rajputana. With the merger of Mewar, Udaipur became the capital of the United State of Rajasthan. The maharana of Udaipur was invested with the title of *rajpramukh* (head of state). Manikya Lal Varma was appointed prime minister of the new state, which was inaugurated on 18 April 1948.

Almost from the outset the prime minister came into opposition with the rajpramukh over the constitution of the state government ministry. Varma wanted to form a ministry of all Congress members. The rajpramukh was keen to install his own candidates from among the *jagirdars*, or feudal lords. Jagirdars traditionally acted as intermediaries between the tillers of the soil (peasants) and the state, taking rent or produce from the tenants and paying tribute to the princely ruler. They were symbols of the old feudal order, for whom millions of inhabitants of Rajputana were held in serfdom. Varma was keen to abolish the age-old system of *jagirdari* and, with Nehru's support, was able to install his own Congress ministry and do away with this feudal relic.

Still retaining their independence from India were Jaipur and the desert kingdoms of Bikaner, Jodhpur and Jaisalmer. From a security point of view, it was vital to the new Indian Union to ensure that the desert kingdoms, which were contiguous with Pakistan, were integrated into the new nation. The princes finally agreed to sign the Instrument of Accession, and the kingdoms of Bikaner, Jodhpur, Jaisalmer and Jaipur were merged in 1949. The maharaja of Jaipur, Man Singh II, was invested with the title of rajpramukh. Jaipur became the capital of the new state of Rajasthan. Heera Lal Shastri was installed as the first premier of Rajasthan.

Later in 1949, the United State of Matsya, comprising the former kingdoms of Bharatpur, Alwar, Karauli and Dholpur, was incorporated into Rajasthan. As a consequence, Rajasthan became the second largest state in India, exceeded in geographical area only by the central Indian state of Madhya Pradesh. It attained its current dimensions in November 1956 with the additions of Ajmer-Merwara, Abu Rd and a part of Dilwara, originally part of the princely kingdom of Sirohi which had been divided between Gujarat and Rajasthan.

The princes of the former kingdoms were constitutionally granted handsome remuneration, privy purses, to assist them in their financial obligations (and to keep them in the style to which they had become accustomed). In 1970, Indira Gandhi (daughter of India's first prime minister, Jawaharlal Nehru), who had come to power in 1966, undertook to discontinue the privy purses, leading to their abolition in 1971.

Many of the former rulers of Rajasthan continue to use the title of maharaja (or similar title) for social purposes. The only power it holds today is as a status symbol. Since the privy purse abolition, the princes have had to financially support themselves. Some hastily sold heirlooms and properties for a pittance, in a desperate attempt to pay bills.

While a handful of princes squandered their family fortunes, others refused to surrender their heritage, and turned to politics business or other vocations. Many converted their palaces into hotels, now prime tourist destinations, such as the Lake Palace Hotel in Udaipur, the Rambagh Palace in Jaipur and the Umaid Bhawan Palace in Jodhpur. The revenue from such hotels has enabled the maharajas to maintain their properties, sustain time-honoured family traditions and continue to lead a comfortable lifestyle.

However, not all palaces are on the tourist circuit and cannot rely on tourism as a source of income. Many palaces and forts are tucked away in remote parts of Rajasthan, and have been reluctantly handed over to the government, because the owners were simply unable to maintain them. Unfortunately, many of these rich vestiges of India's royal past are poorly maintained, and some are in a shocking state of disrepair.

GEOGRAPHY & GEOLOGY

The state of Rajasthan covers some 342,239 sq km in the north-western region of India.

Hills of Rajasthan

The state is dissected by the Aravalli Range, which extends diagonally across Rajasthan from the north-east to the south-west, inhibiting the movement of the Thar Desert eastwards. In places, the Aravalli is over 750m high, although the average elevation of the state falls between 100 and 350m above sea level. The highest point of the range is known as Guru Shikhar (1721m) and is the highest peak of Mt Abu. The Aravalli may be the oldest existing mountain range in the world. There is a second hilly spur, the Vindhyas, in the southernmost regions of Rajasthan.

Rivers

The Aravalli Range effectively divides Rajasthan's two principal river systems. The Chambal, which is the only perennial river in the state, rises in Madhya Pradesh from the northern slopes of the Vindhyas, entering Rajasthan at Chaurasigarh. It forms part of the eastern border between Rajasthan and Madhya Pradesh. Supplemented by its tributaries, the Kali Sindh, Alnia, Kunu, Parbati, Eru, Mej, Chakan and Banas, it flows north-westwards, draining into the Yamuna River which courses across northern India, finally entering the sea at the Bay of Bengal.

The southern region of Rajasthan is drained by the Mahi and Sabarmati rivers, while the Luni, which rises about 7km north of Ajmer in the Aravalli at the confluence of the Saraswati and Sagarmati rivers, is the only river in western Rajasthan. It flows for 482km before draining into the Arabian Sea at the Rann of Kutch in Gujarat. The Luni is seasonal, and comparatively shallow, although at places it is over 2km wide. Its main tributaries are the Lilri, Raipur, Sukri, Bandi, Mitri, Jawai Khari, Sagi and Johari, which all rise in the Aravalli.

Marusthali – Region of Death

The arid desert region in the west of the state is known as Marusthali, or the Region of Death. This sandy wasteland extends between the Aravalli Range to the east and the Sulaiman Kirthar Range to the west. This is the Thar Desert, the eastern extension of the great Saharo-Tharian desert expanse. It encompasses 68% of the state's geographical area and represents 61% of the area covered by desert in India.

In Rajasthan, the arid zone includes the districts of Jaisalmer and Bikaner, the north-western regions of Barmer and Jodhpur districts, the western section of Nagaur and Churu districts, and the southern portion of Ganganagar district. The desert, the greatest part of which lies in Rajasthan, also extends into the neighbouring states of Gujarat, Punjab and Haryana, and across the international border into Pakistan.

The sandy plains are periodically relieved by low, rugged and barren slopes. The sand dunes of Marusthali, which comprise about 60% of the desert region, are formed partly by the erosion of these low eminences and partly from sand carried from the Rann of Kutch in Gujarat by south-westerly winds.

It is hard to imagine that this now desolate region was once covered by massive forests, and was host to various large animals. In 1996, two amateur palaeontologists discovered animal fossils in the Thar Desert which possibly date from some 300 million years ago. They include those of dinosaurs and their primitive ancestors. In the Akal Wood Fossil Park, 16km from Jaisalmer, fossils have been recovered which date from nearly 185 million years ago. Plant fossils as young as 45 million years old indicate that, geologically, the desertification of Rajasthan is relatively recent and an ongoing evolution.

Semi-Arid Transitional Plain

It is difficult to identify exactly where the desert region merges into the semi-arid region, which encompasses about 25% of the geographical area of the state. The semi-arid zone is characterised by a larger distribution of rock protrusions and numerous short water courses. It lies between the Aravalli Range and the Thar Desert, extending westwards from the Aravalli, and encompassing the Ghaggar River Plain, parts of Shekhawati, and the Luni River Basin. The undulating terrain of the Shekhawati region acts to catch and contain rainwater, which is collected in depressions forming salt lakes. The Luni River forms a natural barrier between the desert and semi-arid region, inhibiting the movement of the desert eastwards.

Eastern Plains

The Eastern Plains is a large undulating region to the east of the Aravalli Range, which comprises two distinct areas, the Plain of Mewar, which contains the Banas River Basin, to the north of Udaipur, and the Chappan Plains, to Udaipur's south. The Plain of Mewar encompasses sections of Bhilwara and Bundi, all of Tonk district and most of Ajmer, Jaipur, Sawai Madhopur and Dholpur districts. It is drained by the Banas River and its tributaries which flow south-eastwards before joining the Chambal River on the Madhya Pradesh-Rajasthan border. The Chappan Plains comprises the two southernmost districts of Banswara and Dungarpur, and is drained by the Mahi River and its tributaries, which eventually flow into the Arabian Sea. The region is characterised by various low eminences.

Hadoti Plateau

This zone falls to the east and south-east of the Eastern Plains, and is characterised by hill folds and ridges, most notably around Chittorgarh, Bundi and Ranthambhore. It is the major catchment area for the Chambal River, which is flanked, particularly in the environs of Dholpur, by rugged, precipitous gorges. The region between the Banas and Chambal rivers is scarpland, composed of sandstone, while the area encompassing Jhalawar, Kota, parts of Chittorgarh, Bhilwara and Bundi forms a tableland traversed by the tributaries of the Chambal. The valleys formed by these rivers are rich in black soil.

CLIMATE

The climate of Rajasthan can be neatly divided into four seasons: pre-monsoon, monsoon, post-monsoon and winter.

Pre-monsoon, which extends from April to June, is the hottest season, with temperatures ranging from 32°C to 45°C. There is little relief from the scorching onslaught of the heat, particularly in the arid zone to the west and north-west of the Aravalli Range, where temperatures often climb above 45°C, particularly in May and June. Mt Abu registers the lowest temperatures at this time. In the desert regions, the temperature plummets as night falls. Prevailing winds are from the west and sometimes carry dust storms (known locally as andhis). The only compensation is that the winds are usually accompanied by a slight reduction in temperatures, and sometimes by light showers.

The monsoon is a welcome arrival in late June in the eastern and south-eastern regions of the state, finally falling in mid-July in the desert zones. It is preceded by dust and thunderstorms. Unless the rains are insubstantial, the monsoon is accompanied by a decrease in temperatures, with average maximum temperatures of between 29.5°C to 32.2°C in the south and south-east of Rajasthan, and an average of above 37.7°C in the north and north-western regions. Over 90% of Rajasthan's precipitation occurs during the monsoon period, and humidity is greatest at this time, particularly in August, although the humidity is less evident in the desert zone.

The third season is the post-monsoon. The monsoon has generally passed over the entire state by mid-September. It is followed by a second hot season, with relatively uniform temperatures registered across the state. In October, the average maximum temperature is 33°C to 38°C, and the minimum is between 18°C and 20°C.

The fourth season – of most interest to visitors – is the winter or cold season, from December to March. There is a marked variation in maximum and minimum temperatures, and regional variations across the state. January is the coolest month of the year. Average temperatures at the following centres are as follows (minimums in brackets): Bikaner 22°C (9°C), Jaipur 22.8°C (9°C), Ajmer 22.8°C (7.7°C), Jodhpur 24.4°C (9°C) and Kota 25°C (10.5°C).

JAIPUR

Elevation – 385m/1263ft

mm	Rainfall	in
400		16
300		12
200		8
100		4
0	J FMAMJ JASOND	0

°C	Temperature	°F
50		122
40		104
30		86
20		68
10		50
0	J FMAMJ JASOND	32

JODHPUR

Elevation – 217m/711ft

mm	Rainfall	in
400		16
300		12
200		8
100		4
0	J FMAMJ JASOND	0

°C	Temperature	°F
50		122
40		104
30		86
20		68
10		50
0	J FMAMJ JASOND	32

UDAIPUR

Elevation – 575m/1910ft

mm	Rainfall	in
400		16
300		12
200		8
100		4
0	J FMAMJ JASOND	0

°C	Temperature	°F
50		122
40		104
30		86
20		68
10		50
0	J FMAMJ JASOND	32

There is slight precipitation in the north and north-eastern regions of the state, and light winds, predominantly from the north and north-east. At this time, relative humidity ranges from 50% to 60% in the morning, and 25% to 35% in the afternoon.

There is a wide variation in the distribution of rainfall across the state, with a reduction in the volume of rain as you proceed further west. In the south-east, over 1500mm can be expected, with most rain (about 90% of the annual rainfall) falling during the monsoon period (mid-June to mid-September), and an average of 55 days of rain. At the western extremity of Rajasthan, less than 100mm may be registered in any one year, and rainfall is received on an average of only 15 days in the year.

ECOLOGY & ENVIRONMENT
Desertification

The greatest threat faced by the inhabitants of Rajasthan is desertification. While this is in part a natural phenomenon which has occurred over the ages as geological factors have given rise to warmer and drier climates, the process is exacerbated by the burgeoning human and animal population trying to use ever-diminishing resources. The Thar Desert is the most densely populated desert in the world, with an average of 61 people/sq km, as opposed to only three people/sq km in deserts elsewhere. Further pressure is placed on this fragile region by the density of livestock: while the ratio of livestock to humans elsewhere in the country is 1:05, in the desert, it is 1:2.

An acute shortage of water, salinity, erosion, periodic droughts, overgrazing, overcultivation and overconsumption of scanty vegetation for fuel and timber all either contribute to or are a consequence of the continuing desertification of Rajasthan. As inhabitants scour the landscape for wood fuel, some species of vegetation are severely threatened. The roots of *Calligonum polygonoides*, which is one of the few species found on sand dunes, are used for fuel, and the removal of this plant is severely affecting the stability of the sand dunes. Once common in Jodhpur district, this plant has now completely gone. Rohira has all but disappeared from the arid zone. The wood of this plant, known locally as Marwar teak, is highly prized for furniture construction, and traditionally was used in the carved architraves and window frames of *havelis* (mansions).

A Marwari proverb illustrates the destructive effects of overgrazing on the desert: *Oont chhode Akaro, Bakri chhode Kangro* (The camel consumes everything other than ak [a thorny shrub] but the goat devours even that, leaving only the pebbles.)

Periodic droughts are common in Rajasthan, with their threat of famine. They are caused by the unreliability of the monsoon; in any five years, two may be considered drought years. In the desert regions, it is not uncommon for one in every three years to be stricken by drought. The success of crops is also threatened by scorching heat; sandy soils at best not very fertile, being nutrient deficient, particularly in nitrogen; intermittent dust storms which smother and destroy crops; and few underground water resources. Although Rajasthan is 10.4% of the total Indian area, it has only about 1% of India's available water resources.

In western Rajasthan, even in good years, cultivation barely meets subsistence requirements. The number of rainy days in any year is on average only 15, and there's a high rate of evaporation. The main river system, the Luni, which runs through this region, is not perennial. Ground water is often unfit for animal and human consumption, and irrigation is practically nonexistent.

It is not just the arid zones which are threatened due to over-utilisation of resources. The dense forests which covered the Aravalli Range prior to Independence are thinning rapidly. Before Independence, villagers were forbidden from encroaching on these forests, which were the preserves of the maharajas and barons who hunted large animals here. However, following Independence, huge stands of trees were felled to meet increasing timber, fuel and fodder requirements. This trend is continuing, with a 41.5% reduction in forest cover between 1972 and 1975, and 1980 and 1984.

The alarming disappearance of the forests of the Aravalli has provoked government intervention, and some areas are now closed periodically to enable the forest to regenerate. However, the closed regions are poorly policed by lowly paid guards who are bribed by pastoralists desperate for fodder. Local inhabitants are also entitled to take dry wood from the forests. However, there is simply not enough wood for everyone, so villagers ringbark healthy trees, returning later to remove the dead timber.

Pollution

Pollution and deforestation are damaging many parts of Rajasthan, especially the southern region. Marble mining has been particularly harmful. Industrial waste has caused air, water and noise pollution. To address the issue of water pollution, the government has introduced policies which restrict building and development around lakes and rivers.

It's too late, unfortunately, for the village of Bichri, 15km from Udaipur. Most of the village's canals are contaminated with sulphurous sludge released indiscriminately by chemical plants in the district. Over 350 hectares of prime wetland has been made a desolate wasteland and the water in dozens of wells in the vicinity of the factories is unfit for human consumption. The companies continued to manufacture highly toxic chemicals without official permission. Despite a Supreme Court order to safely store effluents, chemical waste was released into streams or mixed with soil and deposited in various places in a crude attempt to hide it, with the result that these toxic effluents have seeped into the ground water.

Conservation

According to scientists, the most efficient way to combat desertification is afforestation. Not only will afforestation programs provide food, fodder, fuel and timber, but trees stabilise the earth and act as windbreaks, lessening the damage caused by sandstorms. The sparse vegetation in the arid zone is both in a very degraded condition and extremely slow growing, a further cause for alarm.

The first official recognition of the advancement of the Thar Desert and its alarming ramifications for the inhabitants of the arid zone occurred in 1951. As a direct result, the Desert Afforestation Research Station was established in Jodhpur in 1952, which in 1959 became the Central Arid Zone Research Institute, to conduct research into the problems of desertification. This is the most important institute of its type in south Asia.

The institute is stabilising shifting sand dunes; establishing silvipastoral and fuelwood plantations; planting windbreaks to reduce wind speed and subsequent erosion;

rehabilitating degraded forests; and starting afforestation of barren hill slopes, among other endeavours.

Some of the work carried out at the institute has been criticised by conservationists. They claim that, rather than protecting and preserving the desert ecosystem, massive attempts to irrigate and afforest the arid zone alter its fragile composition.

An afforestation project along the Indira Gandhi (Rajasthan) Canal has come under attack. The indigenous *Calligonum polygonoides*, known locally as phog, which has already completely disappeared from some regions in the arid zone, is being uprooted and replaced with fast-growing species such as *Eucalyptus hybrid* and *Acacia tortilis*. Phog, with its deep and widespreading root system, is an important stabiliser of sand dunes. Further, people who have been allocated land in the areas irrigated by the canal have uprooted this shrub to raise crops. This

Indira Gandhi Canal Project

It has been suggested that the massive Indira Gandhi Canal project, which is connected with the Bhakra Dam in Punjab, was concerned more with economics (opening up large arid belts for cash crops managed by wealthy landowners rather than the rural poor) than with ecological concerns and conservation. Indigenous plants have suffered, further adding to the degeneration of the arid zone. Also, critics suggest that the canal has incorporated traditional grazing grounds to which graziers are now denied access, and has been a key factor in the introduction of ecologically unsound cash crops, chemical fertilisers and pesticides. They argue that the command area has been exposed to over-irrigation which has destroyed fragile soil constituents. They suggest that traditional crops, which would provide nourishment and sustenance to local inhabitants and which require less irrigation, and traditional grazing grounds (gochars) could have been established.

has caused heavy silting of a portion of the canal in Jaisalmer district and shifting sand dunes have become prevalent, rendering much of this area a wasteland.

Animal husbandry is the traditional livelihood of the majority of the inhabitants of the 11 desert districts of Rajasthan, forming the major staple of the economy. Intensive planting of non-native species in the name of afforestation reduces traditional grazing grounds. In addition to upsetting the finely balanced desert ecosystem, such species are of little nutritional or practical use to villagers. Environmentalists argue that development should work not counter to, but in harmony with, the desert ecosystem. It should promote the generation and conservation of desert species which are finely attuned and adapted to the fragile environment and provide food, fodder and fuel.

FLORA & FAUNA
Flora
Vegetation in the desert zone is sparse, with only a limited range of very slow-growing thorny trees and shrubs, and grasses, which have adapted to the hostile conditions. The most common tree species are the ubiquitous khejri *(Prosopis cineraria)* and various strains of acacia. Rajasthan also has some dry teak forest, dry mixed deciduous forest, bamboo brakes and subtropical hill forests. Forest stocks are dwindling, however, as inhabitants scour the landscape for fuel and fodder. Forests, most of which are in very poor condition, cover only just over 9% of the state, mostly to the east of the Aravalli Range.

The hardy khejri, held sacred by the Bishnoi tribes of Jodhpur district, is extremely drought resistant, due to its deep root system. The thorny twigs are used for barriers to keep sheep and goats away from crops. The leaves are dried and used for fodder. The bean-shaped fruit can be eaten ripe or unripe. When unripe, it is cooked and eaten as *sangri*. The wood is used to make furniture and the branches burnt for fuel. The twigs are used in the sacred fire burnt at marriage ceremonies.

Conservation Organisations

There are several organisations working in Rajasthan to regenerate the ecosystem and promote environmentally sustainable development:

Bhinasar Gochar Andolan works to promote pasture systems and the use of traditional technology. It argues that every village should be considered a self-sufficient unit and that villagers should make collective decisions about development in their region. It has a philosophy of multi-dimensional development which includes education, health, training, and social and cultural equality. The organisation has had some success growing khejri seedlings in nurseries, one of the most important and useful plants of the desert, but considered for many years by scientists to be too difficult to propagate in nurseries. If you would like more information about Bhinasar Gochar Andolan, contact: Shubhu Patwa (☎ 0151-523205), Journalist, Bhinasar, Bikaner 334403.

Tarun Bharat Sangh (Young India Organisation) is involved in water harvesting projects, constructing small dams to collect rain-fed water. Traditional technology, local labour and materials are used, and dams are shared by communities via small irrigation channels. For further information, write to: Rajendra Singh, Tarun Bharat Sangh, PO Bhikampura Kisori, District Alwar 301022.

Ubeshwar Vikas Mandal is concerned with the afforestation of hilly areas. For more information about their work, write to: 23C Madhuban, near GPO, Udaipur 313001 or call ☎ 0294-560271.

The **Central Arid Zone Research Institute**, in Jodhpur, focuses on the problems of desertification. It has a small pictorial museum, open Monday to Saturday from 10 am to 5 pm, with a photographic exhibition illustrating the work of the institute. For more information, write to Central Arid Zone Research Institute (CAZRI), Jodhpur 342003.

Another tree distributed across the arid zone is rohira *(Tecoma undulata)*: the pods have medicinal value in the relief of abscesses; the wood is used in furniture construction. The Central Arid Zone Research Institute has had some success introducing faster-growing exotic species to the desert zone, including various species of acacia.

Grasses of the arid zone include sewan *(Lasiurus sindicus)*, which is found over large areas, dhaman *(Cenchrus ciliaris)*, boor *(Cenchrus jwarancusa)* and bharut *(Cenchrus catharticus)*. The last of these is abundant in times of drought, when it serves as a staple for the poor.

There are various species of shrubs in the arid zone, including phog *(Cenchrus polygonoides)*. Its root system stabilises sand dunes; the wood is used in construction (when green); branches serve as camel fodder; and the pods, known as lasson, are eaten as vegetables. Other shrub species include the leafless khair *(Capparis decidua)*, ak *(Calotropis procera)* and thor *(Euphorbia caduca)*. Khair not only has strong and durable wood which is resistant to white ants, but produces a fruit which can be eaten fresh or preserved. Ak prospers in sandy soil, and both ak and thor produce a juice which is taken as a cough elixir. The leaves of thor, known as papri, are eaten as a vegetable.

Keoladeo Ghana National Park, in Bharatpur district, has nearly 280 species of plants, including numerous herbs. Common trees found in the park include *Acacia nilotica*, *Acacia leucophloea*, *Prosopis juliflora* and *Prosopis cinerarea*.

Ranthambhore National Park, in Sawai Madhopur district, also has a variety of vegetation, with 306 species identified, including 73 tree species, 13 shrubs and various perennial and annual climbers. There are 30 species of grasses, eight of which are valuable as fodder, and two of which are perennial. Over 100 species of vegetation have medicinal value.

Fauna

Despite the inhospitable terrain, Rajasthan hosts a wide variety of mammals and birds.

The Cult of Conservation

The Bishnoi cult stresses the conservation and protection of all living things, conforming to its 29 (*bishnoi* means 29) conservation principles. It was founded by Guru Jambhoji in the late 15th century in Bikaner district, and now has adherents in Haryana, Gujarat and Uttar Pradesh. It is due to the vigilance of the Bishnoi tribes in the environs of Jodhpur that animals such as the blackbuck are flourishing in this area. For more details, see Around Jodhpur in the Western Rajasthan chapter.

Mammals of the arid zone have adapted to the hostile environment. Some supplement their fluid intake with insects, which are composed of between 65% and 80% water, and water-bearing plants. Others retain water for longer periods. Means of adapting to the extremes in temperature include burrowing in the sand or venturing out only at night, when the temperature plummets.

Antelopes & Gazelles Despite the paucity of blackbuck antelope numbers in most parts of Rajasthan, there are still substantial populations in Jodhpur district, where these animals are afforded special protection by the Bishnoi tribes who live here (see the boxed text above). Blackbucks feature fine spiralling horns, up to 60cm long, in mature males.

It is also partly due to the efforts of the Bishnoi that populations of chinkara, or Indian gazelle, are still found in the arid zone. Chinkaras are slighter than blackbucks, standing some 100cm tall, and live in smaller herds, sometimes with no more than three members. They are very well-adapted to the desert, thriving on wild grasses and various types of shrubs.

Another member of the *Bovidae* family is the nilgai, or bluebull, a large, stocky animal whose front legs are longer than its rear legs, giving it an ungainly, sloping stance. Nilgais are found in most parts of India, and in Rajasthan are found on open plains (although not in the extreme west of the state) and in the foothills of the Aravalli Range.

The Cat Family Tigers were once found along the length of the Aravalli Range. However, hunting by Rajasthan's princely rulers, and animal poachers trading in illegal skins, and the reduction of their habitat means they are now found only at Ranthambhore and Sariska national parks. These parks are both administered by Project Tiger, a government program initiated in 1973-74 to establish a number of protected sanctuaries across India.

The leopard, or panther, is rarely seen, but inhabits rocky declivities in the Aravalli, and parts of Jaipur and Jodhpur districts.

At the start of the 20th century there may have been as many as 40,000 tigers in India.

A much smaller specimen of the cat family is the jungle cat, which is about 60cm long, excluding the tail. It is notable for its long limbs and short tail, and is able to kill animals larger than itself. It is generally nocturnal, but may be seen at the Keoladeo Ghana National Park near Bharatpur.

Smaller than the jungle cat is the Indian desert cat, about the size of a domestic moggie, but covered in spots, other than on the tail, flanks and cheeks, which are striped. The desert cat was once well distributed in the Thar Desert, but is now rarely seen.

The Dog Family The jackal is renowned for its unearthly howling, which enables jackals to locate each other and form packs. Once quite common in Rajasthan, they were found close to villages where they preyed on livestock. Reduction of their habitat and hunting for their skins has drastically reduced their numbers. They are nocturnal, and feed on rodents, lizards, small mammals and carrion.

The wolf once roamed in large numbers in the desert zone, but was hunted almost to the point of extinction by farmers. Over recent decades, they have begun to reappear due to concerted conservation endeavours. Wolves protect themselves from the scorching heat by digging burrows in sand dunes. In the desert zone, they live in pairs rather than packs. Their prey is domestic animals, rodents, small mammals and birds.

The desert fox is a subspecies of the red fox, and was once prolific in the Thar Desert, but its numbers are now drastically reduced. A close cousin of the desert fox is the Indian fox, which used to be found in the arid zone, although not in the extreme west. It is now found in Rajasthan only in national parks.

Rodents The largest rodent in Rajasthan, or in all of India for that matter, is the crested porcupine. In the arid zone, the crested porcupine is found in the environs of hills and near fixed sand dunes. It is seldom seen, as it only ventures out at night, and is herbivorous.

There are several gerbils in the arid zone, including the nocturnal ratod, the blight of farmers as it wreaks havoc on crops. The ratod is the largest gerbil in the Thar Desert, and is widely distributed, although it is not found on sand dunes. It is about the same size as a house rat.

Desert gerbils are smaller but they descend in vast numbers on crops causing untold damage. Their burrowing contributes towards desertification: in the arid zone; between 12,000 and 15,000 burrows have been identified per hectare. Each burrow opening shifts 1kg of soil, which is carried by the high velocity winds, contributing towards soil erosion and dust storms. A distinctive characteristic of the desert gerbil is when it senses danger, it thumps the earth with its hind feet and the entire colony flees to their burrows.

There are various species of rats and mice in the desert region. The mole rat owes its name to its mole-like appearance, accentuated by diminutive ears. It has a short tail and a reddish-brown coat. This destructive little fellow gnaws the bark around the main stems of trees from its underground burrow, eventually killing the tree.

The lesser bandicoot is a relatively new arrival to Rajasthan, having colonised those areas abutting the Indira Gandhi Canal where irrigation has been introduced. It is similar in appearance to the common house rat, although it has a shorter tail, and is a major pest to farmers.

Monkeys Two types of monkey are found in Rajasthan, the rhesus monkey and the more gangly langur. The rhesus is found predominantly in the vicinity of the Aravalli Range. It has a distinctive red face and red rump, and lives in large groups headed by a dominant male. Rhesus monkeys are often found in or near human habitations, upon which they have become dependent for food.

The langur is covered by brownish-grey fur and has a black face with prominent eyebrows. It is herbivorous and, like the rhesus, can be found near human settlements.

The sacred langur which represents Hanuman, the divine monkey chief in Hindu mythology.

Bats Bats found in Rajasthan include a subspecies of the pigmy pipistrelle, the *Pipistrellus mimus glaucillus*, a diminutive bat which lives between the walls of houses or beneath tree bark.

The disconcerting-looking Indian false vampire is a carnivore, living on small rodents, other rats, lizards and small birds. It has enormous ears in proportion to its head, and powerful wings. It is found in eastern Rajasthan.

Insectivores The nocturnal Indian shrew, found throughout Rajasthan, predominantly in the Aravalli Range and the semi-arid Shekhawati region, is also known as a musk rat, but does not belong to the rodent family, and can be distinguished from a rat by its prominent, flexible nose.

Other insectivores include two species of hedgehog: the Indian hedgehog and the desert hedgehog. Both are nocturnal creatures. The desert hedgehog is larger, and is prolific in the desert region. It protects itself from predators by rolling into a ball, with its sharp quills a deterrent to attack.

Other Mammals The wild boar belongs to the pig family and, once prolific in Rajasthan, its numbers are now confined to the south-eastern Aravalli Range, around Mt Abu, and in the vicinity of the new Indira Gandhi Canal. It has tiny eyes, small tusks, a stocky frame and a short, fine tail. The hunting of wild boar was a favourite occupation of the maharajas.

The sloth bear inhabits forested regions, and can be found on the western slopes of the Aravalli Range. It is some 150cm long and stands 75cm at the shoulder. It is covered in long black hair, other than on the muzzle. It feeds on vegetation and insects, although has been known to eat carrion.

The striped hyena resembles a dog but has feline-like features, such as its teeth. It is found in Rajasthan on rocky terrain, and is a nocturnal creature, feeding on carrion and occasionally killing ailing sheep or goats.

The desert hare is found in desert grasslands, and poses a nuisance to farmers, as it feeds on crops. It also ringbarks saplings by tearing the bark near the base of the stem, a bane to conservationists engaged in reafforestation.

Two types of mongoose can be found in Rajasthan: the small Indian mongoose and the Indian grey mongoose, or common mongoose. The small Indian mongoose is found in the arid zone and lives on insects, small rodents, lizards, birds and even snakes. The Indian grey mongoose is larger than its cousin, and enjoys poultry. It also climbs trees to divest nests of eggs.

A civet which is a subspecies of the small Indian civet inhabits the Thar Desert. It is a long, lean animal with an elongated head and short limbs, and is nocturnal. It feeds on poultry, insects, lizards, rodents and eggs.

The Indian hedgehog is commonly found in Jodhpur district and Shekhawati.

Birdlife There is an abundance of birdlife in Rajasthan and no less than 450 species have been identified in the state. The Keoladeo Ghana National Park, near Bharatpur in eastern Rajasthan, is an internationally renowned bird sanctuary.

Birds of the Forests The forests of the Aravalli Range provide a habitat for orioles, hornbills, mynas, kingfishers, swallows, parakeets, warblers, robins, flycatchers, peacocks, quails, doves, barbets, bee-eaters, woodpeckers and drongos, among others.

In the Sitamata-Pratapgarh area can be seen lorikeets, which are found nowhere else in the state. The forests of Darrah are home to the Alexandrine parakeet. Birds of prey include numerous species of owl (great horned, dusky, brown fishing and collared scops, and spotted owlet), eagles (spotted and tawny), white-eyed buzzards, black winged kites and shikras.

Birds of the Wetlands The wetlands in eastern Rajasthan encompass the Keoladeo Ghana National Park. Other wetlands include those encompassed by Sariska and Ranthambhore national parks, Jaisamand Lake in Udaipur district and Sadar Samand Lake in Jodhpur district. The species mentioned here are found at Keoladeo Ghana National Park.

Migratory species include spoonbills, herons, cormorants, storks, openbills, ibis and egrets, among others.

Wintering waterfowl include the common, marbled, falcated and Baikal teal; the pintail, gadwall, shoveler, coot, wigeon, bar-headed and greylag goose; and the common and brahminy pochard. Waders include snipe, sandpipers and plovers. Several terrestrial species include the Siberian crane, which only winters at Keoladeo; the monogamous sarus, which inhabits the park year-round; and the beautiful demoiselle crane. Species resident throughout the year include moorhens, egrets, herons, storks and cormorants.

Birds of prey include many types of eagles (greater spotted, steppe, imperial, Spanish

The peacock is the national bird and is frequently represented in Rajasthani art.

imperial, fishing), vultures (white-backed and scavenger) and owls (spotted, dusky horned and mottled wood). Other birds of prey include the pallid and marsh harrier, sparrowhawk, kestrel and goshawk.

Birds of the Grasslands Some of the better grassland zones to spot birds are the Tal Chhapar Sanctuary in Churu district (northern Rajasthan); Sorsan, near Kota (southern Rajasthan); Sonkalia, near Ajmer (eastern Rajasthan); and in the environs of the Indira Gandhi Canal (western Rajasthan).

Common birds of the grasslands include various species of lark, including the short-toed, crested, sky and crowned finch-lark. Quails, including grey, rain, common and bush, can also be seen, as can several types of shrike (grey, rufous-backed and bay-backed), mynas, drongos and partridges. Migratory birds include the lesser florican, seen during the monsoon, and the houbara bustard, which winters at the grasslands.

Birds of prey include falcons, eagles, hawks, kites, kestrels and harriers.

Birds of the Desert The Thar Desert also has a prolific variety of birdlife. At the small village of Khichan, about 135km from Jodhpur, vast flocks of demoiselle cranes descend on fields in the morning and evening from the end of August to the end of March. Other winter visitors to the desert include houbara bustards and common cranes.

Water is, of course, scarce so water holes attract large flocks of imperial, spotted, pintail and Indian sandgrouse in the early mornings. Other desert dwellers include drongos, common and bush quail, blue tailed and little green bee-eaters and grey partridges.

Birds of prey include eagles (steppe and tawny), buzzards (honey and long-legged), goshawks, peregrine falcons and kestrels. The most notable of the desert and dry grassland dwellers is the impressive great Indian bustard, which stands some 40cm high and can weigh up to 14kg.

Endangered Species While some of Rajasthan's wildlife is perishing as a consequence of encroachment on its habitat, other species are falling at the hands of poachers.

Stalked, Slaughtered & Stuffed

The Rajput is fond of his dog and his gun. The former aids him in pulling down the boar or hare, and with the stalking horse he will toil for hours after the deer.
Colonel James Tod, *Annals & Antiquities of Rajasthan*

The Rajputs, particularly the princes, were once passionate hunters and were greatly admired for their shooting prowess. Hunting *(shikhar)* was considered an important part of an Indian prince's upbringing, right up until the first half of the 20th century. A handful of princesses were even encouraged to excel at this elite sport. Children as young as 10 years old, lugging heavy rifles, would participate in hunts, eager to return to the palace with a creature of some sort.

Indeed, in India hunting was the 'sport of kings' and many princes toured the world in search of new and unusual beasts to add to their prized collection. Stuffed tigers, lion-skin rugs (complete with head), zebra-fur lamps and mounted animal trophies filled many of Rajasthan's palaces. Many palaces still contain a depressing collection of animal 'ornaments'.

Some maharajas argued that hunting was necessary to maintain a crucial balance of wildlife. Others claimed it was their duty to protect their subjects from the many dangerous animals that lurked around villages. But hunting was primarily pursued as a pleasure sport.

Hunting was not the sport of Indian princes alone. The British were voracious hunters and organised elaborate shooting expeditions. During their heyday in India, the British Raj, English lords and other dignitaries often joined the maharajas on bloody killing sprees through the jungles. Trudging through the forest atop elephants, they were mainly in search of the big jungle cats – lions, tigers, panthers and leopards. But almost anything that came in their path was fair game, from wild boar to spotted deer.

Today hunting is illegal in India. Now it is the lucrative international poaching trade that threatens some of India's wildlife with extinction. Sadly, there have been recent reports of hunting animals for sport in Rajasthan – if you do come across any such cases, report them immediately to the local authorities. If they seem unwilling to do anything, contact the Chief Wildlife Warden (☎ 0141-380278), Van Bhawan (near Secretariat), Jaipur.

Tigers It is estimated that since 1990 more than 20 tigers have been slaughtered at Ranthambhore National Park. After its skin is removed, the bones inevitably find their way to China, where they form the basis of 'tiger wine', believed to have healing properties. The penis is coveted for its alleged aphrodisiac powers.

National parks and sanctuaries are proving to be lucrative hunting grounds for poachers. Frequently, only main roads in parks are patrolled by often poorly paid guards, so poachers can trespass without fear of detection. In July 1992, Badia, one of Ranthambhore's more committed trackers, was brutally murdered – allegedly by poachers, who have still not been convicted.

Strict measures have been implemented to stop the international trade in tiger skins and bones, including severe penalties imposed on offenders. According to the chief wildlife warden in Jaipur, it is now almost easier to kill a human being than a tiger at Ranthambhore National Park! Nevertheless, the smaller animals on which tigers prey are still hunted by local villagers, and the survival of this beautiful, endangered animal still hangs in the balance.

Other Fauna Although not necessarily in immediate danger of extinction, large mammals, such as the spotted deer, blackbuck, sambar, chowsingha, bluebull, wild boar and chinkara are hunted for their meat, skins or antlers. Smaller mammals such as mongooses, squirrels, jungle cats, hares and jackals are killed for their fur. The skins of reptiles supply the lucrative handbag, shoe and belt market.

Fish are indiscriminately killed by dynamiting rivers or by poison. Monkeys are trapped and exported to foreign private collectors. Birds and small mammals are captured in nets. Large carnivores such as tigers and leopards are poisoned with baits, or killed or wounded in spring traps. Wild boars are killed by baits which explode inside them.

The habitat of the animals of the Thar Desert is being steadily destroyed by over-grazing and over-utilisation of the desert resources. Some mammals which once thrived in the arid zone have now completely vanished from this region, such as the wolf, cheetah, caracal and wild ass. Several other species are on the endangered list, including the desert fox, jackal, panther, blackbuck (Indian antelope) and chinkara (Indian gazelle).

There has been some reversal in the fate of the great Indian bustard, whose numbers had dwindled alarmingly due to hunting and because its eggs were trampled by livestock. The establishment of the Desert National Park has seen a healthy increase in bustard numbers, and its future is no longer in immediate peril. The population of great Indian bustards in the Desert National Park in western Rajasthan accounts for 50% of the total population (estimated at 1500) in all of India.

NATIONAL PARKS & SANCTUARIES

Rajasthan has several world-renowned sanctuaries and national parks, and numerous other sanctuaries. Some of these, such as Ranthambhore and Sariska, were originally the hunting reserves of the maharajas. Other parks, such as the Desert National Park & Sanctuary in western Rajasthan, have been established to protect and preserve the unique plants and animals found in the arid zone.

Further details about some of the national parks and sanctuaries listed here are provided in their respective chapters.

Eastern Rajasthan

Ranthambhore National Park Ranthambhore was established as a sanctuary in 1955, came under the administration of Project Tiger in 1973 and was declared a national park in 1980. It encompasses an area of 1334 sq km on the eastern edge of the Thar Desert, and within its precincts is an ancient fort.

There is a wide range of fauna, including, apart from the elusive tiger (according to the last census, there are 28 tigers at

Wildlife Conservation Organisations & Resources

Library There is a library at the offices of the Chief Wildlife Warden in Jaipur where visitors are welcome with prior permission. Contact Mr SP Mathur (☎ 0141-380278), Technical Assistant to the Chief Wildlife Warden, Van Bhawan (near Secretariat), Jaipur.

World Wide Fund for Nature (WWF) WWF in Delhi publishes both annual and quarterly journals on issues relating to wildlife conservation in India. Contact World Wide Fund for Nature (☎ 011-4693744 or 4691763, fax 4626837 or 4691226), 172-B Max Mueller Marg, Lodhi Estate, New Delhi 110003.

Bombay Natural History Society The society conducts studies on habits and habitats of birds and wildlife, as well as initiating programs to promote their preservation. For further information contact the society at Hornbill House (☎ 022-2843869, fax 2837615), Dr Salim Ali Chowk, Shaheed Bhagat Singh Rd, Mumbai (Bombay) 400023.

Ranthambhore), chitals, leopards, nilgais (bluebulls), chinkaras (Indian gazelles), sambars (India's largest deer), the threatened wild boar, hyenas, jackals and sloth bears.

The artificial lakes at Rantham-bhore also support a wide variety of birdlife, with no less than 270 species represented, including some migratory visitors. There is an excellent infrastructure in place for visits, including organised safaris, and accommodation to suit all pockets.

The closest town, Sawai Madhopur, is easily accessible by rail, being on the Jaipur to Kota line. Best time to visit: October to April.

Sariska Tiger Reserve & National Park Tigers are also the big attraction at this national park, encompassing 800 sq km of predominantly dry mixed deciduous forest astride the Aravalli Range in Alwar district, 107km from Jaipur and 200km from Delhi. Sariska was once the exclusive hunting ground of the maharajas of Alwar (the royal hunting lodge is now an upmarket hotel). It was established as a sanctuary in 1958, and incorporated into Project Tiger in 1979. As at Ranthambhore, tigers are elusive, but other large mammals at the park include leopards, chitals, chinkaras, chowsinghas (four-horned antelopes), the threatened ratel (honey badger), wild dogs and more. There is also an ancient fort and several old temples.

Safaris can be organised at the Forest Reception Office at the park, and there are three places to stay. The closest large town is Alwar, which lies 35km to the northeast, and is connected to both Delhi and Jaipur by regular train and bus services. Best time to visit: November to June.

Keoladeo Ghana National Park This is India's best known bird sanctuary (usually just called Bharatpur). It features large numbers of breeding waterbirds and thousands of migratory birds, including some from Siberia and China. The network of crossroads and tracks through the sanctuary increases opportunities to see the birds, deer and other wildlife.

There is a good infrastructure in place for visitors, with rickshaw-wallahs trained in bird identification waiting outside the park gates to guide visitors through this beautiful park.

There is accommodation to suit all budgets, both near the park entrance, and in Bharatpur. Bharatpur, only 5km from the sanctuary, is easiest to access from Jaipur by bus. Best time to visit: October to March, July to August (wetlands).

Southern Rajasthan
Jaisamand Wildlife Sanctuary This 62 sq km sanctuary was established in 1957 adjacent to the artificial Jaisamand Lake, which was built in the 17th century by Maharaja Jai Singh.

Apart from the range of wildlife which can be seen here, the lake itself is well worth visiting, with beautiful chhatris, or cenotaphs, around its perimeter. The lake encourages a wide variety of birds, both resident and migratory, and is inhabited by crocodiles, while the dry deciduous forest is home to the chital, leopard, chinkara and wild boar. The sanctuary is 48km south-east of Udaipur. Best time to visit: November to June.

Darrah Wildlife Sanctuary This sanctuary encompasses 250 sq km of dry deciduous forest, 50km from Kota. Mammals which inhabit the sanctuary include leopards, chinkaras, spotted deer, sambars, the threatened wild boar, wolves and sloth bears. Best time to visit: February to May.

National Chambal Wildlife Sanctuary This 548 sq km sanctuary extends into neighbouring Madhya Pradesh, encompassing a sizable stretch of the Chambal River, Rajasthan's only perennial river. The sanctuary was primarily established to protect the rare gharial, a type of thin-snouted fish-eating crocodile. Gharial can be seen basking on the river banks around Kota.

Other wildlife inhabiting the park (but less likely to be observed) are wolves, chinkaras, blackbucks, wild boars and the rare (in Rajasthan, in any case) caracal. The sanctuary is easily accessible from Kota. Best time to visit: October to March.

Kumbhalgarh Wildlife Sanctuary This sanctuary is adjacent to the historic fort of Kumbhalgarh, 84km north of Udaipur, and encompasses 560 sq km in the Aravalli

Range. It is best known for its wolves, which roam in packs of up to 40 animals.

The sanctuary is also the habitat of the rare chowsingha, or four-horned antelope, and also harbours populations of sloth bears, nilgais, wild boars, leopards, panthers, sambars and jackals. It's one of the few reserves that allows people to enter on horseback. Best time to visit: October to June.

Mt Abu Wildlife Sanctuary This 290 sq km sanctuary is the location of the highest peak in the Aravalli, Guru Shikhar (1722m). The sanctuary encompasses both dry mixed deciduous and subtropical forest, and has some large mammals, including wild boars, sambars, chinkaras, (rarely seen) leopards and sloth bears.

It is easily accessible from Mt Abu, 8km distant. The best time to visit: March to June.

Sitamata Wildlife Sanctuary This picturesque sanctuary covers 423 sq km of mainly deciduous forest. A feature is the ancient teak trees. Wildlife includes deer, sambars, leopards, caracals, flying squirrels and wild boars. It is 65km south-east of Udaipur. Best time to visit: March to July.

Northern Rajasthan
Tal Chhapar Wildlife Sanctuary This sanctuary encompasses 70 sq km of grassland 95km to the south-west of Churu. It has populations of blackbuck, chinkara, desert fox and desert cat, and both resident and migratory birds, such as various types of eagle (short-toed, tawny and imperial) and sparrowhawks.

In September, large flocks of harriers visit Tal Chhapar, including Montagu's and marsh harriers, and smaller flocks of hen and pallid harriers. Demoiselle cranes are also winter visitors, Indian rollers can be seen in September and October, and bee-eaters, skylarks, ring and brown doves and crested larks are resident throughout the year. Best time to visit: September to March.

Western Rajasthan

Desert National Park & Sanctuary This national park lies 42km to the south-west of Jaisalmer, and was established in 1980 in order to preserve the fragile desert ecosystem and thus protect the range of drought-resistant species which inhabit it. It encompasses an area of 3162 sq km, an arid zone of sand dunes, thorn forest, scrub and sandy wastelands.

There is a good representative selection of desert dwellers within the park, including blackbucks, chinkaras, nilgais, wolves, desert foxes, desert cats and crested porcupines. There are 43 species of reptiles and numerous bird species, most notable of which is the great Indian bustard, which is thriving in this region as a direct result of the establishment of the national park.

The park should be avoided during the summer months, when temperatures soar to over 50°C. You need to bring a good supply of drinking water at any time. Villagers may let rooms, and there are resthouses in the park environs. Contact the Deputy Director, Desert National Park, Jaisalmer. Best time to visit: September to March.

Dhawa Doli Wildlife Sanctuary This sanctuary lies 40km south-west of Jodhpur on the Barmer road, and has populations of blackbucks, partridges, desert foxes and nilgais. It is possible to visit on tours from Jodhpur. Best time to visit: October to February.

Gajner Wildlife Sanctuary This tiny (10 sq km) sanctuary is 32km from Bikaner on the Jaisalmer road. It has a good representative variety of desert species, including desert cats and desert foxes, as well as chinkaras and blackbucks. Best time to visit: October to March.

Khichan Khichan is a small village which lies only a few kilometres from the large town of Phalodi, between Jodhpur and Jaisalmer, about 135km from the former. It has not yet been listed as a wildlife sanctuary, but bird lovers shouldn't fail to visit.

From late August/early September to the end of March, it's possible to witness the spectacular sight of hundreds of demoiselle cranes descending on the fields around the village, which feed on grain distributed by villagers. See the Western Rajasthan chapter for more details. Best time to visit: September to March.

GOVERNMENT & POLITICS
National

India is a constitutional democracy. There are 25 states and seven union territories and the constitution (which came into force on 26 January 1950) details the powers of the central and state governments as well as those powers that are shared. If the situation in a particular state is deemed to be unmanageable the central government has the controversial right to assume power there. Known as President's Rule, it has been enforced in recent years, either because the law and order situation has gotten out of hand – notably in Punjab from 1985 to 1992, Kashmir in 1990 and in Assam in 1991 – or because there is a political stalemate, such as occurred in Goa, Tamil Nadu, Pondicherry, Haryana and Meghalaya in 1991, and Nagaland in 1992.

Parliament is bicameral; the lower house is known as the *Lok Sabha* (House of the People) and the upper house is known as the *Rajya Sabha* (Council of States).

The lower house has 544 members (excluding the speaker), and elections (using the first past the post system) are held every five years, unless the government calls an election earlier. All Indians over the age of 18 have the right to vote. Of the 544 seats, 125 are reserved for the Scheduled Castes and Tribes.

The upper house has 245 members; members are elected for six-year terms and a third of the house is elected every two years. The president appoints 12 members and the rest are elected by state assemblies using a regional quota system. The president (who's duties are largely ceremonial) is elected by both houses and the state legislatures (the election is held once every five years). The president must act on the advice of a council of ministers, chosen by the prime minister, and may dissolve the lower house but not the upper.

In May 1998 India conducted five nuclear tests in the deserts of Rajasthan. Pakistan responded by conducting its own nuclear tests. The tests brought worldwide condemnation and the fallout for both countries has been economic as donor countries withheld non-humanitarian aid (see Pokaran in the Western Rajasthan chapter).

State
Rajasthan is divided into six administrative zones: Mewat (Alwar region), Marwar (Jodhpur region), Mewar (Udaipur region), Dhundhar (Jaipur region), Hadoti (Kota region) and Shekhawati (Sikar region).

After the formation of the state of Rajasthan, executive and legislative powers were wielded by the rajpramukh, Man Singh II of Jaipur, who was assisted in the execution of his duties by the state ministry, whom he appointed. The chief minister, or premier, was Heera Lal Shashtri. The central government had jurisdiction over defence, external affairs and communications, and retained 'general control' over administration, so the rajpramukh had to accept occasional central government interference.

The ministry headed by Shashtri was replaced by a council of ministers headed by CS Venkatachari in January 1951, which in turn was replaced three months later by that headed by Jainarain Vyas. The ministries were appointed by the rajpramukh, not democratically elected by their constituents. It was not until February 1952 that the first general election to the state assembly was held. Until then, Rajasthanis had been under monarchical rule and had little experience of democratic processes.

The title of rajpramukh was replaced by that of governor in 1956, a position which held little political weight.

After the abolition of the Privy Purse in 1971 by then prime minister Indira Gandhi, a number of maharajas have entered the political arena.

Since Rajasthan has had an elected government, it has been ruled by Congress, the Janata People's Party, and by a coalition of the BJP and the Janata Dal. At various times it has also been subjected to President's Rule. In the 1993 state election, the BJP-Janata Dal coalition led by Bhairon Singh Shekhawat retained power. However, in the 1998 elections, 75% of the seats were won by the Congress Party, and Ashok Gehlot became the new chief minister.

ECONOMY
Prior to Independence, princely rulers derived revenue from rent, customs duty, transit duty imposed on traders and merchants passing through their respective kingdoms, and excise duty on liquor and narcotic drugs. Some maharajas derived revenue from state-owned railways, or from forestry and mining. After the annual tribute payable to the British government was deducted, remaining revenue was spent on maintaining the state's army, on law enforcement, and on sustaining the princes' often extravagant lifestyles. Little of the funds derived from tax and nontax sources were spent on public amenities or civic services such as health and education.

In the immediate post-Independence period, Rajasthan was one of India's poorest states, a situation exacerbated not only by its feudal legacy, but by the ravages wreaked on the region by periodic droughts and famines.

Currently, the per capita income is below the national average.

Agriculture
Today agriculture and animal husbandry form the mainstay of the state's economy, representing around 44% of its revenue. Droughts, which have become more frequent over recent years, are a major drain on state resources. For example, famine relief in 1987-88 exceeded the state's entire proposed budget for that year.

Despite massive expenditure on irrigation, agricultural output has fluctuated dramatically over the years. Actual grain production has increased since 1951 – some years have much greater crop yields than others. The production of oilseeds has increased 24-fold, sugarcane production has more than doubled, and cotton increased from just over 100,000 bales to over one million bales in 1994-95.

The number of livestock has also risen dramatically to some 40 million head – almost double 1951 figures. This represents an alarming trend, as overgrazing is substantially contributing to environmental degradation and desertification. The livestock focus in the current five-year economic plan is to increase productivity and improve livestock health, with improvement in veterinary facilities, rather than increase herds.

Substantial funds have been directed towards afforestation, to inhibit the advancement of desertification and soil erosion, and address the state's fuelwood deficits.

In the 1997-98 Rajasthan budget, the government pledged increased funds to assist farmers with water conservation technology.

Industry
Production of textiles is the most important contributor to the industrial sector, and Rajasthan is one of India's major textile producers. According to the most recent statistics there are 30 textile mills in the state, employing around 50,000 people. The state produces almost half of the total national output of polyester viscose yarn, contributing some Rs 400 million to the national economy.

About 20,000 people are employed in the cement industry, which is the state's largest manufacturing industry, and this industry is continuing to grow. The production of sugar also contributes to the state economy, as does the mining of marble and sandstone, a trade in which the states of Rajputana have been engaged for centuries.

Handicrafts
In order to promote the growth of the handicraft sector and generate employment, the state government has run a large number of training programs in which trainees receive a stipend as an incentive to attend. Over 11,000 people have been trained in carpet weaving under this program. The Rajasthan Small Industries Corporation aims to encourage and promote the local handicraft sector. They operate the Rajasthali showrooms that can be found in Rajasthan and beyond, which sells local handicrafts. For more information, contact the Rajasthan Small Industries Corporation (☎ 0141-380266, fax 380046), Udyog Bhawan, Tilak Mark, Jaipur 302005, Rajasthan.

The state government has exempted most craft items from sales tax, so it is difficult to estimate the revenue earned from this sector as it doesn't go into the state coffers. In 1994, there were over 166,000 small-scale industries, including carpet making, cotton and wool spinning, block-printing, gem cutting and polishing, ivory carving, pottery and brassware production, leather goods production, marble carving and enamelling among others. It is estimated that more than 600,000 people are employed in this sector.

Infrastructure
The Centre for Monitoring Indian Economy (CMIF), attaches a numerical value to the development of infrastructure such as roads, irrigation, education, health, transport and other facilities provided by states (which in turn can gauge the relative prosperity). This measure indicates that Rajasthan is well below the national average in expenditure on infrastructure. It has consistently ranked third lowest out of the 15 major states for the last decade, with only trouble-torn Jammu & Kashmir, and Madhya Pradesh, India's largest state, falling below it on the index.

Tourism
Over recent years, tourism has emerged as one of Rajasthan's prime revenue earners, with the state attracting around one third of the total number of foreign tourists visiting India each year. In 1997, the growth rate of

domestic tourists to Rajasthan was 10%, and 8% for foreign tourists.

POPULATION & PEOPLE

According to the last national census in 1991 (a census is held every 10 years), the population of Rajasthan is 49.7 million, an alarming increase of some 35 million since the first census was conducted in 1951, shortly after Independence. In fact, Rajasthan registered the highest growth rate out of 17 of India's major states, and is well above the national growth rate of 23.5%.

There are various hypotheses for this phenomenal growth. Despite still being periodically ravaged by drought, the population is no longer decimated by famine, as improved transport infrastructure and communications enable the stricken inhabitants to receive aid in the form of grain and fodder. Further, Rajasthan is still a relatively poor state, and there is a correlation between poverty and the size of families. The perpetual desire for 'an heir and a spare' encourages parents to keep trying for two male offspring. The average life expectancy is 61 years of age – a great improvement considering the average was just 47 years of age in 1961.

While the average number of people per sq km is about 130, densities vary drastically according to region (the lowest being in the desert region).

Hindus represent around 89% of the state's population. Scheduled Castes (formerly 'the Untouchables') and Scheduled Tribes form around 17.29% and 12.44% of the state's population respectively.

Almost 8% of Rajasthan's population is Muslim, most of whom are Sunnite. There is a small affluent community of Shi'ite Muslims in south-eastern Rajasthan known as the Bohras.

The Gujjars, who profess Hinduism, dwell in eastern Rajasthan, including Jaipur, Udaipur, Alwar, Kota and Bharatpur. They are divided into two groups, the Laur and the Khari.

The nomadic Rabari, or Raika, are also Hindu. They are divided into two groups, the Marus, who breed camels, and the Chalkias, who breed sheep and goats.

The affluent Oswals hail from Osiyan, near Jodhpur, and are successful in trade and commerce. They are predominantly Jain, although a few profess Vaishnavism. Oswal women are compelled to observe strict purdah, or seclusion.

See the boxed text Tribal People of Rajasthan, over the page, for information on Rajasthan's tribal people.

EDUCATION

Despite the vast improvement in educational facilities in Rajasthan in recent years, Rajasthan has the second lowest literacy rate in India only 38.8%, as compared to the national average of 54%. Only the extremely poor state of Bihar in north-east India has a poorer literacy record.

This depressing state of affairs is worsened when a breakdown of male and female literacy is considered: female literacy is only 20.48% (all-India: 39.3%), which is the lowest percentage of female literacy in *any* of the states and territories of India. In order to improve these statistics, the National Literacy Mission has introduced the Integrated Child Development Scheme (ICDS) in Rajasthan, which has established preschool programs and provides supplementary food to the children to improve their nutrition.

At the formation of the state of Rajasthan, the state possessed only one university, and that was in Jaipur. There are now six universities and the state government has recently decided to establish a Sanskrit university.

Since Independence, five medical colleges have been founded, as well as several technical and engineering colleges. There are currently 166 colleges, of which 97 are private, over 1683 senior higher secondary schools, 3844 secondary schools, 13,546 upper primary schools and 34,098 primary schools. In the 1999 Rajasthan budget, 2675 crores of rupees (one crore is 10 million) was allocated to primary and secondary education.

Tribal People of Rajasthan

The main tribes of Rajasthan, are the Bhils and the Minas, who were the original inhabitants of the area now called Rajasthan, but who were forced into the Aravalli Range by the Aryan invasion. Smaller tribes include the Sahariyas, Damariyas, Garasias and the Gaduliya Lohars.

Bhils The Bhils are an important tribal group and traditionally inhabited the south-eastern corner of the state – the area around Udaipur, Chittorgarh and Dungarpur – although the largest concentrations of them are found in neighbouring Madhya Pradesh.

Legend has it that the Bhils were fine archers, hence their name, which can be traced to the Tamil word *vil*, meaning bow. Bhil bowmen are mentioned in both the *Mahabharata* and the *Ramayana*. They were highly regarded as warriors, and the Rajput rulers relied on them to thwart the invading Marathas and Mughals. In fact, some scholars suggest that the Rajputs owe their warrior propensities to the Bhils, whom they emulated.

Although originally food gatherers, the Bhils these days have taken up small-scale agriculture, or have abandoned the land altogether and taken up city residence and employment. The literacy rate of the Bhils, particularly the women, used to be one of the lowest in the country which made them prime targets for exploitation and bonded labour. This trend is now being reversed, and the fortunes of the Bhils are improving. Several Bhils have even entered state parliament, including, in one instance, a Bhil woman.

Those Bhils who can afford it engage in polygamy. Marriages of love, as opposed to arranged marriages which are the norm in India, are condoned.

The Baneshwar Fair is a Bhil festival held near Dungarpur in January/February each year, and large numbers of Bhils gather for several days of singing, dancing and worship. Holi is another important time for the Bhils.

Witchcraft, magic and superstition are deeply rooted aspects of Bhil culture.

Minas The Minas are the second largest tribal group in the state after the Bhils, and are the most widely spread. They live in the regions of Shekhawati and eastern Rajasthan. Scholars still disagree as to whether the Minas are an indigenous tribe, or whether they migrated to the region from central Asia. The name Mina is derived from *meen* (fish), and the Minas claim descent from the fish incarnation of Vishnu. Originally they were a ruling tribe, but their slow downfall began with the Rajputs and was completed when the British government declared them a 'criminal tribe' in 1924, mainly to stop them trying to regain their territory from the

ARTS

The celebration of beauty in Rajasthan is abundantly evident in its traditional arts and crafts, as well as in everyday domestic items and tools of the Rajputs' trade such as swords and knives.

Traditionally, the maharajas commissioned fine artistic works to adorn their palaces and to convey a degree of opulence befitting their esteemed status; the flourishing of the arts in Rajasthan is due, in a good degree, to the patronage of Rajasthan's princely rulers.

Today the artisans are mainly producing goods for the large number of foreign visitors to Rajasthan, most of whom are less discerning than your average king. Nevertheless, institutions such as the National Awards for Master Craftsmen encourage artisans to strive for artistic excellence and perpetuate Rajasthan's important artistic tradition.

Tribal People of Rajasthan

Rajputs. In their skirmishes with the Rajputs, the Minas resorted to various unorthodox means such as demanding 'protection money' from villagers to curtail their dacoit activities.

Following Independence, their ignominious status as a criminal tribe was lifted, and they took to agriculture. However, their culture was by this time more or less destroyed, and they have been given protection as a Scheduled Tribe.

As with the Bhils, the literacy rate among the Minas was very low, but is improving.

Marriage is generally within the tribe. This is arranged by the parents and most marriages take place when the children are quite young.

Gaduliya Lohars The Gaduliya Lohars were originally a martial Rajput tribe, but these days they are nomadic blacksmiths. Their traditional territory was Mewar (Udaipur) and they fought with the maharana against the Mughals. With typical Rajput chivalry, they made a vow to the maharana that they would only enter his fort at Chittorgarh after he had overcome the Mughals. As he died without achieving this, the clan was forced to become nomadic. When Nehru was in power he led a group of Gaduliya Lohars into the fort at Chittorgarh, with the hope that they would then resettle in their former lands, but they preferred to remain nomadic.

Garasias The Garasias are a small Rajput tribe found in the Abu Road area of southern Rajasthan. It is thought that they intermingled with the Bhils, supported by the fact that bows and arrows are widely used.

The marriage ceremony is curious in that the couple elope, and a sum of money is paid to the father of the bride. If the marriage fails, the bride returns home, with a small sum of money to give to the father. Widows are not entitled to a share of their husband's property, and so generally remarry.

Sahariyas The Sahariyas are thought to be of Bhil origin, and live in the areas of Kota, Dungarpur and Sawai Madhopur in the south-east of the state. They are one of the least educated tribes in the country, with a literacy rate of only 5% and, as unskilled labourers, have been cruelly exploited.

As all members of the clan are considered to be related, marriages are arranged outside the tribe. Their food and worship traditions are closely related to Hindu customs.

Music and dance are integral to all celebrations and festivals, and Rajasthan has a rich tradition of regional folk dances. In some dance performances, whole communities participate; others are performed only by men or by women. There is also the tradition of itinerant performers who interpreted popular or religious myths and legends through song, dance and drama, and who, in the past, received patronage at royal courts and performed for the pleasure of kings and their entourages.

Dance

Many tribal groups in southern Rajasthan have maintained old forms of folk dance. The *ghoomer* is a type of ceremonial dance performed only by women on special occasions, such as festivals or weddings.

continued on page 41

MUSIC

Folk music is a vital part of Rajasthani culture. Through songs the legendary battles of the Rajputs are told. The music engenders both a spirit of identity and provides entertainment as relief from the daily grind of wrenching a living from the inhospitable land.

Folk Songs

Folk songs are commonly ballads which relate heroic deeds or love stories, and religious or devotional songs known as bhajans and banis, and are often accompanied by percussion instruments such as ektaras or dholaks. Various communities specialise in professional singing, such as the Dhadhis, the Dholis, the Mangamars, and the Nats, among others. Hindu prostitutes known as Patars, and Muslim prostitutes known as Kancharis, are renowned for their singing, as are the Muslim Mirasis, who specialise in folk songs called mands which almost approximate classical singing.

Percussion Instruments

The most common instrument found in the villages of Rajasthan is the *dhol*, or drum. Goat skin is stretched over both ends of the dhol, one end being beaten with the hand, and the other with a stick. There is also a smaller version of the dhol, the *dholak*, which is one of the most common instruments of northern India. Another type of drum is the *ektara*, which is played during devotional ceremonies by priests. The ektara is a gourd over which skin is stretched. This membrane is beaten with a finger or with a stick of bamboo.

Matas are played in pairs by two musicians. A mata is an earthenware pot with a skin stretched over the opening. It is a popular instrument of the Bhopas, a caste of professional storytellers. The *chara* is also an earthenware pot, but the mouth is left open, and the musician sometimes blows into this, creating a deep, resonant, booming sound. The sides of the pot are struck with the right hand on which is worn a ring. Sometimes the musician accompanies the performance with dance steps. The chara is traditionally played by the Meghwal caste who are found along the Indo-Pakistan border.

The *naupat* is played during marriage ceremonies, and consists of two drums, a *nagada*, which is the male form of the drum, and the *jheel*, which is the female form.

The tabla is a characteristically northern dual drum used to keep the beat in classical music.

The *chang* is a large drum played generally by one, but sometimes two, musicians. It is frequently played during the festival of Holi. The drummer beats the centre of the drum with his left hand and the rim of the instrument with a stick held in his right hand. The *duff* is also played during Holi. This is a large tambourine with a rim of iron or wood, and a membrane of goat's skin.

The *nagada*, different from the male form of the naupat, consists of two drums of different sizes which are played together. One drum is iron and the other copper. Over the larger of the two is stretched buffalo skin, while the smaller nagada has camel skin. They were traditionally beaten during battles. The *khanzari* is a small drum encircled with brass or iron bells which is traditionally played by Kalbelias. The Kalbelias are a nomadic tribal group who are associated with snake charming. The *tabla* is a pair of drums and is played by classical musicians throughout India.

Stringed Instruments

The two stringed *rawanahattha*, a bowed instrument, is played by Bhopas in honour of their deity, Pabuji. One of the two strings is made of horse hair, the other formed from several thin threads twisted together to form one string. The bowl is made from a coconut shell, and the main body of the instrument from bamboo.

The *kamayacha* is a stringed instrument played by the professional Muslim caste singers known as Manganiyars, who perform in small groups of three of four. The kamayacha is played by means of a bow, drawn across the strings which are made of animal gut. The bowl of the instrument is of wood, with a membrane stretched across it.

A well known stringed instrument is the *sarangi*, of which there are various types. The *Sindhi sarangi* is used to accompany Sarangiya Langas, Muslim singers who perform for Muslim patrons. A smaller version, the *Gujratan sarangi*, is also played by these singers. There is another group of Langas, the Surnayia Langas, who play an oboe-like instrument, but who do not sing. Yet another type of sarangi is the *jogiya sarangi*, traditionally played by snake charmers who hail from Barmer and Jodhpur districts.

The stringed *srimandal* is very rarely seen today, and only a few musicians in Jaisalmer district still excel at this instrument. It is a rectangular board over which are stretched 17 or 18 strings.

The melodic sitar (top) is played throughout India. The sarangi (right), a traditional Rajasthani stringed instrument.

One string, known as the *mandrasa*, is plucked throughout the performance to provide the drone, while the other strings are dexterously plucked to give the melody. Other stringed instruments include the *revaj*, *dusaka*, *apang* and *dilruba*, the last of which is played with a bow.

The five stringed *tandoora* is played by plucking the strings and beating the rhythm on the bowl of the instrument. It is often used to accompany the dance known as the terahtal, which is performed in honour of Ramdev.

The *tambura* is commonly used alongside a main melody instrument such as the violin. This four-stringed instrument provides a secondary melody giving the musicians a constant reference point to follow.

The *sitar*, which is a classical instrument as opposed to a folk instrument, dates from the 12th century and was introduced to India by the Muslims.

Wind Instruments

Wind instruments include the *kariya*, a brass instrument once played in the courts of the maharajas, and also on the battlefield. The *mashak* is a wind instrument played by the Bhopas of Bhaironji. The *surnai* is played by the Jogis of the Bhil areas, the Dholis, and the Langas of Jaisalmer. The mouthpiece contains a jhajoor, or tar-leaf reed.

The *narh* is a four holed flute made from a form of desert grass known as kangore, and was traditionally played by shepherds to amuse themselves on their lonely vigils. Kangore was once obtained from Pakistan, but hostilities with India reduced opportunities to obtain it, so there are few narh players left in Rajasthan.

Another type of wind instrument is the *satara*, consisting of two flutes which are played simultaneously. One of the flutes contains holes which, as with conventional flutes, enables different pitches to be achieved. Holes are absent in the second flute, which gives a steady drone. The satara is a popular instrument with the Bhils and Meghwals, and is played by shepherds.

One of the most well-known instruments of the desert is the *poongi*, also known as a *murli*. This is the traditional snake charmers' flute, the bulge in its centre formed by a gourd. The different pitches are enabled by reeds of different lengths. It is played in the desert regions by folk musicians such as Langas and Manganiyars.

The *bankiya* is found in the Mewar (Udaipur) region, and is a form of trumpet, with sound produced by blowing in small holes at one end of the instrument.

The *morchang* is a small iron instrument held in the mouth by the teeth. Breathing in or out causes the central reed to vibrate, and various tones are achieved by moving the hand along the length of the instrument.

The tambura provides a secondary melody while also creating a drone – a note or chord of unvarying pitch – that other musicians can follow.

Patrons & Performers

Musicians and minstrels play an integral role in Rajasthani society, not only in providing entertainment, but in maintaining a tradition which is deeply rooted in community life. There are various castes and communities of professional musicians such as the Muslim Manganiyars, Langas and Dholis. They belong to subcastes of the lowest caste.

Musicians receive patronage not only from ruling families, but from ordinary people, both high and low caste, who pay for the performers' services with livestock, cash or a portion of the patron's crop. They play an important role in the cultural life and are essential for the ceremonies which accompany birth, marriage and death. The musician's responsibility at a death ceremony includes holding a vigil at the cremation ground for 12 days and reciting lamentations dedicated to the deceased.

As patronage is hereditary, the virtuosity (or lack of it) of the performer does not influence the relationship. A *jajman* (patron) cannot 'fire' a musician who is attached not just to a single family, but to the entire family line. A breakdown in this relationship is detrimental to the cohesiveness of society, so mechanisms have evolved to ensure the continuation of the bond. A patron can endure social stigma if his family's performer withdraws services. A musician can express displeasure with a patron by refusing to recite *subhraj*, poems dedicated to his family. If this fails to bring the patron around, the musician can take the more drastic step of removing the strings from his instrument and symbolically burying them. The worst insult towards a patron by a musician is to make an effigy of him which is tied to the tail of a donkey, paraded through the village and repeatedly beaten with a shoe. The patron is then denied the services of all musicians belonging to that caste, and as musicians are essential at important social functions, the patron is effectively socially ostracised and may, for example, be compelled to marry his children to members of a lower caste.

In addition to receiving patronage from ordinary people, musicians were also patronised, prior to Independence, by the jagirdars, or feudal lords. Most of the musicians who performed for the jagirdars belonged to the Damani caste, a subgroup of the Dholis. Unfortunately, when the jagirdari system was abolished after Independence, the Damanis lost their patrons. Many were compelled to work in fields unrelated to music, spelling the death knell for various forms of traditional music which had formed part of the Damanis' repertoire.

continued from page 37

On the occasion of sacred festivals such as Navratri, women perform the ghoomer for the deities. This dance varies in different communities and regions. In Udaipur, the dancers join a circle and carry sticks which they rhythmically strike together.

The Bhil tribal people of southern Rajasthan perform a special dance during the festival of Holi in February/March known as the *gir*, which is performed only by men, who hold sticks which they beat together. The *gir-ghoomer* is per-formed by both men and women, dressed in traditional costume. At the start of the dance, participants form two circles. The women, in a small inner circle, are encompassed by the men in the larger circle who determine the rhythm of the dance by beating sticks and striking drums. As the dance proceeds, the participants change places, with the men forming the inner circle.

The *dandiya* is performed by both men and women as part of the exuberant Holi celebrations, and is particularly notable in Jodhpur district. Participants form a circle and beat together small sticks accompanied

Karna the Dacoit

The most famous (or infamous) player of the *narh* (flute) was Karna Ram Bheel, who was equally well-known for his enormous moustache, said to be 2.35m long. When not producing sweet melodies on his narh, Karna, to earn his place in the annals of folklore, was a ruthless *dacoit* (bandit) who showed his victims no mercy. He was eventually apprehended for murder and thrown in prison.

He appeared to be a reformed man on his release, being content to play his narh and display his fine moustache, which earned him a place in the *Guinness Book of Records*. However, when his lands were appropriated by a man called Allabaksh, he was so enraged that he tied up the offender and refused to release him. Entreaties on behalf of the captive Allabaksh fell on deaf ears, and when one of Karna's former accomplices, Iliyas, acting in Karna's best interests, freed Allabaksh, Karna, in abject fury, shot him dead.

Iliyas' sons vowed to avenge their father. Karna was ambushed on his camel cart, his head severed and, with magnificent moustache intact, carried off by the sons and placed on their father's grave.

by musicians. Also performed during Holi, in eastern Rajasthan, is the *gindar*, which is danced throughout the night. In an unusual show of tolerance, caste Hindus perform this dance with Dalits, or Untouchables.

The *neja* is danced by the Minas of Kherwara and Dungarpur just after Holi. In this dance, a coconut is placed on a large pole, and while men endeavour to dislodge it, women rhythmically beat sticks and strike the men with whips!

A form of the classical *kathak* dance, which is more commonly associated with Lucknow in Uttar Pradesh, is performed in Jaipur. Traditionally performed by males only, but today it is danced by both boys and girls, the latter dressed as males. Kathak interprets through dance the stories of Krishna and his consort, Radha, and entails dramatic facial expressions, especially through the movement of the eyes and eyebrows, and dexterous movement of the neck and wrists.

The *terahtal*, which is derived from the Hindi word for '13', is performed with the aid of 13 cymbals, fastened to the bodies of the female dancers, who are accompanied by male singers and drummers. It is performed in honour of the local deity, Ramdev, and can be seen at the Ramdevra Festival which is held in August or September at the small village of Ramdevra, near Pokaran in western Rajasthan.

In the region of Marwar (Jodhpur), the *loor*, or *luvar*, is performed only by women who stand opposite each other in two lines. At a given beat of the drum they advance rapidly towards each other singing, and then retreat to their original position.

Performed mostly by the Bhil women of Udaipur, the *gauri* dance depicts legends associated with Shiva and Parvati. Participants form a semicircle and perform a series of steps in time with drum beats.

A nomadic tribal people who are traditionally associated with snake charming, the Kalbelias often complement their performances with dances such as the *shankaria*, which portrays a romantic tale. The Siddha Jats of Bikaner are renowned for their spectacular fire dance, dancing on hot coals which reputedly leave no burns.

A traditional dance of Shekhawati is the *kacchi ghori*. The dancers, all men, ride mock wooden horses and brandish swords in mock battles. They are accompanied by a singer and musicians.

The *ramlila* and the *rasalila* are performed in honour of Rama and Krishna respectively, and are danced to the accompaniment of harmoniums and drums.

Puppetry

The traditional puppeteers, known as *kath-putlis* or *putli-wallahs*, originally hailed from Nagaur district. They emerged in the last century, travelling from village to village to secure their livelihood. The skilled puppeteers relay stories through narration, music and dance. The kathputlis are among the most impoverished of Rajasthan's traditional entertainers, and are often compelled to work as farm labourers.

Many of the kathputlis make their own puppets from wood or clay. Common themes in the stories they re-enact pertain to romance, such as the story of Dhola Maru (see the boxed text The Legend of Dhola Maru in the Northern Rajasthan chapter).

The puppeteer is usually male, but he is generally assisted in his performance by his wife, who plays the dholak, and sings. Today there is less demand for the kathputlis – although the regions of Lunicha, Kuchaman and Khakholi, on the eastern fringes of the Thar Desert, still have a lively tradition of kathputli performers – so they have to go further afield in search of paying audiences, making long journeys throughout northern India in the winter months. Up to a dozen families may set out on these journeys, pitching tents at night and carrying all their possessions on their backs.

Acrobats

Like Rajasthan's puppeteers, its community of acrobats, who belong to the Nat community, are very poor, and often have to resort to begging. The itinerant Nats travel around the countryside performing acrobatic feats such as tightrope walking and balancing on long bamboo poles for the entertainment of villagers. There is still a substantial community of Nats in Chittorgarh district.

Literature

Rajasthan has a tradition of written literature which dates back to the 9th century, at which time it is believed *Khuman Raso*, the tale of a Mewari hero, was written by Dalapat Vijaya. The epic *Prithviraj Raso*, which celebrates the life of Maharaja Prithviraj Chauhan, was written by Chand Bardai in the medieval period. While Rajasthan has produced several talented writers in the post-Independence period, few of their works have been translated into English.

Marwari is the dialect most commonly used by Rajasthani writers. A form of literary Rajasthani, known as Dingal, evolved in the 15th century for the communication of poetry and ballads telling of the exploits of heroes and warriors.

Popular literature is embodied in folk tales related orally by bards down through the centuries. Tales include love stories such as those of Dhola Maru and the tragic tale of the beautiful princess Mumal (see the boxed text Mumal & Mahendra following), tales of heroic exploits, religious legends, fables and stories recounting the dastardly deeds of notorious *dacoits* (bandits), among others.

In addition there are folk songs and ballads, the latter frequently concerned with the virtue and heroism of deified folk heroes such as Pabuji, who died while fulfilling a promise which took him away from his marriage. *Pabuji-ka-phad* is a style of folk poetry performed by the nomadic Bhopas, devotees of Pabuji, who complement the narrative with painted scrolls showing the various events in his life.

Khyals are a form of folk literature. Tales, legends and historical events are communicated through khyals which may include plays, songs, sayings and storytelling. When sung, they are often accompanied by a tambourine-drum known as a *duff*. The most renowned khyals were those performed by the Nautankis of Bharatpur, who incorporated athletic leaps and the beating of drums into their recitations.

The folk literature of Rajasthan, which glorifies heroism, chivalry, virtue and honourable death and sacrifice, has engendered the image in popular consciousness of the brave Rajput warrior.

Painting

The history of painting in Rajasthan can be traced to the prehistoric period, as evidenced by the discovery of paintings in rock

Mumal & Mahendra

Upon first laying eyes on her, Mahendra of Umarkot lost his heart to the beautiful princess Mumal. Every night he raced to her chamber, borne by a swift camel named Chekal. As Mahendra had to travel at night to visit Mumal in the distant village of Lodhruva, he had little energy left to perform his husbandly duties to the satisfaction of his eight wives. Suspecting his nocturnal visits to the princess of renowned beauty, the aggrieved wives beat Mahendra's trusty camel Chekal within almost an inch of his life, rendering him completely lame. Mumal had to use a camel not of the calibre of Chekal, which subsequently lost its way.

In the meantime, Mumal's sister Sumal, of rather more homely appearance, decided to pay a visit to her sister. Sumal was in the habit of wearing men's clothes, and fell asleep next to Mumal who was exhausted from her midnight vigil awaiting Mahendra. When he finally reached Mumal's apartment, he was confronted by the sight of her lying next to what appeared to be another man. Mahendra fled from the chamber, vowing never to lay eyes on her again, and bitterly cursing the inconstancy of women. Mumal waited every night for her absent lover, finally pining away with grief. When Mahendra heard of her death, and of the misunderstanding which had kept him from visiting her, he went mad.

shelters in the Chambal Valley. Fragments of paintings found on pottery shards recovered from Kalibangan, Ahar and Gilund, among other places, indicate the antiquity of its pictorial art tradition.

From the 11th century, pictorial art was recorded on palm leaf, and in subsequent centuries, on paper. These were predominantly religious paintings which illustrated ancient Jain manuscripts. The influence of these early paintings is evident in the paintings of the 15th century. Remnants of paintings dating from this period are evident at the Kumbhalgarh and Chittorgarh forts. Common themes include religious mythology, especially that concerning Krishna and Radha, romance and interpretations of poems written about a musical mode or melody (ragamala).

Miniature Painting The most characteristic paintings of Rajasthan are miniatures, small paintings crammed with detail and executed in vegetable and mineral colours, generally on handmade paper, but also on ivory, marble, wood, cloth and leather. Various schools of miniature painting emerged in the 17th century. Although employing common themes, there were distinct differences in paintings produced in different regions. The most important regional schools of painting were those of Mewar (Udaipur), Marwar (encompassing Bikaner, Jaisalmer and Jodhpur), Amber (Jaipur; also known as the Dhundhar school), Kishangarh (flourished in the 18th century) and Hadoti (Bundi; in 1624 divided into Bundi and Kota).

The Bundi school produced some magnificent work, which other schools tried to emulate, employing rich colours and idealised subject matter, often against a lush jungle background. In the late 18th century, Bundi artists created unusual paintings with half the surface left white, and just a few figures painted against this in pale colours. The Kota school, which emerged in the 19th century, is renowned for its depictions of shikhars, or royal hunts.

Also producing distinctive paintings were the artists of Kishangarh. The Kishangarh school emerged in the second half of the 17th century under the patronage of Raja Man Singh. The school flourished under a later ruler, Sawant Singh, who ascended to the gaddi (throne) in 1706. The portrayal of Krishna's consort, Radha, was a common theme, and it is believed that a local beauty, Bani Thani, who had won the heart of Sawant Singh, was the model for these paintings. The greatest works of the Kishangarh school were produced by the master artist Nihal Chand. The Kishangarh school is also known for its romantic miniatures.

Artists of Amber, and the later capital of Jaipur, received patronage from successive Kachhwaha rulers, so the area was a most prolific centre. Much of the work from Jaipur was influenced by Mughal styles.

In Mewar, the patronage of the royal family and the pursuit of all artistic endeavours afforded a fertile environment for miniature painting to flourish. Mewar is famous for its paintings depicting court life. These were produced for the various maharanas from the early 18th century. The paintings are large and detailed, portraying festivals, ceremonies, elephant fights and hunts. Human faces had distinctive features such as almond-shaped eyes and prominent noses.

The paintings of Jodhpur, belonging to the Marwar school, featured distinctive vivid colours and heroic, bewhiskered men accompanied by dainty maidens. The paintings of Bikaner were greatly influenced by the Mughals, as many master Mughal painters, known as Ustas, were encouraged to attend the Bikaner court.

The Rajasthani painters used colours derived from minerals, ochres and vegetables. The vibrant colours still evident today in miniatures and frescoes in some of the royal palaces were derived from crushed semi-precious stones, while the gold and silver colouring is in fact finely pounded pure gold and silver leaf.

Portrait & Courtly Painting Rajput exposure to the Mughal courts in the first half of the 17th century gave rise to a new mode of painting – the royal portrait. Bikaner, with its close association with the Mughals, was one of the first schools to adopt the new style. Throughout the subsequent evolution of Rajasthani painting, while the Rajputs borrowed from the Mughals and adapted their themes, Rajasthani paintings remained much more idealised, abstract and stylised than their Mughal counterparts.

The 18th century saw less emphasis on religious themes and the illustration of

Miniature painting flourished in Rajasthan during the 18th and 19th centuries.

manuscripts, and more on secular themes. Paintings commonly depicted maharajas engaged in various activities, such as hunting, visiting the zenana, attending the *durbar* (royal court) or fulfilling religious obligations, such as presiding at the Holi celebrations. Mewar became the main centre for the production of these courtly themes.

A distinct difference in the paintings of the Rajputs and those of the Mughals in the 18th century was in the use of colour. While the Mughals used muted colours which gave a sense of shadow and depth, the Rajputs used bold primary colours which rendered their paintings two dimensional and abstract. It is not unusual to see Rajasthani miniatures of this period in which the subjects appear to 'float', captured in limbo between the foreground and background, the earth and the sky.

The 19th century heralded a decline in the execution of portraits in Rajasthan, perhaps reflecting a decline in the relative power of the maharajas as the British began to erode their dominance and, as a consequence, divest them of their heroic status.

Cloth Painting The town of Nathdwara, 48km from Udaipur, is an important centre for the production of *pichwai* paintings, which are religious paintings on home-spun cloth hung behind images of Krishna, who in Nathdwara is worshipped as Sri Nathji. The paintings were introduced by members of a Vaishnavite sect known as the Vallabh Sampradhya.

The large cloths are painted to evoke a particular mood, generally associated with the legends of Krishna, such as the rasalila. In the rasalila, Krishna, in order to please the *gopis* (milkmaids), manifested himself numerous times and was thus able to dance individually beside every maiden (the circular nature of this dance also makes the rasalila a popular theme on the interior of domes in temples and chhatris). Traditionally pichwai paintings were done in colours derived from natural minerals and vegetables, with red and yellow predominating; today, however, they are mass-produced for tourists and are of little artistic value.

Another form of cloth painting is the *phad*, a painted scroll used by the nomadic Bhopas to illustrate legends associated with the deified hero Pabuji. The Bhopa, assisted by his wife, the Bhopi, travels from village to village, dancing, singing and pointing to relevant sections of the scroll at pertinent moments to assist the narrative. The paintings are executed by a subsect of the Chhipa caste, the Joshis, who hail from the regions of Bhilwara and Chittorgarh.

Domestic Painting The region of Shekhawati, in northern Rajasthan, is reputed for its extraordinary painted havelis (see the Architecture section).

The folk art form of *mandana* is also evident in Rajasthan, in which houses are decorated with floral and geometric designs in red chalk, or with vegetation motifs which indicate the various seasons.

Sculpture & Stonework

Rajasthan is known for the fine quality of marble and sandstone extracted from the numerous quarries in the state. This has given rise to a tradition of stonemasons and sculptors. Some of the more famous quarries include those at Makrana, from which the marble used in the Taj Mahal was mined. Also built using marble from these mines were the impressive Dilwara Jain temples at Mt Abu.

The quarries of Dungarpur yield a soft chironatic stone which is used for carving images of the deities. When this stone is oiled, it becomes a rich, lustrous black. Due to their divine subject matter, sculptors producing these images are required to work according to guidelines laid down in the *Shilpa-Shashtra*, an ancient Hindu treatise on sculpture and architecture. In most cases, producing an image of a deity can entail the work of two or more sculptors. An apprentice would be responsible for carving the crude image and liberating it from the stone block, but the fine work which imparts expression and dignity to the image is given to a master sculptor.

The finest sculptors of the day were commissioned to work on the beautiful temples of Rajasthan, and some of the best work can be seen in the temples of the Jains. The Dilwara temples at Mt Abu feature exquisite carvings. No less inspiring are the Jain temples within the fort walls at Jaisalmer, the superb Jain and Hindu temples at Osiyan in western Rajasthan, which date from the 8th to the 12th centuries, and the beautiful 15th century Jain temples at Ranakpur, in southern Rajasthan.

Jaipur is the centre of marble carving. Here artisans create marble images of the deities and domestic utensils such as bowls for grinding spices and kneading dough.

At centres such as Ajmer, Udaipur, Jaipur, Jodhpur and Bikaner can be seen very fine examples of *jali*, or stone tracery, worked on screens and panels in the palaces of these cities. Jali screens offer protection from the elements while allowing ventilation through the intricate geometric patterns. They are frequently found in the windows of the *zenanas*, or women's quarters, enabling the

continued on page 50

ARCHITECTURE

Visitors to Rajasthan will be amazed by the variety and magnificence of the state's architectural heritage. Famous for its majestic forts, intricately carved temples and ornately decorated havelis, Rajasthan is home to some of India's best-known buildings. Many of these reflect the state's long history; the oldest being the Buddhist caves and stupas believed to date from the 5th century BC, and the most eye-catching being the extraordinary forts and palaces of the Rajputs. With its romantic and isolated desert structures, its sacred Jain temples and its colourful crowded cities, Rajasthan is a true paradise for the architecture buff.

Temples

There are temples in south-eastern Rajasthan whose architecture was influenced by the Gupta Empire, which held sway over northern India from the 4th to the 6th centuries. Examples include those at Darrah and Sheetaleshvara Temple at Jhalrapatan.

Around the 8th and 9th centuries, a new style of temple architecture emerged with the consolidation of the Gurjara Pratihara dynasty of Mandore. Temples built at this time include those at Chittorgarh and the exquisitely carved temples at Osiyan, in western Rajasthan. Many feature magnificent sculptural work, such as in the Laxminarayan Temple. A usual feature of these temples is a single *shikhara*, or spire, and a sculpted *mandapa*, or outer chamber, before the inner sanctum. In several cases, the main temple is surrounded by a series of small and finely sculpted shrines. Well-preserved examples are the Kalika Mata and Kumbha Shyam temples in the fort at Chittorgarh.

At Kiradu, to the west of Barmer, a group of five temples conform to the architectural style known as Solanki. The most inspiring is the Someshvara Temple, which has a fine sculpted frieze and a multi-tiered spire.

The 10th century saw the construction of many lovely Jain temples. One of the most impressive and well known groups is the Dilwara group at Mt Abu, renowned for its remarkable and exquisite carving. The Mahavira Temple near Ghanerao in southern Rajasthan is also of note.

Of the later temples, the 15th century temples at Ranakpur, 60km from Udaipur, are the finest. The most important of these is the Chaumukha Temple. It features a series of mandapas adorned with intricate carving, and achieves a breathtaking symmetry. The group of Jain temples in Jaisalmer Fort are also noteworthy. Entrance to the mandapas of some of these temples is through beautifully carved *toranas*, or gateways.

Inset: Detail of elaborate ceiling carvings of the Adinatha Temple at Ranakpur. Photo by: Liz Thompson.

Forts & Palaces

Secular architecture is no less inspiring than religious architecture, as is evident in the massive and beautiful forts and/or palaces of Chittorgarh,

Jodhpur, Jaisalmer, Bikaner, Bundi, Kota, Amber, Jaipur, Alwar, Deeg, Bharatpur, Ranthambhore, Nagaur and Udaipur. These encompass *mahals* (palaces), *zenanas* (women's quarters), *diwan-i-am* (public audience halls) *diwan-i-khas* (private audience halls), *sals* (galleries), *mandirs* (temples) and *baghs* (gardens). The palaces and forts of Rajasthan are the last word in opulence. Sometimes the beauty of the royal edifice was reflected in an artificial pool, or tank, as is evident at Deeg and Alwar. In the later palaces, the Rajputs often borrowed architectural inspiration from the Mughals. The *sheesh mahal*, or mirror palace, which is found in Rajasthan is a Mughal innovation.

Amber Fort was the capital of the Kachhwaha dynasty prior to the foundation of Jaipur. This magnificent fort, dating from the late 16th century, features exquisite tilework, which is evident in many of its chambers. The tradition of fine architecture was maintained when the capital was shifted to Jaipur, evident in the soaring Hawa Mahal, or Palace of the Winds, an impressive edifice which is little more than a facade with hundreds of windows, from which the women of the royal court could watch passing processions. Nearby is the vast City Palace complex, construction of which commenced during the reign of Jai Singh II, founder of Jaipur. Jai Singh II, known as the warrior astronomer, also built the Jantar Mantar, an observatory with a series of huge and amazing devices for observing the celestial bodies and their movements, such as the Samrat Yantra, the largest sundial in the world.

Havelis

The merchants of Rajasthan built ornately decorated residences, known as havelis, and commissioned masons and artists to ensure that they were constructed and decorated in a manner befitting the importance and prosperity of their owners. The Shekhawati district is riddled with havelis, most of which are covered, inside and out, with extraordinarily vibrant murals. The merchants also commissioned the construction of civic buildings such as wells, which benefited the entire community. There are beautiful havelis in Jaisalmer, constructed of sandstone, featuring the fine work of the renowned *silavats* (stonecarvers) of Jaisalmer.

Wells & Tanks

Given the importance of water in a predominantly desert-covered state such as Rajasthan, it is not surprising that wells and reservoirs, often known as tanks or *sagars* (lakes), were frequently beautiful and elaborate edifices. The Mertani *baori* (a well in which a series of steps leads down to the water table), at Jhunjhunu, built in the 18th century, is architecturally a very impressive structure, with a series of chambers built into the side walls, supported by pillars. Also in Jhunjhunu is the beautiful Ajit Sagar, with ornate pavilions around its edges, some featuring painted murals in the domes. In Jaisalmer, in the arid western region of the state, is the Gadi Sagar, which supplied water to the city prior to the

Top Left: Intricately carved drum and dome of the Adinatha Temple at Ranakpur. The central sanctuary of this Jain temple, the Tirthankara, is unsurpassed in its spatial complexity and richness of decoration.

Top Right: Detail of the tower balcony at the Rajmahal at Jaisalmer Fort. This pavilion style tower affords extensive views of the city and surrounding plain.

Middle: Roof decoration detail on one of the seven Jain temples inside Jaisalmer Fort.

Bottom: View of Amber Fort from Lake Mauta. This fortified city on a rocky outcrop was the stronghold of the Rajput rulers prior to the settlement of Jaipur.

BRYN THOMAS

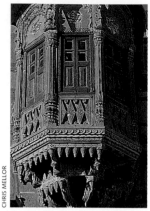

CHRIS MELLOR

CHRIS MELLOR

SARINA SINGH

Top Left: Surya Pol is the second gate into Jaisalmer Fort, surrounded by severe ashlar stonework and topped by a panel of relief carving.

Top Right: This intricately carved balcony of red sandstone is typical of the architecture of Jaisalmer.

Middle: View of the Jaisalmer Fort and city from the Thar Desert. Founded in 1156, the city has an impressive blend of religious and secular architecture, intricately decorated and remarkably intact.

Bottom: Detail of a haveli in Jhunjhunu, Shekhawati. The havelis of this region exhibit a number of richly painted and carved facades.

CHRIS MELLOR

Top: Mool Sagar, on the outskirts of Jaisalmer, is a series of well preserved chhatris of the maharajas of Jaisalmer.

MICHELLE COXALL

Middle: Detail of the paintings on the dome interior of the chhatri of Thakur Sardul Singh, at Parsurampura. This mid-18th century work chronicles the celebrations to welcome home Ram after 10 years in the forest.

Far Right: Facade detail of Patwon ki Haveli, Jaisalmer. The most elaborate and well preserved of the Jaisalmer havelis.

SARINA SINGH

Right: Jaya Stambha, or Tower of Victory at Chittorgarh was erected in 1448 to commemorate victory in battle. The tower is dedicated to Vishnu and other deities whose images adorn the walls. The fifth storey exhibits homages to the architects responsible for the impressive structure.

BRYN THOMAS

Far Right Bottom: Roof detail of one of the Jain temples in Jaisalmer Fort. Elaborate carving adorns the roofs, brackets and columns of each temple.

DAVID ELSE

SARINA SINGH

CHRIS MELLOR

ANDREW LUBRAN

Top: Jagniwas Island, or the Lake Palace Hotel, is the former palace of Maharaja Jagat Singh II of Udaipur. Built in 1754, it is now a luxury hotel.

Middle: The Jal Mahal or Water Palace just out of Jaipur, on the edge of the new city.

Bottom: Meherangarh, Jodhpur, dominates the city with an impenetrable series of walls, ramparts and pols (gateways). It contains various courtyards and palaces clustered around the hill.

construction of the Indira Gandhi Canal. It features pretty, freestanding pavilions in the lake centre, and a series of *ghats* (steps) leading down to the water's edge. Some of the state's most spectacular baoris are at Bundi (southern Rajasthan) and Abhaneri (near Jaipur).

Chhatris

Rajasthan's architectural heritage is also evident in the *chhatris*, or cenotaphs, built to commemorate maharajas, and, as is the case in the Shekhawati district, wealthy merchants such as the Poddars and Goenkas. In rare instances, chhatris also commemorate women, such as the Chhatri of Moosi Rani at Alwar. Although built in honour of Maharaja Bakhtawar Singh, his wife is also commemorated here as she earned herself a degree of immortality with the highest sacrifice – committing herself to the flames of her husband's funeral pyre in an act of *sati* (self-immolation).

A chhatri (which translates as 'umbrella') generally comprises a central dome, supported by a series of pillars on a raised platform, with a series of small pavilions on the corners and sides. In the Shekhawati district, it is not unusual for the inside of the dome to be completely covered with paintings, such as in the Chhatri of Thakur Sardul Singh at Parsurampura, which features battle scenes from the *Ramayana*. There is a series of beautiful chhatris of the Rathore Rajputs at Mandore, the ancient capital of Marwar before Jodhpur was founded. Fine chhatris can also be found in the villages of Dundlod and Ramgarh. Excellent royal chhatris may be seen in Jaipur and flanking Jaisamand Lake, near Udaipur.

Building Conservation

The Indian National Trust for Art & Cultural Heritage (INTACH) is a voluntary organisation that works to conserve and restore Rajasthan's historic monuments. Visitors can help the trust by writing to the chief minister of the Rajasthan state government to advise that the work carried out by INTACH is appreciated. If yo u have a knowledge of architecture, there may be some volunteer work available with INTACH. For more information, write to Dharmendar Kanwar, INTACH, B-14/A Bhawani Singh Rd, Jaipur, 302001, Rajasthan (☎ 0141-382646, fax 381875).

The 12th century Jain marble statue of Saraswati, goddess of learning and music, originating from the Bikaner region.

continued from page 46

women in purdah to view the events of the courts without being seen themselves. Jali screens are sculpted from both sandstone and marble.

Pottery

According to tradition, the first potter was created by Lord Shiva, who required a vessel for ceremonial purposes on the occasion of his wedding to Sati. This potter was named Rudrapal, and it is from him that the potters' caste, known as the Kumbhars, are descended. Many potters today still take the name Rudrapal, in honour of their legendary forebear.

Of all the arts of Rajasthan, pottery has the longest lineage, with fragments of pottery recovered from Kalibangan which date probably from the Harappan era (around 2500 BC). Prior to the beginning of the first millennium, potters in the environs of present-day Bikaner were decorating red pottery with black designs.

Today, different regions of Rajasthan produce different types of pottery, the most famous of which is the blue pottery of Jaipur. Blue glazed pottery originated in China, and later passed to Persia, from where it was introduced to India by the Muslims. The blue glazed work was first evident on tiles which adorned the palaces and cenotaphs of the Mughal rulers. Later the technique was applied to pottery.

In most centres the production of this highly glazed pottery declined during the era of the Mughal emperor Aurangzeb. However, the tradition was revived in Jaipur in the mid-19th century.

The pieces are decorated with images representing legends, ornamental devices and floral motifs, and depictions of animals. They are then painted with a coat of cobalt or copper oxide. After receiving a final coat of glaze, they are baked in a kiln for up to three days.

Most villages in Rajasthan have their own resident potter, who not only produces domestic vessels, but is required to produce clay images of the deities for ceremonial purposes. The most striking of these sacred images are produced in the village of Molela, north of Udaipur in southern Rajasthan. Here potters work with terracotta formed from clay and donkeys' dung, continuing a tradition which dates back to the Harappan era.

Textiles

Rajasthan is famous for its vibrantly coloured textiles. Cotton cloth is produced by the Julaha, or weaver, caste. The cloth from the village of Kaithoon, in Kota district, is the most highly prized. It is known as *masuria*, and is woven from both cotton and silk. Saris made of this cloth fetch top prices around the country.

The basic cloth receives one or several of various treatments to achieve its rich blaze of colour, including dyeing, block-printing and numerous forms of embroidery and appliqué.

Tie-Dyed Cloth Of the dyeing processes, the method producing the most intricate and interesting result is that of *bandhani*, or tie and dye. Basically parts of the fabric are knotted, so that when the fabric is dyed the knotted sections retain their original colour. Alternatively, after the fabric is knotted, it is bleached, so the unknotted sections are paler than the knotted sections.

The intricate work of tying the cloth is the preserve of women and girl children. Different patterns are created by different methods. *Loharia* (which translates as 'ripples') is striped diagonally and is used in saris and turbans. Diagonal patterns of dots are formed by the *jaaldar* and *beldar* processes. *Ekdali* features small circles and squares; *shikari* employs animal and human motifs, which are drawn before the cloth is dyed. In *tikunthi*, circles and squares appear in groups of three; in *chaubasi*, they appear in groups of four; and in *satbandi*, in groups of seven. The dominant colours used in bandhani tie and dye are yellow, red, green and pink.

One of the most intricate designs is where the cloth is first folded, and then pressed with wooden blocks embedded with nails, which causes raised impressions on the cloth. These raised points are then gathered up and tied, and the cloth dyed. The brilliant results are worn as headscarves (*odhnis*). *Pomacha* and *sikari-bandhej* odhnis are also highly sought. The former features lotus motifs against a white or pink background. A yellow background indicates that the wearer has recently given birth. Sikari-bandhej odhnis are produced in Sikar, in the region of Shekhawati, and feature designs of birds and animals.

Printed Cloth There are two forms of printing – block-printing, and reverse or resist printing. In block-printing, wooden blocks known as *buntis* or *chhapas*, on which incisions form the basic design, are dipped in dye and applied directly to the cloth. In the second mode of printing, part of the cloth is covered with a dye-resistant substance such as wax, and the cloth is then dyed. The waxed sections retain their original colour, and the wax is washed off. These original colour sections are then block-printed.

The village of Sanganer, near Jaipur, is famous for its block-printed fabric. The Sanganeri prints, generally featuring floral motifs, are exported around the world. Every day, thousands of metres of fabric can be seen drying in long swathes on the banks of the Saraswati River.

The village of Bagru, near Jaipur, is also renowned for its block-prints, which feature predominantly zigzag motifs. The city of Barmer, in western Rajasthan, produces resist-printed cloth featuring geometric designs in blue and red on both sides which is known as *ajrakh*, and is generally worn only by men as shawls and turbans. Jaisalmer specialises in resist printing, which is only executed at night and in the winter months when it is cold enough.

In Nathdwara, in southern Rajasthan, finely printed cloth depicting religious themes, particularly centred around the life of Sri Nathji, the presiding deity, was used, along with pichwai paintings (see Cloth Painting earlier), to adorn temples. Today, the tradition continues with pilgrims purchasing these cloths as religious mementos.

Dyes Before the introduction of synthetic dyes, all colours were derived from natural sources such as vegetables, minerals and even insects. Yellow was derived from turmeric and buttermilk; green from banana leaves; orange from saffron and jasmine; black from iron rust; blue from the indigo plant; red from sugarcane and sunflowers; and purple from the kirmiz insect. Colours were either fast (*pacca*) or fleeting (*kacha*). Fast colours were generally more muted than fleeting colours, consisting of browns, blues and greens, while the vibrant yellows, oranges and pinks were generally kacha colours.

Appliqué & Embroidery The third method of adorning cloth is embroidery and appliqué, and this usually takes place after the cloth has been printed or tie-dyed. A visit to any of the museums in the palaces of Rajasthan's former princely rulers gives an indication of the superlative quality of the embroidery of this state, evident in the collections of richly brocaded royal vestments. During the period of the Mughals, embroidery workshops known as *kaarkhanas* were established to train artisans so that the royal families would have an abundant supply of richly embroidered cloth. Finely stitched tapestries were also executed for the royal courts, inspired by miniature paintings.

In Bikaner, designs using double stitching result in the pattern appearing on both sides of the cloth. In Shekhawati, the Jats embroider motifs of animals and birds on their odhnis and *ghagharas* (long, gathered skirts). Chainstitch is employed in Alwar district against a bold background. Tiny mirrors are stitched into garments in Jaisalmer, an artistic device widely employed in Gujarat. Beautifully embroidered cloths are also produced for domestic livestock, and ornately bedecked camels are a wonderfully common sight at the Pushkar Camel Fair.

Carpets & Weaving
Before the emergence of the Muslims in India, the tradition of carpet making was unknown in the country. Floor coverings consisted of small mats, called *jajams*, on which only one person could sit. Carpet weaving took off in the 16th century under the patronage of the great Mughal emperor Akbar, who commissioned the establishment of various carpet-weaving factories, including one at Jaipur.

In Jaipur, pile carpets were produced under the tutorship of Persian weavers. Some of these carpets were enormous, requiring the construction of vast looms, in order to produce carpets for the royal durbar halls. There is an exquisite collection of carpets both at the museum in the City Palace, and at the Albert Hall museum, both in Jaipur.

In the 19th century, Maharaja Sawai Ram Singh II of Jaipur established a carpet factory at the Jaipur jail, and soon other jails introduced carpet-making units. Some of the most beautiful *dhurries*, or flat cotton carpets, were produced by prisoners in jails – Bikaner jail was well-known for the excellence of its dhurries.

Following the demise of the princely states, both the quality and quantity of carpets declined, without the patronage of the royal families. However, recent government training initiatives have seen the revival of this craft, and fine quality carpets are being produced in Bikaner, Jodhpur, Jaipur, Kota and other centres.

In the desert regions, where temperatures plummet when the sun goes down, blankets and shawls are vital. Shawls are woven of soft, fine wool, while blankets are woven of coarse, hand-spun wool, and are known as *pattus* or *kheis*. They often feature a special coloured border in a contrasting colour.

Jewellery
In even the poorest villages of Rajasthan, women, and often men, can be seen bedecked in elaborate silver jewellery – bracelets, rings, nose rings, toe rings, ankle bracelets, and pendants worn on the forehead and breast. The quality of the jewellery indicates the relative economic status of the wearer (or more accurately, of her husband) – one woman may wear ornaments weighing up to 5kg! Very rarely are these objects of pure silver. Usually the silver is mixed with copper to make it more malleable, although it is still of a very high grade – generally above 90%. Villagers and tribal groups of different regions can be identified by their ornaments, and these ornaments also indicate the caste to which they belong.

Unfortunately, few antique pieces have survived in their original condition, inevitably being melted down and refashioned into another article according to the dictates of fashion.

The princely rulers invested much of their wealth in ornaments of silver and gold, usually encrusted with precious and semi-precious gems. It was the founder of Amber, Maharaja Man Singh I, who introduced the beautiful *meenakari*, or enamelwork, to Rajasthan, around the end of the 17th century. Man Singh enticed five master meenakari workers from Lahore to his royal court, and established a tradition of fine enamelwork that continues in Jaipur to this day.

The oldest extant example of meenakari work is the Jaipur staff. It is 132cm long and comprises 33 segments of gold upon each of which is exquisite enamelwork featuring floral and animal designs. The handle of the staff is of solid jade. The maharaja bore this staff with him to Delhi when he was summoned to the royal court by Emperor Akbar.

Both silver and gold can be used as a base for meenakari. However, only a limited number of colours, including gold, blue, green and yellow, can be adhered to silver, whereas all available colours can be applied to gold, making it the preferred medium of enamellers.

Jaipur enamellers use the *champlevé* method, in which engravings are made on the object to be enamelled, and these are then flooded with the enamel colour. Each colour has to be individually fired, so those colours which are most resistant to heat are applied first, because they will be re-fired with the addition of each new colour. As a rule, white is the first colour applied, and red the last.

The final piece of art is the product of a succession of master artisans – the *sonar*, or goldsmith; the *chattera*, who engraves the piece; and the *minakar*, or enameller.

Kundan jewellery features precious gems on one side, and meenakari work on the reverse, requiring the expertise of a *kundansaz*, who applies the gems.

Jaipur's meenakari has particularly vibrant colour. The rich ruby red the minakars produce is highly prized. Jaipur is also an important gem cutting and polishing region.

Woodwork

Given the paucity of wood in most parts of Rajasthan, it is not surprising that stone sculpture is more prevalent than woodcarving. Nevertheless, there is a tradition of woodcarving which dates back many centuries. Unfortunately, few of the medieval pieces have survived, having succumbed to Rajasthan's arid climate or to white ants.

Shekhawati was an important centre for woodcarving. Here the woodcarver's talent can be seen in finely wrought doors, and door and window frames. Also in Shekhawati were produced *pidas* – low, folding chairs which feature decorative carving. Bikaner was also an important centre for woodcarving, for its ornately carved doors and lintels, and particularly for latticed screen windows (jalis).

The heads of the puppets of the kathputli were usually carved from wood, and then painted with the requisite (ferocious, heroic, lovelorn) expression. Wooden boxes featuring several layers of lacquer were popular in the 19th century, a craft which was probably introduced from Sind (now in Punjab).

Lacquered ware is produced in Jaipur, Jodhpur, Sawai Madhopur and Udaipur. Jaipur and Jodhpur are known for their lac bangles and bracelets. The wooden item to receive the lacquer treatment is first rubbed with liquid clay, and then, when dry, the design is stencilled with the aid of charcoal. Liquid clay, applied with very fine brushes of squirrel hair, is then used to trace the design, which becomes raised with each successive layer. The surface is then coated with paint, and gold leaf applied.

The village of Bassi, near Chittorgarh, is known for the production of puppets and toys, particularly for images of Ishar and Gauri which feature in the Gangaur Festival. Carved wooden horses, honouring the trusty steed of the deified hero, Ramdevji, are offered at his temple during the annual

Ramdevji Festival. The woodcarvers of Barmer use sheesham and rohira wood. Rohira, known locally as 'Marwar teak' and possessing excellent qualities for carving, has now unfortunately almost vanished from the desert zone.

Ivory Carving

It is believed that the art of ivory carving in India dates back at least to the 2nd century BC. In Rajasthan, the main centres for this art form are Jaipur, Udaipur and Bharatpur, where master carvers were once patronised by the royal courts.

Jaipur was famed in the mid-17th century for its carved ivory hand fans. Jodhpur specialises in ivory bangles, which are worn in great number to cover the entire arm. The bangles increase in size from the wrist to just below the shoulder. The ivory inlaid doors of the Bikaner Palace are famed for their beauty and artisanship.

While carved ivory items can still be purchased in centres such as Jaipur, the export of ivory items from India is illegal. That is, it is illegal to take ivory in any shape or form out of the country.

An exquisitely carved ivory panel, that is used as a palace door inlay.

Leatherwork

Leatherworking has a long history in Rajasthan. As working with leather is considered an 'unclean' profession, it is performed by the lowest caste in the Hindu caste hierarchy, the Sudras. Tanning is carried out by the Chamar caste. Cobblers throughout Rajasthan belong to a caste known as Mochis. Leather shoes known as *jootis* or *mojdis* are produced in Jodhpur and Jaipur, among other centres. Jootis often feature ornate embroidery known as *kashida*: in Jodhpur, the embroidery is applied direct to the leather, while in Jaipur, it is worked on velvet with which the shoes are covered. Embroidery is always done by women. Other ornamentation includes fancy stitching on the uppers, and appliqué. Strangely, there is no 'right' or 'left' foot: both shoes are identical but, due to the softness of the leather, eventually they conform to the shape of the wearer's foot.

Alwar is known for its beautiful leather book bindings, a craft which flourished under Maharaja Banni Singh in the early 19th century. One of the finest covers, for the famous copy of *Gulistan (A Rose Garden)*, by Shekh Muslihud-din-Sadi, can be seen in the Alwar museum at the City Palace complex. Bikaner is known for its production of *kopis*, or camel-hide water bottles.

SOCIETY & CONDUCT
Traditional Culture

Birth The birth of a boy child is greeted with great rejoicing and celebration. The birth is broadcast by an elderly female member of the husband's family who beats a copper *thali* (plate) to inform the neighbours of the good news. However, the birth of a girl child is considered a cause of commiseration, and there is no joyous celebration. A folk saying sums up the typical attitude towards girl children: *Beti bhali no ek* (It is not worth having even one daughter).

In order to ward off evil spirits known as *dakins* or *chureils* who prey on young infants, a ceremony is performed shortly after birth. The death of a newborn child is attributed to the malevolent machinations of these spirits.

Around 20 days following birth, at an hour deemed auspicious by the priest, a ceremony known as *panghat poojan* is performed at the local village well in worship of the water god. The new mother is permitted, after this ceremony, to recommence her domestic duties.

The birth of a girl child is not considered a calamity in all communities. There are several communities, mostly belonging to the Scheduled Castes and Tribes, which demand a bride price, or *reet*, on the marriage of their daughters. Young men who are unable to pay reet are either condemned to bachelorhood, or are compelled to exchange their sisters or female cousins in a multiple marriage transaction.

Adoption Adoption is a common solution in Rajasthan to the problem of a lack of a male heir, and one resorted to in the past by numerous maharajas. The adoption ceremony is performed before a group of representatives from the community. Vermilion is smeared on the forehead of the adoptee, and a turban placed on his head.

Marriage Marriages are, almost without exception, arranged by parents, the engagement being announced after a suitable match is found and the horoscopes of the prospective partners compared by a priest and found to be compatible. The father of the girl traditionally sends her future father-in-law a coconut. Once the coconut has been received, the marriage is inevitable. Cross-caste marriages, once socially taboo, are now performed occasionally, and are generally the result of a love match.

Although outlawed by government, child marriages are not uncommon in rural areas, and the Sahariya tribal people arrange marriages while the child is still in the womb. Often a group of children are married simultaneously, to reduce costs, although the newlyweds return to the family home until they reach maturity. On attaining puberty, girls are given gifts by their parents and then

Female Infanticide

Such is the desire to have male children that the mortality rate of female infants is greater than that of males. The dowry system, which requires the parents of the bride to ply the bridegroom's family with gifts, ensures the continued undesirability of girls, and the lower status of women in Rajasthani society.

The practice of killing newborn female infants was not unknown in Rajasthan prior to Independence, particularly among Rajput families where the dowry, according to tradition, involved paying vast sums of money. Some analysts suggest that female infanticide may still take place. Postnatal care of female infants is less vigilant than that of males. More affluent members of society had, until it was outlawed recently, recourse to tests such as amniocentesis and chorionic villus sampling (CVS) which revealed the sex of a foetus, enabling female ones to be aborted. It is not unlikely that, for the right fee, doctors in large cities could still be persuaded to provide this service.

dispatched with due ceremony to their in-laws' homes. Several days in the year are considered auspicious for marriage, and on such days, thousands of child marriages are performed throughout Rajasthan. The authorities generally turn a blind eye to these proceedings, after receiving baksheesh. Some people who have actively opposed this custom have been violently assaulted.

Spring, especially around the festival of Holi, is a popular time for weddings, although the actual date of marriage is determined by a Brahmin priest. Around Holi in Jaipur, Jodhpur and the other towns and cities of Rajasthan, it's not uncommon to see marriage processions along the busy streets. The groom, resplendent in traditional Rajput warrior costume, is borne aloft on a white horse, surrounded by his friends and family, and the marriage party, known as the *baraat*, is led by a brightly decorated float, on which a singer and musicians blast out the latest Hindi movie love songs through megaphones. Hired helpers carry heavy and ornate fluorescent lights on their shoulders to illuminate the procession.

Traditionally, the bridegroom proceeded to the home of the bride, where he pierced with a sword a shield-shaped device known as a *toran* over the doorway, and thus symbolically 'won' his bride and entered her family home to claim her. This was not necessarily an easy process, as the bride was allowed to fend off her suitor with a sword. If the husband-to-be survived the attack, he could claim her! Today brides strike their future husbands with bunches of sweets rather than sword strokes.

Following the marriage, according to Rajasthani tradition the groom is plied with seemingly nonsensical riddles by his new female in-laws. The main object is to unsettle and embarrass him, and often the riddles have a ribald sexual content.

Polygamy Prior to the dissolution of the princely states, it was not unusual for a maharaja to have at least several wives, who were known as *ranis*. Polygamy flourished during the medieval period when more wives ensured more male progeny, and hence more warriors to fight in the not infrequent battles of the Rajputs.

The ability to support a large harem became a symbol of power and affluence, and even this century, one maharaja boasted more than 300 women, which constituted a vast drain on the state's financial reserves! Gayatri Devi, the jet-setting wife of the last maharaja of Jaipur, Man Singh II, who socialised with, among others, Queen Elizabeth II of England and Prince Philip, was Man Singh's third wife.

Polygamy is still practised by those members of the Bhil and Mina tribes who can afford to maintain more than one wife.

Dowry System Unfortunately, the dowry system is entrenched in Rajasthan, and the parents of girl children can be plunged into terrible debt trying to maintain their honour by sending their daughter to her in-laws' home with appropriate gifts of cash, jewellery, electrical goods such as TVs and radios, and even motor scooters and washing machines.

If the family of the bridegroom believes that the dowry is not adequate, further demands can be made on the bride's family. Bride-burning, or dowry death, is not unknown and, as in other parts of India, the deaths of new brides in 'stove fires' are not uncommon. Some of these are attributed to the greed of in-laws, who kill their daughter-in-law to enable their son to remarry and hence claim another dowry. A poet from Rajasthan has written, 'How is the stove so wise that it distinguishes between a daughter-in-law and mother-in-law?'.

A new law was passed in 1996 prohibiting the demand for dowry by a prospective bride's in-laws. However, it is unlikely that in the short term this will serve to reverse the age-old tradition of dowry, particularly in rural India.

Divorce & Remarriage Traditionally, among the Jats, Gujjars and Scheduled Castes and Tribes, a woman is permitted to remarry following the death of her husband. However, the new husband is required to pay compensation both to the relatives of the former husband and to the bride's parents. Remarriage of widows was once forbidden by the Hindu upper castes, but is gradually becoming more prevalent and accepted. Divorce, also once forbidden, is now also more prevalent among these castes. If a woman wishes for a divorce to marry another man, compensation is payable to the former husband and his family.

Purdah Prior to Independence and the dissolution of the princely states, purdah, or isolation of married women, was prevalent among the upper echelons of society, particularly among the Rajputs. Maintaining a woman in purdah reflected favourably on her husband, as a symbol of his wealth and position.

The women of the royal harems were ensconced in zenanas, rarely venturing beyond the palace precincts, and viewed by no man other than their husband (and the palace eunuchs). If they did leave their cloistered quarters, the women were transported in covered vehicles under heavy escort.

Lower caste women were veiled from the eyes of men by their head scarves. Only the nomads and tribal women were free from the constraints imposed by purdah.

Today purdah is considered a relic of the feudal past and, other than in the Muslim communities and among the Oswal Jains, is generally not observed.

Death Twelve days after cremation, if the deceased was the male head of the family, a symbolic turban-tying ceremony is performed, in which his successor is recognised by his family and the community.

In rural areas, a death feast known variously as *mosar*, *barwa*, *kariyawar* or *terwa* is often held 12 or 13 days after death. The mourning relatives are reminded of their obligations to perform a death feast by community leaders who call on the family three days following the death, regardless of the family's financial ability to discharge this obligation. Frequently these unwelcome visitors are conveniently accompanied by the *bohara*, or village moneylender.

Death feasts can be expensive, elaborate affairs, often plunging those who hold them into debt. It has been known for the bohara to call on the bereaved family shortly after the death feast and seize their possessions in lieu of payment. However, the custom of mosar is entrenched, and to fail in this duty would reflect poorly on both the family and the honour of the deceased person.

In 1922, some 50,000 people were fed at the death feast of Maharaja Madho Singh of Jaipur. Some people celebrate the mosar feast in their lifetime, in case their relatives fail to honour them after their death. The state government has enacted laws to limit the guests at a feast, with little success. Once, an clash between police and mourners at a death feast resulted in scores of deaths.

Very affluent families may erect a *chhatri* (cenotaph) to commemorate the deceased. This practice was common in Shekhawati, where some of the wealthy merchant families, such as the Poddars, have left a legacy of architecturally impressive and beautiful chhatris.

Sati The practice of sati, or voluntary self-immolation by a widow on her husband's funeral pyre, is believed to date from the Vedic era. It is named after Shiva's wife Sati, who self-immolated when her father insulted Shiva by refusing to invite him to a feast. In Rajasthan there are numerous instances of sati, especially among the ruling Rajputs, when the wives of maharajas threw themselves on their husbands' pyres, both to honour their dead husband, and to avoid the ignominy of widowhood.

Widows, rather than being treated with compassion and solicitude on the deaths of their husbands, were divested of their wealth and rich vestments, cursed and hounded, and considered living symbols of misfortune. There are also examples in Rajput history of not only wives but maids, slaves and other domestic hands perishing on the funeral pyre of a deceased ruler.

There are several examples in Rajput's history of sati performed on a mass scale *(jauhar)*, when defeat in battle was imminent and the women of the royal court preferred to face death, rather than dishonour at the hands of the enemy.

In 1846, the princely state of Jaipur was the first state in Rajasthan to outlaw sati after prompting by the British government, and it was soon followed by other states. Mewar resisted the ban, and in 1861 Queen Victoria was compelled to issue a proclamation forbidding the practice of sati. Intermittent cases of sati have taken place over subsequent years.

Traditional Beliefs

Evil spirits, or ghosts, known as *bhuuts* or *dakins*, which possess the minds of their hapless victims, can be dislodged with the assistance of a priest, known as a *jogi* or a

The Death by Fire of Roop Kanwar

On 4 September 1987, India was plunged into controversy when an 18-year-old recently widowed woman, Roop Kanwar, burned to death on her husband's funeral pyre at the village of Deorala in the district of Sikar. According to the dead girl's family and the entire village of Deorala, Roop Kanwar voluntarily ascended the funeral pyre and calmly recited prayers while she was consumed by flames. Sceptics have alleged that the young woman, who had only been married seven months, was drugged and forcibly thrown on the fire.

What is equally as shocking as the fact that a young woman should needlessly perish by fire, whether voluntarily or not, is that in the late 20th century the act of sati was glorified and the victim deified, not just by superstitious rural folk, but by hundreds of thousands of people around the country. Within one week of Roop Kanwar's death, Deorala had become a major pilgrimage site, attracting *half a million* pilgrims, most of whom left substantial donations for a temple to be built in her honour. Among the pilgrims who visited the site of the calamity were several members of both the state and central governments.

On 27 September, Prime Minister Rajiv Gandhi issued a statement declaring the circumstances of the death of Roop Kanwar 'utterly reprehensible and barbaric'. In December 1987, a law was passed by the central government banning sati, with family members of persons committing sati to be divested of their right to inherit her property. Persons charged with 'glorifying' sati would be prohibited from contesting elections. In addition, sati *melas*, or fairs, were banned.

Despite these measures, the incontestable power of the sati still holds sway over the population, both educated and uneducated. Women reverently pay homage at shrines erected in honour of satis, believing that they have the power to make barren women fertile, or cure terminal illnesses. The reverence in which sati is evidently still held is exemplified in the extraordinarily lavish temple of Rani Sati in Jhunjhunu, in Shekhawati, which commemorates the self-immolation of a woman on her husband's funeral pyre in 1595. This temple is said to receive the second highest amount of donations of any temple in India.

---

bhopa (the Bhil name for a priest). Bhuuts and dakins are also blamed for natural disasters such as droughts, famines and crop failure, and are propitiated accordingly to avert calamity. They are known to frequent crossroads. The Balaji exorcism temple, 80km to the east of Jaipur, is visited by those seeking relief from possession by a bhuut or dakin.

Barren women are feared by new mothers, as it is believed that a barren woman will conceive if she secures hair or a fragment of clothing from an infant, who will die as a consequence.

The crossing of a cobra or cat in front of a person is considered a bad omen, as is confronting a goldsmith, a cart laden with firewood, or a woman carrying an empty pitcher. A person setting out on a long journey who is confronted by any of these inauspicious signs would do well to delay their journey.

However, meeting a married woman with a pitcher of water is an auspicious sign, auguring well for a good journey. Also considered good luck is the braying of a donkey or the cheeping of a sparrow. Friday is considered a lucky day, and work commenced on this day is guaranteed success. Monday, however, is not considered a good day for commencing new projects, and journeys to the east are never undertaken on a Monday.

It is considered unlucky to have your hair cut on a Tuesday, and barber stalls generally remain closed on this day throughout the state.

Deceased ancestors are worshipped as *pitars* (men) and *pitaris* (women who die before their husbands). On the anniversary of the death of the pitar or pitari, food must be offered to a Brahmin, a cow, a crow and a dog. These ancestors are also collectively worshipped on a particular fortnight of the year known as Shraddha Paksha.

The Caste System

The caste system, integral to Hinduism, dominates the social organisation of Rajasthan. Although its origins are hazy, it seems to have been developed by the Brahmins, or priest class, to maintain their superiority over the indigenous Dravidians. Eventually, the system became formalised into four distinct castes, each with rules of conduct and behaviour. These, in order of hierarchy, are said to have come from Brahma's mouth (Brahmins; priest caste), arms (Kshatriyas; warrior caste), thighs (Vaisyas; caste of tradespeople and artisans) and feet (Sudras; caste of farmers and peasants). These basic castes are then subdivided into numerous lesser divisions. Beneath all the castes are the Dalits and Scheduled Castes (formerly known as Harijans and Untouchables), who have no caste. A Hindu cannot change their caste – you're born into it and are stuck with it for the rest of your life.

There are variations on the caste system in Rajasthan, the most important being the Rajput caste. The Rajputs are traditionally warriors claiming lineage to the Kshatriyas. Prior to Independence and their merger into the Indian Union, the martial Rajputs wielded the most power. The Rajputs comprised various clans, or *khamps*, according to their dynastic families. Due to the integration of the princely kingdoms into the state of Rajasthan, and the abolition of the system of jagirdari, the Rajputs were nudged from their positions of power by the Brahmins.

The Brahmins can be subdivided into two groups, Chhanayatis and non-Chhanayatis,

between whom intermarriage is traditionally forbidden.

Below the Rajputs in Rajasthan's caste hierarchy, the Vaisyas can be divided into two groups: those who profess Jainism, and those professing Vaishnavism, or worship of the god Vishnu. The Oswals, who hail from Osiyan, fall loosely into this caste classification.

Below the Vaisyas, the Jats today play an active role in the administration and politics of the state. They are generally vegetarian and profess Vaishnavism. There are communities of Jats and Gujjars who are traditionally engaged in farming and animal husbandry. In Rajasthan, the tribal groups, known as Scheduled Tribes, belong to the Dalits, the lowest casteless class for whom all the most menial and degrading tasks are reserved.

Women in Society

Rural women in Rajasthan are one of the most economically and socially disadvantaged groups, unable to hold property in their own right, and receiving little, if any, education. Some measures have been undertaken by the central and state governments to enhance the status of rural women in Indian society. Development of Women & Child in Rural Areas, or DWACRA, is a central government initiative aimed at encouraging and promoting the economic empowerment of women.

In Jaipur, the Women & Child Development Department is administering programs to increase rural women's awareness of issues which directly impinge on them, including child marriage, purdah, dowry, and lack of education for girls. Small meetings known as *jajams* are held at the village level to educate the women.

Legislation has been passed requiring 30% of seats in local elections to *gram panchayats* (one to three villages), *panchayat sammitis* (village clusters) and *zila parishads* (district committees) to be reserved for women across India. The state government of Rajasthan has gone one step further by passing a law that requires 30% of the headpersons of gram panchayats and pan-chayat sammitis to be village women.

There are dozens of voluntary organisa-tions in Rajasthan working towards the eco-nomic and social empowerment of women. Care Rajasthan, the Urmal Trust and Sewa Mandir all run important programs here.

Village Life
Traditional village huts are known as *jhon-pas*. They are generally small, single storey dwellings, with walls of mud and straw, and a thatched roof. The hearth is usually built in part of the *adgaliya*, or verandah, which fronts the dwelling. There are no windows in jhonpas, and the door is generally split bamboo. The floor is packed earth coated with mud and dung. More affluent village members may build houses of stone. Next to the dwelling is a separate building of the same materials, known as a *chhan* or *dogla*. This is where livestock and grain are kept.

Around the hut, and sometimes around the entire village, is a barrier of thorns, to keep wild animals and livestock from wan-dering into the domestic area.

Water, or its absence, is a big problem in the arid zones. Some 24,000 villages in Ra-jasthan have no drinking water, and the bur-den of carrying water, sometimes more than 2 or 3km, belongs to women. A paucity of fuelwood also means villagers have to scour the countryside for a meagre load which is then carried many kilometres back to the hearth. Villagers who own livestock prepare cakes of cow dung in the summer, which is burnt as fuel throughout the year.

Women prepare meals with the aid of a handmill *(chakki)*, a mortar *(okhli)* and pes-tle *(moosal)*. Meals are carried out to the men working in the fields and women also help in the fields during the harvest.

Desert villages are naturally found close to available water sources, and village size is dependent on water availability and land productivity, resulting in small communities which are relatively isolated from each other. To trade their goods and purchase livestock, members of these isolated com-munities attend regular markets and fairs

(melas), which are opportunities for inter-village socialising. These colourful fairs can range from small local gatherings to enor-mous fairs such as the Pushkar Camel Fair.

Dos & Don'ts
Despite the hassles and hardships of travel in India you will generally be accorded great respect. In return you should be sen-sitive to local customs. While you are not expected to get everything right, you should at least exercise common sense and com-mon courtesy. If in doubt about how you should behave, watch what the locals do (eg at a temple), or ask; people are generally happy to explain and delighted that you are taking an interest in their culture.

Religious Etiquette Particular care should be taken when attending a religious place (such as a temple or shrine) or event. Dress and behave appropriately – don't wear shorts or sleeveless tops (this applies to men and women). Do not smoke or hold hands and refrain from kidding around. Re-move your shoes before entering a holy place (sometimes someone is there to take care of the shoes and you should pay that person a couple of rupees when you collect them). Do not touch a carving or statue of a deity. In some places, such as mosques, you will be required to cover your head. For re-ligious reasons, do not touch local people on the head and similarly never direct the soles of your feet at a person, religious shrine or image of a deity. Never touch an-other person with your feet.

Photographic Etiquette You should be sensitive about taking photos of people, es-pecially women, who may find it offensive – always ask first. Taking photos at a death ceremony or a religious ceremony or of people bathing (in public baths or rivers) may cause offence. Photography is prohib-ited at many places of worship.

Guest & Food Etiquette Many Indians, especially urban middle class people, are quite westernised. However, if you spend time with traditional or rural people there are some important things to remember. Don't touch food or cooking utensils that local people will use. You should use your right hand for all social interactions, whether passing money or food or any other item. Eat with your right hand only. If you are drinking from a shared water container, never touch the mouth of the container with your lips; hold the container a little above your mouth and pour. Similarly never touch someone else's food.

If you are invited to dine with a family, take off your shoes if they do and wash your hands before taking your meal. The hearth is the sacred centre of the home, so never approach it unless you have been invited to.

Never enter the kitchen unless you have been invited to do so, and always take your shoes off before you go in. Similarly, never enter the area where drinking water is stored unless you have removed your shoes. Do not touch terracotta vessels in which water is kept – you should always ask your host to serve you.

Bathing Nudity is completely unacceptable and a swimsuit must be worn even when bathing in a remote location. Indian women invariably wear saris to bathe in a river or any place where they are in public view and western women should consider wearing a sari or sarong rather than a bathing suit (unless at a hotel swimming pool, when a swimsuit is perfectly acceptable).

Hotels & Drivers Hotel owners generally do not like taxi/rickshaw drivers being brought onto their premises for a cup of tea or meal. The commission racket has caused headaches for hotel owners, and many refuse to allow drivers to dine at the hotel, even if the guest is paying. Respect the hotel's wishes, as they are the ones who may face problems with the driver long after you have left. If you want to treat your driver to a meal, it is best to take him to an independent restaurant – not one at a hotel. See under Car in the Getting Around chapter for tips about hiring a car and driver.

RELIGION

There is probably more diversity of religions and sects in India than anywhere else on earth. Apart from having nearly all the world's great religions represented, India was the birthplace of Hinduism and Buddhism, a vital supporter of Zoroastrianism (one of the oldest religions) and home to Jainism (an ancient religion unique to India).

Hinduism

Hinduism is the dominant religion of Rajasthan, professed by about 89% of the state's population. It is one of the oldest extant religions, with firm roots extending back to beyond 1000 BC.

Hinduism today has a number of holy books, the most important being the four *Vedas* (Divine Knowledge), which are the foundation of Hindu philosophy. The *Upanishads*, contained within the *Vedas*, delve into the metaphysical nature of the universe and the soul.

Shiv Nataraj – the Cosmic Dancer – is an incarnation of Shiva and believed to encompass creation, preservation and destruction.

Also important is the *Mahabharata* (Great War of the Bharatas), an epic poem containing over 220,000 lines. It describes the battles between the Kauravas and Pandavas, who were descendants of the Induvansa (Lunar Race). In it is the story of Rama, and it is probable that the most famous Hindu epic, the *Ramayana*, was based on this. The *Bhagavad Gita* is a famous episode of the *Mahabharata* where Krishna relates his philosophies to Arjuna.

Hindu Philosophy & Practice The religion postulates that we go through a series of rebirths or reincarnations that eventually lead to *moksha*, the spiritual salvation which frees you from the cycle of rebirths. With each rebirth you can move closer to or further from eventual moksha; the deciding factor is your *karma*, which is literally a law of cause and effect. Bad actions during your life result in bad karma, which ends in a lower reincarnation. Conversely, if your deeds and actions have been good you will reincarnate on a higher level and be a step closer to eventual freedom from rebirth.

Dharma, or the natural law, defines the total social, ethical and spiritual harmony of your life. There are three categories of dharma, the first being the eternal harmony which involves the whole universe. The second category is the dharma that controls castes and the relations between castes. The third dharma is the moral code which an individual should follow.

The Hindu religion has three basic practices. They are *puja*, or worship, the cremation of the dead, and the rules and regulations of the caste system. See the Society & Conduct section of this chapter for details about the caste system.

A *guru* is not so much a teacher as a spiritual guide, somebody who by example or simply by their presence indicates what path you should follow. In a spiritual search one always needs a guru. A *sadhu* is an individual on a spiritual search. They're easily recognised, usually wandering around half-naked, smeared in dust with their hair and beard matted.

Hindu Pantheon Westerners may have trouble understanding Hinduism principally because of its vast pantheon of gods. In fact you can look upon all the different gods simply as pictorial representations of the many attributes of a god. The one omnipresent god usually has three physical representations. Brahma is the creator, Vishnu is the preserver and Shiva is the destroyer and reproducer.

Each god has an animal known as the 'vehicle' on which they ride, as well as a consort with certain attributes and abilities.

Brahma, despite his supreme position, appears much less often than Vishnu or Shiva. Brahma has four arms and four heads, which symbolise his all-seeing presence.

Vishnu, the preserver, is usually shown in one of the physical forms in which he has visited earth. In all, Vishnu has paid nine visits and on his 10th he is expected as Kalki, riding a white horse.

On earlier visits he appeared in animal form, as in his boar or man-lion (Narsingh) incarnations, but on visit seven he appeared as Rama, the personification of the ideal man and the hero of the *Ramayana*.

Durga, the terrible, is the
dark side of Shiva's wife, Parvati.

Rama's consort is Sita. Rama also managed to provide a number of secondary gods including his helpful ally Hanuman, the monkey god, who is one of the most popular deities of Rajasthan.

On visit eight Vishnu came as Krishna, who was brought up with peasants and thus became a great favourite of the working classes. Krishna is widely revered throughout Rajasthan. He is renowned for his exploits with the *gopis* (milkmaids) and his consorts are Radha, the head of the gopis, Rukmani and Satyabhama. Krishna is often blue in colour and plays a flute. Vishnu's last incarnation was on visit nine, as the Buddha. This was probably a ploy to bring the Buddhist splinter group back into the Hindu fold.

When Vishnu appears as Vishnu, rather than one of his incarnations, he sits on a couch made from the coils of a serpent and in his hands he holds two symbols, the conch shell and the discus. Vishnu's vehicle is the half-man half-eagle known as the Garuda. His consort is the beautiful Lakshmi (Laxmi) who came from the sea and is the goddess of wealth and prosperity.

Shiva's creative role is symbolised by the frequently worshipped *lingam* (phallus). Shiva rides on the bull Nandi whose matted hair is said to have Ganga, the goddess of the river Ganges, in it. Some of the most ancient temples in Rajasthan are dedicated to Shiva – the Pratihara dynasty which ruled from the 8th to 10th centuries was Shivaist.

Shiva's consort is Parvati, the beautiful. In Rajasthan she is worshipped during the Teej Festival which celebrates her marriage to Shiva. Parvati has, however, a dark side, when she appears as Durga, the terrible. In this role she holds weapons in her 10 hands and rides a tiger. As Kali, the fiercest of the gods, she demands sacrifices and wears a garland of skulls. The Bhil and Mina tribal people are devotees of Kali. In Rajasthan, she is worshipped by women as Gauri, and honoured during the Gangaur Festival which takes place across Rajasthan just after Holi. Kali usually handles the destructive side of Shiva's personality.

Ganesh is the god of good fortune.

Shiva and Parvati have two children. Ganesh is the elephant-headed god of good fortune, and is probably the most popular of all the gods. Ganesh obtained his elephant head due to his father's notorious temper. Coming back from a long trip, Shiva discovered Parvati in her chambers with a young man. Not pausing to think that their son might have grown up a little during his absence, Shiva lopped his head off. He was then forced by Parvati to bring his son back to life but could only do so by giving him the head of the first living thing he saw – which happened to be an elephant. Ganesh's vehicle is a rat-like creature. Shiva and Parvati's other son is Kartikkaya, the god of war.

In Rajasthan, the most important temple to Ganesh is at the Ranthambhore Fort. Every year thousands of invitations are sent to the elephant god, care of the Fort, to request Ganesh's presence at weddings!

A variety of lesser gods and goddesses make up the Hindu pantheon. Most temples are dedicated to one or other of them, but curiously there are very few Brahma temples – Rajasthan has the honour of being the site of one of only two temples honouring Brahma in the entire country, at Pushkar, in eastern Rajasthan. Most Hindus profess to be either Vaishnavites (followers of Vishnu) or Shaivites (followers of Shiva). The cow is the holy animal of Hinduism.

Worship of the snake god, Sheshnag, is widespread across Rajasthan.

Folk Gods & Goddesses Rajasthan has numerous folk gods and goddesses, many of whom are deified local heroes. As well as these folk deities, every family pays homage to a clan goddess, or *kuldevi*.

The deified folk hero Ramdev has an important temple near Pokaran in western Rajasthan. He is revered for spurning caste distinctions and for his aid to the poor and sick.

Pabuji often features in the stories of the Bhopas, Rajasthan's professional storytellers. According to tradition, Pabuji entered a transaction with a woman called Devalde, in which, in return for a mare, he vowed to protect her cows from all harm. The time to fulfil this obligation came, inconveniently, during the celebration of Pabuji's own marriage. Recalling his vow, Pabuji immediately went to the aid of the threatened livestock. During the ensuing battle, he, along with all the male members of his family, perished at the hands of a villain by the name of Jind Raj Khinchi.

To preserve the family line, Pabuji's sister-in-law cut open her own belly and produced Pabuji's nephew, Nandio, before committing sati on her husband's funeral pyre. An annual festival is held at Kodumand, in Jaisalmer district, the birthplace of Pabuji, at which Bhopas perform Pabuji-ka-phad, poetry recitations in praise of Pabuji.

Gogaji was a warrior who lived in the 11th century and could cure snakebite – victims of snakebite are brought to his shrine by devotees, who include both Hindus and Muslims. Also believed to cure snakebite if propitiated accordingly is Tejaji. According to tradition, while pursuing *dacoits* (villains) who had rustled his father-in-law's cows, Teja was confronted by a snake which was poised to strike him. He pleaded with the snake to let him pass so that he could recover the cows, and promised to return later. The snake relented, and Teja duly returned, bloody and bruised from his confrontation with the dacoits. The snake was reluctant to bite Teja on his wounds, so Teja offered his tongue. So impressed was the snake, that it decreed that anyone honouring Teja by wearing a thread in his name would be cured of snakebite. Other deified heroes include a father and son, Mehaji and Harbhu.

Goddesses, generally incarnations of Devi, or Shakti, the Mother Goddess, include the fierce Chamunda Mata, an incarnation of Durga; Sheetala Mata, the goddess of smallpox, whom parents propitiate in order to spare their children from this affliction; Kela Devi; and Karni Mata, worshipped at Deshnok, near Bikaner.

Aaiji, a 15th century Rajput woman believed to be an incarnation of Shakti, is worshipped at Bilara, in the district of Jodhpur.

Women who have committed sati on their husbands' funeral pyres are also frequently revered as goddesses, such as Rani Sati, who has an elaborate temple in her honour in Jhunjhunu, in Shekhawati.

Barren women pay homage to the god Bhairon, an incarnation of Shiva, at his shrines which are usually found under khejri trees. In order to be blessed with a child, the woman is required to leave a garment hanging from the branches of the tree, and often these can be seen fluttering over shrines to Bhairon. The ubiquitous khejri tree of Rajasthan is worshipped during the festival of Dussehra, and the banyan and peepul trees, both considered sacred, are also worshipped on special days.

Jainism

The Jain religion is contemporaneous with Buddhism and bears many similarities to both it and Hinduism. It was founded around

Hawa Mahal (Palace of the Winds), Jaipur.

A young musician beating the *dhol*, Jaisalmer.

A camel safari throws shadows across the Sam sand dunes, near Jaisalmer.

Henna painters in Pushkar, ready to work intricate patterns on your hands or feet.

Puppets for sale at Jaisalmer Fort. Traditional puppeteers make their own puppets from clay or wood.

500 BC by Mahavira, the 24th and last of the Jain prophets, known as *tirthankars*, or finders of the Path. The Jains tend to be commercially successful and have an influence disproportionate to their actual numbers.

In Rajasthan, Jains number only 1.82% of the population. There are, nevertheless, numerous beautiful Jain temples in this state, as Jainism was for the most part tolerated by the Rajput rulers, some of whom funded the construction of these temples.

The Jain religion originally evolved as a reformist movement against the dominance of priests and the complicated rituals of Brahmanism. It rejected the caste system. Jains believe that the universe is infinite and was not created by a deity. They also believe in reincarnation and eventual spiritual salvation, or moksha, through following the path of the tirthankars. One factor in the search for salvation is *ahimsa*, or reverence for all life and the avoidance of injury to all living things. Due to this belief, Jains are strict vegetarians and some monks cover their mouths with a piece of cloth to avoid accidentally swallowing an insect.

The Jains are divided into two sects, the white-robed Shvetambara and the Digambara. The Digambaras are the more austere sect; their name literally means Sky Clad since, as a sign of their contempt for material possessions, monks sometimes do not wear clothes.

The Jains constructed extraordinary temple complexes, notable for the large number of similar buildings clustered together in one place. While those in Rajasthan are not quite as spectacular as the hilltop 'temple city' at Palitana, in Gujarat, the Jain temple complexes of Mt Abu, Ranakpur and Jaisalmer, and the Jain temples at Osiyan and Bikaner, are known for their beautiful sculpture and architectural symmetry.

Other Religions

Muslims, followers of the Islamic religion, represent 7.28% of the state's population, therefore constituting the second largest religious group in the state. Most Muslims today are Sunnites, followers of the succession from the caliph, while the others are Shias or Shi'ites who follow the descendants of Ali. There is a small community of Shi'ite Muslims, known as Bohras, in south-eastern Rajasthan. The most important pilgrimage site for Muslims in Rajasthan is the Dargah, the tomb of a Sufi saint, Khwaja Muin-ud-din Chishti, at Ajmer.

In Rajasthan, 1.44% of the population professes Sikhism. Most of Rajasthan's Sikhs live in Ganganagar district.

There is a very small population of Christians in Rajasthan, amounting to only 0.12% of the population. They are found predominantly in Ajmer and Jaipur, where there are several Catholic and Protestant churches.

The Buddhist population is negligible in Rajasthan, representing only 0.01% of the population.

Facts for the Visitor

HIGHLIGHTS

While there are plenty of ancient forts and palaces, beautiful temple complexes and fine national parks and sanctuaries in Rajasthan, one of the highlights of a visit to this state is simply travelling through what is probably the most colourful region of India. Rajasthanis adorn themselves in garments of the most astonishingly vibrant colours. Villagers bedeck themselves in chunky and elaborate silver jewellery.

Jaipur

You could easily spend several days in Jaipur itself: arts and crafts from around Rajasthan are assembled in the emporiums of the capital city, and it's a great place to shop. When you've exhausted yourself shopping, a refreshing drink at the luxurious Rambagh Palace hotel's Polo Bar is a perfect way to revive yourself. You could then stroll to the adjacent polo grounds and watch a game of horse polo (during certain times of the winter months), or wander through the artisans' quarters of the old city and watch master craftspeople at work.

In Sanganer, a small village near Jaipur, you can see vast lengths of colourful fabric drying on the riverbanks, or watch yards of it unfurl as it is held at either end by women from the printing and dyeing communities. One of the state's most stunning *baoris* (stepwells) can be seen at Abhaneri, about 95km from Jaipur.

Eastern Rajasthan

Eastern Rajasthan has the state's most important and notable wildlife sanctuaries. Tigers are the attraction at Ranthambhore and Sariska, but even if you miss out on seeing these elusive big cats, you are virtually guaranteed sightings of other large mammals such as chinkaras, sambars, nilgai and wild boars. At Keoladeo Ghana National Park near Bharatpur, you can view at close hand thousands of birds from hundreds of different species in an idyllic wetland setting.

The holy town of Pushkar, also in eastern Rajasthan boasts a beautiful location, with tiny whitewashed buildings and temples along the shore of a small, perfectly round lake. A diminutive hill, with a little temple perched on top of it, serves as a backdrop. The main bazaar is chockablock with shops selling brightly coloured clothes in western styles, funky costume jewellery and various artefacts. There are lots of salubrious places to eat (but no alcohol – this is a holy town), some fantastic second-hand bookshops, and in the evening you can sit on the verandah of your guesthouse, looking out over the lake and listen to the resounding rhythm of drums, beaten by priests to herald the close of the day. In November, Pushkar hosts its annual Camel Fair, and thousands of Rajasthanis throng to the town to trade camels and other livestock.

Alwar and Deeg, also both in eastern Rajasthan, have striking palaces which are not often visited by tourists.

Southern Rajasthan

Udaipur may well be the most romantic city in Rajasthan, if not all of India. Graceful palaces, temples and *havelis* flank the shores of Lake Pichola, in the centre of which is Jagmandir Island and the awesome Lake Palace Hotel, a vision in white. Even if you aren't able to stay at the Lake Palace, there are numerous budget and mid-range guesthouses right on the lake shore which offer superlative views out across the water.

Despite its massive size and historic importance, few travellers make their way to Chittorgarh. Many Rajasthanis consider that the fort at Chittorgarh epitomises the essence of Rajput bravery.

Southern Rajasthan is home to the state's only hill station, Mt Abu. Situated along a 1200m-high plateau, this hill station has the impressive Dilwara Temples, an important

Jain pilgrimage centre. Another beautiful Jain temple can be found at Ranakpur, also in southern Rajasthan, which has 1444 exquisite pillars, no two of which are alike. If you want to step back in time, you can visit Bundi, with its medieval ambience and ramshackle fort complex.

Northern Rajasthan

The remote Shekhawati region of northern Rajasthan is a feast of colour. Here, scores of *havelis* feature paintings on both the internal and external walls. The havelis were built by rich merchants who spared no expense constructing elaborate homes as symbols of their elevated financial and social status. The paintings represent an extraordinary cultural tapestry, recording for posterity the inventions of the day, such as steam locomotives and treadle sewing machines.

Western Rajasthan

Jaisalmer is a travellers' favourite. Its massive fort rises like an apparition after the long bus or train journey across the dead flat desert. Contained within its walls are dozens of cobblestone-lined alleyways concealing temples and bazaars. Up on the ramparts enormous stone balls are perched, once deadly missiles which were pushed down onto the heads of invading enemies. Jaisalmer has dozens of great budget places to stay, plenty of good restaurants and desert panoramas to take your breath away.

The Sam sand dunes, 42km from Jaisalmer, are where even the most jaded seen-it-all traveller will find it hard to resist playing Lawrence of Arabia. Visions of caparisoned camels and their drivers silhouetted against the sun might verge on the clichéd, but this is in fact what you'll see here. Despite the undeniable tourist hype, it is a strangely evocative experience, with musicians playing as the sun sets over the Thar Desert.

Jodhpur's fort is another grand edifice in stone testifying to the warrior spirit of the Rajputs. It's a massive, cannon-ball-pocked monolith which affords brilliant views over the city from its battlements, and its museum houses one of the most fabulous collections of artefacts dating from the days of the maharajas.

Bikaner is a bustling and chaotic desert city. The main attraction here is the city's fine fort, but you can also lose yourself for hours in the labyrinthine streets of the old city, or take a day trip to the Karni Mata Temple at Deshnok. Just when you thought you'd got a handle on Hinduism, this temple will leave you perplexed again, for here, thousands of rats are revered as the incarnate souls of dead storytellers!

Camel & Horse Safaris

If you want the ultimate desert experience you're a perfect candidate for a camel safari. They're possible around Jaisalmer, Bikaner and Pushkar, or in the Shekhawati region. You can also take extended horse safaris in southern Rajasthan. For information, see Activities in this chapter, or the relevant sections in individual chapters.

SUGGESTED ITINERARIES

Although Rajasthan's places of interest are scattered over a vast geographical area, a good rail network means that you can cover large distances very efficiently, and visit many sites in just a few weeks.

Many first-time visitors to India make the mistake of cramming too much into their itinerary, leaving them frazzled at the end of their trip. Take a few days out for serious rest and relaxation; maybe treat yourself to a sojourn at one of the royal abodes off the beaten track, which have been converted into atmospheric hotels. These places are a world away from the hustle and bustle and also offer you a taste of rural life.

Rajasthan's most important sites include Jaipur, the historic fort of Chittorgarh, romantic Udaipur, Ranthambhore National Park, the desert city of Jaisalmer, bustling Jodhpur, and Bharatpur, home of the Keoladeo Ghana National Park. In two weeks or more you could take in all of these, as well as Agra with its Taj Mahal in neighbouring Uttar Pradesh state (see the Agra chapter). A short camel trek in the environs of Jaisalmer, or a visit to the holy town of

Pushkar, or the beautiful palaces of Deeg or Alwar, en route back to Delhi, might also be possible.

In three to four weeks, you could visit all the above places and take in the Shekhawati region of northern Rajasthan, with its magnificent painted havelis, or mansions, as well as the desert city of Bikaner, which has a stunning fort. Bird lovers should stop at Khichan, between Jodhpur and Jaisalmer, to witness the spectacular sight of thousands of demoiselle cranes descending on the fields around this village to feed on grain distributed by villagers.

In four to five weeks you could enjoy an extended camel trek in the environs of Jaisalmer, Bikaner, Pushkar or Shekhawati, a horse safari in southern Rajasthan, and go to Rajasthan's only hill station, Mt Abu, worth visiting especially for its exquisite Jain temples.

PLANNING
When to Go
The best time to visit Rajasthan is in the winter months (December to February), when the days are warm and sunny with average temperatures across the state around 25°C, and the nights are cool. However, hotel prices are at a premium in winter. The days begin to heat up in March, but are generally still quite pleasant. The post-monsoon season, from mid-September to the end of November, is reasonably pleasant, if a little warm, with average maximum temperatures in October around 35°C and an average minimum of around 20°C.

The winter season corresponds with some of Rajasthan's most colourful festivals, such as the Desert Festival in Jaisalmer, the Camel Festival at Bikaner and the Nagaur Cattle Fair. In late February/early March, there's Holi, India's most exuberant festival. Rajasthan's own Gangaur festival is celebrated in March/April, as is Udaipur's Mewar Festival and Jaipur's Elephant Festival. The famous Pushkar Camel Fair takes place in November.

Winter is also a good time to visit Rajasthan's best known wildlife sanctuaries, Keoladeo Ghana National Park, Ranthambhore National Park and Sariska Tiger Reserve & National Park (see National Parks & Sanctuaries in the Facts about Rajasthan chapter, and the Eastern Rajasthan chapter).

Maps
The Discover India Series has a very good map of Rajasthan at a scale of 1:1,200,000, clearly showing rail routes, major highways and roads. Lonely Planet's *India & Bangladesh Travel Atlas* is a handy reference to the entire Indian subcontinent. Its coverage of Rajasthan is excellent, with symbols clearly showing sites of ancient forts, national parks and sanctuaries and other sites of interest.

Many of the tourist offices in Rajasthan sell a good map (Rs 2) of the town in which they are located.

What to Bring
The usual travellers' rule applies – bring as little as possible. It's much better to have to buy something you've left behind than find you have too much and need to get rid of it.

Clothes Light, cool cotton clothes are the best bet for day wear, with a light sweater or pullover for nights which can get surprisingly chilly, especially in the winter months. In some centres, such as Jaipur, Pushkar and Udaipur, western-style clothes can be purchased off the peg at ridiculously low prices, or you can have clothes made to measure in the small tailor shops found in all but the tiniest villages.

Modesty rates highly in India, as in most Asian countries. Although men wearing shorts is accepted as a western eccentricity, they should be a decent length. Unless women want to draw (even greater than usual) attention to themselves, they shouldn't wear shorts or sleeveless tops (see the section on Women Travellers later). A reasonable clothes list would include:

• underwear and swimming gear
• one pair of cotton trousers
• one pair of shorts (men only)
• one long (ankle-length) cotton skirt

- a few T-shirts or lightweight shirts
- a sweater for cold Rajasthani winter nights
- one pair of sneakers or shoes plus socks
- sandals
- thongs (handy to wear when showering in common bathrooms)
- a set of 'dress up' clothes (for dining at the Lake Palace in Udaipur!)
- a straw or cotton hat and sunglasses

Bedding A sleeping bag can be a hassle to carry, but can serve as something to sleep in (also avoiding unsavoury looking hotel bedding), a cushion on hard train seats, a pillow on long bus journeys or a bed top-cover (since cheaper hotels rarely give you one). If you're planning a camel safari, a sleeping bag can come in very handy. If you're sleeping out on the dunes, it can get surprisingly chilly, and the blankets provided on the safaris are rarely warm enough.

A sheet sleeping bag can be very useful, particularly on overnight train trips or if you don't trust the hotel's sheets. Mosquito nets in hotels are rare, so your own sheet or sheet sleeping bag will also help to keep mosquitoes at bay.

Some travellers find that a plastic sheet is useful for a number of reasons, including to bedbug-proof unhealthy-looking beds. Others have recommended an inflatable pillow.

Toiletries Soap, toothpaste and other toiletries are readily available, although hair conditioner often comes in the 'shampoo and conditioner in one' format, so if you don't use this stuff, bring your own conditioner. Astringent is useful for cleaning away the grime at the end of the day. A nailbrush can be extremely useful. Tampons are not readily available in Rajasthan, so bring a supply. Sanitary pads are widely available in larger towns and cities. Bring condoms with you, as the quality of locally made condoms may be suspect.

High-factor sunscreen cream is more widely available, but it's *expensive*! Lip balm is especially useful in the desert regions, where the sun can really pack a punch. Moisture-impregnated disposable tissues are great for your hands and face.

Men can safely leave their shaving gear at home. One of the pleasures of Indian travel is a shave in a barber's shop every few days. With HIV/AIDS becoming more widespread in India, however, choose a barber's shop that looks clean, and make sure that a fresh blade is used. For just a few rupees you'll get the full treatment – lathering, followed by a shave, then the process is repeated, and finally there's the hot, damp towel and sometimes talcum powder. You may also get an invigorating scalp massage thrown in.

Miscellaneous Items For budget travellers, a good padlock is a virtual necessity. Most cheap hotels and quite a number of mid-range places have doors locked by a flimsy latch and padlock. You'll find having your own sturdy lock on the door does wonders for your peace of mind.

A knife (preferably Swiss Army) has a whole range of uses, and can be particularly good for peeling fruit. Some travellers rhapsodise about the usefulness of a miniature electric element to boil water in a cup. A sarong is a handy item – it can be used as a bed sheet, an item of clothing, an emergency towel, and a pillow on trains!

Also handy is insect repellent, a box of mosquito coils or an electric mosquito zapper – you can buy them in most places for about Rs 70; try any medical store. A mosquito net can be very useful, although setting it up might be a problem if it doesn't have its own supports (in which case bring tape with you). Power cuts are not uncommon in Rajasthan ('load shedding' as it is euphemistically known) and there's little street lighting at night so a torch (flashlight) and candles are recommended. A voltage stabiliser is a good idea for travellers bringing sensitive electronic equipment.

Bring along a spare set of specs and your spectacle prescription. If you wear contact lenses, bring enough solution to last your trip. Earplugs are useful for light sleepers, and even heavy sleepers can have difficulty shutting out the din in some hotels. Eye shades can also be handy.

Even in Rajasthan's winter, the sun can really knock you out, so bring plenty of sunscreen and a pair of sunglasses, and use a sun hat. A water bottle should always be by your side, especially in the warmer months (some travellers bring a thermos to keep water cold); and also, if you're not drinking bottled water, have water purification tablets (which also reduces the amount of plastic bottles seen on dumps around India).

A universal sink plug is worth having since few cheaper hotels have plugs. String is very useful as a makeshift clothes line – double-strand nylon is good to secure your clothes if you have no pegs (you can buy small, inexpensive sachets of washing powder almost everywhere). Women should consider bringing a lingerie bag if they intend handing over delicate underclothes for washing, as they can cop quite a battering by both *dhobis* (washerpeople) and laundries at hotels (even five-star ones). It's not only annoying to see that expensive bra ruined, but it's also difficult to buy good quality bras in Rajasthan.

A pair of binoculars may be worth bringing along if you plan to do a lot of birdwatching or wildlife spotting.

Some travellers bring a heavy-duty chain to secure their pack to the luggage racks of trains and buses. Some women carry a high-pitched whistle which may act as a deterrent to would-be assailants.

See the Health section later, for details about medical supplies.

RESPONSIBLE TOURISM

Common sense and courtesy go a long way when you are travelling. Think about the impact you may be having on the environment and on the local people.

If you go on a camel safari, please ensure that you keep any rubbish with you, rather than leaving it to be swept across the desert. Encourage tour operators to do the same.

One way to minimise your impact is to reduce the amount of plastic you use. Buy terracotta cups at train stations rather than the plastic ones; recycle plastic bags; try to recycle plastic drinking bottles – or bring

water purification tablets/solution. Discarded plastic bags are a very serious problem, especially in the cities. These bags are eaten by cows and other creatures, resulting in a slow and painful death.

Avoid buying products that further endanger threatened species and habitats (see under Flora & Fauna in the Facts about Rajasthan chapter). Note that it is illegal to export ivory products or any artefact made from wild animals.

TOURIST OFFICES
Local Tourist Offices

There are Rajasthan Tourism Development Corporation (RTDC) tourist offices (often called Tourist Reception Centres) in most of the places of interest to visitors in Rajasthan, including offices at Jaipur, Ajmer, Alwar, Amber, Bharatpur, Bikaner, Bundi, Chittorgarh, Jaisalmer, Jhunjhunu, Jodhpur, Kota, Mt Abu, Sawai Madhopur and Udaipur. They range from the extraordinarily helpful to the fairly useless. However, you can usually pick up glossy brochures and maps at even the most inefficient of them.

Addresses and further details are given in relevant sections throughout this book. In addition, there are several Rajasthan tourist offices in other Indian cities, including:

Ahmedabad
 (☎ 079-656 0151)
 Rath Hotels & Travels Ltd, 201 Shikhar Complex, Shrimali Society, Navrangpura
Calcutta
 (☎ 033-279740, fax 279051)
 1st Floor Commerce House,
 2 Ganesh Chandra Ave
Chennai (Madras)
 (☎ 044-827 2093)
 28 Commander-in-Chief Rd
Delhi
 (☎ 011-338 3837, fax 338 2823)
 Tourist Reception Centre, Bikaner House, Pandara Rd, New Delhi
Mumbai (Bombay)
 (☎ 022-207 4162, fax 207 5603)
 230 Dr DN Rd

There is a Government of India tourist office in Jaipur (see Information in the Jaipur chapter). The Department of Tourism has a Web site at www.tourisminindia.com.

Government of India tourist offices in the two major international gateways to India used by travellers to Rajasthan are:

Delhi
(☎ 011-332 0008)
88 Janpath, New Delhi
Mumbai (Bombay)
(☎ 022-203 3144, fax 201 4496)
123 Maharshi Karve Rd, Churchgate

Tourist Offices Abroad

The Government of India Department of Tourism maintains a string of tourist offices in other countries where you can get brochures and leaflets which often have high quality information about India so are worth getting. However, some of these foreign offices are not always as useful as those within India. There are also smaller 'promotion offices' in Japan at Osaka and in the USA at Dallas, Miami, San Francisco and Washington DC.

Australia
(☎ 02-9264 4855, fax 9264 4860,
email info@india.com.au)
Level 2, Picadilly, 210 Pitt St,
Sydney NSW 2000
Canada
(☎ 416-962 3787, fax 962 6279)
60 Bloor St West, Suite No 1003, Toronto,
Ontario M4W 3B8
France
(☎ 01 452 33045, fax 452 33345,
email info.fr@india-tourism.com)
8 Blvd de la Madeleine, 75008 Paris
Germany
(☎ 069-242 9490, fax 2429 4977,
email info@india-tourism.com)
Baseler Strasse 48, 60329 Frankfurt-am-Main
Italy
(☎ 02-805 3506, fax 7202 1681,
email info.it@india-tourism.com)
Via Albricci 9, 20122 Milan
Malaysia
(☎ 03-242 5285, fax 242 5301)
Wisma HLA, Lot 203 Jalan Raja Chulan,
50200 Kuala Lumpur
The Netherlands
(☎ 020-620 8991, fax 638 3059,
email info.nl@india-tourism.com)
Rokin 9-15, 1012 KK Amsterdam

Singapore
(☎ 0065-235 3800, fax 235 8677)
United House, 20 Kramat Lane,
Singapore 0922
Sweden
(☎ 08-215081, fax 210186,
email info.se@india-tourism.com)
Sveavagen 9-11, S-III 57, Stockholm 11157
Thailand
(☎ 02-235 2585, fax 236 8411)
KFC Bldg, 3rd floor, 62/5 Thaniya Rd,
Bangkok 10500
UK
(☎ 0171-437 3677, fax 494 1048 (after April
2000 ☎ 020-7437 3677, fax 7494 1048), 24
hour brochure line ☎ 01233-211999)
7 Cork St, London W1X 2LN
USA
(☎ 212 586 4901, fax 301 44 04,
www.tourindia.com)
1270 Avenue of the Americas, Suite 1808,
New York, NY 10020
(☎ 213-380 8855, fax 380 6111)
3550 Wilshire Blvd, Suite 204, Los Angeles
CA 90010

VISAS & DOCUMENTS
Passport
You must have a passport with you all the time. Ensure that it will be valid for the entire period you intend to remain overseas. If your passport is lost or stolen, immediately contact your country's representative (see Embassies & Consulates later).

Visas
Six-month, multiple-entry visas are now issued to most nationals regardless of whether they intend staying that long or re-entering the country. Note that the visa is valid from the date of issue. This means that if you enter India five months after the visa was issued, it will be valid only for one month, not the full six months.

Visas currently cost A\$55 for Australians, UK£19 for Britons, and 200FF for French passport holders. US passport holders may also apply for one-year and 10-year multiple-entry visas, the latter are only available from Indian embassies in the US, Japan and Hong Kong. For US citizens, a six/12 month multiple-entry visa costs US\$50/70, a 10 year multiple entry visa costs US\$120 and a transit visa costs US$25. Passport and visa forms for US citizens are available online from the San Francisco consulate via its Web site www.indianconsulate-sf.org. If you prefer to get your visa en route to India you can pick it up in the following countries:

Pakistan
The high commission in Islamabad is quite efficient, although if there is an Indian embassy in your home country they may have to fax there to check that you are not wanted by the police or in some other way undesirable. The process takes a few days, and of course you have to pay for the fax.
Sri Lanka
The Indian High Commission in Colombo or the Assistant High Commission in Kandy will also make you pay for a fax as well as the visa.
Thailand
It takes four working days for non-Thai nationals to obtain an Indian visa.
Nepal
The Indian embassy in Kathmandu is open Monday to Friday from 9 am to 1 pm and 1.30 to 5.30 pm; visa applications are accepted Monday to Friday from 9.30 am to 12.30 pm and visas are available for collection between 4.45 and 5.30 pm – allow at least seven days for processing.

Visa Extensions Fifteen-day extensions are available from Foreigners' Registration offices in the main Indian cities. You can only get another six months by leaving the country. Some travellers have reported difficulty getting another visa in Nepal.

In Rajasthan, the Foreigners' Registration office (☎ 0141-669391) is located in Jaipur, at the end of the road directly opposite the main entrance to the City Palace Museum. This office is open on weekdays from 10 am to 1.30 pm and 2 to 5 pm.

In Mumbai the Foreigners' Registration Office (☎ 022-262 0111 ext 266) is in Annexe Bldg No 2, CID, 3rd floor, Sayed Badruddin Rd, near the Police Commissioner's Office.

In Delhi, Hans Bhavan, near the Tilak Bridge train station, is where you'll find the Foreigners' Regional Registration Office

(☎ 011-331 9781). The office is open weekdays from 9.30 am to 1.30 pm and 2 to 4 pm.

Onward Tickets

Many Indian embassies and consulates will not issue a visa to enter India unless you hold an onward ticket – sufficient evidence that you intend to leave the country.

Restricted Areas

Due to the hostilities between India and Pakistan, foreigners are prohibited from approaching within 50km of the Indo-Pakistan border. Special permission is required from the Collector's office (☎ 02992-52201) in Jaisalmer to travel to most of Rajasthan west of National Highway No 15, due to its proximity to the Pakistan border, and is only issued in exceptional circumstances. The only places exempted are Amar Sagar, Bada Bagh, Lodhruva, Kuldhara, Akal, Sam, Ramkund, Khuri and Mool Sagar.

Permission is required from the District Magistrate or Superintendent of Police in Barmer to travel to the Kiradu temple complex, about 35km from Barmer near the Pakistan border.

Travel Insurance

A travel insurance policy to cover theft, loss and medical problems is a good idea. Some policies offer lower and higher medical-expense options; the higher ones are chiefly for countries such as the USA, which have high medical costs.

There is a wide variety of policies available, so check the small print. Some specifically exclude 'dangerous activities', which can include scuba diving, motorcycling, or even trekking. A locally acquired motorcycle licence is not valid under some policies. You may prefer a policy which pays doctors or hospitals directly rather than you having to pay on the spot and claim later. If you have to claim later make sure you keep all documentation. Some policies ask you to call back (reverse charges) to a centre in your home country where an immediate assessment of your problem is made. Check that the policy covers ambulances and an emergency flight home.

Driving Licence & Permits

If you are planning to drive in India, get an International Driving Licence from your national motoring organisation. In some centres, such as Delhi, it's possible to hire motorcycles. An International Licence can also be used for other identification purposes, such as bicycle hire.

Other Documents

A health certificate, while not necessary in India, may well be required for onward travel. Student cards are virtually useless these days – many student concessions have either been eliminated or replaced by 'youth fares' or similar age concessions. Similarly, a Youth Hostel (Hostelling International – HI) card is not generally required for India's many hostels, but you do pay slightly less at official youth hostels if you have one.

It's worth having a batch of passport photos for visa applications and for obtaining permits to remote regions. If you run out, Indian photo studios will do excellent portraits at pleasantly low prices.

Photocopies

All important documents (passport data page and visa page, credit cards, travel insurance policy, air/bus/train tickets, driving licence etc) should be photocopied before you leave home. Leave one copy with someone at home and keep another with you, separate from the originals.

EMBASSIES & CONSULATES
Indian Embassies Abroad

India's embassies, consulates and high commissions abroad include the following (unless stated otherwise addresses are for embassies).

Australia
  High Commission
  (☎ 02-6273 3999, fax 6273 1308,
  email hicanb@ozemail.com.au)
  3-5 Moonah Place, Yarralumla, ACT 2600

Bangladesh
  High Commission
  (☎ 02-503606, fax 863662,
  email hcindia@bangla.net)
  120 Road 2, Dhamondi, Residential Area,
  Dhaka
Belgium
  (☎ 02-640 9802, fax 648 9638,
  email eoibru@skynet.be)
  217 Chaussee de Vleurgat, 1050 Brussels
Bhutan
  (☎ 09752-22162, fax 23195)
  India House Estate, Thimpu
Canada
  High Commission
  (☎ 613-744 3751, fax 744 0913,
  email hicmind@ottawa.net)
  10 Springfield Rd, Ottawa,
  Ontario K1M 1C9
China
  (☎ 01-532 1908, fax 532 4684,
  email indebch@ublic3.bta.net.cn)
  1 Ri Tan Dong Lu, Beijing, 100 600
Denmark
  (☎ 045-3118 2888, fax 3927 0218,
  email indemb@euroconnect.dk)
  Vangehusvej 15, 2100 Copenhagen
France
  (☎ 01 40 50 70 70, fax 01 40 50 09 96,
  email culture@indembparis.zee.net)
  15 rue Alfred Dehodencq, 75016 Paris
Germany
  (☎ 228-54050, fax 540 5153,
  email info-indembassy@csm.de)
  Adenauerallee 262-264, 53113 Bonn 1 & 11
  (☎ 30-800178, fax 482 7034,
  email 106071.2115@compuserve.com)
  Majakowskiring 55, 13156 Berlin
Ireland
  (☎ 01-497 0483, fax 497 8074,
  email eoidublin@indigo.ie)
  6 Leeson Park, Dublin 6
Israel
  (☎ 03-510 1431, fax 510 1434,
  email indembtel@netvision.net.il)
  4 Kaufman St, Sharbat House,
  Tel Aviv 68012
Italy
  (☎ 06-488 4642, fax 481 9539,
  email ind.emb@flashnet.it)
  Via XX Settembre 5, 00187 Rome
Japan
  (☎ 03-3262 2391, fax 3234 4866,
  email indembjp@gol.com)
  2-2-11 Kudan Minami, Chiyoda-ku,
  Tokyo 102

Myanmar (Burma)
(☎ 01-282550, fax 289562,
email amb.indembygn@mtpt400.stems.com)
545-7 Merchant St, Yangon (Rangoon)
Nepal
(☎ 071-410900, fax 413132,
email indemb@mos.com.np)
Lain Chaur, PO Box 92, Kathmandu
The Netherlands
(☎ 070-346 9771, fax 361 7072,
email fscom@indemb.nl)
Buitenrustweg 2, 2517 KD, The Hague
New Zealand
High Commission
(☎ 04-473 6390, fax 499 0665,
email hicomind@globe.co.nz)
180 Molesworth St, Wellington
Pakistan
High Commission
(☎ 051-814371, fax 820742,
email hicomind@isb.compol.com)
G5 Diplomatic Enclave, Islamabad
Sri Lanka
High Commission
(☎ 01-421605, fax 446403,
email hicomind@sri.lanka.net)
36-8 Galle Rd, Colombo 3
Thailand
(☎ 02-258 0300, fax 258 4627,
email indiaemb@mozart.inet.co.th)
46 Soi 23 (Prasarnmitr), Sukhumvit Rd,
Bangkok
UK
High Commission
(☎ 0171-836 8484, fax 836 4331 (after April
2000 ☎ 020-7836 8484, fax 7836 4331),
email mailsoction@hicommind.domon.co.uk)
India House, Aldwych, London WC2B 4NA
USA
(☎ 202-939 7000, fax 939 7027,
email indembwash@indiagov.org)
2107 Massachusetts Ave NW,
Washington, DC 20008

Embassies & Consulates in India

Most foreign diplomatic missions are in the
nation's capital, Delhi, but there are also
quite a few consulates in the other major
cities of Mumbai, Calcutta and Chennai
(Madras). As a tourist, it's important to re-
alise what the embassy of the country of
which you are a citizen can and can't do.
Generally speaking, it won't be much help
in emergencies if the trouble you're in is remotely your own fault.

Remember that you are bound by the
laws of the country you are in. Your embassy will not be sympathetic if you end up
in jail after committing a crime locally,
even if such actions are legal in your own
country. In genuine emergencies you might
get some assistance, but only if other channels have been exhausted. For example if
you need to get home urgently, a free ticket
home is exceedingly unlikely – the embassy would expect you to have insurance.
If you have all your money and documents
stolen, it might assist with getting a new
passport, but a loan for onward travel is out
of the question. Embassies used to keep letters for travellers or had a small reading
room with home newspapers, but these
days the mail holding service has been
stopped and newspapers tend to be out of
date.

Unless stated otherwise the following are
embassies in Delhi (the area code for Delhi
is 011):

Australia
(☎ 688 8223, fax 687 4126)
1/50-G Shantipath, Chanakyapuri
Bangladesh
(☎ 683 4668, fax 683 9237)
56 Ring Rd, Lajpat Nagar III
Belgium
(☎ 688 9204, fax 688 5821)
50-N Shantipath, Chanakyapuri
Bhutan
(☎ 688 9807, fax 687 6710)
Chandragupta Marg, Chanakyapuri
Canada
(☎ 687 6500, fax 687 6579)
7/8 Shantipath, Chanakyapuri
China
(☎ 687 1585, fax 688 5486)
50-D Shantipath, Chanakyapuri
Denmark
(☎ 301 0900, fax 379 2019)
11 Aurangzeb Rd
France
(☎ 611 8790, fax 687 2305)
2/50-E Shantipath, Chanakyapuri
Germany
(☎ 687 1831, fax 687 3117)
6/50-G Shantipath, Chanakyapuri
Ireland
(☎ 462 6733, fax 469 7053)
13 Jor Bagh Rd

Israel
(☎ 301 3238, fax 301 4298)
3 Aurangzeb Rd
Italy
(☎ 611 4355, fax 687 3889)
50-E Chandragupta Marg, Chanakyapuri
Japan
(☎ 687 6581, fax 688 5587)
4-5/50-G Shantipath, Chanakyapuri
Myanmar (Burma)
(☎ 688 9007, fax 687 7942)
3/50-F Nyaya Marg, Chanakyapuri
Nepal
(☎ 332 9969, fax 332 6857)
Barakhamba Rd
(☎ 479 1117/1224, fax 479 1410)
1 National Library Ave, Calcutta
The Netherlands
(☎ 688 4951, fax 688 4956)
6/50-F Shantipath, Chanakyapuri
New Zealand
(☎ 688 3170, fax 687 2317)
50-N Nyaya Marg, Chanakyapuri
Pakistan
(☎ 600603, fax 637 2339)
2/50-G Shantipath, Chanakyapuri
Spain
(☎ 379 2085, fax 379 3375)
12 Prithviraj Rd
Sweden
(☎ 687 5760, fax 688 5401)
Nyaya Marg, Chanakyapuri
Switzerland
(☎ 687 8372, fax 687 3093)
Nyaya Marg, Chanakyapuri
UK
(☎ 687 2161, fax 687 2882)
50 Shantipath, Chanakyapuri
USA
(☎ 688 9033, 611 3033, fax 419 0017)
Shantipath, Chanakyapuri

CUSTOMS

The usual duty-free regulations apply for India; that is, 1L bottle of spirits and 200 cigarettes.

You're allowed to bring in all sorts of western technological wonders, but big items, such as videos, are likely to be entered on a 'Tourist Baggage Re-Export' form to ensure you take them out again. This used to be the case with laptop computers, but some travellers say this is no longer necessary. You don't have to declare still cameras, even if you have more than one.

Note that if you are entering India from Nepal you are not entitled to import anything free of duty.

MONEY
Currency

The rupee (Rs) is divided into 100 paise (p). There are coins of 5, 10, 20, 25 and 50 paise, and Rs 1, 2 and 5, and Rs 10, 20, 50, 100 and 500 notes.

In 1996, the Reserve Bank of India decided to stop printing Rs 1, 2 and 5 notes. There are plans to start printing a Rs 1000 note.

You are not allowed to bring Indian currency into or out of the country. You are allowed to bring in unlimited amounts of foreign currency or travellers cheques, but you are supposed to declare anything over US$1000 on arrival.

One of the most annoying things about India is that no one ever seems to have any change, and you'll be left waiting while a shopkeeper hawks your Rs 100 note around

Banknotes

Indian currency notes circulate far longer than in the west and the small notes in particular become very tatty – some should carry a government health warning! A note can have holes right through it (most do in fact, as they are bundled together with staples when new) and be quite acceptable but if it's slightly torn at the top or bottom on the crease line then it's no good and you'll have trouble spending it. Even a missing corner makes a bill unacceptable. The answer to this is to check your change carefully – often the tear can be cleverly concealed beneath a judiciously placed thumb – or simply accept it philosophically or think of clever uses for it. Use damaged notes for official purposes. Some banks have special counters where torn notes will be exchanged for good ones, but who wants to visit banks more than necessary?

other shops. It's a good idea to keep small change handy.

When changing money pay attention to the bills you are getting. Don't accept any ripped ones (staple holes are OK). Also Rs 10 can look very similar to Rs 50. Take your time and check each note even if the wad appears to have been stapled together.

Exchange Rates

To find out the latest exchange rates, visit the Web site www.oanda.com or ask at a bank.

country	unit		rupee
Australia	A$1	=	28.55
Canada	C$1	=	29.48
euro	€1	=	45.25
France	10FF	=	69.00
Germany	DM1	=	23.14
Ireland	IR£1	=	57.44
Israel	ILS1	=	10.51
Japan	¥100	=	36.28
Nepal	10 Nep Rs	=	6.36
Netherlands	f1	=	24.23
New Zealand	NZ$1	=	23.26
UK	UK£1	=	69.10
USA	US$1	=	43.07

Exchanging Money

Outside Rajasthan's main cities, the State Bank of India is usually the place to change money, although you may well be directed to another bank, such as the State Bank of Bikaner & Jaipur or the Bank of Baroda. In the more remote regions (such as parts of Shekhawati), few banks offer exchange facilities, so use the banks in the main tourist centres before heading out into the desert – although you'll have no trouble changing money at Bikaner or Jaisalmer.

Some banks charge an encashment fee, which may be levied for the entire transaction, or on each cheque. Find out how much the bank is going to charge to exchange your cheques before you sign them. Travellers cheques are much more widely accepted than currency.

The wait at most banks can be painstakingly long and the staff brusque.

Cash In Delhi and other gateway cities you can change most foreign currencies – Australian dollars, Deutschmarks, yen or whatever – but in Rajasthan it's best to stick with US dollars or pounds sterling. It pays to have some US$ or UK£ in cash for times when you can't change travellers cheques or use a credit card.

Travellers Cheques All major brands are accepted in India, with American Express and Thomas Cook being the most widely traded. Pounds sterling and US$ are the safest bet; Yen, DM and A$ can be changed in main cities, but not in out-of-the-way places. Not all places take all brands – so it pays to carry more than one type. Charges for changing travellers cheques vary from place to place and bank to bank.

A few simple measures should be taken to facilitate the replacement of travellers cheques, should they be stolen. See Stolen Travellers Cheques in the Dangers & Annoyances section later in this chapter.

Automatic Teller Machines (ATMs) Mumbai, Delhi, plus a limited (but growing) number of smaller centres have ATMs. Any card with a PLUS or CIRRUS symbol is accepted at the following banks' ATMs: Citibank, Hong Kong & Shanghai Bank, ANZ Grindlays and Standard & Chartered.

Credit Cards Credit cards are accepted in most major tourist centres, such as Jaipur and Udaipur, but don't expect to be able to use a card in budget hotels and restaurants.

MasterCard and Visa are the most widely accepted cards, and it might pay to bring both with you. With MasterCard, Japanese Credit Bureau or Visa cards you can obtain cash rupees in Jaipur on the spot. Some other major towns in Rajasthan also issue cash advances on major credit cards. Cash advances on credit cards can be made at Thomas Cook, Bank of Baroda or the Central Bank of India at the Ashok Hotel in Delhi. (It is possible to get US$ from credit cards, debit cards, travellers cheques or money transfers.) Citibank account holders can access their accounts directly with their Citibank card. Bank of America account holders can do the same with their Verateller card and a cheque book. Amex will give a rupee advance on an Amex card.

International Transfers If you run out of money in India, you can have some transferred in no time at all via Thomas Cook's Moneygram service (charges are relatively high as it's only considered an emergency service) or Western Union (via Sita Travels ☎ 011-331 1122, F-12 Connaught Place, Delhi, or DHL).

If you are transferring sums of less than US$1000, Western Union is cheaper than Thomas Cook. Bring your passport when you come to pick up your money.

Black Market The rupee is a fully convertible currency; that is, the rate is set by the market not the government. For this reason there's not much of a black market, although you can get a couple of rupees more for your dollars or pounds cash. In the major tourist centres you will receive constant offers to change money. There's little risk involved (providing you check on the spot that you have received the agreed amount) although it is officially illegal.

Moneychangers Moneychangers are found in quite a few places in Rajasthan and usually open for longer hours than the banks. Their main advantage is their convenience. Of course a caveat applies: always check the bank rates first, and check carefully the money you are given. Never accept very worn or dirty notes.

Encashment Certificates All money is supposed to be changed at official banks or moneychangers, and you are supposed to be given an encashment certificate for each transaction. Some people surreptitiously bring rupees into the country with them – they can be bought at a discount in places such as Singapore or Bangkok. Indian rupees can be brought in openly from Nepal and you can get a slightly better rate there.

Banks will usually give you an encashment certificate, but occasionally they don't bother. It is worth getting them, especially if you want to change excess rupees back into hard currency when you leave India.

The other reason for saving encashment certificates is that if you stay in India longer than four months, you officially have to get an income tax clearance.

Security

The safest place for your money and your passport is next to your skin, either in a money belt around your waist or in a pouch under your shirt or T-shirt. Never, ever carry these things in your luggage. You are also asking for trouble if you walk around with your valuables in a shoulder bag. Bum bags have become quite popular, but be aware that this is advertising that you have something of value on your person; this could make you a target for a mugging. Never leave your valuable documents and travellers cheques in your hotel room. If the hotel is a reputable one, you should be able to use the hotel safe. It is wise to peel off a few hundred dollars and keep them stashed away separately, just in case.

Costs

Whatever budget you decide to travel on, you can be assured that you'll be getting a whole lot more for your money than in most other countries – Rajasthan is great value.

If you stay in luxurious converted forts and palaces, fly between the main cities of Rajasthan, and spend up big in the emporiums in Jaipur, you can spend a lot of money.

At the other extreme, if you stay in dormitories or the cheapest hotels, travel in public buses, and learn to exist on *dhal* (curried lentils) and rice, it is possible to see Rajasthan on about US$7 a day.

Most travellers will probably be looking for something between these extremes. If so, for US$15 to US$25 a day on average, you'll stay in reasonable hotels, eat in regular restaurants but occasionally splash out on a fancy meal, and take auto-rickshaws rather than a bus.

Entry Charges

Most places of interest in Rajasthan (eg museums, monuments) have an entry fee and most levy a charge for still cameras and video cameras. Many places have a lower charge for Indians (residents of India) than for foreigners. In this book the rates for foreigners and Indians are provided separately, where they exist.

In case you're wondering, nonresident Indians (NRIs) are officially meant to be charged the foreigners' rate, although many escape detection and are charged the cheaper residents' rate – quite by accident, of course!

Tipping & Bargaining

In tourist restaurants or hotels, where service is often tacked on anyway, the 10% figure usually applies. In smaller places, where tipping is optional, you need only tip a few rupees, not a percentage of the bill. Hotel porters expect Rs 5 to Rs 10; other tipping levels are Rs 2 for bike-watching, Rs 10 or Rs 15 for train conductors or station porters performing miracles for you, and Rs 5 to Rs 15 for extra services from hotel staff.

While there are fixed-price stores in major cities, in bazaars and markets geared to tourists, you are generally expected to bargain. The trick with bargaining is to know what you should be paying for any given article. You can find out by checking prices at fixed-price stores, asking other travellers what they have paid, and shopping around before settling on a particular vendor. Savvy shoppers have a good eye for quality and are able to make informed judgements. If all else fails, a general rule of thumb is to offer half the original asking price. You will usually end up paying around three-quarters of the original asking price. Bargaining is not a battle to the death; yelling will get you nowhere. See the boxed text The Art of Haggling.

Baksheesh

Baksheesh can be defined as a 'tip', but it is a lot more. Judicious baksheesh will open closed doors, find missing letters and perform other small miracles.

The Art of Haggling

The friendly art of haggling is an absolute must in most parts of Rajasthan, unless you don't mind paying above the market value. Shopkeepers in cities like Udaipur, Jaipur, Jaisalmer, Pushkar and Jodhpur are accustomed to tourists who have lots of money and little time to spend it. This means that when you ask a shopkeeper 'How much?', the reply will probably be 'very good price', but more often than not that price is daylight robbery. How much you're being fleeced usually varies according to how gullible you look. It's not unusual to be charged at least double, or even triple the 'real' price.

So how do you know if you're being overcharged and need to strike back with some serious haggling? Well, you are safe in government emporiums and some larger shops, where the prices are usually fixed (often quite high). But in most other shops that cater primarily to tourists, it's probably worth haggling. The kind of places that usually fall into this category are handicraft, carpet, painting, jewellery, souvenir and clothing shops.

If you have absolutely no idea of what something should really cost, start by slashing the price by at least half. Shopkeepers will probably look frightfully aghast and tell you that this is impossible, as it's the very price they had to pay for the item themselves. This is the usual story. But now the shopkeeper knows that you're not going to be taken for a ride. This is when the battle for a bargain begins and it's up to you and the salesperson to negotiate a price. You'll find that many shopkeepers lower their so-called 'final price' if you proceed to head out of the shop saying you'll 'think about it'.

Usually it's just a matter of time before the price comes tumbling down. And remember, don't be afraid to haggle. It's all part and parcel of shopping in India, and although sometimes downright exhausting, it can also be loads of fun.

Many westerners find this aspect of Indian travel the most trying – the constant demands for baksheesh and the expectations that because you're a foreigner you'll tip. However, from an Indian perspective, baksheesh is an integral part of the system. Take some time to observe how Indians (even those who are obviously not excessively wealthy) deal with baksheesh; they always give something, and it's expected and accepted by both sides.

Although most people think of baksheesh in terms of tipping, it also refers to giving alms to beggars. Wherever you turn you'll be confronted by beggars – many of them (often handicapped or hideously disfigured) genuinely in dire need, others, such as kids hassling for a rupee or a pen, obviously not. All sorts of stories about where travellers' handouts end up do the rounds, many of them with little basis in fact. Stories such as rupee millionaire beggars, people (usually kids) being deliberately mutilated so they can beg, and a beggars' Mafia are common.

It's a personal choice how you approach the issue of beggars and baksheesh. Some people feel it is best to give nothing to any beggar as it 'only encourages them', instead choosing to contribute by helping out at Mother Teresa's or a similar charitable institute; others give away loose change when they have it. Some insulate themselves entirely and give nothing in any way. Whether or not you decide to give to beggars on the street, the 'one pen, one pen' brigade should be firmly discouraged.

POST & COMMUNICATIONS
Sending Mail
The Indian postal and poste restante services are generally excellent. Expected letters almost always are there and letters you send almost invariably reach their destination, although they take up to three weeks. You can buy stamps at larger hotels, saving a lot of queuing in crowded post offices.

Postal Rates It costs Rs 6 to air mail a postcard and Rs 6.50 to send an aerogram anywhere in the world from India. A standard air

mail letter (up to 20g) costs Rs 11. The larger post offices have a speed post service. International rates are Rs 200 for the first 200g and Rs 60 for every additional 200g. Internal rates are Rs 20 for places within 500km and Rs 30 for places beyond 500km.

Posting Parcels Most people discover how to do this the hard way, in which case it'll take half a day. Go about it as described here (which can still take up to an hour).

- Take the parcel to a tailor or to a parcel-stitching-wallah (occasionally found just outside post offices), and ask for your parcel to be stitched up in cheap linen. Negotiate the price first.
- At the post office, ask for the necessary customs declaration forms. Fill them in and glue one to the parcel. The other will be stitched onto it. To avoid excise duty at the delivery end it's best to specify that the contents are a 'gift'. Be careful to declare the value of the contents as less than Rs 1000. If you specify over Rs 1000, your parcel will not be accepted without a bank clearance certificate, which is a hassle to get.
- Have the parcel weighed and franked at the parcel counter.

Books or printed matter can go by bookpost, which is considerably cheaper than parcel post, but the package must be wrapped a certain way: make sure that it can either be opened for inspection, or that it is just wrapped in brown paper or cardboard and tied with string, with the two ends exposed so that the contents are visible. To protect the books, it might be worthwhile first wrapping them in clear plastic. No customs declaration form is necessary.

Rates for air mail bookpost range from Rs 45 for 200g up to Rs 1000 for 5kg, the maximum weight for a bookpost parcel (sea mail costs Rs 175 for 5kg).

Beware of sending parcels COD; the cost may make quantum leaps by the time it reaches its destination. Be cautious with places which offer to mail things to your home after you have bought them. Government emporiums are usually OK. In most other places it pays to post it yourself.

Sending parcels in the other direction (to you in India) is an extremely hit-and-miss affair. Don't count on anything bigger than a letter getting to you. And don't count on a letter getting to you if there's anything of market value inside it.

Parcel post rates from India, using air mail to the USA costs Rs 879 per kilo and Rs 404 for every extra kilo; to the UK it's Rs 880 per kilo and Rs 228 for each additional kilo. As you would expect, sea mail charges are lower. To the USA it's Rs 625 per kilo and Rs 95 for every extra kilo; to the UK it's Rs 770 and Rs 75 per additional kilo.

Receiving Mail

Have letters addressed to you with your surname in capitals and underlined, followed by poste restante, GPO, and the city or town in question. Many 'lost' letters are simply misfiled under given (first) names, so always check under both your names. Letters sent via poste restante are generally held for one month only, after which, if unclaimed, they are returned to the sender. If you want mail to be held for longer, talk to the post master. American Express, in its major city locations, sometimes offers an alternative to the poste restante system.

Telephone

All over India, even in the smallest places, you'll find private STD/ISD/PCO call booths with direct local, interstate and international dialling. Usually found in shops or other businesses, they are easy to spot with large STD/ISD/PCO signs advertising the service. A digital meter lets you see what the call is costing, and gives you a printout at the end. You then just pay the shop owner – quick, painless and a far cry from the not so distant past when a night spent at a telegraph office waiting for a line was not unusual.

Domestic Calls For calls within India, the rates vary depending on the time of day: from 7 to 8.30 pm it's half-rate, cheaper still after 8.30 pm, and 11 pm to 6 am is the cheapest

time of all. On Sundays, calls are half-price throughout the day.

Telephone numbers in Rajasthan have an annoying tendency to change – don't be surprised if a hotel number in this book is no longer the same. If that's the case, call ☎ 197 for local telephone number inquiries. The collect call operator can be reached on ☎ 186.

International Calls A direct international call from a public phone call booth costs Rs 60 per minute to call the UK and Rs 78 per minute to the USA. To make an international call, you will need to dial the following:

00 (international access code from India) + country code (of the country you are calling) + area code + local number

In some centres, STD/ISD/PCO booths may offer a 'call back' service – you ring your folks or friends, give them the number of the booth and wait for them to call you back. The booth operator will charge about Rs 2 to Rs 3 per minute for this service, in addition to the cost of the preliminary call. Advise whoever is going to call you how long you intend to wait at the booth in the event that they have trouble getting back to you. The number your callers dial will be as follows:

(caller's country international access code) + 91 (international country code for India) + area code + local number (booth number)

The Central Telegraph offices/Telecom offices in major towns are usually reasonably efficient. Some are open 24 hours.

Also available is the Home Country Direct service, which gives you access to the international operator in your home country. You can then make a reverse charge (collect) or credit card calls, although this is not always easy. If you are calling from a hotel beware of exorbitant connection charges. You may also have trouble convincing the owner of the telephone that they are not going to get charged for the call. Some countries and numbers to dial are:

Australia	☎ 0006117
Canada	☎ 000167
Germany	☎ 0004917
Italy	☎ 0003917
Japan	☎ 0008117
Netherlands	☎ 0003117
New Zealand	☎ 0006417
Thailand	☎ 0006617
UK	☎ 0004417
USA	☎ 000117

Fax
Fax rates at the telegraph office at the Jaipur central post office are Rs 90 per page for neighbouring countries; Rs 95 per page to other Asian destinations, Africa, Europe, Australia and New Zealand; and Rs 125 to the USA and Canada. This fax office is open 24 hours. Rates within India are Rs 30 per A4 page.

It's possible to receive faxes at telegraph offices. Fax numbers for telegraph offices in Rajasthan, Delhi and Agra are:

Agra	0562-269626, 361146
Ajmer	0145-427004
Alwar	0144-337805
Barmer	02982-20328
Bharatpur	05644-23170
Bikaner	0151-540274
Bundi	0747-22850
Chittorgarh	01472-40072
Jaipur	0141-381525
Jaisalmer	02992-52634
Jodhpur	0291-633194
Kota	0744-451006
Mt Abu	02974-38900
New Delhi	011-331 3411
Pushkar	0145-812282
Udaipur	0294-529922

Many of the STD/ISD/PCO booths also have a fax machine for public use, but some cost between 5% and 30% more than government telegraph offices.

Telegrams
Telegrams can be sent from the telegraph office at the central post office in Jaipur for around Rs 2.50 per word to the USA, and Rs 2 to all other destinations.

Email Access
There are bureaus where you can send and receive email in major cities, such as Jaipur and Udaipur, as well as a growing number of smaller places. While this is the cheapest way to send text, offices may charge more for receiving email than for receiving a fax. Some hotels have email facilities too. Outside the big cities email access rarely exists.

INTERNET RESOURCES
There are online services relevant to Rajasthan, but they come and go with some frequency. The best place to start your Web explorations is the Lonely Planet Web site (www.lonelyplanet.com.au). Here you'll find guidebook updates, travel news, summaries, postcards from other travellers and the Thorn Tree bulletin board, where you can ask questions before you go or dispense advice when you get back. The sub-WWWay section links you to the most useful travel resources elsewhere on the Web.

BOOKS
India is one of the world's largest publishers of books in English. You'll find a great number of interesting, affordable books on India by Indian publishers, which are generally not available in the west.

The following recommendations may be published in different editions in some countries, be hardcover in one place, while readily available in paperback in another. Luckily, bookshops and libraries search by title or author, so a local bookshop or library is best to advise you on their availability.

Lonely Planet
It's pleasing to be able to say that for more information on Rajasthan and its neighbours, most of the best guides come from Lonely Planet! The award-winning *India* is one of Lonely Planet's most popular titles;

this is the most comprehensive guide to the country you'll find. There are also Lonely Planet guides to *Goa*, *Kerala* and *South India*, for travellers spending more time in these regions.

Lonely Planet's handy pocket-sized city guides to *Delhi* and *Mumbai* have more information on these major cities. The Himalaya is well covered, with *Indian Himalaya* and *Trekking in the Indian Himalaya*. The latter is full of practical descriptions and excellent maps of the best trekking routes in the Himalaya. For all your language needs, grab a copy of the *Hindi/Urdu phrasebook*.

In the Journeys travel literature series, *In Rajasthan* by Royina Grewal gives a fascinating insider's view of the people and places encountered in this state. Indian cities are among those featured in *Chasing Rickshaws*, a colourful photographic tribute to cycle-powered vehicles and their drivers. In 1999, Lonely Planet published *Sacred India*, another full-colour book with stunning images of India's diverse religious culture.

Other Guidebooks

While there are numerous glossy, coffee-table books on Rajasthan, there is a paucity of good, practical travel guides. Insight Guides' *Rajasthan* is an attractive volume with fine photographs and excellent essays on the arts, culture and history of Rajasthan. It is, however, a little short on practical travel information, but is a good souvenir to take home with you. Insight also has a book on the 'golden triangle' – *Delhi, Jaipur & Agra*. While the coverage of these cities is good, it's obviously not very helpful if you're planning to get off the main tourist circuit into the heart of the state. In a similar vein is Odyssey Guides' *Delhi, Agra & Jaipur*, and *Delhi, Agra & Jaipur* by Sondeep Shankar & Sumi Krishna Chauhan. Nelles Guides' *Northern India* devotes a small section to Rajasthan.

Travel Writing

Robyn Davidson's *Desert Places* is an account of the author's journey by camel with the Rabari (Rajasthani nomads) on their annual migration through the Thar Desert. It gives a compelling insight into both the plight of the nomads and the solo woman traveller in Rajasthan.

History & Culture

Annals & Antiquities of Rajasthan by Captain James Tod is probably the text most cited by historians writing about Rajasthan. A classic text, it was originally published in 1829-32. It comes in a two or three volume set, published by Oriental Books Reprint Corporation, New Delhi.

Cultural History of Rajasthan by Kalyan Kumar Ganguli is a scholarly text which provides a comprehensive historical and cultural analysis of Rajputana.

Folklore of Rajasthan by DR Ahuja is a handy paperback book which considers the cultural heritage of Rajasthan and its people, with chapters on folk music and dance, customs and traditions, myths and mythology, and more.

For an assessment of the position of women in Indian society, and that of rural women particularly, *May You Be the Mother of One Hundred Sons* by Elizabeth Bumiller offers excellent insights into the subject.

For those interested in the continuing and often shocking and sad story of India's tribal people, there is the scholarly *Tribes of India – the Struggle for Survival* by Christoph von Führer-Haimendorf.

The Idea of Rajasthan, edited by Karine Schomer et al, is a two volume set of contemporary essays by various scholars on the historical and cultural influences which have contributed towards Rajasthani identity.

By My Sword and Shield by E Jaiwant Paul is about the traditional weapons of Indian warriors, especially the Rajputs.

Politics

Rajasthan: Polity, Economy & Society by BL Panagariya & NC Pahariya is a well-written text which concentrates on the formation and composition of the state of Rajasthan in the post-Independence period, the government of the state to the present day, as well as the state's economy, development and cultural heritage.

Princely Rule

A Princess Remembers by Gayatri Devi & Santha Rama Rau is the memoirs of the maharani of Jaipur, Gayatri Devi, wife of the last maharaja, Man Singh II. It's easy reading and provides a fascinating insight into the bygone days of Indian royalty.

A Desert Kingdom: The Rajputs of Bikaner by Naveen Patnaik is a fine hardback volume with magnificent old photos from the collection of Maharaja Ganga Singh of Bikaner, who ascended the throne in 1885. It includes an interesting commentary and historical analysis of his rule.

Maharana by Brian Masters traces the history of the rulers of Udaipur, the world's oldest ruling dynasty, which spans 76 generations.

Maharaja: The Spectacular Heritage of Princely India, with text by Andrew Robinson and superb photos by Sumio Uchiyama, portrays the past and present heritage of princely India and covers a range of royal families, predominantly from Rajasthan.

The House of Marwar by Dhananajaya Singh outlines the history of the royal house of Jodhpur from the first ruler in the early 13th century up to the present maharaja. The book contains a small collection of photos.

Coffee-Table Books

Jaipur: The Last Destination, with text by Aman Nath and beautiful photographs by Samar Singh Jodha, is a magnificent prize-winning hardback volume with extensive historical notes, essays on Jaipur's maharajas and the textiles, arts and crafts of the pink city.

Rajasthan: An Enduring Romance is an attractive hardback by Sunil Mehra.

Rajasthan, text by Gerard Busquet and photos by Pierre Toutain, is predominantly pictorial, reflecting the vibrant places, people and colour of Rajasthan.

Rajasthan: India's Enchanted Land is a finely presented paperback volume with photographs by Raghubir Singh and fore-

word by film director Satyajit Ray. Other attractive souvenir books include *Udaipur – The Fabled City of Romance* by Archana Shankar and *Rajasthan* by Kishore Singh. If you have around Rs 3000, there's the impressive volume *Rajasthan* by Dharmendar Kanwar.

Arts, Crafts & Architecture

Arts & Crafts of Rajasthan, edited by Aman Nath & Francis Wacziarg, is a beautiful hardback volume with photographs accompanied by informative and interesting essays.

Arts & Artists of Rajasthan by RK Vashistha is a hardback volume covering the period from the 7th to the 19th centuries, concentrating on the art centres of Mewar (Udaipur), with numerous photographic plates, extensive notes and short biographies of artists.

The City Palace Museum Udaipur, with text by Andrew Topsfield and photos by Pankaj Shah, provides an interesting visual and historical background to the Mewar paintings at this museum.

Ateliers of the Rajput Courts contains beautiful colour plates of Rajasthani miniatures which are part of the Lalit Khala series (portfolio No 39). The accompanying text is by Raj K Tandan. The prints are loose-leaf, so could be easily framed.

The Royal Palaces of India, with text by George Michell and photographs by Antonio Martinelli, is a comprehensive and detailed guide to the forts and palaces of India. The text is complemented with excellent photographs and some archaeological maps.

The Forts of India by Virginia Fass is a large hardback volume with photographs and substantial historical notes.

The growing interest in the magnificent painted havelis of Shekhawati has spawned a number of books on the region. The definitive one is Ilay Cooper's *The Painted Towns of Shekhawati*. It's not only a practical guide to the region, with maps and notes for easy location and identification of paintings, but has very good essays on the history of the region, painting techniques, layout of the havelis, and more.

Another book on this subject is *Rajasthan: The Painted Walls of Shekhavati* by Francis Wacziarg & Aman Nath.

Flora & Fauna

A classic text on the flora of the arid zone is E Blatter & F Hallberg's *The Flora of the Indian Desert*, first published between 1918 and 1921. This is very much a detailed technical reference, but the notes on traditional uses of the plants of the Thar Desert are interesting.

The Tiger's Destiny, by Valmik Thapar (text) and Fateh Singh Rathore (photographs), deals with the besieged tigers of Ranthambhore National Park.

Specifically dealing with the prolific birdlife of Keoladeo Ghana National Park is *Bharatpur: Bird Paradise*, by Martin Ewans (text) and Thakur Dalip Singh et al (photographs).

Mammals of the Thar Desert by Ishwar Prakash is a small hardback volume with detailed descriptions and field notes accompanied by line drawings. Another good paperback is *A Guide to the Wildlife Parks of Rajasthan* by Dr Suraj Ziddi with photographs by Subhash Bhargava.

Novels

Virgin Princess: An Historical Novel of Mewar (Udaipur, India) – The World's Oldest Dynasty by Jane Richardson is an interesting if badly written romantic tale.

Raj by Gita Mehta is the more convincingly told story of a young Rajput princess contracted in marriage to an arrogant prince. *Inside the Haveli* by Rama Mehta is about a girl from Mumbai who marries into a conservative family in Rajasthan.

FILM

Latcho Drom (Safe Journey), France, 1992/93, was directed by Tony Gatlif. It is a very dramatic movie, as it traces the lives of gypsy dancers and musicians from India to the Middle East, Eastern Europe and Spain. It opens with stunning Rajasthan desert vistas and evocative scenes of traditional music and dance performed by Rajasthani nomads.

CD-ROMS

The following CD-ROMs (which have sections pertaining to Rajasthan) are all available in India but only at major bookstores. *India: A Multimedia Journey* includes videos, slides, maps and travelling tips. *Indian Wildlife* has more than 650 pictures and slides as well as information about more than 30 national parks. *India Festiva* (Rs 1595; Magic Software) includes information on India's numerous festivals. Magic Software (www.magicsw .com) also puts out *India Mystica*, an encyclopedia on Indian culture, *India Musica*, which explains Hindustani music, *Hindi Guru* and *Gujarati Guru* which explain these particular regional cultures, and *Yoga & Meditation*.

NEWSPAPERS & MAGAZINES

English-language dailies include the *Times of India*, the *Hindustan Times*, the *Indian Express* and the *Statesman*; many feel the *Indian Express* is the best of the bunch. The *Economic Times* is for those interested in business and economic analysis.

Weekly news magazines include *Frontline*, *India Today*, *The Week*, *Sunday* and the *Illustrated Weekly of India*. They're widely available at bookshops and train and bus stations. The state tourism department publishes *Rajasthan Atithi*, a bimonthly glossy magazine covering topics of tourist interest. You can get a copy by contacting the Department of Tourism, Art & Culture in Jaipur on ☎ 0141-365256, fax 376362.

The only English-language newspaper published in Rajasthan is *Rajasthan Patrika*. This small daily newspaper predominantly focuses on Rajasthan, but it's extremely difficult to obtain in the English edition. Try contacting its headquarters in Jaipur (☎ 0141-561582).

Time and *Newsweek*, as well as newspapers like the *Herald Tribune* and *Guardian* and magazines like *Der Spiegel* and its English, French and Italian clones, are only available in some major cities and at some expensive hotels.

RADIO & TV

Radio programs can be heard on All India Radio (AIR) which provides the usual interview, music and news features. Details on programs and frequencies are provided in the major English language dailies.

The revolution in the TV network has been the introduction of cable TV. It's amazing to see satellite dishes even in the remotest villages. The result is that viewers can tune in to the BBC and, broadcasting from Hong Kong, Murdoch's Star TV, Prime Sports and V (an MTV-type Hindi music channel). Z TV is a popular local Hindi cable channel. The national broadcaster is Doordarshan.

VIDEO SYSTEMS

Video in India uses the VHS format, although it is possible to convert to and from PAL and NTSC in the larger cities.

PHOTOGRAPHY & VIDEO
Film & Equipment

Colour print film processing facilities are readily available in larger cities. Film is relatively cheap and the quality is usually (but not always) good. A pack of Fuji print film (36 shots) costs about Rs 90; Rs 210 for slide film.

If you're taking slides it's best to bring the film with you. Colour slide film is only available in the major cities; it can be developed in some of the major cities, but quality is not guaranteed. A better bet is to carry your film home with you.

Always check the use-by date on local film stock. Heat and humidity can play havoc with film, even if the use-by date hasn't been exceeded. It's safest to only buy film from reputable stores – and preferably film that's been refrigerated.

Video users can readily get VHS, CVHS, Hi8, Betacam, Umatic (high and low) film in Delhi and Mumbai.

A UV filter permanently fitted to your lens will not only cut down ultraviolet light, but will protect your lens. Spare batteries should be carried at all times. Serious photographers will consider bringing a tripod and fast film (400 ASA) for temple and fort interior shots.

Mahatta & Co (☎ 011-332 9769), M-Block Connaught Place, Delhi, is the sole Indian agent for Canon cameras and can safely repair them.

Exposure

In the desert you should allow for the extreme light intensity, and take care not to overexpose your shots. In general, photography is best done in the early morning and late afternoon. The stark midday sun eliminates shadows, rendering less depth to your photographs.

Protecting Your Camera & Film

Film manufacturers warn that, once exposed, film should be developed as quickly as possible; in practice the film seems to last, even in India's summer heat, without deterioration for months. If you're going to be carrying exposed film for long, consult a specialist photography handbook about ways of enhancing preservation. Try to keep your film cool, and protect it in water and air-proof containers if you're travelling during the monsoon. Silica gel sachets distributed around your gear will help to absorb moisture. Keep your camera and film in the shade as much as possible.

You may like to invest in a lead-lined (X-ray proof) bag, as repeated exposure to airport X-rays (even 'film safe' ones) can damage film. Always keep film in hand luggage. Be aware that in some places customs officers may wish to open every single film canister before you are allowed through.

Video

Properly used, a video camera can give a fascinating record of your holiday. As well as videoing the obvious things – sunsets, spectacular views – remember to record the everyday details of Rajasthani life. Often the most interesting things happen when you're intent on filming something else.

Video cameras these days have amazingly sensitive microphones, and you might be surprised how much sound will be picked up. This can also be a problem if there is a lot of ambient noise. Try to film in long takes, and don't move the camera around too much. Remember you're on holiday, though – don't let the video take over.

Make sure you keep the batteries charged, and have the necessary charger, plugs and transformer. It is worth buying a few film cartridges duty-free before your trip, in case you don't find them in Rajasthan.

Finally, follow the same rules regarding people's sensitivities as for still photography. Always ask permission first.

Restrictions & Photographing People

Be careful what you photograph or video. India is touchy about places of military importance – this can include train stations, bridges, airports, military installations and sensitive border regions. Some temples prohibit photography in the *mandapa* (forechamber) and inner sanctum. If in doubt, ask. Many temples, and numerous forts and palaces, levy a fee to bring a still camera or video camera onto the premises (the prices are given in individual chapters). There's no refund if you decide not to take any pictures after all.

Some people are happy to be photographed, but care should be taken in pointing cameras at women. If in doubt, ask. A zoom is a less intrusive way to take portraits – even when you've obtained permission, keeping a reasonable distance between you and your subject will help reduce your subject's discomfort, giving more natural shots. A zoom is invaluable at festivals when it is difficult to get close to the action.

TIME

India is 5½ hours ahead of GMT/UTC, 4½ hours behind Australian EST and 10½ hours ahead of American EST. It is officially known as IST – Indian Standard Time.

ELECTRICITY
Voltages & Cycles

The electric current is 230-240V AC, 50 cycles. Electricity is widely available in the main towns and cities and tourist destinations, but power cuts are not uncommon – keep a torch or candle handy. Many remote villages still remain without electricity. Those that have electricity usually use it for powering irrigation equipment – very few village homes are electrified.

Plugs & Sockets

Sockets are of a three round-pin variety, similar (but not identical) to European sockets. European round-pin plugs will go into the sockets, but as the pins on Indian plugs are somewhat thicker, the fit is loose and connection is not always guaranteed.

WEIGHTS & MEASURES

Although India is officially metricated, imperial weights and measures are still used in some areas of commerce. You will often hear people referring to lakhs (one lakh = 100,000) and crores (one crore = 10 million) of cars, apples or whatever.

A metric conversion chart is included on the inside back cover of this book.

LAUNDRY

All of the top-end hotels, most of the mid-range hotels and some of the budget hotels and guesthouses offer a laundry service, and costs are reasonable.

Most clothes are washed at dhobi ghats (see the boxed text Dhobi-Wallahs). If you don't think your clothes will stand being beaten clean, then handwash them yourself. Washing powder can be bought cheaply in small sachets anywhere. Women should consider bringing a lingerie bag to protect delicate bras and undies from both washing machines and dhobi ghats.

TOILETS

In five-star hotels and guesthouses geared for foreign tourists, sit-down flush toilets and toilet paper are invariably supplied. Off the beaten track, at train stations (and other public places) and in places that don't specifically cater for foreigners, it's usually squat toilets. In such circumstances it's customary to use your left hand and water, not

Dhobi-Wallahs

After a gruelling day of trekking, riding through sultry deserts on camel-back or climbing to hilltop forts, all you want to do is get out of those grimy clothes. There are no laundromats in Rajasthan but don't despair! You won't have to sacrifice that special meal in a palace-hotel to pay dry-cleaning bills, for there's a *dhobi-wallah* just around the corner.

If you're staying at one of Rajasthan's smaller hotels or guesthouses, there will probably be a knock on your door every other morning and a laundry boy will collect all those dusty, sweaty clothes. The very same clothes will reappear that evening, washed and ironed with TLC for just a few rupees per item. But what happened to your clothes between their departure and return?

Well, they certainly did not get anywhere near a washing machine. First of all they're taken to the *dhobi ghat*. A ghat is a series of steps near a lake or river and a dhobi is a washerperson, so the dhobi ghat is where the dhobis ply their trade.

Upon arrival at the ghat the clothes are separated – all the white shirts are washed together, all the grey trousers, all the black skirts, all the blue jeans. If this was the west, your clothes would be hopelessly lost or you'd need a computer to keep track of them. Your clothes are soaked in soapy water for a few hours, following which the dirt is literally beaten out of them. No multi-programmed miracle of technology can wash as clean as an enthusiastic dhobi, although admittedly after a few visits to the Indian laundry your clothes do look distinctly thinner. Buttons also tend to get shattered, so bring some spare. Zips, lace, bras and underpants sometimes fare likewise.

Once clean, the clothes are strung out on miles of clothesline to quickly dry in the glorious Rajasthani sun. They're then taken to the ironing sheds where primitive irons press your jeans like they've never been pressed before. Not just your jeans – your socks, your T-shirts, even your underwear will come back with knife-edge creases.

Then the Indian miracle takes place. Out of the hundreds, even thousands of items washed that day, somehow your very own brown socks, blue jeans, yellow T-shirts and purple underwear all find their way back together and head for your hotel room. A system of marking clothes, known only to the dhobis, is behind this feat. They say criminals have been tracked down simply by those telltale 'dhobi marks'.

paper. A strategically placed tap (and usually a water container) is available in squat toilets. If you can't get used to the Indian method, carry your own paper (none is supplied, but is widely available to buy). But stuffing paper (and tampons) down the toilet is simply going to further clog an already overloaded sewerage system. Sometimes a bin is provided for the disposal of paper and tampons – use it!

HEALTH

Travel health depends on your predeparture preparations, your daily health care while travelling and how you handle any medical problem that does develop. While the potential dangers can seem quite frightening, in reality few travellers experience anything more than upset stomachs.

One word of advice in Rajasthan – exercise caution in palaces and forts, as there can be some unexpected little steps which, if unseen, can cause a nasty sprain when you trip.

Predeparture Planning

Immunisations Plan ahead for getting your vaccinations: some of them require more than one injection, while some vaccinations should not be given together. It is

Everyday Health

Normal body temperature is 37°C (98.6°F); more than 2°C (4°F) higher indicates a high fever. The normal adult pulse rate is 60 to 100 per minute (children 80 to 100, babies 100 to 140). As a general rule the pulse increases about 20 beats per minute for each 1°C (2°F) rise in fever.

Respiration (breathing) rate is also an indicator of illness. Count the number of breaths per minute: between 12 and 20 is normal for adults and older children (up to 30 for younger children, 40 for babies). People with a high fever or serious respiratory illness breathe more quickly than normal. More than 40 shallow breaths a minute may indicate pneumonia.

recommended you seek medical advice at least six weeks before travel. Be aware that children and pregnant women are often at a greater risk from disease.

Record all vaccinations on an International Health Certificate, available from your doctor or government health department, and carry it with you.

Discuss your requirements with your doctor, but vaccinations you should consider for a trip to India include the following. For more detailed information on the diseases themselves see the individual disease entries later in this section.

Hepatitis A This is the most common travel-acquired illness after diarrhoea. Hepatitis A vaccine (eg Havrix 1440 or VAQTA) provides long-term immunity (possibly more than 10 years) after an initial injection and a booster at six to 12 months. An injection of gamma globulin (ready-made antibody collected from blood donations) also provides protection against hepatitis A. It is effective immediately, unlike the vaccine, but protection is short-lived – two to six months, depending on the dose given – and because it is a blood product there are concerns about its long-term safety. A combined hepatitis A and hepatitis B vaccination, Twinrix, is also available. Three injections over a six month period are required.

Typhoid This is an important vaccination to have where hygiene is a problem. It's available either as an injection or oral capsules.

Diphtheria & Tetanus Both these diseases occur worldwide and can be fatal. Everyone should have these vaccinations which are usually combined. After an initial course of three injections, boosters are necessary every 10 years.

Meningococcal Meningitis Travellers to Rajasthan should consider having this vaccination. A single injection will give protection for three years. Protection may be less effective in children under two years of age.

Hepatitis B Travellers who should consider a hepatitis B vaccination include those visiting countries (including India) where there are high levels of hepatitis B infection, where blood transfusions may not be adequately screened or where sexual contact or needle sharing is a possibility. It involves three injections, the quickest course being over three weeks with a booster at 12 months.

Polio Everyone should keep up to date with this vaccination, which is normally given in childhood. A booster every 10 years maintains immunity.

Rabies This vaccination should be considered by those who will spend a month or longer in the country, especially if they are cycling, handling animals, caving, travelling to remote areas, and for children (who may not report a bite). Pretravel rabies vaccination involves having three injections over 21 to 28 days. If someone who has been vaccinated is bitten or scratched by an infected animal they will require two booster injections of vaccine; those not vaccinated require more.

Japanese B Encephalitis Consider this vaccination if you are spending a month or longer in high-risk areas in India, making repeated trips to a risk area or visiting during an epidemic. It involves three injections over 30 days. The vaccine is expensive and has been associated with serious allergic reactions so the decision to have it should be balanced against the risk of contracting the illness.

Tuberculosis TB risk to travellers is usually very low, unless you will be living with or closely associated with local people in high-risk areas. Vaccination with the BCG vaccine is recommended for children and young adults living in these areas for three months or more.

Malaria Medication Malaria occurs in most parts of India including Rajasthan. Antimalarial drugs do not prevent you from being infected but kill the malaria parasites during a stage in their development and significantly reduce the risk of becoming very ill or dying. Expert advice on medication should be sought, as there are many factors to consider including the area to be visited, the risk of exposure to malaria-carrying mosquitoes, the side effects of medication, your medical history and whether you are a child or pregnant. Travellers to isolated areas in high risk countries may like to carry a treatment dose of medication for use if symptoms occur.

Health Insurance Make sure that you have adequate health insurance. See Travel Insurance under Visas & Documents earlier.

Travel Health Guides If you are planning to be away or travelling in remote areas for a long period of time, you may like to consider taking a more detailed health guide.

CDC's Complete Guide to Healthy Travel, Open Road Publishing, 1997. The US Centers for Disease Control & Prevention recommendations for international travel.
Healthy Travel Asia & India, Dr Isabelle Young, Lonely Planet Publications, 2000. This covers it all from how to treat a nose bleed to finding a doctor.
Staying Healthy in Asia, Africa & Latin America, Dirk Schroeder, Moon Publications, 1994. Detailed and well-organised.
Travellers' Health, Dr Richard Dawood, Oxford University Press, 1995. Comprehensive, easy to read, authoritative and highly recommended, although it's rather large to lug around.
Travel with Children, Maureen Wheeler, Lonely Planet Publications, 1995. Includes advice on travel health for younger children.
Where There is No Doctor, David Werner, Macmillan, 1994. A very detailed guide intended for someone, such as a Peace Corps worker, going to work in an underdeveloped country.

There are also several excellent travel health sites on the Internet. From the Lonely Planet homepage there are links (www.lonelyplanet.com/weblinks/wlprep.htm#heal) to the World Health Organization and the US Centers for Disease Control & Prevention.

Medical Kit Check List

Following is a list of items you should consider including in your medical kit – consult your phamacist for brands available in your country.

☐ **Aspirin** or **paracetamol** (acetaminophen in the US) – for pain or fever.
☐ **Antihistamine** – for allergies, eg hay fever; to ease the itch from insect bites or stings; and to prevent motion sickness.
☐ **Antibiotics** – consider including these if you're travelling well off the beaten track; see your doctor, as they must be prescribed, and carry the prescription with you.
☐ **Loperamide** or **diphenoxylate** – 'blockers' for diarrhoea; **prochlorperazine** or **metaclopramide** for nausea and vomiting.
☐ **Rehydration mixture** – to prevent dehydration, eg due to severe diarrhoea; particularly important when travelling with children.
☐ **Insect repellent, sunscreen, lip balm** and **eye drops**.
☐ **Calamine lotion, sting relief spray** or **aloe vera** – to ease irritation from sunburn and insect bites or stings.
☐ **Antifungal cream** or **powder** – for fungal skin infections such as tinea and thrush.
☐ **Antiseptic** (such as povidone-iodine) – for cuts and grazes.
☐ **Bandages, Band-Aids (plasters)** and other wound dressings.
☐ **Water purification tablets** or **iodine**.
☐ **Scissors, tweezers** and a **thermometer** (note that mercury thermometers are prohibited by airlines).
☐ **Syringes** and **needles** – in case you need injections in a country with medical hygine problems. Ask your doctor for a note explaining why you have them.
☐ **Cold** and **flu tablets, throat lozenges** and **nasal decongestant**.
☐ **Multivitamins** – consider for long trips, when dietary vitamin intake may be inadequate.

Other Preparations Make sure you're healthy before you start travelling. If you are going on a long trip make sure your teeth are OK. If you wear glasses take a spare pair and your prescription.

If you require a particular medication take an adequate supply, as it may not be available locally. Take part of the packaging showing the generic name, rather than the brand, which will make getting replacements easier. It's a good idea to have a legible prescription or letter from your doctor to show that you legally use the medication, to avoid any problems.

Basic Rules

Food There is an old colonial adage which says: 'If you can cook it, boil it or peel it you can eat it ... otherwise forget it'. Vegetables and fruit should be washed with purified water or peeled where possible. Beware of ice cream sold in the street or anywhere it might have been melted and refrozen; if there's any doubt (eg a power cut in the last day or two) steer well clear. Shellfish such as mussels, oysters and clams should be avoided as well as undercooked meat, particularly in the form of mince. Steaming does not make shellfish safe for eating.

If a place looks clean and well-run and the vendor also looks clean and healthy, then the food is probably safe. In general, places that are packed with travellers or locals will be fine, while empty restaurants are questionable. The food in busy restaurants is cooked and eaten quite quickly with little standing around and is probably not reheated.

Water The number-one rule is be careful of the water and especially ice. If you don't know for certain that the water is safe assume the worst. Reputable brands of bottled water or soft drinks are generally fine, although in some places bottles may be refilled with tap water. Only use water from containers with a serrated seal – not tops or corks. Take care with fruit juice, particularly if water may have been added. Milk should be treated with suspicion as it is

---

Nutrition

If your food is poor or limited in availability, if you're travelling hard and fast and therefore missing meals or if you simply lose your appetite, you can soon start to lose weight and place your health at risk.

Make sure your diet is well-balanced. Cooked eggs, tofu, beans, lentils (dhal) and nuts are all safe ways to get protein. Fruit you can peel (bananas, oranges or mandarins, for example) is usually safe (melons can harbour bacteria in their flesh and are best avoided) and a good source of vitamins. Try to eat plenty of grains (including rice) and bread. Remember that although food is generally safer if it is cooked well, overcooked food loses much of its nutritional value. If your diet isn't well-balanced or if your food intake is insufficient, it's a good idea to take vitamin and iron pills.

In hot climates make sure you drink enough – don't rely on feeling thirsty to indicate when you should drink. Not needing to urinate or small amounts of very dark yellow urine is a danger sign of dehydration. Always carry a water bottle with you on long trips. Excessive sweating can lead to loss of salt and therefore muscle cramping. Salt tablets are not a good idea as a preventative, but in places where salt is not used much, adding salt to food can help.

---

often unpasteurised, though boiled milk is fine if it is kept hygienically. Tea or coffee should also be OK, since the water should have been boiled.

Water Purification The simplest way of purifying water is to boil it thoroughly.

Consider purchasing a water filter for a long trip. There are two main kinds of filter. Total filters take out all parasites, bacteria and viruses, and make water safe to drink. They are often expensive, but they can be more cost effective than buying bottled water. Simple filters (which can even be a nylon mesh bag) take out dirt and larger foreign bodies from the water so that chemical solutions work much more effectively; if water is dirty, chemical solutions may not work at all. It's very important when buying a filter to read the specifications, so that you know exactly what it removes from the water and what it doesn't. Simple filtering will not remove all dangerous organisms, so if you cannot boil water it should be treated chemically. Chlorine tablets (eg Puritabs, Steritabs or other brand names) will kill many pathogens, but not some parasites like giardia and amoebic cysts. Iodine is more effective in purifying water and is available in tablet form (such as Potable Aqua). Follow the directions carefully and remember that too much iodine can be harmful.

Medical Problems & Treatment

Self-diagnosis and treatment can be risky, so you should always seek medical help. An embassy, consulate or five-star hotel can usually recommend a local doctor or clinic. Although we do give drug dosages in this section, they are for emergency use only. Correct diagnosis is vital. Because drug brand names vary from country to country we have used their generic names. Check with your pharmacist for brands available locally. Antibiotics should ideally be administered only under medical supervision. Take only the recommended dose at the prescribed intervals and use the whole course, even if the illness seems to be cured earlier. Stop immediately if there are any serious reactions and don't use the antibiotic at all if you are unsure that you have the correct one. Some people are allergic to commonly prescribed antibiotics such as penicillin or sulpha drugs; carry this information (eg on a bracelet) when travelling.

Environmental Hazards

Allergies If you suffer allergies from dust, it is wise to bring a stock of appropriate medication. For those attending animal fairs, such as the Pushkar Camel Fair, it's also a good idea to bring medication if you are allergic to animal hair.

Sunburn In the desert you can get sunburnt surprisingly quickly, even through cloud. Use a sunscreen, hat, and barrier cream for your nose and lips. Calamine lotion or a sting relief spray are good for mild sunburn. Protect your eyes with good quality sunglasses.

Prickly Heat Prickly heat is an itchy rash caused by excessive perspiration trapped under the skin. It usually strikes people who have just arrived in a hot climate. Keeping cool, bathing often, drying the skin and using a mild talcum or prickly heat powder or resorting to an air-conditioned environment may help.

Heat Exhaustion Dehydration and salt deficiency can cause heat exhaustion. Take time to acclimatise to high temperatures, drink sufficient liquids and do not do anything too physically demanding.

Salt deficiency is characterised by fatigue, lethargy, headaches, giddiness and muscle cramps; salt tablets may help, but adding extra salt to your food is better.

Anhidrotic heat exhaustion is a rare form of heat exhaustion that is caused by a person's inability to sweat. It tends to affect people who have been in a hot climate for some time, rather than newcomers. It can progress to heatstroke. Treatment involves shifting away from the area to a place with a cooler climate.

Heatstroke This serious, occasionally fatal, condition can occur if the body's heat-regulating mechanism breaks down and the body temperature rises to dangerous levels. Long, continuous periods of exposure to high temperatures and insufficient fluids can leave you vulnerable to heatstroke.

The symptoms are feeling unwell, not sweating very much (or at all) and a high body temperature (39°C to 41°C or 102°F to 106°F). Where sweating has ceased the skin becomes flushed and red. Severe, throbbing headaches and lack of coordination will also occur, and the sufferer may be confused or aggressive. Eventually the victim will become delirious or convulse. Hospitalisation is essential, but in the interim get victims out of the sun, remove their clothing, cover them with a wet sheet or towel and then fan continually. Give fluids to the patient if they are conscious.

Jet Lag Jet lag is experienced when a person travels by air across more than three time zones (each time zone usually represents a one-hour time difference). It occurs because many body functions (such as temperature, pulse rate and emptying the bladder and bowels) are regulated by internal 24 hour cycles. When we travel long distances rapidly, our bodies take time to adjust to the 'new time' of our destination, and we may experience fatigue, disorientation, insomnia, anxiety, impaired concentration and loss of appetite. These effects will usually be gone within three days of arrival, but to minimise the impact of jet lag:

- Rest for a couple of days prior to departure.
- Try to select flight schedules that minimise sleep deprivation; arriving late in the day means you can go to sleep soon after you arrive. For very long flights, try to organise a stopover.
- Avoid excessive eating (which bloats the stomach) and alcohol (which causes dehydration) during the flight. Instead, drink plenty of non-carbonated, non-alcoholic drinks such as fruit juice or water.
- Avoid smoking.
- Make yourself comfortable by wearing loose-fitting clothes and perhaps bringing an eye mask and ear plugs to help you sleep.
- Try to sleep at the appropriate time for the time zone you are travelling to.

Motion Sickness Eating lightly before and during a trip will reduce the chances of motion sickness. If you are prone to motion sickness try to find a place that minimises movement – near the wing on aircraft, close to midships on boats, near the centre on buses. Fresh air usually helps; reading and cigarette smoke don't. Commercial motion-sickness preparations, which can cause drowsiness, have to be taken before the trip commences. Ginger (available in capsule form) and peppermint (including mint-flavoured sweets) are natural preventatives.

Infectious Diseases

Diarrhoea Changes of water, food or climate can all cause a mild bout of diarrhoea, but a few rushed toilet trips with no other symptoms is not indicative of a major problem. Dehydration is the main danger with any diarrhoea, particularly in children or the elderly as dehydration can occur quite quickly. Under all circumstances fluid replacement (at least equal to the volume being lost) is the most important thing to remember. Weak black tea with a little sugar, soda water, or soft drinks allowed to go flat and diluted 50% with clean water are all good. With severe diarrhoea a rehydrating solution is preferable to replace minerals and salts lost. Commercially available oral rehydration salts (ORS) are very useful; add to boiled or bottled water. In an emergency you can make up a solution of six teaspoons of sugar and a half teaspoon of salt to a litre of boiled or bottled water. You need to drink at least the same volume of fluid that you are losing in bowel movements and vomiting. Urine is the best guide to the adequacy of replacement – if you have small amounts of concentrated urine, you need to drink more. Keep drinking small amounts often. Stick to a bland diet as you recover. Gut-paralysing drugs such as loperamide or diphenoxylate can be used to bring relief from the symptoms, although they do not actually cure the problem. Only use these drugs if you do not have access to toilets, eg if you must travel. Don't use them if you have a high fever or are severely dehydrated. They are not recommended for children under 12 years.

Antibiotics may be needed for diarrhoea: with blood or mucus (dysentery); with fever; that is profuse and watery; that is persistent and not improving after 48 hours; or severe. Any of these suggest a more serious cause of diarrhoea and gut-paralysing drugs should be avoided. In these situations, a stool test may be necessary to diagnose what bug is causing your diarrhoea, so you should seek medical help urgently. Where this is not possible the recommended drugs for bacterial diarrhoea (the most likely cause of severe diarrhoea in travellers) are norfloxacin 400mg twice daily for three days or ciprofloxacin 500mg twice daily for five days. These are not recommended for children or pregnant women. The drug of choice for children would be co-trimoxazole with dosage dependent on weight. It is a five day course. Ampicillin oramoxycillin may be given in pregnancy, but medical care is necessary.

Two other causes of persistent diarrhoea are giardiasis and amoebic dysentery. **Giardiasis** is caused by a common parasite, *Giurdlu lambliu*. Symptoms include stomach cramps, nausea, a bloated stomach, watery, foul-smelling diarrhoea and frequent gas. Giardiasis can appear several weeks after you have been exposed to the parasite. The symptoms may disappear for a few days and then return; this can go on for several weeks. **Amoebic dysentery**, caused by the protozoon *Entamoeba histolytica*, is characterised by a gradual onset of low-grade diarrhoea, often with blood and mucus. Cramping abdominal pain and vomiting are less likely than in other types of diarhoea, and fever may not be present. It will persist until treated and can recur and cause other health problems. You should seek medical advice if you think you have giardiasis or amoebic dysentery, but where this is not possible, tinidazole, or metronidazole are the recommended drugs. Treatment is a 2g single dose of tinidazole or 250mg of metronidazole three times daily for five to 10 days.

Fungal Infections Fungal infections occur more commonly in hot weather and are usually found on the scalp, between the toes (athlete's foot) or fingers, in the groin and on the body (ringworm). You get ringworm (which is a fungal infection, not a worm) from infected animals or other people. Moisture encourages these infections. To prevent fungal infections wear loose, comfortable clothes, avoid artificial fibres, wash frequently and dry yourself carefully.

If you do get an infection, wash the infected area at least daily with a disinfectant or medicated soap and water, and rinse and dry well. Apply an antifungal cream or powder like tolnaftate. Try to expose the infected area to air or sunlight as much as possible and wash all towels and underwear in hot water, change them often and let them dry in the sun.

Hepatitis Hepatitis is a general term for inflammation of the liver. It is a common disease in India, and worldwide. There are several different viruses that cause hepatitis, and they differ in the way that they are transmitted. The symptoms are similar in all forms of the illness, and include fever, chills, headache, fatigue, feelings of weakness and aches and pains, followed by loss of appetite, nausea, vomiting, abdominal pain, dark urine, light-coloured faeces, jaundiced (yellow) skin and yellowing of the whites of the eyes. People who have had hepatitis should avoid alcohol for some time, as the liver needs time to recover.

Hepatitis A is transmitted by contaminated food and drinking water. You should seek medical advice, but there is not much you can do apart from resting, drinking lots of fluids, eating lightly and avoiding fatty foods. **Hepatitis E** is transmitted in the same way as hepatitis A. There are almost 300 million chronic carriers of **Hepatitis B** in the world. It is spread through contact with infected blood, blood products or body fluids; for example, through sexual contact, unsterilised needles and blood transfusions, or contact with blood via small breaks in the skin. Other risk situations include having a shave, tattoo or your body pierced with contaminated equipment.

The symptoms of hepatitis B may be more severe than type A and the disease can lead to long term problems such as chronic liver damage, liver cancer or a long term carrier state. **Hepatitis C** and **D** are spread in the same way as hepatitis B and can also lead to long-term complications. There are vaccines against hepatitis A and B, but there are currently no vaccines against the other types of hepatitis. Following the basic rules about food and water (hepatitis A and E) and avoiding risk situations (hepatitis B, C and D) are important preventative measures.

HIV & AIDS In Rajasthan, there were 78 reported cases of full-blown AIDS in 1998. Udaipur and Ajmer recorded the highest number of cases.

Being infected with the human immunodeficiency virus (HIV) may lead to acquired immune deficiency syndrome (AIDS), which is a fatal disease. Any exposure to blood, blood products or body fluids may put the individual at risk. The disease is often transmitted through sexual contact or dirty needles – vaccinations, acupuncture, tattooing and body piercing can be potentially as dangerous as intravenous drug use. HIV/AIDS can also be spread through infected blood transfusions.

If you do need an injection, ask to see the syringe unwrapped in front of you, or take a needle and syringe pack with you. Fear of HIV infection should never preclude treatment for serious medical conditions.

Intestinal Worms These parasites are most common in rural tropical areas. The different worms have different ways of infecting people. Some may be ingested on food such as undercooked meat (eg tapeworms) and some enter through your skin (eg hookworms). Infestations may not show up for some time, and although they are generally not serious, if left untreated some can cause severe health problems later. Consider having a stool test when you return home to check for worms.

Meningococcal Meningitis This serious disease can be fatal. There are recurring epidemics in northern India and Nepal. A fever, severe headache, sensitivity to light and neck stiffness which prevents forward bending of the head are the first symptoms. There may also be purple patches on the skin. Death can occur within a few hours, so urgent medical treatment is required. The disease is spread by close contact with people who carry it in their throats and noses and spread it through coughs and sneezes; they may not even be aware that they are carriers. Treatment is large doses of penicillin given intravenously, or chloramphenicol injections.

Sexually Transmitted Diseases HIV/AIDS and hepatitis B can be transmitted through sexual contact – see the relevant sections earlier. Gonorrhoea, herpes and syphilis are among these diseases; sores, discharges, blisters or rashes around the genitals or pain when urinating are common symptoms. In some STDs, such as wart virus or chlamydia, symptoms may be less marked or not observed at all, especially in women. Chlamydia can cause infertility in men and women before any symptoms are noticed. Syphilis symptoms eventually disappear completely but the disease continues and can cause severe problems in later years. While abstinence from sexual contact is the only 100% effective prevention, using condoms is also effective. The different sexually transmitted diseases each require specific antibiotic treatments.

Travellers to Rajasthan should consider bringing along condoms from their own country, which may be more reliable than local brands.

Typhoid Typhoid fever is a dangerous gut infection caused by contaminated water and food. Medical help must be sought. In its early stages sufferers may feel they have a bad cold or flu on the way, as early symptoms are a headache, body aches and a fever which rises a little each day until it is around 40°C (104°F) or more. The victim's pulse is often slow relative to the degree of fever present – unlike a normal fever where the pulse increases. There may also be vomiting, abdominal pain, diarrhoea or constipation. In the second week the high fever and slow pulse continue and a few pink spots may appear on the body; trembling, delirium, weakness, weight loss and dehydration may occur. Complications such as pneumonia, perforated bowel or meningitis may occur.

Insect-Borne Diseases

Filariasis, leishmaniasis, Lyme disease, and typhus are all insect-borne diseases, but they do not pose a great risk to travellers. For more information on them see Less Common Diseases at the end of this section.

Malaria This serious and potentially fatal disease is spread by mosquito bites. If you are travelling in endemic areas it is extremely important to avoid mosquito bites and to take tablets to prevent this disease. Symptoms range from fever, chills and sweating, headache, diarrhoea and abdominal pains to a vague feeling of ill-health. Seek medical help immediately if malaria is suspected. Without treatment it can rapidly become more serious and can be fatal. If medical care is not available, malaria tablets can be used for treatment. You need to use a malaria tablet which is different from the one you were taking when you contracted malaria. The standard treatment dose of mefloquine is two 250mg tablets and a further two six hours later. For Fansidar, it's a single dose of three tablets. If you were previously taking mefloquine and cannot obtain Fansidar, then other alternatives are Malarone (atovaquone-proguanil; four tablets once daily for three days), halofantrine (three doses of two 250mg tablets every six hours) or quinine sulphate (600mg every six hours). There is a greater risk of side effects with these dosages than in normal use if used with mefloquine, so medical advice is preferable. Also, halofantrine is no longer recommended by the WHO as emergency standby treatment because of side effects, so should only be used if no other drugs are available. Travellers are advised to prevent mosquito bites at all times. The main messages are:

- Wear light-coloured clothing.
- Wear long trousers and long-sleeved shirts.
- Use mosquito repellents containing the compound DEET on exposed areas (prolonged overuse of DEET may be harmful, especially to children, but its use is considered preferable to being bitten by disease-transmitting mosquitoes).
- Avoid perfumes or aftershave.
- Use a mosquito net impregnated with mosquito repellent (permethrin) – it may be worth taking your own.
- Impregnating clothes with permethrin effectively deters mosquitoes and other insects.

Dengue Fever This viral disease is transmitted by mosquitoes and occurs mainly in tropical and subtropical areas of the world, including India. Generally, the risk to travellers is small except during epidemics, which are usually seasonal (during and just after the rainy season). The *Aedes aegypti* mosquito which transmits the dengue virus is most active during the day, unlike the malaria mosquito, and is found mainly in urban areas, in and around human dwellings.

Signs and symptoms of dengue fever include a sudden onset of high fever, headache, joint and muscle pains (hence its old name 'breakbone fever') and nausea and vomiting. A rash of small red spots appears three to four days after the onset of fever. Dengue is commonly mistaken for other infectious diseases, including influenza. You should seek medical attention if you think you may be infected, although there is no specific treatment. Infection can be diagnosed by a blood test. Aspirin should be avoided, as it increases the risk of haemorrhaging. Recovery may be prolonged, with tiredness lasting for several weeks.

Severe complications are rare in travellers, but include dengue haemorrhagic fever (DHF), which can be fatal without prompt medical treatment. DHF is thought to be a result of a second infection due to a different strain (there are four major strains), and usually affects residents of the country rather than travellers. There is no vaccine against dengue fever. The best prevention is to avoid mosquito bites at all times. If you have had dengue before, you are at higher risk of complications if you get infected again, so check with your doctor before you go.

Japanese B Encephalitis This viral infection of the brain is transmitted by mosquitoes. Most cases occur in rural areas as the virus exists in pigs and wading birds. Symptoms include fever, headache and alteration in consciousness. Hospitalisation is needed for correct diagnosis and treatment. There is a high mortality rate among those who have symptoms; of those who survive many are intellectually disabled.

Cuts, Bites & Stings

See Less Common Diseases for details of rabies, which is passed through animal bites.

Bedbugs & Lice Bedbugs live in various places, but particularly in dirty mattresses and bedding, evidenced by spots of blood on bedclothes or on the wall. They leave itchy bites in neat rows. Calamine lotion or a sting relief spray may help. All lice cause itching and discomfort. They make themselves at home in your hair (head lice), your clothing (body lice) or in your pubic hair (crabs). You catch lice through direct contact with infected people or by sharing combs, clothing and the like. Powder or shampoo treatment will kill them and infected clothing should be washed in very hot, soapy water and left in the sun to dry.

Bites & Stings Bee and wasp stings are usually painful rather than dangerous, but for people who are allergic to them severe breathing difficulties may occur and require urgent medical care. Calamine lotion or a sting relief spray will ease discomfort and ice packs will reduce pain and swelling. There are some spiders with dangerous bites but antivenenes are available. Scorpion stings are notoriously painful and can be fatal. Scorpions often shelter in shoes or clothing.

Cuts & Scratches Wash well and treat any cut with an antiseptic such as povidoneiodine. Where possible avoid bandages and Band-Aids, which can keep wounds wet.

Leeches & Ticks Leeches may be present in the forests; they attach themselves to your skin to suck your blood. Trekkers often get them on their legs or in their boots. Salt or a lighted cigarette end will make them fall off. Do not pull them off, as the bite is then more likely to become infected. Clean and apply pressure if the point of attachment is bleeding. An insect repellent may keep them away.

You should always check all over your body if you have been walking through a potentially tick-infested area as ticks can cause skin infections and other more serious diseases. If a tick is found attached, press down around the tick's head with tweezers, grab the head and gently pull upwards. Avoid pulling the rear of the body as this may squeeze the tick's gut contents through the attached mouth parts into the skin, increasing the risk of infection and disease. Smearing chemicals on the tick will not make it let go and is not recommended.

Snakes To minimise your chances of being bitten always wear boots, socks and long trousers when walking through undergrowth where snakes may be present. Don't put your hands into holes and crevices, and be careful when collecting firewood.

Snake bites do not cause instantaneous death and antivenenes are usually available. Immediately wrap the bitten limb tightly, as you would for a sprained ankle, and then attach a splint to immobilise it. Keep the victim still and seek medical help, if possible with the dead snake for identification. Don't attempt to catch the snake if there is a possibility of being bitten again.

Tourniquets and sucking out the poison are now comprehensively discredited.

Women's Health

Gynaecological Problems Antibiotic use, synthetic underwear, sweat and contraceptive pills can lead to fungal vaginal infections, especially in hot climates. Fungal infections are characterised by a rash, itch and discharge, and can be treated with a vinegar or lemon-juice douche, or with yoghurt. Nystatin, miconazole or clotrimazole pessaries or vaginal cream are the usual

Rajasthani girls in traditional dress. Jewellery is an essential part of their everyday attire.

LIZ THOMPSON

MICHELLE COXALL

A musician with his *tambura*, Jaisalmer.

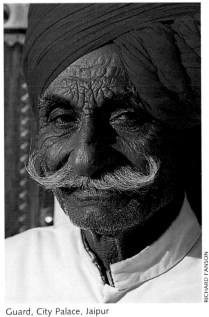

RICHARD I'ANSON

Guard, City Palace, Jaipur

RICHARD I'ANSON

Elephant below Amber Fort, near Jaipur.

SARINA SINGH

Village potter, near Jodhpur.

GREG ELMS

The sun's rays add to the brilliance of the clothes in this crowd scene, Jaisalmer.

treatment. Maintaining good personal hygiene, and wearing loose-fitting clothes and cotton underwear may help prevent these infections.

Sexually transmitted diseases are a major cause of vaginal problems. Symptoms include a smelly discharge, painful intercourse and sometimes a burning sensation when urinating. Medical attention should be sought and male sexual partners must also be treated. Remember that in addition to these diseases HIV or hepatitis B may also be acquired during exposure. Besides abstinence, the best thing is to practise safe sex using condoms.

Pregnancy It is not advisable to travel to some places while pregnant as some vaccinations normally used to prevent serious diseases are not advisable in pregnancy (eg yellow fever). In addition, some diseases are much more serious for the mother (and may increase the risk of a stillborn child) in pregnancy eg malaria.

Most miscarriages occur during the first three months of pregnancy. Miscarriage is not uncommon, and can occasionally lead to severe bleeding. The last three months should be spent within reasonable distance of good medical care. A baby born as early as 24 weeks stands a chance of survival, but only in a good modern hospital.

Pregnant women should avoid all unnecessary medication, although vaccinations and malarial prophylactics should still be taken where needed. Extra care should be taken to prevent illness and particular attention should be paid to diet and nutrition. Alcohol and nicotine, for example, should be avoided.

Less Common Diseases
The following diseases pose a small risk to travellers, and so are only mentioned in passing. Seek medical advice if you think you may have any of these diseases.

Cholera This is the worst of the watery diarrhoeas and medical help should be sought. Outbreaks of cholera are generally widely reported, so you can avoid such problem areas. Fluid replacement is the most vital treatment – the risk of dehydration is severe as you may lose up to 20L a day. If there is a delay in getting to hospital then begin taking tetracycline. The adult dose is 250mg four times daily. It is not recommended for children under nine years nor for pregnant women. Tetracycline may help shorten the illness, but adequate fluids are required to save lives.

Filariasis This is a mosquito-transmitted parasitic infection found in India and other parts of Asia. Possible symptoms include fever, pain and swelling of the lymph glands, inflammation of lymph drainage areas, swelling of a limb or the scrotum, skin rashes and blindness.

Treatment is available to eliminate the parasites from the body, but some of the damage already caused may not be reversible. Medical advice should be obtained promptly if the infection is suspected.

Leishmaniasis This is a group of parasitic diseases transmitted by the bite of sandflies which are found in India and other parts of the world. Cutaneous leishmaniasis affects the skin tissue causing ulceration and disfigurement, and visceral leishmaniasis affects the internal organs.

Seek medical advice as laboratory testing is required for diagnosis and correct treatment. Avoiding sandfly bites is the best precaution and yet another reason to cover up and apply repellent.

Lyme Disease This is a tick-transmitted infection which may be acquired in India. The illness usually begins with a spreading rash at the site of the tick bite and is accompanied by fever, headache, extreme fatigue, aching joints and muscles and mild neck stiffness. If untreated, these symptoms usually resolve over several weeks but over subsequent weeks or months disorders of the nervous system, heart and joints may develop. Treatment works best early in the illness. Medical help should be sought.

Rabies This fatal viral infection is found in many countries, including India. Many animals can be infected (eg dogs, cats, bats and monkeys) and it is their saliva which is infectious. Any bite, scratch or even lick from an animal should be cleaned immediately and thoroughly. Scrub with soap and running water, and then apply alcohol or iodine solution. Medical help should be sought promptly to receive a course of injections to prevent the onset of symptoms and death.

Tetanus This disease is caused by a germ which lives in soil and the faeces of horses and other animals. It enters the body via breaks in the skin. The first symptom may be discomfort in swallowing, or stiffening of the jaw and neck; this is followed by painful convulsions of the jaw and whole body. The disease can be fatal. It can be prevented by vaccination.

Tuberculosis (TB) TB is a bacterial infection usually transmitted from person to person by coughing but may be transmitted through consumption of unpasteurised milk. Milk that has been boiled is safe to drink, and the souring of milk to make yoghurt or cheese also kills the bacilli. Travellers are usually not at great risk as close household contact with the infected person is usually required before the disease is passed on. You may need to have a TB test before you travel as this can help diagnose the disease later if you become ill.

Typhus This disease is spread by ticks, mites or lice. It begins with fever, chills, headache and muscle pains followed a few days later by a body rash. There is often a large painful sore at the site of the bite, and nearby lymph nodes are swollen and painful. Typhus can be treated under medical supervision. Seek local advice on areas where ticks pose a danger and always check your skin carefully for them after walking in a danger area such as a tropical forest. An insect repellent can help, and walkers in tick-infested areas should consider having their boots and trousers impregnated with benzyl benzoate and dibutylphthalate.

WOMEN TRAVELLERS
Attitudes Towards Women
India is generally perfectly safe for women travellers, even for those travelling alone. Having said that, foreign women have been hassled, stared at, spied on in hotel rooms, and often groped, although the situation was rarely threatening. Rajasthan is, unfortunately, no exception, and women travelling alone will find themselves constantly the centre of unsolicited male attention.

Being a woman also has some advantages. There is often a special ladies' queue for train tickets or even a ladies' quota and ladies' compartments. One woman wrote that these ladies' carriages were often nearly empty – another said that they were full of screaming children. Special ladies' facilities are also sometimes found in cinemas and other places.

Safety Precautions
Staying safe is a matter of common sense. Close attention to standards of dress will go a long way to minimising problems for female travellers. The light cotton drawstring skirts that many foreign women pick up in Rajasthan are really sari petticoats and to wear them in the street is rather like going out half dressed. Ways of blending into the background include avoiding sleeveless blouses, shorts, skimpy, short or tight-fitting clothing and the bra-less look.

The *salwar kameez* (traditional Punjabi shirt and pyjama combination) is becoming increasingly popular among western women travellers because it's practical and cheap and, most of all, it's considered respectable attire. A cotton salwar kameez is also surprisingly cool in a hot climate and keeps the burning sun off your skin. A scarf, or the *dupatta* that is worn with the salwar kameez, is handy if you visit a shrine that requires your head to be covered.

Getting stared at is something you'll have to get used to. Walk confidently and don't return male stares, as this may be considered a come-on; just ignore them. Dark glasses can help. Other harassment likely to be encountered includes obscene comments, touching-up and jeering, particularly by groups of youths. Taking a book to a restaurant is a good way of avoiding eye contact. Be courteous yet firm when dealing with male service staff, especially in hotels.

Getting involved in inane conversations with men is often considered a turn-on. Keep discussions down to a necessary minimum. If you get the uncomfortable feeling he's encroaching on your space, the chances are that he is. A firm request to keep away is usually enough.

On trains and buses, firmly return any errant limbs, put some item of luggage in between you and if all else fails, find a new spot. You're also within your rights to tell him to shove off!

Make it a point to arrive in towns before it gets dark and if you go out at night it's a good idea to inform someone at the hotel where you are going and when you intend to return.

GAY & LESBIAN TRAVELLERS
While overt displays of affection between members of the opposite sex, such as cuddling and hand-holding, are frowned upon in India, it is not unusual to see Indian men holding hands with each other or engaged in other close affectionate behaviour. This does not necessarily suggest that they are gay. The gay movement in India is confined almost exclusively to larger cities and Mumbai is really the only place where there's a gay 'scene'.

As with relations between heterosexual western couples travelling in India – both married and unmarried – gay and lesbian travellers should exercise discretion and refrain from displaying overt affection towards each other in public.

Legal Status Homosexual relations for men are illegal in India. Section 377 of the national legislation forbids 'carnal intercourse against the order of nature' (that is, anal intercourse). The penalties for trans-gression can be up to life imprisonment. There is no legislation forbidding lesbian relations.

Publications & Organisations *Bombay Dost* is a gay and lesbian publication available from 105 Veena Beena Shopping Centre, Bandra (W) Mumbai; The People Tree, 8 Parliament St, New Delhi; and Classic Books, 10 Middleton St, Calcutta.

Support groups include Bombay Dost (address above); Pravartak, Post Bag 10237, Calcutta, West Bengal 700019; Sakhi (Lesbian Group), PO Box 3526, Lajpat Nagar, New Delhi 110024; and Sneha Sangama, PO Box 3250, RT Nagar, Bangalore 560032.

DISABLED TRAVELLERS
Travelling in Rajasthan has some fairly rigorous challenges, even for the able-bodied traveller – long bus trips in crowded vehicles between remote villages and endless queues in the scorching heat at bus and train stations can test even the hardiest traveller. For the mobility-impaired traveller, these challenges are increased many-fold. Few buildings have wheelchair access; toilets have certainly not been designed to accommodate wheelchairs; footpaths, where they exist (only in larger towns), are generally riddled with potholes and crevices, littered with obstacles and packed with throngs of people, severely restricting mobility.

Nevertheless, increasing numbers of disabled travellers are taking on the challenge. Seeing the mobility-impaired locals in the city of Jaipur whizz through the traffic at breakneck speed in modified hand-powered bicycles might even serve as inspiration! If your mobility is restricted you will require a strong, able-bodied companion to accompany you, and it would be well worth considering hiring a private vehicle and your own driver.

Organisations One organisation that may be able to assist with information on travel practicalities in India for disabled people is the Royal Association for Disability and Rehabilitation (RADAR; ☎ 0171-250 3222, fax 250 0212 (after April 2000 ☎ 020-7250 3222, fax 7250 0212), email radar@radar. org.uk) at 12 City Forum, 250 City Rd, London EC1V 8AF, UK.

SENIOR TRAVELLERS

Unless you are incapacitated, or your mobility or vision is impaired, and if you're are in reasonable health, there is absolutely no reason why the senior traveller should not consider India as a holiday destination. Travelling in India can be exhausting, so give yourself some time just to relax. It may be helpful to discuss your proposed trip with your local GP.

TRAVEL WITH CHILDREN

The numbers of intrepid souls travelling around India accompanied by one, or even two, young children, seems to be on the increase. Children can often enhance your encounters with local people, as they often possess little of the self-consciousness and sense of the cultural differences which can inhibit interaction between adults. Nevertheless, travelling with children can be hard work, and ideally the burden needs to be shared between two adults.

If you are travelling with children, make sure you take along enough sunscreen lotion as the midday sun can pack quite a punch in Rajasthan (even in the winter) and their skin is easily burnt.

For more information, see the Health section earlier in this chapter, and get hold of a copy of Lonely Planet's *Travel with Children* by Maureen Wheeler.

A good Web site for a personal account of travelling in India with children is www .southwest.com.au/~lockley. Lonely Planet's Thorn Tree (www.lonelyplanet com.au) has a subdirectory on travelling with children.

DANGERS & ANNOYANCES

Common sense and caution are your best weapons against the risk of theft or worse. There's no need to be paranoid – talk to other travellers, and pay heed to suggestions any reliable staff at hotels and guesthouses tell you.

Warning

❗ Lonely Planet recommends that travellers do not burn charcoal or other fuels as a means of heating in hotel rooms. Tragically, a number of people have died, including two young English people in Darjeeling in 1996, of carbon monoxide poisoning because they've used fires in their poorly ventilated hotel room. Ask the proprietor for more blankets if you need to get warm.

Theft

You should never leave those most important valuables (passport, tickets, health certificates, money, travellers cheques) in your room; they should be with you at all times. Either have a stout leather passport wallet on your belt, a passport pouch under your shirt, or simply extra internal pockets in your clothing. On trains at night keep your gear near you; padlocking a bag to a luggage rack can be useful, and some of the newer trains have loops under the seats which you can chain things to. Never walk around with valuables casually slung over your shoulder. Take extra care in crowded public transport.

Thieves are particularly prevalent on train routes where there are lots of tourists. The Delhi-Agra *Shatabdi Express* service is notorious; Delhi to Jaipur, Jaipur to Ajmer and Jodhpur to Jaisalmer are other routes to take care on. Train departure time, when the confusion and crowds are at their worst, is the time to be most careful. Just as the train is about to leave, you are distracted by someone while their accomplice is stealing your bag from by your feet.

Airports are another place to be careful, especially when international arrivals take place in the middle of the night, when you are unlikely to be at your most alert.

Beware also of your fellow travellers. Unhappily there are more than a few backpackers who make their money go further by helping themselves to other people's.

Finally, a good travel insurance policy helps. If you do have something stolen, you're going to have to report it to the police. You'll also need a statement proving you have done so if you want to claim on insurance. Insurance companies, despite their rosy promises of full protection and speedy settlement of claims, are just as disbelieving as the Indian police and will often attempt every devious trick in the book to avoid paying out on a baggage claim. Note that some policies specify that you must report an item stolen to the police within a limited amount of time of finding it missing.

Stolen Travellers Cheques If you're unlucky enough to have travellers cheques stolen, some precautions can ease the pain. The most important one is to keep an emergency cash-stash in a totally separate place. In that same place you should keep a record of the cheque serial numbers, proof of purchase slips, encashment vouchers and your passport number.

American Express makes considerable noise about 'instant replacement' of their cheques but a lot of people find, to their cost, that without taking these precautions 'instant' can take longer than you think. If you don't have the receipt you were given when you bought the cheques, rapid replacement will be difficult. The receipt should be kept separate from the cheques, and a photocopy in yet another location doesn't hurt either. Chances are you'll be able to get a limited amount of funds on the spot, and the rest will be available when the bank has verified your initial purchase of the cheques. American Express has a 24 hour number in Delhi (☎ 011-687 5050) which you must ring within 24 hours of the theft.

Holi Festival

The Hindu festival of Holi is usually a lot of fun, but unfortunately some merrymakers can go a bit too far. The festival is celebrated in India in late February/early March with much zeal (see the boxed text Festivals of Rajasthan later) and the last day is marked by the exuberant and excessive

---

Diarrhoea With Your Meal, Sir?

Scams designed to part tourists from their money are many and varied. The nastiest scam of all involves poisoning diners to make money from subsequent medical treatment. There are variations on this theme, but essentially a guest at a hotel is targeted, and when they eat at the hotel restaurant their meal is deliberately adulterated. The victim becomes quickly and violently ill with a stomach complaint. The hotel then arranges for a 'doctor' to come around and/or for the victim to be sent to a private clinic. Either way, the victim pays for treatment and a tidy profit is made.

Usually, the poisoning scam is combined with a medical insurance fiddle, through which the clinic claims for expensive treatments under the victim's travel insurance, rather than getting the victim to pay directly. In this instance the clinic will insist the victim be hospitalised and undergo extensive (and perhaps unnecessary) treatment, such as being hooked up to an intravenous drip, to bump up the charge. Sometimes the insurance scam is offered all by itself: you will be encouraged to fraudulently sign for medical treatment even if you haven't been ill, perhaps in return for free lodging or a cash sum.

The poisoning scam became public knowledge in late 1998 when several victims complained about it to the authorities and two Irish backpackers allegedly died as a result of it. Now that the matter has been investigated by the police, it is to be hoped that the perpetrators will be scared off. Nevertheless, it's wise to seek local advice from other travellers.

---

throwing of coloured powder and water. Foreign visitors are considered fair game for a dousing – especially in tourist spots such as Udaipur, Jaipur and Jodhpur. There have been several reports of toxic substances being mixed with the water thrown at people during this high-spirited festival.

Female travellers have also reported being groped by drunken men. It's advisable for women to avoid venturing onto the streets alone on the last day of Holi, when this festival reaches its climax.

Contaminated Food & Drink

From time to time drugging episodes are reported. Travellers meet somebody on a train or bus or in a town, start talking and are then offered a cup of tea or something similar. Hours later they wake up with a headache and all their gear gone. Don't accept drinks or food from strangers no matter how friendly they seem, particularly if you're on your own. (See boxed text on previous page.)

The drink *bhang lassi*, which is laced with marijuana, can pack more of a punch than the hapless traveller would reasonably expect – see the boxed text Bhang Lassi Warning in the Drinks section, later in this chapter.

LEGAL MATTERS

If you find yourself in a sticky legal predicament, contact your embassy immediately. You should carry your passport with you at all times.

In the Indian justice system it seems the burden of proof is on the accused, and proving one's innocence is virtually impossible. The police forces are often corrupt and will pay 'witnesses' to give evidence.

Drugs

For a long time India was a place where you could indulge in all sorts of illegal drugs (mostly grass and hashish) with relative ease and safety – they were cheap, readily available and the risks were minimal. These days things have definitely changed. Although dope and hashish are still widely available, penalties for possession, use and trafficking in illegal drugs are strictly enforced. If convicted on a drugs-related charge, sentences are long (minimum of 10 years), even for minor offences, and there is no remission or parole. In some cases it has taken almost three years just to get a court hearing.

BUSINESS HOURS

Government offices are open from 10 am to 5 pm, Monday to Saturday, and are closed every second Saturday. Banks are open from 10 am to 2 pm Monday to Friday, and 10 am to noon on Saturday – although there are variations, so it pays to check. Travellers cheque transactions usually cease 30 minutes before the official bank closing time. In some tourist centres there may be foreign exchange offices that stay open longer (eg Thomas Cook is open Monday to Saturday 9.30 am to 6 pm). In most of the state capitals, the main post office is open until around 7 pm daily.

Shops and offices are usually closed on Sunday and public holidays. In popular tourist areas such as Udaipur, Jaisalmer and Pushkar, many shops open at around 9 am, and close at around 7 pm. About half close on Sunday.

PUBLIC HOLIDAYS & SPECIAL EVENTS

India has a great number of holidays and festivals. Most of them follow either the Indian lunar calendar (a highly complicated system determined chiefly by astrologers) or the Islamic calendar (which is about 11 days shorter than the Gregorian (western) calendar; 12 days shorter in leap years), and therefore changes from year to year according to the Gregorian calendar. Local tourist offices should be able to provide specific dates. Most tourist attractions, such as museums and monuments, are closed on public holidays.

Festivals in Rajasthan generally take one of three forms: purely religious festivals; tourist-oriented festivals; and *melas*, or fairs, such as the Pushkar Camel Fair, which provide opportunities for villagers from remote regions to trade livestock and socialise. In this last category, fairs can also have a religious element – people attending the Pushkar Camel Fair, for example, take advantage of their visit to this holy town by taking some time to bathe in the sacred lake, worship and present offerings and *pujas* (prayers) at the temples.

Hindu Lunar Months

The months of the Hindu lunar calendar *(vikram samvat)* and their Gregorian equivalents are as follows:

Chaitra	March-April
Vaishaka	April-May
Jyaistha	May-June
Asadha	June-July
Sravana	July-August
Bhadra	August-September
Asvina	September-October
Kartika	October-November
Aghan	November-December
Pausa	December-January
Magha	January-February
Phalguna	February-March

ACTIVITIES
Camel Safaris

Just about everyone in Rajasthan is offering camel safaris these days. Apart from hotels, there are specialist operators. A favourite is the Jaisalmer region, in western Rajasthan, where it's possible to take a safari lasting from one day up to a week or more. Prices vary according to what is provided Basic safaris start at about Rs 350 per person per day, which includes meals. You pay more for greater comfort. The Pushkar area is also popular, and a couple of operators in Shekhawati offer camel treks around towns with interesting painted havelis in this semi-arid region. Several operators in Bikaner (western Rajasthan) also offer good camel safaris and one has just set up in Jodhpur. See the relevant chapters for more details.

Regional Festival Calendar

Descriptions of regional festivals are included at the beginning of individual chapters of this book. The following is a quick reference for dates of the major regional fairs and festivals up to the year 2003.

festival/fair	lunar calendar	2000	2001	2002	2003
Bikaner Camel Festival	Pausa 14-15	20-21 Jan	8-9 Jan	27-28 Jan	17-18 Jan
Nagaur Fair	Magha 7-10	12-15 Feb	31 Jan-3 Feb	19-22 Feb	8-11 Feb
Jaisalmer Desert Festival	Magha 13-15	17-19 Feb	6-8 Feb	25-27 Feb	14-16 Feb
Jaipur Elephant Festival	Phalguna 15	19 Mar	9 Mar	28 Mar	17 Mar
Gangaur Fair, Jaipur	Chaitra 3-4	7-8 Apr	28-29 Mar	15-16 Apr	4-5 Apr
Mewar Festival, Udaipur	Chaitra 3-4	7-8 Apr	28-29 Mar	15-16 Apr	4-5 Apr
Teej Fair, Jaipur	Sravana 3-4	2-3 Aug	23-24 Jul	11-12 Aug	1-2 Aug
Marwar Festival, Jodhpur	Asvina 14-15	12-13 Oct	31 Oct-1 Nov	19-20 Oct	8-9 Oct
Pushkar Camel Fair	Kartika 12-15	9-11 Nov	27-30 Nov	16-19 Nov	5-8 Nov
Dussehra Mela, Kota	Asvina 8-10	5-7 Oct	24-26 Oct	13-15 Oct	3-5 Oct
Chandrabhaga Fair, Jhalawar	Kartika 14	10-12 Nov	29 Nov-1 Dec	18-20 Nov	7-9 Nov

Festivals of Rajasthan

These festivals are celebrated across the entire state of Rajasthan and many are nationwide celebrations. For exact dates, see the boxed text Regional Festival Calendar. Descriptions of regional festivals are included at the beginning of individual chapters.

February-March

Shivaratri – This day of fasting is dedicated to Lord Shiva; his followers believe that it was on this day he danced the *tandava* (the Dance of Destruction). Processions to the temples are followed by the chanting of mantras and anointing of *lingams* (phallic symbols).

Holi – This is one of the most exuberant Hindu festivals, with people marking the end of winter by throwing coloured water and *gulal* (powder) at one another. On the night before Holi, bonfires are built to symbolise the destruction of the evil demon Holika. Rajasthanis celebrate Holi with particular enthusiasm, and foreign visitors are considered fair game for a dousing with gulal. It's great fun, and your best bet is just to give yourself up to the revelry, wear your oldest clothes, and expect to look like a *gulab jamun* (red sticky sweet) at the end of the day. Udaipur and Jaisalmer are both excellent venues to celebrate Holi (but in some places the festivities can get a bit out of control – see the Dangers & Annoyances section of this chapter).

March-April

Gangaur – This festival is a celebration of love – that between Shiva and his consort Gauri, or Parvati – and is a favourite with the women of Rajasthan. Unmarried girls pay homage to Gauri in the hope that they will be blessed with a good husband. Married women pray for the long life and health of their husbands. Images of Gauri are garbed in colourful vestments and carried through the streets in processions. Women perform the *ghoomer* dance, and married women try to be at their husbands' sides during the festival. Jaipur, Bikaner, Jodhpur, Nathdwara and Jaisalmer all host colourful celebrations of Gangaur.

Ramanavami – In temples across India the birth of Rama, incarnation of Vishnu and hero of the *Ramayana*, is celebrated on this day. In the week previous to Ramanavami, the *Ramayana* is widely read and performed.

April-May

Baisakhi – This Sikh festival commemorates the day that Guru Govind Singh founded the Khalsa, the Sikh brotherhood, which adopted the five *kakkars* (means by which Sikh men recognise each other) as part of their code of behaviour. The *Granth Sahib*, the Sikh holy book, is read through at *gurdwaras* (Sikh temples). Feasts and dancing follow in the evening.

July-August

Teej – Also known as the Festival of Swings, a reference to the flower-bedecked swings which are erected at this time, Teej celebrates the onset of the monsoon, and is held in honour of the marriage of Shiva and Parvati.

Naag Panchami – This festival is dedicated to Ananta, the serpent upon whose coils Vishnu rested between universes. Offerings are made to snake images, and snake charmers do a roaring trade.

Raksha Bandhan (Narial Purnima) – On the full-moon day of the Hindu month of Sravana, girls fix amulets known as *rakhis* to their brothers' wrists to protect them in the coming year. The brothers give their sisters gifts. A woman can gain the brotherly protection of a man who

Festivals of Rajasthan

is not actually her brother by giving him a rakhi. Political expediency encouraged the maharani of Chittorgarh to honour the Emperor Humayun in this manner. The emperor was then compelled to try to save the fort of Chittorgarh from the sultan of Gujarat.

Janmashtami – The anniversary of Krishna's birth is celebrated with happy abandon in tune with Krishna's own mischievous moods.

Independence Day – This holiday on 15 August celebrates the anniversary of India's independence from Britain in 1947. The prime minister delivers an address from the ramparts of Delhi's Red Fort.

August-September

Ganesh Chaturthi – This festival, held on the fourth day of the Hindu month Bhadra, is dedicated to Ganesh, the god of good fortune. It is considered to be the most auspicious day of the year, but to look at the moon on this day is considered unlucky.

Shravan Purnima – After a day-long fast, high-caste Hindus replace the sacred thread which they always wear looped over their left shoulder.

September-October

Dussehra – Dussehra is celebrated by Hindus all over India in the month of Asvina. Kota, in southern Rajasthan, celebrates Dussehra with a large *mela*. Dussehra celebrates the victory of Lord Rama over the demon king Ravana.

Gandhi Jayanti – This is a solemn celebration of Mahatma Gandhi's birthday on 2 October.

October-November

Diwali (Deepavali) – This is the happiest festival of the Hindu calendar, celebrated on the 15th day of Kartika. At night countless oil lamps are lit to show Lord Rama the way home from his period of exile. Fireworks are used to celebrate this five-day festival. Diwali has also become the Festival of Sweets. Giving sweets is now as traditional as lighting lamps and firecrackers.

Govardhana Puja – This is a Hindu festival dedicated to that holiest of animals, the cow.

Nanak Jayanti – The birthday of Guru Nanak, the founder of the Sikh religion, is celebrated with prayer readings and processions.

November-December

Christmas Day – The anniversary of the birth of Christ is an Indian public holiday.

MUSLIM HOLIDAYS

The dates of the Muslim festivals are not fixed; they fall about 11 days earlier each year.

Ramadan – This most important Muslim festival is a 30 day dawn-to-dusk fast. It was during this month that the prophet Mohammed had the Quran revealed to him in Mecca. Ramadan falls between December and January.

Id-ul-Fitr – This day celebrates the end of Ramadan.

Id-ul-Zuhara – This is a Muslim festival commemorating Abraham's attempt to sacrifice his son. It is celebrated with prayers and feasts.

Muharram – Muharram is a 10 day festival commemorating the martyrdom of Mohammed's grandson, Imam Hussain.

Horse Safaris

Horse safaris are a good way of exploring the region. Some hotels can arrange horse safaris, and there are also a number of specialised operators such as Shalivahan Stud & Stables (see Organised Tours in the Jodhpur section of the Western Rajasthan chapter), Pratap Country Inn (see Places to Stay under Udaipur, in the Southern Rajasthan chapter), Ghanerao Tours and Aravali Safari & Tours (see Other Tours in the Jaipur chapter). The Dundlod Fort (see Dundlod in the Northern Rajasthan chapter) can arrange horse safaris around the Shekhawati region.

For most horse safaris, you are required to bring your own riding hat and boots. The best time to ride is during the cooler months (between mid-October and mid-March).

Cycling

Ramesh Jangid (see Nawalgarh in the Northern Rajasthan chapter) can organise cycling tours around the villages of Shekhawati, including informative commentaries on the remarkable paintings of this region. Butterfield & Robinson offers more upmarket organised bicycle tours (see Bicycle in the Getting Around chapter).

Alternatively, you can independently hire a bicycle from one of the numerous rental places found in the larger towns of Rajasthan and tour on your own.

Trekking

Various operators can organise treks in the Aravalli Range of Rajasthan. Ramesh Jangid (see Cycling) organises treks which include a guide, all meals, transport and accommodation in village homes, tents and *dharamsalas* (pilgrims' lodgings).

Aravali Safari & Tours in Jaipur can also organise treks in the Aravalli Range. Registhan Tours Pvt Ltd in Jaipur organises treks in the Udaipur region. See the Jaipur chapter for details.

Golf

It is possible to play golf (equipment is available for hire) in Jaipur and Jodhpur – see the relevant chapters for details.

Tennis

Few places in Rajasthan offer tennis facilities. Some of the top-end hotels may allow nonguests to play on their courts for a charge. In Jaipur, you can play at the Jai Club for Rs 200 per couple per hour – see the Jaipur chapter.

Ten-Pin Bowling

Bowling has tickled the fancy of Jaipurians. See Entertainment in the Jaipur chapter for details about the two bowling alleys in the capital.

Swimming

Some of the upmarket hotels, including the Hotel Jaipur Ashok in Jaipur, the Shiv Niwas Palace Hotel in Udaipur, the Ajit Bhawan in Jodhpur, the Sawai Madhopur Lodge near the Ranthambhore National Park, and the Gorbandh Palace Hotel in Jaisalmer, allow nonguests use of their swimming pool. Expect to pay anywhere from Rs 100 to Rs 300 for this privilege, which should include a towel.

Boating

Pedal and row boats can be hired at the lake at Ramgarh, situated about 35km from Jaipur.

In Eastern Rajasthan, you can have a boat ride at the Keoladeo Ghana National Park (Bharatpur), and at the Ana Sagar in Ajmer.

In southern Rajasthan, boats can be rented at Nakki Lake in Mt Abu, at Kishore Sagar in Kota, at Lake Bagela in Nagda, and at Fateh Sagar in Udaipur. Despite rumours several years ago, water sports have not been developed on the placid Lake Pichola in Udaipur – thank goodness! However, regulated organised boat rides are available and are recommended.

Polo & Horse Riding

You can learn polo and other equestrian skills at the Dundlod Fort hotel in Dundlod, in the Shekhawati region (see the Northern Rajasthan chapter). The Pratap Country Inn, near Udaipur, has horse riding lessons for beginners. See Places to Stay under Udaipur in the Southern Rajasthan chapter.

COURSES
Meditation Retreats
The Dhammathali Vipassana Meditation Centre near Jaipur runs courses in meditation for both beginners and more advanced students throughout the year at its centre near Galta, about 3km east of Jaipur (see the Jaipur chapter).

The Brahma Kumaris Spiritual University is at Mt Abu, and has introductory courses in raja yoga meditation. Residential courses are also offered, but these need to be organised through one of the 4500 or so overseas branches of the university before arrival in India (see Mt Abu in the Southern Rajasthan chapter).

Ramesh Jangid can organise on request supervised yoga meditation, nutrition and fasting courses for groups at his Apani Dhani (Eco Farm). See Nawalgarh in the Northern Rajasthan chapter for his contact details.

Yoga
Yoga courses are available at a number of places in Rajasthan, including Prakaritic Chikitsalya and Madhavanand Ashram, both in Jaipur (see the Jaipur chapter).

Astrology
Those fascinated by the mysterious future can take lessons in astrology, held by Dr Vinod Shastri, the General Secretary of the Rajasthan Astrological Council & Research Institute. There are lessons for beginners for Rs 3000 per person; advanced courses are available on application. The Jaipur chapter has more details.

Music & Dance
It is possible to learn traditional music and dance at the Maharaja Sawai Mansingh Sangeet Mahavidyalaya in Jaipur. See the Jaipur chapter for details.

Painting & Pottery
In Jhunjhunu, in the heart of the Shekhawati region, you can learn traditional Shekhawati painting from a local artist. See Jhunjhunu in the Northern Rajasthan chapter for details.

Stretch out and embrace all Rajasthan has to offer with a yoga course.

In Jaipur, Mr Kripal Singh gives lessons in Indian painting and pottery (see the Jaipur chapter).

VOLUNTEER WORK
Numerous charities and international aid agencies have branches in India and, although they're mostly staffed by locals, there are some opportunities for foreigners. Though it may be possible to find temporary volunteer work when you are in India, you'll probably be of more use to the charity concerned if you write in advance and, if they need you, stay for long enough to be of help. A week on a hospital ward may salve your conscience, but you may not do much more than get in the way of the staff there.

For information on specific charities in India, contact the main branches in your own country. For long-term posts, the following organisations may be able to help or offer advice and further contacts:

Australian Volunteers Abroad:
  Overseas Service Bureau Programme
  (☎ 03-9279 1788, fax 9416 1619)
  PO Box 350, Fitzroy, Vic 3065, Australia

Co-ordinating Committee for
  International Voluntary Service
  (☎ 01 45 68 27 31)
  c/o UNESCO, 1 rue Miollis, F-75015
  Paris, France
Council of International Programs (CIP)
  (☎ 703-527 1160)
  1101 Wilson Blvd Ste 1708, Arlington VA
  22209, USA
International Voluntary Service (IVS)
  (☎ 0131-226 6722)
  St John's Church Centre,
  Edinburgh EH2 4BJ, UK
Peace Corps of the USA
  (☎ 202-606 3970, fax 606 3110)
  1990 K St NW, Washington, DC 20526, USA
Voluntary Service Overseas (VSO)
  (☎ 0181-780 2266, fax 780 1326; after April
  2000 ☎ 020-8780 2266, fax 8780 1326)
  317 Putney Bridge Rd,
  London SW15 2PN, UK

Help in Suffering

Help in Suffering is an animal hospital in
Jaipur funded by the World Society for the
Protection of Animals (London) and Ani-
maux Secours, Arthaz, France. The philosophy of Help in Suffering is to create a
'friendly, rabies-free, healthy street dog
population'. It also treats sick animals, and
does a tremendous job to help creatures
great and small, from puppies to buffaloes.
If you see an animal in distress in Jaipur,
this is the place to call.

Qualified vets interested in working with
Help in Suffering in a voluntary capacity
should write to: Help in Suffering, Maharani
Farm, Durgapura, Jaipur, Rajasthan 302018,
(☎ 0141-550203, fax 548044). Your efforts
will be most beneficial if you stay for at least
a month. Donations are also gratefully accepted, and can be forwarded to: Help in
Suffering, 12 East View St, Greenwich,
NSW 2065, Australia.

SOS Worldwide

SOS, which has its headquarters in Vienna,
runs over 30 programs across India and celebrated its 30th year in India in 1995. The
society looks after orphaned, destitute and
abandoned children, cared for by unmarried
women, abandoned wives and widows. In
Jaipur, SOS has a garden-surrounded property, and cares for over 150 children and
young adults aged from birth to 25 years.
Children live in 'families' of up to 10 children with a 'mother' in semi-detached
homes on the grounds, and are all provided
with education.

Volunteers are welcome there to teach
English, help the children with their home-
work and simply join in their games. Mon-
etary donations are also gratefully accepted,
as are clothes in good condition, games, and
sporting equipment. It is also possible to
sponsor a child. Prospective sponsors
should specify the age and sex of a child
they would like to sponsor, and will receive
details of the child, progress reports and a
photograph. For more information write to
SOS Children's Village, Opposite Pital
Factory, Jhotwara Rd, Jaipur, 302016, Rajasthan (☎ 0141-202393, fax 200140).

Mother Teresa Home

The Mother Teresa Home (☎ 0141-365804)
is located near St Xavier's School at C-
Scheme in Jaipur. For information about
volunteer work, speak to the sister-
in-charge, Sister Theotina. Donations can
be sent to: The Missionaries of Charity,
Mother Teresa Home, PO Box 36, Jaipur,
Rajasthan.

Les Amis du Shekhawati

The aim of the Friends of Shekhawati is to
safeguard and preserve Shekhawati's rich
artistic heritage including both the remarkable paintings of this region, and the havelis
themselves. The society's work includes
educating local villagers about the social
and artistic importance of the paintings of
Shekhawati, as well as undertaking restoration work and promoting the region.
Ramesh Jangid (see Nawalgarh in the
Northern Rajasthan chapter) is the president
of the association, and he welcomes volunteers. For more information, or if you'd like
to become a member, contact: Friends of
Shekhawati, c/o Ramesh Jangid, Nawalgarh, 333042, Rajasthan (☎ 01594-24060,
fax 24061).

Urmul Trust

This trust was founded by Mr Sanjay Ghosh in 1986. The main aims of the trust are to provide primary health care and education to the people of the remote villages of Rajasthan; raise awareness among the women of the desert of their rights and privileges in society; and promote the handicrafts of rural artisans and cut out middlemen and commissions, with profits going directly to artisans.

Those interested in volunteer work with the trust should contact the secretary at the Urmul Trust (☎/fax 0151-523093), which is inside Urmul Dairy, Ganganagar Rd, Bikaner (adjacent to the bus station). There is work available in social welfare, teaching English, health care, and other projects. Even if you don't have skills in these areas, Urmul may have positions to implement and oversee projects. A high level of commitment is required. Donations are also gratefully accepted.

ACCOMMODATION

There is accommodation in Rajasthan to suit all pockets, from budget guesthouses at less than US$5 per night to some of India's most luxurious hotels, many of which have been converted from forts and palaces. In the desert village of Khuri, 40km from Jaisalmer, it's possible to stay in a *jhonpa*, a traditional mud hut with a thatched roof; in Pushkar, one place offers accommodation in treehouses; or you can always sleep under the stars on the Sam sand dunes.

Hotels can change from wonderful to awful in a matter of days, so explore a few options before deciding, or speak to other travellers to find out the current state of affairs. Be warned that these days the word 'palace' or 'castle' has been tacked onto literally hundreds of hotel names in Rajasthan, but most are not authentic royal abodes.

Check-out procedure can take ages at some hotels; to save time, ask reception to tally up your bill a day before you intend leaving. Room service (even at some of the expensive hotels) can also take an agonizingly long time; when placing your order, make a point of asking when it will be ready. Most hotels firmly discourage your driver from using the guest facilities (see Society & Conduct in the Facts About Rajasthan chapter).

Throughout India, hotels are defined as 'western' or 'Indian'. The differentiation is meaningless for the tourist, although expensive hotels are always western, because the acid test is the toilet. 'Western' hotels have a sit-up-style toilet; 'Indian' ones usually (but not always) have the traditional Asian squat style. In this book, the squat toilets are referred to as Indian-style toilets. You can find modern, well-equipped, clean places with Indian toilets and dirty, dismal dumps with western toilets. Some places even have the weird hybrid toilet, which is basically a western toilet with footpads on the edge of the bowl!

Most budget hotels offer either shared or private (attached) bathrooms. Most mid-range and all top-end hotels only have rooms with a private bathroom.

Accommodation tariffs will have risen by the time you read this (the increase could be anything from 5% to as much as 50%).

Tourist Bungalows

The Rajasthan Tourism Development Corporation (RTDC) has a good network of hotels (commonly referred to as 'tourist bungalows') throughout the state. Once they were great value, but these days, the conditions and services of most are below average. Nevertheless, many offer cheap dormitory accommodation (around Rs 50 per person per night). There are also usually three types of rooms available, all with attached bathroom: ordinary rooms (the cheapest option apart from the dormitory) have ceiling fans and sometimes only have cold water (hot water comes by the bucket); deluxe rooms have air coolers; and super-deluxe rooms are usually carpeted and have air-conditioning. Generally there is a non-veg restaurant (with filling thalis) on the premises, and sometimes a bar. Frequently the local tourist office (often known as the

Tourist Reception Centre) is also on the same premises – handy for information.

Railway Retiring Rooms

Railway retiring rooms are like regular hotels or dormitories except they are at the train stations. To stay here you are generally supposed to have a train ticket or Indrail Pass. The rooms are extremely convenient if you have an early train departure, although they can be noisy if it is a busy station. They are often very cheap and in some places also excellent value. In Jaisalmer, a portion of the railway retiring rooms are in a cluster of small jhonpas, opposite the train station. Retiring room details are at the end of the budget hotel section of each town.

Cheap Hotels

There are cheap hotels all over Rajasthan, from filthy, uninhabitable dives (with prices at rock bottom) to quite reasonable places. Ceiling fans, mosquito nets, private toilets and bathrooms are all possibilities, even in rooms which cost Rs 150 or less per night for a double. Many of the cheaper hotels have hot water in a bucket; some may have showers, but most are mere trickles.

Although prices are generally for singles and doubles, most hotels will put an extra bed in a room for about an additional 25%. In smaller hotels it's often possible to bargain a little if you want to. On the other hand, these places will often put their prices up if there's a shortage of accommodation.

Single women travellers may feel uneasy staying at a rock-bottom place, as they are often seedy, male-dominated joints. If you feel uncomfortable, ease your mind by moving on to another hotel.

Although rare in Rajasthan, some of the ultra-cheap, very basic places won't take foreigners because of the hassle of the foreign registration C forms (these have to be submitted to the local police station within 24 hours of the foreigner checking in).

Expensive Hotels

Rajasthan has a disproportionate number of expensive hotels, largely due to its tourist appeal. As well, many former maharajas have been compelled to convert their beautiful forts and palaces into swanky hotels to bring in the tourist dollars. In Jaipur and some other major centres, there are also five-star hotels belonging to international groups such as the Holiday Inn and Sheraton. The Oberoi Group has recently opened a very exclusive boutique hotel in Jaipur, and is planning to open similar hotels in Udaipur and Jaisalmer.

While the top-end hotels in India are certainly comfortable, the service at some leaves a little to be desired, especially considering the high tariffs. The staff can be rather indifferent and you sometimes feel more like a number than a name.

Palaces, Forts & Castles

Rajasthan is famous for its delightful palace hotels. The most well known are the Lake Palace and Shiv Niwas Palace hotels in Udaipur, the Rambagh Palace in Jaipur and the Umaid Bhawan Palace in Jodhpur (where the best suite will set you back a mere US$990 *per night*). But you don't have to spend a fortune to stay in a palace – there are plenty of other erstwhile royal abodes which are more moderately priced.

As palaces and forts were not originally designed for tourism purposes, the size and quality of rooms can vary wildly. If possible, try to look at a few rooms before checking-in.

Throughout the state there are many finely appointed historical buildings which have been converted into tourist accommodation. They are known as Heritage Hotels and include havelis, forts and former royal hunting lodges. Many of the RTDC's tourist offices have a brochure that lists Heritage Hotels, or you can contact the Heritage Hotels Association of India (☎ 0141-374112, fax 372084) in Jaipur.

Homestay/Paying Guest House Scheme

Staying with an Indian family can be an enriching education. It's a change from dealing with tourist-oriented people, and a good opportunity to experience everyday Indian life.

Rajasthan's homestay program, known as the Paying Guest House Scheme, operates in most major towns of Rajasthan. The cost is from Rs 50 per night upwards, depending on the level of facilities offered, but most cater to the budget end of the market. Meals are usually available with prior notice.

The scheme is administered by the RTDC, and tourist offices have comprehensive lists of the participating families. The Tourist Reception Centre in Jaipur sells a handy booklet (Rs 5) listing all the paying guest houses in Rajasthan.

Geysers

Many places to stay have geysers as the source of water. These are small hot water tanks. Some geysers at budget and mid-range hotels may have to be switched on an hour or so before use.

Taxes & Service Charges

The state government imposes a variety of taxes on hotel accommodation (and restaurants). At most rock-bottom hotels you won't have to pay any taxes. At the better budget places, and all mid-range hotels, you can assume that room rates over about Rs 250 will attract a 10% (sometimes just 5%) tax. Most mid-range and all luxury hotels attract a 10% loading.

Another common tax, additional to the above, is a service charge pegged at 10%. In some hotels this is only levied on food, room service and use of telephones, not on the accommodation costs. At others, it's levied on the total bill. If you're trying to keep costs down, don't sign up meals or room service to your room bill and keep telephone use to a minimum if you know that the service charge is levied on the total bill.

It is always worthwhile asking before you check-in whether you will be taxed, and by how much, to prevent an unpleasant shock when you get the bill. Rates quoted in this book are the basic rate only unless otherwise indicated. Taxes and service charges are extra.

Seasonal Variations

In the winter months (December to March) most hoteliers crank up their prices to two to three times the low-season price. In some locations and at some hotels, there are even higher rates for the brief Christmas/New Year period, or during major festivals such as the Camel Fair in Pushkar.

Conversely, in the low season (May to August) prices at even normally expensive hotels can be surprisingly reasonable.

Touts

Hordes of accommodation touts operate in many towns in Rajasthan – Jaipur, Ajmer, Pushkar, Udaipur and Jaisalmer, in particular – and at any international airport terminal. Very often they are the rickshaw-wallahs who meet you at the bus or train station. They earn a fat commission from hoteliers for taking you to their hotel. Some very good cheap hotels simply refuse to pay the touts and you'll then hear stories about the hotel you want being 'full', 'closed for repairs', 'no good any more' or even 'burnt down'. On one occasion, a traveller was informed that the hotel of their choice had been bombed! It hadn't.

Touts do have a use though – if you arrive in a town when some big festival is on, or during peak season, they will know where there are rooms available.

DRINKS
Nonalcoholic Drinks

Tea & Coffee Indian *chai* (tea) is much loved in Rajasthan and the sharing of this hot beverage is often a part of social and business gatherings. At train stations it is often served in small clay pots, which you then smash on the ground when empty. Unfortunately, these days chai-wallahs are increasingly using plastic cups which are not environmentally friendly.

Many travellers like Indian chai, but some people find it far too sweet. If you ask for 'tray tea', you will be given the tea, the milk and the sugar separately, allowing you to combine them as you see fit. Unless you specify otherwise, tea is 'mixed tea' or

Rajasthani Cuisine

Considering the paucity of fresh fruit and vegetables in the arid zones, Rajasthan has a surprising variety of regional dishes.

These days, quite a few restaurants have adapted Rajasthani dishes to cater to western tastes and you will only find authentic Rajasthani cuisine in the villages or at family homes.

Local restaurants, known elsewhere in the country as *dhabas*, are known here as *bhojanalyas*, from *bhojan* (food or meal), and *alya* (place). These simple eateries are great if you're on a tight budget, but make sure you get food that has been freshly cooked, not reheated. Many of these fast-food joints, especially omelette stalls, can be found around bus stands.

Thalis are the traditional all-you-can-eat meal, a combination of curry dishes, relishes, papadams, yoghurt, puris or chapatis and rice. Thali is actually the name of the plate on which the meal is served. Most of the RTDC hotels, for example, serve a decent thali at a reasonable price.

Rajasthan has interesting vegetarian dishes including *govind gatta*, a lentil paste with dried fruit and nuts which is rolled into a sausage shape, sliced and deep fried; *papad ki sabzi*, which is simply a papadam with vegetables and *masala* (mixed spices); and *alu mangori*, which is a ground lentil paste that is dried in the sun and then put in a curry with potatoes *(alu)* – once rolled by hand, it is now often forced through a machine in the same way as macaroni. A common vegetarian snack is *alu samosa*, pastry cones stuffed with spicy potato.

Mogri is a type of desert bean and it is creatively made into a curry known as *mogri mangori*. A sweeter version is *methi mangori* – methi is the leaf of a green desert vegetable. Another type of desert bean is *sangri*, which forms part of the dish *kair sangri*. *Kachri* is a type of desert fruit which is made into a chutney. *Dana methi* is small pea-shaped vegetables *(dana)* and methi boiled and mixed with sugar, masala and dried fruit. *Cheelra ka saag* is a gram (legume) flour paste *chapati* (unleavened bread) which is chopped up, fried, and then added to a curry.

Hunting or *shikhar* was an important Rajput tradition and this introduced a variety of game to the dinner table, including venison, quail, duck and wild boar. Nonveg dishes include *sule*, which is barbecued meat (usually mutton), and *khade masala ka keema*, which is minced meat *(keema)* with whole spices. *Hari mirch ka keema* is minced meat with green chillies. Some meat dishes are cooked in a *handi*, an earthenware pot.

Cereal dishes include *kabooli Jodhpuri,* which has meat, vegetables such as cauliflower, cabbage and peas, and fried gram paste balls. *Khichri* is a mix of cereals including millet which is added to meat dishes. *Dalia ki khichri* is wheat porridge mixed with masala, a little *gur* (jaggery, or raw sugar) and *ghee* (clarified butter). *Ghaat* is a corn porridge served with yoghurt.

Breads *(roti)* include *sogra*, a millet chapati; *makki roti*, a thick corn chapati; and *dhokla*, maize flour which is steamed and formed into balls and cooked with green coriander, spinach and mint, and eaten with chutney. A *purat roti* is a type of Rajasthani filo pastry. The roti is repeatedly coated with oil and folded so that when it is cooked it is light and fluffy. *Bati* is a popular Rajasthani bread, traditionally buried in the sand and left to bake in the scorching desert sun. *Saadi bati* is a baked ball of wheat flour paste. *Bafle bati* is steamed wheat flour balls. *Cheelre* is a gram powder paste chapati. *Masala bati* is wheat balls stuffed with masala, peas and peanuts.

Pickles and chutneys, known as *achars*, include *goonde achar*. Goonde is a green fruit that is boiled and mixed with mustard oil and masalas. *Kair achar* is a pickle with desert bean as its base. *Lahsun achar* is an onion pickle. *Lal mirch* is a garlic-stuffed red chilli. *Kamrak ka achar* is a pickle with kamrak, a type of desert vegetable with a pungent, sour taste. *Bathua raita* is a *raita* with the leaves of bathua used like spinach – boiled, rinsed, and into a paste with yoghurt.

Rajasthani Cuisine

There is no dearth of desserts in this desert state, including *lapsi*, which is jaggery with a wheat flour porridge; *kheer*, or rice pudding with cardamom and saffron, a favourite in north India; and *maalpua*, a small chapati made from wheat flour, rolled in sugar and fried.

Badam ki barfi is a type of almond fudge made from sugar, powdered milk, almonds and ghee. *Chakki* is a piece of *barfi* (a milk-based fudge) made from gram flour, sugar and milk cake. *Churma* is a sweet of gram flour, sugar, cardamom, ghee and dried fruits. *Ghewar* is a paste of *urad* cereal, a Rajasthani favourite. *Firni* is a ball-shaped sweet made from urad cereal, deep fried and then dipped in syrup. *Sooji halwa* is semolina pudding. *Meetha chaval* is sweet boiled rice. *Alu ki jalebi* is mashed potato, sugar, saffron and arrowroot. The mixture is made into spirals and fried in hot oil, then soaked in a warm sugar syrup. This sweet is served hot.

Paan

An Indian meal should properly be finished with *paan* – a collection of spices and condiments chewed with betel nut. Found throughout eastern Asia, betel is a mildly intoxicating and addictive nut, but by itself it is quite inedible. After a meal you chew paan as a mild digestive.

Paan sellers have little containers in which they mix either *saadha* (plain) or *mithaa* (sweet) paans from the betel nut itself, lime paste (the ash not the fruit), the powder known as *catachu*, various spices and even a dash of opium in a pricey paan. The concoction is folded in a piece of edible leaf which you chew. Then, spit the leftovers out and add another red blotch to the pavement. Paan will turn your teeth red-black over time and even addict you to the betel nut, but trying one won't do any harm.

Popular Dishes

Kair sangri is served with a mango pickle. Kair is a small, round desert fruit which grows on a prickly shrub and is a favourite of camels, and sangri is dried wild leaves. The seeds and leaves are soaked overnight in water, boiled and then fried in oil with various masalas, dried dates, red chillies, turmeric powder, shredded dried mango, salt, coriander and cumin seeds.

Bati is coarse wheat flour mixed with ghee and water then kneaded into a soft dough. Cinnamon and nutmeg powders are sprinkled into the dough, then into round balls and boiled in water, with a dash of turmeric powder. The balls are then roasted until they turn brown, deep fried in ghee and served with dhal. The dhal is urad lentils boiled in water then cooked with *garam* (hot) masala, red chillies, cumin seeds, salt, oil and fresh coriander.

Safed Maas (white meat) is a traditional Rajasthani delicacy. The secret is in the gravy – onion, ginger, garlic paste, salt, pepper, cashew nut paste and cardamom. Chunks of mutton (with bones) are cooked in this gravy and fresh cream is added just before serving.

Maas ka sule, a favourite meat dish among the Rajputs, can be made from partridge, wild boar, chicken, mutton and fish. Marinate chunks of meat in a paste of turmeric powder, coriander powder, ginger and garlic paste, salt, red chilli powder, mustard oil and yoghurt. Cook the chunks on skewers in a *tandoor*, then glaze with melted butter and a tangy masala.

Moong dhal halwa is a popular dessert of finely ground moong dhal, fried with ghee, sugar, cinnamon and cardamom powder until the mixture turns a light brown. Raisins, chopped cashew nuts and almonds are added before serving.

Ghewar is a paste of urad cereal which is crushed, deep fried and then dipped in a sugar syrup flavoured with cardamom, cinnamon and cloves. It is served hot and topped with a thick layer of unsweetened cream and garnished with rose petals.

'milk tea', which means it has been made by putting cold water, milk, sugar and tea into one pot and bringing the whole concoction to the boil, then letting it stew for a long time.

It's almost impossible to get a decent cup of coffee in the north. Even in an expensive restaurant instant coffee is almost always used; however, some top-end hotels in Rajasthan are now thankfully introducing cappuccinos to their menu! The branches of the Indian Coffee House (there's one in Jaipur) are one of the few places with reasonable coffee. In Udaipur, the El Parador restaurant makes excellent percolated coffee that really hits the spot.

Water Some travellers drink the water everywhere and never get sick; others are more careful and still get hit with a bug. Basically, you should not drink the water unless you know it has been boiled, and definitely avoid the street vendors' carts everywhere. Even in the better class of hotel and restaurant, the water is usually only filtered and not boiled. The local water filters remove solids and do nothing towards removing any bacteria. Water is generally safer in the dry season than in the monsoon when it really can be dangerous.

Water-purifying tablets are not available in India; bring them with you. See the Health section earlier.

Mineral Water Most travellers to India these days avoid tap water altogether and stick to mineral water. It is available virtually everywhere, and comes in 1L plastic bottles (a few now come in glass bottles). The price ranges from Rs 12 to Rs 40 (the top-end hotels charge the most), with Rs 20 being about the average.

Virtually all the so-called mineral water available is actually treated tap water. A recent reliable survey found that 65% of the available mineral waters were less than totally pure, and in some cases were worse than what comes out of the tap! Generally, though, if you stick to bottled water, any gut problems you might have will be from other sources. (See Basic Rules in the Health section earlier.) Before buying a bottle of mineral water, make sure the lid is properly sealed. Crush the bottle before disposing of it, to ensure that it cannot be refilled with tap water then resold.

Soft Drinks Soft drinks are a safe substitute for water. Coca-Cola got the boot from India a number of years back for not cooperating with the government, but both they and Pepsi Cola are back with a vengeance. There are many similar indigenous brands with names like Thums Up, Limca, Gold Spot or Mirinda. They are reasonably priced at around Rs 8 for a 300ml bottle (more in restaurants and hotels). They're very sweet.

Juices & Other Drinks You can get small boxes of fruit juices for about Rs 7. These are refreshing, if a little sweet. Freshly squeezed orange juice is usually available at bus and train stations.

Another alternative to soft drinks is soda water. It costs around Rs 4.50 for a 300ml bottle. With soda water you can get excellent, and safe, lemon squash sodas.

Falooda is a popular drink made with milk, nuts, cream and vermicelli strands. Finally there's *lassi*, that oh so cool, refreshing iced *curd* (yoghurt) drink. *Makhania lassi* is a delicious saffron-flavoured version.

Rajasthani Drinks *Chach* is a thin, salted lassi. *Jaljeera* is a mix of masalas and water. *Kairi chach* is unripe mango juice with water and salt, widely available in summer and allegedly a good remedy for sunstroke.

Alcoholic Drinks

Alcohol is relatively expensive – a bottle of Indian beer can cost anything from Rs 35 up to Rs 170 in a flashy hotel; Rs 40 to Rs 60 is the usual price range. Indian beers have delightful names such as Golden Eagle, Cannon Extra Strong, Bullet, Black Label, Knock Out, Turbo, Kingfisher, Guru or Punjab. At the time of writing, the government of Rajasthan was phasing out the sale

Bhang Lassi Warning

Although it's rarely printed in their menus, many restaurants in Rajasthan serve *bhang lassi*, a yoghurt and iced-water beverage laced with bhang, a derivative of marijuana. Usually called 'special lassi', this often potent concoction does not agree with everyone. Some travellers have been stuck in bed for several miserable days after drinking it; others have been robbed while lying in a state of delirium.

of beer from restaurants and beer bars. However, beer is still available in hotel bars and it is quite possible that the ban on beer could be temporary – check the situation out locally.

Beer and other Indian interpretations of western alcoholic drinks are known as IMFL – Indian Made Foreign Liquor. They include imitations of whisky and brandy under a plethora of different brand names. The taste varies from hospital disinfectant to passable imitation whisky. Always buy the best brand. If you fancy a rum and cola, the Indian rum Old Monk is not bad at all.

With the continuing freeing up of the economy, it is likely that well-known foreign brands of beer and spirits will become available.

Local drinks are known as country liquor and include *toddy*, a mildly alcoholic extract from the coconut palm flower, and *feni*, a distilled liquor produced either from fermented cashew nuts or from coconuts. The two varieties taste quite different.

Arak is what the peasants (and bus drivers' best boys) drink to get blotto. It's a clear, distilled rice liquor and it creeps up on you without warning. Treat with caution and only ever drink it from a bottle produced in a government-controlled distillery. *Never, ever* drink it otherwise – hundreds of people die or are blinded every year in India as a result of drinking arak produced in illicit stills. You can assume it contains methyl alcohol (wood alcohol).

ENTERTAINMENT

When it comes to pubs and bars, nightclubs and other activities you may take for granted, Rajasthan isn't a hive of activity (indeed this is part of the appeal for many tourists). Major cities such as Mumbai and Delhi are about the nearest you'll come to finding them. But one thing India is well endowed with is cinemas. There are many thousands all over the country. Entry is inexpensive, and if you haven't seen a Bollywood blockbuster before, you should try to see at least one during your trip. Jaipur's Raj Mandir Cinema, decked out in 1920s style, would have to be one of the most atmospheric places to see a Hindi film (see Entertainment in the Jaipur chapter).

Puppet shows or traditional Rajasthani music and dance performances are held at many hotels.

The Department of Tourism (☎ 0141-370180) in Jaipur can often arrange cultural programs for visitors. In Jaipur, for example, they can put on a traditional Rajasthani banquet followed by performances of folk dances.

SPECTATOR SPORTS
Cricket

India's national sport (obsession almost) is cricket. In recent years, Jaipur's Sawai Mansingh Stadium (☎ 0141-514732) has been the venue for several World Cup cricket matches (winter only). Tickets generally go on sale 10 days prior to the match, and matches are advertised in English-language papers. Telephone the stadium for details of forthcoming events.

Tennis

Some international tennis tournaments are held at the Jai Club, off MI Rd in Jaipur (near Panch Batti). Matches are generally well advertised, and tickets can often be obtained from sponsors.

Polo

Polo matches are played at the Rajasthan Polo Club (☎ 0141-383580), Bhawani Singh Rd, near the Rambagh Palace hotel,

Polo

Horse polo was very popular among the maharajas, especially during the British Raj, and they often provided polo ponies, facilities and training to talented players. Some of them were among the top players in the world, such as Maharaja Man Singh of Jaipur, whose polo team was champion on the European polo circuit in the 1930s. The maharaja had a stable of some 40 ponies, which were shipped over to England. The team was accompanied by a carpenter (to keep them supplied with polo sticks). Man Singh actually died playing the sport he loved, at a polo match in England in 1970.

Emperor Akbar was believed to have been the first person to introduce rules to the game, but polo, as it is played today, was introduced by a British Cavalry Regiment stationed in India during the 1870s. A set of international rules was implemented after WWI.

The game flourished in India until Independence, when patronage decreased and the game became less popular. Today there is a renewed interest in polo, and Rajasthan produces some of the nation's finest players. The Mewar (Udaipur) polo team has been one of the country's most successful both in India and abroad.

The Polo Bar at the Rambagh Palace hotel in Jaipur is dedicated to this sport of kings, and has photos of some great Indian polo players.

in Jaipur, and also at the polo ground in Ramgarh, about 35km from Jaipur (see Around Jaipur in the Jaipur chapter). Matches are also sometimes held at the polo ground in Jodhpur.

The horse polo season extends over winter with the most important matches usually played in March.

During Jaipur's Elephant Festival in March, matches of elephant polo are played. For more details, contact the tourist office in Jaipur.

SHOPPING

Rajasthan really is one of the easiest places to spend money – there are so many colourful arts and crafts, busy bazaars, gorgeous fabrics, miniature paintings, and much more. The cardinal rule when purchasing handicrafts is to bargain and bargain hard. You can get a good idea of what is reasonable in quality and price by visiting the Rajasthan state emporium, Rajasthali, in either New Delhi or Jaipur. Because prices are fixed, you will get an idea of how hard to bargain when you purchase similar items from regular dealers.

Be careful when buying items which include delivery to your home country. You may well be given assurances that the price includes home delivery and all customs and handling charges. Inevitably this is not the case, and you may find yourself having to collect the item yourself from your country's main port or airport, and pay customs charges (which could be as much as 20% of the item's value) and handling charges levied by the airline or shipping company (which could be up to 10% of the value). If you can't collect the item promptly, or get someone to do it on your behalf, exorbitant storage charges may also be charged.

Unfortunately, the quality of Rajasthan's handicrafts is not always what it could be, particularly in paintings, which are produced in great numbers for tourist buyers. Sellers may claim that the paintings are antiques – they rarely are, but a proficient artist should be able to produce a good reproduction of an old miniature. Udaipur has some good shops specialising in modern reproductions of those painted in Mewar from the early 18th century. These are produced on many different surfaces such as cloth, paper and marble. Other good buys in Udaipur include jewellery, block-printed fabrics, *dhurries* (cotton rugs), lac bangles and wooden handicrafts.

The heavy folk-art jewellery of Rajasthan has particular appeal for westerners. Traditional silver folk jewellery, which is quite chunky, is sold by weight in the bazaars of towns and cities. In Ajmer, you can buy

A Warning!

In touristy places such as Jaipur, take extreme care with the commission merchants – these guys hang around waiting to pick you up and cart you off to their favourite dealers where whatever you pay will have a hefty margin built into it to pay their commission. Stories about 'my family's place', 'my brother's shop' and 'special deal at my friend's place' are just stories and nothing more.

Whatever you might be told, if you are taken by a rickshaw driver or tout to a place, be it a hotel, craftshop, market or even restaurant, the price you pay will be inflated. This can be by as much as 50%, so try to visit these places on your own. And don't underestimate the persistence of these guys. We heard of one ill traveller who virtually collapsed into a cycle-rickshaw in Agra and asked to be taken to a doctor – he ended up at a marble workshop, and the rickshaw-wallah insisted that, yes, indeed a doctor did work there!

Another trap occurs when using a credit card. You may be told that if you buy the goods, the merchant won't forward the credit slip for payment until you actually received them, even if it is in three months time – this is total bullshit. No trader will be sending you as much as a postcard until they have received the money, in full, for the goods you are buying. What you'll find in fact is that within 48 hours of your signing the credit slip, the merchant has telexed the bank in Delhi and the money will have been credited to their account.

Also beware of any shop which takes your credit card out the back and comes back with the slip for you to sign. Sometimes while out of sight, the vendor will imprint a few more forms, forge your signature, and you'll be billed for items you haven't purchased. Have the slip filled out right in front of you.

If you believe any stories about buying anything in India to sell at a profit elsewhere, you'll simply be proving (once again) that old adage about separating fools from their money. Precious stones and carpets are favourites for this game. Merchants will tell you that you can sell the items in Australia, Europe or the USA for several times the purchase price, and will even give you the (often imaginary) addresses of dealers who will buy them. You'll also be shown written statements, from other travellers, documenting the money they have made – it's all a scam. The stones or carpets you buy will be worth only a fraction of what you pay. Don't let greed cloud your judgement. It seems that with every book we make the warnings longer and more explicit, and yet we still get letters from people with tales of woe and they usually concern scams we specifically mention.

While it is a minority of traders involved in dishonest schemes, virtually all are involved in the commission racket, so shop with care – take your time, be firm and bargain hard. Good luck!

---

other silver items such as cigarette and pill boxes. Pushkar is lined with shops selling silver jewellery, much of it designed with western tastes in mind. A good buy in Pushkar is painted and glass beads, good for making into necklaces. Also in Pushkar you can buy silk blouses at cheap prices. They're very light and don't take up much space in your pack. But be warned: after several washes they fray at the seams.

Pushkar sells good cassettes featuring traditional, contemporary or fusion music.

Dhurries can be good buys. Medium-fine quality knotted carpets have 150 to 160 knots per square inch, and cost around Rs 350 per square foot.

Jaipur is renowned for its blue-glazed pottery featuring floral and geometric motifs. Its *meenakari* enamelwork, likewise, is beautifully crafted. Filigree animals and birds are richly coloured in ruby reds, blues, greens and whites. Also in Jaipur you can buy Sanganeri block-print fabrics produced in the nearby village of Sanganer. Other Rajasthani textiles can be purchased in the bazaars, such as *bandhani* tie-dye prints. It's worth visiting the Anokhi showroom in Jaipur, where printed fabrics in traditional and contemporary designs are made into fashionable western garments and home accessories (cushion covers and table cloths).

Kota is best known for its saris, while Mt Abu has a jumble of things to buy, including carpets, bronze Hindu deities, curios and wooden items.

Colourful wooden and papier-mâché puppets make excellent gifts, and are ridiculously cheap. They can be found in most of the major towns.

Some travellers bring home a pair of *jootis*, the traditional leather shoes of Rajasthan, some of which feature embroidery and curled-up toes.

Wall hangings made from segments of intricately embroidered fabric, some with the beautiful mirrorwork for which Rajasthan (and neighbouring Gujarat) is famous, are popular buys. Pieces can range from small cushion-sized squares to bedspread-sized pieces. Prices range from a couple of hundred rupees up to several thousand. Barmer, south of Jaisalmer, is famous for its embroidery.

For more about the handicrafts of Rajasthan, see Arts in the Facts about Rajasthan chapter. Note that it is illegal to export ivory or any artefacts made from wild animals.

Antiques

In Jodhpur there are several showrooms specialising in antiques. Most of the good

Rajasthan's tradition of fine quality embroidery endures and makes the perfect gift.

merchandise has been picked over by dealers, but the showrooms are still fascinating places to visit, and you can purchase some excellent antique reproduction furniture, or have it made to order.

Articles over 100 years old are not allowed to be exported from India without an export clearance certificate. If you have doubts about any item and think it could be defined as an antique, you can check with branches of the Archaeological Survey of India. In New Delhi, contact the Director, Antiquities, Archaeological Survey of India, Janpath (☎ 011-301 7220).

Getting There & Away

No international airlines fly directly to Rajasthan, so getting there is a two part journey. Therefore, the first part of this chapter deals with travel from international destinations to India. For people travelling to Rajasthan, Delhi and Mumbai (Bombay) are the two main entry points. The second section of this chapter concentrates on travel from Delhi and Mumbai into Rajasthan.

Individual chapters devoted entirely to Delhi, Mumbai and Agra can be found at the end of this book.

India

AIR

The plane ticket will probably be the single most expensive item in your budget, and buying it can be an intimidating business. There is likely to be a multitude of airlines and travel agents hoping to separate you from your money, and it is always worth putting aside a few hours to research the current state of the market.

Start early: some of the cheapest tickets have to be bought months in advance, and some popular flights sell out early. Talk to other recent travellers, look at the ads in newspapers and magazines (not forgetting the press of the ethnic group whose country you plan to visit), consult reference books and watch for special offers. Then phone around travel agents for bargains. (Airlines can supply information on routes and timetables; however, except at times of inter-airline war they do not supply the cheapest tickets). Find out the fare, the route, the duration of the journey and any restrictions on the ticket. Then sit back and decide which is best for you.

You may discover that those impossibly cheap flights are 'fully booked, but we have another one that costs a bit more ...'. Or the flight is on an airline notorious for its poor safety standards and leaves you in the world's least favourite airport in mid-journey for 14 hours. Or they claim only to have the last two seats available for that country for the whole of November, which they will hold for you for a maximum of two hours. Don't panic – keep ringing around.

Use the fares quoted in this book as a guide only. They are approximate and based on the rates advertised by travel agents at the time of going to press. Quoted air fares do not necessarily constitute a recommendation for the carrier. If you are travelling from the UK or the USA, you will probably find that the cheapest flights are being advertised by obscure bucket shops whose names haven't yet reached the telephone directory. Many such firms are honest and solvent, but there are a few rogues who will take your money and disappear, to reopen elsewhere a month or two later under a new name. If you feel suspicious about a firm, don't give them all the money at once – leave a deposit of 20% or so and pay the balance when you get the ticket. If they insist on cash in advance, go somewhere else. And once you have the ticket, ring the airline to confirm that you are actually booked on the flight.

You may decide to pay more than the rock-bottom fare by opting for the safety of a better-known travel agent. Firms such as STA Travel, which has offices worldwide, Council Travel in the USA or Travel CUTS

Reconfirmation

It is essential to reconfirm your return flight home at least 72 hours prior to departure. Some travellers have reported that failure to do so resulted in cancelled seats and several anxious days, trying to secure new seats for their return journey – not a pleasant way to end a holiday in India!

in Canada are not going to disappear overnight, leaving you clutching a receipt for a nonexistent ticket, but they do offer good prices to most destinations.

Round-the-World (RTW) fares are very competitive and are a popular way to travel to India (see the boxed text Air Travel Glossary).

Once you have your ticket, write down its number, together with the flight number and other details, and keep the information somewhere separate. If the ticket is lost or stolen, this will help you get a replacement. It's sensible to buy travel insurance as early as possible. If you buy it the week before you fly, you may find, for example, that you're not covered for delays to your flight caused by industrial action.

International Airports

Most people who visit Rajasthan arrive at either the Delhi or Mumbai international airports. For important information about the Delhi and Mumbai airports, see those individual chapters at the end of this book.

International Airlines

See the Getting There & Away sections of the Delhi and Mumbai chapters for the contact details of international airline offices in each of those cities.

Travellers with Special Needs

If you have special needs of any sort – you've broken a leg or you're vegetarian, taking the baby, terrified of flying – you should let the airline know as soon as possible so they can make arrangements accordingly. You should remind them when you reconfirm your booking (at least 72 hours before departure) and again when you check in at the airport. It may also be worth ringing round the airlines before you make your booking to find out how they can handle your particular needs.

Airports and airlines can be surprisingly helpful, but they do need advance warning. Most international airports will provide escorts from check-in desk to plane where needed, and there should be ramps, lifts, accessible toilets and reachable phones. Aircraft toilets, on the other hand, are likely to present a problem; travellers should discuss this with the airline at an early stage and, if necessary, with their doctor.

Guide dogs for the blind will often have to travel in a specially pressurised baggage compartment with other animals, away from their owner; smaller guide dogs may be admitted to the cabin. All guide dogs will be subject to the same quarantine laws (six months in isolation etc) as any other animal when entering or returning to countries currently free of rabies such as Australia.

Deaf travellers can ask for airport and in-flight announcements to be written down for them.

Children under two travel for 10% of the standard fare (or free, on some airlines), as long as they don't occupy a seat. They don't get a baggage allowance either. 'Skycots' should be provided by the airline if requested in advance; these will take a child

---

Warning

The information in this chapter is particularly vulnerable to change: prices for international travel are volatile, routes can be introduced or cancelled, schedules change, special deals come and go, and rules and visa requirements are amended. Airlines and governments seem to take a perverse pleasure in making price structures and regulations as complicated as possible. You should check directly with the airline or a travel agent to make sure you understand how a fare (and ticket you may buy) works. In addition, the travel industry is highly competitive and there are many lurks and perks.

The upshot of this is that you should get opinions, quotes and advice from as many airlines and travel agents as possible before you part with your hard-earned cash. The details given in this chapter should be regarded as pointers and are not a substitute for your own careful, up-to-date research.

weighing up to about 10kg. Children between two and 12 can usually occupy a seat for half to two-thirds of the full fare and do get a baggage allowance. Pushchairs can often be taken as hand luggage.

Departure Tax
Departure tax is Rs 500 which can be paid on purchase of some tickets or at the airport. There is a Rs 250 tax to neighbouring countries (Sri Lanka, Pakistan, Bangladesh and Nepal).

Cheap Tickets in India
Although you can get cheap tickets in Mumbai and Calcutta, it is in Delhi that the real wheeling and dealing goes on. There are a number of bucket shops around Connaught Place, but inquire with other travellers about their current trustworthiness. And if you use a bucket shop, double-check with the airline itself that the booking has been made. Fares include:

from	to	price range
Delhi	London	Rs 13,000-20,000
Delhi	New York	Rs 22,000-30,000
Delhi	Los Angeles	Rs 28,000-35,000
Delhi	Hong Kong	Rs 17,000-19,000
Delhi	Bangkok	Rs 12,000-13,575
Delhi	Lahore	US$100
Delhi	Karachi	US$180
Calcutta	Hong Kong	Rs 17,000-19,000
Calcutta	Bangkok	Rs 9500-9730
Calcutta	Rangoon	Rs 6160
Calcutta	Kathmandu	US$96

The USA
The *New York Times*, the *LA Times*, the *Chicago Tribune* and the *San Francisco Examiner* all produce weekly travel sections in which you'll find any number of travel agents' ads. Council Travel and STA Travel have offices in major cities nationwide. The magazine *Travel Unlimited* (PO Box 1058, Allston, MA 02134) publishes details of the cheapest air fares and courier possibilities for destinations all over the world from the USA. The high season for flights from the US to India is June to August and again from December to January. Low season runs from March to around mid-May and from September to November.

High season fares from the east coast to Mumbai range from US$1650 (Air India via Delhi) to US$2300 (TWA/Air France via Paris). To Delhi fares are US$1500 (Delta Airlines via Frankfurt). Low season fares to Mumbai and Delhi are US$1500 (Alaska Airlines) and US$1400 (Lufthansa) respectively. Aeroflot consistently offers the lowest fares: US$900 to Mumbai from either coast during the high season. Singapore Airlines also has some very good deals.

Canada
Travel CUTS has offices in all major cities. The Toronto *Globe & Mail* and *Vancouver Sun* carry travel agents' ads. The magazine *Great Expeditions* (PO Box 8000-411, Abbotsford, BC V2S 6H1) is useful.

Vancouver to Mumbai fares are CA$1600 (Swissair or Lufthansa) in the low season and CA$1700 (Canadian Air via Chicago) in the high season. During the high season all flights from Vancouver are routed through the US. Montreal to Mumbai flights cost CA$1600; with Swissair or Lufthansa in the low season and KLM/Northwest (via Amsterdam) or Lufthansa (via Frankfurt) in the high season.

Australia
STA Travel and Flight Centres International are major dealers in cheap air fares. Check the travel agents' ads in the *Yellow Pages* and ring around.

The low season is 1 February to 21 November. Advance purchase tickets from the east coast of Australia to India range from A$1200 to A$1700 depending on the season and the destination in India. Fares are slightly cheaper from Darwin or Perth. Fares from Australia to the UK via India range from A$1950 to A$2250.

New Zealand
As in Australia, STA Travel and Flight Centres International are popular travel agents.

Air Travel Glossary

Baggage Allowance This will be written on your ticket and usually includes one 20kg item to go in the hold, plus one item of hand luggage.

Bucket Shops These are unbonded travel agencies specialising in discounted airline tickets.

Bumped Just because you have a confirmed seat doesn't mean you're going to get on the plane (see Overbooking).

Cancellation Penalties If you have to cancel or change a discounted ticket, there are often heavy penalties involved; insurance can sometimes be taken out against these penalties. Some airlines impose penalties on regular tickets as well, particularly against 'no-show' passengers.

Check-In Airlines ask you to check in a certain time ahead of the flight departure (usually one to two hours on international flights). If you fail to check in on time and the flight is overbooked, the airline can cancel your booking and give your seat to somebody else.

Confirmation Having a ticket written out with the flight and date you want doesn't mean you have a seat until the agent has checked with the airline that your status is 'OK' or confirmed. Meanwhile you could just be 'on request'.

Courier Fares Businesses often need to send urgent documents or freight securely and quickly. Courier companies hire people to accompany the package through customs and, in return, offer a discount ticket which is sometimes a phenomenal bargain. In effect, what the companies do is ship their freight as your luggage on regular commercial flights. This is a legitimate operation, but there are two shortcomings – the short turnaround time of the ticket (usually not longer than a month) and the limitation on your luggage allowance. You may have to surrender all your allowance and take only carry-on luggage.

Full Fares Airlines traditionally offer 1st class (coded F), business class (coded J) and economy class (coded Y) tickets. These days there are so many promotional and discounted fares available that few passengers pay full economy fare.

ITX An ITX, or 'independent inclusive tour excursion', is often available on tickets to popular holiday destinations. Officially it's a package deal combined with hotel accommodation, but many agents will sell you one of these for the flight only and give you phoney hotel vouchers in the unlikely event that you're challenged at the airport.

Lost Tickets If you lose your airline ticket an airline will usually treat it like a travellers cheque and, after inquiries, issue you with another one. Legally, however, an airline is entitled to treat it like cash and if you lose it then it's gone forever. Take good care of your tickets.

MCO An MCO, or 'miscellaneous charge order', is a voucher that looks like an airline ticket but carries no destination or date. It can be exchanged through any International Association of Travel Agents (IATA) airline for a ticket on a specific flight. It's a useful alternative to an onward ticket in those countries that demand one, and is more flexible than an ordinary ticket if you're unsure of your route.

No-Shows No-shows are passengers who fail to show up for their flight. Full-fare passengers who fail to turn up are sometimes entitled to travel on a later flight. The rest are penalised (see Cancellation Penalties).

On Request This is an unconfirmed booking for a flight.

Air Travel Glossary

Onward Tickets An entry requirement for many countries is that you have a ticket out of the country. If you're unsure of your next move, the easiest solution is to buy the cheapest onward ticket to a neighbouring country or a ticket from a reliable airline which can later be refunded if you do not use it.

Open Jaw Tickets These are return tickets where you fly out to one place but return from another. If available, this can save you backtracking to your arrival point.

Overbooking Airlines hate to fly empty seats and since every flight has some passengers who fail to show up, airlines often book more passengers than they have seats. Usually excess passengers make up for the no-shows, but occasionally somebody gets bumped. Guess who it is most likely to be? The passengers who check in late.

Point-to-Point Tickets These are discount tickets that can be bought on some routes in return for passengers waiving their rights to a stopover.

Promotional Fares These are officially discounted fares, available from travel agencies or direct from the airline.

Reconfirmation At least 72 hours prior to departure time of an onward or return flight, you must contact the airline and 'reconfirm' that you intend to be on the flight. If you don't do this the airline can delete your name from the passenger list and you could lose your seat.

Restrictions Discounted tickets often have various restrictions on them – such as needing to be paid for in advance and incurring a penalty to be altered. Others are restrictions on the minimum and maximum period you must be away, such as a minimum of 14 days or a maximum of one year.

Round-the-World Tickets RTW tickets give you a limited period (usually a year) in which to circumnavigate the globe. You can go anywhere the carrying airlines go, as long as you don't backtrack. The number of stopovers or total number of separate flights is decided before you set off and they usually cost a bit more than a basic return flight.

Stand-by This is a discounted ticket where you only fly if there is a seat free at the last moment. Stand-by fares are usually available only on domestic routes.

Travel Agencies Travel agencies vary widely and you should choose one that suits your needs. Some simply handle tours, while full-services agencies handle everything from tours and tickets to car rental and hotel bookings. If all you want is a ticket at the lowest possible price, then go to an agency specialising in discounted tickets.

Transferred Tickets Airline tickets cannot be transferred from one person to another. Travellers sometimes try to sell the return half of their ticket, but officials can ask you to prove that you are the person named on the ticket. This is less likely to happen on domestic flights, but on an international flight tickets are compared with passports.

Travel Periods Ticket prices vary with the time of year. There is a low (off-peak) season and a high (peak) season, and often a low-shoulder season and a high-shoulder season as well. Usually the fare depends on your outward flight – if you depart in the high season and return in the low season, you pay the high-season fare.

There are no direct flights between India and New Zealand so most airlines offer stopovers in Asia. Air fares to Delhi from Auckland with Malaysian Airlines cost from NZ$1745 return (NZ$1945 between November and January). There are a few cheaper combinations with Air India and Garuda.

The UK & Ireland

Various excursion fares are available from London to India, but you can get better prices through London's many cheap-ticket specialists. *Trailfinders* in west London produces a lavishly illustrated brochure which includes air fares. STA Travel also has branches in the UK. Look in the Sunday papers and *Exchange & Mart* for ads. Also look out for the free magazines available in London – start by looking outside the main train stations.

Most British travel agents are registered with the Association of British Travel Agents (ABTA). If you have paid for your flight to an ABTA-registered agent which then goes out of business, ABTA will guarantee a refund or an alternative. Unregistered bucket shops are riskier but also sometimes cheaper.

The Globetrotters Club (BCM Roving, London WC1N 3XX) publishes a newsletter called *Globe*, which covers obscure destinations and can help in finding travelling companions.

From London to Delhi fares are approximately £290 to £380. KLM, Air India, Air Lanka and the Middle East airlines all offer very competitive fares. Lufthansa also offers good deals to Delhi, although you can't change your flight dates on the cheapest tickets. London-Mumbai fares cost from £300 to £400. There are also a few packages including charter flights between London and Agra. If you want to stop in India en route to Australia expect to pay around £556 (although some tickets cost £900).

Fares from Belfast to Mumbai or Delhi cost from £439. If you stop over in Mumbai en route to Australia expect to pay £700.

Continental Europe

NBBS (Amsterdam) is a popular agent. Paris to Mumbai or Delhi costs about 3600FF.

Africa

There are plenty of flights between East Africa and Mumbai due to the large Indian population in Kenya. Typical one-way fares from Mumbai to Nairobi are US$420.

Bangladesh

Bangladesh Biman and Indian Airlines fly between Calcutta and Dhaka (US$80) and between Calcutta and Chittagong (US$106) in Bangladesh.

Malayasia

The one-way economy fare from Kuala Lumpur to Delhi is US$435.

The Maldives

Thiruvananthapuram-Malé (Trivandrum-Malé) costs US$70 one way. It's cheaper to go to the Maldives from Colombo in Sri Lanka.

Myanmar

There are no land crossing points between Myanmar and India (or between Myanmar and any other country). If you want to visit Myanmar your only choice is to fly there. Myanmar Airways flies Calcutta-Yangon (Rs 12,990); Bangladesh Biman flies Dhaka-Yangon.

Nepal

Royal Nepal Airlines Corporation (RNAC) and Indian Airlines share routes between India and Kathmandu. RNAC has two flights daily; Indian Airlines has one. Both airlines give a 25% discount to those under 30 years of age on flights between Kathmandu and India. No student card is needed.

Delhi is the main departure point for flights between India and Kathmandu. The one hour flight from Delhi to Kathmandu with Royal Nepal Airlines is US$142, and Mumbai to Kathmandu US$165. If you want to see the mountains as you fly into Kathmandu from Delhi, you must sit on the left side.

Pakistan

Pakistan International Airlines (PIA) and Air India operate flights from Karachi to

Delhi for US$180 and Lahore to Delhi for US$100.

Singapore

The one-way economy fare from Singapore to Delhi is US$586.

Sri Lanka

There are flights between Colombo and Mumbai, Chennai, Tiruchirappalli or Thiruvananthapuram (Trivandrum). Fares from Chennai to Colombo are Rs 3655.

Thailand

Bangkok is a popular departure point from South-East Asia into Asia proper. Bangkok to Kathmandu with Thai International is 5240B one way, 8300B return for a ticket valid for three months and 9700B for a ticket valid for one year. Bangkok to Calcutta via Yangon (Myanmar) can by done for 10,060B by combining a Thai International ticket from Bangkok to Yangon with an Indian Airlines ticket from Yangon to Calcutta (this ticket must be ordered three days in advance). Bangkok to Calcutta one way costs 5200B with Thai International.

LAND

Bangladesh

The situation with crossings between India and Bangladesh is vague. The main crossings are at Benapol/Haridispur (near Jessore, on the Calcutta route), Chilahati/Haldibari (in the far north, on the Siliguri-Darjeeling route) and more recently along the entire eastern border with India (eg at Tamabil/Dawki, in the north-east corner of the Shillong route, and east of Brahmanbaria on the route to Agartala in the Tripura region). If officials say you cannot cross elsewhere, be sceptical because we have letters to the contrary from travellers.

In recent years, travellers have crossed at Bhurungamari/Chengrabandha (in the north, well east of Chilahati, an alternative route to Siliguri and Darjeeling), Hili/Balurghat (north-west of Bogra) and Godagari/Lalgola (west of Rajshahi on the Padma River, an alternative route to Calcutta). It may also be possible to pass at Satkhira (south-west of Khulna).

The problem is that these lesser crossings have so few westerners passing through (maybe only twice a year) that everyone assumes it's impossible. Getting the correct story from Indian and Bangladeshi officials is virtually impossible. The truth is probably that crossing at these points is simply more variable and never certain. If you do use one of the minor crossings, be sure you don't leave the border without a stamp in your passport, otherwise you may run into problems when leaving the country.

No exit permit is required to leave Bangladesh. But if you enter Bangladesh by air and leave by land you do need a road permit, from the Passport & Immigration office, 2nd floor, 17/1 Segunbagicha Rd, Dhaka. It's open from 8 am to 1 pm Thursday to Saturday. Two passport photos are required but there is no fee. The process takes about 24 hours. If you are driving from Bangladesh in your own vehicle, two permits are required: one from the Indian High Commission (☎ 02-504879), House 120, Road 2, Dhanmoni, Dhaka; and one from the Bangladesh Ministry of Foreign Affairs (☎ 02-883260/883261), Pioneer Rd, facing the Supreme Court in Segun Bagicha (in the city centre).

Dhaka to Calcutta The Dhaka to Calcutta route is the one used by the majority of land travellers between Bangladesh and India. Coming from Dhaka it's wise to book your seat on the bus at least a day in advance. The buses that operate overnight between Dhaka (departing between 8 and 11 pm) and the border are direct; they reach Benapol (the Bangladeshi border town) at dawn. From Benapol to the border, it's about 10 minutes by cycle-rickshaw (Tk 6). There are no buses in the daytime between the border and Benapol. Crossing the border takes an hour or so with the usual filling in and stamping of forms. From the border at Haridaspur (India) it's about 10km (20 mins, Rs 17/90 by cycle/auto-rickshaw) to Bangaon. It's possible to change money at

Bangaon, where the rate is better than at the border. Alternatively, you can take a Coaster (minibus) from Jessore to Benapol (Tk 14), from where you can proceed to the border and India.

Chilahati to Darjeeling The Bangladesh border point is at Chilahati, and this can be reached by train, although it's much quicker to take the bus. From Chilahati to Haldibari (the Indian border checkpoint), it's a 7km walk along a disused railway line. The train trip from Haldibari to New Jalpaiguri takes two hours and costs Rs 11. From New Jalpaiguri to Darjeeling you can take the fast buses or the slower, more picturesque toy train (if running). Note that changing money in Chilahati is virtually impossible. There are moneychangers at Haldibari.

Siliguri to Bhurungamari This northern border crossing is rarely used by travellers. Getting to the Indian border town of Chengrabandha from Siliguri is easy. There are buses every 45 minutes between 6 am and 1 pm for the 70km trip (2½ hrs, Rs 24). The Indian immigration office opens at 9 am. Outside you can change your Indian rupees into taka. Bhurugamari is 1km from the border. It's a tiny village and if you're caught here for the night your only option may be to sleep on the floor of one of the bus offices. You can take buses direct to Rangpur (5½ hrs), Bogra (8 hrs) or Dhaka (15 hrs).

Sylhet to Shillong It takes 2½ hours to get to Tamabil from Sylhet by bus from where it's a 15 minute hike to the border. It is then a further 1.5km walk to Dauki in India, from where buses run to Shillong (3½ hrs).

Nepal

Political and weather conditions permitting, there are three main land entry points into Nepal. The most popular crossing points from India are Sunaulai/Bhairawa (south of Pokhara), Raxaul Bazaar/Birganj (south of Kathmandu) and Kakarbhitta (near Siliguri and Darjeeling in the far east). If you are travelling to or from Delhi or elsewhere in western India the route through Sunauli/Bhairawa is the most convenient. There's an ordinary bus to Sunauli from Varanasi (10 hrs, Rs 105). There are bus/train packages to/from Agra.

There are direct buses from Delhi, but these generally get bad reports from travellers. It's cheaper and more satisfactory to organise the trip yourself.

You can also enter at Mahendranagar in the far west of Nepal, although it's a much more difficult route. When the Mahendra Highway is completed, the route will be open all year, but until then it is a dry season-only proposition, strictly for the hardy. There are daily buses from New Delhi to Banbassa in Uttar Pradesh, the nearest Indian village to the border (11 hrs). Banbassa is also connected by rail to Bareilly and by bus with the hill station Almora. There are direct buses from Mahendranagar to Kathmandu but they take a gruelling 22 hours. It's better to do the whole trip during daylight and to break the journey at Nepalganj. There are plenty of night and day buses from Nepalganj to Kathmandu (14 hrs).

Pakistan

At present, due to the continuing unstable political situation between India and Pakistan, there's only one border crossing open and that remains hostage to Pakistan-India relations. However, there have been signs that cross-border links will be strengthened with the introduction of a direct bus link between Delhi and Lahore – get current information before heading off.

Lahore to Amritsar The only legal overland crossing between India and Pakistan is at Wagah, just east of Lahore (Attari on the India side), by rail and road; you can also drive your own vehicle across here. On each side you clear immigration, customs and further security checks and walk across 100m of neutral territory. The border is open daily from 9 am to 3 pm (9.30 am to 3.30 pm India time). Daily express trains link Lahore with Amritsar in India. The *Amritsar Express* leaves Lahore City station at

11 am and reaches Amritsar about 3 pm. The return trip leaves Amritsar at 9.30 am, arriving at Lahore about 2 pm. Sometimes border delays can make the trip much longer. There are also slower daily Lahore-Wagah trains. Buses are quicker and more frequent, though the trip still takes nearly half a day. There are no direct buses but plenty to and from the border on both sides.

A Lahore-Delhi bus service began in early 1999. The route takes in Wagah, Attari, Amritsar and Sirhind. It runs four days a week but it's only for people with relatives on the other side.

South-East Asia

In contrast to the difficulties of travelling overland in central Asia, the South-East Asian overland trip is still wide open and as popular as ever. From Australia the first step is to Indonesia – Timor, Bali or Jakarta. Although most people fly from an east coast city or Perth to Bali, there are also flights from Darwin and from Port Hedland in the north of Western Australia. The shortest route is the flight between Darwin and Kupang on the Indonesian island of Timor.

From Bali you head north through Java to Jakarta, from where you can travel by ship, fly to Singapore or continue north through Sumatra then cross to Penang in Malaysia. After travelling around Malaysia, you can fly from Penang to Chennai in India or, more popularly, continue north to Thailand and eventually fly out from Bangkok to India, perhaps with a stopover in Myanmar. Unfortunately, crossing by land from Myanmar to India (or indeed to any other country) is forbidden by the Myanmar government.

An interesting alternative route is to travel from Australia to Papua New Guinea and from there cross to Irian Jaya, then to Sulawesi in Indonesia. There are all sorts of travel variations possible in South-East Asia; the region is a delight to travel through, it's good value for money, the food is generally excellent and healthy, and all in all it's an area of the world not to be missed. For full details see the Lonely Planet guide *South-East Asia on a shoestring*.

Europe

A steady trickle of people drive their own motorcycles or vehicles overland from Europe. There are some interesting, though difficult, routes to India through Eastern Europe and the republics that were once a part of the USSR. An international carnet is required.

Many people combine travel to the subcontinent with the Middle East by flying from India or Pakistan to Amman in Jordan or one of the Gulf states. A number of the London-based overland companies operate bus or truck trips across Asia on a regular basis. See Organised Tours later for companies that do overland trips.

For more detail on the Asian overland route see the Lonely Planet guides to *Pakistan*, *Iran* and *Turkey*.

SEA

There is no longer a ferry service running between Rameswaram and Talaimannar in Sri Lanka. The service between Chennai and Penang (Malayasia) ended some years ago. The shipping services between Africa and India only carry freight (including vehicles), not passengers.

INSURANCE

Regardless of how you plan to travel to India, it's worth taking out travel insurance. For more information, see Visas & Documents in the Facts for the Visitor chapter.

ORGANISED TOURS

In addition to companies that provide more standard tours, there are numerous foreign ecotourism and adventure-travel companies which can provide unusual and interesting trips. There are too many to include them all here; check newspapers and travel magazines for advertisements, and journals such as *Earth Journal* (USA) for listings. Several companies which have special-interest tours exclusively to Rajasthan are listed under Organised Tours in the Getting Around chapter. Companies that organise tours to various parts of India include the following:

Australasia

One World Travel
  (☎ 03-9650 3322, fax 9650 4254)
  3rd Floor, 227 Collins St, Melbourne, Vic 3000, Australia
One World Tours
  (☎ 08-8232 2727,
  email bwitty@ozemail.com.au)
  99 Hay St, Subiaco, Perth, WA 6008, Australia
Peregrine Adventures
  (☎ 03-9663 8611)
  258 Lonsdale St, Melbourne, Vic 3000, Australia (offices in Sydney, Brisbane, Adelaide, Perth and Hobart)
Venturetreks
  (☎ 09-379 9855, fax 377 0320)
  164 Parnell Rd (PO Box 37610), Parnell, Auckland, New Zealand
Window to the World
  (☎/fax 02-6493 8595)
  36 Fieldbuckets Rd, Quamma, NSW 2550, Australia
World Expeditions
  (☎ 02-9264 3366, fax 9261 1974)
  3rd Floor, 441 Kent St, Sydney, NSW 2000, Australia
  (☎ 03-9670 8400, fax 9670 7474)
  1st Floor, 393 Little Bourke St, Melbourne, Vic 3000, Australia

UK

Encounter Overland
  (☎ 020-7370 6845, fax 7244 9737,
  email adventure@encounter.co.uk,
  www.encounter-overland.com)
  267 Old Brompton Rd, London SW5 9JA
Exodus Expeditions
  (☎ 020-8673 0859, fax 8673 0779,
  email sales@ exodustravels.co.uk,
  www.exodustravels.co.uk)
  9 Weir Rd, London SW12 OLT
Imaginative Traveller
  (☎ 020-8742 3113, fax 8742 3045,
  email info@iaginative-traveller.com
  www.imaginative-traveller.com)
  14 Barley Mow Passage, Chiswick, London W4 4PH

USA

Adventure Center
  (☎ 800-227 8747,
  emailtripinfo@adventure-center.com)
  1311 63rd St, Suite 200, Emeryville, CA 94608
All Adventure Travel, Inc.
  (☎ 303-440 7924)
  PO Box 4307, Boulder, CO 80306
Asian Pacific Adventures

  (☎ 800-825 1680,
  email travelasia@earthlink.net)
  826 Sierra Bonita Ave, Los Angeles, CA 90036
Geographic Expeditions
  (☎ 415-922 0448, fax 346 5535,
  email info@geoex.com, www.geoex.com)
  2627 Lombard St, San Francisco, CA 94123

Rajasthan

AIR

India's major domestic airline, the government-run Indian Airlines, operates flights between major towns in Rajasthan – see individual chapters for details. During the tourist season (from around mid-October to mid-April) some private airlines (eg UP Airways) also charter flights, but their timetables are erratic so it's best to check the current situation with a travel agent.

Although there has been a deregulation of the Indian skies, Indian Airlines still has a monopoly on domestic air services in Rajasthan. At the time of writing, Jet Airways was the only private domestic carrier operating flights to Rajasthan (for details, see the boxed text Jaipur Air Services in the Jaipur chapter); however, other private operators may have introduced services by now.

Note that all domestic airline prices are expected to increase by around 10% in late 1999. Expect similar annual increments thereafter.

Domestic Airlines & Air Services

For the contact details of domestic airline offices in Delhi and Mumbai, see the Getting There & Away sections of those chapters.

Flights operate to four cities in Rajasthan – Jaipur, Udaipur, Jodhpur and Jaisalmer. See the Getting There & Away sections of those places for details.

Reservations

Indian Airlines has computerised booking at all but the smallest offices, so getting flight information and reservations is relatively simple – it's just getting to the head of the queue that takes the time. Nevertheless,

A Rajasthani chhatri: sculpted pillars define a line of symmetry beneath an elaborate ceiling.

Village girl with kid, near Jodhpur.

Hawker food being cooked in Jaipur.

Spices used in Rajasthani cuisine.

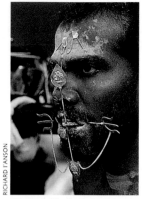

RICHARD I'ANSON

LIZ THOMPSON

Pilgrim with ritual piercing.

Religious objects used for worship.

JOHN HAY

Garlands of flowers used as *mala*, or temple offerings.

RICHARD I'ANSON

Sadhus, or holy ones, come to Pushkar to seek enlightenment.

flights during the tourist season can fill up in a flash, so you should try to plan as far in advance as possible.

For most airlines, tickets must be paid for with foreign currency or by credit card, or rupees backed up by encashment certificates. Change is given in rupees.

Indian Airlines offers a 25% discount for passengers from 12 to 30 years of age (foreigners only). Infants up to two years old travel at 10% of the adult fare, but only one infant can travel at this fare per adult. Children two to 12 years old travel at 50% fare. Indian nationals aged 65 and over also qualify for a 50% discount.

Refunds on adult tickets attract a charge of Rs 100 and can be made at any office. There are no refund charges on infant tickets. If a flight is delayed or cancelled, you cannot get a refund on the ticket. If you fail to show up 30 minutes before the flight, this is regarded as a 'no-show' and you forfeit the full value of the ticket. All domestic airlines require that you reconfirm your flight 72 hours before departure.

Indian Airlines accepts no responsibility if you lose your tickets. It absolutely will not refund lost tickets, but at its discretion may issue replacements.

For information about flight schedules and special offers (such as package deals), see the Indian Airlines Web site at www.nic.in/indian-airlines/.

Check In

Check-in time is one hour before departure. The baggage allowance for domestic airlines is 20kg for economy seats and 30kg for business class. Remember to get hand luggage tags or else you'll be sent back to the check-in counter to get them.

As a security measure on some internal routes, you are required to identify your checked-in baggage on the tarmac immediately prior to boarding. Note that any batteries discovered by security guards in your hand luggage will be confiscated to prevent using them to detonate incendiary devices during the flight. Put batteries (even cells

used for camera flashguns) in your checked baggage.

It's wise to make your domestic flight booking at least a day ahead of your international flight out of India – some travellers have missed international connections due to the sudden delay/cancellation of their domestic flight.

BUS

Apart from the gateway cities of Delhi and Mumbai, there are also regular bus services between other major Indian cities and Rajasthan, such as Agra, Aurangabad and Ahmedabad.

Details of buses operating from Delhi and Mumbai are provided in the Getting There & Away sections of individual chapters in this book. For more general information on travelling by bus in India, see Bus in the Getting Around chapter.

TRAIN

Comprehensive information on travelling in India by train is in the Getting Around chapter. Details of trains operating between Rajasthan and Delhi/Mumbai are provided in the Getting There & Away sections of individual chapters.

For details about the *Palace on Wheels*, a luxury escorted train journey which departs from Delhi and takes in Agra and the major tourist sights of Rajasthan, see the boxed text in the Getting Around chapter.

CAR & MOTORCYCLE

Few people bring their own vehicles to India. If you do decide to bring a car or motorcycle to India it must be brought in under a carnet, a customs document guaranteeing its removal at the end of your stay. Failing to do so will be very expensive.

For information about organised motorcycle and bicycle tours in Rajasthan, see the Getting Around chapter.

Rental

Self-drive car rental in India is not widespread, but it is possible. If you don't feel confident about driving on Indian roads, it's best to hire a car and driver – see the Getting Around chapter for details.

There are several places that offer self-drive car hire. Europcar (☎ 0141-362762, fax 363993) at G-2 Shri Gopal Tower, Ashok Marg, C-Scheme, Jaipur charges Rs 750 per day for a Maruti 800cc with a 150km mileage limit (each kilometre above that costs Rs 4). For unlimited mileage, the charge is Rs 900 per day. A better rate is offered if you hire the car for at least a week.

Hertz maintains offices in Jaipur, Delhi and Mumbai, as well as several other Indian cities. It also offers chauffeur drive rates. Hertz charges Rs 2000 per day to hire a self-drive Maruti 1000cc (larger than the Maruti 800cc), or Rs 1900 per day if you hire for at least seven days. This allows a mileage of 200km per day; it costs an additional Rs 12 for each kilometre clocked up after that.

Fuel is in addition to the above rates, and you will also be required to pay a deposit of up to Rs 15,000 (returnable if there's no damage whatsoever to the car – a scratch constitutes 'damage').

Addresses of Hertz offices are:

Delhi
  (☎ 011-687 7188)
  Ansal Chambers, Bhikaji Cama Place
Jaipur
  (☎ 0141-635000)
  Holiday Inn hotel, Amber Rd
Mumbai
  (☎ 022-492 1838)
  Autoriders International, 139 Autoworld, Tardeo Rd, Tardeo

Getting Around

AIR
Domestic Air Services
There are operational airports in Rajasthan at Jaipur, Jodhpur, Udaipur and Jaisalmer. In addition to flights serving Rajasthan from other Indian cities (see Air in the Getting There & Away chapter), there are several air services between the cities of Rajasthan. Information on booking domestic flights is in the Getting There & Away chapter.

BUS
The state government bus service is called Rajasthan Roadways. Often, there are privately owned local bus services and luxury private coaches between major cities, that can be booked with travel agencies.

Types
Generally bus travel is crowded, cramped, slow and uncomfortable.

Ordinary buses usually have five seats across – three on one side of the aisle, two on the other – although if there are only five people sitting in them consider yourself lucky! There are usually mounds of baggage in the aisles, occasionally chickens under seats, and in some more remote places there'll be people travelling 'upper class' (ie on the roof) as well. These buses tend to be frustratingly slow, are often in an advanced state of decrepitude and stop frequently – often for seemingly no reason – and for long periods.

Express buses are a big improvement in that they stop far less often. They're still crowded, but at least you feel like you're getting somewhere. The fare is usually a few rupees more than on an ordinary bus – well worth the extra.

Deluxe buses have only four seats across and these will usually recline. Super-deluxe buses offer even greater comfort and have air-conditioning.

Unlike state-operated bus companies, private operators are keen to maximise profits; their priority is therefore speed rather than maintenance – traveller beware.

The thing that many foreigners find hardest to cope with on the buses is the incessant music. Hindi pop music is usually played at maximum volume and seems to screech on and on without end. Just as bad are the video machines found on many deluxe buses, which are also usually pumped up at full volume.

Getting a Seat
If you are travelling with someone, work out a bus boarding plan so one of you can guard the gear while the other storms the bus in search of a seat. Another accepted method is to pass a newspaper or article of clothing through the window and place it on an empty seat, or ask a passenger to do it for you. Having made your 'reservation' you then board the bus after things have simmered down. This method rarely fails.

At many bus stations there is a separate women's queue. You may not notice this because the sign (if it exists) will not be in English and there may not be any women queuing. Usually the same ticket window will handle the male and female queues, taking turns. This means that women can usually go straight up to the front of the queue (beside the front of the male queue) and get almost immediate service.

Baggage
Baggage is generally carried free on the roof, so it's an idea to take precautions. Make sure your bag's tied on properly and that nobody dumps a tin trunk on top of it.

Theft is sometimes a problem, so keep an eye on your bags at chai (tea) stops and carry your valuables on board with you. Having a large, heavy-duty bag into which your pack will fit can be a good idea, not only for bus travel but also for air travel.

If someone carries your bag onto the roof, expect to pay them a few rupees.

131

Toilet Stops

On long-distance bus trips, chai stops can be far too frequent or, conversely, agonisingly infrequent. Long-distance trips can be a real hassle for women travellers as toilet facilities are generally inadequate to say the least. Forget about modesty and do what the local women do – wander a few yards off or find a convenient bush.

TRAIN

The Indian Railways system is the world's fourth largest with a route length of over 60,000km. Every day over 7000 passenger trains carry over 10.5 million passengers and connect 7100 stations. Indian Railways is the world's largest single employer with a shade over 1.6 million employees!

For details about Indian train timetables etc, see the following Web sites: www .india-travel.com/table.htm and www.indi a-travel.com/indrail.htm and www.trainweb .com/indiarail/ttable.htm

Timetables

The first step in coming to grips with Indian Railways is to get a timetable. *Trains at a Glance* is a handy, 100 page guide covering all of the main routes and trains. It is usually available at major train stations, and sometimes on news stands in the larger cities.

There is also the 300 page *Indian Bradshaw*, which covers every train service throughout the country. It is more detailed than most people need and it can be frustratingly difficult to find things, but for any serious exploring, Indian Bradshaw is invaluable. Published monthly, it's not widely available but you can usually find it on the bookstalls at major city train stations.

Thomas Cook's *Overseas Timetable* has good train timetables for India, although it's not available in India.

Train schedules often seem to change in Rajasthan, so it's a good idea to double check the details provided in this book.

Classes

There are generally two classes – 1st and 2nd – but there are a number of subtle variations on this basic distinction. For instance, there is 1st class and 1st class air-con. The air-con carriages only operate on the major trains and routes. The fare for 1st class air-con is more than double the fare for normal 1st class. A slightly cheaper air-con alternative is the air-con two-tier sleeper, which costs about 25% more than 1st class. These carriages are a lot more common than 1st class air-con, but are still only found on the major routes.

Types

What you want is a mail or express train. What you do not want is a passenger train. No Indian train travels very fast, but at least the mail and express trains keep travelling more of the time.

Air-con 'superfast' express services operate on certain main routes, and because of tighter scheduling and fewer stops they are much faster. A separate fare structure applies to them as meals are included. The *Shatabdi Express*, which operates between Delhi and Jaipur, and Mumbai and Ahmedabad, is such a service.

Gauge

There are three gauge types in India: broad, metre and narrow. What you want nearly as much as a mail or express train is broad gauge. In broad gauge the rails are 1.676m apart; metre gauge is, as it says, one metre wide; narrow gauge is either 0.762m (two feet six inches) or 0.610m (two feet).

Broad gauge has a major advantage: it is much faster. It also gives a smoother ride. The carriages are much the same between broad gauge and metre gauge, but on the narrow gauge they are much, much narrower and the accommodation is very cramped. In areas where there are no broad-gauge lines, it may be worth taking a bus, which will often be faster then the metre-gauge trains.

Some of the narrow-gauge lines in Rajasthan are currently being converted to broad gauge, which means you may be subject to long delays or cancellations on some services.

Life on Board

It's India for real on board the trains. In 2nd class, unreserved travel can be a nightmare since the trains are often hopelessly crowded. Combined with the crowds, the noise and the confusion there's the discomfort. Fans and lights have a habit of failing at prolonged stops when there's no air moving through the carriage, and toilets can get a bit rough towards the end of a long journey. Worst of all are the stops. Trains seem to stop often, interminably and for no apparent reason. Often it's because somebody has pulled the emergency stop cable because they are close to home. Still, it's all part of life on the rails.

In 2nd class reserved it's a great deal better since, in theory, only four people share each bench. However, there's inevitably the fifth, and sometimes even the sixth, person who gets the others to bunch up so they can get at least part of their bum on the seat. This normally doesn't happen at night or in 1st class, where there are either two or four people to a compartment, and the compartment doors are lockable.

Costs

Fares operate on a distance basis. The timetables indicate the distance in kilometres between the stations and from this it is simple to calculate the cost between any two stations. If you have a ticket for at least 400km, you can break your journey at the rate of one day per 200km so long as you travel at least 300km on the first sector. This can save a lot of hassle buying tickets and also, of course, result in a small saving.

The Indian Rail Fares table in this section indicates fares for set distances. In most chapters of this book, fares for specific trains have been individually provided.

Reservations

The cost of reservations is nominal – it's the time it takes to make the reservation that hurts, although this is getting better as computerised reservation becomes more widespread. At the moment this is limited to the major towns and cities. There is a special computerised reservation counter for foreign tourists at the Jaipur reservation office.

Reservations for some trains can be made up to 60 days in advance. Other trains only accept bookings 30 days prior to travel, and some only seven days in advance. Your reservation ticket will indicate which carriage and berth you have, and when the train arrives you will find a sheet of paper fixed to each carriage listing passenger names beside their appropriate berth number. Usually this information is also posted on notice boards on the platform. It is Indian rail efficiency at its best.

Indian Rail Fares in Rupees						
distance (km)	1st class (air-con)	1st class	air-con chair	2nd class express	2nd class express (sleeper)	2nd class passenger (seat)
50	406	122	100	76	22	10
100	542	173	114	76	32	16
200	725	230	171	76	54	29
300	943	361	231	105	73	39
400	1156	455	277	129	90	48
500	1333	531	323	152	107	55
1000	2155	862	492	245	174	77
1500	2908	1156	658	311	219	94
2000	3616	1435	800	360	253	111

As at many bus stations, there are separate women's queues, usually with a sign saying 'Ladies' Queue' (see Getting a Seat in the Bus section).

Rail reservations incur a booking fee of Rs 15 to Rs 50, depending on the class.

If the train you want is fully booked, it's often possible to get an RAC (Reservation Against Cancellation) ticket. This entitles you to board the train and have seating accommodation. Once the train is moving, the TTE (Travelling Ticket Examiner) will find a berth for you, but it may take an hour or more. This is different from a wait-listed ticket, which does not give you the right to actually board the train (should you be so cheeky you can be 'detrained and fined'). The hassle with RAC tickets is that your group will probably get split up.

If you plan your trip well ahead, you can avoid all the hassles by booking from abroad. A good Indian travel agent will book and obtain tickets in advance and have them ready for you on arrival. As an alternative to buying tickets as you go along, it's possible to buy a ticket from A to Z with all the stops along the way pre-booked. It might take a bit of time sitting down and working it out at the start, but if your time is limited and you can fix your schedule rigidly, this can be a good way to go.

Refunds

Booked tickets are refundable but cancellation fees apply. If you present the ticket more than one day in advance, a fee of Rs 10 to Rs 50 applies, depending on the class. Up to four hours before, you lose 25% of the ticket value; up to three to 12 hours after departure (depending on the distance of the ticketed journey) you lose 50%. Any later than that and you can keep the ticket as a souvenir.

Tickets for unreserved travel can be refunded up to three hours after the departure of the train, and the only penalty is Rs 10 per passenger.

When refunding your ticket, you are officially entitled to go straight to the head of the queue (if there isn't a dedicated window for refunds), the rationale being that the spot you are surrendering may be just the one required by the next person in the queue.

Sleepers

There are 2nd class and 1st class sleepers, although by western standards 1st class is not luxurious. Bedding is only available on certain 1st class and air-con two-tier services, and then only if arranged when booking your ticket. First class sleepers are generally private compartments with two or four berths in them, sometimes with a toilet as well. Usually the sleeping berths fold up to make a seating compartment during the day. First class air-con sleepers are more luxurious, and much more expensive, than regular 1st class sleepers.

Second class sleepers are known as three-tier. They are arranged in sections without doors, each of six berths. During the day, the middle berth is lowered to make seats for six or eight people. At night they are folded into position, everybody has to bed down at the same time, and a TTE ensures that nobody without a reservation gets into the carriage.

Broad-gauge, three-tier sleeping carriages also have a row of narrow two-tier (upper and lower) berths along one side. These are not only narrower than the 'inside' berths, they are about 20cm shorter, so the average person cannot stretch right out. When reserving 2nd class berths, always write 'inside' on the 'Accommodation Preference' section of the booking form. Sleeping berths are only available between 9 pm and 6 am.

For any sleeper reservation, you should try to book at least several days ahead. There is usually a board or computer screen in each station indicating what is available or how long before the next free berth/seat comes up on the various routes. Once you've selected a particular train and date, you must fill in a reservation form. Do this before you get to the front of the queue. The forms are usually found in boxes around the reservation hall. The demand for 1st class sleepers is generally far less than for 2nd class.

On timetables and state-of-reservation boards at train stations, trains are often listed without destinations. This is where your *Trains at a Glance* or *Indian Bradshaw* comes in. If you don't have one, you'll have to ask – and that will soak up time. Tourist offices can usually suggest the best trains but there isn't always a tourist office. It's something you'll have to come to terms with.

Getting a Space Despite Everything

If you want a sleeper and there are none left, then it's time to try and break into the quotas. Ask the stationmaster (often a helpful man who speaks English) if there is a tourist quota, station quota or a VIP quota. The last of these is often a good bet because VIPs rarely turn up to use their quotas.

If all that fails then you're going to be travelling unreserved and that can be no fun at all. To ease the pain get yourself some expert help. For, say, Rs 10 baksheesh (although you may have to pay a bit more) you can get a porter who will absolutely ensure that you get a seat if it's humanly possible. If it's a train starting from your station, the key to success is to be on the train before it arrives at the departure platform. Your porter will do just that, so when it rolls up you simply stroll on board and take the seat he has warmed for you. If it's a through train then it can be a real free-for-all, and you can be certain he'll be better at it than you are – he'll also not be encumbered with baggage or backpacks.

Women can ask about the Ladies' Compartments that many trains have and that are often a refuge from the crowds in other compartments.

Left Luggage

Most stations have a left-luggage facility (quaintly called a cloakroom) where backpacks can be left for around Rs 2 per day. This is a very useful facility if you're visiting (but not staying in) a town, or if you want to find a place to stay, unencumbered by gear. The regulations state that any luggage left in a cloakroom must be locked, although this is not strictly enforced.

Special Trains

The luxurious *Palace on Wheels* train makes a regular circuit of Rajasthan. For more details see the boxed text Palace on Wheels in this chapter.

Indrail Passes

Indrail passes permit unlimited travel on Indian trains for the period of their validity, but they are expensive and not really good value. To get the full value out of any of the passes, you need to travel around 300km per day; with the speed of Indian trains that's at least six hours travelling! If you are only planning to travel to and within Rajasthan, they're not really worth considering. Lonely Planet's *India* guidebook has more details about Indrail passes.

CAR
Rental

Self-Drive Hertz is the main car rental operator in Rajasthan offering self-drive (see Car & Motorcycle in the Getting There & Away chapter for rates). Given Rajasthan's crazy driving conditions it's far better, and much more straightforward, to hire a car and driver (see following). By western standards the cost is quite low, certainly cheaper than a rent-a-car (without driver) in the west.

Car & Driver Long-distance car hire with driver is an increasingly popular way to get around Rajasthan. Spread among, say, four people it's not overly expensive and you have the flexibility to go where you want when you want.

Almost any local taxi will quite happily set off on a long-distance trip in Rajasthan. Inquiring at a taxi rank or travel agency is the easiest way to contact one, or you can ask your hotel to book one for you, although this will probab-ly cost more. Try to get a driver who can speak English and who is knowledgeable about the areas you plan to travel to.

Official rates for a car and driver with the Rajasthan Tourism Development Corporation are Rs 4.40/km for a non air-con car, and an expensive Rs 8/km for an air-con car, with the usual 250km minimum hire charge per day. More competitive rates are offered by some travel agencies in Jaipur – see Getting There & Away in the Jaipur chapter.

If you hire a car and driver to tour around Rajasthan, it is imperative to set the ground rules. With so many tourists visiting Rajasthan, unfortunately a lot of drivers have got away with bullying their passengers. Many travellers have complained of having their holiday dictated by the driver. To avoid this, let the driver know that you are the boss from the very beginning. Other travellers have shelled out much more money than they should, paying for the driver's accommodation and meals (and booze!) even though this cost had already been factored into their fee.

Make sure you understand the accommodation/meal arrangement for drivers before paying the car rental company (also shop around for the best deal before deciding which rental company to go with). In most cases, what you pay includes an allowance for the driver's accommodation and meals – but many travellers are unaware of this. And when it comes to accommodation, it should not be your headache where the driver stays – that is totally up to him to decide.

Some hotels (especially in remote areas) will provide free lodging for drivers, as there is nowhere else to stay. If you follow the above advice, the relationship between you and your driver is far more likely to be a happy one. A tip at the end of the trip is the best way of showing your appreciation for good service.

For safety reasons, it is best to avoid travelling after dark (see following).

Most hotels do not allow drivers to stay or eat in guest areas, even if you insist on paying – see Dos & Don'ts in the Society & Conduct section of the Facts about Rajasthan chapter.

Road Conditions

Because of the extreme congestion in the cities and the narrow bumpy roads in the country, driving is often a slow, stop-start process – hard on you, the car and fuel economy. Service is so-so in India; parts and tyres are not always easy to obtain, although there are plenty of puncture-repair places. All in all, driving is no great pleasure except in rural areas where there's little traffic.

Road Safety

In 1951 the number of motorised vehicles on India's roads totalled 300,000. The figure had climbed to 5.4 million by 1981 and shot to 26.5 million in 1996.

In India there are an estimated 70,000 road deaths a year – an astonishing total in relation to the number of vehicles on the road. In the USA, where there is more than 20 times the number of vehicles, there are about 43,000 road fatalities per year.

The reasons for the high death rate in India are numerous and many of them are fairly obvious – starting with the congestion on the roads and the equal congestion in vehicles. When a bus runs off the road there are plenty of people stuffed inside to get injured, and it's unlikely too many of them will be able to escape in a hurry. One newspaper article stated that 'most accidents are caused by brake failure or the steering wheel getting free'!

Many of those killed are pedestrians involved in hit-and-run accidents. The propensity to disappear after the incident is not wholly surprising – lynch mobs can assemble remarkably quickly, even when the driver is not at fault!

Most accidents are caused by trucks, for on Indian roads might is right and trucks are the biggest, heaviest and mightiest. You either get out of their way or get run down. As with so many Indian vehicles, they're likely to be grossly overloaded and not in the best of condition. Trucks are actually licensed and taxed to carry a load 25% more than the maximum recommended by the manufacturer. It's staggering to see the number of crumpled trucks by the sides of the national highways: and these aren't old accidents, but ones that have obviously happened in the last 24 hours or so. If they haven't been killed, quite often the driver and crew will be sitting around, wondering what to do next.

If you are driving yourself, you need to be extremely vigilant at all times. At night there are unlit cars and ox carts, and in the daytime there are fearless cyclists and hordes of pedestrians. Day and night there are crazy truck drivers to contend with. Indeed, at night, it's best to avoid driving at all along any major truck route unless you're prepared to get off the road completely every time a truck is coming in the opposite direction! The other thing you have to contend with is the eccentric way in which headlights are used – a combination of full beam and totally off (dipped beams are virtually unheard of). A loud horn definitely helps since the normal driving technique is to put your hand firmly on the horn, close your eyes and plough through regardless. Vehicles always have the right of way over pedestrians and bigger vehicles always have the right of way over smaller ones.

MOTORCYCLE

Travelling around India by motorcycle has become increasingly popular in recent years, and it certainly has its attractions – motoring along the back roads through small untouristy villages, picnics in the wilds, the freedom to go when and where you like – making it the ideal way to get to grips with the vastness that is India.

You'll still get a sore bum; you'll have difficult and frustrating conversations; and you'll get fed up with asking directions, receiving misleading answers and getting lost; but you'll also have adventures not available to the visitor who relies on public transport.

Some places in Rajasthan hire out motorbikes on a daily, weekly or monthly basis (see individual Getting Around chapters for details), however the range of machines available is rather limited (Delhi, for instance, has a much broader range).

Most people who buy a motorcycle, do not confine their journey just to Rajasthan. Lonely Planet's *India* guidebook has a comprehensive section devoted entirely to motorcycle travel, including details of renting, what to bring, buying & selling, ownership papers, insurance & tax, types of bikes available, repairs & maintenance and lots of other useful tips. The Getting Around sections of the Delhi and Mumbai chapters have some details about where motorcycles can be purchased in those cities.

Organised Motorcycle Tours

Following are some organised motorcycle operators who offer tours of Rajasthan. Contact them for details about the various tours they offer and the current prices.

Ferris Wheels (☎/fax 61 02-9904 7419, email safari@ferriswheels.com.au, www.ferriswheels.com.au), PO Box 743, Crows Nest, NSW 2065, Australia, organises tours through Rajasthan and the Himalaya on classic Enfields. In Rajasthan, the standard tours are for three weeks, but tailor-made packages for groups are also possible. These tours operate during the cooler winter months.

Classic Bike Adventure (☎ 0832-273351, fax 276124, 277343), Casa Tres Amigos, Socol Vado No 425, Assagao, Bardez, Goa, is a German company that also organises bike tours on Enfields. Tours last two to three weeks and cover Rajasthan, the Himalaya between Kullu-Manali and Gangotri, and the south from Goa.

Indian Motorcycle Adventures (☎ 09-372 7550, email gumby@ihug.co.nz), at 40 O'Brien Rd, Rocky Bay, Waiheke Island, New Zealand, does 20-day tours of Rajasthan in November, January and February.

BICYCLE

If you are considering extensive travel by bicycle, see Lonely Planet's *India* guidebook, which contains a comprehensive section devoted to this mode of travel. There are details about using your own bike, spare parts, road conditions, buying & selling a bike in India, and plenty of other useful tips.

Organised Bicycle Tours

These are yet to take off in a big way. Ramesh Jangid in Nawalgarh can organise cycle tours around the *havelis* (painted houses) of Shekhawati (northern Rajasthan). See that chapter for details.

If you want to splash out, Butterfield & Robinson offer biking expeditions through Rajasthan. In 13 days, you cover from around 25 to 35km daily and also do from 5 to 15km of walking each day. Expect to pay at least US$5750 per person (US$6425 for singles), which includes all hotel accommodation, flights, trains and mini-van support vehicles, most meals, guides, all entry charges, custom 21-speed Trek bicycles, maps, a water bottle and luggage transportation. For further details call ☎ 416-864 1354 or 180-0678 1147, fax 416-864 0541, email info@butterfield.com or visit their Web site at www.butterfield.com

HITCHING

Hitching is never entirely safe in any country in the world, and we don't recommend it. Travellers who hitch should understand that they are taking a small but potentially serious risk. People who do choose to hitch are safer if they travel in pairs and let someone know where they are planning to go.

In India hitching is not a realistic option. There are not that many private cars streaking across India so you are likely to be on board trucks. You are then stuck with the old quandaries: 'Will the driver expect to be paid?'; 'Will they be unhappy if I don't offer to pay?'; 'Will they be unhappy with the amount I offer or will they simply want too much?'.

However, it is a very bad idea for women to hitch. Remember: India is a developing country with a patriarchal society far less sympathetic to rape victims than the west, and that's saying something. A woman in the cabin of a truck on a lonely road is perhaps tempting fate.

LOCAL TRANSPORT

Although there are comprehensive local bus networks in most major towns, unless you

have time to familiarise yourself with the routes, you're better off sticking to taxis, auto-rickshaws, cycle-rickshaws and hiring bicycles. The buses are often so hopelessly overcrowded that you can only really use them if you get on at the starting point and get off at the terminus.

Setting a Fare A basic rule applies to any form of transport where the fare is not ticketed, fixed or metered: agree on the fare beforehand. If you fail to do that you can expect enormous arguments and hassles when you get to your destination. And agree on the fare clearly – if there is more than one of you make sure it covers all of you (the price quoted should be per vehicle, not per person). If you have baggage make sure there are no extra charges, or you may be asked for more at the end of the trip. If a driver refuses to use the meter, or insists on an extortionate rate, simply walk away – if he really wants the job the price will drop. If you can't agree on a reasonable fare, find another driver.

To/From the Airport

There are often official buses, operated by the government, Indian Airlines or some local cooperative, to major airports in India. Where there aren't any, there will be taxis or auto-rickshaws.

Taxi

There are taxis in most towns in Rajasthan, and many of them (certainly in the major cities) are metered. Getting a metered fare is a different situation. First of all the meter may be 'broken'. Threatening to get another taxi will usually fix it immediately, except during rush hours.

Secondly, the meter will almost certainly be out of date. Fares are adjusted upwards so much faster and more frequently than meters are recalibrated that drivers almost always have 'fare adjustment cards' indicating what you should pay compared to what the meter indicates. This is, of course, wide open to abuse. You have no idea if you're being shown the right card or if the taxi's meter has actually been recalibrated and you're being shown the card anyway.

The only answer to all this is to try and get an idea of what the fare should be before departure (ask information desks at the airport or your hotel). You'll begin to develop a feel for what the meter says, what the cards say and what the two together should indicate.

Auto-Rickshaw

An auto-rickshaw is a noisy three-wheel device powered by a two-stroke motorcycle engine with a driver up front and seats for two (or sometimes more) passengers behind. They don't have doors and have just a canvas top. They are also known as scooters or autos.

They're generally about half the price of a taxi, are usually metered and follow the same ground rules as taxis.

Because of their size, auto-rickshaws are often faster than taxis for short trips and their drivers are decidedly nuttier. Hair-raising near-misses are guaranteed and glancing-blow collisions are not infrequent; thrill seekers will love them!

Tempo

Somewhat like a large auto-rickshaw, these ungainly looking three-wheel devices operate rather like minibuses or share taxis along fixed routes. Unless you are spending large amounts of time in one city, it is generally impractical to try to find out what the routes are. You'll find it much easier and more convenient to go by auto-rickshaw.

Cycle-Rickshaw

This is effectively a three-wheeler bicycle with a seat for two passengers behind the rider. They can be found in many of Rajasthan's towns and are a cheaper (if slower) alternative to auto-rickshaws. They are also much more environmentally friendly.

Fares must always be agreed on in advance. Avoid situations where the driver says: 'As you like'. He's punting on the fact that you are not well acquainted with correct fares and will overpay. No matter what you pay in situations like this, it will in-

variably be deemed too little and an unpleasant situation often develops. This is especially the case in popular tourist destinations, such as Agra and Jaipur. In these places the riders can be as talkative and opinionated as any New York cabby.

It's quite feasible to hire a rickshaw-wallah by time, not just for a straight trip. Hiring one for a day or several days can make good financial sense. Ensure that your watches are synchronised before you set out!

Hassling over the fares is the biggest difficulty. Rickshaw-wallahs will often go all out for a fare higher than it would cost you by taxi or auto-rickshaw. Nor does actually agreeing on a fare always make a big difference; there is a greater possibility of a post-travel fare disagreement when you travel by cycle-rickshaw than when you go by taxi or auto-rickshaw – metered or not.

Tonga

In some smaller regional towns such as Nawalgarh in Shekhawati, you'll come across horse-drawn carriages known as tongas. Prices are generally comparable with cycle-rickshaws.

Bicycle

India is a country of bicycles – it's an ideal way of getting around the sights in a city or even for making longer trips (see Organised Bicycle Tours earlier). Even in the smallest towns there is usually a shop that rents some sort of bicycle. They charge from around Rs 3 to Rs 5 per hour or Rs 15 to Rs 25 per day. Shops in tourist traps such as Jaisalmer, however, can charge much more (up to Rs 40 per day). In some places they may be unwilling to hire to you since you are a stranger, but you can generally get around this by offering some sort of ID card as security (such as a passport), or by paying a deposit (usually Rs 300 to Rs 500). If you do leave your passport, don't forget to get it back!

If you should be so unfortunate as to get a puncture, don't worry: you'll soon spot men sitting under trees with puncture-repair outfits at the ready and it'll cost just a couple of rupees to fix.

If you're travelling with small children and would like to ride a lot, consider getting a bicycle seat made. If you find a shop making cane furniture they'll probably be able to make up a child's bicycle seat from a sketch. Get it made to fit on a standard-size rear carrier and it can be securely attached with a few lengths of cord.

ORGANISED TOURS
RTDC Tours

In most of the larger cities and places of tourist interest in Rajasthan, including Jaipur, Jodhpur, Udaipur and Jaisalmer, the RTDC operates city tours or tours to places of interest in the environs. These tours are usually very good value, particularly where the tourist sights are spread out over a wide area, as in Jaipur.

The big drawback is that many of these tours try to cram far too much into too short a period of time. Nevertheless, they're normally worthwhile, and you can always return to places of interest at your leisure later on. It's also possible to arrange an English-speaking guide at most RTDC tourist offices (see Organised Tours in the Jaipur chapter for prices).

The RTDC also offers a range of package tours. These include a six day Mewar tour, which leaves Delhi every Saturday and takes in Jaipur, Chittorgarh, Ranakpur,

Palace on Wheels

The RTDC *Palace on Wheels* is a special tourist train service which operates weekly tours of Rajasthan, departing from Delhi every Wednesday from September to the end of April. The itinerary takes in Jaipur, Chittorgarh, Udaipur, Sawai Madhopur (for Ranthambhore National Park), Jaisalmer, Jodhpur, Bharatpur (for the Keoladeo Ghana National Park) and Agra. It's a hell of a lot of ground to cover in a week, but most of the travelling is done at night.

Originally this train used carriages which had belonged to various maharajas, but these became so ancient that new carriages were built to look like the originals. They were also fitted with air-conditioning. The result is a very luxurious mobile hotel and it can be a memorable way to travel. The train has two dining cars and a well stocked bar. Each coach, which is attended by a splendidly costumed captain and attendant, contains four coupés (either double or twin share) which have attached bath with running hot and cold water.

The cost includes tours, entry fees, accommodation on the train plus all meals. Rates per person per day from October to March are US$260 for triple occupancy (the third person sleeps on a fold-away bed) and US$325/460 for a double/single. In September and April the tariff is lower: US$215/270/370. It's a very popular service and bookings must be made in advance at RTDC's Tourist Reception Centre, Bikaner House, Pandara Rd, New Delhi, 110011 (☎ 011-338 1884, fax 338 2823), or at RTDC's Hotel Swagatam Campus, Near Railway Station, Jaipur, 302006, Rajasthan (☎ 0141-203531, fax 201045, www.palace onwheels.net).

Udaipur, Ajmer and Pushkar (Rs 5000 per person); a three day Golden Triangle tour, which leaves Delhi every Friday and takes in Siliserh, Sariska, Jaipur, Bharatpur, Fatehpur Sikri and Agra (Rs 2800 per person); a three day Hawa Mahal tour, which leaves Delhi every Tuesday and takes in Agra, Fatehpur Sikri, Bharatpur, Deeg, Sariska and Jaipur (Rs 2800 per person); the seven day desert circuit tour, which leaves Delhi every Monday and takes in Bikaner, Jaisalmer, Jodhpur, Ajmer and Pushkar (Rs 5600 per person); a four day wildlife tour, which leaves every Thursday and visits Sariska, Ranthambhore and Bharatpur (Rs 3650 per person); and the 15 day Rajasthan tour, which leaves on the first and third Thursday of every month and covers the entire state (Rs 11,100 per person). The tariff includes transport, accommodation (usually at RTDC hotels), sightseeing, guide and entry charges. The tariff for children is lower. There must be a minimum of four people for these tours to operate. For more information, contact RTDC's Tourist Reception Centre, Bikaner House, Pandara Rd, New Delhi, 110011 (☎ 011-338 1884 or 338 3837, fax 338 2823).

Other Tours

There is a plethora of travel agents offering various excursions in Rajasthan. Ask other travellers for current advice on good operators, and shop around to get the best deals. See the Organised Tours section in individual chapters of this book for some options.

Below are a few operators, mainly based in Jaipur.

Amber Tours (☎ 0141-381543), which has a counter at the Rambagh Palace hotel in Jaipur, operates chauffeur-driven day tours to Sariska and Ranthambhore wildlife sanctuaries. For costs, see Other Tours in the Jaipur chapter.

Registhan Tours Pvt Ltd (☎/fax 0141-380824), at E-141 Sadar Patel Marg (near the Rajmahal Palace) in Jaipur arranges camel and horse safaris, treks in the Udaipur area and jeep safaris. The camel saf-aris are run in the Jaisalmer and Shekhawati districts. For more information, see Other Tours in the Jaipur chapter. Aravali Safari & Tours (☎ 0141-373124, fax 365345) is opposite the Rajputana Palace Sheraton on Palace Rd. It can arrange luxury camel treks in Jaisalmer and its environs, and horse safaris in the Udaipur region. Ghanerao Tours (☎/fax 0141-201 209), B-11/302 Kamal Apartments, Bani Park, Jaipur, also organises horse treks in southern Rajasthan.

Alternative Travels (☎ 01594-22239, fax 24061), Apani Dhani, Nawalgarh, Shekhawati, is one of the few outfits in Rajasthan that promotes sustainable cultural tourism. Ramesh Jangid of Alternative Travels can organise camel and cycling trips around the painted towns of Shekhawati, treks in the Aravalli Range and homestays with villagers. For more details, see Organised Tours in the Nawalgarh section of the Northern Rajasthan (Shekhawati) chapter.

Jaipur

*Je na dekkhyo Jaipario
to kal main akar kaai kario?*
If one has not seen Jaipur,
what is the point of having been born?

• **pop 1.8 million**   ☎ **0141**

Although Jaipur is today among the most tumultuous and polluted places in the state, this vibrant capital of Rajasthan rarely disappoints the first-time visitor. It is a city of contrasts, where camels wait at traffic lights with auto-rickshaws and Ambassador cars. And film hoardings depicting many times larger-than-life mustachioed heroes, their faces contorted into desperate grimaces as they battle their adversaries, loom down over luxury car showrooms, while artisans engage in such traditional crafts as block-printing, gem cutting and polishing, puppet making, and *dhurrie* (carpet) weaving. Women resplendent in iridescent lime green, hot pink, and sunflower-coloured saris thread their way through the crowded bazaars of the old city. Providing stunning backdrops are the ancient forts of Amber, Nahargarh, Jaigarh and Moti Dungri, dramatic testaments to a bygone era which lend a lingering romance to this chaotic city.

Among Jaipur's highlights is the fascinating City Palace, which has a fine museum with priceless exhibits dating from the successive reigns of the Kachhwaha rulers. Nearby is the Jantar Mantar, the observatory built by the founder of Jaipur, Jai Singh II, in the second quarter of the 18th century. It looks more like an outdoor exhibition of modern art than an observatory, but astrologers and astronomers still consult the strange devices here to make their celestial calculations.

The old city is a fascinating place to wander around, with its colourful bazaars and artisans' quarters. As it is laid out on a grid pattern, it's fairly easy to orient yourself here. The *chaupars*, or three main squares in the old city, are great places to be at sunset, when the pink walls give off a rosy hue and

Highlights

- **Bazaars and Emporiums** – lively places, stacked with handicrafts
- **City Palace Complex** – a maze of courtyards, gardens and buildings
- **Amber Fort** – a stunning example of Rajput architecture, 11km from Jaipur
- **Sanganer** – a village outside Jaipur, famous for its block-printed fabrics and handmade paper

you can sit and watch the chaos unfold around you as vendors make their way home.

History

The city of Jaipur is named after its founder, the great warrior-astronomer Maharaja Jai Singh II (1693-1743), who came to power at the age of 12 upon the death of his father, Maharaja Bishan Singh. The maharaja had been informed by astrologers upon his son's birth that the boy would achieve great things in his lifetime, and Bishan Singh ensured that he received the very best education in the arts, sciences, philosophy and military affairs.

At 15 years old the prodigal prince matched his wits against the Mughal emperor, Aurangzeb, who summoned the lad to the Mughal court to explain why he had failed to report to the Deccan to fight the Marathas as he had been ordered. When the emperor grasped the lad's hand the youth retorted that, as the emperor had extended the traditional gesture of protection offered by a bridegroom to his new wife by taking his hand, it was incumbent upon Aurangzeb to protect the young ruler and his kingdom in a similar fashion. Impressed by his wit and pluck, Aurangzeb conferred on Jai Singh the title 'Sawai', meaning 'one and a quarter', a title which was proudly borne by all of Jai Singh's descendants.

Jai Singh could trace his lineage back to the Rajput clan of Kachhwahas, who consolidated their power around the 12th century and built the impressive Amber Fort which lies about 11km to the north-east of present-day Jaipur. The dominion of the Kachhwahas spread, eventually encompassing a large area which abutted the kingdoms of Mewar (Udaipur region) and Marwar (Jodhpur region).

The Kachhwahas recognised the expediency of aligning themselves with the powerful Mughal empire, and enjoyed the patronage of the Mughal emperors. However, Jai Singh incurred the displeasure of Aurangzeb's successor, Bahadur Shah, who came to power following Aurangzeb's death in 1707.

Bahadur Shah's accession was contested by his younger brother, Azam Shah, and Jai Singh unfortunately supported Azam's bid for power. Bahadur Shah responded by demanding his removal from Amber Fort, and he installed Jai Singh's younger brother Vijay Singh in his place. This naturally rankled with Jai Singh, who eventually dislodged his brother. Soliciting the support of other large Rajput states, Jai Singh formed a formidable front against the Mughal ruler, and eventually reconsolidated his rule.

The wealth of the kingdom increased exponentially, and this, plus the need to accommodate the burgeoning population and a paucity of water at the old capital at Amber, prompted the maharaja in 1727 to commence work on a new city which he named after himself – Jaipur.

It was a collaborative effort using his vision and the impressive expertise of his chief architect, Vidyadhar. Jai Singh's strong grounding in the sciences is reflected in the precise symmetry of the new city which, unlike the many unplanned and labyrinthine cities in North India at the time, was laid out according to strict principles of town planning set down in the *Shilpa-Shastra*, an ancient Hindu treatise on architecture. The small villages which lay in the vicinity were incorporated into the new city, which was dissected by wide boulevards flanked by stalls of equal size forming seven rectangles, called *mohallas*, of varying size.

The most central of the seven rectangles comprises the city palace complex containing the palace itself, the administrative quarters, the Jantar Mantar (Jai Singh's remarkable observatory) and the *zenana mahals*, or the women's palaces. Here the maharaja's 28 wives and several concubines were installed – he held the dubious honour of maintaining more wives and concubines than any of his predecessors, although most of these alliances were motivated more by political expediency than by amorous compulsions.

The city was not just an aesthetic triumph; its stout walls protected its inhabitants from would-be invaders, encouraging merchants and tradespeople to flock here and further serving to enhance the city's growth and prosperity. Jai Singh's interest in the arts, sciences and religion fostered their development in Jaipur, and the royal court became a centre of intellectual and artistic endeavour.

Maharaja Jai Singh II. This precocious maharaja came to power at the age of 12.

Festivals of Jaipur District

Several important festivals are unique to Jaipur. For statewide and nationwide festivals, see the boxed text 'Festivals of Rajasthan' in the Facts for the Visitor chapter.

March-April

Gangaur – Women across the state celebrate the love between Lord Shiva and his consort Parvati (Gauri) during this much adored festival. It commences on the day following Holi, and continues for 18 days. Wooden images of Gauri are bedecked in beautiful costumes and jewels and worshipped. An elaborately garbed image of Gauri is carried on a palanquin from the Tripolia, at the City Palace, through the streets of the old city.

Elephant Festival – During Jaipur's elephant festival, gaily caparisoned elephants lumber through the streets, and matches of elephant polo are held at the polo ground near the Rambagh Palace. One of the more bizarre spectacles is a tug-of-war between elephants and men.

Sheetala Ashtami – This festival is held in honour of the goddess of smallpox, Sheetala Mata, at the village of Chaksu, near Jaipur where the goddess receives special prayers petitioning her to spare young children from smallpox.

July-August

Teej – This festival heralds the onset of the monsoon, and is celebrated across Rajasthan in honour of the marriage of Lord Shiva and Parvati. It is a favourite with Rajasthani women. At this time, flower-bedecked swings are hung from trees, and songs celebrating love are sung by maidens.

Following Jai Singh's death in 1744, power struggles between his many offspring laid the kingdom open to invasion by neighbouring Rajput kingdoms, who encroached on and appropriated large tracts of territory. The kingdom maintained good relations with the British Raj, although the British gradually began to undermine the independence of the state, exercising greater control over its administration.

In 1876, Maharaja Ram Singh had the entire old city painted pink, traditionally a colour associated with hospitality, to welcome the Prince of Wales (later King Edward VII) to the city. This tradition has been maintained, and today all residents of the old city are compelled by law to preserve the pink facade. Maharaja Ram Singh also built Ramgarh Lake to supply water to the ever growing city.

During the 19th and 20th centuries, the spacious and carefully planned city contained within Jai Singh's original city walls could not contain the population, and the city spread beyond its walled perimeters.

In 1922, Man Singh II, Jaipur's last maharaja, took the throne following the death of his adoptive father, Sawai Madho Singh II. During his reign, civic buildings such as schools, hospitals and the vast Secretariat complex were built outside the original walls.

Following Independence in 1947, the status of the princely state was to change forever. In March 1949, Jaipur merged with the Rajput states of Jodhpur, Jaisalmer and Bikaner, becoming the Greater Rajasthan Union. Jaipur was honoured above the other former states when the title Rajpramukh, meaning head of state, was conferred on Man Singh II, invested with administrative supervision of the new province. The title was later revoked, and Man Singh II was posted as Indian ambassador to Spain. In 1956, Jaipur became the capital of the state of Rajasthan.

The population has expanded from some 300,000 in 1950 to close to two million today, and while the city remains prosperous and retains vestiges of its former grandeur, unplanned urban sprawl has disfigured what was possibly one of the most beautiful cities in India. All of the seven original gates into the old city remain, but unfortunately much of the wall itself has been torn down for building material. There is now a preservation order on the remainder.

FESTIVALS & CEREMONIES

Rajasthan hosts some of India's most spectacular *melas* (fairs) and festivals. The sight of thousands of colourfully garbed villagers assembled in one place is spectacle enough, but these melas and celebrations often feature vibrant and intricate dances involving dozens of participants, further contributing to the spectacle. See the boxed text Festivals of Rajasthan later in this chapter.

Fairs and festivals may be purely commercial in nature, such as the Nagaur Fair; purely religious, such as Gangaur, which commemorates the love between Shiva and Parvati; a combination of both, such as the Pushkar Camel Fair, which is held at the sacred Pushkar Lake; or seasonal, celebrating the seasons. Whatever their impetus, fairs and festivals afford an integral social function, enabling villagers from remote regions to meet and mingle, marriage alliances to be contracted, livestock deals to be struck and rural issues (for example, market prices, drought control measures) to be discussed.

At all festivals, as much attention to detail in dress is accorded the animal participants as the human ones. Camels are adorned with colourful tassels and bridles, magnificently embroidered or mirrored rugs and ornaments known as *gorbandhs*, which are made by new brides for their husbands' camels.

Rajasthan's oldest, most well known and arguably most spectacular festival is the Pushkar Camel Fair, which is held annually in November at the small town of Pushkar, near Ajmer. This fair fulfils both a religious and commercial role, enabling thousands of devotees from around the country to bathe in the sacred Pushkar Lake on the auspicious date of Kartik Purnima, while also providing a temporary marketplace for traders in livestock to parade their elaborately bedecked and groomed beasts before potential buyers. It is a spectacle *par excellence*, with thousands of participants, Ferris wheels, a 'tent city' and, of course, plenty of cool camels.

Inset: 'Mr Desert' Jaisalmer Desert Festival. Photo: Sarina Singh.

Right: Jaipur boy playing the role of Hanuman, monkey god and Rama's ally.

Far Right: Dancing girl, Pushkar.

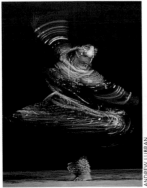

RICHARD I'ANSON

Some festivals have been established purely to attract overseas visitors, such as Jaisalmer's Desert Festival, which is held each year in January/February, corresponding with the peak tourist season. Despite its blatant rupee-driven impetus, if you're within camel's spit of Jaisalmer, it's an occasion which shouldn't be missed, with villagers and townspeople donning traditional garb, dozens of elaborately caparisoned camels, traditional dances and music, camel polo matches and more. This is an ideal time to visit the Sam sand dunes near Jaisalmer, when traditional musicians attempt to outdo each other in musical virtuosity, and camel races take place across the dunes. The Mr Desert competition attracts a swag of mustachioed hopefuls.

Festivals which are celebrated nationwide, such as Holi and Diwali, appear, when celebrated in this state, to be injected with that curiously Rajasthani element of verve and zest which sets them apart from the rest of the country. Holi, for example, the Festival of Colours, which

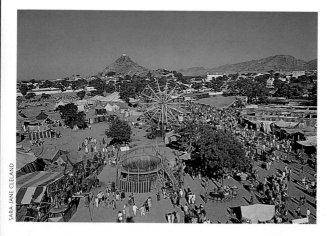

SARA-JANE CLELAND

Top: Camels at sunset, Pushkar.

Left: Pushkar Camel Fair from the air.

takes place in late February/early March, truly lives up to its name in Rajasthan, where the flinging of coloured dye achieves new heights of spirited abandon. In the days of the princely states, subjects gleefully threw coloured water at their maharajas, and princes played Holi with the ladies of the *zenana* (women's quarters).

Westerners are, of course, not immune to the revelry, and your best bet, should you find yourself in Rajasthan at this time, is to don your oldest clothes and resign yourself to being completely drenched with wet and often indelible colour. Men and women, old and young, rich and poor – everyone enters into the spirit of Holi, with faces, hair and clothes smeared in pink, yellow and green dye. Even the cows lumbering through the streets are an unsettling and vibrant pink!

Weddings are also celebrated with typical Rajasthani enthusiasm. During the peak wedding season – around February and March – marriage parties, known as *baraats*, parade through the streets of towns and villages across the state, led by a motorised or hand-pulled 'stage' on which a singer waxes lyrical upon the virtues of love (despite the

Top Left: Dancing at the Pushkar Camel Festival.

Top Right: Ready for a ceremony in Udaipur.

Right: Camel traders and camels at sunset, Jaisalmer Desert Festival.

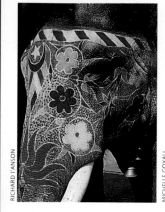

RICHARD I'ANSON

MICHELLE COXALL

fact that most marriages are arranged!), his voice amplified 100-fold through a bank of loudspeakers. Astride a white horse, the groom is borne to a gaily decorated *mandap* (pavilion), usually at the bride's house, where the vows are made and the guests are entertained by hired entertainers such as musicians, *hijras* (eunuchs who dress effeminately) and singers.

Traditional dances play a large role in the celebration of religious festivals such as Navratri and Dussehra, during both of which women dance the *ghoomer*. During Holi, the Bhil tribal people dance the *gir*. In either August or September, in the small village of Ramdevra in western Rajasthan, female dancers perform the *terahtal* in honour of the local deity Ramdevji.

LIZ THOMPSON

Top Left: Elephant decorated for festival, Amber.

Top Right: Hijras make appearances at births and weddings.

Left: Preparing food for pilgrims at a Jain temple, Ranakpur.

Orientation

The walled 'pink city' is in the north-east of Jaipur; the new parts have spread to the south and west. The city's main tourist attractions are in the old part of town. The principal shopping centre in the old city is Johari Bazaar, the jewellers' market. Unlike some retail centres in narrow alleys elsewhere in Asia, this one is broad and open.

There are three main interconnecting roads in the new part of town – Mirza Ismail Rd (MI Rd), Station Rd and Sansar Chandra Marg. Along or just off these roads are most of the budget and mid-range hotels and restaurants, the main train station, the bus terminal, many of the banks and the modern shopping centre.

Information

Tourist Offices There's an Rajasthan Tourism Development Corporation (RTDC) tourist office (☎ 315714) on platform No 1 at the train station. It's open daily from 7 am to 6 pm. The main Tourist Reception Centre (☎ 365256) is in the RTDC's Tourist Hotel compound on MI Rd and is open daily except Sunday from 10 am until 5 pm. The staff are quite helpful, especially Madan Singh. You can buy a range of literature including a good map of Jaipur (Rs 2) and even posters (Rs 15). They also sell a handy booklet listing all families who have registered with the Paying Guest House Scheme in Jaipur (Rs 2), as well as one which covers all of Rajasthan (Rs 5).

Also in the RTDC's Tourist Hotel compound are Gujarat Tourism Development Corporation offices (☎ 362017), open Monday to Saturday from 10 am to 5 pm; and Garhwal (northern Uttar Pradesh) Tourism Development Corporation (☎ 378892), open Monday to Saturday from 10 am to 1 pm and 1.30 to 5 pm (until noon on Sunday).

The Government of India tourist office (☎ 372200) is located in the grounds of the Hotel Khasa Kothi, near the train station. It has lots of glossy brochures, but is otherwise of limited help. Its office is open on weekdays from 9 am to 6 pm and on Saturday from 9 am to 1.30 pm.

Bookings for RTDC hotels around Rajasthan, accommodation in the tourist village during the Pushkar Camel Fair, and reservations for the *Palace on Wheels* train (see the boxed text in the Getting Around chapter) can be made at the RTDC's Central Reservations Office, (☎ 203531, fax 201 045), Hotel Swagatam Campus, Near Railway Station, Jaipur, 302006.

Applications for visa extensions can be lodged at the Foreigners Registration Office (☎ 669391), located in the City Palace complex – see Visas & Documents in the Facts for the Visitor chapter for more details.

Money Thomas Cook (☎ 360940), 1st floor, Jaipur Towers, MI Rd, changes travellers cheques and major currencies. An encashment fee of Rs 20 is payable on travellers cheques other than Thomas Cook. It's open Monday to Saturday from 9.30 am to 6 pm.

The little Bank of Rajasthan (☎ 381416) at the Rambagh Palace changes travellers cheques and currency, and is conveniently open daily from 7 am to 8 pm.

The Central Bank of India (☎ 317419), Anand Building, Sansar Chandra Marg, can do cash advances on MasterCard and Visa. The minimum amount is US$100. It also changes travellers cheques and major currencies. The Andhra Bank (☎ 369606), MI Rd, gives cash advances on MasterCard, Visa and JCB (Japanese Credit Bureau) cards. Your account must have a credit balance if you wish to use this facility.

The Tripolia Bazaar branch of the Bank of Baroda (☎ 314079) only changes major currencies and travellers cheques.

Post & Communications The telegraph office is in the same building as the main post office (☎ 368740) on MI Rd. The fax number at the main post office is 381525. It costs Rs 10 to receive faxes (up to three pages). Make sure that your sender clearly marks your name at the top of the fax. The cost for sending a fax varies from country to country; to Australia and the UK it costs Rs 95 per page and to the USA it's Rs 110 per page.

JAIPUR

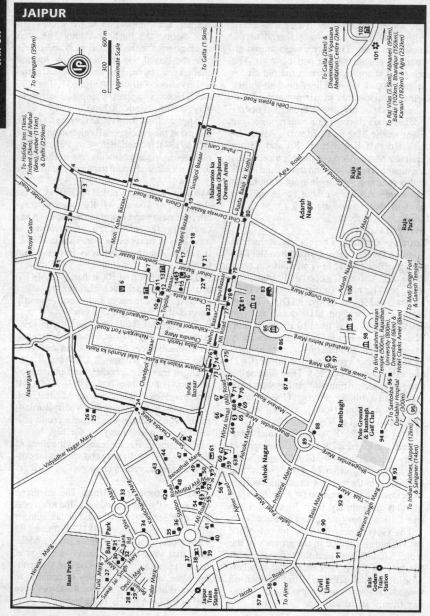

To Ramgarh (35km)

To Holiday Inn (1km),
Trident (5km), Jai Mahal
(6km), Amber (11km)
& Delhi (259km)

To Galta (2km) &
Dhammathali Vipassana
Meditation Centre (2km)

To Raj Vilas (3.5km), Abhaneri (95km),
Balaji (102km), Bharatpur (150km),
Karauli (182km) & Agra (232km)

To Galta (1.5km)

0   300   600 m
Approximate Scale

Delhi Bypass Road

Royal Gaitor

Nahargarh

Amber Road

Moti Katra Bazaar

Sireedeori Bazaar

Tripolia Bazaar

Chaura Rasta

Ganpaur Bazaar

Nahargarh Fort Road

Babe Harish Chandra Marg

Khajane Walon ka Rasta

Jalal Munshi ka Rasta

Chandpol Bazaar

Indra Bazaar

Sansar Chandra Marg

Vidyadhar Nagar Marg

Bani Park

Niwan Marg

Tulsi Marg

Sawai Jai Singh Hwy

Devji Marg

Kabir Marg

Station Road

Sindhi Camp Rd

Bank Marg

Motilal Atal Marg

Banasthali Marg

MI Road

Ajmer Road

Jaipur Train Station

To Ajmer

Jacob Rd

Civil Lines

Bais Godam Train Station

To Indian Airlines, Airport (12km)
& Sanganer (14km)

Sadar Patel Marg

Bhawani Singh Marg

Tilak Marg

Bajaj Marg

Ashok Nagar

Prithviraj Marg

Bhagwandas Marg

Mahavir Road

Rambagh

Polo Ground
& Rambagh
Golf Club

Sawai Ram Singh Marg

To Birla Lakshmi Narayan
Temple (500m), Rajasthan
University (800m),
Dronelandia (6km) &
Hotel Clarks Amer (8km)

To Santokha
& Durlabhji Hospital

Jawaharlal Nehru Marg

Moti Dungri Marg

Adarsh Nagar Marg

To Moti Dungri Fort
& Ganesh Temple

Adarsh
Nagar

Raja
Park

Govind Marg

Agra Road

Mahavaton ka
Mohalla (Elephant
Owners' Area)

L Rasta Balaji ki Kothi

Surajpol Bazaar

Pahar Ganj

Chat Darwaja Bazaar

Ghora Nikas Road

Ramganj Bazaar

Johari Bazaar

Hapu Bazaar

Nehru Bazaar

Kishanpol Bazaar

Chaura Rasta

MI Road

PLACES TO STAY

3	Samode Haveli
17	Hotel Kailash
23	Hotel Sweet Dream
25	Hotel Bissau Palace; Divya Drishti
26	Hotel Khetri House
27	Hotel Meghniwas
28	Tirupati Guest House
29	Shapura House
30	Madhuban; Madhavanand Ashram
31	Umaid Bhawan Guest House; Sajjan Niwas Guest House
32	Pipalda House
33	Jaipur Inn
34	Hotel Jaipur Ashok
35	RTDC's Hotel Teej
37	RTDC's Hotel Swagatam; RTDC's Central Reservations Office
38	Rajputana Palace Sheraton; Bookwise; Kaalbelia disco
40	Hotel Khasa Kothi; Government of India Tourist Office
41	RTDC's Hotel Gangaur
44	Jai Mangal Palace
45	Alsisar Haveli
46	Hotel Arya Niwas
47	Hotel Mangal
49	Mansingh Hotel; Central Bank of India
50	Hotel Neelam; Karni Niwas
53	Atithi Guest House; Aangan Guest House
57	Jai Mahal Palace Hotel
59	RTDC's Tourist Hotel; Tourist Reception Centre
63	Evergreen Guest House; Hotel Pink Sun; Ashiyana Guest House
84	Nana-ki-Haveli
87	Hotel Diggi Palace
91	Rajmahal Palace
93	Youth Hostel
94	Rambagh Palace; Bank of Rajasthan; Rajasthan Tours
96	Narain Niwas Palace Hotel
100	Rajasthan Palace Hotel

PLACES TO EAT

21	Royal's
22	LMB Hotel & Restaurant
51	Ganpati Plaza; Swaad; Pizza Hut; Celebrations; Baskin 31 Robbins; Hot Breads; Rajasthan Travel Service; Air India
56	Rainbow Restaurant
60	Copper Chimney
62	Handi Restaurant
66	Chanakya Restaurant
67	Lassiwala; Goyal Colour Lab; Charmica
70	Golden Dragon Restaurant; Bake Hut
71	Niro's; Surya Mahal; Jal Mahal; Natraj Restaurant
74	Indian Coffee House

OTHER

1	Samrat Gate
2	Zorawar Gate
4	Gangapol (Gate)
5	Char Darwaja (Gate)
6	Govind Devji Temple
7	Jantar Mantar (Observatory)
8	City Palace & Maharaja Sawai Mansingh II Museum; Foreigners Registration Office
9	Choti Chaupar
10	Iswari Minar Swarga Sal
11	Dr Vinod Shastri (Astrologer)
12	Tripolia Gate; Atishpol (Stable Gate)
13	Hawa Mahal
14	Bank of Baroda
15	Gopalji ka Rasta
16	Jama Masjid
18	Haldio ka Rasta
19	Ramganj Chaupar
20	Surajpol (Gate)
24	Chandpol (Gate)
36	Sita World Travels
39	Aravali Safari & Tours
42	Mewar Cyber Café & Communication
43	Main Bus Terminal
48	Polo Victory Cinema
52	Cathay Pacific
54	British Airways
55	Jaipur Towers (Thomas Cook & Airline Agents)
58	Soma
61	Main Post Office; Philatelic Museum
64	DHL Worldwide Express
65	Andhra Bank
68	Books Corner
69	Raj Mandir Cinema
72	Books & News Mart
73	Singhpol (Gate)
75	Rajasthali Emporium; Rajasthan Handloom House
76	Ajmeri Gate
77	New Gate
78	Lufthansa; Singapore Airlines
79	Sanganeri Gate
80	Ghat Gate
81	Ram Niwas Public Gardens
82	Ravindra Rangmanch Gallery
83	Zoo
85	Central Museum (Albert Hall)
86	Maharaja College
88	Birla Planetarium
89	Statue Circle
90	Registhan Tours
92	Anokhi Showroom
95	Rambagh Circle
97	Sawai Mansingh Hospital
98	Dolls Museum
99	Museum of Indology
101	Vidyadharji ka Bagh
102	Sisodia Rani Palace & Gardens

There's a handy parcel packing service in the foyer of the post office and a speedy desk handling parcel postage daily, except Sunday, from 10 am to 5.30 pm. Inside the main post office, there's a **Philatelic Museum** with a collection of old stamps (some for sale). It's open Monday to Saturday from 10 am to 1.30 pm and 2 to 5 pm. Free entry.

It is not unusual for telephone numbers to change in Rajasthan. Jaipur has tackled this problem by offering an excellent automated Jaipur 'changed telephone number' service in English (☎ 1952) and in Hindi (☎ 1951). For local telephone number inquiries call ☎ 197. The collect call operator can be reached on ☎ 186.

There are plenty of local/long-distance telephone booths scattered around Jaipur, which are usually cheaper than the hotels.

DHL Worldwide Express (☎ 362826, fax 368852), in a small lane off MI Rd at C-scheme, G-7A Vinobha Marg, can arrange air freight. The office is open Monday to Saturday from 9 am to 7.30 pm.

Email & Internet Access Internet outlets are rapidly cropping up in Jaipur, so by the time you read this there should be many more – find out which is the closest to you. One fairly central place where you can snack while you surf is the Mewar Cyber Café & Communication (☎ 206172, email mewar@jp1.dot.net.in), near the main bus terminal on Station Rd.

Travel Agencies The capital has plenty of travel agencies and many arrange local sightseeing. Sita World Travels (☎ 203626, fax 205479), Station Rd, can book domestic and international air tickets, cars and drivers and hotels, and can organise freight cargo (both air and sea). See Getting There & Away, later in this chapter, for details of car and driver rates. Registhan Tours Pvt Ltd (☎/fax 380824) is at E-141 Sardar Patel Marg (near the Rajmahal Palace), and also has car and driver packages.

Jetair Tours (☎ 375430, fax 374242), 112/113 Jaipur Towers, MI Rd, books various tours in Rajasthan. It is a part of Jetair Ltd which is an agency for many international and domestic airlines.

Amber Tours Pvt Ltd (☎ 381543) and Rajasthan Tours (☎ 381041) both have a counter at the Rambagh Palace. They offer a variety of services, including the hire of cars and drivers.

Aravali Safari & Tours (☎ 373124, fax 365345) is opposite the Rajputana Palace Sheraton, Palace Rd. This IATA accredited agency specialises in tours of Rajasthan and can also book cars.

Bookshops National English-language dailies and a good selection of maps, magazines, postcards and books on India (with particular emphasis on Rajasthan) can be found at Books Corner, MI Rd, near Niro's restaurant. There are some French-language books for sale too. Here you will also find the monthly publication *Jaipur Vision* (Rs 20), a small informative booklet for tourists. If you can't find a copy, call the Jaipur Vision office at ☎ 622185. In the same block as Books Corner, heading towards the old city, is the Books & News Mart which also has a fair selection of books on Rajasthan. There is an excellent selection of books about India, including an extensive collection of titles pertaining to Rajasthan, at the bookshop in the Rambagh Palace hotel, as well as at Divya Drishti (Hotel Bissau Palace) and Bookwise (Rajputana Palace Sheraton hotel). Barwara Book House, out at Civil Lines, also has quite a good collection. You can buy and exchange second-hand books at some of the budget hotels.

Film & Photography For reliable film processing try Goyal Colour Lab on MI Rd, opposite the Natraj restaurant (they also have a branch in Nehru Bazaar). They can develop print film in one hour at a cost of Rs 135 for 24 prints. It takes about two days to develop slide films and costs Rs 200 for 36 slides (including mounting). Star Colour Lab, at Nehru Bazaar in the old city, is another film processing outlet.

Medical Services The Sawai Mansingh Hospital (☎ 560291) is on Sawai Ram Singh Marg. The Santokba Durlabhji Hospital (☎ 566251) is on Bhawani Singh Marg. Most hotels can arrange a doctor on site.

Emergency

Police	☎ 100
Fire	☎ 101
Ambulance	☎ 102

These numbers apply to most other towns in Rajasthan too.

Dangers & Annoyances Travellers have reported problems with commission merchants. See the boxed text A Warning! in the Shopping section of the Facts for the Visitor chapter.

Old City (Pink City)

The old city is partially encircled by a crenellated wall pierced at intervals by gates – the major gates are Chandpol ('pol' means gate), Ajmeri and Sanganeri. Broad avenues, over 30m wide, divide the pink city into neat rectangles, each of which is the domain of a particular group of artisans or commercial activities.

Chandpol is the entrance to the bustling **Chandpol Bazaar**. This is crossed by Khajane Walon ka Rasta, where you can see Jaipur's marble workers. At the intersection of Chandpol Bazaar and Kishanpol Bazaar you will find the **Choti Chaupar**, where villagers from outlying regions come to sell and trade their produce. **Kishanpol Bazaar** is famous for textiles, particularly tie-dye cloth, and you can see the artisans engaged in their work here, producing two forms of tie-dye, *bandhani* and *loharia*.

Continuing west beyond Choti Chaupar brings you to **Tripolia Bazaar**, also known as Maniharon ka Rasta. Here you are confronted by stall after stall crammed with domestic kitchen utensils, textiles, trinkets and ironware. The stalls are closed on Sunday.

On the north side of Tripolia Bazaar is the **Iswari Minar Swarga Sal** (Heaven Piercing Minaret), an apt name as this is the highest structure in the old city. The minaret was erected by Iswari Singh, who succeeded Jai Singh. Lacking the military prowess and courage of his warrior father, Iswari Singh took his own life rather than confront the advancing Maratha army. His ignominious end was overshadowed by the sacrifice of his 21 wives and concubines, who performed *jauhar* by immolating themselves upon his funeral pyre.

A short distance farther west is **Tripolia Gate**, the triple-arched gate after which the bazaar takes its name. This is the main entrance to the City Palace and Jantar Mantar (see later), but only the maharaja's family is permitted entrance via its portals. The public entrance to the palace complex is via the less ostentatious **Atishpol**, or Stable Gate, to the left. To the north of the City Palace is the **Govind Devji Temple**, surrounded by gardens. Here is an image of Govinda Deva which Jai Singh installed as the patron deity of his family.

Proceeding east along Tripolia Bazaar you will come to another major intersection. To the south, **Johari Bazaar** leads to the Sanganeri Gate. Johari Bazaar (closed for part of Sunday and Tuesday) and the small laneways which dissect it are where you will find Jaipur's jewellers and gold and silversmiths. Of particular interest are the artisans doing enamelling, or *meenakari*. This highly glazed and intricate work in shades of ruby, bottle green and royal blue is a speciality of Jaipur. On Johari Bazaar you can also find cotton merchants, with their bolts of white cloth. Interspersed with the uniform shop fronts are the grand *havelis* or homes of Jaipur's wealthy merchants. If you turn right before exiting the Sanganeri Gate you'll reach **Bapu Bazaar** and farther west, **Nehru Bazaar** which extends between Chaura Rasta and Kishanpol Bazaar on the inside of the southern wall. Brightly coloured bolts of fabric, shoes of camel skin, trinkets and aromatic perfumes make this bazaar a favourite destination for Jaipur's women.

The northern extension of Johari Bazaar, to the north of the large square known as **Badi Chaupar**, is **Siredeori Bazaar**, also known as Hawa Mahal Bazaar. The latter name is derived from the extraordinary **Hawa Mahal**, or Palace of the Winds (see later), a short distance to the north along the bazaar on the left-hand side.

Back on Tripolia Bazaar, if you proceed farther east beyond **Ramganj Chaupar**, you'll pass through **Ramganj Bazaar** where you can see shoemakers at work. Farther east is **Surajpol Bazaar**. The area to the south is known as **Mahavaton ka Mohalla**, traditionally the quarters of elephants and their *mahoots* (elephant masters). Surajpol Bazaar leads to the Surajpol, the main exit from the old city in the eastern wall.

Tie-Dye

In the bandhani form of tie-dye, a pale background is covered with large splotches. This effect is achieved by knotting the dyed cloth and then bleaching it, with the knotted sections retaining their colour. A worker in this form of tie-dye is known as a Bandhej.

The second form of tie-dye, called loharia, features diagonal motifs in contrasting colours. Loharia pieces are named according to the number of colours employed: *panchrangi* features five colours (from *panch*, meaning five), and *satrangi* features seven different colours. The cloth is worn as turbans and saris.

City Palace In the heart of the old city, the City Palace complex occupies a large area divided into a series of courtyards, gardens and buildings. The outer wall was built by Jai Singh, but other additions are more recent, some dating to the start of the 20th century. Today the palace is a blend of Rajasthani and Mughal architecture. The son of the last maharaja and his family still live in part of the palace.

Before the palace proper lies the **Mubarak Mahal**, or Welcome Palace, built in the late 19th century by Maharaja Sawai Madho Singh II as a reception centre for visiting dignitaries. It now forms part of the **Maharaja Sawai Mansingh II Museum** (no smoking allowed), and contains a collection of royal costumes and superb shawls including Sanganeri block prints, royal shawls, Kashmiri *pashmina* (goats' wool) shawls, folk embroideries and Benares silk saris. One remarkable exhibit is a set of the voluminous clothes of Sawai Madho Singh I (reigned 1750-68), who was over 2m tall, 1.2m wide and weighed 250kg!

The **Maharani's Palace** (apartments of the queen) now houses a collection of weaponry. Note the extraordinary frescoes on the ceiling of this room: the colours were derived from semi-precious jewel dust and are beautifully preserved. The priceless collection of weapons dates back to the 15th century, and includes the gruesome Rajput scissor-action daggers – when the dagger enters the body, the handles are released to spread the blades. The dagger is withdrawn, virtually disembowelling the hapless victim.

Other exhibits include swords with pistols attached to their blades; beautiful crystal, ivory and silver-handled daggers; armour of chain mail, one complete set of which can weigh up to 35kg; and a ruby and emerald encrusted sword presented by Queen Victoria to Maharaja Sawai Ram Singh, the ruler of Jaipur from 1835-80. There is also an assortment of guns, including some which also serve as walking sticks, a gun the size of a small cannon for use on camel back, and double barrelled pistols which held bullets made of lead dipped in poison and packed with gunpowder.

Between the armoury and the art gallery is the **diwan-i-khas**, or hall of private audience. In its marble-paved gallery stand two silver vessels which Maharaja Madho Singh II took to London filled with holy Ganges water. As a devout Hindu, the maharaja was reluctant to risk ritual pollution by imbibing English water. These enormous vessels each have a capacity of over 9000L, stand 160cm tall, and are the largest sterling silver objects in the world. There are a number of crystal chandeliers hanging from the ceiling, however these are covered with plastic to protect them from dust and pigeon droppings. They are only uncovered on certain festive occasions.

The art gallery is housed in the former **diwan-i-am**, or hall of public audience, beyond and to the right of the diwan-i-khas. It retains a beautifully preserved painted ceiling, on which the original semi-precious stone colours have barely faded and from which is suspended an enormous crystal chandelier. Exhibits include a copy of the entire *Bhagavad Gita*, handwritten in tiny script, and miniature copies of other holy Hindu Scriptures small enough to be easily hidden in the event that Aurangzeb tried to destroy the sacred texts. There are also beautiful handwritten books in Persian and

Sanskrit; early manuscripts on palm leaf; miniature paintings of the Rajasthani, Mughal and Persian schools depicting religious themes, most notably scenes from the *Ramayana*; various ornate howdahs (elephant saddles); and exquisitely detailed paper cuttings incised with a thumbnail.

The **Chandra Mahal** is still occupied by the royal family, but you can visit the ground floor, which only has a few exhibits. Note the exquisite **Peacock Gate** in the courtyard outside.

The palace and museum are open daily between 9.30 am and 4.45 pm. Entry is Rs 35/110 for Indians/foreigners; Rs 20/75 for children between the age of five and 12. The ticket includes entry to Jaigarh (see Around Jaipur), but is only valid for two days from purchase. Photography opportunities are limited because cameras and videos are prohibited inside the palace museums. If you're still interested, a video costs Rs 100 for everyone, but a Rs 50 camera fee is only levied on Indians! There are guides for hire inside the palace complex for Rs 150.

Jantar Mantar Next to the entrance to the City Palace is the Jantar Mantar, or observatory (Jantar Mantar means instrument of calculation), begun by Jai Singh in 1728. Jai Singh's passion for astronomy was even more notable than his prowess as a warrior. Before commencing the Jantar Mantar, he sent scholars abroad to study foreign observatories. The Jaipur observatory is the largest and the best preserved of the five he built, with 13 different instruments for calculating the movement of celestial bodies. It was restored in 1901. Others are in Delhi (the oldest, dating from 1724), Varanasi and Ujjain. The fifth observatory, at Mathura, has now disappeared.

At first glance, Jantar Mantar appears to be a curious if somewhat compelling collection of sculptures. In fact, each construction has a specific purpose, for example measuring the positions of the stars, altitude and azimuth, and calculating eclipses.

The most striking instrument is the **Brihat Samrat Yantra** sundial, an imposing edifice

to the far left of the observatory complex which has a 27m high gnomon arm set at an angle of 27°. The shadow this casts moves up to 4m in an hour, and aids in the calculation of local and meridian pass time and various attributes of the heavenly bodies, including declination (the angular distance of a heavenly body from the celestial equator) and altitude. It is still used by astrologers today, and is the focus of a gathering of astrologers during the full moon days of June and July, when it is used to help predict the monsoon rains, and subsequent success or failure of crops.

Immediately to the left as you enter the compound is the **Laghu Samrat Yantra**, or small sundial. This does not measure as precisely as the Brihat Samrat Yantra, but also serves to calculate the declination of celestial bodies, and the shadow cast by its gnomon enables local time to be determined. Nearby is the **Dhruva Darshak Yantra**, an instrument which is used to determine the location of the Pole Star.

The large hemispherical shaped object nearby, known as the **Narivalaya Yantra**, is actually two small sundials. The two faces of the instrument represent the northern and southern hemispheres, and enable calculation of the time within a minute's accuracy.

The two large disks suspended from wooden beams nearby are the **Yantra Raj**, a multipurpose instrument which, among other things, can help determine the positions of constellations. A similar looking instrument, the **Unnatansha Yantra**, lies in the northeastern corner of the observatory complex. The disk is divided into segments by horizontal and vertical lines. A hole where these lines intersect, in the centre of the instrument, aids in the calculation of the altitude of celestial bodies.

Nearby is the **Dakhinovrith Bhitti Yantra**, which serves a similar function to the Unnatansha Yantra in helping to determine placement of heavenly bodies.

Near the southern wall of the observatory is a cluster of 12 instruments known as the **Rashi Yantras**. Each rashi, or individual instrument, represents one of the 12 zodiac

Jantar Mantar is an extraordinary observatory built by Maharaja Jai Singh II in 1728 and is still used by astrologers today. It has 13 different instruments to calculate the movement of celestial bodies.

signs. The gradient of each rashi differs in accordance with the particular sign represented and its position in relation to the ecliptic.

The two concave structures on a plinth in the western section of the observatory compound are the **Kapali Yantra**. The eastern Kapali Yantra is inscribed with lines to which astronomers refer in their deliberations; it is used more for graphical analysis than calculation, as opposed to the western Kapali Yantra, which is used to determine the position of a celestial body.

The **Jai Prakash Yantra** was the last instrument installed at the observatory and was invented by Jai Singh, after whom it is named. The two marble bowls which comprise the instrument aid not only in celestial observations, but can be used to verify the calculations determined with the other instruments at the observatory.

Two other impressive instruments are the **Ram Yantras**, which are formed from 12 upright slabs and 12 horizontal slabs. They are used in the calculation of the altitude and azimuth of celestial bodies. Another instrument which is used for calculating azimuth, particularly of the sun, is the **Digansha Yantra**.

It can also be used to determine the time of sunrise and sunset.

The observatory is open daily from 9 am to 4.30 pm. Admission is Rs 4 (free on Monday) and a camera costs Rs 20/50 for Indians/foreigners, while a video is Rs 50/100.

Those interested in the theory behind the construction of these monumental instruments should try to hunt out *A Guide to the Jaipur Astronomical Observatory* by BL Dhama. It may be tough to find as it's now out of print.

Hawa Mahal Built in 1799, the Hawa Mahal, or Palace of the Winds, is one of Jaipur's major landmarks, although it is actually little more than a facade. This five-storey building, which looks out over the main street of the buzzing old city, is a stunning example of Rajput artistry with its pink, delicately honeycombed sandstone windows, of which there are 953. It was originally built to enable ladies of the royal household to watch the everyday life and processions of the city. You can climb to the top of the Hawa Mahal for a view over the city. The palace was built by Maharaja Sawaj

Pratap Singh and is part of the City Palace complex. There's a small archaeological museum (closed Saturday) on the same site.

Most people come here to see the beautiful facade of the Hawa Mahal, but if you want to go inside, entrance is from the rear of the building. To get there, go back to the intersection on your left as you face the Hawa Mahal, turn right and then take the first right again through an archway. It's open daily from 9 am to 4.30 pm. There's an entry fee of Rs 2. The camera charge is Rs 10/30 for Indians/foreigners, and a video camera costs Rs 20/70.

North of the Old City

Nahargarh, the Tiger Fort, overlooks the city of Jaipur from a sheer ridge to the north and is floodlit at night. The fort was built in 1734 by Jai Singh and extended in 1868. An 8km road runs up through the hills from Jaipur, and the fort can be reached along a zigzagging 2km path which starts from the north-west of the old city. The glorious views fully justify the effort, and the entry fee is only Rs 2, plus Rs 30/70 for a camera/video. There's a cafeteria here, with a toilet (see Places to Eat).

Royal Gaitor is a beautiful, peaceful place just outside Jaipur's old city walls, accessible via the Zorawar or Samrat gates in the northern wall. It contains the cenotaphs of the maharajas of Jaipur, from Jai Singh II, the founder of Jaipur, to that of the last maharaja, Man Singh II. The more ancient cenotaphs, including that of Jai Singh, are in a walled compound to the rear. A caretaker may be required to open the gate for you here. Behind Maharaja Madho Singh II's carved cenotaph is another commemorating his 13 sons who died of malaria. Beside the entrance to the Royal Gaitor, steps lead to a Ganesh temple (20 minutes).

Entrance to the Royal Gaitor is free, but there's a Rs 10/20 camera/video charge.

East of the Old City

Sisodia Rani Palace & Gardens & Vidyadharji ka Bagh Six kilometres from the city on Agra Rd (leave by the Ghat Gate), and surrounded by terraced gardens, this palace was built for Maharaja Jai Singh's second wife, the Sisodia princess. The outer walls are decorated with murals depicting hunting scenes and the Krishna legend. Entry to the palace gardens (open daily from 8 am to 6 pm) costs Rs 3. Video cameras are not permitted.

Vidyadharji ka Bagh, a garden built in honour of Jai Singh's chief architect and town planner, Vidyadhar, is about 200m before Sisodia Rani Palace on Agra Rd. The garden is open daily from 8 am to 6 pm and entry is Rs 2 (videos are not allowed).

Getting There & Away Regular local buses leave from the front of the main train station and from Ghat Gate for the Sisodia Rani Palace (15 minutes, Rs 5). You could ask the bus driver to drop you at the Vidyadharji ka Bagh, and then continue on to the palace. You can get a good view over the gardens without entering the complex by continuing along the road past the entrance and driving to the back of the gardens. This road continues to the temple of the sun god at Galta (following). Above the palace, a steep zigzag staircase leads to a Jain temple.

Galta The temple of the sun god at Galta is 100m above Jaipur to the east, a 2.5km climb from Surajpol (see Jaipur map). A deep temple-studded gorge stands behind the temple and there are fine views over the surrounding plains. Very heavy rains in 1991 destroyed many of the original frescoes. Restoration has been done, although unfortunately the new work has little of the artistic skill of the original frescoes. In the temple are images of Brahma, Vishnu, Garlo Rishi, Shankaracharya, Parvati and Ganesh. The temple is fronted by pools into which some daring souls jump from the adjacent cliffs. The water is claimed to be 'several elephants deep'.

There are some original frescoes in reasonable condition in the chamber at the end of the bottom pool, including those depicting athletic feats, the maharaja playing polo, and the exploits of Krishna and the *gopis* (milkmaids). On the ceiling are swirl motifs, and it is possible to make out faces which are not initially evident on first viewing. Galta is perched between the cliff faces of a rocky valley, and is a fairly desolate and barren, if somewhat evocative, place.

There are regular local buses from Jaipur (25 mins, Rs 5.50).

New City

By the mid-19th century it became obvious that Jai Singh's well-planned city could not accommodate the growing population. During the reign of Maharaja Ram Singh (1835-80) the city spread beyond its walls and civic facilities such as a postal system and piped water were introduced. The maharaja commissioned the landscaping of the **Ram Niwas Public Gardens**, on Jawaharlal Nehru Marg, and the construction in the gardens of impressive **Albert Hall**, which now houses the Central Museum (see later).

These civic improvements were continued by Jaipur's last maharaja, Man Singh II, who can be credited with the university, the Secretariat, residential colonies, schools, hospitals and colleges. Unfortunately unplanned urban growth is now spoiling this once beautiful city, with private interests and political expediency outweighing aesthetic considerations. Buildings are being constructed with little regard for Jaipur's rich architectural heritage.

There is a small **zoo** in the Ram Niwas Public Gardens with a collection of unhappy looking animals. It's open daily except Tuesday from 8 am to 5 pm; entry is Rs 2. Nearby, an old theatre houses Jaipur's **Modern Art Gallery**, on the first floor of the Ravindra Rangmanch building. You can view the small collection daily except Sunday from 10 am to 5 pm (free admission). A short distance away is the **Maharaja College**, founded in 1845 for the study of Urdu and Persian. For excellent contemporary paintings, go to the **Juneja Art Gallery** (see the Shopping section later).

The rather ramshackle **Museum of Indology** is a mind-boggling private collection of rare folk art objects and other bits and pieces

of interest – there's everything from a map of India painted on a rice grain, to manuscripts (one written by Aurangzeb), old stamps, tribal ornaments, fossils, tantric art, currency notes, clocks, old nut-cutters, a 200-year-old mirrorwork swing from Bikaner and much more. The museum is a private home (although the living quarters have been swallowed up by the collection), and is signposted off J Nehru Marg, south of the Central Museum. It's open daily from 8 am to 6 pm. Entry is Rs 40 (including a guide). Cameras and videos are not allowed.

Sadly, many artefacts are crammed into cupboards due to lack of display space. The owner is planning to open another museum – donations are appreciated and make you a life member of the museum. Close to the Museum of Indology, in the Deaf, Dumb & Blind compound on J Nehru Marg, is the little **Dolls Museum**. The collection includes dolls wearing traditional costumes from around the world, including two leprechauns from Ireland! It's open daily from 10 am to 5 pm (entry is Rs 2). Stamp enthusiasts may be interested in the small **Philatelic Museum** at the main post office (see Post & Communications earlier).

Farther south down J Nehru Marg, looming above the road to the left, is the small and romantic fort of **Moti Dungri**. It has also served as a prison, but today remains in the possession of the erstwhile royal family, and entry is prohibited.

The **Birla Lakshmi Narayan Temple** is a large, modern marble edifice at the foot of Moti Dungri Fort. The wealthy industrialist, Birla, born in Palani, Rajasthan, bought the land on which the temple now stands from the maharaja for a token Rs 1. Stained glass windows depict scenes from Hindu Scriptures. Ganesh, the protector of households, is above the lintel, and the fine quality of the marble is evident when you enter the temple and look back at the entranceway – Ganesh can be made out *through* the marble, which is almost transparent. The images of Lakshmi and Narayan are carved from one piece of marble. Many of the deities of the Hindu pantheon are depicted inside the temple, and on the outside walls great historical personages and religious figures from other religions are shown, including Socrates, Zarathustra, Christ, Buddha and Confucius. There is a small **museum** next to the temple, which is open daily from 8 am to noon and 4 to 8 pm (free entry). The collection includes household objects and clothing of the Birla family. English-speaking guides can explain aspects of the temple's architecture and of Hinduism free of charge.

Not far away is the **Ganesh Temple**, open daily from 5 am to noon and 4 to 8.30 pm (until 11.30 pm on Wednesday). If you don't like crowds avoid the temple on Wednesday (the auspicious day), when there are throngs of devotees. Remove your shoes at the bottom of the steps leading up to the temple. Photography is not allowed. You can buy ladoos to offer Lord Ganesh at the sweet stalls outside the temple.

The **Birla Planetarium** at the BM Birla Science & Technology Centre, near Statue Circle, is open daily (except the last Wednesday of every month) from 10 am to 8 pm. Most shows (one hour) are in Hindi (11 am, 1, 3, 5, 7 and 8 pm). An English commentary is only given in a 6 pm session. Entry is Rs 13. Next door, there's a science museum (admission is Rs 7).

About 3km south-west of the old city is the **Rambagh Palace**, now one of India's most prestigious hotels. Nowhere is the encroachment of the new city more evident than here – once maintained by Maharaja Ram Singh as a hunting lodge, well beyond the limits of the city centre, the Rambagh is now surrounded by sprawling suburbs. However, its spacious and beautifully maintained gardens still engender a sense of luxurious isolation. Man Singh, the last maharaja of Jaipur, converted the former lodge into a magnificent home for his third wife, Gayatri Devi, a glamorous princess from the small state of Cooch Behar. Now in her seventies, Gayatri Devi in her heyday was regarded as one of the world's most beautiful women. She is in the *Guinness Book of World Records* for obtaining the largest victory margin (a staggering 175,000 votes) in

a democracy, when she contested the national elections in 1962. The Man Singhs were renowned for their lavish hospitality, and at Rambagh they entertained some of the world's rich and famous people, including Eleanor Roosevelt and Jackie Kennedy. It was a fairy-tale romance and a fairy-tale life, evocatively recounted in her autobiography, *A Princess Remembers*. Today Gayatri Devi retains residential quarters at the Rambagh Palace, which became a hotel (see Places to Stay) in 1958.

Central Museum This somewhat dusty collection is housed in the architecturally impressive Albert Hall in the Ram Niwas Public Gardens, south of the old city. Entry to the museum is Rs 5/30 for Indians/foreigners (free on Monday). It is open daily except Friday, from 10 am to 4.30 pm. No photography is permitted.

Exhibits include a natural history collection, models of yogis adopting various positions, tribal ware, dioramas depicting various Rajasthani dances, and sections on the decorative arts, costumes, drawings, musical instruments and tribal costumes.

To the right of the Albert Hall is the **Durbar Hall**, which is usually closed, but the caretaker may open it on request (a little baksheesh helps). This hall houses a collection of old carpets, some 400 years old.

Beauty Parlours

Jaipur has lots of beauty parlours for women and some for men. Many feature *kayakalp* treatments – a beauty therapy system using traditional *ayurvedic* (herbal) creams. Treatments include face packs, facial massages and henna designs for hands and feet. The cost for a one hour treatment including a facial massage is approximately Rs 175. To get *mehndi* (henna) applied costs Rs 50 per hand.

For a bit of pampering, go to the Bindiya beauty parlour at the Rajputana Palace Sheraton (see Places to Stay). A 40 minute coconut oil body massage is Rs 495. If that breaks the budget, there's a heavenly 20 minute head massage for Rs 175.

Astrology

It costs Rs 300 for a 20 minute consultation with Dr Vinod Shastri (☎ 663338 or 551117), the General Secretary of the Rajasthan Astrological Council & Research Institute. You need your exact time and place (city or town) of birth to get a computerised horoscope. A five year prediction costs Rs 900, while a 30 year prediction is a hefty Rs 3000! Dr Shastri can be found in his shop near the City Palace, Chandani Chowk, Tripolia Gate. It's highly advisable to make an advance appointment.

Dr Shastri also gives astrology lessons for beginners. The charge is Rs 3000 per person for 10 one-hour lectures over a period of five days (minimum of five people needed). More advanced lessons are also available.

These days, many hotels are cashing in on foreigners' interest in fortune telling.

Meditation

Vipassana is one of India's oldest forms of meditation, which is 'a logical process of mental purification through self-observation that strives to achieve real peace of mind and lead you to a happy, useful life.'

The Dhammathali Vipassana Meditation Centre (☎ 641520) runs courses (for a donation) in meditation for both beginners and more advanced students throughout the year. Courses are for a minimum of 10 days. This serene meditation centre is tucked away in the hilly countryside near Galta (temple of the sun god), about 3km east of the city centre. Accommodation is provided in single rooms (some with attached bath) and vegetarian meals are available. Ring the centre to find out when courses are held.

Yoga

There are several places which conduct yoga classes, including the Prakaritic Chikitsalya (☎ 510590), at the Nature Cure Centre, Bapu Nagar (near the Rajasthan University), which also offers natural therapies. For yoga, a minimum of 10 days is recommended (there is no charge, but a donation is appreciated). The classes are held daily from 6.30 to 7.30 am (winter); 6 to 7 am (summer). If you take a course for at least 10 days, you can stay in the accommodation on site; a single room with common bath is Rs 60, and a double with private bath is Rs 150. Veg meals are available. Meditation and naturopathy courses can also be arranged.

Another option for yoga is the Madhavanand Ashram (☎ 200317), at C-19 Behari Marg in Bani Park (next door to the Madhuban guesthouse). It offers group courses for beginners and advanced students (all courses are a minimum of one week and involve around one hour per day). The courses here are also run on donations. For private classes (Rs 500 per week) contact the yoga instructor, Mr Sahah (☎ 305063).

Music & Dance Classes

Music and dance are taught at the Maharaja Sawai Mansingh Sangeet Mahavidyalaya, at Chandani Chowk, behind Tripolia Gate. The sign is in Hindi – ask locals to point you in the right direction. Tuition is given in traditional Indian instruments such as tabla, sitar and flute, as well as Rajasthani folk instruments. It costs around Rs 200 per month in a small group for regular students. Individual tuition costs about Rs 1000 per month. There is also tuition in classical Indian dance (kathak), and Rajasthani folk dances. Vocal tuition can also be undertaken. For details contact the principal, Mr Shekhawat, on ☎ 601406 or ☎ 661397.

Painting & Pottery Classes

Mr Kripal Singh (☎ 201127), B-18A Shivamarg, Bani Park, is highly respected and offers lessons in Indian painting, including miniatures and frescoes. The charge is Rs 1000 per person per day (including materials). He gives lessons in pottery (Rs 500 per person per day) and has an excellent range for sale. Advance bookings are essential.

Golf

Rambagh Golf Club (☎ 384482), near the Rambagh Palace, charges Rs 100/600 for Indians/foreigners per day, plus Rs 100 for equipment and Rs 50 for a caddie. You have to buy the balls.

Tennis

For tennis, there's the Jai Club (☎ 362052), off MI Rd, which charges Rs 200 per couple per hour (bookings essential). Rackets are provided but you have to buy the balls.

Organised Tours

Jaipur & Around It's possible to book approved government day tours of the city and environs with English-speaking guides. The tours visit the Hawa Mahal, Amber Fort (see Around Jaipur later), Jantar Mantar, City Palace, Birla Lakshmi Narayan Temple and the Central Museum (closed Friday).

The half-day tours are a little rushed but otherwise OK. Times are 8 am to 1 pm, 11.30 am to 4.30 pm and 1.30 to 6.30 pm. The full-day tours are from 9 am to 6 pm, with a lunch stop at Nahargarh. The half-day tour is Rs 75, and the full-day tour is Rs 115 (entrance fees to monuments are extra). Tours depart daily from the tourist office at the main train station throughout the year according to demand, picking up passengers en route at RTDC hotels. Ring ☎ 375466 for more details. Bookings can be made either at the tourist office at the train station, or at the Tourist Reception Centre at the RTDC's Tourist Hotel (see Information earlier).

Approved guides for local sightseeing can be hired through the tourist officer at the Tourist Reception Centre. A half-day (four hour) tour for up to four people is Rs 230. A full-day (eight hour) tour for up to four people is Rs 345. An extra fee of Rs 100 for both tours is levied for French, German, Italian, Japanese or Spanish speaking guides.

The Rajasthan Travel Service (☎ 365408) is on the first floor of the Ganpati Plaza on MI Rd. It offers a half/full-day tour of Jaipur for Rs 75/125 per person, which includes a free pick-up from most hotels. It also has a 'Jaipur by Night' tour for Rs 300 per person, including dinner.

There are RTDC tours (minimum of 10 people) to Nahargarh for Rs 150, including dinner. There are also daily RTDC tours to Chokhi Dhani, a kitsch and contrived restaurant near the airport, which has evening traditional folk performances and Rajasthani veg cuisine (Rs 125). Chokhi Dhani also has cottage-style accommodation which ranges from Rs 1950 to Rs 3000.

Other Parts of Rajasthan If you want a taste of rural Rajasthan, the Hotel Bissau Palace (☎ 304391, fax 304628) organises tours to their erstwhile hunting pavilion, 'The Retreat' (where Prince Charles and Princess Diana once visited). It is located about 27km from Jaipur. From here you are whisked away by camel cart to nearby villages. It costs Rs 500 per person (for a minimum of six people) or Rs 750 per person (for groups of five or less). This includes transport, the village tour and lunch. Advance bookings essential.

For details of the these tour operators, see Travel Agencies earlier in this chapter.

Sita World Travels books tours and excursions including elephant and bicycle polo matches.

Registhan Tours can arrange camel and horse safaris, trekking in the Udaipur area, jeep expeditions and tailor-made tours. Its horse safaris start at Rs 6000 per day per person, including all meals and tent accommodation. The camel safaris are run in the Jaisalmer and Shekhawati districts. Prices start at Rs 1800 per person per day, including tents and meals. Transport to and from these districts is extra. Aravali Safari & Tours has luxury camel treks in Jaisalmer, and horse safaris in the Udaipur region. Ghanerao Tours (☎/fax 201209), B-11/302 Kamal Apartments, Bani Park, organises tailor-made horse safaris in southern Rajasthan.

Amber Tours offers chauffeur-driven day tours to Sariska and Ranthambhore wildlife sanctuaries. A day excursion to Sariska costs Rs 1750 for an Ambassador (non air-con), Rs 2500 for an air-con vehicle. To Ranthambhore, it's Rs 2080 in an Ambassador, Rs 3200 in an air-con vehicle.

Places to Stay

Getting to the hotel of your choice in Jaipur can be a headache. Auto-rickshaw drivers besiege almost every traveller who arrives by train (less so if you come by bus). If you don't want to go to a hotel of their choice, they will either refuse to take you at all or they'll demand at least double the normal fare. If you do go to the hotel of their choice, you'll pay through the nose for accommodation because the manager will be paying them a commission of at least 30% (and the charge won't go down for subsequent nights). The way to get around this 'Mafia' is to go straight to the prepaid autorickshaw stands, which have been set up at both the bus and train stations, where rates are set by the government.

Most hotels give discounts of 25% to 40% in the low season. The Tourist Reception Centre (see Information, earlier) has a list of places participating in the Paying Guest House Scheme in Jaipur. The cost ranges from around Rs 125 to Rs 1000 per night.

Places to Stay – Budget

Hotel Diggi Palace (☎ *373091, fax 370359)*, just off Sawai Ram Singh Marg, less than 1km south of Ajmeri Gate, is a popular travellers' hang-out. Bare but acceptable doubles with common bath (hot water free by the bucket) are Rs 100 and Rs 125. With attached bath and geyser, they start at Rs 250. There's a good restaurant and lovely lawn area for chilling out. The building is the former residence of the *thakur* (similar to a lord or baron) of Diggi.

Jaipur Inn (☎ *201121, fax 204796, email jaipurinn@hotmail.com, B-17 Shiv Marg, Bani Park)*, run by retired Wing Commander RN Bhargava and his son, is another favourite. Beds in the rather cramped dorm are Rs 100; to camp on the lawn (own tent required) is Rs 50 per person with use of bathroom facilities. Spartan singles/doubles with common bath (Rs 20 per bucket of hot water) go for Rs 200/250; rooms with attached bath start at Rs 300/350. The better rooms range from Rs 400/500 to Rs 500/700. You can hire a bicycle/mozzie net for Rs 25/15 per day and it's Rs 100 to use the washing machine. The restaurant (see Places to Eat) sports fine views.

Pipalda House (☎ *201925, D-240A Bank Rd)*, also in Bani Park, has rooms with bath from Rs 150/250 a single/double.

Tirupati Guest House (☎ *201801, D-152 Durga Marg, Bani Park)* is a simple family home run by affable Manish Sharma. Spartan and rather dark doubles with bath are just Rs 100 and basic veg meals are available. New rooms may be built soon which are expected to cost from Rs 150 to Rs 200.

Atithi Guest House (☎ *378679, fax 379496, email tanmay@jp1.dot.net.in, 1 Park House Scheme Rd)*, opposite All India Radio, between MI and Station Rds, is run by the helpful Shukla family. It offers fresh, clean singles/doubles with attached bath from Rs 300/350 to Rs 600/650. There are home-cooked veg meals and the rooftop is a great place to kick back with a good book. Next door is the similarly priced *Aangan Guest House* (☎ *373449, fax 364596)*, which is reasonably good.

Karni Niwas (☎ *365433, fax 375034, email karniniwas@hotmail.com, C-5 Motilal Atal Marg)* is close to the Polo Victory Cinema and in a lane behind Hotel Neelam. It's a homey place run by a nice family, with clean singles/doubles with attached bath from Rs 275/325 to Rs 650/700. Many rooms have a balcony; meals are available.

Hotel Arya Niwas (☎ *372456, fax 364 376, email aryahotl@jp1.dot.net.in)* behind Amber Tower, just off Sansar Chandra Marg, is another popular travellers hang-out, which is well-maintained and managed. This large hotel has singles/doubles with private bath from Rs 300/400 to Rs 500/650. Meals are taken at the rather impersonal self-service veg restaurant.

Hotel Mangal (☎ *375126, Sansar Chandra Marg)* is not far from the bus stand. Rates are from Rs 300/350 to Rs 800 for a suite (the cheaper rooms are better value). There's 24 hour room service, a restaurant and beauty parlour.

Jai Mangal Palace (☎ *378901, fax 361236, Station Rd)* is right opposite the bus stand. There's a swimming pool here (summer only), as well as a restaurant. Standard singles/doubles are Rs 300/350, air-cooled rooms are Rs 400/450, and air-con rooms are Rs 650/700. The rooms are OK, but nothing flash.

Evergreen Guest House (☎ 363446, fax 204234) is just off MI Rd in the area known as Chameliwala Market. It's a good place to meet other backpackers but the cleanliness and service are erratic. Amenities include a small swimming pool, and reasonably priced restaurant. Rooms start at Rs 150/175 with private bath and free bucket hot water. The best air-con singles/doubles are Rs 400/490. Checkout is an ungenerous 10 am. A few steps away is the slightly cheaper but less impressive *Hotel Pink Sun* (☎ 370385). The bathrooms here could be better and some travellers have complained about the noise.

Ashiyana Guest House (☎ 375414), nearby, is better value with rooms with common bath for Rs 70/150; Rs 175 for a double with bath and Rs 200 for the best room. Hot water is Rs 10 per bucket. There's a small snack shop, but no meals are available.

Hotel Kailash (☎ 565372, fax 566195, Johari Bazaar), opposite the Jama Masjid, is one of the few places to stay within the old city. It's nothing fancy but is friendly, offering small singles/doubles with common bath for Rs 150/175, with attached bath for Rs 215/240, and larger rooms for Rs 250/300. Veg meals can be arranged with advance notice.

Devi Niwas (☎ 363727, Dhuleshwar Bagh, Sardar Patel Marg) is an unpretentious little place with just a handful of rooms with private bath for Rs 300 a double.

Hotel Sweet Dream (☎ 314409, Nehru Bazaar) is just inside the city walls. The small and slightly dishevelled ordinary rooms have attached bath with cold water for Rs 230/300 (some rooms are better than others so look at a few first). Air-cooled rooms are Rs 330/400 and have hot water. Better air-con rooms are also available for Rs 550/625. There's a veg rooftop restaurant here.

Hotel Khetri House (☎ 303941), outside Chandpol, not far from the Hotel Bissau Palace, was built for the maharaja of Khetri and is now in a state of dusty decay. There's no signboard for the hotel – it's a pale yellow building set back from a garden. Some people will love this extraordinary place and some will find it downright spooky. Rooms are enormous, with tatty old Art Deco furniture and claw-feet baths, and the otherworldly atmosphere is enhanced by a creaky caretaker. All rooms have air-coolers and running hot water, and doubles range in price from Rs 320 to Rs 500. Meals are available.

The *Youth Hostel* (☎ 701405, Bhagwandas Rd) is a bit out of town and not really wonderful value for money. Doubles with common bath cost Rs 150 (Rs 100 for members). Breakfast is Rs 15 and lunch/dinner is Rs 25.

Retiring rooms at the train station are reasonable. Singles/doubles with common bath are Rs 100/250. An air-con double with bath is Rs 400.

RTDC Places Near the main post office, the *Tourist Hotel* (☎ 360238, MI Rd) has a certain faded appeal, although it's looking quite shabby these days. Ordinary singles/doubles with bath (many with Indian-style toilet) start at Rs 175/225. Meals are available.

Hotel Swagatam (☎ 200595, MI Rd), at the west end near the train station, has a rather institutional feel to it. Drab standard rooms with bath go for Rs 275/350 and deluxe air-cooled rooms are Rs 400/550. Dorm beds cost Rs 50. The rates include breakfast and bed tea.

Places to Stay – Mid-Range

Madhuban (☎ 200033, fax 202344, email madhuban@usa.net, D-237 Behari Marg, Bani Park), about 1km north of the train station, is perfect if you're looking for a homey atmosphere with no hassles whatsoever. Run by the helpful Dicky Singh and his family, it has singles/doubles ranging from Rs 400/500 to Rs 850/950. The more expensive rooms have fine antique furnishings. Ring ahead to arrange a free pick-up from the bus or train station. There's an indoor restaurant, or you can eat out in the pleasant garden where there's a puppet show most evenings. For your dessert try the thin and crispy fried Rajasthani maalpuas – delectable!

Alsisar Haveli (☎/fax 368290, Sansar Chandra Marg) is a gracious 19th century mansion set in well-manicured gardens. Although more pricey than other mid-range places, it's still an excellent choice, with quaintly furnished rooms for Rs 1195/1550 a single/double. A suite is Rs 1800. There's a restaurant and a relaxing garden area.

Hotel Meghniwas (☎ 202034, fax 201 425, C-9 Sawai Jai Singh Hwy, Bani Park) is another marvellous choice, run by the charming Mrs Indu Singh. Singles/doubles (all air-con) start at Rs 950/1000. Room Nos 201 and 209 are like mini-apartments and are ideal for long-term guests (Rs 1495 a double). There's a good restaurant and a pool to splash in.

Umaid Bhawan Guest House (☎ 206 426, D1-2A Bani Park), behind the Collectorate via Bank Rd, is a family-run place with rooms ranging from Rs 350/450 a single/double to Rs 1500 for the 'Regal suite'. Meals are available.

Sajjan Niwas Guest House (☎ 311544, fax 201494, D1-2B Bani Park), next door, is very good value for money with spacious, airy rooms from Rs 300/400 to Rs 850/950 a single/double. Meals are available.

Hotel Bissau Palace (☎ 304391, fax 304628, email sanjai@jp1.dot.net.in) is an option if you want to stay in an old palace but can't afford the Rambagh and its ilk. There's a swimming pool, tennis court, lovely wood-paneled library and two restaurants (one on the rooftop with splendid views; residents only). The cheapest rooms are Rs 600/750 (some are quite small), while better air-con singles/doubles go for Rs 900/990. Suites cost Rs 1800. Village tours can be arranged (see Organised Tours earlier in this chapter).

Shahpura House (☎ 202293, fax 201494, D-257 Devi Marg, Bani Park) has well-kept double rooms from Rs 600 to Rs 1000, and a restaurant.

Nana-ki-Haveli (☎ 665502, fax 605481, Fateh Tiba), just off Moti Dungri Marg, is a friendly place with a homey touch. Rooms are Rs 1095/1195 and meals are available; the set lunch or dinner is Rs 225.

Chirmi Palace Hotel (☎ 365063, fax 364462, Dhuleshwar Bagh, Sardar Patel Marg) has decent singles/doubles for Rs 1050/1195; some rooms have more character than others (room No 9 even has a rocking chair) so try to have a look at a few first. There's a cute restaurant and local sightseeing trips can be arranged (Rs 190/310 for two/four hours).

LMB Hotel (☎ 565844, fax 562176, Johari Bazaar) is in the old city above the well-known restaurant of the same name (see Places to Eat). Standard singles/doubles are Rs 975/1275. The rooms are not anything spectacular, but acceptable.

Hotel Neelam (☎ 372215, fax 367808, A-3 Motilal Atal Marg), near the Polo Victory Cinema, has average singles/doubles from Rs 750/900. There's a veg restaurant.

Narain Niwas Palace Hotel (☎ 561291, fax 561045, Narain Singh Rd), in Kanota Bagh, just south of the city, is comfortable enough but looking a bit faded around the edges. The cheapest rooms cost Rs 1195/1750, while suites are Rs 2350. There's a pool, garden and restaurant (the set lunch or dinner is Rs 300). The owners also operate the *Royal Castle Kanota*, 14km south-east of Jaipur.

Rajasthan Palace Hotel (☎ 661542, fax 602114, 3 Peelwa Garden, Moti Dungri Marg) has doubles from Rs 300 to Rs 1500. The cheaper rooms are good value.

Shahar Palace (☎ 382961, fax 214356, Ajmer Rd, Barwada Colony, Civil Lines) is a family-run guest house set in a beautiful garden. Air-cooled rooms with attached bathroom are Rs 400, while the air-con rooms are Rs 1000. The cheaper rooms (request one upstairs) are much better value. Meals are available and the couple who run this place are nice.

At the *Nahargarh*, above the old city, there is one basic double room on offer for a hefty Rs 500. Reservations should be made with the Tourist Reception Centre (☎ 365256).

ANDREW LUBRAN

Elaborate decorations for the Jaipur Elephant Festival.

RICHARD I'ANSON

Hawa Mahal detail, Jaipur.

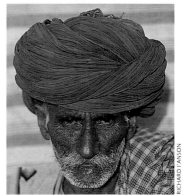

RICHARD I'ANSON

Rajput man.

RICHARD I'ANSON

Jaipur street scene, with the background of pink buildings adding a rosy hue.

Early morning, Jaipur, and the pink walls of the city are tinged with gold.

A snake charmer plays the *poongi* in Jaipur.

City Palace guards at the Peacock Door, Jaipur.

RTDC Places *Hotel Gangaur (☎ 361233)* is just off MI Rd. Rooms start at Rs 500/650. There's a good nonveg restaurant here, and a coffee shop.

Hotel Teej (☎ 205482, Collectorate Rd) is opposite the Moti Mahal Cinema. Dorm beds are Rs 50, deluxe air-cooled rooms are Rs 450/550, and air-con super deluxe rooms are Rs 600/700.

Places to Stay – Top End

Jaipur has plenty of top-notch hotels, but considering the price, the service at many is not up to scratch. Sometimes you get the distinct feeling that you're a number, not a name.

Raj Vilas (☎ 640101, fax 640202, email reservations@rajvilas.com, Goner Rd), just 8km from the city centre, scores top marks when it comes to attentive, yet unobtrusive service. This would have to be the slickest hotel in Jaipur, if not Rajasthan. Run by the Oberoi Group, it has 71 rooms yet still manages to retain a personal touch. Set in 32 acres, all rooms are immaculate and tastefully appointed. Deluxe singles/ doubles are US$260/280, luxury tents are US$300 and villas (each with their own pool) range from US$600 to US$1000. Ayurvedic treatments are available in the health centre. There's a pricey restaurant serving 'fusion cuisine' (a combination of Asian and continental food). Nonguests have to pay Rs 350 to visit, which is deducted from any food or drink purchased.

Trident (☎ 630101, fax 630303), north of the city (opposite Jal Mahal – the Water Palace; see Around Jaipur), is also run by the Oberoi Group. It is not as upmarket as the Raj Vilas, but is still exceptionally well kept and managed. Attractive rooms cost Rs 3600/3900 a single/double.

Samode Haveli (☎ 632370, fax 632407), in the north-east corner of the old city, is one of the most interesting places to stay. This 200-year-old building was once the town house of the *rawal* (nobleman) of Samode, who was also the prime minister of Jaipur. Several of the suites are truly astonishing, featuring intricate mirrorwork,

ornate paintings, tiny alcoves and recesses and soaring arches. Ordinary singles/doubles are Rs 1195/2200, and suites are Rs 2395.

Rambagh Palace (☎ 381919, fax 381098, Bhawani Singh Marg) was previously the palace of Maharaja Man Singh II of Jaipur, and the maharani still lives in separate quarters in the hotel grounds. Standard singles/doubles are US$185/205, superior rooms are US$220/240, the Maharaja suite is US$475, and the Royal suite is US$675. Nonguests are welcome to dine in the restaurant with advance notice or take tea on the verandah without notice. There's also a good bar (see Places to Eat). The set breakfast is US$6, lunch is US$10, and dinner is US$15.

Jai Mahal Palace Hotel (☎ 371616, fax 365237, cnr Jacob Rd and Ajmer Marg), south of the train station, has fine gardens and offers gracious hospitality. Standard singles/doubles are US$155/175. There's a restaurant, coffee shop, pool, and you can get your future told by the astrologer in the evening (Rs 200).

Rajmahal Palace (☎ 381625, fax 381 887, Sardar Patel Marg), in the south of the city, is a more modest edifice than either the Rambagh or Jai Mahal. There are 21 appealing rooms and suites, a restaurant, badminton courts, swimming pool and jogging track. This was formerly the British Residency, and was also temporarily the home of Maharaja Man Singh II and the maharani after their residence, the Rambagh Palace, was converted into a luxury hotel. Standard singles/doubles are US$70/80 and suites range from US$125 to US$250.

Mansingh Hotel (☎ 378771, fax 377582), off Sansar Chandra Marg in the centre of town, has good rooms for Rs 1995/3000, and large two-bedroom suites for Rs 10,000. There are two restaurants featuring veg and nonveg cuisine, a bar, swimming pool, spa and health club.

Holiday Inn (☎ 635000, fax 635608, Amber Rd) is in rather bleak surroundings about 1km north of the old city. Comfortably appointed standard rooms are Rs 2000/3200. This includes a buffet breakfast.

There's a swimming pool, coffee shop, bar, restaurants and a car hire desk.

Rajputana Palace Sheraton (☎ 360011, fax 367848) is a swanky hotel between Station and Palace Rds, near the train station. The entrance is on Palace Rd. Amenities include several restaurants, a swimming pool, health club, 24 hour coffee shop and a disco (see Entertainment, later in this chapter). Rooms start at US$130/140 a single/double and shoot up to US$700 for the sumptuous Presidential suite.

Hotel Clarks Amer (☎ 550616, fax 550013) is a bit inconveniently located about 10km south of the town centre. The rooms cost Rs 1195/4000 and there's a swimming pool, coffee shop and restaurant.

Hotel Jaipur Ashok (☎ 204491, fax 202099, Jai Singh Circle, Bani Park) is about 1km north of the train station. It's not as glitzy as some of its more modern competitors, but is nicely appointed with air-conrooms for Rs 1500/2500. There's a pool (open to nonguests for Rs 100), a coffee shop, restaurant and bar.

Places to Eat

Jaipur has a very good range of restaurants, many offering a mishmash of Indian, continental and Chinese cuisine. If you feel like lashing out, there are plenty of fine restaurants at the top-end hotels.

Niro's on MI Rd, was established in 1949 and is well worth a try. It's so popular that you may have to wait for a table, especially on weekends, but fortunately you can book ahead *(☎ 374493)*. There's an extensive menu offering hearty veg and nonveg Indian, Chinese and continental food. Hot sellers include the chicken tikka butter masala (Rs 130) and the chicken pepper steak sizzler (Rs 130). An American ice cream soda will set you back a cool Rs 60.

Surya Mahal, nearby, is less upmarket than Niro's, but still a good place to eat. There is a range of south Indian dishes, and specials such as the delicious makki ki roti sarson ka saag (Rs 46).

Jal Mahal, next door, is a little takeaway ice cream parlour. A cone of mango tango is

Rs 16, and a virgin pink waffle sundae is Rs 25. It also has espresso coffee (Rs 10) and Italian thickshakes (Rs 12).

Natraj Restaurant, farther east up MI Rd towards the old city, is a very good vegetarian place, with an extensive menu featuring north Indian and Chinese cuisine. The vegetable bomb curry (Rs 70) is a blast, and there are tempting Indian sweets to take away.

Golden Dragon Restaurant is down a lane next to Niro's and specialises in Chinese food. Singapore noodles are Rs 70 and chicken sweet and sour is Rs 100. There are also some Indian dishes. The food here is OK but nothing to write home about.

Bake Hut (☎ 369840), nearby, offers sweet treats including chocolate donuts (Rs 8), nougat pastry (Rs 15) and little lemon tarts (Rs 10). Birthday cakes are baked to order. The ***Venus Bakery*** on Subhash Marg, just off MI Rd, also sells pastries.

Lassiwala, opposite Niro's on MI Rd, with its name in brass, is a simple little place that whips up a mighty good lassi. A thick, creamy glassful is Rs 10/20 for a small/jumbo.

Chanakya Restaurant, farther west down MI Rd, on the opposite side to Niro's is a pleasant place that gets rave reports from travellers. The food is indeed very good at this pure veg restaurant and the staff will helpfully explain the various menu items. Continental dishes range from Rs 65 to Rs 150, and Indian cuisine ranges from Rs 45 to Rs 130. The filling Rajasthani thali is Rs 150.

Handi Restaurant, on MI Rd, set back from the road at the Maya Mansions building, is nothing fancy inside but cooks up tasty eats. BBQ dishes are the speciality; seekh kebab is Rs 55, paneer tikka is Rs 65. In the evenings, it's possible to get cheap takeaway kebabs at the entrance to the restaurant.

Copper Chimney is a short distance to the east, and has satiating veg and nonveg Indian, continental and Chinese cuisine. Main Indian veg dishes range from Rs 50 to Rs 100, and nonveg ranges from Rs 85 to

Rs 200. Try the Rajasthani dish lal maas – mutton in a thick spicy gravy – for Rs 85.

Swaad, at the swanky Ganpati Plaza on MI Rd, is recommended for a minor splurge. It serves interesting Indian, continental and Chinese cuisine in pleasant surroundings. Travellers' favourites include the subz malaai kofta-palak gravy (cottage cheese and herbs with a spinach gravy, Rs 60) and the sizzlers (Rs 95 to Rs 165). Desserts go from Rs 45 to Rs 105 for the baked Alaska. Go downstairs for a beer.

Celebrations, also at the Ganpati Plaza, is not quite as stimulating as Swaad, but certainly above average in terms of food and decor. It serves veg cuisine, including some south Indian specialities such as idli sambar (Rs 28) and masala dosa (Rs 32). For something different, try the chhach dakhini (Rs 18), an unusual ginger and onion flavoured buttermilk beverage with curry leaves.

Pizza Hut, also in the Ganpati Plaza, is a cool, clean haven and is the place to come if you're hanging out for *real* pizza. There are traditional western-style pizzas, as well as 'fusion' creations such as chicken tikka pizza. They come in three sizes – regular, medium or large. Other goodies are on offer such as garlic bread (Rs 25), spaghetti bolognese (Rs 100) and brownie fudge sundaes (Rs 50). You can eat in, take away, or opt for the free delivery service (☎ 388627). After a pizza pig-out, what better place to satisfy your sweet tooth than at *Baskin 31 Robbins*, also in the Ganpati Plaza. One scrumptious scoop of ice cream is Rs 25; Rs 30 for a cone. There is a bounty of flamboyant flavours such as 'kiss me nut'.

Hot Breads, yet again at the Ganpati Plaza, has Jaipur's widest range of freshly baked fare, including black forest cake (Rs 18 per slice) and lemon tarts (Rs 20). It also sells a selection of fast foods such as pizzas and hot dogs; you can eat in or take away.

Rainbow Restaurant, also on MI Rd, just opposite the Ganpati Plaza, offers Indian, continental and Chinese cuisine – the food is OK but not great. The Rainbow Special, a vegetable sizzler, costs Rs 60.

LMB is a *sattvik* (pure vegetarian) air-con restaurant in Johari Bazaar, near the centre of the old city, which has been going strong since 1954. The 50s decor is looking slightly jaded, and the food and service get mixed reports from travellers. Main dishes range from Rs 35 to Rs 80.

Royal's, diagonally opposite the LMB, has cheap vegetarian fast food and specialises in south Indian cuisine.

Indian Coffee House on MI Rd, off the street, next to Arrow menswear, is good if you are suffering withdrawal symptoms from lack of a decent cup of coffee. It has a somewhat seedy ambience, like a place where shady deals are consummated. On the plus side, it has good, cheap south Indian dishes.

Four Seasons (D-43A Subhash Marg, C-Scheme) is not centrally located, but the food gets good reports. This multicuisine vegetarian restaurant has moderately priced food served in nice surroundings. A speciality is the rava dosa (ground rice and semolina south Indian pancake with fresh coconut, onions, carrots and green chillies) for Rs 35. Other menu items include burgers (Rs 27 to Rs 40), pizzas (Rs 38 to Rs 50) and a Rajasthani thali (Rs 55).

Jaipur Inn (see Places to Stay) boasts one of the city's only rooftop restaurants, with superlative views over the capital. The Indian veg buffet dinner costs Rs 100 (nonresidents should book in advance).

The small *Durg Cafeteria*, at the Nahargarh just north of the old city, is open daily from 10 am to 10 pm. A veg thali is Rs 55 and a cheese sandwich is Rs 23.

Polo Bar at the Rambagh Palace (see Places to Stay) is Jaipur's most atmospheric watering hole, but you'll pay for the privilege of drinking here. A bottle of beer is Rs 150 and a 'polo special' cocktail is Rs 235. A few token nibbles are available, such as crispy fried baby corn, for a giant Rs 130.

Entertainment

Despite being the capital, entertainment is surprisingly limited. There's the upmarket *Kaalbelia* disco at the Rajputana Palace

Sheraton, but it's only open to residents of the hotel. Many hotels put on some sort of evening music, dance or puppet show.

Raj Mandir Cinema (☎ 379372), just off MI Rd, is *the* place to go if you're planning to take in at least one Hindi film. This opulent cinema is a Jaipur tourist attraction in its own right and is usually full, despite its immense size. Bookings can be made one day in advance (between 4 and 5 pm – this timing may have changed). This is your best chance of securing a seat. Ask for the manager if you face a problem – you may get priority if you say you will not be in Jaipur for long. Tickets are split into various categories: pearl (Rs 15), ruby (Rs 30), emerald (Rs 34) and diamond (Rs 46); avoid the cheaper tickets, which are very close to the screen. There are occasionally English-language movies screened at some cinemas in Jaipur – check the newspapers for details.

Bowling alleys seem to be the latest rage with Jaipurians, who mainly flock here on Sunday and during the evening. The best alley is at *Dreamland (☎ 546608)*, somewhat inconveniently located in Malviya Nagar at Gaurav Tower, Bardiya Shopping Centre. This modern complex also has various video games, the *New Yorker* veg fast-food eatery, and the rather lifeless *Space Station* disco, which closes at 11.30 pm (no alcohol allowed). Entry to Dreamland is Rs 30 per person and the bowling fee is Rs 100 for 10 rounds (20 balls). There's even a fortune teller here (Rs 100 for 15 minutes).

Kin Pin (☎ 623029), on the 3rd floor of Centre Point (opposite AC Market) in Raja Park, is not as impressive as Dreamland. It's open daily from 11 am to 11pm and entry is Rs 25 (deducted from the bowling fee of Rs 50 per round – 20 bowls). A game of billiards costs Rs 100 for 45 minutes and video games are also available. There's a *Wimpy* hamburger joint downstairs, where you can eat in or take away. Their speciality is the spicy chicken burger (Rs 48).

Spectator Sports

Maharaja Man Singh indulged his passion for polo by building an enormous **polo** ground next to the Rambagh Palace, which is still the site of polo matches today. The royal team, led by their flamboyant maharaja, sailed for England in 1933 accompanied by 39 horses and their own personal carpenter (to keep the team in a constant supply of polo sticks), and stunned the opposition players and spectators with their equestrian flair, winning every important match in the tournament. Sadly the maharaja's passion was to prove fatal, and he died during a polo match in England in 1970. The polo season extends over winter, with the most important matches played during March.

During Jaipur's elephant festival in March (for dates see the boxed Regional Festival Calendar in the Facts for the Visitor chapter) you can see elephant polo matches at the ground. Telephone the Polo Club on ☎ 383580 for details.

Polo matches also take place at the polo ground in Ramgarh (see Around Jaipur).

Tennis and cricket matches are held in Jaipur. For details and more information about polo, see Spectator Sports in the introductory Facts for the Visitor chapter.

Shopping

Jaipur is *the* place to shop until you drop! It has a wild and wonderful array of handicrafts ranging from grimacing papier-mâché puppets to exquisitely carved furniture. You'll have to bargain hard though – this city is accustomed to tourists with lots of money and little time to spend it. Shops around the tourist traps, such as the City Palace and Hawa Mahal, tend to be more expensive. For useful tips on bargaining, see the boxed text, The Art of Haggling under Money in the Facts for the Visitor chapter. At some shops, such as government emporiums, you cannot haggle as the prices are fixed.

The state government emporium, Rajasthali, is opposite Ajmeri Gate on MI Rd. There's a good selection of artefacts and crafts from all over the state, including enamelwork, embroidery, pottery, woodwork, jewellery, puppets, block-printed sheets, miniatures, brassware, mirrorwork and more. Next door is Rajasthan Handloom House, where there's a fine selection of the state's textiles.

It's worth visiting the Anokhi showroom at 2 Tilak Marg, near the Secretariat. It has a terrific range of high quality textiles, such as block-printed fabrics, tablecloths, bed covers, cosmetic bags, scarves and clothing. Soma, out at 5 Jacob Rd in Civil Lines, sells similar fare at competitive prices.

Kripal Kumbh, B-18A Shivamarg in Bani Park, is a great place to buy Jaipur's famous blue pottery. Neerja, S-19 Bhawani Singh Rd at C-Scheme, also sells blue pottery. For good quality *jootis* (traditional Rajasthani shoes), go to Charmica (opposite the Natraj restaurant) on MI Rd; a pair of jootis ranges from Rs 150 to Rs 350, and the adorable baby jootis cost Rs 40. They also sell sandals for men and women.

The Juneja Art Gallery at the Lakshmi Complex on MI Rd (not far from the main post office) has a fabulous range of contemporary paintings by predominantly Rajasthani artists. Prices range from Rs 100 to Rs 50,000. Ask the helpful Sangeeta Juneja to show you around.

The cutting, polishing and selling of precious and semi-precious stones is centred around the Muslim area of Pahar Ganj, in the Surajpol Bazaar area. Silver jewellery is also made here. There are numerous factories and showrooms strung along the length of Amber Road between Zorawar Gate and the Holiday Inn. Here you'll find hand-block prints, blue pottery, carpets and antiques.

Many rickshaw-wallahs are right into the commission business and it's almost guaranteed that they'll be getting a hefty cut from any shop they take you to. Many unwary visitors get talked into buying things for resale at inflated prices. Beware of these 'buy now to sell at a profit later' scams – see the boxed text A Warning! under Shopping in the Facts for the Visitor chapter.

Shops in Jaipur are usually all open by 10.30 am and close at around 7.30 pm. Most are shut on Sunday.

Getting There & Away

Air Many of the international airlines which serve India are represented by two agencies based at the conveniently located Jaipur Towers building on MI Rd (in the same building as Thomas Cook).

Jetair Ltd (☎ 375430, fax 374242) is open Monday to Saturday from 9.30 am to 1 pm and 2 to 5.30 pm. It represents Air France, Royal Jordanian Airlines, Austrian Airlines, Gulf Airways, Air Canada, Biman Bangladesh and Jet Airways.

Interglobe Air Transport (☎ 361487, fax 361886) is in the same building and is open Monday to Saturday from 9 am to 1 pm and 2 to 5.30 pm. It represents United Airlines, South African Airways, SAS, Syrian Airways, Pakistan International Airlines (PIA), Tarom, Canadian Pacific, Ansett Australia, Air New Zealand, and Varig.

Thai is represented by Delhi Express Travels (☎ 360188).

At the time of writing, only Indian Airlines offered services to and between destinations in Rajasthan. Private airlines may operate during the busy tourist season, so check with a travel agent. Domestic airlines can be booked through most travel agents, such as Satyam Travels & Tours (☎ 378794, fax 375426), ground floor, Jaipur Towers, MI Rd. Satyam has a computer link with Indian Airlines, so there's no need to visit the Indian Airlines office, which is some distance from the centre of the city on Tonk Rd. Satyam is open Monday to Saturday from 10 am to 6 pm.

Addresses of airlines in Jaipur are as follows:

Air India (☎ 368569) Ganpati Plaza (1st floor)
Alitalia (☎ 369120) opposite HMT Showroom, MI Rd
British Airways (☎ 370374) near All India Radio, MI Rd
Cathay Pacific (☎ 375625) opposite Hotel Neelam, Motilal Atal Marg
Indian Airlines (☎ 514500) Nehru Place, Tonk Rd
Kuwait Airways (☎ 372896) Jaipur Towers, MI Rd
Lufthansa & Singapore Airlines (☎ 561360) 126-7 Sarogi Mansion, MI Rd

Air Fares

Airline schedules can be erratic, so check that the information below is still current. A few private airlines, such as UP Airways, sometimes operate flights during the peak tourist season – check with a travel agent. Prices for all airlines will have risen by the time you read this.

flight	service	departs	arrives	cost (US$)
Indian Airlines				
Delhi-Jaipur	IC491	daily 5.45 am	6.25 am	55
Delhi-Jaipur	IC473	Wed, Fri, Sun 10.30 am	11.10 am	55
Jaipur-Delhi	IC492	daily 9.15 pm	9.55 pm	55
Jaipur-Delhi	IC474	Tues, Thurs, Sat 2.55 pm	3.35 pm	55
Jaipur-Udaipur	IC491	daily 6.55 am	7.40 am	70
Jaipur-Jaisalmer	IC473	Wed, Fri, Sun 11.40 am	12.35 pm	110
Jaipur-Mumbai	IC491	daily 6.55 am	10.20 am	140
Jaipur-Mumbai	IC269	Mon, Wed, Fri 7.15 pm	9.45 pm	140
Jaipur-Aurangabad	IC491	daily 6.55 am	9.10 am	125
Jaipur-Ahmedabad	IC269	Mon, Wed, Fri 7.15 pm	8.15 pm	95
Jaipur-Calcutta	IC270	Mon, Wed, Fri 7.20 pm	9.25 pm	200
Jaipur-Jodhpur	IC493	Mon, Wed, Fri, Sun 12.35 pm	1.00 pm	70
Jodhpur-Jaipur	IC493	Mon, Wed, Fri, Sun 3.00 pm	3.30 pm	70
Jet Airways				
Delhi-Jaipur	9W721	daily 4 pm	4.40 pm	58
Jaipur-Delhi	9W722	daily 5.10 pm	5.50 pm	58
Jaipur-Mumbai	9W374	daily 8.35 am	10.05 am	144
Jaipur-Mumbai	9W372	daily 7.20 pm	8.50 pm	144

Bus Rajasthan State Transport Corporation (RSTC) buses all leave from the main bus terminal on Station Rd, and stop to pick up passengers at Narain Singh Circle (you can also buy tickets from here). Some services are deluxe (essentially non-stop). There is a left-luggage office at the main terminal (Rs 5 per bag for 12 hours), and a prepaid autorickshaw stand.

The deluxe buses all leave from platform No 3, which is tucked away in the right-hand corner of the bus terminal. These deluxe buses should be booked in advance at the reservation office which is open 24 hours daily, is also at platform 3 (before leaving the office, make sure the departure date on your ticket is correct).

It's best to get an express or deluxe bus – private buses are generally not as reliable when it comes to schedules. For express bus

inquiries ring ☎ 206143; for deluxe buses call ☎ 205621.

There are no direct RSTC services to Mumbai or Baroda; so you will need to change at Udaipur. There are numerous private agencies operate direct services to these cities. There is one direct RSTC service to Ahmedabad.

There are numerous private travel agencies in Jaipur which book deluxe (two seat by two seat) services to major cities (generally services run overnight). There is a cluster of these offices along Motilal Atal Marg, near the Polo Victory Cinema.

Train The computerised railway reservation office (☎ 201401) is reasonably efficient. It is in the building to your right as you exit the main train station and is open Monday to Saturday from 8 am to 2 pm and 2.15 to

RSTC Bus Services from Jaipur

destination	duration (hours)	cost (Rs) express	cost (Rs) deluxe
Abu Rd	12	186.00	-
Agra	5	92.50	112.00
Ajmer	2½	52.50	63.00
Alwar	4	61.00	75.50
Bharatpur	4½	70.50	87.00
Bikaner	8	137.50	168.00
Bundi	5	81.50	111.00
Chittorgarh	7	114.00	152.00
Delhi	5½	102.50	190.00
Jaisalmer	15	245.00	286.00
Jodhpur	7	129.00	160.00
Kota	5	97.00	120.00
Mt Abu	13	–	246.00
Pushkar	3½	57.00	–
Sawai Madhopur	4½	45.00	–
Udaipur	10	165.50	200.00
Shekhawati District			
Churu	6	80.00	98.50
Jhunjhunu	6	70.50	87.00
Nawalgarh	3	–	71.00
Pilani	7½	89.50	110.00
Sikar	2	45.50	–

8 pm, on Sunday from 8 am to 2 pm, and is for advance reservations only. Join the queue for 'Freedom Fighters and Foreign Tourists' at counter 769.

For same-day travel, you'll need to buy your ticket at the train station. For metre-gauge trains, the booking office is on platform No 6. The railway inquiries number is ☎ 131.

Some bookshops sell a small booklet for Rs 5, called 'Jaipur Time Table', which contains details about train and bus schedules. Double check the train schedules given in the boxed text in this chapter, as they may have changed by now. There's a prepaid auto-rickshaw stand at the train station.

Many of the lines into Jaipur have been converted to broad gauge. As other parts of the state's railway are converted expect disruptions to services.

Car Cars and drivers can be hired through numerous travel agencies, including Sita World Travels (☎ 203626) on Station Rd. Costs at Sita are Rs 4.50/km (minimum 250km per day) for a non air-con car, Rs 7.50 for an air-con car; the overnight charge is an extra Rs 75 per day.

Registhan Tours (☎/fax 380824) hires out vehicles for similar prices. Rates with the RTDC are Rs 4.40/km for a non air-con car, and an expensive Rs 8/km for an air-con car, with the usual 250km minimum per day.

If you're game, self-drive rental cars can be hired at the Hertz office (☎ 635000, fax 609090) which has a desk at the Holiday Inn hotel on Amber Road. For self-drive rates, see the Car & Motorcycle section in the introductory Getting There & Away chapter.

Jaipur Train Services

train & service	departs	arrives	2nd class	1st class	chair
2015 *Shatabdi Express*					
New Delhi-Jaipur	6.15 am	10.30 am	–	910	465
Jaipur-New Delhi (via Alwar)	5.55 pm	10.15 pm	195	375	–
2414 *Delhi-Jaipur Superfast*					
Delhi Junction-Jaipur	5.15 am	11 am	–	–	102
Jaipur-Delhi Junction	4.30 pm	9.50 pm	–	–	102
Intercity Express					
Old Delhi-Jaipur	4.40 pm	10.00 pm	92	261	-
Jaipur-Old Delhi (via Alwar)	6 am	11.20 am	92	261	-
9615 *Chetak Express*					
Jaipur-Udaipur	10.10 pm	10.25 am	161	515	-
Udaipur-Jaipur	6.30 pm	6.00 am	161	515	-
2465 *Intercity Express*					
Jaipur-Jodhpur	5.30 pm	10 pm	104	292	-
Jodhpur-Jaipur	5.45 pm	10.35 am	104	292	-
2461 *Mandore Express*					
Jaipur-Jodhpur	2.45 am	7.55 am	153	628	-
Jodhpur-Jaipur	7.30 pm	12.30 am	153	628	-
2308 *Howrah Jodhpur Express*					
Jaipur-Agra	11.20 pm	6.35 am	160	672	-
Agra-Jaipur	7.15 pm	3.45 am	160	672	-
Jaipur-Jodhpur	4.05 am	10.00 am	153	628	-
9106 *Ahmedabad Mail*					
Jaipur-Abu Road	4.40 am	12.55 pm	161	725	-
Abu Road-Ahmedabad	1.10 pm	5.30 pm	96	452	-
2956 *Bombay Superfast*					
Jaipur-Kota	1.40 pm	5.10 pm	130	532	-
Kota-Jaipur	9 am	12.20 pm	130	532	-
Kota-Mumbai	5.20 pm	8 am	275	1162	-
Regular Passenger Services					
Jaipur-Kota	–		67	–	
Jaipur-Sawai Madhopur	–	–	60	–	
2468 *Intercity Express*					
Jaipur-Bikaner	2.55 pm	9.30 pm	104	310	-
Bikaner-Jaipur	6.00 am	noon	104	310	-
4737 *Bikaner Express*					
Jaipur-Bikaner	9.05 pm	7.00 am	103	497	
Bikaner-Jaipur	8.25 pm	7.00 am	103	497	
9734 *Shekhawati Express*					
Jaipur-Sikar	5.45 pm	9.15 pm	–	–	96

Getting Around

To/From the Airport There is currently no scheduled bus service between the airport and the city. Taxi/auto-rickshaws will cost at least Rs 200/150 for the 15km journey into the city centre. Share with others to cut the cost.

Auto-Rickshaw There are prepaid auto-rickshaw stands at the bus and train stations. Rates are fixed by the government, which means you don't have to haggle. In other cases you should be prepared to bargain hard. If you wish to hire an auto-rickshaw for a half-day sightseeing tour (including Amber), expect to pay around Rs 200; Rs 300 for a full day. This price is per rickshaw, not per person and don't let drivers tell you otherwise. Make sure you fix a price before setting off to avoid a scene later. A slower, but cheaper and more environmentally friendly, option is to hire a cycle-rickshaw.

Bicycle Bicycles can be hired from most bike shops, including that to the right as you exit the main train station, a few steps past the reservation office. They charge Rs 2/24 per hour/day. Some hotels can also arrange bicycle hire or direct you to the nearest rental place.

Around Jaipur

Jaipur is an excellent base from which to visit some of the ancient sites and interesting towns and villages in the precincts. A comprehensive network of local buses makes getting to these regions relatively simple, or it's possible to join an organised tour run by the RTDC which includes a commentary on the various sites visited. See Organised Tours earlier in this section for more details.

AMBER

Situated about 11km out of Jaipur on the Delhi to Jaipur road, Amber was once the ancient capital of Jaipur state.

This stonework inlay is typical
of the intricate work seen at Amber Fort.

The Kachhwahas originally hailed from Gwalior, in present-day Madhya Pradesh, where they reigned for over 800 years. The marital alliance between a Kachhwaha prince, Taj Karan, and a Rajput princess resulted in the granting of the region of Dausa to the prince, by the princess' father.

Taj Karan's descendants coveted the hilltop on which Amber Fort was later built, recognising its virtue as a potential military stronghold. The site was eventually prised from its original inhabitants, the Susawat Minas, and the Minas were granted guardianship of the Kachhwahas' treasury in perpetuity.

The Kachhwahas, despite being devout Hindus belonging to the Kshatriya (warrior) caste, recognised the expediency of aligning themselves with the powerful Mughal empire. They paid homage at the Mughal court, cemented the relationship with marital alliances and defended the Mughals in their various skirmishes. For this they were handsomely rewarded. With war booty they financed construction of the fortress-palace at Amber, which was begun in 1592 by Maharaja Man Singh, the Rajput commander

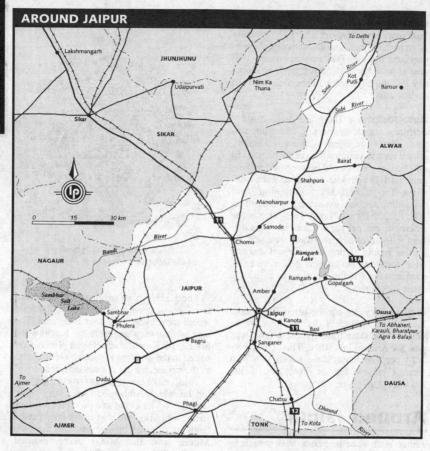

AROUND JAIPUR

of Akbar's army. It was later extended and completed by the Jai Singhs before the move to Jaipur on the plains below. The fort is a superb example of Rajput architecture, stunningly situated on a hillside and overlooking a lake which reflects its terraces and ramparts.

You can climb up to the fort from the road in about 10 minutes, and cold drinks are available within the palace if the climb is a hot one. A seat in a jeep up to the fort costs Rs 15 return. Riding up on elephants is popular, though daylight robbery at Rs 400 per elephant return (including a so-called 'elephant tax'). Each elephant can carry up to four people. A quick ride around the palace courtyard costs about Rs 20.

An imposing stairway leads to the **diwan-i-am**, or public audience hall, with a double row of columns each topped by a capital in the shape of an elephant, and latticed galleries above. Here the maharaja held audience and received the petitions of his subjects.

Steps to the right lead to the small **Kali Temple**, where every day from the 16th century until 1980 (when the government banned the practice) a goat was sacrificed. It's a beautiful temple, entered by gorgeous silver doors featuring repoussé work. Before the image of Kali lie two silver lions. According to tradition, Maharaja Man Singh prayed to the goddess for victory in a battle with the ruler of Bengal. The goddess came to the maharaja in a dream advising that if he won the battle he should retrieve her image which was lying at the bottom of the sea. After vanquishing his foes, the maharaja recovered the statue and installed it in the temple as Shila Devi. *Shila* means slab, and the image is carved from one piece of stone. Above the lintel of the temple is the usual image of Ganesh, this one carved from a single piece of coral.

The maharaja's apartments are on the higher terrace – you enter through a gateway decorated with mosaics and sculptures. The **Jai Mandir**, or hall of victory, is noted for its inlaid panels and glittering mirror ceiling. Regrettably, much of this was allowed to deteriorate during the 1970s and 80s but restoration is now proceeding.

Opposite the Jai Mandir is the **Sukh Niwas**, or hall of pleasure, with an ivory-inlaid sandalwood door and a channel running right through the room which once carried cooling water, acting as an ingenious early air-cooling system. Not a single drop of water was wasted, with the overflow passing through conduits to the palace gardens. From the Jai Mandir you can enjoy the fine views from the palace ramparts over the lake below.

The zenana, or **women's apartments**, are to the rear of the complex. The rooms have been cleverly designed so that the maharaja could embark on his nocturnal visits to their respective chambers without the knowledge of the other wives and concubines, as the chambers are all independent of each other but open onto a common corridor.

Amber Palace is open daily from 9 am to 4.30 pm and entry costs Rs 4. To use a still camera costs Rs 20/50 for Indians/foreign-ers, and a video camera is Rs 50/100. You'll probably be assailed by persistent hawkers shoving souvenirs in your face – just keep your cool and ignore them. If you find your own way to the fort, as opposed to joining one of the RTDC city tours, it's possible to hire a RTDC guide at the small tourist office (open daily except Sunday from 10 am to 4.30 pm) at the fort entrance, who can explain the salient features. It costs Rs 75 for a 1½ hour excursion (up to four people), Rs 230 for a half-day excursion, and Rs 345 for a full day.

Getting There & Away
There are regular buses from both the train station and near the Hawa Mahal in the old city (25 minutes, Rs 4).

JAIGARH
This imposing fort, built in 1726 by Jai Singh, was only opened to the public in mid-1983. It's within walking distance of Amber and offers a great view over the plains from the Diwa Burj watchtower. The fort served as the treasury of the Kachwha-has, and some people are convinced that at least part of the royal treasure is still secreted somewhere among its corridors. It's a remarkable feat of military architecture, in a fine state of preservation. The fort, with its water reservoirs, residential areas, puppet theatre and enormous cannon, Jaya Vana, is open daily from 9 am to 5 pm. Admission costs Rs 15 (free if you have a ticket to Jaipur's City Palace which is less than two days old), plus Rs 20/100 for a camera/video. Car entry charge is Rs 50.

JAL MAHAL
Between Jaipur and Amber, the Jal Mahal (Water Palace) is situated in the middle of a lake and reached by a causeway. Farther south on Amber Road are the cenotaphs of the maharanis of Jaipur.

SANGANER & BAGRU
The small village of Sanganer is 16km south of Jaipur and is entered through the ruins of two *tripolias*, or triple gateways. In

addition to its ruined palace, Sanganer has a group of Jain temples with fine carvings to which entry is restricted. The town is noted for its handmade paper and block printing (most shops can be found on or just off the main drag, Stadium Rd), and a highlight of a visit here is to walk down to the riverbank (on the right as you enter the town) to see the brightly coloured fabrics drying in the sun. Salim's Paper, on Gramodyog Rd, is the largest handmade paper factory in India and claims to be one of the biggest in the world. Here you can see the paper production process and there's also a beautiful range of paper products for sale in their showroom – great (and light) gifts for friends back home. Another large (but less ostentatious) handmade paper manufacturer is AL Paper House, near the tempo stand. For block-printed fabrics, there are a number of shops, including Sakshi which also has a tremendous range of blue pottery (downstairs).

About 20km west of Sanganer is the little village of Bagru, also known for its block printing, particularly of colourful designs featuring circular motifs (but you won't see as much here as in Sanganer).

Getting There & Away

There are buses to Sanganer (30 mins, Rs 5.50). Alternatively, buses and tempos leave from the Ajmeri Gate for Sanganer every few minutes (30 mins, Rs 5.50). To Bagru, there are daily buses from Jaipur (45 mins, Rs 7).

SAMODE

The small village of Samode is nestled among rugged hills about 50km north of Jaipur. Really, the only reason to visit is if you can stay at the **Samode Palace** (although strictly speaking it's not actually a palace, as it wasn't owned by a ruler, but by one of his noblemen). Like the Samode Haveli in Jaipur, this building was owned by the rawal of Samode. It's an interesting building built on three levels, each with its own courtyard. The highlight is the exquisite diwan-i-khas, which is covered with original paintings and mirrorwork.

Places to Stay

Samode Palace (☎ *01423-4114, fax 4123*) or book through Samode Haveli in Jaipur (☎ *0141-632370, fax 632 407*) has attractive doubles from Rs 2750 to Rs 3750. Breakfast/lunch/dinner costs Rs 250/375/425. Palace entry for nonguests is Rs 100 (deducted if you have a meal).

Samode Bagh (☎ *01423-44113*) has similarly priced luxurious tented accommodation (with attached modern bathrooms replete with flush toilets and hot water). It is 3km away – a very relaxing place, with lovely gardens and a swimming pool (open to guests of the Samode Palace).

Hotel Maharaja Palace (☎ *01423-44151*) is an alternative if you can't stay at the palace or tents – although it's absolutely no match. The kitsch rooms are way overpriced for what you get. They're Rs 1350 for a deluxe double, or Rs 1900 for a super deluxe. The best room costs Rs 2450.

Getting There & Away

There are four daily direct buses to Samode (1½ hrs, Rs 13.50) and also every 30 minutes to Chomu (1 hr, Rs 8.50), where you get another bus to Samode (30 mins, Rs 5).

BAIRAT

Continuing beyond Amber, 52km north of Jaipur and only a short distance to the east of the main Jaipur-Delhi road, is the ancient Buddhist centre of Viratnagar, or Bairat. Archaeological evidence – the discovery of ancient coins, the remains of a Buddhist monastery, and several rock-cut edicts, a legacy of the great 3rd century BC Buddhist convert Ashoka – indicate that this was once an important centre of Buddhism.

RAMGARH

This green oasis, about 35km north-east of Jaipur, has a pretty lake (boating available) and a picturesque polo ground (call the HRH office in Jaipur on ☎ 0141-374791/94 to find out when matches are being played). There's also an ancient Durga temple – remove your shoes at the bottom of the steps that lead up to this temple.

Ramgarh Lodge (☎ 01426-552217, fax 381098), the one-time royal hunting lodge overlooking Ramgarh Lake, is the best place to stay. Run by the Taj Group, airy singles/doubles cost Rs 1600/2300 and the best room is Rs 2950. Inside the lodge, there are a number of stuffed beasts, including a bear holding a tray and a tacky elephant's trunk pot plant holder! Billiards, squash, tennis and boating are available. Night jeep safaris to view wildlife cost Rs 500 per jeep for one hour.

RTDC's Jheel Tourist Village (☎ 01426-52370), farther away from the lake, is cheaper at Rs 300/350 for a single/double room with attached bath. An extra bed is Rs 100. An entry fee of Rs 10 is levied on non-residents who wish to visit. There's a small dining area that serves fare such as veg pakora (Rs 22) and mutton curry (Rs 55). They can arrange boating on Ramgarh Lake; a pedal boat is Rs 40 per half-hour.

Buses travel daily between Jaipur and Ramgarh (1 hr, Rs 9).

ABHANERI

About 95km from Jaipur on the Agra road, this village has one of Rajasthan's most awesome *baoris* (stepwells). Flanking the mammoth baori is a small crumbling pal-ace, now inhabited by pigeons and bats. Entry is free but the caretaker may like a little baksheesh (Rs 10 perhaps) to show you around. You can usually see about 11 levels of steps down to the stagnant water of the baori, but there are believed to be many more levels beneath that. You are allowed to take photos of the baori, but not of the statues.

Getting There & Away

From Jaipur, catch a bus to Sikandra, from where you can hire a jeep for the 10km trip to Abhaneri (Rs 200 return, including a 30 minute stop). Alternatively, you can get a bus from Jaipur to Gular from where it's a 5km walk to Abhaneri.

BALAJI

The extraordinary Hindu exorcism temple of Balaji is about 1.5km off the Jaipur to Agra road, about 1½ hours by bus from Bharatpur. The exorcisms can be violent and many of those treated will discuss their experiences. To view the exorcisms, go upstairs, where you may see people shaking, and others chained up – they have been exorcised and the chains represent the chaining of the evil spirit. Most exorcisms take place on Tuesday and Saturday. Take off your shoes before entering the temple and you may like to cover your head with a scarf as a mark of respect. No photography is permitted. The often disturbing scenes at this temple may upset some.

Getting There & Away

From Jaipur daily local buses go to Balaji (2½ hrs, Rs 26) and express buses (Rs 42).

KARAULI

Located 182km south-east of Jaipur, Karauli was founded in 1348 and has some important Krishna temples.

The **old city palace** was constructed over different periods of time and the oldest portion is about 600 years old. The durbar hall has some particularly fine paintings. This palace, which was occupied by the Karauli royal family until around the 1950s, is in need of restoration. Today it is occupied by naughty monkeys and a gaggle of geese. In the old days, geese were used to sound the alert if an intruder entered the palace grounds (they certainly can make one hell of a racket!). There's a Krishna temple in the palace compound which is open daily from 5 am to noon and 5.30 to 8 pm. Entry to the palace is Rs 5/20 for Indians/foreigners and it is open daily from sunrise to sunset.

Bhanwar Vilas Palace (☎ 07464-20024, or Jaipur 0141-211532, fax 210512), owned by Maharaja Krishna Chandra Pal, is more like a large country manor than a palace. Comfortable rooms cost US$29/32 a single/double and meals are available. Excursions to nearby points of interest, including the old city palace can be organised.

There are buses running between Jaipur and Karauli (5 hrs, Rs 45).

Eastern Rajasthan

The sites and cities of eastern Rajasthan are all easily accessible from Jaipur, and this region hosts a vast array of attractions. For those who wish to steep themselves in history, there are beautiful palace complexes at Alwar and Deeg, and fine forts at Bharatpur and Ranthambhore. Wildlife and bird enthusiasts are well catered for, with tiger spotting possibilities at both Ranthambhore National Park and the Sariska Tiger Reserve; both are administered by Project Tiger. Keoladeo Ghana National Park is India's premier bird sanctuary, with an astonishing population of resident and migratory birds in a picturesque wetland setting.

The holy Hindu pilgrimage town of Pushkar, set around a small lake, is one of the most popular travellers' centres in India. You can stay in one of the dozens of tiny whitewashed guesthouses, dine in any one of numerous vegetarian restaurants, have a priest perform a *puja* on your behalf, or shop in the fascinating market where you'll find colourful clothes designed to western tastes. Pushkar is most famous for the Camel Fair that it hosts annually in November. Ajmer, close to Pushkar, is an important pilgrimage centre for Muslims, who pay homage at the Dargah, a tomb to the Sufi saint, Khwaja Muin-ud-din Chishti. Ajmer is also the site of the prestigious institution of Mayo College, where many of Rajasthan's young princes were educated.

HISTORY

Alwar, in north-eastern Rajasthan, is possibly the oldest kingdom in kingdom-studded Rajasthan. In 1500 BC it formed part of the Matsya territories of Viratnagar (present-day Bairat), which also encompassed Bharatpur, Dholpur and Karauli.

History blends into mythology, as it was here in the ancient kingdom of Matsya that the Kauravas went cattle rustling, precipitating the war between them and their kinsfolk, the Pandavas. This great battle forms

Highlights

- **Keoladeo Ghana National Park** – World Heritage-listed bird sanctuary
- **Ranthambhore National Park and Sariska Tiger Reserve** – spot tigers and other wildlife in wilderness regions
- **Pushkar** – beautiful temple town around a small lake; home of the famous Camel Fair
- **Palaces** – fine complexes at Deeg and Alwar
- **The Dargah in Ajmer** – tomb of an important Muslim Sufi

the basis of the *Mahabharata*. The city of Alwar is believed to have been founded by a member of the Kachhwaha family from Amber, but control was wrested from the Kachhwahas by the Nikumbhas. They in turn lost the city to the Bada Gurjara Rajputs of Machari. It then passed to the Khanzadas, under Bahadura Nahara of Mewat, who converted from Hinduism to Islam to win the favour of Emperor Tughlaq of Delhi. At this time, Alwar and Tijara were part of the kingdom of Mewat.

In 1427, descendants of Bahadura Nahara of Mewat bravely defended the Alwar fort against the Muslims. Although the Mewati leader professed the Muslim faith, he chose to ally himself with the Rajputs as opposed to the Muslims in Delhi. As Alwar was located on the strategic south-western frontier of Delhi, this rankled with the Mughals, who mounted military forays into the region, only conquering it after great difficulty. Alwar was later granted to Sawai Jai Singh of Jaipur by Aurangzeb, but the emperor took it back when he visited the city and saw the strategic virtues of its forts.

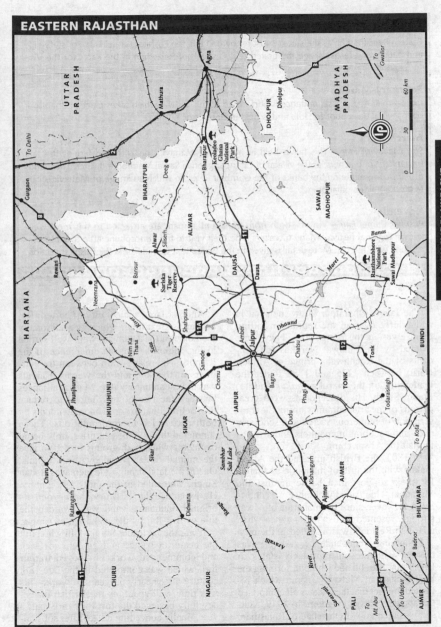

Festivals of Eastern Rajasthan

Eastern Rajasthan hosts the state's most renowned fair, the Pushkar Camel Fair. For statewide and nationwide festivals, see the boxed text Festivals of Rajasthan in the Facts for the Visitor chapter.

February-March

Brij Festival – The *Rasalila* dance is performed at this festival which takes place in Bharatpur over several days prior to Holi, and is held in honour of Krishna.

March-April

Shri Mahavirji Fair – This fair is held in honour of Mahavir, the 24th and last of the Jain *tirthankars*, or teachers, at the village of Chandangaon in Sawai Madhopur district. Thousands of Jains congregate on the banks of the Gambhir River, to which an image of Mahavir is carried on a golden palanquin.

November

Pushkar Camel Fair – Visitors, both from India and abroad, are attracted to this most well-known regional festival. Many travellers time their visit to the atmospheric little town to correspond with the fair. More detail is given in the boxed text Camel Fair in the Pushkar section.

The Jats of Bharatpur threw their hat in and briefly overran the region, installing themselves in the Alwar fort. They were evicted by the Lalawat Narukas (descendants of the Kachhwaha prince of Amber, Naru) between 1775 and 1782 under the leadership of the Naruka *thakur* (noble) Pratap Singh. His descendants were great patrons of the arts, commissioning the transcription of numerous sacred and scholarly texts and encouraging painters and artisans to visit the Alwar court.

In 1803, the British invested the Alwar thakur with the title of maharaja as thanks for their support in a battle against the Marathas. This friendly alliance was short-lived, however, since the maharaja of Alwar strongly resented British interference when a British Resident was installed in the city.

Following Independence, Alwar was merged with the other princely states of Bharatpur, Karauli and Dholpur, forming the United State of Matsya, a name which reflected the fact that these states all comprised the ancient Matsya kingdom. In 1949, Matsya was merged with the state of Rajasthan.

Another large ancient city of eastern Rajasthan is Bharatpur, which is traditionally the home of the Jats, who were well settled in this region before the emergence of the Rajputs. The relationship between the Jats, tillers of the soil, and the warrior Rajputs was at best an uneasy one. Marital alliances between the two groups helped to reduce the friction, but territorial encroachments by both parties led to confrontations. These simmered through the centuries, only being overcome when both groups turned to face the mutual threat posed by the Mughals. One of the Jats' strongest leaders was Badan Singh, who ruled in the mid-18th century. He expanded Jat territory far beyond its original boundaries, and was awarded the title of Brij-Raj by the maharaja of Amber.

It was the Jat leader Suraj Mahl who built the beautiful palace and gardens at Deeg and commenced work on the Bharatpur fort, which was completed in the late 18th century after nearly 60 years of work. This was time well spent, as the British unsuccessfully besieged the fort for nearly half a year, finally conceding defeat after substantial losses. The rulers of Bharatpur were the first to enter into an agreement with the East India Company.

The massive fort at Ranthambhore predates that at Bharatpur by many centuries, having been founded in the 10th century by the Chauhan Rajputs. Ranthambhore was held in reverence by the Jains, and several temples here were of great spiritual importance. Over the centuries Ranthambhore was subjected to numerous assaults by the Muslims, and in the 14th century the first *jauhar*, or collective sacrifice, was declared in Rajasthan when the women thought their ruler, Hammir Deva, had died on the battlefield.

The Mughal emperor Akbar negotiated a treaty with Surjana Hada, a Bundi ruler who purchased the fort of Ranthambhore from Jhunjhar Khan, and the fort passed to Jagannatha, under whose leadership the Jain religion flourished. The fort was taken by the Mughals under Aurangzeb, with whom it remained until the 18th century, when it was granted to the maharaja of Jaipur.

Ajmer was also founded by the Chauhans, three centuries earlier than Ranthambhore. In the late 12th century it passed to Mohammed of Ghori, and remained a possession of the sultanate of Delhi until the second decade of the 14th century. Fought over by various neighbouring states over subsequent centuries, it later passed to the Mughals, was briefly taken by the Rajput Rathores, was restored to the Mughals under Akbar, later passed to the Scindias, and came under direct British rule in 1818.

BHARATPUR & KEOLADEO GHANA NATIONAL PARK
• pop 1,646,500   ☎ 05644

Bharatpur is famous for its World Heritage-listed bird sanctuary, the Keoladeo Ghana National Park, the main entrance to which lies 5km from the train station. Many travellers rate this beautiful bird park as a highlight of their visit to India and if you're a bird-watching enthusiast, you should spend at least a few days here. According to a recent report, 354 species of birds have been identified at the park (see later).

In the 17th and 18th centuries, Bharatpur was an important Jat stronghold. The Jats maintained a high degree of autonomy, both because of their prowess in battle and their chiefs' marriage alliances with Rajput nobility. They successfully opposed the Mughals on more than one occasion and their fort at Bharatpur, constructed in the 18th century, withstood an attack by the British in 1805 and a long siege in 1825. The siege led to the first treaty of friendship between the states of north-west India and the East India Company.

The town itself, which was once surrounded by an 11km-long wall (now demolished), is of little interest. Bring along mosquito repellent as the little bloodsuckers can be tenacious here.

Orientation
The Keoladeo National Park lies 5km to the south of the city centre, and is easily accessed by cycle-rickshaw. There is a good selection of hotels both in the town centre and closer to the park.

Information
Tourist Office The helpful Tourist Reception Centre (☎ 22542) is at Rajasthan Tourism Development Corporation's (RTDC) Hotel Saras, about 700m from the park entrance – but at the time of writing there were plans to shift it across the road from the RTDC. It's open daily (except Sunday and every second Saturday of the month) from 10 am to 5 pm. The office provides tourist literature and maps of Bharatpur (Rs 2).

Money There are currency exchange facilities at the State Bank of Bikaner & Jaipur, near the Binarayan Gate.

Post The main post office, near Gandhi Park, is open daily except Sunday from 10 am to 1 pm and 2 to 5 pm.

Bookshops There is a small bookshop at the checkpost, 1.5km from the main gate inside the park, which has a selection of titles on Indian animal and bird life, and also sells

EASTERN RAJASTHAN

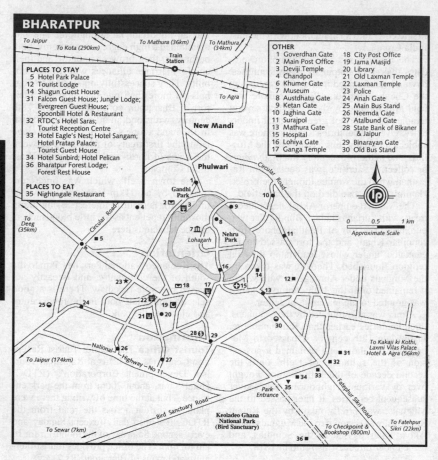

BHARATPUR

To Jaipur
To Kota (290km)
To Mathura (36km)
To Mathura (34km)
Train Station
To Agra

PLACES TO STAY
5   Hotel Park Palace
12 Tourist Lodge
14 Shagun Guest House
31 Falcon Guest House; Jungle Lodge;
    Evergreen Guest House;
    Spoonbill Hotel & Restaurant
32 RTDC's Hotel Saras;
    Tourist Reception Centre
33 Hotel Eagle's Nest; Hotel Sangam;
    Hotel Pratap Palace;
    Tourist Guest House
34 Hotel Sunbird; Hotel Pelican
36 Bharatpur Forest Lodge;
    Forest Rest House

PLACES TO EAT
35 Nightingale Restaurant

OTHER
1   Goverdhan Gate
2   Main Post Office
3   Deviji Temple
4   Chandpol
5   Khumer Gate
7   Museum
8   Austdhatu Gate
9   Ketan Gate
10 Jaghina Gate
11 Surajpol
13 Mathura Gate
15 Hospital
16 Lohiya Gate
17 Ganga Temple
18 City Post Office
19 Jama Masjid
20 Library
21 Old Laxman Temple
22 Laxman Temple
23 Police
24 Anah Gate
25 Main Bus Stand
26 Neemda Gate
27 Atalbund Gate
28 State Bank of Bikaner
    & Jaipur
29 Binarayan Gate
30 Old Bus Stand

New Mandi

Phulwari

Gandhi Park

Circular Road

Nehru Park

Lohagarh

To Deeg (35km)

To Jaipur (174km)

National Highway – No 11

Park Entrance

Bird Sanctuary Road

To Sewar (7km)

Keoladeo Ghana National Park (Bird Sanctuary)

To Checkpoint & Bookshop (800m)

To Kakaji ki Kothi, Laxmi Vilas Palace Hotel & Agra (56km)

Fatehpur Sikri Road

To Fatehpur Sikri (22km)

0   0.5   1 km
Approximate Scale

---

postcards. The bookshop is open daily from 6 am to 6 pm.

Lohagarh

Lohagarh, also known as the Iron Fort, was built in the early 18th century and took its name from its supposedly impregnable defences. Maharaja Suraj Mahl, the fort's constructor and the founder of Bharatpur, built two towers within the ramparts, the Jawahar Burj and Fateh Burj, to commemorate his victories over the Mughals and the British.

The fort occupies an entire small artificial island in the centre of the town, and the three palaces within its precincts are in an advanced state of decay. In fact, the entire fort has a forlorn, derelict feel, and is in need of restoration. The main entrance is the **Austdhatu Gate**. *Austdhatu* means 'eight metals', a reference to the spikes on the gate which are reputedly made of eight different metals.

Museum The government museum is housed in the former *durbar* (maharaja's meeting hall) in the fort. Unfortunately, some areas of the museum are poorly lit and many of the exhibits are not well captioned. There's a display of sculpture which spans the ages, some pieces dating from the 2nd century AD. There's a well-preserved 7th century carving of Shiva and Parvati which was recovered from Kama (near Deeg), and a fine carving of Shiva as Nataraja, the cosmic dancer, dating from the 10th century.

In a separate hall, but also part of the museum's collection, is a gallery featuring portraits and old photographs of the maharajas of Bharatpur (shoes have to be removed here). Other exhibits include weaponry, an Australian sheep hide and an assortment of dusty stuffed beasts including a couple of pitiful baby bear cubs. The museum is open from 10 am to 4.30 pm daily except Friday. Entry is Rs 3 (free on Monday) and the camera/video charge is Rs 10/20.

Jawaharbij This viewing point is a short walk to the north-east of the museum along a steep path. It was from here that the maharajas surveyed their city. It's a nice place capturing the cool breezes in a series of pavilions, the ceilings of which feature badly deteriorating frescoes – scenes of elephants and chariots can be made out. As you would expect, the views down over the city are superlative.

Nehru Park From the museum to Nehru Park is a five minute walk. Nehru Park is between the museum and the main gate (Austdhatu Gate) of the fort. There are pleasant lawns and flower beds.

Ganga Temple
Just outside the Lohiya Gate is this temple dedicated to the goddess Ganga. On the laneway leading up to the temple, vendors sell mattress stuffing made of Punjabi wool. Construction of the temple commenced in 1845 during the reign of Maharaja Balwant Singh, but it was not completed until 1937, during the reign of Maharaja Brijendra Sawai. The two storey temple, made of sandstone, features a black and white chequered floor and ornately carved arches. The edges of the terrace on which the temple stands, overlooking the busy streets below, are not stable. Do not approach them too closely.

Keoladeo Ghana National Park
This beautiful sanctuary, which has now been denoted a national park, came into being in the 18th century. Maharaja Suraj Mahl of Bharatpur converted a low-lying swamp formed by the confluence of the Gambhir and Banganga rivers into a reservoir, the Ajun Bund. Flooding during subsequent monsoons soon inundated the surrounding region, creating a shallow wetland ecosystem, the perfect habitat for an astonishing variety of birds.

The maharaja did not have conservationist motives, but wanted a ready supply of waterfowl, affording fine shooting (and dining) possibilities. Indeed, Keoladeo continued to supply maharajas' tables until as late as 1965. An inscription on a pillar near the small temple in the park bears testimony to the penchant for hunting. On one day alone, over 5000 ducks were shot.

A fence was built around the forests of the wetlands in the latter part of the 19th century to stop feral cattle roaming through the area. From 1944-64, afforestation policies were pursued, with the plantation of stands of acacias.

The post-Independence period was one of great turmoil. Local communities were keen to divert the canals which feed the swamplands for irrigation, and to convert the wetlands into crop lands. Fortunately, the conservationists won the day, and in 1956 the region was declared a sanctuary. In 1982, it was denoted a national park, encompassing a small area of some 29 sq km, of which one third is submerged during the annual monsoon.

Today Keoladeo is recognised as one of the most important bird breeding and feeding grounds in the world. Please keep the birds happy by disposing of rubbish properly, and keeping noise to a minimum.

Siberian Cranes

Park authorities at Keoladeo were concerned when the endangered Siberian crane *(Grus leucogeranus)* failed to appear during two successive winter seasons in 1994 and 95. In 1996, on the first day of winter, ornithologists around the world heaved a collective sigh of relief when four of these magnificent birds flew into the park, nearly two months after their usual arrival. In 1998, two birds came to the park.

It is believed that the total population of Siberian cranes wintering in Iran and India is only 15; an estimated 100 of these birds have perished over the last 12 years during their 5000km-long journey from the Orb River basin in Siberia over inhospitable terrain. There are two other populations of Siberian cranes which hail from the Orb River. The most substantial population, numbering almost 3000, winters at the Yangtze River in China. A small population of about a dozen flies to winter grounds along the south coast of Iran's Caspian Sea. The tiny remaining population makes its annual winter journey to India, and it is this group that is hosted at Keoladeo. About 30 years ago more than 200 sibes, as they are known, wintered at Keoladeo, and this sharp drop in numbers raises grave fears about their survival as a species. They have been termed 'critically endangered' by the International Union of Conservation of Nature.

Tragically, it is not the natural rigours of the long migration which are blamed for the critical depletion of sibe numbers, but the Afghanistan war, with sibes being slaughtered for meat by Afghanis. They are also believed to fall prey to hunters in Pakistan, who shoot them for sport. Unfortunately, efforts to install a transmitter on one of the sibes which arrived at Keoladeo in 1996 failed, due to various problems, including bureaucratic delays. The transmitter would have provided conservationists and scientists with invaluable information about the birds' migratory route, habitats and breeding range. The transmitter would have sent signals through the Argos satellite launched jointly by the USA and France. Conservationists can now only wait and hope that these brave journeyers will return to their winter grounds, hopefully in replenished numbers, in future seasons.

Keoladeo Fauna During the monsoon period (July/August), and for a month or so following the monsoon, the park is home to vast colonies of birds which come here to breed and feed on the wetland's rich aquatic species. Some of the species which nest at this time include storks, moorhens, herons, egrets and cormorants. Keep your eyes peeled for storks spreading their wings to shield their chicks from the hot sun. Around October the bird population increases with the arrival of wintering migratory birds who usually seem to stay until around the end of February. Among these birds is the highly endangered Siberian crane, which is found in India and only at this park (see the boxed text). This is the best time of the year to visit the sanctuary.

The migratory birds have mostly left by the end of March. At the beginning of April, when the waters begin to recede, there is still a substantial population of birds of prey (vultures), some kingfishers, and smaller birds such as robins, wagtails and mynas. Many of these birds feed at the few pools, teeming with fish, that remain in the park during the dry summer months. During the height of summer, when the waters have all but disappeared, the sanctuary is carpeted in dry grasslands which afford habitat to a variety of fauna such as the deer (spotted, sambar, bluebull), jackals, jungle cats, blackbucks, hares and mongoose.

Visiting the Park The park is open from 6 am to 6 pm daily. Only one sealed road goes through, but a series of raised embankments thread their way between the shallow wetlands. Walking or cycling along them affords unique opportunities to observe the rich birdlife at close quarters.

Entry to the park costs Rs 20/100 for Indians/foreigners and entitles you to enter as many times as you like on that day. A still camera is free, but it costs Rs 200 for a video camera. There's also an entry fee for bicycles (Rs 3) and cycle-rickshaws (Rs 5). Motorised vehicles are prohibited beyond the checkpost, 1.5km inside the park, so the only way of getting around is by foot, bicycle or cycle-rickshaw.

Only cycle-rickshaws authorised by the government (recognisable by the yellow plate bolted onto the front) are allowed in – beware of anyone who tells you otherwise! Although you don't pay entry fees for the drivers, you'll be up for Rs 30 per hour if you take one. A cycle-rickshaw can take a maximum of two people (if you hire a guide, he follows on foot/bicycle). It's worthwhile hiring one of these government-approved rickshaw-wallahs, as they have been trained in bird identification – one of them, Runghu Singh, first observed the four Siberian cranes which returned to the park in 1996 after two years absence, thrilling ornithologists. Not only are you encouraging local employment, they really do know their birds. After hiring a guide once, you can then ramble around the park at leisure unaccompanied. Guides can be organised at the park entrance. Official government prices are Rs 35 for one to five people per hour, and Rs 75 for five to 10 people.

Boats can be hired for Rs 80 per hour (maximum four people). They are a very good way of getting close to the wildlife. A horse-drawn tonga costs Rs 60 per hour (maximum six people).

If you hire a guide, most have a pair of binoculars which you can use. Otherwise it's worth hiring binoculars (many hotels rent them out); try to get some with a strap so you can conveniently hang them around your neck. Most hotels can also arrange a packed lunch.

After your initial visit to the park with a rickshaw-wallah or trained guide, a fantastic way to see the park on subsequent visits is to hire a bicycle. These can be hired at the park entrance for Rs 20 per day. Having a bike allows you to easily avoid the bottlenecks, which inevitably occur at the nesting sites of the larger birds. It's just about the only way you'll be able to watch the numerous kingfishers at close quarters – noise or human activity frightens them away. Some of the hotels rent bicycles (see Places to Stay). If you plan to visit the national park at dawn (one of the best times to see the birds), you'll have to hire a bicycle the day before.

The southern reaches of the park are virtually devoid of *humanus touristicus*, and so are much better than the northern part for serious bird-watching.

There's a small snack bar about halfway through the park, next to the tiny Keoladeo Temple. You can also get a bite to eat at the Bharatpur Forest Lodge (see Places to Stay), located in the park.

A small display at the main entrance to the park has a range of stuffed birds, map of the park, nests of various species, examples of aquatic species found in the park's lakes and a photographic display. Entry is free.

Places to Stay & Eat

For details about guesthouses registered with the Paying Guest House Scheme, contact the Tourist Reception Centre (see Information earlier). The price ranges from Rs 100 to Rs 300 per night.

Many hotels have bicycles and binoculars for hire and can organise a packed lunch. Most slash tariffs in the low season. The commission system has reared its ugly head in Bharatpur – don't be pressured into accommodation by touts at the train station or bus stand.

Park Precincts The following places are all within easy walking distance (within 1km) of the main entrance to the national park. The lodgings here are the most popular with travellers, so can fill up fast.

RTDC's Hotel Saras (☎ 23700, cnr Fatehpur Sikri and Bird Sanctuary Rds) has slightly shabby singles/doubles for Rs 300/350 with attached bath and geyser. Deluxe air-cooled singles/doubles are Rs 450/550, and the super deluxe rooms, with air-con and TV, cost Rs 600/700. Beds in the dusty dorm cost Rs 50. There's a restaurant which has a wide selection of veg meals and a few token nonveg dishes; chicken biryani is Rs 70.

Spoonbill Hotel & Restaurant (☎ 23571) is just behind the RTDC's Hotel Saras and is popular with travellers. It has one double room with common bath for Rs 150, or rooms with attached bath (hot water by the bucket for Rs 5) for Rs 150/200. There are also dorm beds for Rs 50. The restaurant features both veg and nonveg cuisine including Rajasthani dishes such as churma (Rs 15), the royal dish of Rajasthan – sugar, cheese and dried fruit fried in butter. There's a campfire in winter, bike hire is Rs 30 per day (mountain bikes are Rs 40), binoculars are from Rs 50 per day, and there's a bird spotter's guide available for loan for Rs 20 per day.

Falcon Guest House (☎ 23815), nearby, is a peaceful and homey place, run by the friendly Mrs Rajni Singh. Her husband, Tej, is an ornithologist and is happy to answer questions when he comes home from work. There are good-sized singles/doubles with attached bath for Rs 150/200, or Rs 350/400 for a bigger room with a softer mattress and private balcony. There's a restaurant in the little marigold garden where you can get home-cooked food such as egg curry (Rs 30) and veg thalis (Rs 60). Bikes are available for hire and there's a 50% low-season discount.

Evergreen Guest House (☎ 25917) nearby, has four rooms with private bath for Rs 100/200 a single/double. Meals are available and there are bikes and binoculars for hire.

Jungle Lodge (☎ 25622), nearby, has small but comfortable rooms with bath and hot water (Rs 100/200) which open onto a shady verandah. There are also larger rooms for Rs 200/300. There's a nice lawn area and discounts up to 50% in the low season. There are rental bikes/binoculars for Rs 30/75 per day, and a lending library. Meals are available.

Hotel Sangam (☎ 25616, Fatehpur Sikri Rd) is directly opposite the RTDC's Hotel Saras. Ordinary singles/doubles downstairs with cold water are Rs 150/200, and upstairs fairly plain rooms with hot water cost Rs 300/400. There's a veg and nonveg restaurant with dishes such as spaghetti (Rs 30 to Rs 40) and banana paratha (Rs 12).

Hotel Eagle's Nest (☎ 25144, Bird Sanctuary Rd) is nearby. Rooms with fan and hot water by the bucket are Rs 250/350. Air-cooled rooms with geyser are Rs 500/650. This is a clean, comfortable place, and a 25% discount is offered between mid-April and mid-September. There's a large nonveg restaurant, which serves Indian and Chinese food at reasonable prices.

Hotel Sunbird (☎ 25701) is a short distance farther down this road, heading towards the sanctuary, and is a popular choice. Rooms with private bath range from Rs 150/250 to Rs 400/500. The **Tandoor Restaurant** here whips up a good selection of dishes, such as Kashmiri biryani (Rs 35). Bikes are available for hire (Rs 50 per day).

Hotel Pelican (☎ 24221) is nearby on the same road. Tiny but airy singles/doubles with common bath (hot water by the bucket for Rs 3) are only Rs 40/75. With attached bath, rooms cost Rs 100/125 or Rs 150/200 for a bigger room with air-cooling. The restaurant has continental, Indian and Chinese cuisine. Rental bikes and binoculars cost Rs 30 each for 24 hours.

Nightingale Restaurant (☎ 27022, fax 24351) is in a eucalyptus grove and offers small two person tents from Rs 80 to Rs 200. The campsite is open from around 15 October to 15 February. Bring mosquito repellent as the mozzies can be a real hassle. The restaurant serves cheap eats; palak paneer is Rs 30.

Hotel Pratap Palace (☎ 24245, fax 25093, Bird Sanctuary Rd) is also close to the park entrance. Ordinary singles/doubles with an attached bath and geyser are Rs

200/300, carpeted deluxe rooms are Rs 600/700, and deluxe air-con rooms with TV are Rs 900/1050. The cheaper rooms aren't bad value, but the more expensive ones are a bit overpriced. There are also some rooms with common bath for Rs 100/150. A 30% discount is offered between mid-April and mid-September. Breakfast costs Rs 85, and lunch and dinner are Rs 180.

Tourist Guest House (Bird Sanctuary Rd) has large spartan singles/doubles for Rs 100/150 with attached bath and hot water. A single with common bath is Rs 60 and a bed in the small dorm is Rs 30.

Shubham Guest House (☎ 26670, B-173 Jawahar Nagar) is a short distance up the road opposite the park entrance. The rooms aren't the greatest, but this place is in a handy location near the park. Singles/doubles with bath cost Rs 125/150.

Bharatpur Forest Lodge (☎ 22760, fax 22864) is about 1km beyond the entrance gate and 8km from the Bharatpur train station. This ITDC (Indian Tourism Development Corporation) hotel is looking a little faded. Rooms are certainly comfortably appointed but not really luxurious. However, you have to pay for the privilege of staying in the national park itself. Singles/doubles cost Rs 1700/2500. A buffet breakfast is Rs 140, and lunch/dinner costs Rs 250. The restaurant is open to nonresidents and is handy if you feel peckish while in the park. There are light bites such as sandwiches (around Rs 35) as well as more substantial meals. A hot chocolate is Rs 30 and a bottle of cold beer is Rs 100.

Forest Rest House (☎ 22777), also inside the park, rents out rooms if they are not being occupied by government officials. Simple doubles with attached bathroom cost Rs 600, including all meals.

Bharatpur *Tourist Lodge (☎ 23742)*, close to the Mathura Gate and near the old bus stand, is an unpretentious guesthouse with basic rooms at just Rs 50/80 for singles/ doubles with common bath, and Rs 75/100 with attached bath. The best double is Rs 150. Meals are available and there's a good

balcony area. Bikes and binoculars are on hire for Rs 40 each per day.

Shagun Guest House (☎ 29202) is down a laneway just inside Mathura Gate and is nothing flash, but is excellent if you're strapped for cash. There are primitive grass huts for a meagre Rs 46/66 which have mosquito nets and lights; singles/doubles with common bath for Rs 56/76; and rooms with attached bath and hot water Rs 68/86. Bike hire is Rs 28 per day, and electric fans are available. You can get basic meals here, and the owner, Rajeev, is friendly and has a wealth of knowledge on the park and Bharatpur.

Laxmi Vilas Palace Hotel (☎ 23523, fax 25259) is at Kakaji ki Kothi on the old Agra road, about equidistant between the national park and the town centre. Standard singles/doubles are Rs 1195/1250, and suites cost Rs 2250. The hotel was originally built for the younger son of Maharaja Jaswant Singh. The standard rooms are nothing special, and the small deluxe rooms are also not sizzling hot value. The restaurant is open to nonresidents; the buffet lunch or dinner is Rs 250.

Hotel Park Palace (☎ 23783), which is the closest hotel to the bus stand, near the Khumer Gate, is a possibility if you've got an early morning bus to catch. The cheapest rooms go for Rs 200/250 with bath and hot water. Some rooms can cop a fair bit of traffic noise. There's a restaurant and bar.

Getting There & Away

Bus There are local buses to Deeg (1 hr, Rs 15), to Jaipur (4½ hrs, Rs 70) and to Agra (1½ hrs, Rs 22), every 30 minutes. There are also regular services to Fatehpur Sikri (1 hr, Rs 10). These buses all leave from the main bus stand.

There are no direct buses to Sawai Madhopur (for Ranthambhore National Park). All services require a change at Dausa. The train is a far better option.

Train Bharatpur is on the Delhi to Mumbai broad-gauge line. A good service between Delhi and Bharatpur is the *Firozpur Janta*

Express. It leaves New Delhi station at 2 pm, arriving in Bharatpur at 6.15 pm (175km, Rs 96/245 in 2nd/1st class). It leaves Bharatpur at 8 am, arriving back at the capital at 12.30 pm. There are several good services to Sawai Madhopur (182km, Rs 96/258), which go on to Kota (290km, Rs 72/361) and Mumbai (1210km, Rs 200/1004). To Agra, there's a passenger train in the morning and afternoon (1½ hrs, Rs 11).

Getting Around

Bharatpur has auto-rickshaws, cycle-rickshaws and tongas. An excellent way to zip around is by bicycle, which costs Rs 20 to Rs 50 per day (the more expensive bikes are in better condition).

DEEG

• pop 40,000   ☎ 05641

Very few travellers ever make it to Deeg, about 36km north of Bharatpur. This is a shame, because this small town with its massive fortifications, stunningly beautiful palace and busy market is much more interesting than Bharatpur (excluding the bird park) itself. It's an easy day trip from Bharatpur, or from Agra or Mathura, both in the adjacent state of Uttar Pradesh.

Built by Suraj Mahl in the mid-18th century, Deeg was formerly the second capital of Bharatpur state. The Bharatpur maharajas ruled from both Bharatpur and Deeg. At Deeg, the maharaja's forces successfully withstood a combined Mughal and Maratha army of some 80,000 men. Eight years later, the maharaja even had the temerity to attack the Red Fort in Delhi! The booty he carried off included an entire marble building which can still be seen.

Suraj Mahl's Palace (Gopal Bhavan)

Suraj Mahl's Palace, the **Gopal Bhavan**, built by Maharaja Suraj Mahl between 1756 and 1763, has to be one of India's most beautiful and delicately proportioned buildings. Built in a combination of Rajput and Mughal architectural styles, it is in an excellent state of repair and, as it was used by the maharajas until the early 1970s, most of the rooms still contain their original furnishings. These include chaises longues, plenty of antiques, a stuffed tiger which was shot by a maharaja, elephant feet stands, and fine china from China and France.

The mostly two storey palace is three and four storeys high in places. The eastern facade is fronted by imposing arches to take full advantage of the early morning light. On either side of the palace are two exquisite pavilions. In the northern pavilion is a throne of black marble, while that in the southern pavilion is of white marble. In an upstairs room at the rear of the palace is an Indian-style dining table – a raised, horseshoe-shaped affair. Guests sat on both sides. In the maharaja's bedroom is an enormous (3.6 by 2.4m) bed.

The palace is flanked by two tanks, to the east the **Gopal Sagar**, and to the west the **Rup Sagar**. The magnificently maintained gardens and flower beds are fed by water from these reservoirs. In the gardens the **Keshav Bhavan**, or Summer Pavilion, a single storey edifice with five arches along each side. An arcade runs around the interior of the pavilion over a type of canal with hundreds of fountains, many of which are still functional, and turned on occasionally (including local festivals). Deeg's massive walls (up to 28m high) and 12 bastions, some with their cannons still in place, are also worth exploring.

On the north side of the palace grounds is the **Nand Bhawan**, an oblong hall enclosed by a grand arcade.

The palace is open daily from 8 am to 5 pm; admission is free.

Laxmi Mandir

This very old temple is presided over by a *mataji*, or female priest. There are alcoves on three sides enshrining images of Durga, Hanuman and Gada, and a small shrine to Shiva to one side. The temple is on Batchu Marg, 20 minutes walk from the palace.

Places to Stay & Eat

Few travellers stop overnight at Deeg and there's only one place worth staying: *RTDC's Motel Deeg* (☎ 21000). It's five minutes walk from the bus stand and the palace, and has just a handful of rooms, all with attached bath (bucket hot water). They cost Rs 250/300/400 a single/double/triple, or if you have your own tent you can pitch it on the lawn for Rs 30 per person (which includes use of bathroom facilities). Meals are available; a veg thali is Rs 55, a cheese sandwich is Rs 27 and a cup of tea is Rs 5.

Getting There & Away
There are numerous buses between Deeg and Alwar (2½ hrs, Rs 22/28 for local/express). There's a bus to Mathura (1¼ hrs, Rs 12/15). Buses for Bharatpur leave every 30 minutes (1 hr, Rs 12/15). From Agra, there is one direct daily express bus (Rs 45).

ALWAR
- **pop 250,000**   ☎ 0144

Alwar was once an important Rajput state, which gained pre-eminence in the 18th century under Pratap Singh, who pushed back the rulers of Jaipur to the south and the Jats of Bharatpur to the east, and who successfully resisted the Marathas. It was one of the first Rajput states to ally itself with the fledgling British empire, although British interference in Alwar's internal affairs meant that this partnership was not always amicable. Beautiful palace buildings, hunting lodges at Sariska, and the extraordinary collection of *objets d'art* in the government museum at the palace bear testament to the wealth of this erstwhile state.

Orientation
The city palace and museum are in the north-west of the city, about 1km north of the bus stand. There is a collection of budget hotels a short distance to the east of the bus stand. The main post office is about midway between the bus stand and the train station, the latter on the eastern edge of the town.

Information
Tourist Office Near the train station, the Tourist Reception Centre (☎ 21868) is not far from the Hotel Aravali. It's open daily

except Sunday from 10 am to 5 pm (closed for lunch from 1.30 to 2 pm). It can organise guides for local sightseeing and they also sell a good map of Alwar (Rs 2).

Money You can change money at the State Bank of Bikaner & Jaipur, near the bus stand.

Bala Quila
This huge fort, with its 5km of ramparts, stands 300m above the city. Predating the time of Pratap Singh, it's one of the very few forts in Rajasthan constructed before the rise of the Mughals. Unfortunately, because the fort now houses a radio transmitter station, you can only see inside with special permission from the superintendent of police (☎ 337453).

Palace Complex
Below the fort is the large, imposing city palace complex, its massive gates and tank lined by a beautifully symmetrical chain of *ghats* with four pavilions on each side and two at each end. Today, most of the complex is occupied by government offices, but there is a museum (see later), housed in the former city palace. To gain access to the tank and its ghats, take the steps on the far left-hand side when facing the palace. Just outside the palace you can see clerks busily clacking away on typewriters for their lawyer bosses (who have outdoor 'offices' here). The lawyers can be distinguished by their white shirts and black jackets.

Cenotaph of Maharaja Bakhtawar Singh This double storey edifice resting on a platform of sandstone was built in 1815 by Maharaja Vinay Singh in memory of his father. The cenotaph is also known as the Chhatri of Moosi Rani, as one of the wives of Bakhtawar Singh who performed *sati* (self-immolation) on his funeral pyre. Every day several women can be seen paying homage to the maharani at the cenotaph by pouring holy water over raised sculpted footprints of the deceased royal couple. There is fine carving on the interior of the cenotaph (shoes should be removed), but

EASTERN RAJASTHAN

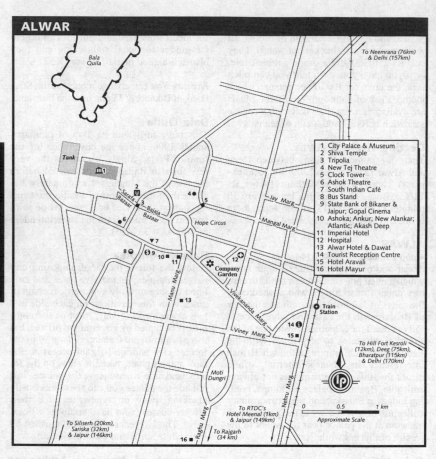

ALWAR

1 City Palace & Museum
2 Shiva Temple
3 Tripolia
4 New Tej Theatre
5 Clock Tower
6 Ashok Theatre
7 South Indian Café
8 Bus Stand
9 State Bank of Bikaner & Jaipur; Gopal Cinema
10 Ashoka; Ankur; New Alankar; Atlantic; Akash Deep
11 Imperial Hotel
12 Hospital
13 Alwar Hotel & Dawat
14 Tourist Reception Centre
15 Hotel Aravali
16 Hotel Mayur

Bala Quila

Tank

Sarafa Bazaar

Bajaja Bazaar

Hope Circus

Jay Marg

Mangal Marg

Company Garden

Manu Marg

Vivekananda Marg

Viney Marg

Moti Dungri

Raghu Marg

Nehru Marg

Train Station

To Neemrana (76km) & Delhi (157km)

To Hill Fort Kesroli (12km), Deeg (75km), Bharatpur (115km) & Delhi (170km)

To RTDC's Hotel Meenal (1km) & Jaipur (149km)

To Siliserh (20km), Sariska (32km) & Jaipur (146km)

To Rajgarh (34 km)

0   0.5   1 km
Approximate Scale

unfortunately the frescoes on the ceiling are almost indiscernible.

Museum The excellent and comprehensive collection housed in this government museum includes royal vestments in beautiful brocades, including an enormous bear; Kashmiri lacquer work; and stone sculptures which include an 11th century sculpture of Vishnu. There are some extraordinary exhibits testifying to the wealth of the maharajas of Alwar, including

a pair of ivory slippers and a silver dining table with lions' feet legs. Other exhibits include miniature models depicting various themes; one shows two red-haired British men in negotiation with the maharaja. There are also tiny potters, *chai-wallahs* and fruit vendors.

There's a fine collection of traditional instruments, including a sitar in the shape of a peacock, and a standard of the Alwar royal house presented to Raja Mangal Singh by Queen Victoria (whose bust stands nearby).

A separate exhibition hall has a collection of paintings including a lovely depiction of Krishna and Radha featuring gold leaf, and miniatures on ivory. There is a copy of *Gulistan (A Rose Garden)* by Shekh Muslihuddin-Sadi, originally written in 1258. This copy was commissioned by Maharaja Vinay Singh of Alwar in 1858, and the scribes spent over 12 years meticulously copying the text which features beautiful calligraphy. There is also a painting of a seated Christ, and scrolls of the *Bhagavad Gita* and *Mahabharata* in miniature script. The armoury section has a stunning collection of weapons and armour.

The museum is open daily except Friday from 10 am to 4.30 pm; entry is Rs 3 (free on Monday). Photography is not permitted.

Places to Stay

Finding a budget place to stay is not a problem in Alwar. Contact the Tourist Reception Centre (see Information, earlier) for details about the Paying Guest House Scheme, which offers accommodation from Rs 100 to Rs 350 per night.

Ankur (☎ 333025), *Atlantic (☎ 21581)*, *New Alankar (☎ 20027)*, *Ashoka (☎ 21780)* and *Akash Deep (☎ 22912)* are a cluster of cheap hotels which face each other around a central courtyard, about 500m east of the bus stand, set back from Manu Marg. All the hotels begin with 'A' and are each owned by one of five brothers. Without wishing to upset any of the brothers, the Ashoka seems to be the best, with singles/doubles with attached bath (hot water by the bucket for Rs 3) for Rs 100/150 and Rs 200/250, or Rs 400/450 with air-con. However, there's really not much difference between them; their prices are comparable.

Imperial Hotel (☎ 21438, 1 Manu Marg) is at the start of the laneway which leads to the five As. Somewhat musty singles/doubles with attached bath and air-cooler start at Rs 140/220. This place could be a little noisy, as it fronts a busy street. There's a good restaurant here (see Places to Eat).

Hotel Aravali (☎ 332883, fax 332011), is an option if you have an early morning rail departure. Located near the train station, it is run by the Kakkar family (the owner's son, Achal, and his wife, Anika, are helpful and can be contacted through reception). Dorm beds cost Rs 100 and singles/doubles with private bath start at Rs 200/250 (request these prices). Suites are Rs 2500. Some rooms can be a bit noisy, so ask for a quiet one. There's a restaurant (see Places to Eat), bar and pool (summer only).

RTDC's Hotel Meenal (☎ 22852) is a respectable mid-range place, charging Rs 350/450 for a tidy deluxe single/double, and Rs 500/600 for a super deluxe room. There's a little dining hall; a veg/nonveg thali costs Rs 55/68.

Alwar Hotel (☎ 20012, fax 332250, 26 Manu Marg), set in a leafy garden, has decent rooms from Rs 300/450 with private bath to Rs 600/700 with air-con. There's a good restaurant (see Places to Eat).

Hotel Mayur (☎ 337222), south of the town centre, is in need of restoration, with tatty singles/doubles with bath from Rs 250/300 for an economy room, to Rs 600/650 for a deluxe room. The restaurant is not bad; half a tandoori chicken is Rs 55.

Vijay Mandir Palace, located about 7km from Alwar, is a stunning royal property overlooking a lake. There were rumours that it may soon be converted into a hotel – ask at the Tourist Reception Centre (see Information, earlier) if you're interested.

Retiring rooms at the train station have beds for Rs 40 per person. No meals are available.

Places to Eat

Narula's, near the Ganesh Talkies, whips up Indian, Chinese and continental cuisine. This pleasant restaurant, which is down a stairway, offers a good choice of dishes, including veg sizzlers (Rs 45), half a butter chicken (Rs 80), French fries (Rs 20) and strawberry milkshakes (Rs 25).

Hotel Aravali, near the train station, serves moderately priced veg and nonveg fare at its restaurant. For dessert, ask for one hot gulab jamun served with vanilla ice cream (Rs 35) – a delicious combination of hot and cold. For a drink, go to the hotel's *Guftgu* bar, where you can guzzle beer (Rs 80 per bottle) and chew on chicken tikkas (Rs 45) while admiring the lilac chairs.

Imperial Hotel (Manu Marg) has vegetarian fare and specialises in south Indian cuisine. Most dishes are under Rs 30; a masala dosa is Rs 16 and a vegetable pakora is Rs 14.

Dawat (Alwar Hotel, Manu Marg) serves Indian, continental and Chinese food. Menu includes paneer tikka (Rs 50), veg chow mein (Rs 35) and chicken sandwiches (Rs 32).

South Indian Cafe is opposite the Gopal Cinema, on the road leading to the bus stand. It has cheap and decent dishes such as masala dosas.

Getting There & Away

Bus Buses for Sariska leave every 30 minutes throughout the day (1 hr, Rs 8/13 for local/express). There are also buses every 30 minutes to Jaipur (4 hrs, Rs 45/61). There are regular buses to Deeg (2½ hrs, Rs 23/30), and to Bharatpur for Keoladeo Ghana National Park (local 4½ hrs, Rs 29; express 3½ hrs, Rs 45).

Train To Delhi, there's the *Shatabdi Express* (3 hrs, Rs 320 in air-con chair car). The *Intercity* leaves Alwar at 8.50 am, arriving in Delhi at 11.30 am (Rs 47 in 2nd class; no 1st class). To Jaipur the *Shatabdi Express* departs Alwar at 8.37 am, arriving into Jaipur at about 11 am (Rs 290 in air-con chair car), and Ajmer at about 1.30 pm (Rs 446). The *Intercity* leaves at 7.33 pm, arriving in Jaipur at 10 pm (Rs 46).

Getting Around

There are cycle-rickshaws, auto-rickshaws, tempos and some tongas. A cycle-rickshaw from the train station to the town centre should cost around Rs 10. Bicycles can be hired near the train station (Rs 10/20 per half/full day).

AROUND ALWAR
Siliserh

At Siliserh, which lies 20km south-west of Alwar off the road to Sariska Tiger Reserve, is a restored palace which was built by the Alwar maharaja Vinay Singh, and is situated in a dramatic location overlooking a tranquil lake. Inevitably, it is now a hotel: *RTDC's Hotel Lake Palace (☎ 0144-86322)*. This property is beautiful, but unfortunately the cleanliness and service is erratic. It has rooms with attached bath from Rs 200/300 to Rs 750/850. There's a bar and restaurant; a veg/nonveg thali is Rs 70/90.

Kesroli

Hill Fort Kesroli (☎ 0144-81312, Delhi ☎ 011-4616145, fax 4621112), 12km from Alwar in Kesroli village is run from the Neemrana Fort Palace (see following). Double rooms in the 14th century fort are from Rs 1500 to Rs 4000. From the fort you can see brightly clad villagers working in the fields. The buffet lunch/dinner is Rs 150/200 (nonresidents must book one day ahead). The hotel can arrange Alwar sightseeing (Rs 1500 per jeep including a guide; maximum four people).

Neemrana

This small village lies about 75km north of Alwar on the main Delhi-Jaipur highway, a short distance to the south of the Haryana border. There's not much of interest in the village itself, but 2km away is the restored fortress palace. Dating from 1464, it was from here that the Rajput maharaja Prithviraj Chauhan III reigned. In usual Rajasthan style, it has been converted into a luxury hotel: *Neemrana Fort Palace (☎/fax 01494 -46005)*. Bookings must be made at Delhi (☎ 011-4616145, fax 4621112, email neem rana@fwacziarg.com). Suitably luxurious rooms start at Rs 1500/2500 (some rooms are better than others and several even have loos with views of the countryside). Camel rides are available for Rs 300 per hour. Every weekend between October and March there is a Rajasthani folk music program, and to complete the picture, the hotel has its own helipad. Nonguests can visit for Rs 100, but there's no entry charge if you eat at the restaurant; the buffet lunch/dinner is Rs 350/400.

Getting There & Away Buses on the main Delhi-Jaipur route generally stop at Behror, 14km from Neemrana, and a farther 2km from the hotel. A taxi from Behror to the hotel will cost about Rs 200.

SARISKA TIGER RESERVE & NATIONAL PARK
☎ 0144

Situated 107km from Jaipur and 200km from Delhi, the sanctuary is in a wooded valley surrounded by barren hills. It covers 800 sq km (including a core area of 498 sq km) and has bluebulls, sambars, spotted deer, wild boars and, of course, tigers. Project Tiger has been in charge of the sanctuary since 1979.

This park contains ruined temples as well as a fort and pavilions built by the maharaja of Alwar. The sanctuary can be visited year-round, although during July and August your chance of spotting wildlife is minimal, as the animals move to higher ground. The best time is between November and June. The last census was in 1996, and numbers of tigers were determined by pug marks (like fingerprints, each pug mark is different). According to the census, there are more than 24 tigers in the park. In the prior census (1995), the rusty spotted cat (*Poionailusrus rubiginosus*) was identified for the first time at Sariska. There are over 300 species of birds in the park.

You'll see most wildlife in the evening, though tiger sightings are becoming more common during the day. To spot a tiger you should plan on two or three safaris.

Wildlife Safaris

While it is possible to take private cars into the park, they are limited to sealed roads only, minimising the chances of spotting wildlife. The best way to visit the park is by jeep. Diesel/petrol jeeps cost Rs 500/600 per jeep, and can take up to five people. There's an entry fee of Rs 125 per jeep, and an additional park entry fee of Rs 20/100 for Indians/foreigners for three hours. Entry for Indians is free on Tuesday and Saturday (from 8 am to 3 pm), so try to avoid visiting on these days as the park can get crowded. A still camera is free but there's a video fee of Rs 200. Guides are available (Rs 50 per hour; maximum of five people).

Bookings can be made at the Forest Reception Office (☎ 41333) on Jaipur Rd (directly opposite the Hotel Sariska Palace) which is where buses will drop you. The park is open in winter (October to the end of February) from 7 am to 4 pm, and during the rest of the year from 6.30 am to 5 pm.

Places to Stay & Eat

Forest Rest House has a guesthouse next door to the Forest Reception Office. It has three double rooms, but bookings should be made in advance through the Chief Wildlife Warden, Van Bhawan (near Secretariat), Jaipur (☎ 0141-380278).

RTDC's Tiger Den Sariska (☎ 41342), nearby, has a nice garden area, but the rooms are a bit run-down and the service is variable. The cheapest option is the nine-bed dorm (Rs 50). Rooms with attached bath and air-cooling go for Rs 550/600 a single/double, air-con rooms are Rs 700/825 and a suite is Rs 950/1200. Several travellers advise that you should bring mosquito repellent or a net. There's a bar and restaurant; the veg/nonveg thali is Rs 65/85. Jeep hire can be arranged.

Hotel Sariska Palace (☎ 41322, fax 41323), which is over 100 years old, is located at the end of a long sweeping driveway directly opposite the Forest Reception Office. It's not a glitzy palace, rather a modest but comfortable and serene erstwhile royal hunting lodge, set on 37 hectares. The Aravalli Range affords a fine backdrop, and the grounds are traversed by the Ruparail River. It is possible to take short horse and camel rides around the grounds. The drawing room has an assortment of stuffed beasts, and the dining room is replete with antiques. There's a small lending library and Rajasthani dance programs at night. A bonfire is lit in winter.

Singles/doubles cost Rs 2000/3000, and suites are Rs 3750. Meals cost Rs 175 for breakfast and Rs 350 for lunch or dinner. Nonguests are welcome to dine here with

EASTERN RAJASTHAN

one hour's advance notice. Jeep hire can be organised.

Getting There & Away

Sariska is 35km from Alwar, which is a convenient town from which to approach the sanctuary. There are direct buses to Alwar from Delhi and Jaipur. Though some people attempt to visit Sariska on a day trip from Jaipur, this option is expensive and largely a waste of time. There are numerous buses between Sariska and both Alwar (1 hr, Rs 14) and Jaipur (3 hrs, Rs 48). Buses stop out the front of the Forest Reception Office.

AJMER

• pop 477,000   ☎ 0145

South-west of Jaipur is Ajmer, a burgeoning town on the shore of the Ana Sagar, flanked by barren hills. Situated in a valley, Ajmer is a major religious centre for Muslim pilgrims during the fast of Ramadan, and has some superb examples of early Muslim architecture. It is famous for the tomb of Khwaja Muin-ud-din Chishti, a venerated Sufi saint who founded the Chishtiya order, which still exists as the prime Sufi order in India today.

The British selected Ajmer as the site for Mayo College (see the boxed text in this section), a prestigious school opened in 1875 exclusively for Indian nobility. Today it is open to all boys (who can afford the fees). Other monuments which stand as reminders of Ajmer's colonial past are the Edward Memorial Hall, Ajmer Club and Jubilee Clock Tower.

The main streets of Ajmer are crammed with traffic, pedestrians and busy bazaars. One street sells nothing but silver items. But Ajmer doesn't really have the same rustic charm or panache as other Rajasthani towns and is more of a pilgrimage centre than a tourist destination. This is reflected in the dearth of good accommodation and eating places.

Although it does have some impressive architecture, an ancient fort (Taragarh) overlooking the town, and is an important religious centre, Ajmer is really just a stepping stone to nearby Pushkar for most travellers. If you are unable to find accommodation in Pushkar, which is often the case during the Camel Fair, Ajmer can make a convenient base – if all the hotels in Ajmer are booked out at this time, contact the tourist office (see Information, later in this section) to find out about paying guesthouse options.

History

The town of Ajmer has always had great strategic importance due to its secure position, protected by the Aravalli Range, and its location on the major trade route between Delhi and the ports of Gujarat. It was founded by Ajaipal Chauhan in the 7th century. He constructed a hill fort and named the place Ajaimeru, or invincible hill. Ajmer was ruled by the Chauhans until the late 12th century, when Prithviraj Chauhan lost it to Mohammed of Ghori. It became part of the sultanate in Delhi and remained so until 1326. After that Ajmer was continually fought over by surrounding states including the sultans of Delhi and Gujarat and the rulers of Mewar and Marwar.

Later in its history, Ajmer became a favourite residence of the great Mughals. One of the first contacts between the Mughals and the British occurred in Ajmer when Sir Thomas Roe met with Emperor Jehangir here in 1616.

The city was subsequently taken by the Scindias and, in 1818, was handed over to the British, becoming one of the few places in Rajasthan controlled directly by the British rather than being part of a princely state.

Orientation

The main bus stand is close to the RTDC's Hotel Khadim on the east side of town. The train station and most of the hotels are on the west side of town. North of the main post office is Naya Bazaar (known for its silver jewellery and tie-dye fabrics) and Agra Gate. Farther north is the large artificial lake Ana Sagar.

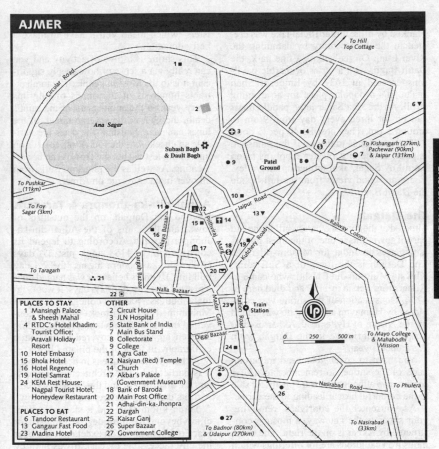

AJMER

Ana Sagar

Subash Bagh
& Dault Bagh

Patel
Ground

To Pushkar
(11km)

To Foy
Sagar (3km)

Circular Road

Naya Bazaar

Dargah Bazaar

To Taragarh

Prithviraj Marg

Jaipur Road

Railway Colony

Kutchery Road

Madar Gate

Station Road

Nalla Bazaar

Diggi Bazaar

Train
Station

To Hill
Top Cottage

To Kishangarh (27km),
Pachewar (90km)
& Jaipur (131km)

To Mayo College
& Mahabodhi
Mission

To Nasirabad
(33km)

Nasirabad Road

To Phulera

To Badnor (80km)
& Udaipur (270km)

0   250   500 m

PLACES TO STAY	OTHER
1 Mansingh Palace	2 Circuit House
& Sheesh Mahal	3 JLN Hospital
4 RTDC's Hotel Khadim;	5 State Bank of India
Tourist Office;	7 Main Bus Stand
Aravali Holiday	8 Collectorate
Resort	9 College
10 Hotel Embassy	11 Agra Gate
15 Bhola Hotel	12 Nasiyan (Red) Temple
16 Hotel Regency	14 Church
19 Hotel Samrat	17 Akbar's Palace
24 KEM Rest House;	(Government Museum)
Nagpal Tourist Hotel;	18 Bank of Baroda
Honeydew Restaurant	20 Main Post Office
	21 Adhai-din-ka-Jhonpra
PLACES TO EAT	22 Dargah
6 Tandoor Restaurant	25 Kaisar Ganj
13 Gangaur Fast Food	26 Super Bazaar
23 Madina Hotel	27 Government College

Information

Tourist Offices The main tourist office
(☎ 52426) is in the RTDC's Hotel Khadim
compound and is open Monday to Saturday
from 8 am to noon and 3 to 6 pm. There's
also a small tourist information counter at
the train station, open daily except Sunday
from 10 am to 5 pm.

Money You can change money at the State
Bank of India, opposite the Collectorate,
but they don't do cash advances on credit

cards. The Bank of Baroda on Prithviraj
Marg, opposite the main post office, does
issue cash advances on Visa and Master-
Card but only changes travellers cheques.

Post & Communications The main post
office is less than half a kilometre from the
train station. It is open daily except Sunday
from 10 am to 5 pm. There are numerous
telephone booths throughout the town, including one in the same grounds as the
tourist office.

Ana Sagar

Flanked by hills, this artificial lake was created in the 12th century by damming the River Luni. On its bank is a fine park, the **Dault Bagh**, with a series of marble pavilions erected in 1637 by Emperor Shah Jahan. It's a popular place for an evening stroll. At the Ana Sagar jetty, paddle boats can be for hired every day from 9 am to around 5 pm. They cost Rs 40 per ½ hour.

The lake tends to dry up if the monsoon is poor, so the city's water supply is taken from Foy Sagar, 3km farther up the valley. There are good views from the hill beside the Dault Bagh.

The Dargah

Situated at the foot of a barren hill in the old part of town, this is one of the most important places in India for Muslim pilgrims. The Dargah is the tomb of a Sufi saint, Khwaja Muin-ud-din Chishti, who came to Ajmer from Persia in 1192 and died here in 1236. Construction of the shrine was completed by Humayun and the gate was added by the Nizam of Hyderabad. Akbar used to make the pilgrimage to the Dargah from Agra once a year.

You have to cover your head in certain parts of the shrine, so remember to take a scarf or cap although there are plenty for sale at the colourful bazaar leading to the shrine.

As you enter the courtyard, removing your shoes at the gateway, a mosque constructed by Akbar is on the right. The enormous iron cauldrons are for offerings which are customarily shared by families involved in the shrine's upkeep. In an inner court there is another mosque built by Shah Jahan. Constructed of white marble, it has 11 arches and a Persian inscription running the full length of the building.

The saint's tomb is in the centre of the second court. It has a marble dome and the actual tomb inside is surrounded by a silver platform. The horseshoes nailed to the shrine doors are offerings from successful horse dealers! Beware of 'guides' hassling for donations around the Dargah using the standard fake donation books. Don't be bu!-

lied into signing any books or 'visitors registers' which mean you'll have to make a hefty donation.

This shrine is a hive of activity and you can really get a sense of how deeply significant it is to the Muslim people. The tomb attracts hundreds of thousands of pilgrims every year on the anniversary of the saint's death, the Urs, in the seventh month of the lunar calendar, Jyaistha (the dates are variable so check with the tourist office). It's an interesting festival but the crowds can be suffocating. As well as the pilgrims, Sufis from all over India converge on Ajmer.

Adhai-din-ka-Jhonpra & Taragarh

Beyond the Dargah, on the outskirts of town, are the ruins of the Adhai-din-ka-Jhonpra mosque. According to legend its construction, in 1153, took just 2½ days (Adhai-din-ka-Jhonpra means 'the 2½ day building'). Others believe it was named after a festival that lasted for 2½ days. It was originally built as a Sanskrit college, but in 1198 Mohammed of Ghori took Ajmer and converted the building into a mosque by adding a seven arched wall covered with Islamic calligraphy in front of the pillared hall.

Although the mosque is in need of repair, it is particularly fine architecture. The pillars are all different and the arched 'screen', with its damaged minarets, is noteworthy.

Three kilometres and a steep 1½ hour climb beyond the mosque, the Taragarh, or Star Fort, commands an excellent view over the city (accessible by car). It was built by Ajaipal Chauhan, the town's founder. The fort was the site of much military activity during Mughal times and was later used as a sanatorium by the British.

Akbar's Palace (Government Museum)

Back in the city, not far from the main post office, this imposing building was constructed by Akbar in 1570 and today houses the Government Museum. Exhibits in the limited collection include old weapons, miniature paintings, ancient rock inscriptions and stone sculptures which date back to the

8th century AD. It is open daily except Friday from 10 am to 4.30 pm. Entry is Rs 3 (free on Monday). A camera costs Rs 5/10 for Indians/foreigners and a video is Rs 10/20.

Nasiyan (Red) Temple

The Red Temple on Prithviraj Marg is a Jain temple built in 1865. Its double storey hall contains a series of large, gilt wooden figures from Jain mythology which depict the Jain concept of the ancient world. The hall is decorated with gold, silver and precious stones. It's unlike any other temple in Rajasthan and is worth a visit. The temple is open daily from 8.30 am to 4.30 pm and entry costs Rs 3.

Mayo College

The very first pupil to attend Ajmer's Mayo College was the maharaja of Alwar, who arrived in grand style in 1875 on an elephant, accompanied by a formidable entourage of servants, trumpeters, horses, camels and other elaborate trimmings. This prestigious primary and secondary school was founded by Lord Mayo, a viceroy of India, and was open only to the sons of Indian aristocracy. The school premises were certainly fit for a king, with well-maintained gardens

SANJAY SINGH BADNOR

EASTERN RAJASTHAN

and beautiful buildings. Some princes even had their own lavish house built on the extensive school compound, named after the state ruled by their family.

The Mayo coat of arms was designed by Rudyard Kipling's father and this 'Eton of the East' was based on the English public school system. At Mayo, the young Indian princes were groomed to be proper gentlemen, and possibly continue to Oxford or Cambridge universities. These elite English institutions have been paramount in educating the sons of nobility and continue to be so today.

However, for many of the princes academic results were not high on their list of priorities. Education was simply considered a fashionable accessory for their future role as king.

In the past, royalty did not have to work as they derived their wealth from the taxation of land. Many royal families had other sources of revenue too. This all changed after Independence in 1947, when the princes merged their states with the Indian Union.

Today Mayo College is no longer exclusively for the sons of kings. It has opened its gates to boys from all walks of life (if, of course, their parents can afford the school fees). Mayo is one of India's leading educational institutions and is geared towards academic excellence. After graduating from Mayo, most students pursue tertiary studies and enter a range of vocations from medicine to commerce.

The school has retained its old-world charm and still takes great pride in its illustrious history. Even though British rule ended in India over five decades ago, a flavour of the British Raj still lingers at Mayo. The walls proudly display austere portraits of former English headmasters and British lords once on the school's governing council.

EASTERN RAJASTHAN

Places to Stay

Most of Ajmer's budget hotels are typical Indian boarding houses of similar standard. They offer basic essentials and are OK for a night, but those in Pushkar are far preferable. Many of the hotels cater to the large number of Muslim pilgrims that visit Ajmer each year. When leaving the train station you'll probably be accosted by cycle and auto-rickshaw drivers all keen to take you 'anywhere' for Rs 10 or less – unfortunately 'anywhere' usually means to a hotel where they get commission.

A good and often cheaper alternative to hotels are the homes participating in Ajmer's Paying Guest House Scheme, which give you the interesting opportunity to live with an Indian family. Rates range from around Rs 50 to Rs 800 per night depending on the facilities provided. The tourist office (see Information earlier) has details about these paying guesthouses.

Hill Top Cottage (☎ 623984, 164 Shastri Nagar), behind the shopping center, is definitely one of the most homey places to stay in Ajmer. Far removed from the crowds and dust, it's not a cottage as the name suggests, but a family-run house on an elevated site. The rooftop sports panoramic views. Clean singles/doubles/triples with attached bath go for Rs 400/500/600. There are also cheaper, but smaller, rooms for Rs 300/400. Breakfast is Rs 30 and a veg lunch or dinner is Rs 50.

Hotel Regency (☎ 620296), close to the Dargah, is a good choice in a town starved of hotel talent. Single/double rooms with attached bath cost Rs 380/400, or Rs 670/690 with air-con. There's a good veg restaurant (see Places to Eat).

Hotel Embassy (☎ 623859, Jaipur Rd) is a fairly new property with nice singles/doubles for Rs 500/800. A restaurant was in the pipeline at the time of writing.

King Edward Memorial Rest House (☎ 429936, Station Rd), known locally as 'KEM', is to the left as you exit the train station. Don't let the grand name fool you. This place is run-down and has lax service. Very few travellers seem to stay here.

Rooms with bath range from Rs 65 for a basic '2nd class' single to Rs 100/150 for '1st class' singles/doubles, and Rs 125/200 for deluxe rooms.

Nagpal Tourist Hotel (☎ 429503), nearby, is a far more salubrious option. The cheapest singles with bath are small but OK and cost Rs 175. Doubles go from Rs 300 to Rs 1200 for a better air-con room. Although this hotel is more expensive than the King Edward Memorial Rest House, it's leaps and bounds better. Go next door to the Honeydew Restaurant for a feed.

Bhola Hotel (☎ 432844), opposite the church near Agra Gate, has no-frills singles/doubles for Rs 125/175 with private bath. Self-service buckets of hot water are available (no charge). There's a good vegetarian restaurant here (see Places to Eat).

RTDC's Hotel Khadim (☎ 52490) is not far from the bus stand. There's a range of nondescript rooms with private bath priced from Rs 320/500 to Rs 670/850. Dorm beds are available for Rs 50. A veg thali in the restaurant is Rs 45.

Aravali Holiday Resort (☎ 52089), next door, is more homey with just eight simple rooms; a single/double with attached bath (bucket hot water) costs Rs 150/200. No meals are available.

Hotel Samrat (☎ 621257, Kutchery Rd) is just a few minutes walk from the train station. The rooms are small and a bit musty, but it's very convenient for early morning departures with the private bus companies, as many have their offices nearby. Singles/doubles with bath (some with Indian-style toilets) cost Rs 180/300, or Rs 700/1000 with air-con. Some rooms can cop a lot of traffic noise so ask for a quiet room at the back. Only room service meals are available.

The *Mansingh Palace* (☎ 425702, fax 425858, Circular Rd), overlooking Ana Sagar, is the only top end hotel in Ajmer – and it capitalises on this by charging high rates. Rooms are comfortable enough, but not crash hot value at Rs 1995/3000 a single/double, or Rs 4500 for a suite. There's also a bar and restaurant (see Places to Eat).

Places to Eat

Ajmer has a paucity of decent independent restaurants, probably because the town attracts relatively few tourists.

Bhola Hotel, located at the top of a seedy staircase, has a good and reasonably priced vegetarian restaurant. There are delicious thalis for Rs 35, and a range of other dishes such as paneer kofta (Rs 40).

Honeydew Restaurant, next door to the KEM Rest House, offers Indian, Chinese and continental veg and nonveg fare. There's also a variety of fast food such as hot dogs (Rs 18), pizzas (around Rs 40), chocolate milkshakes (Rs 22), and for the adventurous, brain pakoras (Rs 40). A favourite with travellers is the banana lassi (Rs 20). There's seating indoors and out.

Gangaur Fast Food off Kutchery Rd, serves the usual selection of fast food including pizzas (about Rs 45) and ice cream sodas (around Rs 35). There are also south Indian specialities such as butter masala dosa (Rs 25), and some Chinese dishes.

Tandoor Restaurant (Jaipur Rd) is a little out of town and slightly expensive but the food is good. It offers a wide selection of dishes; a tandoori chicken costs Rs 90 and a masala dosa is Rs 15. There's seating indoors and out.

Hotel Regency, near the Dargah, serves vegetarian Indian, Chinese and some continental food in its pleasant restaurant. Menu items include soups (around Rs 20), veg sizzlers (Rs 78) and kaju curry (Rs 48). If you feel like drinkies after a visit to the Dargah, there's a tiny bar at this hotel where you can knock back a beer (Rs 75 a bottle).

Madina Hotel is handy if you're waiting for a train (the station is directly opposite). This very simple eatery cooks up cheap fare, specialising in mutton korma, chicken mughlai and rumali roti.

Sheesh Mahal, at the Mansingh Palace hotel, is the top restaurant in town. Pricey Indian, continental and Chinese dishes are on offer. Menu includes veg sizzlers (Rs 140), chicken tikka masala (Rs 160) and pudina paneer (Rs 95). Desserts hover around Rs 60.

Getting There & Away

Bus The inquiry number for Roadways is ☎ 429398. There are buses from Jaipur to Ajmer every 30 minutes, some nonstop (131km, 2½ hrs, Rs 52). From Delhi, there are state transport buses which run daily in either direction (9 hrs, Rs 152).

Buses leave every few minutes throughout the day for Pushkar (½ hr, Rs 5). The trip usually takes a bit longer during the fair, when roads can become congested.

State transport buses also go to:

destination	distance (km)	cost (Rs)
Abu Road	356	137
Ahmedabad	536	185
Alwar	280	108
Bharatpur	305	122
Bhopal	560	204
Bikaner	277	108
Bundi	165	65
Chittorgarh	191	72
Indore	514	189
Jodhpur	210	80
Kota	200	62
Nagaur	165	65
Ranakpur	237	100
Sawai Madhopur	230	65
Sikar	191	65
Udaipur	303	132

In addition, buses leave for Agra (385km, Rs 140.50) and for Jaisalmer (490km, Rs 175).

Also, there are private buses to Ahmedabad, Udaipur, Jodhpur, Jaipur, Mt Abu, Jaisalmer, Bikaner, Delhi and Mumbai. Most of the companies have offices on Kutchery Rd. If you book your ticket to one of these destinations through an agency in Pushkar, they should provide a free jeep transfer to Ajmer to start your journey.

Train The inquiry number for the railway is ☎ 131. Ajmer is on the Delhi-Jaipur-Marwar-Ahmedabad-Mumbai line and most trains stop at Ajmer. The 135km journey from Jaipur costs Rs 40 in 2nd class.

To Udaipur, there's a fast express (7½ hrs, Rs 370/564 in 2nd/1st class). The comfortable *Shatabdi Express* travels daily, except Sunday, between Ajmer and Delhi

(Rs 580/1125 in ordinary/executive class) via Jaipur (Rs 290/555). Refreshments and meals are included in the ticket price. The train leaves Delhi at 6.15 am and arrives in Ajmer at 12.40 pm. Going in the other direction, the train leaves Ajmer at 3.30 pm and arrives in Delhi at 10.15 pm.

The *Jaipur-Bandra Express* travels between Ajmer and Mumbai (Rs 245).

Getting Around

There are plenty of auto-rickshaws, some cycle-rickshaws and tongas. To travel anywhere in town by auto-rickshaw should cost you around Rs 15.

AROUND AJMER
Kishangarh

Kishangarh is 27km north-east from Ajmer and was founded in the early 17th century by Kishan Singh, a Rathore prince. Since the 18th century, Kishangarh has had one of India's most famous schools of miniature painting. Among its renowned paintings is that of Krishna's consort, Radha, depicted as a beautiful woman with enchanting almond-shaped eyes. Today local artists are trying to revive this magnificent school of painting by making copies of the originals on various surfaces such as wood, stone and cloth. The original paintings were done on paper.

Kishangarh town is divided into the old city which still has an old-world charm, and the new city which is mainly commercial. Pollution is steadily increasing along with the growing number of marble factories and textile mills.

Places to Stay *Roopangarh Fort (☎ 01 497-20217, fax 42001)* or Delhi *(☎ 011-6220031, fax 6220032)*, about 25km out of town, has been converted into an evocative hotel by the maharaja and maharani of Kishangarh. Roopangarh was the capital of this province for about 100 years and was never conquered despite being repeatedly attacked by neighbouring states. The fort was founded in 1653 by Maharaja Roop Singh, the fifth ruler of Kishangarh. He was inspired to make this site his capital after

watching a mother sheep gallantly protect her lambs from a pack of hungry wolves. The road to the fort passes through an interesting village where you get a glimpse of everyday life as it was long ago. The hotel can arrange village tours, bird-watching and camel, horse or jeep safaris.

The tariff for smaller rooms is Rs 750, while bigger rooms cost Rs 1190/1575, or Rs 2500 for a suite. All rooms have a character of their own, such as Room No 7 which has an awesome bed. Go up to the rooftop to soak up the sunset.

Phool Mahal Palace, in town, should now be up and running as an upmarket hotel. Contact Roopangarh Fort for details.

Getting There & Away There are frequently run daily buses between Ajmer and Kishangarh (Rs 11).

Pachewar

This little village, about 90km north-east of Ajmer, can be a handy stopover between Ajmer and Jaipur/Sawai Madhopur. There's a lake in the village which attracts migratory birds in the winter.

Pachewar Garh (☎ 01437-28756) or Jaipur *(☎/fax 0141-601007)* is not as flash as many of Rajasthan's other fort-hotels, but is still comfortable enough. Singles/doubles with attached bath cost Rs 650/800. The set breakfast/lunch/dinner is Rs 120/180/220. The hotel can arrange jeep safaris; a half-day safari is Rs 250 per person (minimum six people).

Badnor

About 80km south-west of Ajmer is Badnor, best known for its imposing fort which is more than 500 years old. Badnor is a small fortified town surrounded by 10 lakes that fill during the monsoon. Badnor's historic fort was home to a former feudal family until 1962. Today it belongs to the government and is poorly maintained. This sleepy little town, off the beaten track, is a good place to visit if you want to see a small rural community that encounters very few tourists and is virtually untouched by modernisation.

Lunch can be organised (minimum of 10 people; advance bookings essential) at the Jal Mahal, a lakeside property belonging to the thakur of Badnor; the cost is Rs 250 per person. To arrange a visit to the fort, or lunch, contact the thakur of Badnor who resides in Ajmer (☎ 0145-52579).

PUSHKAR
- **pop 13,000**   ☎ **0145**

Pushkar is a very important pilgrimage centre and devout Hindus should visit it at least once in their lifetime. The town attracts a large number of *sadhus* (individuals on a spiritual search) who mainly congregate around the lake and temples. Unfortunately, after a poor monsoon the lake doesn't fill up. This is a pity, as it is a big factor in the town's appeal and is of great religious importance. Situated right on the edge of the desert, Pushkar is only 11km north-west of Ajmer but separated from it by Nag Pahar, the Snake Mountain.

Pushkar has become a major tourist hotbed. Many travellers who visit the place fall so deeply in love with it that they stay much longer than anticipated. Despite having a distinctly tourist and commercial ambience these days, Pushkar still has a certain appeal – although many travellers who find it too much of a scene have skipped it in favour of more mellow destinations.

Pushkar is world famous for its spectacular Camel Fair which takes place here in the Hindu lunar month of Kartika (see the boxed text Camel Fair for exact dates). If you're anywhere within striking distance at the time, it's an event not to be missed.

During this period, the town is jampacked with tribal people from all over Rajasthan, pilgrims from all over India and film-makers and tourists from all over the world. And of course there are plenty of camels and other livestock (it's best to arrive a few days before the official commencement date to see the most livestock).

Being a holy place, alcohol, meat and even eggs are banned. Even though drugs are prohibited, bhang lassis are served at some restaurants in Pushkar – see the boxed text Bhang Lassi Warning! in the Drinks section of the Facts for the Visitor chapter.

It is unknown how old Pushkar actually is. According to legend, the sacred lake of Pushkar sprang up at the spot where Brahma dropped a lotus flower from the sky. Brahma, Lord of Creation, wanted to perform a *yagna*, or holy sacrifice, at the lake on a full moon night. Since his wife, Savitri, did not attend, he impetuously married another woman named Gayatri. Savitri felt terribly betrayed when she found out and bitterly vowed that Brahma would not be worshipped anywhere other than in Pushkar. Since then, this Brahma temple at Pushkar has remained one of the only ones in the world dedicated to Brahma and allegedly the only one in India. On two hills near Pushkar Lake are temples, one dedicated to Savitri and the other to Gayatri.

Orientation
The desert town clings to the side of the small but beautiful Pushkar Lake with its many bathing ghats and temples. Pushkar town is a maze of narrow streets filled with interesting little shops, food stalls, hotels and temples. Fortunately there's virtually no traffic in the main bazaar, making it a pleasurable place to explore at leisure. The town is very tourist friendly and most people speak some English, so you should have no problem finding your way around.

Information
There is no tourist office in Pushkar, but there are lots of travel agents (although the service at some can be downright unenthusiastic) and it's easy to find your way around. The helpful owner of the Hotel Venus (see Places to Stay) is happy to point tourists in the right direction.

Money The State Bank of Bikaner & Jaipur only changes travellers cheques (not currency) – you may also find the wait irritatingly long and the staff brusque. Currency (and travellers cheques) can be changed at the moneychangers scattered along Sadar Bazaar Rd.

EASTERN RAJASTHAN

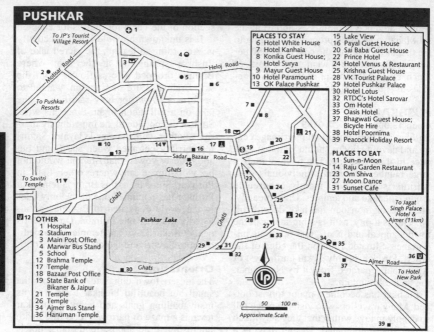

PUSHKAR

PLACES TO STAY
6 Hotel White House
7 Hotel Kanhaia
8 Konika Guest House;
    Hotel Surya
9 Mayur Guest House
10 Hotel Paramount
13 OK Palace Pushkar
15 Lake View
16 Payal Guest House
20 Sai Baba Guest House
22 Prince Hotel
24 Hotel Venus & Restaurant
25 Krishna Guest House
28 VK Tourist Palace
29 Hotel Pushkar Palace
30 Hotel Lotus
32 RTDC's Hotel Sarovar
33 Om Hotel
35 Oasis Hotel
37 Bhagwati Guest House;
    Bicycle Hire
38 Hotel Poornima
39 Peacock Holiday Resort

PLACES TO EAT
11 Sun-n-Moon
14 Raju Garden Restaurant
23 Om Shiva
27 Moon Dance
31 Sunset Cafe

OTHER
1 Hospital
2 Stadium
3 Main Post Office
4 Marwar Bus Stand
5 School
12 Brahma Temple
17 Temple
18 Bazaar Post Office
19 State Bank of
    Bikaner & Jaipur
21 Temple
26 Temple
34 Ajmer Bus Stand
36 Hanuman Temple

Pushkar Lake

To JP's Tourist Village Resort
To Pushkar Resorts
To Savitri Temple
Heloj Road
Matsar Road
Sadar Bazaar Road
Ghats
Ajmer Road
To Jagat Singh Palace Hotel & Ajmer (11km)
To Hotel New Park

0   50   100 m
Approximate Scale

Post The main post office is just south of the hospital. There's also a more convenient smaller post office in the main bazaar (it only sells stamps). Both places are open Monday to Saturday from 10 am to 4 pm.

Email & Internet Access On Sadar Bazaar Rd, there are a number of places offering Internet access. The usual charge is around Rs 35 for 10 minutes to surf the Net, or Rs 200 per hour. To send an email costs upwards of Rs 3 per minute.

Temples
Pushkar boasts temples, though few are as ancient as you might expect at such an important pilgrimage site, since many were destroyed by Aurangzeb in the 17th century and subsequently rebuilt. The most famous is the **Brahma Temple**. It's marked by a red spire, and over the entrance gateway is the

hans, or goose symbol, of Brahma, who is said to have personally chosen Pushkar as the temple's site.

The one hour trek up to the hilltop **Savitri Temple** overlooking the lake is best made early in the morning; the view is magnificent.

Ghats
Numerous ghats run down to the lake and pilgrims are constantly bathing in the lake's holy waters. If you wish to join them, do it with respect – remove your shoes, don't smoke, refrain from kidding around and don't take photographs.

Camel Safaris
There are quite a few people in Pushkar who offer camel rides and safaris. It's best to ask your hotel, a travel agent, or other travellers to recommend somebody who organises good safaris. The usual price is

Camel Fair

The exact date on which the Camel Fair is held depends on the lunar calendar but, in Hindu chronology, it falls on the full moon of Kartik Purnima, when devotees cleanse away their sins by bathing in the holy lake. Each year, up to 200,000 people flock to Pushkar for the Camel Fair, bringing with them some 50,000 camels and cattle for several days of pilgrimage, livestock trading, horse dealing and spirited festivities. There are camel races, street theatre and a variety of stalls selling handicrafts. The place becomes a flurry of activity with musicians, mystics, comedians, tourists, traders, animals and devotees all converging on the small town. It's truly a feast for the eyes, so don't forget to bring your camera. This fair is the only one of its kind on the planet and has featured in numerous magazines, travel shows and films.

It's strongly recommended that you get to the fair several days *prior* to the official commencement date, to see the camel and cattle trading at its peak. For some reason, the number of camels significantly declines from the official commencement date!

Although Pushkar is transformed into a carnival, the Camel Fair is taken very seriously by livestock owners, who come from all over the country with the sole intent of trading. A good camel can fetch tens of thousands of rupees and is a vital source of income for many villagers.

Be warned that it can get noisy at night (and in the early morning when loud devotional music is often played), so if you're a light sleeper, bring along earplugs. Carry appropriate allergy medication if you are affected by dust and/or animal hair. Keep your valuables in a safe place – a moneybelt worn under the clothes is recommended.

Dates of the fair in forthcoming years are as follows:

2000	9 to 11 November
2001	27 to 30 November
2002	16 to 19 November
2003	5 to 8 November

about Rs 50 per hour or Rs 300 per day, but you may be able to bargain these down. Most organisers are happy to tailor-make a safari and have good suggestions about places of interest in and around Pushkar. Camel safaris are a splendid way of taking in the sights and experiencing the rugged beauty of the desert. If it's your first time on a camel, take it easy and avoid galloping!

Places to Stay

The bulk of Pushkar's budget hotels are nothing fancy (many budget places are spartan and have Indian-style toilets), but they're generally clean and freshly white-washed. You should ask to see a few rooms before deciding on one, as many have a cell-like atmosphere due to the small or nonexistent windows.

Although the town is dominated by budget hotels, there are several upmarket accommodation options. But be warned that during the Camel Fair when demand for rooms is high, most hotels have ridiculously inflated prices. Unfortunately there isn't much you can do about this, as it's usually a case of get what you can before it's all gone.

With thousands of tourists visiting each year, Pushkar has been exposed to the 'wicked ways of the west' and many hotels display prominent warning signs such as: 'In Pushkar, holding hands or kissing in public are not permitted'; 'Ladies and men should dress appropriately'; 'Drugs, alcohol and meat are not permitted'.

Hotel Pushkar Palace (☎ *72001, fax 72226)*, near the lake, is an old favourite with travellers and a nice place to stay. Once belonging to the maharaja of Kishangarh, these days it's a fairly upmarket hotel that also has some budget rooms at Rs 150/200 with common bath. These rooms are tiny and a little dark but right by the lake. Smart rooms with air-cooling, attached bath and hot water cost Rs 550/600, or Rs 1100/1195. There's a pleasant outdoor sitting area overlooking the lake and a very good, though slightly pricey, restaurant (see Places to Eat).

EASTERN RAJASTHAN

Pushkar Passports

You can recognise travellers who've been to the ghats in Pushkar by the red ribbons (the 'Pushkar Passport') tied around their wrists. Getting one can be an expensive procedure if you allow yourself to be bullied into a more generous donation than you wanted to give. Priests, some genuine, some not, will approach you near the ghats and offer to do a puja. At some point during the prayers they'll ask you to tell Brahma how much you're going to give him, Rs 100 to Rs 400 being the suggested figure (although some travellers have even been asked for US dollars!). Don't fall for this emotional blackmail – if you want to give just Rs 10, that's fine, although some 'priests' may tell you it doesn't even cover the cost of their 'materials'. It's best to say in advance how much you will give. Many visitors cop an ear full of abuse if they do not shell out the cash demanded – keep your cool and don't let the pushy priest ruin your visit to the lake. Some travellers put on a red ribbon prior to visiting the lake to avoid being approached by a priest altogether.

A current scam involves 'priests' offering travellers a flower, or petals. Once you take this, you are asked to throw it into the holy lake – for a pretty price! It is best to firmly refuse any flowers that may be offered.

Obviously there are still some genuine, friendly priests in Pushkar, but unfortunately more and more travellers are reporting problems with the 'other half'. If you feel strongly about it, try lodging a written complaint with the tourist office in nearby Ajmer.

RTDC's Hotel Sarovar (☎ 72040) is set in its own spacious grounds at the far eastern end of the lake and with a restaurant, next to the Hotel Pushkar Palace, but approached from a different entrance. It's better value than the RTDC hotel in Ajmer, although some travellers have complained about the cleanliness and service here. Ordinary singles/doubles cost Rs 125/200 with common bath, or Rs 250/300 with attached bath. Air-cooled deluxe rooms are Rs 300/350, and the best rooms overlooking the lake cost Rs 325/500. There are also dorm beds for Rs 50.

VK Tourist Palace (☎ 72174), in the same area, is a popular cheapie with reasonable rooms from Rs 75/150 with common bath, or Rs 150/250 with attached bath. There's also a good rooftop restaurant.

Hotel Venus (☎ 72323), nearby, is run by Himmat Singh who will enthusiastically answer any questions you may have about Pushkar. The hotel has singles/doubles with attached bath for Rs 100/150. There's a popular restaurant upstairs (see Places to Eat).

Krishna Guest House (☎ 72091), also in this area, has bare but cheap rooms with common bath for Rs 80/100, or Rs 100/150 with private bath. Meals are available.

The **Om Hotel** (☎ 72672), nearby, is not a bad choice. Singles/doubles with common bath are Rs 50/100, and doubles with bath are Rs 200.

Payal Guest House (☎ 72163) is a laidback place right in the middle of the main bazaar, complete with its own resident rabbit. It has decent singles/doubles starting from Rs 50/100 with common bath, or Rs 100/150 with attached bath. There's a cool, banana tree shaded courtyard and this place is more like a home than a hotel. Meals are available and there's even a small bakery.

Lake View (☎ 72106), across the street, does have some rooms with good views of the lake. Doubles with common bath are Rs 100, or Rs 150 with private bath.

Hotel Paramount (☎ 72428) is nearby and has excellent views over the lake. Double rooms cost Rs 100 with common bath. The best rooms here are Nos 106, 108, 109 and 111, each with a small balcony and an attached bath (around Rs 450).

Hotel White House (☎ 72147), north of the lake, is run by a Brahmin family and is a popular choice with travellers. Clean singles/doubles with common bath cost Rs 80/150, or Rs 200/300 with attached bath.

There are good views from the rooftop restaurant, which serves a wide variety of reasonably priced Indian and continental food. Their mango tea is refreshing.

Hotel Poornima (☎ 72254), near the Ajmer bus stand, has rooms with attached bath for Rs 60/100.

Bhagwati Guest House (☎ 72423) is an option if you're going through a cash crunch. Small but acceptable rooms with common bath go for just Rs 40/60. Larger doubles with attached bath range from Rs 80 to Rs 125. The owner, Chandu, is a friendly guy. There's also a good restaurant with stuff like cheeseburgers (Rs 40), banana pancakes (Rs 25) and pizzas (Rs 45).

Oasis Hotel (☎ 72100) is across the road, with comfortable singles/doubles with attached bath for Rs 125/150 and air-con rooms for Rs 650/750. There's a restaurant, swimming pool and the rooftop terrace is popular for sunbaking (don't forget to slap on the sunscreen).

Peacock Holiday Resort (☎ 72093, fax 72516), on the outskirts of town, is in a pleasant setting but gets mixed reports from travellers. There's a shady courtyard and swimming pool with a slide. Standard singles/doubles cost Rs 300/450.

Hotel New Park (☎ 72464, fax 72244), nearby, is better value for money. It is surrounded by tranquil flower gardens and wheat fields, and has its own swimming pool and restaurant. Clean singles/doubles with attached bath range from Rs 100/150 to Rs 650/750.

Prince Hotel (☎ 72674), closer to the lake, has a small courtyard and very basic singles/doubles for Rs 50/80 with common bath. Double rooms with attached bath go for Rs 100.

Sai Baba Guest House, in the same area, is a possibility if you're low on rupees. Simple and somewhat gloomy rooms with common bath cost a mere Rs 40/70 a single/double.

Konika Guest House, not far away, has five clean doubles with private bath from Rs 100. The *Hotel Surya*, next door, is similar in price and standard.

Hotel Kanhaia (☎ 72146) is a fine choice, with clean doubles without/with private bath for Rs 100/200. Meals are available.

Mayur Guest House (☎ 72302) has rooms with common bath for Rs 40/60 and rooms with bath for Rs 80/100. Only breakfast is available.

OK Palace Pushkar (☎ 72868) offers singles/doubles with common bath for a low Rs 40/80, or doubles with bath for Rs 100. The *Hotel Lotus* (☎ 72824), in a quiet location on the south side of the lake, is another cheapie, but very basic.

Jagat Singh Palace Hotel (☎ 72953, fax 72952), a little out of the main town area, is terrific if you like your creature comforts. Designed like a fort it has well furnished singles/doubles for around Rs 1500/1700. There's a large garden area and a restaurant. A pool is planned.

Pushkar Resorts (☎ 72017, fax 72946, email pushkar@pushkarresorts.com), about 5km out of town, is also suitably luxurious. There are 40 modern cottages which are certainly clean and comfortable, although a little lacking in character. All have air-con and TV and cost Rs 1695/1995 a single/double. There's a dining hall (residents only), a swimming pool, billiard table and two telescopes for stargazing. Camel cart picnics and camel/jeep safaris can be organised.

JP's Tourist Village Resort (☎ 72067, fax 72026) is about 2km from the centre of town and has comfortable doubles from Rs 400 to Rs 750. For those who want to relive their childhood, treehouse accommodation is available for Rs 150 per person. There's also a restaurant and swimming pool.

Tourist Village During the Camel Fair, the RTDC and many private operators set up a sea of tents near the *mela* (fair) ground. It can get cold at night, so bring something warm to wear. A torch (flashlight) may also be useful. Demand for tents is high so you're strongly urged to book well ahead.

Royal Tents, owned by the maharaja of Jodhpur, seem to be the most luxurious tents available in Pushkar, but you'll pay for

EASTERN RAJASTHAN

this privilege. They cost US$175/225 a single/double with private bathroom (bucket hot water), including all meals. Reservations should be made in advance at the Umaid Bhawan Palace in Jodhpur (☎ 0291-433316, fax 635373).

Royal Desert Camp, farther away from the fairground, is another good option, with tents for US$90/100 with private bath (which even have showers). There are also some cheaper tents with shared bathroom. The price includes all meals and a 'camel shuttle service' to and from the fair. Book well ahead through the Hotel Pushkar Palace in Pushkar (☎ 72001, fax 72226).

RTDC's Tourist Village (☎ 72074) has dormitory tents for US$7 per person, and standard tents with singles/doubles and common bath for US$69/84, including all meals. There are also more upmarket tents with attached bath for US$105/119 and deluxe huts for US$119/132, including meals. These huts are open all year round, and are available for just Rs 250/350 when the fair is not on. To make a booking, contact the General Manager, Central Reservations, RTDC's Hotel Swagatam Campus, Near Railway Station, Jaipur, 302006, Rajasthan (☎ 0141-202586, fax 201045). Full payment must be received 45 days in advance to be sure of accommodation.

Places to Eat

Pushkar is one of those towns in which everyone has a favourite restaurant, and there's plenty to choose from. There are quite a few rooftop and garden restaurants which are ideal for a leisurely meal. Strict vegetarianism that forbids even eggs rather limits the range of ingredients that can be used, but the cooks make up for this with imagination. You can even get an eggless omelette in some places!

Buffet meals are popular, with many places offering all-you-can-eat meals for Rs 25 to Rs 40. It's safest to eat buffet meals at the busiest places where the food is more likely to be freshly cooked for each meal, rather than reheated. German bakeries seem to be the latest rage around town.

Hotel Pushkar Palace (see Places to Stay) is a pleasant place to dine, and you can eat in the restaurant or out in the relaxing garden. There's a buffet (Rs 100) or you can opt for à la carte; palak paneer is Rs 60, cheese naan is Rs 30 and mango lassi is Rs 25. There's also a small bakery on the premises; a croissant costs Rs 10 and there are various cakes for around Rs 30 per slice.

Sunset Cafe, nearby, has long been a popular hang-out with travellers – a good place to swap stories about Goa, Kathmandu and beyond. This simple cafe offers the usual have-a-go-at-anything menu, which includes dosas (Rs 20) and sizzlers (from Rs 50 to Rs 75). There's a German bakery; the lemon cake is pretty good (Rs 20 per slice). The location by the lake shore is delightful, especially at sunset, but the service can be sluggish.

Om Shiva, near the State Bank of Bikaner & Jaipur, on the north-east side of the lake, is below par when it comes to service, but they cook up quite a tasty buffet for lunch and dinner (Rs 40 each).

VK Tourist Palace (see Places to Stay) has a rooftop restaurant which offers a good buffet for Rs 40.

Venus Restaurant, at the Hotel Venus, is a great place to just kick back and watch the world go by. It whips up reasonably good Indian, Chinese, Italian and continental food. A veg thali costs Rs 30 and a banana lassi is Rs 10. They also squeeze refreshing fruit juices for around Rs 12.

Moon Dance is a laid-back garden retreat which serves a wide range of food, including good Indian, Mexican, Italian and even Thai dishes. A spinach mushroom enchilada is Rs 45, as is a Kashmiri burger, and a cup of cinnamon tea is Rs 5. There's also a German bakery.

Raju Garden Restaurant offers a mishmash of western, Chinese and Indian fare. The prices are a little high, but the selection is good. If your tummy is screaming for something simple, try the baked potatoes (Rs 45). Birthday cakes can be ordered here (with advance notice); they range from a meek Rs 65 to a mind-blowing Rs 1000!

Sun-n-Moon, not far from the Brahma Temple, has tables around a bo tree, and there's a soothing calm about this place. It offers a variety of western and Indian food such as Kashmiri burgers (Rs 45), veg pizzas (Rs 45), and tantalising roasted banana with chocolate and honey (Rs 40).

Shopping
Pushkar has cashed in on the droves of tourists that come here. There's something to suit all tastes and pockets, though you'll have to haggle over prices. The shopkeepers are used to tourists who accept the first price, so there's the usual nonsense about 'last price' quotes which aren't negotiable. Take time and visit a few shops.

There is a wide selection of handicraft places throughout the main bazaar and it's hard to resist buying something. Pushkar is not a bad place to pick up gifts for family and friends back home.

A lot of what is stocked here actually comes from the Barmer district south of Jaisalmer and other tribal areas of Rajasthan. There are scores of silver shops and a number of places where you can choose your own beads and get them strung on a leather strap into a bracelet or necklace. It's also good for embroidered fabrics such as wall hangings, bed covers, cute cushion covers, scarves and groovy shoulder bags.

In between are the inevitable clothing shops, many catering to styles which were in vogue in Goa and Nepal at the end of the 1960s. You may find occasional timeless items, but most of it is pretty clichéd.

The music shops, on the other hand, are well worth a visit if you're interested in picking up some examples of traditional, contemporary or fusion music.

There are a number of bookshops in the main bazaar selling an excellent range of second-hand novels in various languages, and they'll buy them back for 50% of what you pay.

Getting There & Away
Frequent buses leave Ajmer for Pushkar (Rs 5; only Rs 4 when going *from* Pushkar *to*

Ajmer because of the road toll – for private cars the toll is Rs 25). It's a spectacular climb up and over the hills and you never know quite what to expect around each turn.

There are a number of travel agencies in Pushkar offering tickets for private buses to various destinations – shop around for the best price. Most of these buses leave from Ajmer, but the agencies should provide you with free transport to Ajmer in time for the departures. See the Ajmer section for destinations. Some travel agencies will also book rail tickets for services leaving from Ajmer, for an additional booking fee (usually around Rs 50), which saves you the hassle of going down to the Ajmer station.

Getting Around
Fortunately, there are no auto-rickshaws in the town centre – it's a breeze to get around by foot. Bicycle is a great way to buzz around – there are hire places next to the Bhagwati Hotel (Rs 4/25 per hour/day). It's possible to get a wallah to carry your luggage on a hand-drawn cart to or from the bus stand for a small fee (Rs 10 is fine).

TONK
You may well find yourself in this town, 95km to the south of Jaipur, en route to Sawai Madhopur, gateway to the Ranthambhore National Park. To the north of the modern new town is the original walled city, which was built in the mid-17th century. Tonk was originally ruled by a tribe of Afghani Pathans, and their prosperous Muslim descendants have left a legacy of fine mansions, a testament to the wealth they accumulated when they ruled as nawabs from this region. Tonk also served as an important administrative centre during the era of the Raj, and the British have left behind some well-preserved colonial buildings.

Attractions in Tonk include the early 19th century **Sunehri Kothi**, with its beautiful coloured glass and inlay work; and the imposing **Jama Masjid**, an important place of worship. At the **Arabic & Persian Research Institute**, a rare collection of old Arabic and Persian manuscripts and books is housed.

EASTERN RAJASTHAN

Places to Stay

The *Natraj Hotel (☎ 01432-42266, Patel Circle)*, about 2.5km from the bus stand, is the best option if you do find yourself stuck in Tonk for the night. The hotel name is written in Hindi (it's a pale yellow building). A double room with attached bath costs Rs 120. A cycle-rickshaw from the bus station to the hotel should cost you about Rs 14.

Getting There & Away

There are many buses from Jaipur's main bus stand which pass through Tonk (2½ hrs, Rs 26) en route to Kota. There are numerous buses between Tonk and Sawai Madhopur for Ranthambhore National Park (2½ hrs, Rs 20).

SAWAI MADHOPUR & RANTHAMBHORE NATIONAL PARK
☎ 07462

Situated near the town of Sawai Madhopur, midway between Bharatpur and Kota, Ranthambhore National Park is one of the prime examples of Project Tiger's conservation efforts in Rajasthan. Sadly, it also demonstrates the program's overall failure; for it was in this park that government officials were implicated in the poaching of tigers for the Chinese folk medicine trade.

Not only tigers, but all species of the cat family inhabiting the park are threatened, as well as other animals such as the ratel, or honey badger *(Mellivora capensis)*, a nocturnal beast and member of the weasel family.

Prior to Independence, the park was the preserve of Jaipur's maharajas, who mounted elaborate big game shoots, or *shikhars*, here. The Queen and Prince Philip were the special guests of Maharaja Man Singh. They stayed in the erstwhile hunting lodge (now a hotel, the RTDC's Castle Jhoomar Baori – see Places to Stay), and the Duke of Edinburgh proved himself as a hunter, bagging a large tiger.

In 1955 the game park was declared a wildlife sanctuary, and in 1973 was one of nine sanctuaries that were selected as part

Ranthambhore Revival

In the last few years, eco-development on the park peripheries has established fodder production plots and fuel-wood plantations – some 90% of which are acacias. The viability of the project will become more evident when the forests are ready for harvesting, which will be eight to 10 years after planting. Veterinary services are provided free to villages, including artificial insemination and vaccination. The goal is to vaccinate 100% of the cattle, as diseased cattle can potentially contaminate water sources which are vital to the animal inhabitants of the national park.

Much of this conservation work is due to the commitment of workers and volunteers of the Ranthambhore Foundation. It was inaugurated in 1987 as a nonprofit society for the creation of natural integration and harmony between the park's human dwellers, vegetation and wildlife. Its programs include the dissemination of knowledge at the village level regarding health, medicine and family planning; the revival of traditional arts and crafts, which provide alternative forms of income for villagers; the introduction of stall-fed cattle, such as buffaloes, to reduce the negative impacts of grazing; the establishment of nurseries and seed collection as a regreening initiative; education focused on environmental awareness; research into animal habitats, including a study of water resources; the establishment of 'green groups' in villages to raise environmental awareness; introduction and research into alternative forms of energy, such as biogas in place of firewood; facilitating village relocation from sensitive park areas and aiding villagers in this relocation; and integrating traditional wisdom with modern science in regenerating ecosystems and ensuring a healthy habitat for its animals.

For more information on the work of the foundation, write to: Ranthambhore Foundation, 19 Kautilya Marg, Chanakyapuri, New Delhi, 110021 (☎ 011-301 6261, fax 011-301 9457).

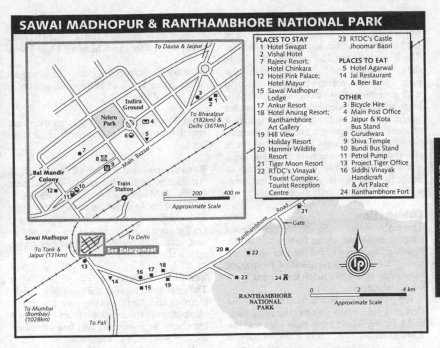

SAWAI MADHOPUR & RANTHAMBHORE NATIONAL PARK

PLACES TO STAY
1 Hotel Swagat
2 Vishal Hotel
7 Rajeev Resort;
   Hotel Chinkara
12 Hotel Pink Palace;
   Hotel Mayur
15 Sawai Madhopur
   Lodge
17 Ankur Resort
18 Hotel Anurag Resort;
   Ranthambhore
   Art Gallery
19 Hill View
   Holiday Resort
20 Hammir Wildlife
   Resort
21 Tiger Moon Resort
22 RTDC's Vinayak
   Tourist Complex;
   Tourist Reception
   Centre

23 RTDC's Castle
   Jhoomar Baori

PLACES TO EAT
5 Hotel Agarwal
14 Jai Restaurant
   & Beer Bar

OTHER
3 Bicycle Hire
4 Main Post Office
6 Jaipur & Kota
   Bus Stand
8 Gurudwara
9 Shiva Temple
10 Bundi Bus Stand
11 Petrol Pump
13 Project Tiger Office
16 Siddhi Vinayak
   Handicraft
   & Art Palace
24 Ranthambhore Fort

EASTERN RAJASTHAN

of the Project Tiger program. It was designated a national park in 1980, and in 1984 the forests to the south and north-east of the original park were declared the Sawai Man Singh and Keladevi sanctuaries respectively. In 1991, Project Tiger was extended to include the Keladevi Sanctuary. The park now covers 1334 sq km.

The most recent census, conducted in 1996, reported 28 tigers in the park, but since then there are believed to be 25 tigers and nine cubs. Other animals inhabiting Ranthambhore include the endangered caracal, also a member of the cat family, the leopard and jungle cat; several members of the dog family such as hyena, fox and jackal; the sloth bear and varieties of deer, including the chital (spotted deer) and the sambar, India's largest deer. There are also two species of antelope: the chinkara (Indian gazelle) and nilgai (bluebull).

As well as its animal population, Ranthambhore boasts over 270 species of birds, including a number of migratory birds which visit the park either in winter or during the monsoon. Birdlife includes various types of owl, such as the brown fish owl and the great Indian horned owl and other birds of prey such as Bonelli's eagle and the crested serpent eagle. There are also migratory populations of kingfishers, geese and storks.

The vegetation of the park is primarily deciduous, and the dominant species is the hardy dhok *(Anogeissus pendula)*. Its leaves are used for animal fodder. In April, when the brilliant flame of the forest blooms, it creates a spectacular vision of fiery red across the park precincts. Around the four lakes of Ranthambhore are various tree species including gurjan *(Lannea coromandelica)*, with its grey trunk, gums *(Sterculia urens)* and salar *(Boswellia serrata)*.

Villagers compete for land in both the national park and its buffer zones. They need land both for cultivation and wood-felling. There are between 150 and 200 villages in the buffer areas, and four villages within the park. These four will eventually be relocated with government assistance. Most of the villages are directly dependent on the park for fodder and fuel, and represent a population of some 100,000 people and an equal number of cattle. Although it is illegal to graze stock within the core national park area, some villagers have been compelled to break the law as overgrazing has left them with no grazing grounds at all.

Orientation

The main bazaar in Sawai Madhopur runs roughly east-west, about 100m north of the train station. Many of the cheaper hotels are strung along the eastern end of the bazaar (turn right when you reach the bazaar from the train station).

It's 10km from Sawai Madhopur to the first park gate where you pay the entry fees, and a farther 3km to the main gate and the Ranthambhore Fort. There is mid-range and top end accommodation strung all the way along the road from Sawai Madhopur to the park. Advance booking is essential during the busy Christmas and New Year periods.

Information

Tourist Office The Tourist Reception Centre (☎ 20808) is open daily except Sunday from 10 am to 5 pm (closed for lunch from 1.30 to 2 pm). It's located in the grounds of the RTDC's Vinayak Tourist Complex. It has a good map of Sawai Madhopur (Rs 2) for sale. For information about safari timings, and to make bookings, you'll need to go to the Project Tiger office (following). There are plans to open a crafts village here, similar to Shilpgram in Udaipur (see the Southern Rajasthan chapter).

Project Tiger Office The Project Tiger office (☎ 20223) is currently tucked away half a kilometre west of the train station; however there are plans to shift it to the Tourist Reception Centre, so check first. The office is open daily except Sunday from 10 am to 5 pm (closed for lunch between 1 and 2 pm).

Money You can change travellers cheques at the State Bank of Bikaner & Jaipur, in Sawai Madhopur.

Post The main post office is on the street which runs parallel to and north of the main bazaar.

Bookshops Siddhi Vinayak Handicraft & Art Palace, on the Ranthambhore road near the Sawai Madhopur Lodge, has a small collection of books on Indian birds and wildlife, with particular emphasis on Ranthambhore. On the same road, near the Hotel Anurag Resort, is the Ranthambhore Art Gallery which sells a similar range of books.

Wildlife Safaris

The best time to visit the park is between October and April, and the park is actually closed during the monsoon from 1 July to 1 October. Early morning and late afternoon are the best times to view wildlife.

There's a reasonable chance of spotting a tiger, but you should plan on two or three safaris. Other game, especially the larger and smaller herbivores, are more numerous. Even if you don't see a tiger, it's worth being there for the scenery alone: in India it's not often you get the chance to visit such a large area of virgin bush.

A good network of four gravel tracks crisscrosses the park and on each safari two or three jeeps take each trail. There are also large trucks (open-topped) called canters which seat 20 people, but they're limited to only two of the trails. The jeeps are opensided. If you've ever been on safari in Africa, you might think this is unduly risky but the tigers appear unconcerned by garrulous tourists toting cameras only metres away from where they're lying. No one has been mauled or eaten – yet!

If you are taking photos, it's worthwhile bringing some 400 or 800 ASA film, as the undergrowth is dense and surprisingly dark in places. The prime time for photography is March and April and jeeps are better suited to photography than the canters.

Entry to the park costs Rs 20/100 for Indians/foreigners. A still camera is free, but it's Rs 200 if you've got a video camera. You'll also have to pay the entry fee of Rs 125 per jeep (the entry fee for canters is included in the ticket price). Jeeps and canters must be booked at the Project Tiger office (☎ 20223), or the Tourist Reception Centre (☎ 20808) if it has moved. A seat in a canter costs Rs 80, and you can arrange to be picked up if your hotel is on the road between the town and the park. Jeeps cost Rs 600 per trip and this can be shared by up to five people. This includes all kilometre charges, so if you're staying farther from the park entrance the trip isn't going to cost more. A guide is included in the ticket price for canters but not for jeeps. As a guide is compulsory, you'll have to pay Rs 100 for one if you take a jeep. Many guides speak English and there's currently one, Yadvendra Singh (☎ 34042, fax 21212), who is also semi-fluent in German.

A maximum of 10 jeeps (two of which are reserved for government VIPs) is permitted in the park at any one time. Seven of these can be booked up to one month in advance – contact the Project Tiger Office (or Tourist Reception Centre) for further details. Bookings for morning trips can be made between 4 and 5 pm on the afternoon prior, and between 11 am and noon for the afternoon safari (but check these timings in case they have changed).

In winter (October to February), both canters and jeeps leave at 7 am and 2.30 pm; the safari takes three hours. In summer (March to June), they leave at 6.30 am and 3.30 pm. If you're taking a morning safari in winter it's a good idea to bring something warm to wear, as it can get quite cold. According to several guides, red clothing should be avoided as it apparently irritates tigers! Take a hat and a bottle of water. Mosquito repellent is also recommended, particularly in October and November. Some guides have binoculars which you

Miniature paintings often portrayed the Rajasthani rulers or the British hunting tigers.

may be able to use, but at the time of writing there were no places where they could be hired.

Some travellers have reported that local entrepreneurial types are in a scam with the Project Tiger office where they buy all the jeeps and canters available for hire each day and offer them to the top-end hotel guests for two to four times the normal price. Although this was not this author's experience, it is a good idea to be prepared for any eventuality.

Ranthambhore Fort

The ancient Ranthambhore Fort, in the heart of the national park, is believed to have been built by the Chauhan Rajputs in the 10th century AD, only a few years before the invasion of India by Mohammed Ghori. According to tradition, the fort was erected over the site at which two princes were engaged in a boar hunt. The boar eluded the princes and dived into a lake. Not to be thwarted, the princes prayed to Shiva to restore the boar. This Shiva deigned to do, on condition that the princes build a fort in his honour at the spot.

However, it is Ganesh who is most revered at the fort, and a temple in his honour can be found overlooking its southern ramparts. Traditionally when a marriage is to take place, invitations are forwarded to Lord Ganesh before any other guests. The temple at the fort receives hundreds of letters each week addressed to the elephant god, some of which include money to enable him to pay for his fare to the marriage celebration!

The fort is believed to be the site at which the first jauhar (collective suicide) in Rajput history was performed. In the early 14th century, the ruler of the fort, Hammir Deva, was engaged in a protracted battle with the Muslim forces. Although Hammir repulsed the Muslim invaders, the women who were installed in the fort for their safety heard that he had succumbed on the battlefield. In usual Rajput style, preferring death to dishonour, they committed mass suicide. When confronted with the grisly news, the victorious Hammir beheaded himself before the image of Shiva in the temple at the fort.

From a distance, the fort is not an imposing edifice, being almost indiscernible on its hilltop looking out over the lake of Padam Talab. However, it affords very fine views from the disintegrating walls of the Badal Mahal, on its north side, and its seven enormous gateways are still intact. Inside the fort there are three Hindu temples, dedicated to Ganesh, Shiva and Ramlalaji, and a Jain temple. They date from the 12th and 13th centuries and are constructed of impressive blocks of red Karauli stone. Constructed of the same stone are a number of cenotaphs which can be seen in the precincts of the fort. The fort is open daily from 6 am to 6 pm and entry is free.

Places to Stay & Eat

Most travellers prefer to stay on Ranthambhore Rd, which has impressive hotels and is a more peaceful area than Sawai Madhopur. However, cheaper lodgings can be found in Sawai Madhopur. Many hotels offer hefty low-season discounts (up to 50%).

Ranthambhore Rd All of the places below offer fixed-price meals, and some also offer an à la carte selection.

Sawai Madhopur Lodge (☎ 20541, fax 20718) is 3km from the train station, the first and most upmarket place to stay on Ranthambhore Rd (coming from Sawai Madhopur). The lodge formerly belonged to the maharaja of Jaipur and is now managed by the Taj group. It is suitably luxurious, with a lending library, bar, restaurant, pool (open to nonresidents for Rs 300), tennis court and beautiful garden. Rooms are Rs 2500/3500 a single/double, and a suite is Rs 4900. Luxury tents (with private bath) cost Rs 2800 a double. Nonguests are welcome to dine at the restaurant with advance notice; the buffet lunch is Rs 265, and dinner is Rs 285.

Ankur Resort (☎ 20792, fax 20697) is the next place to stay, heading towards the national park. Rooms are cool and clean, and there's a pleasant garden area. Singles/doubles cost Rs 400/550 with attached bath and there are also cottages for Rs 600/750. It costs Rs 100 for vegetarian meals, and Rs 150 for nonveg meals.

Hotel Anurag Resort (☎/fax 20451) has ordinary singles/doubles with bath for Rs 400/500, and deluxe rooms for Rs 500/600. Dorm beds are Rs 75, and it's possible to camp here (in your own tent) for Rs 100 per camp site, which includes access to toilets and bathroom facilities. Breakfast is Rs 70, lunch/dinner is Rs 100 (veg) or Rs 150 (nonveg).

Hill View Holiday Resort (☎ 22173, fax 20423) is somewhat overpriced considering the below-average rooms and service. A single/double with bath costs Rs 400/500, and cottages are Rs 1200 a double. Meals are available.

RTDC's Castle Jhoomar Baori (☎ 20495) is about 6km from the train station, where there is a turn-off which leads 1km in to it. This former royal hunting lodge is in a fine position perched on a hilltop, and although the rooms are not super luxurious, they do have character. There's a lounge, open rooftop areas and a bar. Deluxe air-cooled rooms are Rs 700/800, the air-con Panther suite is Rs 900/1100, and the Tiger and Leopard suites, also with air-con, are Rs 1200/1500. Fixed price nonveg continental lunch or dinner is Rs 220, and veg meals are Rs 180. There are also veg/nonveg thalis for Rs 80/90. Breakfast is Rs 120, and there is also à la carte. This is a quiet place to stay, and the staff are friendly.

Hammir Wildlife Resort (☎ 20562, fax 20697) is a rather neglected place, 7km from the train station. Rooms are comfortable, if a little tatty and bare, and cost Rs 450/550. The cottages (Rs 750 a double) are not much better. The veg/nonveg meals are Rs 100/130.

RTDC's Vinayak Tourist Complex (☎ 21 333) is also 7km from the train station. Comfortable carpeted rooms are Rs 550/650, all with air-cooling. There's a very nice lawn area and a campfire is lit in winter. There's a dining hall; the veg/nonveg thali is Rs 70/85.

Tiger Moon Resort Sawai Madhopur *(☎/fax 52042);* Mumbai *(☎ 022-643 3622, fax 640 6399)* is at the end of Ranthambhore Rd, 11km from the train station. This place has an appealing jungle lodge ambience with its cottages scattered under a canopy of trees. It costs US$54 per person, including breakfast. Their 'Jungle Plan' includes accommodation, meals and a morning and evening safari (US$92 per person). There's a good restaurant and swimming pool (residents only).

Jai Restaurant & Beer Bar, on Ranthambhore Rd, claims to sell the cheapest beer in town; Rs 50 per bottle, or Rs 60 for a Thunderbolt – a more powerful brew. It serves snacks indoors, up on the terrace, or in the little garden. Indoors, there are some 'cabins' designed to maximise privacy.

Sawai Madhopur

As few travellers choose to stay in Sawai Madhopur, the accommodation options are limited and lacklustre. However, an upmarket Oberoi hotel may soon be opening – contact the New Delhi corporate office for details on ☎ 011-291 4841, fax 292 9800.

Hotel Chinkara (☎ 20340, 13 Indira Colony, Civil Lines) is a very good choice in Sawai Madhopur. It offers large rooms with bath for Rs 200/300. Meals are available with advance notice.

Rajeev Resort (☎ 21067, 16 Indira Colony, Civil Lines), just a few doors away, has decent singles/doubles with private bath for Rs 200/300. A continental lunch or dinner is Rs 90.

Vishal Hotel (☎ 20504), in the main bazaar, has a range of reasonable rooms, some with balconies. Singles/doubles with attached bath (hot water free by the bucket) downstairs are Rs 50/80. The larger upstairs rooms are Rs 150 a double. Only breakfast is available.

Hotel Swagat (☎ 20601), farther east, is not as good as the Vishal Hotel, and single female travellers may feel uncomfortable at this seedy flophouse. Primitive and rather grubby rooms with attached bath (hot water by the bucket) go for Rs 60/80; Rs 80/125 gets you a slightly better room.

Hotel Pink Palace (☎ 20722, plot A1, Bal Mandir Colony) is on the west side of the overpass. Basic rooms cost Rs 125/150 with attached bath (buckets of hot water), or Rs 200/300 with geyser. There's also one single room with common bath for Rs 50. Meals are available.

Hotel Mayur (☎ 20909), next door, has rooms with bath for Rs 125/200 and meals are available with advance notice. A room with four beds and private bath costs Rs 350. The rooms here could be cleaner, but the owner, Lalit Sharma, is nice.

Retiring rooms at the train station cost Rs 110 for a double with attached bath. Dorm beds are Rs 35.

Hotel Agarwal is a small dhaba in the main bazaar which has a variety of cheap vegetarian eats.

Getting There & Away

Bus There are buses every hour to Jaipur via Dausa between 5.30 am and 3.30 pm (4½ hrs, Rs 45), and buses to Kota (4 hrs, Rs 45). To get to Bharatpur you change at Dausa (3 hrs from Sawai Madhopur), from where there are many buses on to Bharatpur (Rs 60). All these buses leave from the main bus stand, about two minutes walk north of the main bazaar. Buses to Bundi leave from the Bundi bus stand, at the west end of the main bazaar (2 hrs, Rs 40).

Train Sawai Madhopur is on the main Delhi-Mumbai broad-gauge railway line. There are rail connections to various destinations including Agra, Kota and Jaipur. Ask your hotel or the Tourist Reception Centre (see Information earlier) if you require the latest details.

Getting Around
Bicycle hire is available at the shops just outside the main entrance to the train station,

and at the east end of the main bazaar. The cost is around Rs 15 per day.

DHOLPUR
Situated almost midway between Agra (Uttar Pradesh) and Gwalior (Madhya Pradesh), on an eastward thrusting spur of Rajasthan, is Dholpur. It was near here that Aurangzeb's sons fought a pitched battle to determine who would succeed him as emperor of the rapidly declining Mughal empire. The Shergarh fort in Dholpur is very old and is now in ruins.

Dholpur, located on National Highway 3, is most easily reached from either Agra or Gwalior, and there are regular rail and bus connections from both of these cities, as well as from Dausa.

Southern Rajasthan

Bordering Gujarat and Madhya Pradesh, southern Rajasthan is one of the state's most fertile regions. It has a varied topography, with rolling hills, lush valleys and desolate plains. The region is also dotted with many lakes, including Jaisamand, one of the biggest artificial lakes in Asia. The south boasts some of Rajasthan's most important forts, including the huge hilltop fort of Chittorgarh. This sprawling fort occupies a paramount place in the annals of Rajput valour, for this was where tens of thousands of Rajput men, women and children perished in the name of honour. The imposing 15th century fort of Kumbhalgarh is the second most significant in the Mewar (Udaipur) region, after Chittorgarh.

Southern Rajasthan has one of the best known palace-hotels in India: the breathtaking Lake Palace Hotel in Udaipur. Superbly situated in the middle of a lake, this enchanting white palace once served as the royal summer residence.

Kota is one of the state's major industrial centres and has seen an increasing rate of industrialisation and pollution. This trend is not limited to Kota: over the past decade, many cities and towns in southern Rajasthan have suffered a rising level of pollution, largely because of industrial growth and urban sprawl. Marble mining has burgeoned in the south and contributed to denuding the landscape of vegetation; it's not unusual to see quarries and piles of rubble strewn across the countryside. Although the government has taken measures to curtail industrial waste, a handful of historic monuments are believed to have already been adversely affected by pollution.

Southern Rajasthan has the state's only hill station, Mt Abu. Situated along a 1200m-high plateau, hordes of people throng here during summer to escape the sweltering heat. Like many other hill stations in India, Mt Abu is very popular with honeymooners and young families. The Brahma Kumaris Spiritual University is located here and attracts a large number of devotees from all around the world. Mt Abu also has the superb Dilwara Temples, which are an important Jain pilgrimage centre. These temples have some of the most amazing marble carvings in Rajasthan, if not India. Another impressive and important Jain temple at Ranakpur is renowned for its 1444 exquisite pillars, no two of which are alike.

This part of the state is rich in antiquities with potentially many more undiscovered. Jhalawar, for instance, is an archaeologist's heaven, with historic relics being continually unearthed at a rare assortment of ancient sites, including extraordinary Buddhist caves and stupas atop a hill.

Historically, Rajasthan has been a flourishing centre of art and culture, with many of India's finest schools of miniature painting. Former rulers were great patrons of the arts and employed local artists to develop unique styles. The famous Bundi school of painting had Mughal influences and specialised in hunting and palace scenes. Kota,

Highlights

- **Udaipur** – possibly India's most romantic city: whitewashed temples and grand palaces surround a lake from the depths of which rises the stunning Lake Palace

- **Jain temples at Mt Abu & Ranakpur** – among the most exquisite in all of India

- **Chittorgarh** – Rajasthan's most historically significant fort, where tens of thousands of men, women and children died in the name of honour

- **Bundi** – a little town with a ramshackle fort and medieval ambience

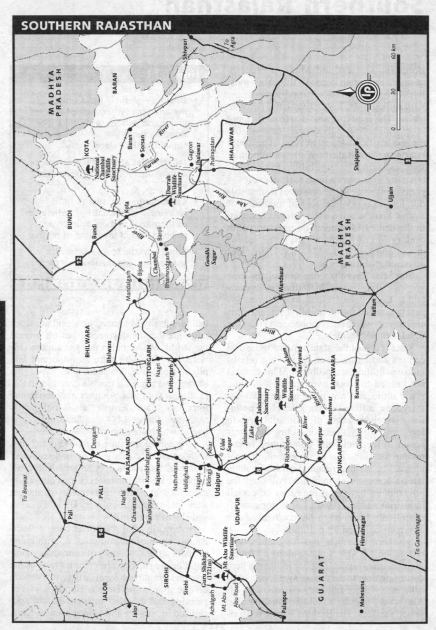

SOUTHERN RAJASTHAN

Mewar's Most Honoured Mother

In Udaipur there is a woman who has been immortalised for her astounding loyalty to the royal family. Her name is Panna dhai and her story is one of immense personal sacrifice and bravery, altruism and tragedy.

In Mewar, it was not unusual to ask a woman who was nursing her baby to supplement the feeding of another baby whose mother was unable to do so. Such a woman was known as a *dhai* (foster mother) and only a privileged few were selected, when necessary, for babies of the Mewar royal family.

In 1535, the then Maharana of Mewar, Vikramaditya, was assassinated by a man called Banbir. At the time, the rightful successor of the throne, Prince Udai Singh II, was just a baby. Prince Udai Singh II had a dhai called Panna, who had her own infant son, Chandan. Banbir wanted control of the Mewar kingdom and would eliminate any impediments in his quest. Panna dhai was aware of his sinister plot and took extra care to protect the little heir to the throne, Prince Udai Singh II.

One night, Banbir managed to break into the prince's bedroom, determined to kill the sleeping baby. Panna dhai had already suspected his wicked intentions and had placed her own child in the prince's cradle. When he demanded to know which child was the prince, Panna dhai pointed to the prince's cradle where her own son slept. Banbir whipped out his sword and slaughtered the child.

Soon after the murder, Panna dhai hid Prince Udai Singh II in a basket and fled to the fort at Kumbhalgarh. She told the nobles and people of Mewar what had happened and Prince Udai Singh II was promptly crowned, ensuring the unbroken lineage of the Mewar dynasty.

The current maharana of Udaipur has honoured the memory of Panna dhai by including a special award in the annual Maharana Mewar Foundation Awards ceremony. The Panna dhai award is given to an individual who 'ventures beyond the call of duty and sets an example in society of permanent value through sacrifice'.

once surrounded by dense forests which were popular hunting grounds for the local nobility, produced miniature paintings in the early 19th century that are acclaimed for their eloquent depictions of hunting and have featured at many international exhibitions. Mewar also developed its own style and was especially known for its highly detailed court scenes. Created from the early 18th century for the Mewar rulers, some of these paintings can be seen at the City Palace Museum in Udaipur. Also noteworthy are the vivid Nathdwara *pichwai* paintings, which were produced in the 17th century after the image of Vishnu was brought here from Mathura. Other small towns, mostly those with royal connections, also had their own school of painting.

Many traditional tribal folk dances and songs have survived from southern Rajasthan's colourful past. A prime example is that of the Bhil tribal people, who often perform their vibrant dances during special festivals, such as Holi.

There are a handful of wildlife reserves in southern Rajasthan and abundant birdlife around the many lakes, particularly at Udaipur, Jaisamand, Dungarpur and Deogarh.

HISTORY

Southern Rajasthan's history is dominated by the region of Mewar, which was wracked with bloodshed and acts of astounding valour. The events at Chittorgarh, the former capital of Mewar, were undoubtedly the most catastrophic and poignant in all of Rajasthan,

Festivals of Southern Rajasthan

Several colourful festivals are celebrated in southern Rajasthan. For statewide and nationwide festivals, see the boxed text 'Festivals of Rajasthan' in the Facts for the Visitor chapter.

January-February

Baneshwar Fair – celebrated by thousands of Bhil people at Baneshwar, in Dungarpur district, this festival is in honour of Vishnu who is worshipped as Kalki. Festivities include acrobatic performances and cultural programs, and a silver image of Kalki is paraded through the village on horseback. See Baneshwar in the South of Udaipur section for more details.

February-March

Holi – celebrated across India in late February/early March. Udaipur is the place to be in Rajasthan during this happy celebration. Holi marks the end of winter and the beginning of spring. It symbolises the victory of divine power over demonic strength. It is also known as the festival of colours, because of the exuberant throwing of coloured powder and water on the last day.

The Udaipur royal family hosts an elaborate function at the City Palace to celebrate Holi. There's an evening procession with decorated horses, a band, local nobility in traditional attire and, of course, the royal family. After performing an ancient religious ceremony, the royal family lights a huge sacred fire signifying the triumph of good over evil. Tribal people then commence a traditional dance. Afterwards, you get the chance to rub shoulders with nobility at a reception held in the *Zenana Mahal* at the City Palace. Tickets cost Rs 1200 per person, including dinner, and can be obtained at the Shiv Niwas Palace Hotel (☎ 0294-528016, fax 528006) in Udaipur.

March-April

Gangaur – essentially a festival for women, it is dedicated to the goddess Gauri (Parvati) and celebrated by women across Rajasthan. Wives pray for their spouses and unmarried women pray for good husbands. The Garasia tribes of the Mt Abu region add an interesting element to the festivities: they celebrate Gangaur for an entire month, and the image of Gangaur is carried aloft from village to village. Young unmarried youths and maidens are able to meet without social sanction and select marriage partners, with whom they elope. In Bundi, Kota and Jhalawar, unmarried girls collect poppies from the fields and make them into wreaths for the goddess.

Mewar Festival – In late March/early April, Udaipur hosts its own colourful version of the Gangaur Festival. People dressed in traditional costumes sing and dance in a lively procession which goes through the town to Gangaur Ghat at Lake Pichola. Idols of Gauri and Lord Shiva, who represent the perfect couple, are carried in the procession. There are also cultural programs.

June

Summer Festival – takes place in Mt Abu, which registers the coolest temperatures in the state at this scorching time of the year, so is not a bad place to be. The festival takes place over three days (1-3 June each year) and includes classical and traditional folk cultural programs.

August-September

Kajli Teej – The onset of the monsoon, eight days before Janmashtami, Lord Krishna's birthday.

October-November

Chandrabhaga Fair – a large cattle fair taking place on the last day of the Hindu month of Kartika on the banks of the Chandrabhaga River near Jhalrapatan. Attracting villagers from Rajasthan and neighbouring states, it includes livestock trading and colourful stalls. The religious element involves pilgrims at this time bathing in a sacred part of the river known as Chandrawati.

for it was here that countless Rajput men, women and children chose death over defeat. Chittorgarh was sacked three times in its history and each defeat ended in immense carnage. While the men died in battle, the women committed *jauhar* (collective sacrifice) by throwing themselves into the flames of huge pyres to avoid the infamy of capture. The first defeat took place in 1303, when a Pathan king of Delhi seized the fort: the men of Rajput gallantly fought a far stronger enemy and the women committed jauhar. The same grim outcome occurred in 1535, when the sultan of Gujarat besieged the fort, and finally in 1568, when Chittorgarh was seized by the Mughal emperor, Akbar. After the third attack, Mewar's ruler, Maharana Udai Singh II, decided to leave Chittorgarh and establish his new capital in Udaipur.

Geographically, Udaipur was shielded by thick forests and the Aravalli Range, and was therefore far less vulnerable than the exposed Chittorgarh. But this did not stop invaders from trying to lay siege to the new capital of Mewar, and Udaipur also had its share of battles. These power struggles ended in the early 19th century when the British signed an alliance pledging to protect the Mewar rulers.

Historically, the rulers of the Mewar region have occupied the top of the Rajput hierarchy, making this an important part of Rajasthan. This dynasty is believed to be one of the oldest in the world, reigning in unbroken succession for over 1400 years. The rulers of Mewar come from the illustrious Sisodia Rajput clan, which traces its descent from the sun. They staunchly defied foreign domination of any kind and were the only Hindu princes who refused to intermarry with the once influential Mughal emperors. For them, honour, heritage and independence were of paramount importance, even if they meant deprivation and suffering.

Other princely states in southern Rajasthan, such as Kota and Bundi, were formed long after the region of Mewar. For example, the remote princely state of Jhalawar was only created in 1838.

BUNDI
- pop 77,000   ☎ 0747

Visiting Bundi is like stepping back in time. It's a picturesque and captivating little town which has more or less retained a medieval atmosphere. Located only 39km north-west of Kota, it's more pleasant to stay here and visit Kota on a day trip.

Bundi is not a major tourist tramping ground, which is a big part of its appeal. The only place you may get a little hassled (by small children) is on the way up to the palace. In the evening, people throng to the colourful and bustling markets that meander through the town's lanes. Unlike many other places in Rajasthan, in Bundi you're unlikely to be hounded by persistent shopkeepers.

The Rajput legacy is well-preserved in the shape of the massive Taragarh (fort), which broods over the town in its narrow valley below, and the palace which stands beneath it. In this palace are found the famous Bundi murals. The old city has a number of blue-coloured houses, similar to those found in Jodhpur.

Bundi has a collection of interesting historic sites, but sadly many are in a crumbling state of disrepair.

History
Conquered in 1241 by Rao Deva Hara, Bundi was the capital of a major princely state during the heyday of the Rajputs. Kota was part of Bundi, deemed as the land grant of the ruler's eldest son. But in 1624, Kota was made into a separate state at the instigation of the Mughal emperor, Jehangir. Although Bundi's importance dwindled with the rise of Kota during Mughal times, it maintained its independence until its incorporation into the state of Rajasthan after Independence.

Orientation
It's relatively easy to find your way to the palace on foot through the bazaar – once you pass through the city gate, there are only two main roads through town and the palace is visible from many points. The bus stand is at the Kota (south-east) end of town.

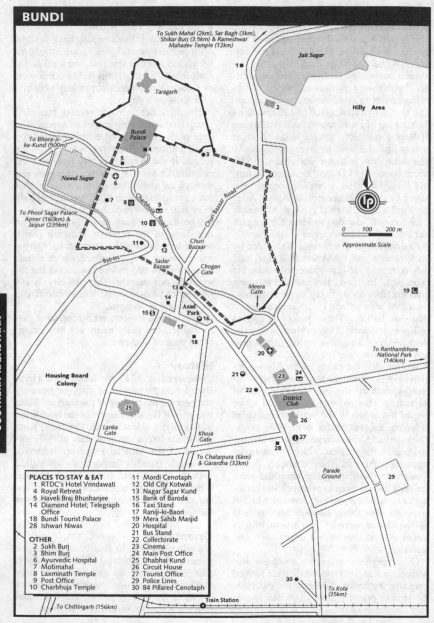

BUNDI

To Sukh Mahal (2km), Sar Bagh (3km),
Shikar Burj (3.5km) & Rameshwar
Mahadev Temple (12km)

Jait Sagar

Hilly Area

Taragarh

Bundi Palace

To Bhora-ji-
ka-Kund (500m)

Nawal Sagar

To Phool Sagar Palace,
Ajmer (160km) &
Jaipur (235km)

Charbhuja Road

Churi Bazaar Road

Churi
Bazaar

0   100   200 m
Approximate Scale

Bypass

Sadar
Bazaar

Chogan
Gate

Meera
Gate

Azad
Park

Housing Board
Colony

To Ranthambhore
National Park
(140km)

District
Club

Lanka
Gate

Khoja
Gate

To Chatarpura (6km)
& Garardha (32km)

Parade
Ground

To Kota
(35km)

PLACES TO STAY & EAT
1   RTDC's Hotel Vrindawati
4   Royal Retreat
5   Haveli Braj Bhushanjee
14 Diamond Hotel; Telegraph
    Office
18 Bundi Tourist Palace
28 Ishwari Niwas

OTHER
2   Sukh Burj
3   Bhim Burj
6   Ayurvedic Hospital
7   Motimahal
8   Laxminath Temple
9   Post Office
10 Charbhuja Temple

11 Mordi Cenotaph
12 Old City Kotwali
13 Nagar Sagar Kund
15 Bank of Baroda
16 Taxi Stand
17 Raniji-ki-Baori
19 Mera Sahib Masjid
20 Hospital
21 Bus Stand
22 Collectorate
23 Cinema
24 Main Post Office
25 Dhabhai Kund
26 Circuit House
27 Tourist Office
29 Police Lines
30 84 Pillared Cenotaph

To Chittorgarh (156km)

Train Station

SOUTHERN RAJASTHAN

Information

Tourist Office There's a small tourist office (☎ 22697) in the grounds of the Circuit House. It's open Monday to Saturday from 10 am to 1.30 pm and 2 to 5 pm. It sells a good map of Bundi for Rs 2. Mukesh Mehta, at the Haveli Braj Bhushanjee hotel (conveniently situated near the palace), is also a terrific source of information and is happy to point tourists in the right direction. He is planning to offer email facilities for tourists.

Money The Bank of Baroda, opposite Raniji-ki-Baori, changes major currency travellers cheques, but not currency. At the time of writing, no banks in Bundi issued cash advances on credit cards.

Post & Communications The main post office is near the cinema and there's a smaller post office opposite the Charbhuja Temple in the old city. Faxes can be sent and received at the telegraph office, opposite Raniji-ki-Baori.

Ayurvedic Hospital If you're feeling a little off colour, you may like to drop in at the Ayurvedic Hospital (☎ 22708) at Balchand Pada (opposite the Haveli Braj Bhushanjee), which prescribes natural plant-based remedies. There are medicines for all sorts of ailments, from upset tummies to arthritis. In winter, the hospital is open Monday to Saturday from 9 am to 3 pm and on Sunday from 9 to 11 am. In summer, it's open Monday to Saturday from 8 am to 2 pm and on Sunday from 8 to 10 am.

Taragarh

Also known as the Star Fort, Taragarh was built in 1354, and is a great place to ramble around. The fort (free entry) is reached by a steep road leading up the hillside to an enormous gateway topped by rampant elephants. This rather ramshackle fort, with its overgrown vegetation and resident monkeys, is thankfully free of the souvenir shops and touts found at so many of Rajasthan's tourist attractions. Inside are huge reservoirs carved out of solid rock and the Bhim Burj, the largest of the battlements, on which is mounted a famous cannon. The views over the town and surrounding countryside are magical, especially at sunset. It's just a pity that the national broadcaster, Doordarshan, decided to build a ghastly concrete transmission tower right next to the fort – it's a real eyesore.

Bundi Palace

The palace itself is reached from the northwestern end of the bazaar, through a huge wooden gateway and up a steep cobbled ramp. Only one part of the outer perimeter of the palace, known as the Chittra Shala is officially open to the public (free entry). If you want to see the renowned **Bundi murals** (found in the Chattra Mahal and Badal Mahal), you could try contacting the secretary of the maharaja of Bundi (☎ 32812), or ask at your hotel. Photography is officially prohibited. From a distance, the palace looks beautiful when it is illuminated at night.

Baoris & Water Tanks

Bundi has scores of beautiful *baoris* (stepwells), some right in the centre of town. The very impressive **Raniji-ki-Baori** is 46m deep and has some superb carving. One of the largest of its kind, it was built in 1699 by Rani Nathavatji. The **Nagar Sagar Kund** is a pair of matching stepwells outside the Chogan Gate to the old city, in the centre of town.

Visible from the fort is the square artificial lake of **Nawal Sagar**. In the centre is a temple to Varuna, the Aryan god of water. Also worth a look is the **Bhora-ji-ka-Kund**, which is located opposite one of Bundi's oldest Shiva temples, the Abhaynath Temple. This 16th century tank attracts a variety of birdlife after a good monsoon, including kingfishers and hummingbirds. The **Dhabhai Kund**, not far from the Raniji-ki-baori, is another imposing tank.

Other Attractions

Try to slot in time to visit the vibrant **sabzi (vegetable) market**, situated between the Raniji-ki-Baori and Nagar Sagar Kund. There are marvellous photo opportunities at this market, so don't forget your camera.

SOUTHERN RAJASTHAN

Bundi's other attractions are all out of town and are difficult to reach without transport. The modern palace, known as the **Phool Sagar Palace**, has a charming artificial tank and gardens, and is several kilometres out of town on the Ajmer road. The tank is a good place for bird-watching, especially from November to February. This palace was closed to the public, mainly because of a dispute between the current maharaja and his sister. It seems he sold it to the Oberoi hotel chain, but his sister is claiming her share of the proceeds. Until the dispute is settled (if it is in fact settled), it is likely the palace will remain closed.

There's another palace, the smaller **Sukh Mahal**, closer to town on the edge of Jait Sagar, where Rudyard Kipling once stayed. It's now the Irrigation Rest House. The nearby, rather neglected **Sar Bagh** has a collection of royal cenotaphs, some with beautifully carved statues. **Shikar Burj** is a small erstwhile royal hunting lodge and picnic spot on the road which runs along the north side of Jait Sagar – a picturesque lake flanked by hills and strewn with pretty lotus flowers during the monsoon and winter months.

South of town is the stunning **84 Pillared Cenotaph** (Chaurasi Khambon ki Chhatri), which is lit up at night. It's set among well-maintained gardens, and this architecturally impressive monument with its 84 pillars is certainly worth a look.

Just beyond Bundi's Ganesh ghati, there are six tiny **villages** in the pristine countryside – a brilliant way to explore them is by bicycle (for bicycle hire see Getting Around later). It's a good idea to take a picnic lunch. The first village you'll come to is Dalapura and the last is Akoda (around 8km from Bundi). About 3km beyond Akoda village is the Rameshwa Mahadev, a 16th century Shiva temple.

About 32km from Bundi at the village of Garardha, you can see some ancient red-coloured **rock paintings**. Found on some of the boulders flanking the river, these are believed to be about 15,000 years old. There's a curious depiction of a man riding a huge bird as well as some hunting scenes. There are also some stick figures of people holding hands – this is apparently how villagers crossed rivers long ago and is still practised today in some regions. To make the most of the trip out here, it's best to come with a local guide – contact Mukesh Mehta at the Haveli Braj Bhushanjee (see Places to Stay) for more information. For a half-day return trip in an Ambassador car, it costs around Rs 450 and an additional Rs 200 for an English-speaking guide. Carry water and wear strong shoes (so you can easily scramble across the rocks). Mukesh has some photos of the rock paintings if you can't go out there.

Festivals

About 10km north-west of Bundi, in the little village of Bharodia, there's a festival held in honour of Ghans Bheru (a Hindu god), the day after Diwali (October/November). Unknown to most tourists, this colourful festival attracts thousands of villagers from the Bundi district, who converge on the village to celebrate a prosperous harvest. To find out the exact dates, contact the tourist office in Bundi (see Information earlier).

Places to Stay & Eat

You won't find any five-star hotels in Bundi. There are only budget and mid-range accommodation options (which are also the best places to eat). There are some good budget places operating under Bundi's Paying Guest House Scheme, with prices ranging from Rs 50 to Rs 350 per night – ask the tourist office for details.

The commission racket operates in Bundi so don't feel pressured into staying at a place of your taxi or auto-rickshaw driver's choice.

Haveli Braj Bhushanjee (☎ *32322, fax 32142*), opposite the Ayurvedic Hospital just below the palace, is a popular hang-out with travellers and deservedly so. This funky, 150-year-old haveli is run by the helpful Braj Bhushanjee family (ancestors of former prime ministers of Bundi), and has a cosy feel to it. The views from the rooftop terrace are splendid, especially at night when the palace is illuminated. Clean rooms with private bath start at Rs 250/300 and wholesome, but expensive, set veg meals are Rs 250. If you arrive after hours when the shop is closed, just ring the doorbell. They do free pick-ups from the bus stand and train station (advance notice appreciated). And just so you can see what you're missing, ask to see their photos of the Bundi murals which were taken inside the closed part of the palace.

Royal Retreat (☎ 34426), ideally situated in the palace compound, is also a popular place, set around a quiet open-air courtyard. There are two small double rooms with common bath for Rs 250, and several larger rooms with attached bath for Rs 550/750. The vegetarian restaurant (open also to non-residents) is reasonably priced, with Indian dishes ranging from Rs 20 to Rs 40. You can even get beer here (Rs 80 per bottle). There's an interesting collection of handicrafts for sale in their shop.

The *Ishwari Niwas* (☎ 32414, fax 32486, 1 Civil Lines), opposite the tourist office, is a family-run hotel with royal associations. It's a pleasant place, although a little more expensive than the other hotels in town. Rooms are set around a lovely courtyard and cost Rs 600/1200. A suite is Rs 1500. Sightseeing excursions can be arranged.

Bundi Tourist Palace (☎ 32650), opposite Azad Park, is nothing fancy, but ideal if you're strapped for cash. There are six rooms with common bath for Rs 60/120; hot water costs Rs 5 per bucket. The rooms are tiny but OK. No meals are available.

Diamond Hotel (☎ 22656), in the bustling bazaar area, has somewhat grimy singles/doubles with bath from Rs 75/150. The restaurant serves veg dishes at nominal prices; a Kashmiri pulao is Rs 25.

RTDC's Hotel Vrindawati (☎ 32473), out by Jait Sagar, has seven rooms with bath for Rs 275/350, or Rs 325/400 for a deluxe carpeted room. The cheaper rooms are better value than the deluxe rooms. There's a small dining hall where you can get a veg/nonveg thali for Rs 60/90.

Shopping

Bundi does not really have anything special to buy, but the shop-lined streets of the old city are a wonderful place to soak in the medieval ambience. A visit to the colourful vegetable market is also recommended (see Other Attractions earlier).

Getting There & Away

Bus There are express buses to multiple destinations in Rajasthan including:

destination	duration (hrs)	cost (Rs)
Ajmer	5	60
Kota	1	15
Sawai Madhopur	4½	50
Udaipur	8½	120
Jodhpur	10	150
Bikaner	10	150
Jaipur	5	80

Some buses also go to places in neighbouring Madhya Pradesh state, such as Indore (12 hours, Rs 160) and Shivpuri (10 hours, Rs 125).

Train There are rail connections between Bundi and Agra, Chittorgarh and Kota. From Kota, you can catch a connecting train to various destinations (see Kota for details).

There's an overnight train to Agra: the *Agra Fort Passenger.* It comes from Chittorgarh (leaves daily at 2.30 pm), arrives and leaves Bundi at 6 pm and arrives in Kota at 6.45 pm. It leaves Kota at 9 pm arriving in Agra at 7.30 am. The same train leaves Agra at 7.30 pm and arrives in Bundi at 8 am, then continues to Chittorgarh arriving at 11.30 am.

Getting Around

Taxi & Auto-Rickshaw Taxis can be hired from the stand near the Raniji-ki-Baori. Auto-rickshaw drivers will quote around Rs 15 to take you from the bus stand to the Bundi Palace. For local sightseeing, expect to pay around Rs 50 per hour for an auto-rickshaw.

Bicycle Bicycles are an ideal way to get around and can be cheaply rented near the old city kotwali (police station). The charge is around Rs 10 per day.

SOUTHERN RAJASTHAN

KOTA

- **pop 640,000**   ☏ **0744**

Kota is one of Rajasthan's less inspiring cities and today serves as an army headquarters. It is also Rajasthan's prime industrial centre (mainly chemicals), powered by the hydroelectric plants on the Chambal River – the only permanent river in Rajasthan – and a nearby nuclear plant that made headlines in 1992 when it was revealed that levels of radioactivity in the area were way above 'safe' levels. Kota also has one of Asia's largest fertiliser plants.

Growing industrialisation has led to increasing levels of pollution. Black smoke belches into the air from two huge chimneys across the river. Fortunately, there are a few leafy parks scattered throughout the town and an artificial lake with an enchanting palace on a little island in the middle.

Kota is well known for its saris, which are woven at the nearby village of Kaithoon. Known as *Kota doria* saris, they are made of cotton or silk in an assortment of colours, many with delicate golden thread designs. The Kota miniature paintings are also noteworthy, particularly the hunting scenes. These present a vivid and detailed portrayal of hunting expeditions in the once thickly wooded forests in and around Kota.

History

Following the Rajput conquest of this area of Rajasthan in the 12th century, Bundi was chosen as the capital, with Kota as the land grant of the ruler's eldest son. In 1624 Kota became a separate state and remained so until it was integrated into Rajasthan after Independence.

Building of the city began in 1264 following the defeat of Koteya, a Bhil chieftain. He was beheaded and on that very spot the foundation stone of the fort was laid. Kota didn't reach its present size until well into the 17th century, when Rao Madho Singh, a son of the ruler of Bundi, was made ruler of Kota by the Mughal emperor, Jehangir. Subsequent rulers have all added to the fort and palaces, and each also contributed to making Kota a flourishing centre of art and culture.

Orientation

Kota is strung out along the east bank of the Chambal River. The train station is well to the north; the RTDC's Hotel Chambal, a number of other hotels and the bus stand are in the middle; and Chambal gardens, the fort and the Kota Barrage are to the south.

Information

Tourist Office The Tourist Reception Centre (☏ 327695) is in the grounds of the RTDC's Hotel Chambal. It's open Monday to Saturday from 10 am to 5 pm.

Money The State Bank of Bikaner & Jaipur at Industrial Estate (opposite Rajasthan Patrika) changes travellers cheques and currency. The State Bank of India only changes American Express travellers cheques, as well as major currencies.

Post The main post office is located on Station Rd and is open daily except Sunday from 10 am to 1.30 pm and 2 to 5 pm.

City Palace & Fort

Standing beside the Kota Barrage and overlooking the Chambal River, the City Palace and fort is one of the largest such complexes in Rajasthan. The palace itself was the former residence of the Kota rulers and used to be the centre of power. The treasury, courts, arsenal, soldiers and various state offices were all located here. Some of its buildings are now occupied by schools. Entry is from the south side through the **Naya Darwaza**, or New Gate.

The **Rao Madho Singh Museum**, in the City Palace, is impressive. It's on the right-hand side of the complex's huge central courtyard and is entered through a gateway topped by rampant elephants. Inside, there are displays of weapons, old costumes and some of the best preserved murals in Rajasthan. There's also a collection of animal trophies and portraits of past rulers. The pieces are well displayed and it's an enjoyable place to take in the history of the region. The museum is open daily except Friday from 10 am to 4.30 pm. Admission is Rs

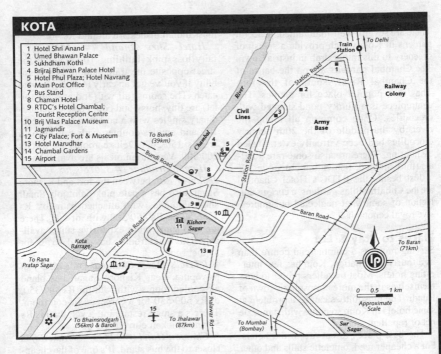

KOTA

1 Hotel Shri Anand
2 Umed Bhawan Palace
3 Sukhdham Kothi
4 Brijraj Bhawan Palace Hotel
5 Hotel Phul Plaza; Hotel Navrang
6 Main Post Office
7 Bus Stand
8 Chaman Hotel
9 RTDC's Hotel Chambal;
   Tourist Reception Centre
10 Brij Vilas Palace Museum
11 Jagmandir
12 City Palace; Fort & Museum
13 Hotel Marudhar
14 Chambal Gardens
15 Airport

SOUTHERN RAJASTHAN

7/50 for Indians/foreigners, Rs 50/75 for a camera/video.

After visiting the museum, wander around the rest of the complex just to appreciate how magnificent it must have been in its heyday. Unfortunately, a lot of it is falling into disrepair and the gardens are no more, but there are some excellent views over the old city, the river and the monstrous industrial complex across the river. Pollution is believed to be contributing to the deterioration of the fort. Some of the exterior murals are fading, which is a great pity.

Jagmandir

Between the City Palace and the RTDC's Hotel Chambal is the picturesque artificial tank of Kishore Sagar, constructed in 1346. Right in the middle of the tank, on a small island, is the beguiling little palace of Jagmandir. Built in 1740 by one of the mahara-

nis of Kota, it's best seen early in the morning but is exquisite at any time of day. It's not currently open to the public but you could get a closer look by going on a boat (daily except Monday from 10 am to 5 pm). It costs Rs 60 to hire an entire boat for a 15 minute ride.

Brij Vilas Palace Museum (Government Museum)

The government museum is in a small, plain palace near the Kishore Sagar. It has a collection of stone idols and other such fragments, mainly from the archaeological sites at Baroli and Jhalawar. There are also some weapons, paintings and old manuscripts. Neither the museum nor the palace are of great interest, though. The museum is open daily except Friday from 10 am to 4.30 pm; entry is Rs 3 (free Mondays). Photography is not allowed.

Gardens

There are several well-maintained, peaceful gardens in Kota which provide a splash of greenery to this rather drab industrial town. The **Chambal gardens** are on the banks of the Chambal River, south of the fort. They're a popular place for picnics. The centrepiece is a murky pond stocked with crocodiles. Once common all along the river, by the middle of the 20th century crocodiles had been virtually exterminated by hunting. There are also some rare gharials (thin-snouted, fish-eating crocodiles).

Just beside the RTDC's Hotel Chambal are the **Chhattar Bilas gardens**, a curious collection of somewhat neglected but impressive royal cenotaphs.

Places to Stay & Eat

Serving more as a commercial centre than as a tourist destination, Kota has few interesting hotels. Most travellers prefer to base themselves in the more atmospheric town of Bundi. The mosquitoes can be a problem at some hotels in Kota, so come with a mozzie net or repellent.

The best places to eat are in the hotels. For a cheaper feed, omelette stalls and other small eateries set up in the early evening on the footpath outside the main post office. If you do eat here, select food that has been freshly cooked, not reheated.

Hotel Navrang (☎ *323294, fax 450044)*, near the main post office, is one of the best mid-range choices in Kota. Don't be deceived by the front of the hotel, which looks rather run-down. The rooms all have attached bath and are arranged around an inner courtyard. Singles/doubles cost Rs 350/400 with air-cooling, or Rs 450/660 with air-con. Some rooms have more character than others, so try to have a look at a few first. There's a reasonably priced restaurant serving Indian, continental and Chinese cuisine.

Hotel Phul Plaza (☎ *329350, fax 322 614)*, next door, is also quite good. It has ordinary singles/doubles with attached bath and air-cooling for Rs 275/350, or Rs 450/550 with air-con. Suites cost Rs 1000/1100.

There's also a good vegetarian restaurant; most Indian dishes are around Rs 40.

Hotel Shri Anand (☎ *441157)*, a fairyfloss pink building 100m along the street opposite the train station, is a possibility if you've got an early morning train to catch. The rooms (all with Indian-style toilet) are tiny, noisy and could be cleaner. Ordinary singles with a common bath cost Rs 100 and singles/doubles with private bath are Rs 150/200. Deluxe rooms go for Rs 200/300. Vegetarian meals are available.

Hotel Marudhar (☎ *326186, fax 324415, Jhalawar Rd)*, between the fort and Kishore Sagar, also has a pale pink paint job. Small singles/doubles with attached bath cost Rs 225/250, or Rs 450/500 with air-con. There are also some more expensive suites available. This hotel fronts a busy road, so ask for a quiet room.

RTDC's Hotel Chambal (☎ *326527)* at Nayapura, near Kishore Sagar, has bland air-cooled rooms with bath for Rs 300/350, or Rs 500/550 for a carpeted air-con room. There's a small restaurant; a veg thali is Rs 55 and chicken curry is Rs 60.

Chaman Hotel (☎ *323377, Station Rd)* is closer to the bus stand. It's one of the cheapest hotels in town, but be prepared for grubby sheets and rooms the size of cupboards. Single female travellers are advised to give this place a miss. Singles/doubles with bath cost Rs 80/120. You can get a veg thali for Rs 30.

The modest *Brijraj Bhawan Palace Hotel* (☎ *450529, fax 450057)*, Civil Lines, is an atmospheric palace, which was once the former British residency. Situated on an elevated site overlooking the Chambal River, the hotel has been named after the current maharao of Kota, Brijraj Singh, who converted part of this property into a hotel in 1964. Today the maharao and his family live in one portion of the palace. There are well-maintained gardens, a tennis court and an elegantly furnished lounge filled with pictures of former rulers and various dignitaries. Comfortable rooms cost Rs 1050/1450, or Rs 1800 for a magnificent suite. There's an intimate dining room (residents only), that unlike most palaces is homey, not grand. Set lunch or dinner is Rs 240.

Umed Bhawan Palace (☎ 325262, fax 451110, Station Rd) is more grandiose than the Brijraj Bhawan Palace; however while it looks OK, closer inspection reveals lack of attention to detail. Surrounded by sprawling gardens, this gracious palace has a restaurant, bar and billiard room. The cheapest singles/doubles cost Rs 1190/1790. There are also luxury rooms for Rs 1390/2190 and the royal chamber for Rs 1690/2490.

Sukhdham Kothi (☎ 320081, fax 327 781), nearby, is over 100 years old and was once the home of the British resident's surgeon. Set in 3 acres of lovely gardens, this place has singles/doubles for Rs 950/1195. The set breakfast/lunch/dinner is Rs 110/200/225. The hotel can arrange jeep safaris to places of interest around Kota.

Getting There & Away

Air There used to be flights to and from Kota, but these were discontinued a few years back. Flights may be rescheduled in the future, so ask a travel agent or at any airport.

Bus There are express bus connections to:

destination	duration (hrs)	cost (Rs)
Ajmer	6	75
Alwar	8	110
Bikaner	12	175
Chittorgarh	6	73
Jaipur	6	95
Jodhpur	11	175
Mt Abu	12	160
Udaipur	6	90

For Jaisalmer, you'll have to change buses at Ajmer or Bikaner. Buses leave for Bundi every half hour (50 mins, Rs 15). If you're heading into Madhya Pradesh, several buses a day go to such places as Gwalior, Ujjain, Bhopal and Indore.

Train Kota is on the main broad-gauge Mumbai-Delhi line via Sawai Madhopur, the gateway to the Ranthambhore National Park, so there are plenty of trains going to: Sawai Madhopur (108km, 2 hrs, Rs 76/112 in 2nd/1st class), Agra Fort (343km, Rs 105/361), Jaipur (5 hrs, Rs 90/313), and to Delhi (10 hrs, Rs 160/546). There's a line linking Kota with Chittorgarh via Bundi; the daily train departs at 6.30 am, arriving in Bundi at 8 am (Rs 8) and gets into Chittor at 11.30 am (Rs 51).

Getting Around

Minibuses link the train station and bus stand (Rs 2). An auto-rickshaw should cost Rs 15 for this journey, although naturally you'll be asked for more. A cheaper alternative is to take a cycle-rickshaw.

AROUND KOTA
Wildlife Sanctuaries

The 250 sq km **Darrah Wildlife Sanctuary** is located about 50km from Kota. Here there are spotted deer, wild boars, bears, sambars, leopards, panthers and antelopes. It is open daily from sunrise to sunset, but is sometimes closed during the monsoon (usually from early July to mid-September). You need to get permission to visit from the local forest ranger, or contact the District Forest Office (☎ 0744-321263) in Kota – if that all fails, ask at the Tourist Reception Centre (☎ 0744-327695) in Kota. Entry costs Rs 10/40 for Indians/foreigners, plus Rs 125 per jeep (maximum of six people). Also accessible from Kota is the **National Chambal Wildlife Sanctuary**, which extends into neighbouring Madhya Pradesh. This 549 sq km reserve is best known for its gharials which inhabit the Chambal River, but blackbucks, chinkaras, wolves and the rarely seen caracals can also be found here.

About 45km east of Kota, flanking the main canal of the Chambal and Parvan rivers, are the **Sorsan grasslands**. Covering 35 sq km, these grasslands are rich in insects during the monsoon and attract a good variety of resident and migratory birds, including the great Indian bustard – a reluctant flier which is more commonly seen stalking through the grasslands on its sturdy legs. Other birds of Sorsan include mynas,

orioles, quails, partridges, flycatchers, bul-
buls, chats, drongos, shrikes, larks, robins
and weavers. Flocks of migrants, such as
warblers, flycatchers, larks, starlings and
rosy pastors, winter at Sorsan between October and March. Indian rollers can be seen
in early winter. The nearby canal and lakes
attract waterfowl, such as bar-headed and
greylag geese, common pochards, common
teal and pintails.

Baroli
One of Rajasthan's oldest temple complexes is at Baroli, 56km south-west of
Kota on the way to Rana Pratap Sagar. Set
in a peaceful area, many of these 9th century temples were vandalised by Muslim
armies but much remains. The main temple
is the **Ghateshvara Temple** which features
impressive columns. Although it is one of
the best preserved temples here, some of the
figures have been damaged. Many of the
sculptures from the temples are displayed in
the government museum in Kota.

There are hourly buses from Kota to
Baroli (1½ hrs, Rs 15). These leave from the
Gumanpura bus stand, near the petrol pump.

Bhainsrodgarh
Not far from Baroli is the picturesque
Bhainsrodgarh. This 14th century fort was
never besieged by an enemy force. Perched
on a ridge overlooking the Chambal River,
it is still occupied by descendants of a feudal family. You must get permission to visit
the fort – inquire at the Tourist Reception
Centre (☎ 0744-327695) in Kota.

JHALAWAR
☎ 07432
Situated 87km south of Kota, at the centre of
an opium-producing region, Jhalawar was
the capital of a small princely state created
in 1838. This town is well and truly off the
main tourist circuit, and only attracts a small
number of travellers. During winter, many
of the fields in this region are carpeted with
picturesque pink and white poppies.

In the centre of town is the **Jhalawar Fort**,
built by Maharaja Madan Singh in 1838.

Today it houses the government offices and
is run-down. There's also the small **Government Museum** which has a collection of 8th
century sculptures, gold coins, weapons and
old paintings. It's open every day except Friday from 10 am to 4.30 pm and entry is free.

The annual **Chandrabhaga Fair** is held on
the banks of the Chandrabhaga River, just
outside Jhalrapatan (see Around Jhalawar).
The fair takes place in the Hindu lunar
month of Kartika (for exact dates, see the
Regional Festival Calendar in the Facts for
the Visitor chapter), when thousands of
devotees take a holy dip. Apart from the cattle trading, a number of little shops and food
stalls are set up for the fair.

Information
Tourist Office The tourist office (☎ 30081)
is located at the RTDC's Hotel Chandrawati
(see Places to Stay). It is open daily except
Sunday from 10 am to 5 pm, but is not really
geared up for tourists so is of limited help.

Money Carry enough rupees with you, as
no banks in Jhalawar changed money at the
time of writing.

Post The main post office is near the bus
stand and is open daily except Sunday from
10 am to 1 pm and 2 to 6 pm.

Places to Stay & Eat
Attracting just a smattering of tourists, Jhalawar has very limited accommodation. The
best places to eat are in the hotels.

Purvaj Hotel (☎ 30951), at Mangalpura
near the clock tower, is the most homey
place to stay. This simple 200-year-old
haveli (mansion) has basic but cheap rooms
and the owner, Dileep Singh Jhala, is
friendly. It has more character than the other
hotels in Jhalawar. Ordinary singles/doubles
with attached bath (bucket hot water) cost
Rs 100/200, or deluxe doubles with views
over the town cost Rs 300. A bed in the tiny
dorm costs Rs 50. Meals are available.

*RTDC's Hotel Chandrawati (☎ 30015,
Jhalrapatan Rd)* has somewhat tatty rooms
with bath from Rs 175/200 to Rs 275/325.

There's also a small restaurant where you can get a veg thali for Rs 60.

Hotel Dwarika (☎ 22626), in the same area, is better than the RTDC hotel. It has reasonably good singles/doubles with bath (bucket hot water) for Rs 170/190. Deluxe rooms with constant hot water cost Rs 200/240. There's a vegetarian restaurant.

Getting There & Away

There are frequent buses from Kota to Jhalawar (2½ hrs, Rs 34). From there, buses go to most major towns in Rajasthan, including Jaipur (8 hrs, Rs 150) and Udaipur (11 hrs, Rs 140), Ajmer (6½ hrs, Rs 100), Jodhpur (11 hrs, Rs 150) and Alwar (12 hrs, Rs 175).

The nearest train station is 25km away and a jeep taxi to/from the station costs about Rs 160.

Getting Around

Jeep If you plan to visit the historic sites out of town, it's best to hire a jeep because many of the roads are in a state of bumpy disrepair. Expect to pay around Rs 700 to hire a jeep for eight hours. Inquire at your hotel about jeep hire places.

Auto-Rickshaw To travel anywhere in town by auto-rickshaw should cost Rs 15.

Bicycle Bicycle is a good way of making your way around. Available from near the Purvaj Hotel for Rs 2/10 per hour/day.

AROUND JHALAWAR
Jhalrapatan

Seven kilometres south of Jhalawar on the Kota road is **Jhalrapatan** (City of Temple Bells). This walled town once had more than 100 temples, although far fewer remain. The best known is the huge 10th century Surya Temple, which contains magnificent sculptures and one of the best preserved idols of Surya (the sun god) in India. There's also the 12th century **Shantinath Jain Temple**, a colourful and well-maintained temple with intricately carved statues and two huge stone elephants. Outside Jhalrapatan, the 7th-century **Chandrabhaga Temple** is set in gardens

on the banks of the Chandrabhaga River. There's also a small baori (stepwell) here.

Getting There & Away There are regular daily buses from Jhalawar to Jhalrapatan (20 mins, Rs 4).

Gagron Fort

While you're in this area, you should also look at the impressive Gagron Fort, 10km from Jhalawar. Very few tourists even suspect its existence and if you like to explore in peace and quiet this place is perfect. Within the fort walls there's a small village and the shrine of the Sufi saint, Mittheshah. From the ramparts there are good views of the surrounding countryside. The fort is situated at the confluence of two rivers. Though not as famous as others like Chittorgarh, Jodhpur and Jaisalmer, the huge fort occupies a prominent place in the annals of Rajput chivalry and has been fought over for centuries. Gagron Fort is open daily from sunrise to sunset and admission is free.

Other Attractions

Jhalawar's other attractions are farther out of town and difficult to reach without transport (a jeep is best as the roads are rough). About 54km from Jhalawar at **Dalhanpur** are some temple ruins believed to be hundreds of years old. Located near the Chhapi River, this small collection of ruins includes some carved pillars with erotic figures. Take care not to damage the fragments of pillars and statues that have fallen over. About 11km from Dalhanpur, at **Kakuni**, are the ruins of an old township. There's also a small temple with a huge idol of Lord Ganesh. Beyond Kakuni is the large **Fort of Manohar Thana**, once of great strategic importance. There are several small temples within its walls and a reforestation program has filled the compound with vegetation and birdlife.

There are ancient **Buddhist caves and stupas** atop a desolate hill near the town of Kolvi, about 90km from Jhalawar. It's a short climb to the top, where you'll find several enormous figures of Buddha. A narrow path winds past large stupas and numerous bat-filled meditation chambers. These re-markable caves are believed to date back to the 5th century and some contain weathered sculptures of Buddha – sadly, they are ne-glected and deteriorating.

CHITTORGARH (CHITTOR)
• pop 84,500   ☎ 01472

The massive hilltop fort of Chittorgarh is one of the most historically significant in Rajasthan and epitomises the whole roman-tic, doomed ideal of Rajput chivalry. Three times in its long history, Chittor was sacked by a stronger enemy and, on each occasion, the end came in textbook Rajput fashion: jauhar was declared in the face of impossi-ble odds. The men donned the saffron robes of martyrdom and rode out from the fort to certain death, while the women immolated themselves on a huge funeral pyre. Honour was always more important than death and Chittor still holds a special place in the hearts of many Rajputs.

The only real reason to come to Chittor is to see the fort – the town itself is quite crowded and really not of much interest. In and around Chittorgarh there are an increas-ing number of industries, some of which can be seen from the fort. Hopefully the pollu-tion that usually comes with industrial growth will not affect the fort.

Despite the rugged fort's impressive lo-cation and colourful history, Chittor is well and truly off the main tourist circuit and sees surprisingly few visitors. If you're pressed for time, it's possible to squeeze in a visit to Chittor on a day trip from Udaipur. It's well worth the detour.

History
Chittor's first defeat occurred in 1303 when Ala-ud-din Khilji, the Pathan king of Delhi, besieged the fort in order to capture the beautiful Padmini, wife of the Rana's uncle, Bhim Singh. When defeat was inevitable the Rajput noblewomen, including Padmini, committed jauhar and Bhim Singh led the orange-clad noblemen out to their deaths.

In 1535 Bahadur Shah, the sultan of Gu-jarat, besieged the fort and, once again, the medieval dictates of chivalry determined the outcome. This time, the carnage was im-mense. It is said that 13,000 Rajput women and 32,000 Rajput warriors died following the declaration of jauhar.

The final sack of Chittor came 33 years later, in 1568, when the Mughal Emperor Akbar took the town. The fort was defended heroically, against overwhelming odds. The women performed jauhar, the fort gates were flung open and 8000 orange-robed warriors rode out to their deaths. On this oc-casion, Maharana Udai Singh II fled Chittor for Udaipur, where he re-established his capital. In 1616, Jehangir returned Chittor to the Rajputs but there was no resettlement.

Orientation
The fort stands on a 280 hectare site on top of a 180m-high hill, which rises abruptly from the surrounding plain. Until 1568 the town of Chittor was also on the hilltop, within the fort walls, but today's modern town, known as Lower Town, sprawls to the west of the hill. A river separates it from the bus stand, rail-way line and the rest of the town.

Information
Tourist Office The Tourist Reception Cen-tre (☎ 41089) is near the train station and is open Monday to Saturday from 10 am to 5 pm (closed for lunch between 1 and 2 pm).

Money Money can be changed at the State Bank of Bikaner & Jaipur, a short distance north of the main post office.

Post The main post office is located less than a kilometre south of the bus stand. It is open every day except Sunday from 10 am to 1 pm and 2 to 5 pm.

Fort
According to legend, Bhim, one of the Pan-dava heroes of the *Mahabharata*, is credited with the fort's original construction. All of Chittor's attractions are within the fort. A zigzag ascent of over 1km leads through seven gateways to the main gate on the western side, the **Rampol** (*pol* means gate).

CHITTORGARH (CHITTOR)

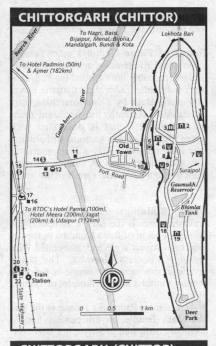

CHITTORGARH (CHITTOR)

PLACES TO STAY
11 Bhagwati Hotel
13 Natraj Tourist Hotel
16 Hotel Pratap Palace
21 Shalimar Hotel
22 Hotel Chetak

OTHER
1 Mahavir Temple; Tower of Fame
2 Fateh Prakash Palace
3 Archaeological Museum & Office
4 Rana Kumbha Palace
5 Chhatris of Jaimal & Kalla
6 Kumbha Shyam Temple; Meera Temple
7 Temple of Neelkanth Mahadev
8 Tower of Victory
9 Mahasati Temple; Sammidheshwar Temple
10 Rawat Bagh Singh Memorial
12 Bus Stand
14 State Bank of India
15 State Bank of Bikaner & Jaipur
17 Main Post Office
18 Kalika Mata Temple
19 Padmini's Palace
20 Tourist Reception Centre

On the climb, you pass two **chhatris**, memorials marking spots where Jaimal and Kalla, heroes of the 1568 siege, fell during the struggle against Akbar. The main gate on the eastern side of the fort is the **Surajpol**. Within the fort, a circular road runs around the ruins and there's a **deer park** at the southern end.

There are good views over the town, countryside and the huge cement factory from the western end of the fort; there's even a small village located here.

Today, the fort of Chittor is a virtually deserted ruin, but impressive reminders of its grandeur still stand. The main sites in the fort can all be seen in half a day (assuming you're not walking) but, if you like the atmosphere of ancient sites, then it is definitely worth spending longer as this is a very mellow place.

Entry to the fort is Rs 2/50 for Indians/foreigners. A still camera is free, but there's a video charge of Rs 25 in the Tower of Victory. Car entry is free, but if there is just one passenger there is a Rs 25 charge.

English-speaking guides are available inside the fort, usually at the Rana Kumbha Palace. The guides charge around Rs 200 for four people. Make sure you get a government-approved guide (they carry a guide licence).

Rana Kumbha Palace Entering the fort and turning right, you come almost immediately to the ruins of this 15th century palace. It contains both elephant and horse stables and a Shiva temple. One of the jauhars is said to have taken place in a vaulted cellar. Across from the palace is the **archaeological office** and **museum**, and the **treasury building** or Nau Lakha Bhandar. Close by is the **Singa Chowri Temple**.

Fateh Prakash Palace This palace is just beyond the Rana Kumbha Palace, and is much more modern (Maharana Fateh Singh died in 1930). It is closed except for a small **museum** which is open daily except Friday from 10.30 am to 4.30 pm. Entry costs Rs 3 (free Monday).

Tower of Victory The Jaya Stambh, or Tower of Victory, was erected by Rana Kumbha between 1458-68 to commemorate his victory over Mahmud Khilji of Malwa in 1440. It rises 37m in nine storeys and you can climb the narrow stairs to the eighth storey. Entry is Rs 3 (free on Friday) and opening hours are 8 am to 7 pm. Watch your head on the lintels! Hindu sculptures adorn the outside of the tower, but the dome was damaged by lightning and repaired during the 19th century.

Close to the tower is the **Mahasati**, an area where the ranas were cremated during Chittorgarh's period as the Mewar capital. There are many *sati* stones (stones to commemorate women who committed sati, by throwing themselves on their husbands' funeral pyres) here. The **Sammidheshwar Temple** stands in the same area.

Gaumukh Reservoir Walk down beyond the temple and, at the very edge of the cliff, you'll see this deep tank. The reservoir takes its name from a spring which feeds the tank from a cow's mouth carved in the cliff-side. The opening here leads to the cave in which Padmini and her compatriots are said to have committed jauhar.

Padmini's Palace Continuing south, you come to Padmini's Palace, built beside a large lotus pool with a pavilion in its centre. Legend relates that, as Padmini sat in this pavilion, Ala-ud-din was permitted to see her reflection in a mirror in the palace. This glimpse was the spark that convinced him to destroy Chittor in order to possess her.

The bronze gates in this pavilion were carried off by Akbar and can now be seen in the fort at Agra. Near Padmini's Palace is a small prison where captured invaders were kept and a sultan of Malwa and of Gujarat were once locked up.

Not far away are the former military training grounds for Rajput soldiers, today a helipad for visiting dignitaries. Continuing round the circular road, you pass the deer park, the **Bhimlat Tank**, the **Adhbudhnath Shiva Temple**, the **Surajpol** and

the **Neelkanth Mahadev Jain Temple** before reaching the Tower of Fame.

Tower of Fame Chittor's other famous tower, the Kirti Stambha, or Tower of Fame, is older (probably built around the 12th century) and smaller (22m high) than the Tower of Victory. Built by a Jain merchant, it is dedicated to Adinath, the first Jain *tirthankar* (prophet), and is decorated with naked figures of the various tirthankars, thus indicating that it is a Digambara, or 'sky clad', monument. A narrow stairway leads through the seven storeys of the tower to the top.

Other Buildings Close to the Fateh Prakash Palace is the **Meera Temple**, built during the reign of Rana Kumbha in the ornate Indo-Aryan style and associated with the mystic-poetess Meerabai. The larger temple in this same compound is the 15th century **Kumbha Shyam Temple**, or Temple of Varah.

Across from Padmini's Palace is the **Kalika Mata Temple**, an 8th century temple originally dedicated to Surya, but later converted to a temple to the goddess Kali. At the northern tip of the fort is another gate, the **Lokhota Bari**, while at the southern end is a small opening from which criminals and traitors were hurled into the abyss.

Places to Stay & Eat

Hotel standards in Chittor are generally disappointing; the cleanliness and service is usually below average and many of the cheaper places have miserable bathrooms (many budget places have an Indian-style toilet). Another alternative is available by employing the services of the Paying Guest House Scheme, which operates in Chittor (ask at the Tourist Reception Centre – see Information earlier).

Shalimar Hotel (☎ *40842*), opposite the train station, has dull singles/doubles for Rs 80/100 with common bath, or Rs 125/200 with bath attached. Hot water is by the bucket (no charge). Air-con rooms with constant hot water cost Rs 400/450.

Hotel Chetak (☎ *41588)*, nearby, is somewhat better, with rooms from Rs 150/250 with private bath. Deluxe rooms cost Rs 250/350, or Rs 450/550 with air-conditioning. There's a restaurant serving veg Indian, south Indian and Chinese food. A vegetarian thali costs Rs 32.

Hotel Meera (☎ *40266)*, in the same area, is a good option in this town low on hotel talent. Singles/doubles with private bath range from Rs 300/350 to Rs 600/700. Meals are available.

Natraj Tourist Hotel (☎ *41009)* right by the bus stand, is very basic but undeniably cheap. Small, dark rooms with common bath cost Rs 40/60, or Rs 60/100 with bath; but you'll probably have to get them to change the sheets. No meals are available.

Bhagwati Hotel (☎ *46226)*, just over the river, is better than the Natraj, but still not that great. Simple and rather noisy double rooms with common bath go for Rs 70, or Rs 60/80 with attached bath. Most rooms have hot water by the bucket.

RTDC's Hotel Panna (☎ *41238)* is closer to town (ie farther away from the fort). Dorm beds are Rs 50, and slapdash singles/doubles with bath start at Rs 175/225. The best rooms are Rs 475/575. The hotel has a seedy little bar and a restaurant (the veg/nonveg thali is Rs 45/55).

Hotel Pratap Palace (☎ *40099, fax 41 042)* is one of the most popular places to stay. Air-cooled rooms with attached bathroom cost upwards of Rs 200/250 a single/double. There's a restaurant near the pleasant garden; a half tandoori chicken costs Rs 80, malai kofta is Rs 30. Village safaris can be arranged, and visits to their castle in Bijaipur (see Around Chittorgarh).

Hotel Padmini (☎/*fax 41718)* is a little out of town near the Bearch River, but is the most upmarket place in Chittor. There are some rooms for Rs 400/500 with bath, or better air-con singles/doubles for Rs 800/1000. The veg restaurant serves Indian and Chinese food; palak paneer is Rs 35.

Retiring rooms at the train station cost Rs 100 for a double or Rs 200 for an air-con room. Simple veg thali available for Rs 16.

Getting There & Away

Bus Express buses travel to various destinations including Delhi (12 hrs, Rs 224), Ajmer (4 hrs, Rs 73) and Jaipur (8 hrs, Rs 125). It's possible to take an early morning bus from Udaipur to Chittorgarh (3 hrs, Rs 44), spend about three hours visiting the fort (by auto-rickshaw or tonga), and then take a late afternoon bus to Ajmer, but this is definitely pushing it.

Train The *Chetak Express* travels to Ajmer (Rs 96/258 in 2nd/1st class), Jaipur (Rs 133/313) and Delhi (Rs 207/667). The *Neemach Agra* connects Chittor and Kota (Rs 28). There are also rail connections to Ahmedabad and Udaipur.

Getting Around

It's about 6km from the train station to the fort, less from the bus stand, and 7km around the fort itself, not including the long southern loop out to the deer park. Auto-rickshaws charge around Rs 100 for a trip around the fort compound, and this includes waiting time at the various sites.

Bicycles can be rented near the train station (Rs 30 per day) to visit the fort but, as many Indian bikes lack gears, you may have to push the machine to the top. Still, they're great on the top and for the journey back down – but check the brakes first!

AROUND CHITTORGARH
Bijaipur

Castle Bijaipur, 40km south of Chittor, is a rustic 16th century palace in the village of Bijaipur. It's an ideal place to kick back with a good book, do yoga, meditate, walk or do absolutely nothing! Traditionally decorated singles/doubles in this peaceful castle cost Rs 800/850. If you want to lash out, the best rooms will set you back Rs 1350/1500. There's a pleasant garden courtyard and an airy restaurant serving Rajasthani food – set lunch/dinner is Rs 175/300.

There are some good walks in the pretty countryside around the castle. The friendly owners can arrange jeep safaris to places of interest around Bijaipur, such as the nearby

Bhil tribal village, or a visit to their cool jungle property, known as *thanderiberi*. Tribal folk singing and dancing can also be organised at the castle with advance notice, or you can see local craftspeople at work in **Bassi** village, 12km from Bijaipur – they specialise in wooden handicrafts. Bookings for the castle should be made through Hotel Pratap Palace (☎ *01472-40099, fax 41042*) in Chittorgarh. Nonguests can dine at the castle with advance notice.

Getting There & Away Frequent buses travel daily to Bijaipur from Chittorgarh (1½ hrs, Rs 20). A jeep taxi can be organised through the Hotel Pratap Palace in Chittor for Rs 400 (one way).

Menal & Bijolia

On the Bundi to Chittorgarh road, 48km from Bundi, Menal is a complex of Shiva temples built in the Gupta period. After a good monsoon, there's an impressive waterfall in this area that is also a big attraction.

Bijolia, 16km from Menal, was once a group of 100 temples. Most of these were destroyed by Mughal invaders and today only three are left standing, one of which has a huge figure of Ganesh.

Mandalgarh

A detour between Menal and Bijolia takes you to Mandalgarh. It is the third fort of Mewar built by Rana Kumbha – the others are the great fort of Chittorgarh and the fort at Kumbhalgarh.

Nagri

One of the oldest towns in Rajasthan, Nagri is 17km north of Chittor. Hindu and Buddhist remains from the Mauryan to the Gupta periods have been found here. Many old copper coins and sculptures discovered in Nagri are now at museums in Chittorgarh and Udaipur.

Jagat

At this small town, 20km south of the road between Udaipur and Chittorgarh, is a small 10th century **Durga Temple**. There are some fine carvings, including a couple of small erotic carvings which have inspired some people to call the town the Khajuraho of Rajasthan (total nonsense!).

UDAIPUR

- pop 366,000   ☎ 0294

Possibly no city in Rajasthan is quite as romantic as Udaipur, even though the state is replete with grandiose palaces, fantastic hilltop forts and gripping legends of chivalry and heroism. The French Impressionist painters would have loved this place, called the 'Venice of the East'. Indeed, with its bewitching palaces surrounded by serene lakes and rolling hills, Udaipur looks as though it has been lifted straight from the pages of a fairytale book. In the *Annals & Antiquities of Rajasthan*, Colonel James Tod describes Udaipur as 'the most diversified and most romantic spot on the continent of India'.

This 'oasis' in the desert has become a jewel of India's tourism industry and thousands of people flock here each year. Consequently, Udaipur has no dearth of hotels – there are places to suit all tastes and pockets, from simple guest houses to incredible palaces. And there has to be more rooftop restaurants than any other place in India. So sit back, relax and take in the picturesque views. There are also brilliant views of Udaipur from the Monsoon Palace (Sajjan Garh), situated on a nearby mountain.

Udaipur rivals the famous creations of the Mughals with superbly crafted elegance and the Rajput love of the whimsical. The Lake Palace is the best late example of this cultural explosion, but Udaipur is full of palaces, temples and havelis ranging from the modest to the extravagant. And, since water is relatively plentiful in this part of the state (in between the periodic droughts), there are plenty of green parks and gardens, many of which line the lake shores.

Udaipur is proud of its heritage as a centre for crafts and the performing arts, and its school of miniature painting is noteworthy. These paintings were produced for the maharanas of Udaipur from the early 18th to the mid-20th centuries and many examples can be seen at the City Palace Museum.

Until recently the higher, uninhabited parts of the city were covered in forests; as elsewhere, most of these have been turned into firewood, but there is a movement afoot to reverse this. The city was once surrounded by a wall and, although the gates and much of the wall over the higher crags remain, a great deal of it has disappeared. It's sad that this fate should have befallen such a historic place, but its essence remains.

In common with most Indian cities, Udaipur's urban and industrial sprawl spreads beyond the city's original boundaries and pollution of various kinds can be discouraging. This will be your first impression of Udaipur if you arrive at the train or bus stations. Ignore it and head for the old city, where a different world awaits you.

History

Udaipur was founded in 1568 by Maharana Udai Singh II following the final sacking of Chittorgarh by the Mughal emperor, Akbar. According to legend, Udai Singh II found the site of his new capital some years before the last assault on Chittor, after coming across a holy man meditating on a hill near Lake Pichola. The old man advised the maharana to establish his capital on that very spot and that's how Udaipur came into existence. Surrounded by forests, lakes and the protective Aravalli Range, the new capital of Mewar was certainly in a less vulnerable location than Chittor. (For information about Udaipur's royal coat of arms, see the boxed text Sons of the Sun in the Facts about Rajasthan chapter.)

Maharana Udai Singh II died in 1572 and was succeeded by his son, Pratap, who bravely defended Udaipur from subsequent Mughal attacks, and gallantly fought at the battle of Haldighati in 1576 (see the North of Udaipur section, later). Unlike many other rulers in Rajasthan, the rulers of Mewar refused to be controlled by foreign invaders, even though they were constantly attacked. After struggling against the Mughals, Udaipur was later attacked by the Marathas.

An end to bloody battles and instability came with British intervention in the early 19th century, when a treaty was signed which pledged to protect Udaipur from invaders. This umbrella of protection ended when India gained independence from the British. Along with all the other princely states, Udaipur surrendered its sovereignty and became part of a united India.

Orientation

The old city, bounded by the remains of a city wall, is on the east side of Lake Pichola. The train station and bus stand are both just outside the city wall to the south-east.

Information

Tourist Offices The Tourist Reception Centre (☎ 411535) is located in the Fateh Memorial Building near Surajpol, less than 1km from the bus stand. The office is open Monday to Saturday from 10 am to 1.30 pm and 2 to 5 pm. Smaller tourist information counters operate at the train station and airport. An independent information counter operates at the southern end of the City Palace complex.

Money You can change money at a number of places including the Vijaya Bank and Thomas Cook, both in the City Palace complex (near the museum). At Chetak Circle, the State Bank of Bikaner & Jaipur changes money. There's also the Bank of Baroda, the Bank of Rajasthan and the Punjab National Bank, all in Bapu Bazaar.

Post & Communications The main post office is north of the old city, at Chetak Circle; poste restante is at the post office at Shastri Circle. There's also a small post office (called the Palace Extension Counter) in the quadrant outside the City Palace Museum. It's open daily except Sunday from 10.30 am to 1 pm and 1.30 to 4.30 pm.

The DHL Worldwide Express office (☎ 414388) is at 380 Ashok Nagar, Shree Niketan Building (near Ayer Bridge). This office is open daily except Sunday from 9.30 am to 5 pm. It can arrange air freight around the world.

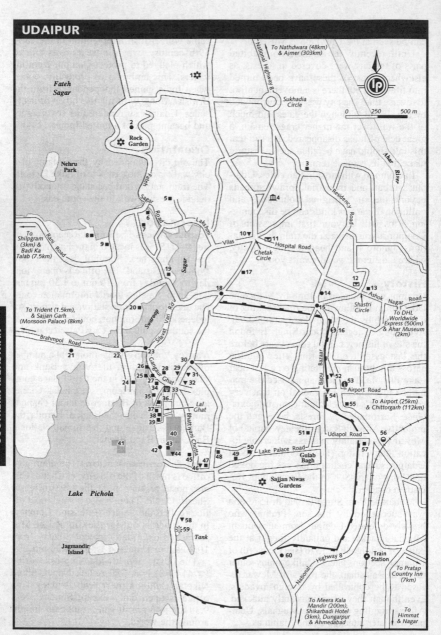

UDAIPUR

To Nathdwara (48km)
& Ajmer (303km)

National Highway 8

*Fateh
Sagar*

1 ✴

Sukhadia
Circle

0   250   500 m

2 ●

✿ Rock
Garden

*Nehru
Park*

3 ■

Residency Road

Ahar River

Fateh Sagar Road

5 ■

🏛 4

6 ■
7 ■

Lakshmi

10 ▼
11 ✉

Hospital Road

To Shilpgram
(3km) &
Badi Ka
Talab (7.5km)

8 ■
9 ●

Vilas

*Chetak
Circle*

Rani Road

19 ■

Sagar

17 ■

12 ✉
13 ■

Ashok

Nagar Road

14 ■

18 ■

Shastri
Circle

To Trident (1.5km),
& Sajjan Garh
(Monsoon Palace) (8km)

20 ■

Swaroop

15 ●

To DHL
Worldwide
Express (500m)
& Ahar Museum
(2km)

Brahmpol Road

Silawat Vati Rd

16 💲

21 ●

22 ●

23 ●

30 ●

26 ●
27 ▼
25 ■
34 ■
35 ●

28 ▼
29 ▼
31 ▼
32 ▼
33 🅟

Bapu Bazaar

52 ▼
53 ■

ℹ

Airport Road

24 ■

36 ■
37 ■
38 ■
39 ■

*Lal
Ghat*

Bhattyani Chotta

Gangaur Ghat

54 ●
55 ■

To Airport (25km)
& Chittorgarh (112km)

40

41

42 ●
43 ■
44 ▼

45 ●
46 ■
47 ▼

48 ■
49 ■

50 ■

51 ■

Lake Palace Road

*Gulab
Bagh*

Udiapol Road

56 ●

57 ■

Lake   Pichola

✿ Sajjan Niwas
Gardens

*Jagmandir
Island*

58 ▼
59 ✴

Tank

60 ●

National Highway 8

Train
Station

To Pratap
Country Inn
(7km)

To Meera Kala
Mandir (200m),
Shikarbadi Hotel
(3km), Dungarpur
& Ahmedabad

To
Himmat
& Nagar

SOUTHERN RAJASTHAN

UDAIPUR

PLACES TO STAY		
3	Mewar Inn	
5	Laxmi Vilas Palace Hotel;	
	Hotel Anand Bhawan	
6	Hotel Gulab Niwas	
7	Hotel Hilltop Palace	
8	Hotel Lakend	
9	Hotel Ram Pratap Palace	
13	RTDC's Hotel Kajri	
17	Ajanta Hotel	
19	Pahadi Palace	
20	Hotel Natural	
24	Wonder View Palace;	
	Lake Pichola Hotel;	
	Lake Shore Hotel;	
	Udai Kothi;	
	Ambrai Restaurant	
25	Jheel Guest House	
26	Nukkad Guest House	
27	Hotel Gangaur Palace	
28	Hotel Badi Haveli & Heera	
	Cycle Store; Lehar Guest	
	House; Anjani Hotel	
34	Jag Niwas Guest House	
35	Hotel Caravanserai; Lalghat	
	Guest House; Evergreen	
	Guest House & Restaurant	
	Natural View	
36	Lake Ghat Guest House;	
	Ratan Palace Guest House	

37	Kankarwa Haveli; Jagat	
	Niwas Palace Hotel;	
	Rainbow Guest House	
38	Hotel Sai-Niwas;	
	Shiva Guest House	
39	Lake Corner Soni Paying	
	Guest House	
41	Jagniwas Island (Lake Palace	
	Hotel)	
43	Shiv Niwas Palace Hotel;	
	Fateh Prakash Palace Hotel	
45	Hotel Raj Palace	
47	Rang Niwas Palace Hotel	
48	Ranjit Niwas Hotel	
49	Hotel Mahendra Prakash;	
	Hotel Shambhu Vilas	
50	Haveli Hotel	
51	Hotel Vishnupriya (Quality	
	Inn); Chirag Restaurant &	
	Beer Bar	
55	Apsara Hotel	
57	Hotel Welcome	

PLACES TO EAT		
10	Berry's Restaurant	
29	Maxim's Café	
31	Anna Restaurant	
32	Mayur Café	
44	Sunset View Terrace;	
	Samor Bagh	

46	Roof Garden Café	
52	Park View	
54	16 Chef Restaurant; Surajpol	
58	Café Hill Park	

OTHER		
1	Saheliyon ki Bari	
2	Pratap Smarak (Moti Magri)	
4	Bhartiya Lok Kala Museum	
11	Main Post Office	
12	Poste Restante	
14	Indian Airlines	
15	Delhi Gate	
16	Bank of Baroda;	
	Punjab National Bank;	
	Bank of Rajasthan	
18	Hathipol	
21	Brahmpol	
22	Ambapol	
23	Chandpol	
30	Clock Tower	
33	Jagdish Temple	
40	City Palace; Museums;	
	WWF; Banks; Comfort	
	Travels & Tours	
42	Bansi Ghat (City Palace Jetty)	
53	Tourist Reception Centre	
56	Bus Stand	
59	Sunset Point	
60	Kishanpol	

SOUTHERN RAJASTHAN

Internet Resources At the time of writing, the Hotel Raj Palace (see Places to Stay) and the Comfort Travels & Tours office (☎ 419746), in the courtyard outside the City Palace Museum, were the only places with email facilities.

Travel Agencies Udaipur has scores of small travel agencies (concentrated in the tourist-laden old city), all promising the best deals in town. Shop around for the best price, as most will try to match or better the prices quoted to you by other agencies.

Bookshops There's a particularly good array of bookshops in the old city, as this is Udaipur's biggest tourist hang-out. Most of these shops sell titles pertaining to Rajasthan and some have interesting books on spirituality. Many of these bookshops also sell a small collection of music cassettes.

Ayurvedic Hospital The government-run Madan Mohan Malvai Ayurvedic College & Hospital (☎ 525392) at Ambamata Scheme, near Fateh Sagar, prescribes natural medicines and conducts courses in ayurveda. This hospital was opened in 1944 and specialises in joint pains, paralysis and neurological disorders. It's open daily from 9 am to 3 pm in the winter, and from 8 am to 2 pm in the summer.

Lake Pichola

The beautiful Lake Pichola was enlarged by Maharana Udai Singh II after he founded the city. He built a masonry dam, known as the Badipol, and the lake is now 4km long and 3km wide. Nevertheless, it remains fairly shallow and can actually dry up in severe droughts. At these times, you can walk to the island palaces from the shore. Fortunately, this doesn't happen often. A handful

Tie The Knot With An Exotic Twist

Getting married? If you want to play prince and princess on your special day, you couldn't do much better than Udaipur, with its whimsical palaces. This 'Venice of the East' has become a favourite wedding venue for foreigners – many have travelled thousands of miles to tie the knot in this dreamy destination.

Situated in the middle of Lake Pichola, the gorgeous Lake Palace was once the exclusive summer residence of Udaipur's maharanas, but is today accessible to anyone (who can afford it!). If you like the thought of celebrating your marriage at one of the sets of *Octopussy*, then the Lily Pond may appeal to you. This is an inner open-air courtyard at the Lake Palace Hotel, replete with lily ponds and fountains. It can accommodate up to 200 people.

If you would prefer something more intimate but still at the Lake Palace Hotel, there's the Mewar Terrace, which can hold up to 80 people.

There's also a smaller reception area, the Mayur Mahal, located on the shores of Lake Pichola near the City Palace. This is a 400-year-old courtyard which is not as swanky as the Lake Palace, but has an old-world charm. It can only hold about 40 people.

For those who like the idea of getting married on the move, there's the Gangaur Boat, an old royal barge belonging to the maharana of Udaipur. There's no motor, so it is rowed by men dressed in traditional attire, worn long ago when the maharanas reigned. It can take up to 30 guests. If it's too tough deciding on just one venue, you can opt for several – for instance, cocktails on the Gangaur Boat followed by dinner at the Lily Pond.

Whatever venue you choose, all arrangements are made by the Lake Palace Hotel. The staff are happy to tailor a wedding to suit your needs, and they can cook up a variety of cuisines, ranging from Rajasthani to Italian (except the royal barge which only serves Indian food). Flowers, music, fireworks and a photographer can also be organised.

Most types of wedding ceremonies are possible, as long as you give the Lake Palace Hotel plenty of notice. If you intend getting married by a Christian priest, you must send a 'No Objection Certificate' (issued by a church in your country of residence) to Udaipur at least a month prior to your wedding date. If you opt for a Hindu ceremony, all arrangements can be made by the Lake Palace Hotel, including advice on where to get traditional Rajasthani wedding clothes. You will even get a certificate of marriage.

You're advised to make a reservation at least a year ahead, to ensure you get the venue of your choice. The most pleasant time to get married is during the cooler months between November and March.

The cost varies depending on the venue and individual requirements. For prices and further information, contact the General Manager, Lake Palace Hotel (☎ 0294-527961/527973, fax 527974), Post Box 5, Udaipur 313001, Rajasthan.

In Udaipur, it's also possible to have weddings at the beautiful Shiv Niwas Palace Hotel (see Places to Stay), the grandiose durbar hall (see the boxed text Durbar Hall) and the evocative Jagmandir Island. For these venues, you must contact the Sales & Marketing Manager, HRH Group of Hotels, City Palace (☎ 0294-528016/528019, fax 528006), Udaipur, 313001, Rajasthan. If possible, have a look at all the venues before making a choice. Good luck!

of crocodiles are believed to live in the more remote parts of the lake, near uninhabited sections of the shore. Unfortunately

the lake occasionally gets choked with that insidious weed, the water hyacinth. The City Palace extends a considerable distance along the east bank. South of the palace, a pleasant garden runs down to the shore. North of the palace, you can wander along the shore to some interesting bathing and *dhobi* (laundry) ghats.

Out in the lake are two islands – Jagniwas and Jagmandir. **Boat rides**, which leave regularly from the City Palace jetty (known as Bansi Ghat), are enjoyable and cost Rs 75 per person for 30 minutes and Rs 150 per person for one hour; the latter includes a stop at Jagmandir Island. Boat rides are available every hour from 10 am to 4 pm daily.

Jagniwas Island (Lake Palace Hotel)
Jagniwas, the Lake Palace island, is about 1.5 hectares in size. The palace was built by Maharana Jagat Singh II in 1754 and covers the whole island. Once the royal summer palace, it was converted into a hotel in the 1960s by Maharana Bhagwat Singh. It is the ultimate in luxury hotels, with courtyards, fountains, restaurants and even a swimming pool. The gleaming white Lake Palace Hotel was largely responsible for putting Udaipur on the international tourist map. Its unparalleled location, majestic interior and exquisite architecture have placed it among the most exotic hotels in the world today. It's a magical place but casual visitors are discouraged. Nonguests can only come over for lunch or dinner – and then only if the hotel is not full, which it often is (for details see Places to Eat). Hotel launches cross to the island from the City Palace jetty. The Lake Palace and two other palaces in Udaipur, the Shiv Niwas Palace and the Monsoon Palace (Sajjan Garh), appeared in the James Bond film *Octopussy*.

Behind Jagniwas is a much smaller island known as **Arsi Vilas**. It was built by a former maharana of Udaipur to watch the sunset. There's a landing attached to this island, which has been used as a helipad in the past.
Jagmandir Island The other island palace, Jagmandir, was commenced by Maharana Karan Singh, but takes its name from Maharana Jagat Singh (1628-52), who made a number of additions to it. It is said that the Mughal emperor, Shah Jahan, derived some

of his ideas and inspiration for the Taj Mahal from this palace after staying here in 1623-24 while leading a revolt against his father, Jehangir. The island has some beautiful stone carvings, including a row of huge elephants that look as though they are guarding the island. An intricately carved chhatri made of grey-blue stone is also impressive. There are trees, flowers and courtyards on this ancient island palace, which has recently been the venue for moonlight piano concerts and other special events, including weddings. The view across the lake from the southern end, with the city and its glorious palace rising up behind the island palaces, is a scene of rare beauty.

City Palace & Museums
The huge City Palace, towering over the lake, is the largest palace complex in Rajasthan. Although it's a conglomeration of buildings added by various maharanas, the palace manages to retain a surprising uniformity of design. Building was started by Maharana Udai Singh II. The palace is surmounted by balconies, towers and cupolas and there are wonderful views over the lake and the city from the upper terraces.

The palace is entered from the northern end through the Baripol of 1600 and the Tripolia Gate of 1725, with its eight carved marble arches. It was once a custom for maharanas to be weighed under the gate and their weight in gold or silver distributed to the populace.

The main part of the palace is now preserved as the **City Palace Museum** with a large and varied collection of artefacts. Downstairs from the entrance is an armoury section, sporting a collection of old weapons including a lethal two-pronged sword. The museum includes the Mor Chowk with its beautiful mosaics of peacocks, the favourite Rajasthani bird. The Manak (or Ruby) Mahal has glass and mirrorwork while Krishna Vilas has a remarkable collection of miniatures (no photography is permitted here). In the Bari Mahal there is a fine central garden with good views over the old city. The Moti Mahal has beautiful mirrorwork and the

Chini Mahal is covered in ornamental tiles. The Surya Chopar has a huge, ornamental sun – the symbol of the Mewar dynasty, which traces its origin to the sun. More paintings can be seen in the Zenana Mahal. Note the large tiger-catching cage near the Zenana Mahal entrance; a helpless goat or buffalo would be tied up inside the cage to lure the tiger in – gruesome. Nearby is a tiny WWF shop (open daily from 10 am to 5 pm) – the greeting cards (Rs 10) and pack of playing cards (Rs 53) sold here are lovely.

Enter the City Palace Museum through the Ganesh Deori, which leads to the Rajya Angan, or Royal Courtyard. The museum is open daily from 9.30 am to 4.30 pm. Admission is Rs 25, or Rs 15 for children under the age of 12 and Rs 50/300 for a camera/video. If you enter the museum from the Lake Palace side (past the Fateh Prakash Palace Hotel and the maharana's private residence), the entry fee is higher (Rs 75) – although this is not always policed. An English-speaking guide costs Rs 95 (maximum five people), Rs 120 (maximum 10 people), or Rs 150 (maximum 15 people); the knowledgeable Kishan Das speaks French, English, Hindi and is currently learning Spanish. In the winter months (prime tourist season), the museum can get particularly crowded, so try to visit before 11 am to avoid the rush. There's a Rajasthani art school in the museum complex where you can see live demonstrations of miniature painting.

There's a **Government Museum** (closed Friday) which costs Rs 3 (free Mondays) within the palace complex; no photography is allowed. The museum exhibits a collection of weapons, sculptures and paintings, plus a stuffed kangaroo that's coming apart at the legs, a freaky stuffed monkey holding a small lamp, and a Siamese-twin deer. The large rectangular courtyard outside the City Palace Museum has some shops selling rather pricey handicrafts, a small kiosk, places where you can buy film for your camera, and a money-exchange facility.

The other part of the palace is up against the lake shore and has been partly converted into two luxury hotels known as the Shiv Niwas Palace and the Fateh Prakash Palace hotels (see Places to Stay).

The **Crystal Gallery**, at the Fateh Prakash Palace Hotel in the City Palace complex, is breathtaking. This rare collection of Osler's crystal was ordered from England by Maharana Sajjan Singh in 1877, although the maharana never saw the crystal because of his untimely death. Items include crystal dressing tables, lamps, chairs, crockery, table fountains and even beds! There's an exquisite antique jewel-studded carpet, which has to be seen to be believed. This gallery is open daily from 10 am to 1 pm and 3 to 8 pm (winter); from 9 am to noon and 3 to 8 pm (summer). Entry (Rs 200 per person) includes a soft drink, tea or coffee. Photography is strictly prohibited. The Crystal Gallery overlooks the grandiose **durbar hall** (see boxed text p. 239).

Jagdish Temple

Located only 150m north of the entrance to the City Palace, this fine Indo-Aryan temple was built by Maharana Jagat Singh in 1651 and enshrines a black stone image of Vishnu as Jagannath, Lord of the Universe. There is a brass image of the Garuda in a shrine in front of the temple and the steps up to the temple are flanked by elephants. Hopefully the ugly scaffolding will have been removed from the temple by the time you read this. The temple is open daily from 5 am to 2 pm and 4 to 10 pm.

Fateh Sagar

North of Lake Pichola, this lake has become a popular hang-out as night falls, for lovestruck local youth. Overlooked by a number of hills, it was originally built in 1678 by Maharana Jai Singh, but reconstructed by Maharana Fateh Singh after heavy rains destroyed the dam. A pleasant drive winds along the east bank and in the middle of the lake is Nehru Park, a popular garden island with a boat-shaped cafe. You can get there by boat from near the bottom of Moti Magri for Rs 5. Pedal boats (Rs 40/80 for half/one hour) are also available.

An auto-rickshaw from the old city to Fateh Sagar should charge around Rs 20 (one way).

Pratap Smarak (Moti Magri)

Atop the Moti Magri, or Pearl Hill, overlooking Fateh Sagar, is a **statue** of the Rajput hero Maharana Pratap, who frequently defied the Mughals. The path to the top traverses elegant **gardens**, including a Japanese rock garden. The park is open daily from 7.30 am to 7 pm and admission is Rs 10. Car/rickshaw/motorbike/bicycle entry is Rs 15/5/3/1.

Bhartiya Lok Kala Museum

The interesting collection exhibited by this small museum and foundation for the preservation and promotion of local folk arts includes dresses, turbans, dolls, masks, musical instruments, paintings and – its high point – puppets. The museum is open daily from 9 am to 6 pm and admission costs Rs 10, plus Rs 10 for a camera and Rs 50 for a video camera. Regular 15 minute puppet shows are held daily (usually every half hour) and are included in the admission charge. From 6 to 7 pm there's a Rajasthani dance and puppet show for Rs 30. Call ☎ 529296 for more details. An auto-rickshaw from the old city should cost Rs 20 (one way).

Saheliyon ki Bari

The Saheliyon ki Bari, or Garden of the Maids of Honour, is north of the city. This small ornamental garden is well-maintained, with fountains, kiosks, marble elephants and a delightful lotus pool. It's open daily from 9 am to 6 pm and entry is Rs 2. They may ask for Rs 2 to turn the fountains on.

Shilpgram

Shilpgram, a crafts village 3km west of Fateh Sagar, was inaugurated by Rajiv Gandhi in 1989. Although rather contrived, it's an interesting place with traditional houses from four states – Rajasthan, Gujarat, Goa and Maharashtra – and there are daily demonstrations by musicians, dancers or artisans from the various states. Although

it's much more animated during festival times (usually in early December, but check with the Tourist Reception Centre), there's usually something happening. Camel rides are available here. It's open daily from 11 am to 7 pm and entry is Rs 5/10 for Indians/foreigners.

The *Shilpi Restaurant* right next to the site serves snacks and good Indian, continental and Chinese food. Main Indian veg dishes range from Rs 38 to Rs 70 and non-veg between Rs 40 and Rs 140. It also has a swimming pool (Rs 100), open every day from 11 am to 4 pm. Not too far away is the less impressive *Woodland Restaurant*, that serves Indian, continental and Chinese fare.

A return auto-rickshaw trip (including a 30 minute halt) from the old city to Shilpgram is Rs 80.

Ahar Museum & Cenotaphs

About 2km east of Udaipur are the remains of an ancient city. There's a **museum** here, where you'll find a limited, but very old collection of earthen pottery, sculptures and other archaeological finds. Some pieces date back to 1700 BC and there's a beautiful 10th century metal figure of Buddha. The museum is open daily except Friday from 10 am to 4.30 pm and entry is Rs 3 (free on Monday). Photography is not allowed.

Nearby is an impressive cluster of **cenotaphs** of the maharanas of Mewar, which have recently been restored. A total of around 19 former maharanas were cremated here. The most striking cenotaph is that of Maharana Amar Singh who ruled from 1597 to 1620.

Monsoon Palace (Sajjan Garh)

On the distant mountain range, visible from the city, is the former maharana's Monsoon Palace, also known as Sajjan Garh. It was built by Maharana Sajjan Singh in the late 19th century. This deserted and run-down palace is today owned by the government and closed to the public (although a little baksheesh to the caretaker may open doors). Nonetheless, this place is worth visiting just for the stunning views from the mountain on

SOUTHERN RAJASTHAN

which it is sited. From here, you can really appreciate how huge the City Palace complex is. This is a splendid place to kick back with a picnic lunch and simply soak up the views. The palace is illuminated at night and from a distance looks like something out of a fairytale.

The round trip takes about one hour by car. The return trip by auto-rickshaw/taxi should cost around Rs 100/300 (including a 30 minute halt), but you'll probably be asked for more – bargain hard.

Other Attractions

The huge **fountain** in the centre of Patel or Sukhadia Circle, north of the city, is illuminated at night. **Sajjan Niwas Gardens** has pleasant lawns (beware of the unfriendly dogs here) and a zoo. Beside it is the Rose Garden, or **Gulab Bagh**. Don't confuse the **Nehru Park** opposite Bapu Bazaar with the island park of the same name in Fateh Sagar. The city park has some strange topiary work, a giant cement teapot and children's slides with an elephant and a camel. **Sunset Point**, not far from the Café Hill Park, is indeed delightful at sunset (entry is Rs 5; Rs 2 for children under 12), with dazzling views over Lake Pichola, Jagmandir Island and the Monsoon Palace. There's a musical fountain, which plays a merry tune each evening from 6 to 6.30 pm, 6.45 to 7.15 pm. 7.30 to 8 pm and 8.15 to 8.45 pm.

Almost 5km beyond Shilpgram is **Badi Ka Talab**, also called Tiger Lake. This mammoth artificial lake, flanked by hills, is a pleasant picnic spot. The lake is at its most impressive after monsoon. Crocodiles lurk in parts of the lake, so swimmers beware! Near the lake there's a small Shiva and Hanuman temple. An auto-rickshaw to the lake should cost Rs 100 (one way), or Rs 200 return (with a one hour halt).

Festivals

Both Holi and Gangaur are celebrated with much pageantry and colour in Udaipur. See the boxed text Festivals of Southern Rajasthan at the beginning of this chapter for more details.

Organised Tours

A five hour tour starts at the RTDC's Hotel Kajri at 8 am each day. It costs Rs 50 (excluding entry charges to sites) and takes in all the main city sights. Depending on demand, an afternoon tour (2 to 7 pm) goes out to Eklingji, Haldighati and Nathdwara (see the North of Udaipur section); it costs Rs 80. Contact the Tourist Reception Centre (☎ 411535) for more details. See the Lake Pichola section (earlier) for information about boat rides.

Places to Stay – Homestays

Udaipur pioneered the Homestay/Paying Guest House Scheme in Rajasthan, and there are now over 75 families in it. Expect to pay Rs 100 to Rs 600 per night, depending on the level of comfort and facilities you want. The Tourist Reception Centre (see Information earlier) has a list detailing all the places and the services offered.

Places to Stay – Budget

There are several main clusters of budget hotels in Udaipur, but those around the Jagdish Temple are definitely preferable to the others. Next best are those between the City Palace and the bus stand, along Lake Palace Rd and Bhattiyani Chotta. Another cluster is along the main road between the bus stand and Delhi Gate. This is a very noisy and polluted road, and you'd have to be desperate or totally lacking in imagination to stay here.

Watch out for check-out times, which vary greatly in Udaipur, and note that many places whack a 10% service charge on the room rates they advertise. If you're booking a hotel near Lake Pichola, ask for a lake-facing room (they usually cost a bit more, though). At many of the budget hotels, if nobody is at reception when you arrive, go to the restaurant, up to the rooftop, or just yell out 'hello'.

Owing to cut-throat hotel competition, the commission system is in place with a vengeance. Many rickshaw drivers will try to drag you to a place of their choice rather than yours, especially if you want to go to the Lal Ghat area (near Lake Pichola). If that's the case, just ask for Jagdish Temple,

Durbar Hall

Many palaces in India have a durbar hall, or hall of audience. Historically, it was used by India's rulers for official occasions such as state banquets. It was also used to hold formal or informal meetings.

The restored durbar hall at the Fateh Prakash Palace Hotel, in the City Palace complex in Udaipur, is undoubtedly one of India's most impressive, with a lavish interior – just wait until you feast your eyes on the massive chandeliers. The walls display royal weapons and striking portraits of former maharanas of Mewar (a most distinguished-looking lot). The illustrious Mewar rulers come from what is believed to be the oldest ruling dynasty in the world, spanning 76 generations.

The foundation stone was laid in 1909 by Lord Minto, the Viceroy of India, during the reign of Maharana Fateh Singh. As a mark of honour to Lord Minto, it was originally named the Minto Hall. The top floor of this high-ceilinged hall is surrounded by viewing galleries, where ladies of the palace could watch in veiled seclusion what was happening below. Nowadays, there is a brilliant Crystal Gallery up here (see City Palace & Museums for more information).

The durbar hall in Udaipur is open to visitors. It still has the capacity to hold hundreds of people and can even be hired for conferences or social gatherings – for details, contact the Fateh Prakash Palace Hotel (☎ 0294-528016, fax 528006).

Entry to the durbar hall is Rs 50 (free for the residents of the Fateh Prakash Palace and Shiv Niwas Palace hotels, and for those visiting the Crystal Gallery).

COURTESY OF THE CITY PALACE, UDAIPUR

as all the guest houses in that area are within easy walking distance of the temple. An auto-rickshaw from the bus stand to the Jagdish Temple should cost about Rs 15. Some really tenacious drivers may even claim that the hotel you wish to go to has suddenly closed, burned down, or the owner died in a freak accident! Don't be fooled by these far-fetched stories.

Jagdish Temple Area You'll pay a little more for a hotel in this area, but there is

hardly any traffic noise, most places have fabulous views over the lake and the central location is ideal. As it's the most popular area to stay, you get a lot of the 'yes have a look! change money! buy something!' from the touts and shop owners, but this is not Agra.

Hotel Gangaur Palace (☎ 422303, 3 Gangaur Ghat Rd) is a terrific choice in this area. It has large, clean doubles with attached bath from Rs 150 to Rs 350 for lake view rooms. There are also some rooms with common bath for Rs 60/80. The rooftop restaurant serves Indian and continental food.

Hotel Badi Haveli *(☎ 412588, Gangaur Ghat Rd)* has plain but neat rooms for Rs 100/150 with common bath, or Rs 180 for a double with attached bath. For Rs 250 you get the best room at the top. This little labyrinth has narrow staircases, terraces, a courtyard and two rooftops with great views over the lake and old city. There's a vegetarian restaurant with thalis for Rs 51.

Lehar Guest House *(☎ 417651, 86 Gangaur Ghat Rd)*, run by Manju, has doubles with attached bath for Rs 80, or Rs 150 for a better view over the town. There's a small rooftop restaurant, with good views, which serves Indian and continental food. If nobody is at reception when you get here, just go up to the restaurant.

Anjani Hotel *(☎ 421770, 77 Gangaur Ghat Rd)* has decent rooms with private bath from Rs 100. There's a reasonably priced rooftop restaurant.

Lalghat Guest House *(☎ 525301, fax 418508, 33 Lal Ghat)*, right by the lake, is popular with travellers. The rooftop areas have excellent views over the lake and there's a back terrace which overlooks the ghats. A variety of rooms are available, ranging from dorm beds for Rs 50, small rooms with common bath for Rs 75/100, larger doubles for Rs 150, or Rs 200/250 for rooms with attached bath. The best room costs Rs 350 a double. All the rooms have fans and mosquito nets. There is a small kitchen for self-caterers and a little shop. The rooftop terrace is popular for sunbaking (remember to be sun smart!)

Lake Ghat Guest House *(☎ 521636, fax 520023)*, across the road from the Lalghat Guest House, is a popular choice. Singles/doubles/triples with bath are Rs 150/200/250, with lake views from the rooftop. There's a good restaurant; a veg thali is Rs 40.

Jag Niwas Guest House *(☎ 422067, 21 Gangaur Ghat Rd)* is a little place with singles/doubles with attached bathroom for Rs 80/150. The rooftop has a veg restaurant.

Evergreen Guest House *(☎ 421585, 32 Lal Ghat)* has fairly clean rooms around a small courtyard, and a popular restaurant (see Places to Eat). There are just seven double rooms for Rs 100 with common bath, Rs 150 with attached bath and Rs 250 for the finest room.

Rainbow Guest House *(☎ 417030, 27-28 Lal Ghat)* has just three basic rooms; one single (Rs 100) and two doubles (Rs 150). All rooms have a private bathroom and hot water is by the bucket (no charge).

Lake Corner Soni Paying Guest House, in the Lal Ghat area, has doubles with common bath for Rs 100, or Rs 150 with attached bath (many rooms with Indian-style toilet). This place is nothing fancy, but the elderly couple who run it are lovely. There are fantastic views from the rooftop.

Shiva Guest House *(☎ 421952, 74 Navghat)* is a possibility if you're on a tight budget. Singles/doubles with common bath cost Rs 50/100, or Rs 100/150 with private bath.

Jheel Guest House *(☎ 421352, 56 Gangaur Ghat Rd)* is right at the bottom of the hill by the ghat, and is housed in an old haveli. Rooms with common bath go for around Rs 80/150, or Rs 200 for a larger room with bath attached. The newer annexe across the road has better (more expensive) rooms and a rooftop restaurant overlooking the lake.

Nukkad Guest House *(56 Ganesh Ghati)*, run by the friendly Trilok and Kala, has very basic but cheap rooms. Doubles without/with bath cost Rs 60/80. The best double is Rs 100. Meals are available.

Lake Palace Rd Area This area is central but farther away from Lake Pichola than the hotels in the Jagdish Temple area.

Hotel Mahendra Prakash *(☎ 522993)* has decent doubles with attached bath ranging from Rs 150 to Rs 600. There's also a sparkling clean swimming pool, a restaurant and a rooftop with views of the City Palace.

Hotel Shambhu Vilas *(☎ 421921)*, a few doors away, has singles/doubles with bath from Rs 200/350. Nearby is the rather dishevelled *Haveli Hotel* *(☎ 421351)*.

Ranjit Niwas Hotel *(☎ 525774)*, not far away, is nothing flash but reasonably cheap.

Sunrise at Bharatpur's famous bird sanctuary, the Keoladeo Ghana National Park.

ANDREW LUBRAN

BRYN THOMAS

Pushkar Lake, a holy place for ritual bathing.

SARA-JANE CLELAND

Women on balcony overlooking Pushkar Lake.

RICHARD I'ANSON

Late afternoon at Pushkar Camel Fair. Rajasthani folk music will play into the night.

Temple offerings, Ranakpur.

Temple decorations.

Temple sweepers in the beautiful Jain temple complex, Ranakpur.

View of Udaipur City Palace from Lake Pichola.

Jagmandir, Kishore Sagar, Kota.

Dorm beds are Rs 50, mundane rooms with common bath are Rs 100/150, or Rs 150/250 with attached bath.

Bus Stand Area For people catching an early-morning bus, there are several humdrum options in this uninspirational area.

Apsara Hotel (☎ 420400), north of the bus stand, is a huge and somewhat dreary place set back from the road. The rooms front onto an internal courtyard, making them relatively quiet. There are dorm beds for Rs 50 and double rooms from Rs 200 to Rs 600, all with private bath.

Hotel Welcome (☎ 485375) is opposite the bus stand and offers basic singles/doubles with attached bath for Rs 95/125. Deluxe rooms cost Rs 250/300 and there's also a vegetarian restaurant.

Elsewhere If you don't mind staying away from the heart of the old city, there are some good budget options.

Lake Shore Hotel is across from the City Palace, on the opposite side of Lake Pichola. Situated south of Chandpol, this is a laid-back place which is good if you want to escape from the hustle and bustle. It's fairly basic but OK, with just a few rooms, and a terrace with fine views over the water. Singles/doubles with common bath are Rs 100/200; Rs 350 gets you a larger double with attached bath and a view over the lake. The best room costs Rs 500. There's a very good restaurant; baked potatoes with garlic cheese are Rs 40.

Hotel Natural (☎ 527879, 55 Rang Sagar) is farther away from Lake Pichola, but is good if you want to abscond from the tumult. Basic doubles with attached bath (bucket hot water) are Rs 150, while a double with constant hot water is Rs 200 (some rooms have Indian-style toilets). There's good veg food cooked with tender loving care by Ritu, and a slice of cake, just like grandma used to bake, costs Rs 25.

Pahadi Palace (☎ 420099, 18 Ambargarh, Swaroop Sagar), not far away, has spotlessly clean rooms and is great value for money. Well-kept doubles with private bath range

from Rs 100 to Rs 750. This pleasant place is run by the affable Ansar Ahmed.

Mewar Inn (☎ 522090, 42 Residency Rd) is not in a thrilling location, but may be worth considering if you're strapped for cash. Basic singles/doubles with common bath go for a mere Rs 30/40. The rooms with attached bath start at Rs 69/79. A discount is given to YHA members. There's a rooftop veg restaurant and bicycles for hire (Rs 15 per day).

Ajanta Hotel (☎ 528914, fax 525769) is set around a courtyard between Chetak Circle and Hathipol and is more popular with domestic tourists. The well-maintained rooms range from Rs 300/400 to Rs 700/800, all with private bath and hot water.

Pratap Country Inn (☎ 583138, fax 583058) is a serene and secluded country retreat at Titaradi village, about 7km outside Udaipur. Run by the charming Maharaj Narendra Singh, it has doubles with attached bath from Rs 200 to Rs 1200. Horse riding is available (lessons for learners are Rs 150 per day) and longer safaris can be organised (from US$100 per person per day). It can be tough getting a rickshaw out here (Rs 50), but the hotel can pick you up from Udaipur with advance notice.

Places to Stay – Mid-Range

Jagdish Temple Area There is a very good selection of mid-range hotels in the Jagdish Temple area, near Lake Pichola. It's wise to book ahead, as these places can fill up fast during the tourist season.

Kankarwa Haveli (☎ 411457, fax 521403, 26 Lalghat), run by the helpful Janardan Singh, is a family-run haveli which is a wonderful place to stay. Squeaky-clean doubles range from Rs 400 to Rs 1200; the more expensive rooms overlook Lake Pichola. There's no restaurant, but with prior notice they can arrange breakfast and dinner (veg only). Or you can just pop next door to the Jagat Niwas Palace Hotel for a feed.

Jagat Niwas Palace Hotel (☎ 420133, fax 520023, 25 Lalghat), right on the lake shore, has long been a popular hang-out with travellers. This charming converted haveli has a great restaurant (see Places to Eat) with tremendous lake views. Double rooms range from Rs 350 to Rs 1400.

Hotel Sai-Niwas (☎/fax 524909, 75 Navghat Marg), just down the hill towards the ghat from the City Palace entrance, is also heartily recommended. The seven double rooms are imaginatively decorated (even the toilet!) and range from Rs 800 to Rs 1000. There's a cute restaurant which serves Indian and continental food; veg curry is Rs 45, lentil soup is Rs 40.

Ratan Palace Guest House (☎ 561153, 21 Lalghat) offers good double rooms with private bathroom from Rs 250 to Rs 450. The terrace has lake views and meals are available.

Hotel Caravanserai (☎ 411103, fax 521252, 14 Lalghat) is modern with well-kept rooms from Rs 300 to Rs 1195. The food at the rooftop restaurant is only average, but is compensated for by the lake views and live Indian classical music in the evening.

Lake Palace Rd Area *Rang Niwas Palace Hotel* (☎ 523890, fax 527884), on Lake Palace Rd, is one of the best mid-range options in Udaipur. Set in lovely gardens with a swimming pool, it's a very relaxed hotel and you'll have no hassles here whatsoever. There's accommodation in the old building, formerly a royal guesthouse, and also rooms in the new building. Comfortable doubles with attached bathroom range from Rs 500 to Rs 2000. There are also a couple of budget doubles with common bath (Rs 350). The restaurant gets mixed reports from travellers.

Hotel Raj Palace (☎ 527092, fax 410395, 103 Bhattiyani Chotta) is another very good place to stay. It has a small dorm (Rs 75) and double rooms from Rs 250 to Rs 950. There's a lush courtyard restaurant which is a great place to chill out with a beer. The restaurant whips up delicious food – like their chicken masala.

Near Gulab Bagh, *Hotel Vishnupriya (Quality Inn)* (☎ 421313, fax 420314, 9 Garden Rd) has standard rooms for only Rs 995/1495, and deluxe rooms for Rs 1195/1895. Although this place is comfortable enough, it lacks the panache of the other two hotels.

Fateh Sagar Area There are some options around Udaipur's other major lake, Fateh Sagar. These are a little inconvenient, away from the old city, but on the plus side, they're far removed from the tumult and touts.

Hotel Ram Pratap Palace (☎ 528701, fax 528700, 5B Alkapuri) is an elegant modern haveli overlooking the lake, and a splendid choice in this area. Double rooms cost Rs 985, or Rs 1185 for a deluxe lake-facing room. There's a good restaurant and the rooftop terrace has romantic views.

Hotel Lakend (☎ 415100, fax 523898) nearby, is a huge hotel which has comfortable single/double rooms from Rs 550/750. Amenities include a swimming pool and restaurant.

Hotel Anand Bhawan (☎ 523256, fax 523247) offers standard rooms for Rs 700/900. The restaurant serves veg and non-veg dishes.

Nearby, *Hotel Gulab Niwas* (☎/fax 523644) is an old lodge set in a pleasant garden. Ordinary rooms cost Rs 575/675, but the rooms in the old building (Rs 975/1175) have much more character.

Elsewhere These hotels are on the opposite side of Lake Pichola to the City Palace.

Wonder View Palace (☎ 522996, fax 415287), south of Chandpol, has singles/doubles from Rs 400/500 to Rs 800/1000. These are OK but some of the bathrooms in the cheaper rooms could be better.

Udai Kothi (☎ 524002), nearby, was on the last leg of construction at the time of writing and will boast Udaipur's *only* rooftop swimming pool! Doubles are expected to range between Rs 600 to Rs 800.

Places to Stay – Top End
Lake Pichola Hotel (☎ 421197, fax 410575), south of Chandpol and across the lake from the City Palace, boasts superlative

views – go up to the rooftop terrace to really soak these up. It's a modern building in the traditional style, with singles/doubles for Rs 975/1000. But it's worth paying Rs 1150/1195 to get a deluxe room, which has a balcony and lake view. There's a good bar and restaurant and this hotel is the best of the lower priced top-end hotels.

Trident (☎ *419393, fax 419494*) is rather out on a limb, beyond Chandpol, but is Udaipur's slickest hotel when it comes to service and attention to detail. Hidden in the hills, this modern property is part of the Oberoi Group and offers smart singles/doubles from US$125/140. The multicuisine restaurant (nonresidents welcome) is excellent and even has frothy cappuccinos. Other amenities include a swimming pool, bar, beauty parlour and health club. Don't miss the wild boar feeding frenzy – a truly awesome sight! The Oberoi Group is planning to open an upmarket boutique hotel in Udaipur (similar to the Raj Vilas in Jaipur) – contact their Delhi corporate office for details on ☎ 011-2914841, fax 2929800.

Laxmi Vilas Palace Hotel (☎ *529711, fax 526273*) is between Swaroop Sagar and Fateh Sagar, up on the hill. It's a pleasant four star ITDC place where air-con rooms cost from US$115/130 to US$250 for the Maharani suite. There's a bar, restaurant and swimming pool.

Hotel Hilltop Palace (☎ *521997, fax 525106*) is a modern hotel atop another hill in the same area. Clean rooms start at Rs 1350/2100 and there's a pool, bar and restaurant. Although the ambience here is somewhat sterile, its rooftop terrace is probably the best place in town to get a 360° view of Udaipur, and nobody seems to mind if you come here just for the views.

Lake Palace Hotel (☎ *527961/527973, fax 527974*) which appears to be floating in the middle of Lake Pichola, is one of the world's most spectacular hotels. It looks like something lifted straight out of a romantic novel and few people would pass up an opportunity to stay here. This swanky white palace has a bar, restaurants (see Places to Eat), little shopping arcade, open air courtyards, lotus ponds, and a small, mango tree-shaded swimming pool. The cheapest doubles are US$210 (no lake view); US$245 gets you a lake view. Sumptuous suites cost US$325 to US$550. Needless to say, you will need to book well in advance.

Shikarbadi Hotel (☎ *583201, fax 584841*) or book at Shiv Niwas Palace Hotel, is out of town on the Ahmedabad road. Once a royal hunting lodge, it is set in wilderness and has a swimming pool and relaxing gardens. Attractive singles/doubles cost Rs 1195/2395. A stud farm on the premises offers short horse rides (Rs 250 for 45 minutes) and longer safaris (a half-day safari with breakfast is Rs 1500). Sip tea while you watch the wild boars gorge at 4 pm each day (not far from the pool area).

Part of the City Palace complex, *Shiv Niwas Palace Hotel* (☎ *528016/528019, fax 528006, email resv@hrhindia.com*) is another atmospheric palace-hotel. The cheapest rooms (US$100 a double) aren't really crash hot value – it's much better to get a room around the pool which start from US$250 a double (room No 16 has fine views over the lake). For a real splurge there are some lavish suites; the lotus suite (room No 19, US$600) doesn't have much of a lake view but is very romantic – it even has a small fountain near the dreamy four poster bed! There's a good restaurant (see Places to Eat), bar, holistic health centre and marble pool (open to nonresidents for Rs 240 including a towel). A small bagpipe (!) band strikes up a merry tune each evening. It is recommended that advance bookings are made.

Fateh Prakash Palace Hotel (☎ *528016/528019, fax 528006*), also in the City Palace complex, was built in the early 1900s during the reign of Maharana Fateh Singh. The cheapest double rooms are US$100, but these are not in the main palace wing. Far more ornate rooms furnished with traditional palace pieces cost US$200/250 a single/double (some with a lake view). The intimate *Gallery Restaurant* (see Places to Eat) has brilliant views across the lake.

Places to Eat

Udaipur has scores of sun-kissed rooftop cafes catering to budget travellers, as well as fine dining at the top-end hotels. Many restaurants also boast terrific lake views. At places offering multicuisine menus, the chefs generally do a better job of the Indian food. Some restaurants in Udaipur serve bhang lassi – see the boxed text Bhang Lassi Warning in the Drinks section of the Facts for the Visitor chapter.

Many of the budget restaurants try to lure customers by putting on a nightly screening of the James Bond movie *Octopussy*, which was partly filmed in Udaipur. These days, contemporary cult movies are also screened – when this author visited, the hot favourites were *Pulp Fiction* and *Trainspotting*.

Sunset View Terrace, ideally situated on a terrace overlooking Lake Pichola, is *the* place to be at sunset. Located near the Fateh Prakash Palace Hotel in the City Palace complex, this place is worth visiting for the views alone (don't forget your camera). Live Indian classical music is played in the late afternoon and the menu offers a range of light bites such as pizzas (Rs 110), burgers (Rs 90), veg samosas (Rs 75), masala tea (Rs 35) and milkshakes (Rs 50).

Ambrai is also worth visiting for its superb location. It is located just past the Lake Pichola Hotel, beyond Chandpol, and is a great place to kick back with a cold beer or hot masala tea. The beauty about this outdoor restaurant is that, unlike other places to eat, it sits right at water level. You can get Indian, Chinese and continental cuisine; chicken saagwala is Rs 80 and ice cream is Rs 40.

El Parador, out in the Fateh Sagar area (opposite the Ayurvedic College & Hospital on Ambamata Rd, at Ranaji Chowk), is a cosy little place which is heartily recommended. It is one of the only places in Rajasthan which make *real* percolated coffee (Rs 60 per heavenly pot)! Run by a friendly family, this homey place whips up a range of moderately priced Italian, Greek, Mexican and French cuisine.

Mayur Café by the Jagdish Temple has long been popular, but these days travellers have mixed reports about the food and service. There are south Indian dishes and western alternatives such as spaghetti with cheese (Rs 30).

Nearby, *Maxim's Café* is better value and not as indifferent to travellers as the Mayur Café. Menu items include paneer tikka (Rs 20) and Rajasthani pizza (Rs 22).

Anna Restaurant, not far away, is also good for cheap chow. The menu consists of Indian, continental and Chinese food, and includes a selection of cakes (around Rs 30) – perfect with a cup of mint tea (Rs 7).

Samor Bagh, at the Lake Palace Rd entrance to the City Palace, has slightly pricey Indian, Chinese and continental food. Its speciality is paneer pasanda (Rs 50). Other menu items include chicken steak sizzlers (Rs 85) and hakka noodles (Rs 40). You can sit in the large 'hut' or out in the garden.

Restaurant Natural View, on the rooftop of the Evergreen Guest House, has fine lake views but is a tad overpriced considering what you get. It serves Indian, Chinese and continental fare; chicken palak is Rs 55 and fish curry is Rs 50.

Roof Garden Café, just around the corner from the Rang Niwas Palace Hotel, facing the City Palace, looks like the Hanging Gardens of Babylon. The setting is more stimulating than the Indian, continental and Chinese food on offer. Menu items include chicken curry (Rs 45) and cool banana lassi (Rs 12).

Café Hill Park, south-west of the Sajjan Niwas Gardens on a hill overlooking Lake Pichola, attracts people for its views rather than its food. This rather ramshackle café offers Indian, continental and Chinese fare, including cheese burgers (Rs 30) and chicken curry (Rs 40). Eating outside is more pleasant than indoors.

Park View, one of Udaipur's oldest restaurants, is opposite the park in the main part of town but there's absolutely no view. This dimly lit place is particularly good for its north Indian cuisine and is often packed with middle-class Indian families. A half tandoori chicken is Rs 57 and fish curry is Rs 47.

16 Chef Restaurant (16 Gyan Marg), inside Surajpol, is a possibility if you're low on dough. It has cheap vegetarian Indian, Chinese and some continental fare. Most main dishes are below Rs 35; the dum aloo Kashmiri is Rs 32, garlic naan is Rs 10 and a veg grill sizzler is Rs 30.

Berry's Restaurant, at Chetak Circle, has a sterile feel to it but cooks up pretty good Indian food and is quite popular with the locals. The butter chicken is a hot seller (Rs 85 for half a bird) and there are also sizzlers (from Rs 75 to Rs 115).

Chirag Restaurant & Beer Bar, next door to the Hotel Vishnupriya (Quality Inn), has a wide menu offering Indian, Chinese and continental food. A plate of chicken curry is Rs 45.

Hotel Natural has a menu offering a mishmash of veg Indian, Chinese, Mexican, Tibetan and Italian food. They also bake home-made birthday cakes for around Rs 100 – ring Ritu (☎ 529573) to place your order.

Jagat Niwas Palace Hotel (☎ 420133) has an absolutely delightful restaurant with superlative lake views – great for a minor splurge. Its western dishes are a little pricey, but the Indian food is cheaper; palak paneer is Rs 50 and spaghetti bolognese is Rs 95. It's wise to book ahead (especially for dinner), as this place can fill up in a flash.

Shiv Niwas Palace Hotel (☎ 528016) is highly recommended for a dose of pampering and is most captivating in the evening. There's seating indoors or in the pleasant open-air courtyard by the pool. Their Indian food is best – try the aloo chutneywale, potatoes stuffed with Indian cottage cheese in a mango and mint chutney for Rs 75. Indian classical music is performed each evening by the pool-side, creating a magical ambience. Nonresidents are welcome, but it's wise to book ahead, especially for dinner.

Before dinner, treat yourself to a little drinkie at the plush pool-side *Paanera Bar*, which has soft sofas to sink into. If it's been a tough day, there's tequila (Rs 180 a shot), or if you're in the mood, go wild on a bottle of bubbly – the Moet costs a cool Rs 5000!

Gallery Restaurant, at the Fateh Prakash Palace Hotel, serves a set continental lunch/dinner for Rs 500/600. Although the food

here is nothing to write home about, this elegant little restaurant has beguiling views across Lake Pichola. For a really romantic evening, come here at sunset for a drink, then enjoy the live Indian classical music while you dine. For something more moneybelt friendly, there's an afternoon tea served daily between 3 and 5 pm. A 'full cream tea' costs Rs 125, homemade biscuits and cakes cost Rs 100 and a pot of chocolate served with whipped cream is Rs 65.

Lake Palace Hotel is, of course, the ultimate dining experience, although there's no guarantee you'll get in since it is usually only possible to get a table when the hotel is not full. The buffet lunch/dinner costs Rs 500/600 (including the boat crossing) and before your meal, you can take a drink at the sophisticated bar. Special Rajasthani thalis are available with advance notice – they're mighty filling, so make sure you go on an empty stomach. Reservations are essential, and reasonably tidy dress is expected. For something different, ask about their tiny *floating pontoon* on Lake Pichola, which arranges lunch/dinner for US$40 (maximum four people). If you don't want a waiter hanging around, you can request a cordless phone to be left in case you need anything. Wear something warm if you are dining at night in the winter.

Entertainment

Meera Kala Mandir (☎ 583176, Sector 11, Hiran Magari), near the Pars Theatre has one-hour Rajasthani folk dance and music performances daily (except Sunday) at 7 pm from August to April. It costs Rs 60 per person. It has a range of tribal folk dances. An auto-rickshaw to the auditorium from the City Palace area costs around Rs 25.

Many hotels stage their own entertainment for guests – usually puppet shows or Rajasthani music/dance performances.

Shopping

Udaipur has oodles of small shops selling a jumble of items from funky western clothing to exquisite antique jewellery. There are all sorts of local crafts, especially miniature paintings in the Rajput-Mughal style. The miniatures are painted on cloth, marble, wood, paper and even leaves. This is one of the best places to buy them, as the range is vast and prices will suit all budgets. They make great gifts for friends back home and have the bonus of being light to carry. Other things to buy in Udaipur include jewellery, carpets, block-printed fabrics, marble items, wooden figures and papier mâché. There's a good cluster of shops on Lake Palace Rd, near the Rang Niwas Palace Hotel, and also around the Jagdish Temple. Shops are open daily from 9.30 am to 7.30 pm.

Be warned that shops in Udaipur are used to tourists with lots of money to spend and little time to spend it, so be prepared to bargain hard (for some useful tips on bargaining, see the boxed text The Art of Haggling in the Facts for the Visitor chapter).

Getting There & Away

Air Indian Airlines has at least one flight a day to Delhi (US$95), Jaipur (US$70), Jodhpur (US$55), Mumbai (US$110) and Aurangabad (US$105). The Indian Airlines office (☎ 410999) at Delhi Gate is open Monday to Saturday from 10 am to 1 pm and 2 to 5 pm; Sunday from 10 am to 2 pm.

You are strongly advised to make flight bookings well in advance during the busy tourist season.

Bus Frequent RSTC buses run from Udaipur to other regional centres, as well as to Delhi and Ahmedabad. If you use these buses, take an express since the ordinary buses take forever, make innumerable detours to various towns off the main route and can be very uncomfortable. For long-distance travel, use deluxe or express buses (book ahead). Destinations served by deluxe bus include:

destination	duration (hrs)	cost (Rs)
Ajmer	6	110
Chittorgarh	3	50
Jaipur	9	200
Jodhpur	8	110
Kota/Bundi	6	100
Mt Abu	7	100

There are quite a few private bus companies which operate to such places as:

destination	duration (hrs)	cost (Rs)
Ahmedabad	6	80
Delhi	14	200
Indore	10	150
Jaipur	9	120
Jodhpur	9	70
Kota	6	80
Mt Abu	5	70
Mumbai	16	200
Vadodara	8	120

It's easiest to book these buses through a travel agent (for a Rs 20 to Rs 50 service charge).

Train Lines into Udaipur are currently metre gauge only, so there are very limited train services – you're better off getting a bus to most destinations. Nobody seems to know when the conversion to broad gauge will take place.

The *Chetak Express* goes to Chittorgarh (Rs 76/184 in 2nd/1st class), Ajmer (Rs 125/370), and Jaipur (Rs 161/515) and on to Delhi (20 hrs, 233/718). The *Mewar Fast Express* also travels to Chittorgarh (Rs 36/184).

Taxi If you hire a taxi, the drivers will show or quote you a list of 'official' rates to places like Mt Abu and Jodhpur. Shop around for the most competitive rate. Taxis usually charge return trip fares even if you're only going one way. For useful tips on hiring a taxi and driver, see the Car section in the Getting Around chapter.

Getting Around

To/From the Airport The airport is 25km from the city. There's no airport bus; a taxi/auto-rickshaw costs around Rs 190/150.

Auto-Rickshaws Auto-rickshaws are unmetered, so you should agree on a fare before setting off. The standard fare for tourists anywhere in the city appears to hover around Rs 20, and you'll be lucky to get it for less since too many tourists pay the first price asked. An auto-rickshaw charges around Rs 130/250 for a half/full day of local sightseeing.

Bicycle & Motorcycle A cheap and environmentally friendly way to buzz around is by bike. Hire them all over town for around Rs 25 per day. Heera Cycle Store (☎ 523525) near Hotel Badi Haveli in the old city rents mopeds/motorcycles for Rs 150/300 per day.

NORTH OF UDAIPUR
Eklingji & Nagda
The interesting village of Eklingji – only 22km and a short bus ride north of Udaipur – has a number of ancient temples. The **Shiva temple** in the village itself was originally built in 734, although its present form dates from the rule of Maharana Raimal between 1473 and 1509. The walled complex has an elaborately pillared hall under a large pyramidal roof and features a four faced Shiva image of black marble. The temple is open daily at odd hours – 4.15 to 6.45 am, 10.30 am to 1.30 pm and 5.15 to 7.45 pm (check times in case they have changed). Photography is not allowed. Avoid the temple on Monday (an auspicious day for devotees) as it can get very crowded. The maharana of Udaipur pays a private visit to the temple on Monday evening.

At Nagda, about 1km off the road and 1km before Eklingji, are three 10th century temples. The Jain temple of **Adbudji** is essentially ruined, but its architecture is interesting. The nearby **Sas Bahu**, or Mother and Daughter-in-Law group, has very fine and intricate carvings including some erotic figures. You can reach these temples most conveniently by hiring a bicycle in Eklingji itself. There are also some small temples submerged in a nearby lake.

Places to Stay & Eat *Heritage Resorts* (☎ *0294-440382, fax 527549)*, at Lake Bagela in Nagda, is set in lovely grounds and offers singles/doubles for Rs 1540/ 2900. There is a restaurant (nonguests are

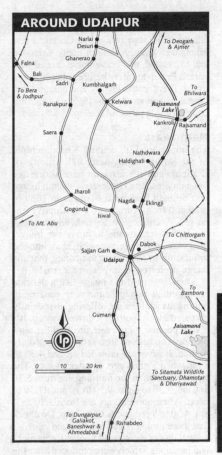

AROUND UDAIPUR

welcome) which charges Rs 275 for the buffet lunch or dinner. There's a small pool, and horse rides are available for Rs 50. A boat ride is Rs 30 per person for 30 minutes.

Getting There & Away Local buses run from Udaipur to Eklingji every hour from 5 am to 9 pm (40 mins, Rs 15).

Haldighati
This site, 40km north of Udaipur, is where Maharana Pratap defied the superior Mughal

SOUTHERN RAJASTHAN

forces of Akbar in 1576. The site is a battle-field and the only thing to see is the small chhatri to the warrior's horse, Chetak, a few kilometres away. Although badly wounded and exhausted, this brave horse carried Maharana Pratap to safety before collapsing and dying. It is for this loyalty and courage that Chetak is honoured. The site has a beautiful courtyard in a peaceful setting.

Nathdwara

The important 18th century Vishnu temple of **Sri Nathji** stands here, 48km north of Udaipur, and it's an important shrine for Vaishnavites. The black stone Vishnu image was brought here from Mathura in 1669 to protect it from Aurangzeb's destructive impulses. According to legend, when an attempt was later made to move the image, the getaway vehicle, a wagon, sank into the ground up to the axles, indicating that the image preferred to stay where it was!

Attendants treat the image like a delicate child, getting it up in the morning, washing it, putting its clothes on, offering it specially prepared meals, putting it down to sleep. It's a very popular pilgrimage site, and the temple opens and closes around the image's daily routine. It gets very crowded around 4.30 to 5 pm when Vishnu gets up after a siesta. The temple timings in the morning are from 5.30 to 6 am, 7.30 to 8 am, 9.30 to 10 am, 11.30 to noon. Afternoon timings are from 3.30 to 4 pm, 4.30 to 5 pm and 6.30 to 7 pm. Do check that these timings have not changed.

Nathdwara is also well known for its pich-wai paintings, which were produced after the image of Vishnu was brought to the town. These bright paintings, with their rather static images, were usually done on hand-spun fabric. As with many other schools of painting, numerous inferior reproductions of the pichwai paintings are created specifically for the lucrative tourist trade.

Places to Stay & Eat The *RTDC's Hotel Gokul* (☎ 02953-30917) is surprisingly good considering it's an RTDC establishment. It's set in quiet gardens and offers air-cooled rooms for Rs 300/400, and dorm beds for Rs

50. There's also a bar and a restaurant where vegetarian thalis cost Rs 50.

Shriji Resort (☎ 02953-40341) has deluxe doubles for Rs 890 and super deluxe doubles for Rs 990. The restaurant serves Indian vegetarian food.

Getting There & Away There are frequent daily RSTC buses from Udaipur to Nathdwara (1½ hrs, Rs 20).

Kankroli & Rajsamand Lake

At Kankroli, Dwarkadhish (an incarnation of Vishnu) has a **temple** similar to the temple at Nathdwara, and opening hours are similarly erratic.

Nearby is the large Rajsamand Lake, created by a dam constructed in 1660 by Maharana Raj Singh, who ruled from 1652-80. There are many ornamental arches, and picturesque chhatris along the huge *bund* (embankment). It also has several interesting old inscriptions.

There are frequent RSTC buses from Udaipur (2½ hrs, Rs 30).

Kumbhalgarh

Kumbhalgarh, 84km north of Udaipur, is the most important fort in the Mewar region after Chittorgarh. It was here that the rulers of Mewar retreated in times of danger, and where a baby prince of Mewar was hidden from an assassin (see the boxed text Mewar's Most Honoured Mother earlier). It's an isolated and fascinating place, built by Maharana Kumbha in the 15th century. Because of its inaccessibility – at 1100m on top of the Aravalli Range – it was taken only once in its history. Even then, it took the combined armies of the Mughal emperor, Akbar, and of Amber and Marwar to breach its defences. The thick walls of this mighty fort stretch some 36km and enclose many temples, palaces, gardens and water storage facilities. The fort was renovated in the 19th century by Maharana Fateh Singh. It's worth taking a leisurely walk in the large compound, which has some interesting ruins and is very peaceful. The fort is open daily from 9 am to 5 pm and entry is free.

There's also the **Kumbhalgarh Wildlife Sanctuary** here, known for its wolves. The scarcity of waterholes between March and June makes this the best time to see animals, including chowsinghas (four-horned antelopes), leopards, panthers, sloth bears and various bird species. The best time for wildlife spotting is in the early morning or late afternoon. The Aodhi Hotel (see Places to Stay & Eat) can arrange horse and jeep hire for guests. Entry to the sanctuary costs Rs 20/40 for Indians/foreigners plus Rs 50 for a camera and a hefty Rs 300 for a video. You need to get permission to enter the reserve from the forest department in nearby Kelwara, or from the Deputy Chief Wildlife Warden in Udaipur (☎ 0294-421361), but if you're staying at the Aodhi Hotel, they will organise it for you.

Places to Stay & Eat The *Aodhi Hotel* (☎ 02954-4222) or book through Shiv Niwas Palace Hotel in Udaipur (☎ 0294-528016, fax 528006) is the best hotel in Kumbhalgarh – an ideal place to just read a book or play a leisurely game of cards. Built on the side of a hill, rooms are decorated in a wilderness theme and cost Rs 1195/2395. Suites are Rs 4500. Nonresidents can dine in the restaurant; the set lunch/dinner is Rs 275/350, or you can dine à la carte (menu items include pasta with spinach and cream sauce for Rs 90 and safed maas for Rs 110). There's also a little bar (a bottle of beer is Rs 100) and an inviting swimming pool. It's a short walk from the hotel to the fort and horse safaris are available (Rs 500 per person for three hours, or Rs 1500 for a full day including lunch). Visits to nearby tribal villages can also be arranged.

Kumbhalgarh Fort Hotel (☎ 02954-42372, fax 0294-525106), nearby, is a new hotel with comfortable singles/doubles from Rs 1195/2395. The set breakfast/lunch/dinner is Rs 175/275/325 and a pool is being planned.

Hotel Ratnadeep (☎ 02954-42217) in nearby Kelwara is a bit farther away from the fort, but is an option if you can't afford the above two hotels. Ordinary rooms with attached bath (most with Indian-style toilets) start at Rs 400 and dorm beds cost Rs 100. There's also a small restaurant. Near this hotel is a Jain temple.

Thandiberi Forest Guest House is in the sanctuary, but bookings need to be made in advance through the Deputy Chief Wildlife Warden in Udaipur (☎ 0294-421361).

Getting There & Away There are several daily RSTC buses from Udaipur (3½ hrs, Rs 28), but not all leave from the bus stand – some go from Chetak Circle. Express buses only leave in the morning (Rs 35) – some stop in Kelwara and others go directly to Kumbhalgarh. If you want to hire a jeep, it's a good idea to come here as part of a small group and share the cost.

Ranakpur

One of the biggest and most important Jain temples in India, the extremely beautiful Ranakpur complex is well worth seeing. It is tucked away in a remote and quiet valley of the Aravalli Range 60km from Udaipur.

The main temple is the **Chaumukha Temple**, or Four-Faced Temple, dedicated to Adinath, the first tirthankar. Built in 1439, this huge, superbly crafted and well-kept marble temple has 29 halls supported by 1444 pillars – no two are alike. Within the complex are two other Jain temples – to **Neminath** and **Parasnath** – and, a short distance away, a **Sun Temple**. The **Amba Mata Temple** is 1km from the main complex.

The temple complex is open daily to non-Jains from 11 am to 5 pm (Jains can visit from 6 am to 8.30 pm). Shoes and all leather articles must be left at the entrance. Admission to the temple is free, but there's a Rs 25/125 camera/video camera charge.

Places to Stay & Eat Staying overnight at Ranakpur breaks up the long trip between Udaipur and Jodhpur.

Maharani Bagh Orchard Retreat (☎ 02934-85151) or book through the Umaid Bhawan Palace in Jodhpur (☎ 0291-433 316, fax 635373) is set in a lush mango orchard 4km from Ranakpur. It offers modern cottage-style accommodation for Rs 1190/2100 a single/double. Meals are available; the buffet lunch or dinner costs Rs 300 (nonresidents welcome). This is the most upmarket place to stay in Ranakpur.

The Castle (☎ 02934-85133) is set in large grounds and has good singles/doubles for Rs 600/700. There's a restaurant which serves Indian, continental and Chinese food; potato curry is Rs 35 and half a tandoori chicken is Rs 80.

RTDC's Hotel Shilpi (☎ 02934-85074) is conveniently situated near the temple, and has ordinary singles/doubles for Rs 200/250, deluxe rooms for Rs 300/350, and dorm beds for Rs 50. Vegetarian thalis are available in the dining room for Rs 55.

Dharamsala (☎ 02934-85019) is pilgrims' lodgings within the temple complex, offering very basic accommodation for a donation. At meal time you can get a veg thali in the dining hall for just Rs 12. The rooms are simple (with common bath) and the amount you pay depends entirely on you.

Roopam Restaurant (☎ 02934-3921) has a few nice rooms for Rs 550/650. The restaurant offers a buffet (Rs 150) or à la carte dining (Rs 35 to Rs 60 for a main dish). A bottle of beer is Rs 80.

Getting There & Away Ranakpur is 39km from Falna Junction on the Ajmer-Mt Abu rail and road routes. From Udaipur there are frequent buses (3 hrs, Rs 35/45 by express/deluxe). Although it's just possible to travel through from Ranakpur to Jodhpur or Mt Abu on the same day, it's hardly worth it since you'll arrive well after dark. It's better to stay for the night and continue the next day. There's also a daily express bus from Mt Abu (7 hrs, Rs 80).

Narlai

Narlai can make an ideal base for exploring the various attractions around Udaipur.

Rawla Narlai, book through the Ajit Bhawan in Jodhpur (☎ 0291-437410, fax 637774) is well kept with appealing single/doubles for Rs 1190/1795. Meals are available (set breakfast/lunch/dinner is Rs 150/250/300). Opposite the hotel is a mammoth single granite rock with a small temple on top.

There's also a good **baori** in Narlai where you can have dinner around a bonfire with folk dances for Rs 550 per person (advance bookings essential); several old temples and lots of quiet walks.

There are RSTC buses from Udaipur (4 hrs, Rs 60) and a deluxe bus (3½ hrs, Rs 70).

Ghanerao

About 7km from Narlai is the little town of Ghanerao, which has a castle that has been converted into a hotel.

Ghanerao Royal Castle (☎ 02934-84035) has recently renovated its rooms; they cost Rs 1250/1500. Suites are Rs 2000. A set meal in the dining room costs Rs 125/200/250 for breakfast/lunch/dinner. There's a pavilion in a central courtyard of the castle where palace musicians used to perform. Near the castle are the cenotaphs of former rulers. The hotel can arrange jeep excursions; a three hour safari is Rs 500 per person.

Take an RSTC bus from Udaipur to Ghanerao (4 hrs, Rs 50) or a deluxe bus to Sadri (Rs 70) or Desuri (Rs 70), then a jeep taxi (about Rs 75) from there to Ghanerao.

Deogarh

The attractive little town of Deogarh (pronounced Dev-gar), or 'castle of the gods', is 135km north of Udaipur. Surrounded by lakes, hills and rugged countryside, it's an ideal place to take a break from the rigours of travelling on the Indian roads. It makes a good stopover if you're on your way from Udaipur to Ajmer/Jaipur/Jodhpur, or between Kota and Jodhpur.

Deogarh has lots of pleasant walks and is known for its school of miniature painting. While here, you should visit **Anjaneshwar Mahadev**, a small cave temple dedicated to Lord Shiva. It's believed to be around 2000 years old and is unusually situated on the side of a hill. From the top of this hill there are good views of the countryside. One of the attractions of Deogarh is its castle, which has been converted into an atmospheric hotel.

Places to Stay The delightful *Deogarh Castle* (☎ *02904-52777, fax 52555, email deogarh@hotmail.com*) is a family-run hotel with appealing double rooms from Rs 2050 to Rs 3500. This well-managed castle has a good restaurant – request the rarely found palak ka halwa, a dessert made from spinach which sounds awful, looks awful, but tastes great (kind of like semi-burnt toffee). The hotel offers a 2½ hour 'rural ramble' jeep excursion for Rs 350 per person, including refreshments. Bird-watching, trekking and picnic outings can be arranged. Bicycles are for hire for Rs 100 per person per day.

Getting There & Away There's a deluxe bus from Udaipur (3 hrs, Rs 60).

There are railway connections between Udaipur and Deogarh (5 hrs, Rs 24/150 in 2nd/1st class). This train leaves Udaipur at 5.30 am and 4.30 pm. From Deogarh, the train leaves at 4.30 am (taking 6 hrs), or at 5 pm (arriving at 10 pm).

Bera

About 145km from Udaipur, Bera is a good place for spotting leopard and other wildlife. The best times for wildlife spotting are from 6 to 10 am and 4 to 8 pm.

Leopards Lair (☎/fax 02933-43479) has comfortable modern cottages for Rs 4000/ 4500 a single/double per night – price includes all meals and two wildlife safaris with the amicable thakur of Bera, Devi Singh.

SOUTH OF UDAIPUR
Rishabdeo

A 15th century Jain temple of Lord Rishabdeo is in this village, located about 65km south of Udaipur. Lord Rishabdeo is a reincarnation of Mahavir, the 24th and last of the Jain prophets, who founded Jainism around 500 BC and is also worshipped as a reincarnation of Vishnu. The temple, which is an important pilgrimage centre, has the Lord's image, some beautiful carvings and two large black stone elephants at the temple's

entrance. A short walk through a lane lined with small shops leads you there.

There are irregular buses to Rishabdeo from Udaipur (3½ hrs, Rs 45).

Jaisamand Lake

Located in a stunning site 48km south-east of Udaipur, Jaisamand Lake is one of the largest artificial lakes in Asia. It was built by Maharana Jai Singh in the 17th century and created by damming the Gomti River; today it measures 14km long and 9km wide. There are beautiful marble chhatris around the embankment, each with an elephant in front. The summer palaces of the Udaipur maharanis are also here. The lake features a variety of birdlife and the nearby **Jaisamand wildlife sanctuary** is home to leopards, deer, wild boar and crocodiles. The sanctuary is open daily and entry is free. The forests here used to be a favourite hunting ground for the former rulers of Mewar and elaborate hunting expeditions would frequently take place here.

Places to Stay *Jaisamand Island Resort* (☎ *02906-2222*) or book through the Hotel Lakend in Udaipur (☎ *0294-415100, fax 523898*) is a modern hotel in an isolated position 20 minutes by boat across the lake. Comfortable singles/doubles cost Rs 1150/ 2700, all with views over the water. Meals are available and trips to nearby tribal villages can be arranged. Nonguests can visit the resort for Rs 150.

Forest Guest House is a cheaper option at Jaisamand. You must contact the Deputy Chief Wildlife Warden, Udaipur (☎ *0294-421361*) for reservations.

Tourist Bungalow (☎ *02906-7833*), on the shores of the lake, has four ordinary rooms for Rs 450/700 with attached bath.

Getting There & Away Hourly RSTC buses travel from Udaipur to Jaisamand (1½ hrs, Rs 15).

Bambora

About 45km south-east of Udaipur, this sleepy little village has a 250-year-old fort that has been converted into an impressive hotel.

Karni Fort has smart singles/doubles from Rs 2000/2500. The best room (on the second floor) has a blissfully soft round bed with panoramic views; it costs Rs 3750. There's a good restaurant, secret tunnel, and an alluring swimming pool which has four water-spurting marble elephants and a central pavilion. Book at Jodhpur's Hotel Karni Bhawan (☎ *0291-432220, fax 433495).*

Sitamata Wildlife Sanctuary

Located 65km south-east of Udaipur, the Sitamata Wildlife Sanctuary covers 423 sq km of mainly deciduous forest (see National Parks & Sanctuaries in the Facts about Rajasthan chapter). Not many tourists make it out this way, which is part of the region's appeal. If you're in search of picturesque countryside, peace and plenty of fresh air, this place is ideal and there are two very different accommodation options available, described in the following two sections.

Dhamotar

Teekhi Magri Resort, situated about 22km from the village of Dhamotar (160km from Udaipur), is highly recommended for those seeking a secluded jungle retreat. The accommodation and facilities are fairly simple, but this is part of the charm. The silence is like music to the ears and you won't get touts shoving souvenirs and postcards in your face. There are just three basic brick-clay cottages which were constructed by local tribals; these cost Rs 1100 a double (lighting is by lantern). The jungle surrounding the cottages is home to a variety of wildlife, including leopards (look for paw prints in the morning). Meals are available and the stargazing is superb. In the winter, it can get very cold at night, so bring warm clothing.

This remote resort is run by the thakur of Dhamotar, Digvijay Singh, and his son Brijraj, who accompany guests on tribal village safaris and other excursions, in their amazing 1945 American jeep. You can visit their 17th century castle at Dhamotar – it's not nearly as glitzy as many of the other palaces

in Rajasthan, but it has a certain old-world charm. You can visit Sitamata wildlife sanctuary, picnic by a bubbling brook and visit the tiny Sitamata temple. You may like to see *lekha bhata* (written rock), rock carvings situated along a dry creek bed (wear strong shoes). This small collection of weathered rock carvings are believed to date back to the Mesolithic era (10,000 to 5000 years BC). There are also some interesting temples in the area, including the crumbling Nahar Singh Khera temple, an evocative 8th century Hindu temple with some erotic carvings, and the Madura Talab tribal temple.

Bookings are essential. Contact Dhamotar House, 21 Surendra Pal Colony, New Sanganer Rd, Jaipur, 302019 (☎ *0141-212235).*

Dhariyawad

Fort Dhariyawad (☎ *02950-20050)* or call Jaipur (☎ *0141-201180)* is also in the Sitamata sanctuary area, 120km from Udaipur. Although it does not have the same remote jungle appeal as the Teekhi Magri Resort just described, it is certainly recommended for those who prefer their creature comforts. This well-kept fort offers comfortable rooms for Rs 1100 a double. The restaurant serves tasty food; the set breakfast/lunch/dinner is Rs 175/250/350. Horse and jeep safaris can be arranged to places of interest in the area. The owners can also arrange tented accommodation for the Baneshwar fair (see Baneshwar later).

There are RSTC buses from Udaipur to Dhariyawad (4 hrs, Rs 31).

Dungarpur

Situated about 110km south of Udaipur, Dungarpur, the City of Hills, was founded in the 13th century. Between 9 am and 4 pm daily, you can visit the deserted old palace, **Juna Mahal**, after obtaining a ticket (Rs 100) from the Udai Bilas Palace (see Places to Stay). Built in stages between the 13th and 18th centuries this crumbling, seven storey palace is filled with old frescoes and paintings. The Aam Khas, or main living room, has impressive mirrorwork and glass inlays. The former royal hunting lodge, on a nearby hilltop, has sensational views over the town and its many temples.

Other points of interest in Dungarpur include the **Government Museum**, near the hospital, with pieces dating back to the 6th century. They are well displayed but the captions are in Hindi. The museum is open daily except Friday from 10 am to 5 pm. Admission is Rs 3 (free on Monday). The beautiful **Deo Somnath Temple**, about 25km out of town, dates back to the 12th century. Note the amazing banyan tree opposite the temple, which must be hundreds of years old.

Places to Stay Interesting *Udai Bilas Palace (☎ 02964-30808, fax 31008)* is an 18th century palace which has partly been converted into a hotel by Maharaj Kumar Harshvardhan Singh of Dungarpur. Constructed of *pareva* (Dungarpur's blue-grey stone), everything at this palace seems to have been left just as it was in those unhurried days before socialist India swept aside the princely states. A feature of this hotel is the intricately carved Ek Thambia Mahal (one pillared palace). The property is ideally located near Gaibsagar (lake), which is a good place for bird-watching.

On the lake is a small Shiva temple built in the 1920s. Singles/doubles at the palace cost Rs 1450/1900 and many rooms are decorated in Art Deco style (some have a private balcony with lake views). Suites cost Rs 2600 – suite No 5 has an awesome old shower. Meals are taken at the long dining room table, with stuffed beasts watching your every bite – note the exquisite ceiling made from Burmese teak. Bicycle hire and bird-watching excursions can be organised.

Hotel Pratibha Palace (☎ 02964-30775, Shastri Colony) is the best budget hotel in town, with tiny singles/doubles with bath (Indian-style toilet and bucket hot water) from Rs 50/100 to Rs 150/250. Some rooms are quite small but otherwise OK considering the tariff. No meals are available but there are several cheap dhabas nearby.

Getting There & Away Frequent RSTC buses travel to Dungarpur from Udaipur

(3 hrs, Rs 35). There's also a slow train between Dungarpur and Udaipur (Rs 78/184 in 2nd/1st class).

Galiakot

About 50km south-east of Dungarpur is an important Muslim pilgrimage centre at Galiakot. This town is famous for the tomb of Saint Fakruddin, who spread the word of Mohammed in the 10th century. Each year, thousands of local and international Bohra Muslim pilgrims flock here to pay homage to the saint.

There are three daily buses from Udaipur (3 hrs, Rs 36).

Baneshwar

Baneshwar is at the confluence of three holy rivers: the Mahi, Som and Jakham. In January/February the week-long **Baneshwar Fair** is held at the Baneshwar Temple, about 80km from Dungarpur. It attracts thousands of Bhil tribals. The dates for this fair are 16-19 Feb in 2000, 4-8 Feb in 2001, 23-27 Feb in 2002 and 12-16 Feb in 2003.

Tents with attached bathroom (minimum of 10 tents; Rs 5500 a double including all meals) can be arranged through Fort Dhariyawad (see earlier).

MT ABU

- **pop 18,000**   ☎ 02974

Rajasthan's only hill station sprawls along a 1200m-high plateau in the south of the state, close to the Gujarat border. It's a popular hot season retreat from the plains of both Rajasthan and Gujarat, but you won't find many western travellers here – apart from those studying at the Brahma Kumaris Spiritual University. Indian visitors include starry-eyed honeymooners who come to enjoy the pleasant climate and easy-going pace. Like most hill stations, it's best to avoid Mt Abu in summer, when hordes of people come to escape the heat although it is not as cool as it used to be, due to increased development, predominantly for tourism. Vegetation has been cleared for the many hotels that continue to crop up. Nonetheless, it has retained a green charm.

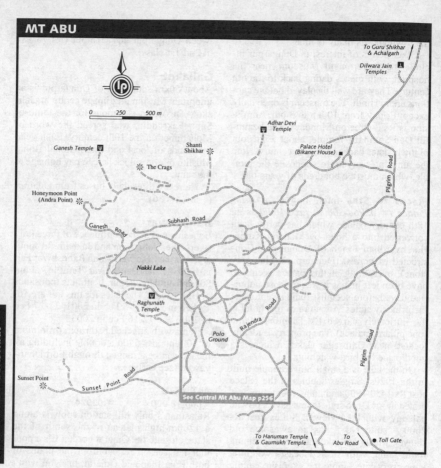

MT ABU

To Guru Shikhar
& Achalgarh

Dilwara Jain
Temples

Adhar Devi
Temple

Palace Hotel
(Bikaner House)

Pilgrim Road

Shanti
Shikhar

Ganesh Temple

The Crags

Honeymoon Point
(Andra Point)

Subhash Road

Ganesh Road

Nakki Lake

Raghunath
Temple

Rajendra Road

Polo
Ground

Pilgrim Road

Sunset Point

Sunset Point Road

See Central Mt Abu Map p256

To Hanuman Temple
& Gaumukh Temple

To
Abu Road

Toll Gate

0   250   500 m

SOUTHERN RAJASTHAN

Mt Abu also has a number of noteworthy temples, particularly the breathtaking Dilwara group of Jain temples, 5km away. This is a very important pilgrimage centre for Jains and the temples' superb marble carvings are among the best in Rajasthan, if not India. Also, like many hill stations, Mt Abu has its own lake, which is the hub of activity.

When or how Mt Abu came into existence is fraught with various myths and legends. According to one, Mt Abu is as old as the Himalaya. It was named after Arbuda, a mighty serpent who saved Lord Shiva's revered bull, Nandi, from plunging into an abyss. Another legend relates that in Mt Abu, the four Rajput fire clans, the Chauhans, Solankis, Pramaras and Pratiharas, were created from a fire pit by Brahmin priests.

Orientation

Mt Abu is a good place to simply wander around at leisure. It is on a hilly plateau about 22km long by 6km wide, 27km from the nearest train station at Abu Road. The main part of the town extends along the road in from Abu Road, down to Nakki Lake.

Information
Tourist Office The Tourist Reception Centre (☎ 43151) is opposite the bus stand. It is open Monday to Saturday from 10 am to 1.30 pm and 2 to 5 pm.

Money The State Bank of Bikaner & Jaipur, situated in the same area as the main post office, changes travellers cheques and currency. The Bank of Baroda, near the southern part of the polo ground, only changes currency. The State Bank of India also only changes currency.

Post & Communications The main post office is on Raj Bhavan Rd. Local and long-distance calls can be made from the numerous telephone booths in the Nakki Lake area.

Nakki Lake
Legend has it this small lake, virtually in the centre of Mt Abu, was scooped out by a god using only his nails, or *nakh*. Some Hindus thus believe it to be a holy lake. The lake is surrounded by hills, parks and strange **rock formations**. The best known, Toad Rock, looks just like a toad about to hop into the lake. Others, like Nun Rock, Nandi Rock or Camel Rock, require more imagination. The 14th century **Raghunath Temple** stands beside the lake. Several maharajas built lavish summer houses around Nakki Lake; the maharaja of Jaipur's former summer palace is perched on a hill overlooking the water.

Nakki Lake is the heart of all activity in Mt Abu. It's a short and easy stroll around it and there are juice stalls, ice cream parlours, balloon vendors, shops and small food stalls. You'll probably have to plough through the persistent photographers eager to take a happy snap of you by the water, and the honeymooners are often approached by innovative sellers offering a range of aphrodisiacs that 'make big difference'.

On the lake is a dilapidated, concrete boat-shaped snack bar. A one hour horse ride costs

Rs 100 and from around 8 am to 7 pm daily, you can hire your own boat (Rs 25 per person for 30 minutes).

Viewpoints
Of the various viewpoints around town, **Sunset Point** is the most popular. Hordes stroll out here every evening to catch the setting sun, the food stalls and all the usual entertainment. Other popular spots include **Honeymoon Point**, which also offers a view of the sunset, **The Crags** and **Robert's Spur**. You can follow the white arrows along a rather overgrown path up to the summit of **Shanti Shikhar**, west of Adhar Devi Temple, where there are panoramic views.

The best spot is the terrace of the maharaja of Jaipur's former **summer palace**. No one minds if you climb up for the view a photo.

Adhar Devi Temple
Three kilometres north of town, around 365 steps lead to this ancient Durga temple built in a natural cleft in the rock. You have to stoop to get through the low entrance to the temple. There are nice views over Mt Abu from up here.

Brahma Kumaris Spiritual University & Museum
The Brahma Kumaris teach that all religions lead to God and so are equally valid, and the principles of each should be studied. The university's stated aim is the establishment of universal peace through 'the impartation of spiritual knowledge and training of easy raja yoga meditation'. There are over 4500 branches in about 70 countries around the world and followers come to Mt Abu to attend courses at the spiritual university.

To attend one of these residential courses, contact your local branch and arrange things in advance. You can, however, arrange for someone to give you an introductory course (seven lessons) while you're in Mt Abu; this would take a minimum of three days. There's no charge – the organisation is entirely supported by donations, as is the accommodation.

CENTRAL MT ABU

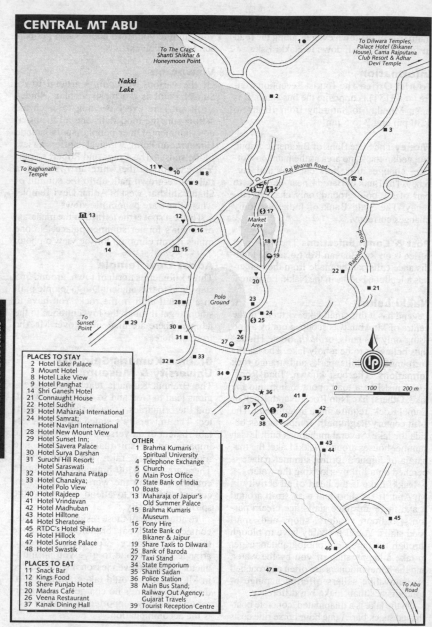

PLACES TO STAY
2 Hotel Lake Palace
3 Mount Hotel
8 Hotel Lake View
9 Hotel Panghat
14 Shri Ganesh Hotel
21 Connaught House
22 Hotel Sudhir
23 Hotel Maharaja International
24 Hotel Samrat;
   Hotel Navijan International
28 Hotel New Mount View
29 Hotel Sunset Inn;
   Hotel Savera Palace
30 Hotel Surya Darshan
31 Suruchi Hill Resort;
   Hotel Saraswati
32 Hotel Maharana Pratap
33 Hotel Chanakya;
   Hotel Polo View
40 Hotel Rajdeep
41 Hotel Vrindavan
42 Hotel Madhuban
43 Hotel Hilltone
44 Hotel Sheratone
45 RTDC's Hotel Shikhar
46 Hotel Hillock
47 Hotel Sunrise Palace
48 Hotel Swastik

PLACES TO EAT
11 Snack Bar
12 Kings Food
18 Shere Punjab Hotel
20 Madras Café
26 Veena Restaurant
37 Kanak Dining Hall

OTHER
1 Brahma Kumaris
   Spiritual University
4 Telephone Exchange
5 Church
6 Main Post Office
7 State Bank of India
10 Boats
13 Maharaja of Jaipur's
   Old Summer Palace
15 Brahma Kumaris
   Museum
16 Pony Hire
17 State Bank of
   Bikaner & Jaipur
19 Share Taxis to Dilwara
25 Bank of Baroda
27 Taxi Stand
34 State Emporium
35 Shanti Sadan
36 Police Station
38 Main Bus Stand;
   Railway Out Agency;
   Gujarat Travels
39 Tourist Reception Centre

Nakki Lake

To The Crags,
Shanti Shikhar &
Honeymoon Point

To Dilwara Temples,
Palace Hotel (Bikaner
House), Cama Rajputana
Club Resort & Adhar
Devi Temple

To Raghunath
Temple

Raj Bhavan Road

Rajendra Road

Market
Area

To Sunset
Point

Polo
Ground

To Abu
Road

0   100   200 m

SOUTHERN RAJASTHAN

There's a museum (free) in the town outlining the university's teachings and offering meditation sessions. It's open daily from 8 am to 8 pm.

Dilwara Temples

These remarkable Jain temples are Mt Abu's main attraction and among the finest examples of Jain architecture in India. The complex includes two temples with marble carvings which are exquisite – the art must surely have reached unsurpassed heights here.

The older of the temples is the **Vimal Vasahi**, built in 1031 and dedicated to the first tirthankar, Adinath. The central shrine has an image of Adinath, while around the courtyard are 52 identical cells, each with a Buddha-like cross-legged image. Forty-eight elegantly carved pillars form the entrance to the courtyard. In front of the temple stands the **House of Elephants**, with figures of elephants marching in procession to the temple.

The later **Tejpal Temple** is dedicated to Neminath, the 22nd tirthankar, and was built in 1230 by the brothers Tejpal and Vastupal. Like Vimal, they were ministers in the government of the ruler of Gujarat. Although the Tejpal Temple is important as an extremely old and complete example of a Jain temple, its most notable feature is the intricacy and delicacy of the marble carving. It is so fine that, in places, the marble becomes almost transparent. In particular, the lotus flower which hangs from the centre of the dome is an incredible piece of work. It's difficult to believe that this huge lace-like filigree started as a solid block of marble. The temple employs several full-time stonecarvers to maintain and restore the work.

There are three other temples in the enclosure, but they all pale beside the Tejpal and Vimal Vasahi. There's a local festival at the Dilwara temples in June (dates vary according to the lunar calendar – ask at the Tourist Reception Centre).

The complex is open for non-Jains from noon to 6 pm (Jains can visit from sunrise to sunset). Entry is free. Photography is not allowed, and bags are searched to prevent cameras being taken in. As at other Jain temples, all articles of leather (such as shoes and belts) have to be left at the entrance (where you pay a few rupees when collecting them).

You can stroll out to Dilwara from the town in less than an hour, or take a share taxi for Rs 3 per person (one way) from just opposite the Madras Café in the centre of town.

Organised Tours

The RTDC offers daily tours of all the main sites. They leave from the main bus stand (opposite the Tourist Reception Centre) and cost Rs 35. This does not include entry or camera charges. Tour times are 8.30 am to 1.15 pm and 1.30 to 6 pm (later in summer). The afternoon tour finishes at Sunset Point.

Places to Stay

There are plenty of hotels to choose from, with new ones springing up each year. Most are along or just off the main road through to Nakki Lake. The high season lasts from around mid-April to mid-November. As most hotel owners raise prices to whatever the market will bear at those times, Mt Abu can be an expensive place to stay. During the five days of Diwali (October/November), rooms are ridiculously expensive and virtually unobtainable without advance booking. Avoid the place at this time, when it is transformed from a quiet retreat to a congested and noisy hive of activity.

In the low season (with the exception of Christmas and New Year), discounts of up to 50% are available and mid-range accommodation can be an absolute bargain. Most places are definitely open to a bit of bargaining, and the rates get cheaper the longer you stay. Most of the budget hotels usually have an ungenerous 9 am checkout time.

At all times of the year there are plenty of touts working the bus and taxi stands. In the low season you can safely ignore them; at peak times they can save you a lot of legwork as they'll know exactly where the last available room is. Hot water can be erratic at the budget places and the service is rather unenthusiastic at most places.

Mt Abu operates the Paying Guest House Scheme, which gives you the opportunity to live with a local family – contact the Tourist Reception Centre (see Information earlier) for details.

Places to Stay – Budget

Hotel Lake View (☎ 38659) overlooks picturesque Nakki Lake but, although the views are certainly good, it's only an average hotel. In winter, doubles with attached bath range from Rs 200 to Rs 350. Hot water is available between 7 and 11 am, and there's a pleasant terrace. Meals are served.

Hotel Panghat (☎ 38886), close by, is also good if you want to be where the action is – Nakki Lake. There are rooms with a lake view, attached bathroom and TV for Rs 150. Hot water is available from 7 to 10 am.

Shri Ganesh Hotel (☎ 43591), up the hill towards the maharaja of Jaipur's old summer palace, is a popular place. The location is quiet and the rooms are not bad considering the price (although some lack windows). As this place is a little farther from the centre of things, the high-season rates tend to be a little more sensible than elsewhere, and bargaining is possible. Low-season rates are around Rs 100 for a double room with a bath, while high-season rates are Rs 350.

Hotel Rajdeep (☎ 43525) is right opposite the bus stand, so can get a bit noisy. It's an old building with rooms with bath from around Rs 150 in the low season. There's a small restaurant at the front of this hotel which doubles as reception.

Hotel Vrindavan (☎ 43147) is a pleasant place near the bus stand (set back from the main road, making it relatively quiet) with good rooms from Rs 250 to Rs 450 with attached bath. There's a vegetarian restaurant with thalis for Rs 45.

Hotel Sudhir (☎ 43311) offers basic doubles with attached bath and constant hot water for Rs 250. The best room costs Rs 450. There are good views from the terrace and veg meals are available.

RTDC's Hotel Shikhar (☎ 38944), back from the main road and up a steepish path, is one of the biggest places in Mt Abu. Although fairly popular, it's certainly not the best value in town and the service leaves a little to be desired. Singles/doubles with bath start at Rs 200/275. A dorm bed is Rs 50.

Hotel Chanakya (☎ 43438) charges Rs 450 (doubles only) in the low season for a comfortable room with attached bath and constant hot water. In the high season the tariff shoots up to Rs 950. The nearby *Hotel Polo View* (☎ 43487) and the *Hotel Surya Darshan* (☎ 43165), both charge around Rs 300 for a room with attached bath.

Hotel New Mount View (☎ 38279) is an older building and the no-frills rooms cost Rs 300 a double with private bath (hot water from 7 to 10 am).

Nearby *Hotel Saraswati* (☎ 38887, fax 38337) is pretty good value. There are clean doubles for Rs 100 with attached bath, and a range of other rooms from Rs 150 to Rs 350 with hot water from 7 to 11 am. It's well run and a popular place to stay. There's a vegetarian restaurant that serves Gujarati thalis for Rs 40.

Places to Stay – Mid-Range

Mount Hotel (☎ 43150), run by the affable Jehangir Bharucha (fondly known as 'Jimmy') is a homey place in a tranquil location along the road to the Dilwara temples. It once belonged to a British army officer and has changed little since those days. The handful of rooms are a bit worn and weary, but you'll have no hassles whatsoever. Doubles range from Rs 400 to Rs 600. Vegetarian meals (Rs 90) are available with advance notice and Jimmy can organise horse safaris. His dog, Spots, is a friendly creature.

Hotel Lake Palace (☎ 43254) makes the most of its excellent location – just across from Nakki Lake – with rather high prices. Singles/doubles/triples are Rs 600/750/900 in the high season; but if you bargain hard in the low season and you should be able to get at least 30% off these prices. Indian food is available.

Hotel Sunset Inn (☎ 43194, fax 43515), on the western edge of Mt Abu, is a modern hotel that's well run. There are good doubles from Rs 650 to Rs 1100 for an air-con super deluxe family room. There's a 30% low-season discount and the restaurant serves Punjabi and Gujarati food.

Hotel Savera Palace (☎ 43354), nearby, is similarly priced but not as good. Humdrum singles/doubles cost Rs 880/990. There's a restaurant and swimming pool.

Suruchi Hill Resort (☎ 43577) is at the bottom end of the polo ground. Singles/doubles cost Rs 490/690 in the high season, and there's a 50% low-season discount. It has an Indian restaurant.

Hotel Maharana Pratap (☎ 38667, fax 38900), at the end of this road, is a smart place with decent double rooms from Rs 500 in the low season. There's a restaurant which serves Indian, Chinese and continental cuisine.

Hotel Sheratone (☎ 43544, fax 38900), not far from the main bus stand, has large, airy double rooms from Rs 400 to Rs 750 in the low season; Rs 900 to Rs 1250 in the high season. It has good views from the rooftop terrace and meals are available.

Hotel Madhuban (☎ 38822), nearby, has doubles ranging from Rs 400 to Rs 1350 (low season); all rooms have hot water from 7 to 11 am. There are only snacks available here.

Hotel Samrat (☎ 43153) and *Hotel Navijan International (☎ 43173)*, on the main road, are basically the same hotel, although they appear to be separate. Low-season rates in the Samrat start at Rs 250/550 for rooms with hot water from 6 am to noon; the Navijan is a smidgen cheaper, but not quite as good.

Directly opposite, *Hotel Maharaja International (☎ 38114)* is a little more up-market, but not remarkable. Doubles cost Rs 590 (low season) and Punjabi and Gujarati food is cooked here.

Hotel Swastik (☎ 83752), farther away from the lake on the road to Abu Rd, has reasonably good doubles from Rs 890 to Rs 1090. There's also an Indian vegetarian restaurant.

Places to Stay – Top End

Palace Hotel (Bikaner House) (☎ 38673, fax 38674) is a worthwhile treat and a very pleasant place to chill out. The hotel was once the summer residence of the maharaja of Bikaner and is now run by the maharaja's amiable son-in-law (who shuttles between Mt Abu and Mumbai). The hotel is in a picturesque location near the Dilwara Temples and has shady gardens, a private lake, two tennis courts, and pony rides by arrangement. There are 38 comfortable rooms, including 13 capacious suites. The cost is a reasonable Rs 1095/1350, or Rs 1195/2000 for a suite. Tasty meals are available in the dining room (see Places to Eat).

Cama Rajputana Club Resort (☎ 38205, fax 38412), nearby, was once a private club but now a large hotel. Set in its own gardens, ordinary doubles cost Rs 1800, deluxe rooms cost Rs 2000, and suites are Rs 3000. There's a good restaurant serving Chinese, continental and Punjabi food. A buffet lunch or dinner costs Rs 250.

Connaught House (☎ 38560) or book through the Umaid Bhawan Palace in Jodhpur (☎ 0291-433316, fax 635373) belongs to the maharaja of Jodhpur and has a relaxing atmosphere. It's more like an English cottage than a hotel and is set in shady gardens. The rooms in the old building are Rs 1190/1950 a single/double, and have more character than those in the new wing, which cost Rs 1190/1750. Meals are available but should be ordered in advance; the set lunch/dinner is Rs 150/200.

Hotel Sunrise Palace (☎ 43573, fax 38775), at the southern end of Mt Abu, is yet another former summer residence of a Rajput maharaja (this time the maharaja of Bharatpur). Although it lacks the panache of Connaught House and the Palace Hotel, it's a very tranquil hotel with fabulous views. The rooms are well furnished and range from Rs 650 to Rs 1450. The restaurant has excellent views; set lunch/dinner is Rs 135.

Hotel Hilltone (☎ 38391, fax 38395) is centrally located and is quite a good choice. Within the modern complex there's a swimming pool, restaurant, bar and sauna. Decent doubles range from Rs 1300 to Rs 2400, and there are two cottages for Rs 2800. There's a 30% discount in the low season. The restaurant has an extensive menu; Russian salad is Rs 40, murg makhani is Rs 95 and desserts range from Rs 25 to Rs 45.

Hotel Hillock (☎ 38463, fax 38467) is a large, swanky place – spotlessly clean and well decorated. The comfortable rooms cost Rs 1790 to Rs 3790; and an extra bed costs Rs 390. A 30% discount is offered in the low season. There's a restaurant serving Indian, Chinese and continental food, a bar, swimming pool and pleasant gardens.

Kesar Bhavan Palace (☎ 38647) was under construction at the time of writing. Rooms are expected to cost Rs 900 for a deluxe room, and Rs 1150 for a superior room.

Places to Eat

Kanak Dining Hall, near the main bus stand, is a popular place to eat. The all-you-can-eat Gujarati thalis are perhaps the best in Mt Abu (Rs 45); there's seating indoors and outdoors.

Veena Restaurant is farther uphill, next to the junction at the bottom end of the polo ground. Its refillable Gujarati thalis (Rs 40) are also excellent.

Shere Punjab Hotel, in the bazaar area, has reasonably priced Punjabi and Chinese food. They take delight in their brain preparations (brain pakoda is Rs 30). There are also some more conventional creations such as chicken curry (Rs 35).

Madras Café, also in this area, is a pure veg place with an assortment of Indian and western fare. There are even Jain pizzas (no garlic, onion or cheese) for Rs 30. Masala dosas are Rs 25 and a glass of lassi is Rs 15. Meat eaters are catered for upstairs.

Kings Food, on the road leading down to the lake, has the usual have-a-go-at-anything menu and is good for a light bite.

Palace Hotel (Bikaner House) is the best place to go for a special meal. The set lunch or dinner costs Rs 235 (veg), Rs 295 (non-veg). It's best to make advance reservations.

Shopping

Around Nakki Lake there are lots of colourful little shops and stalls flogging all sorts of kitsch curios. In the evening, the town really comes to life and this is an enjoyable time to do some leisurely browsing and people watching.

Getting There & Away

As you enter Mt Abu, there's a toll gate where bus and car passengers are charged Rs 5, plus Rs 5 for a car. If you're travelling by bus, this is an irksome hold-up, as you have to wait until the collector painstakingly gathers the toll from each and every passenger (keep small change handy).

Bus Regular buses make the 27km climb from Abu Road up to Mt Abu (1 hr, Rs 15) – you never know quite what to expect as the bus spirals up the mountain. Some RSTC buses go all the way to Mt Abu, while others terminate at Abu Road, so make sure you get the one you want.

The bus schedule from Mt Abu is extensive, and for many destinations you will find a direct bus faster and more convenient than going down to Abu Road and waiting for a train. Deluxe buses go to:

destination	duration (hrs)	cost (Rs)
Ahmedabad	6	100
Ajmer	8	120
Baroda	8	160
Jaipur	11	130
Jodhpur	8	100
Surat	10	180
Udaipur	5	70

Bus tickets can be bought from travel agents, such as Gujarat Travels (☎ 43554) (near the bus stand), which is open daily from 6 am to midnight. Gujarat Travels can also arrange local sightseeing (a half/full day costs Rs 40/80 per person).

Train Abu Road, the railhead for Mt Abu, is on the broad-gauge line between Delhi and Mumbai via Ahmedabad.

In Mt Abu there's a 'Railway Out Agency' (☎ 38697) near the main bus stand (opposite the police station) which has quotas on most of the express trains out of Abu Road. It's open daily from 10 am to 1 pm and 2 to 4 pm (only until noon on Sunday).

From Abu Road, direct trains run to various destinations including Ajmer, Jodhpur, Jaipur, Ahmedabad and Agra. For Bhuj and the rest of the Kathiawar peninsula in Gujarat, change trains at Palanpur, 53km south of Abu Road.

Taxi A taxi, which you can share with up to five people, costs about Rs 200 from Abu Road. To hire a jeep for local sightseeing costs around Rs 800 per day (bargain hard and you just may bring it down). Many hotels can arrange jeep hire, or they can be rented in the town centre.

Getting Around

Buses from the bus stand go to the various sites in Mt Abu, but it takes a little planning to get out and back without too much hanging around. For Dilwara it's easier to take a share taxi, and these leave when full from opposite the Madras Café in the centre of town; the fare is Rs 3 per person.

There are no auto-rickshaws in Mt Abu, but it's relatively easy to get around on foot. Porters with trolleys can be hired for a small charge to transport your luggage – weary travellers can even be transported on the trolley!

AROUND MT ABU
Achalgarh

The Shiva temple of **Achaleshwar Mahandeva** in Achalgarh, 11km north of Mt Abu, has a number of interesting features, including a toe of Shiva, a brass Nandi and, where the Shiva lingam would normally be, a deep hole said to extend all the way to the underworld.

Outside, by the car park, three stone buffaloes stand around a tank while the figure of a king shoots at them with a bow and arrows. A legend states that the tank was once filled with ghee, but demons in the form of buffaloes came down and polluted the ghee – until the king shot them. A path leads up the hillside to a group of colourful **Jain temples** with fine views out over the plains.

Guru Shikhar

At the end of the plateau, 15km from Mt Abu, is Guru Shikhar, the highest point in Rajasthan at 1722m. A road goes almost all the way to the summit. At the top is the **Atri Rishi Temple**, complete with a priest and good views all around.

Mt Abu Wildlife Sanctuary

This 290 sq km wildlife sanctuary, 8km north-east of Mt Abu, is home to panthers, bears, sambars, foxes, wild boars and birds. It encloses forested hills and includes Guru Shikhar and **Trevor's Tank**, a small reservoir named after an English engineer.

A sign at the sanctuary gives the following advice: 'Use your eyes to observe the plants, birds and animals, use your ears to hear birds and animals call, use your legs to walk – the more you walk the more you see and hear'.

The sanctuary is open daily from 8 am to 5 pm. Entry costs Rs 5/40 for Indians/foreigners. Vehicle entry is Rs 125 for cars and jeeps, or Rs 15 for motorbikes.

Gaumukh Temple

Down on the Abu Road side of Mt Abu, a small stream flows from the mouth of a marble cow, giving the shrine its name. There is also a marble figure of the bull Nandi, Shiva's vehicle. The tank here, Agni Kund, is said to be the site of the sacrificial fire, made by the sage Vasishta, from which four of the great Rajput clans were born. An image of Vasishta is flanked by figures of Rama and Krishna.

ABU ROAD

This station down on the plains is the rail junction for Mt Abu. The train station and bus stand are right next to each other on the edge of town.

Although there are RSTC buses from Abu Road to other cities such as Jodhpur,

Jaipur, Udaipur and Ahmedabad, there is little point in catching them from here as they are all available from Mt Abu itself. Alternatively, buses that are operated by private companies also run from Mt Abu to several destinations.

There is a sprinkling of cheap hotels at Abu Road and most are only a short walk from the train station. These places are satisfactory and OK for a night, but those available in Mt Abu are far preferable in terms of comfort and price.

Retiring rooms at the train station are available for a charge of Rs 120 for a double room; an extra bed costs Rs 60. Veg thalis are sold for Rs 35.

Northern Rajasthan (Shekhawati)

The semi-desert Shekhawati region lies in the triangular area between Delhi, Jaipur and Bikaner. Around the 14th century, a number of Muslim clans moved into the area and the towns which developed became important trading posts on caravan routes from the ports of Gujarat. The name of the region and its inhabitants can be traced to a 15th century Rajput Kachhwaha chieftain by the name of Rao Shekha.

Although the towns have long since lost their importance, they have not lost the amazing painted *havelis*, or traditional mansions with internal courtyards, built by the merchants of the region. Most of the buildings date from the 18th century to early 20th century, and such is their splendour that the area has been dubbed by some as the 'open-air gallery of Rajasthan'. There are also the obligatory (for Rajasthan) forts, a couple of minor castles, distinctive wells, *baoris* (stepwells), *chhatris* (cenotaphs) and a handful of mosques.

The major towns of interest in the region are Nawalgarh, Fatehpur, Mandawa, Ramgarh and Jhunjhunu, although at least a few havelis survive in virtually every town. Shekhawati sees fewer tourists than many other parts of Rajasthan, so facilities at most places can be limited. Having said that, there are some places (such as Mandawa and Nawalgarh), where you may find yourself hounded by persistent children, or 'guides', insisting they show you around.

HISTORY

As the Mughal empire fell into decline after the death of Aurangzeb in 1707, the descendants of Rao Shekha, who had already installed themselves in the area to the east of the Aravalli Range, encroached on the regions to the north and west. Covering an area of approximately 30,000 sq km, today the Shekhawati region encompasses the

---

Highlights

- **Painted havelis** – especially the well-preserved examples at Nawalgarh and Jhunjhunu
- **The architecture** – visit numerous wells, stepwells and cenotaphs
- **Khetri Mahal in Jhunjhunu** – an intricate series of arches and columns
- **Malji ka Kamra at Churu** – go searching for this extraordinary building

---

administrative districts of Churu, Jhunjhunu and Sikar.

The chieftains of the region retained a nominal loyalty to the Rajput states of Jaipur and Amber, who in turn honoured them with hereditary titles known as *tazimi sardars*. It was probably exposure to the courts of Jaipur and Amber which encouraged the chieftains, known as *thakurs*, or barons, to commission the first of the thousands of murals to decorate their havelis.

By 1732, two of these chieftains, Sardul Singh and Shiv Singh, had overthrown the nawabs of Fatehpur and Jhunjhunu and carved their territories up between them. Their descendants, particularly the sons of Sardul Singh, installed themselves in surrounding villages, where they commanded the allegiance and respect of the villagers. Their coffers were filled by heavy taxes imposed on the poor farmers of the area and duties levied on the caravans carrying goods from the ports of Gujarat overland to northern India and the countries bordering India to the north, north-west and north-east. The merchants travelled via Shekhawati because the Rajput royal states on either side imposed even greater levies on

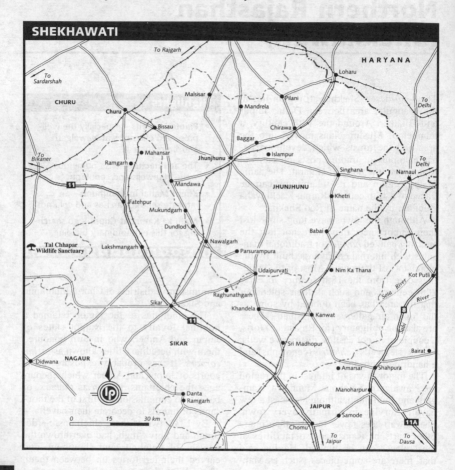

traders than those of the Shekhawats. The arid region of Shekhawati thus saw a great deal of transit trading activity, encouraging merchants to establish themselves here.

The rise of the British Raj following the eclipse of the Mughal empire could have sounded the death knell for Shekhawati. The British ports at Mumbai (Bombay) and Calcutta were able to handle a much greater volume of trade than those at Gujarat. Pressure by the British East India Company compelled Jaipur state to drastically reduce its levies, and it became no longer necessary for traders to travel via Shekhawati. However, the Shekhawat merchants had received a good grounding in the practices and principles of trade, and were reluctant to relinquish what was obviously a lucrative source of income.

Towards the end of the 19th century, the menfolk emigrated en masse from their desert homes to the thriving trading centres emerging on the ports of the Ganges. Their business acumen was unparalleled, and

Festivals of Northern Rajasthan

Festivals peculiar to the Shekhawati region are given below. For statewide and nationwide festivals, see the boxed text 'Festivals of Rajasthan' in the Facts for the Visitor chapter.

March
Nawalgarh Fair – This fair is a relatively recent innovation promoted by the RTDC. Frankly, it's not wildly exciting: it features sports matches and displays on civic accomplishments with captions in Hindi. Given Rajasthan's propensity for spectacle, it may become more colourful in time.

September-October
Bissau Festival – Ten days before the festival of Dussehra, Bissau hosts dramatic performances of the *Ramayana*. The actors wear costumes and masks made locally, and the performance takes place in the bazaar at twilight.

some of the richest merchants of Calcutta hailed from the tiny region of Shekhawati on the other side of India. Some of India's wealthiest industrialists of the 20th century, such as the Birlas, were originally Marwaris (as the people of Shekhawati became known).

THE HAVELIS

The merchants lived frugally in their adopted homes in the trading centres, sending the bulk of their vast fortunes back to their families in Shekhawati to be used to construct grand havelis commensurate with their new stations in life: symbols of their success and increasing prosperity. Merchants competed with one another to build ever more grand edifices – homes, temples, stepwells – and these were richly decorated, both inside and out, with thousands of painted murals.

Many of the artists, masons and craftsmen, known as *chajeras,* were commissioned from beyond Shekhawati – particularly from Jaipur, where they had been employed decorating the palaces of the new capital – and others flooded into the region to offer their skills. There was a cross-pollination of ideas and techniques, with local artists learning skills from the new arrivals and adopting their designs.

The Buildings

The popular design was a building which from the outside was relatively unremarkable; rather the focus was on one or more internal courtyards which provided security and privacy for the women and offered some relief from the fierce heat which grips the area in summer. The plain exteriors also made the houses easy to defend.

The main entrance is a large wooden gate, which is usually locked. In this gate is a smaller doorway which gives access to a small outer courtyard. Often an enormous ramp leads to the entrance, up which a prospective groom could ascend in appropriate grandeur on horse or, in some cases, elephant back. Above the entrance can usually be seen one or more small shield-shaped devices called *torans*. These are generally wrought of wood and silver, and often feature a parrot – the bird of love. In a mock show of conquest, the groom was required to pierce the toran with his sword before claiming his bride. Each toran represents the marriage of a female from the household.

To one side of the outer courtyard is the *baithak*, or salon, in which the merchant could receive guests. In order to impress visitors, this room was generally the most elaborately crafted and often featured marble or mock marble walls. Here the merchant and his guests reclined against bolsters as they discussed their business.

Between the outer and inner courtyard is a type of vestibule, traversed by a blank wall in which is a small window. Through this window the women of the household, who were kept in strict *purdah* (isolation), could peep at prospective guests. Entry into the inner courtyard was restricted to women, members of the family and, very occasionally, privileged guests. Access was gained on either side of the partitioning wall. This courtyard was the main domestic arena – the walls are smoke-stained walls by countless kitchen fires. Rooms off this courtyard served as bedrooms or store rooms, and staircases led to upper levels mostly comprised of bedrooms. The largest of the mansions had as many as four courtyards and were up to six storeys high.

The Paintings

The early Mughal influence, manifested in floral arabesques and geometric designs – according to the dictates of their religion, the Mughals never created a representation of an animal or human – gave way to influences from the Rajput royal courts. Later the walls were embellished with paintings of the new British technological marvels to which the Shekhawat merchants were exposed in centres such as Calcutta. Many of the pictures of motor cars and steam trains which adorn the buildings of Shekhawati were painted by artisans who had probably never even seen a motorised vehicle!

Originally the colours used in the murals were all ochre-based, but in the 1860s artificial pigments were introduced from Germany. The predominant colours are blue and maroon, but other colours such as yellow, green and indigo are also featured.

The major themes used by artists, who were known as *chiteras*, were scenes from Hindu mythology, history, folk tales, eroticism (many of these works have been defaced or destroyed), and – among the most interesting – foreigners and their modern inventions such as trains, planes, telephones, gramophones and bicycles. Animals and landscapes were also popular. The colourful paintings were a response to the arid landscape, and served both an educational and entertainment purpose. Religious themes mostly featured the legends of lords Krishna and Rama, and were used as moral teachings where good prevailed over evil.

The paintings also served as social documents depicting the concerns of the day. The advent of photography and exposure to European art had a dramatic influence on the execution of art in Shekhawati. Previously, subjects were depicted two-dimensionally, with little emphasis on anatomical accuracy or shading for perspective, and more emphasis on the imagination. With the influence of photography, artists sought a more faithful rendering of their subjects.

The paintings of Shekhawati are thus an extraordinary synthesis of eastern and western influences. An haveli in Fatehpur perfectly illustrates this cultural collision: in one painting, Krishna is depicted playing a gramophone for his consort Radha. Some of the paintings of the early 20th century exhibit an extraordinary technical expertise; others are florid, grotesque and executed in lurid colours. But all are interesting.

RESPONSIBLE TOURISM

The tourist boom has still not really caught up with Shekhawati, but with so much to see, and some interesting places to stay, it's an area well worth exploring. The best plan is to just wander at random through these small, dusty towns. There's no chance of getting lost, and there are surprises around every corner. While tourism can play a positive role in promoting interest in Shekhawati's great legacy of beautifully painted buildings, therefore generating the political will to preserve them, this is both an ecologically and culturally sensitive region. There is a basic infrastructure to accommodate the increasing number of foreign visitors, but tourism here is still in its infancy.

Camel safaris are a popular way to visit the local villages. Visitors can help minimise the potentially destructive nature of these expeditions by ensuring that all rubbish is carried out and insisting on kerosene fires instead of using the already beleaguered sources of wood upon which locals depend. It is also possible to stay in village homes: Ramesh Jangid from Nawalgarh has some interesting homestay programs (see Organised Tours in the Nawalgarh section).

Ramesh is also a terrific source of information on the havelis. He is the president of Les Amis du Shekhawati (The Friends of Shekhawati) – for more information about the society and its endeavours to protect the paintings of Shekhawati, see Volunteer Work in the Facts for the Visitor chapter. Ramesh has initiated some visionary conservation measures at his Eco Farm in Nawalgarh.

Another good source of information on the painted havelis of Shekhawati is Laxmi Kant Jangid, at the Hotel Shiv Shekhawati in Jhunjhunu.

These days most of the havelis are not inhabited by their owners, who find the small towns in rural Rajasthan have little appeal. Many are occupied just by a single *chowkidar* (caretaker), while others may be home to a local family. None are open as museums or for display, and consequently many are either totally or partially locked up. While locals seem tolerant of strangers wandering into their front courtyard, be aware that these are private places, so tact and discretion should be used. Local custom dictates that shoes should be removed when entering the inner courtyard of an haveli.

One unfortunate aspect of the tourist trade is also beginning to manifest itself here – the desire for antiques. A couple of towns have antique shops chock-a-block with items ripped from the havelis – particularly doors and window frames, but anything that can be carted away is fair game. Investing in these antiques is tantamount to condoning this desecration.

One last note: flashes from cameras can damage the paintings. In many instances, you may not be forbidden to use flash photography, but don't!

The Legend of Dhola Maru

One of the most popular paintings to be seen on the walls of Shekhawati havelis depicts the legend of Dhola Maru, the Shekhawati equivalent of Romeo and Juliet.

The princess Maru hailed from Pugal, near Bikaner, and Dhola was a young prince from Gwalior. When Maru was two years old there was a bad drought in Pugal, so her father, the maharaja, shifted to Gwalior where his friend, the maharaja there and father of Dhola, ruled. He stayed for three years, returning to Pugal when he learned that the drought had broken. Before he left, as a token of friendship between the two rulers, a marriage alliance was contracted between their children. However, after 20 years the promise had been forgotten and Maru was contracted to marry a man by the name of Umra.

Wedding plans would have proceeded but a bard, who had travelled from Pugal to Gwalior, sang at the royal court of the childhood marriage of Dhola and Maru. In this way Dhola came to hear of the beautiful Maru, with whom he immediately fell in love after simply hearing her virtues described, and resolved to meet her. Of course, when Maru laid eyes on her champion she fell in love with him, and they decided to flee together.

Her betrothed, Umra, heard of their flight and set chase with his brother, Sumra. They pursued the camel-borne lovers on horseback, and the brave Maru fired at them with arrows, which proved of little use against the brothers, who had guns. They were able to temporarily elude the brothers and took shelter in a forest. However, Dhola was bitten by a snake and succumbed on the spot. Maru, thus thwarted by death, proceeded to weep for her lost lover, and her lamentations were heard by Shiva and Parvati who were walking nearby. Parvati beseeched Shiva to restore the dead Dhola to life and the couple was reunited.

GUIDEBOOKS

For a full rundown on the history, people, towns and buildings of the area, it's well worth investing in a copy of *The Guide to the Painted Towns of Shekhawati*, by Ilay Cooper. It gives details of buildings of interest in each town, precise locations of interesting paintings and fine sketch maps of the larger tours of the area.

GETTING THERE & AWAY

Access to the region is easiest from Jaipur or Bikaner. The towns of Sikar (gateway to the region, but with no notable havelis) and Fatehpur are on the main Jaipur to Bikaner road and are served by many buses. Churu is on the main Delhi to Bikaner railway line, while Sikar, Nawalgarh and Jhunjhunu have several daily passenger train links with Jaipur and Delhi. Shekhawati is also easily accessible by train from Delhi. For more details, see the relevant Getting There & Away sections.

GETTING AROUND

The Shekhawati region is crisscrossed by narrow bitumen roads and all towns are served by government or private buses. Local services to the smaller towns can get very crowded and riding 'upper class' (on the roof!) is quite acceptable – and often necessary. Many of the roads are in poor condition, so be prepared for a bumpy journey at times.

If you have a group of four or five, it is worth hiring a taxi for the day to take you around the area. It's easy to arrange in the towns which have accommodation, although finding a driver who speaks English is more of a challenge. The official rate for a taxi is Rs 4/km with a minimum of 300km per day. Some of the larger towns have auto-rickshaws and tongas.

A number of operators are now offering camel safaris in the Shekhawati region. See Organised Tours in the Nawalgarh and Dundlod sections for details.

NAWALGARH

☎ 01594

Nawalgarh was founded in 1737 by Nawal Singh, one of the five sons of the Rajput ruler Sardul Singh. The arrival of merchants from Jaipur increased the town's prosperity, and some of India's most successful merchants hailed from Nawalgarh, including the wealthy Goenka family, who built many havelis. The township is built in a depression where a number of rivers terminate. The accumulated silt carried by these rivers was used in the bricks for the havelis here, making some that are the best preserved in Shekhawati.

Information

The best source of information on Nawalgarh and its painted havelis is Ramesh Jangid at Ramesh Jangid's Tourist Pension (see Places to Stay). He is actively involved in the preservation of Shekhawati's havelis, and has initiated educational programs to raise local awareness about the rich cultural legacy they represent. Ramesh can speak Hindi, English, French and German.

Money You can change money at the State Bank of Bikaner and Jaipur, situated in the old fort.

Things to See

Bala Qila The main building in this town is the fort, founded in 1737. Today it is largely disfigured by modern accretions. It houses government offices and two banks. One room in the south-eastern quarter of the fort retains paintings on its ceiling which depict street scenes of both Jaipur and Nawalgarh from the mid-19th century.

The Havelis To the west of the Bala Qila is a group of six havelis known as the **Aath Havelis**. The incongruous name – *aath* means 'eight' – refers to the fact that originally eight havelis were planned. The paintings are not technically as proficient as some others in this town, but they illustrate the transition in painting styles over the decades. As you approach the group from the road, the first haveli to the left is a case in point: there are older paintings on the front of the side external wall, while newer paintings, with the synthetic colours, are at

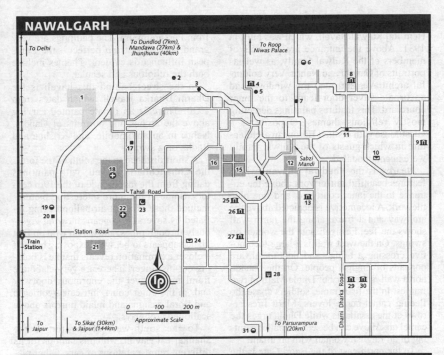

NAWALGARH

PLACES TO STAY
1 Apani Dhani (Eco Farm)
17 Ramesh Jangid's Tourist
   Pension
20 Nawal Hotel

OTHER
2 Well
3 Mandi Gate
4 Hem Raj Kulwal Haveli
5 Khedwal Bhavan
6 Dundlod Bus Stand
7 Baori Gate

8 Bhagton ki Haveli
9 Anandi Lal Poddar Haveli
10 Central Post Office
11 Poddar Gate
12 Fort (Bala Qila);
   Bank of Baroda;
   State Bank of Bikaner
   & Jaipur
13 Chhauchharia Haveli
14 Nansa Gate
15 Aath Havelis
16 Murarka Haveli
18 Maur Hospital

19 Main Bus Stand
21 Poddar College
22 Eye Hospital
23 Mosque
24 Post Office
25 Jhunjhunuwala Haveli
26 Geevrajka Haveli
27 Shankar Lal Haveli
28 Ganga Mai Temple
29 Parsurampura Haveli
30 Dharni Dharka Haveli
31 Parsurampura
   Bus Stand

the rear. The front section depicts a steam locomotive, while the back section has monumental pictures of elephants, horses and camels.

Opposite this group of havelis is the **Murarka Haveli**, which has some very fine

paintings including, above the entrance, miniatures depicting the Krishna legends. The haveli is no longer inhabited, but is hired for marriage celebrations. Unfortunately, unless a marriage is taking place, the richly painted inner courtyard is usually locked.

About 10 minutes walk to the north is the **Hem Raj Kulwal Haveli**, which was built in 1931. Above the entrance are portraits of members of the Kulwal family, as well as portraits of Gandhi and Nehru. Very colourful architraves surround the windows and an ornate silver door leads to the inner courtyard. This features paintings depicting mostly religious themes. Opposite is a guesthouse with distinct European architecture in which guests of the Kulwal family were accommodated.

Nearby is the **Khedwal Bhavan**, which features beautiful mirrorwork above the entrance to the inner courtyard, and fine blue tilework. A locomotive is depicted above the archway and a frieze along the north wall shows the Teej Festival: note the women on swings. On the west wall is a large locomotive crossing a bridge and underneath are portraits of English people. On the outside north wall is the story of Dhola Maru in two frames. In the first frame, soldiers chase the fleeing camel-borne lovers. Maru fires arrows at the assailants while Dhola urges the camel on. Above can be seen a smaller painting of an English woman with an infant.

To the north-east of the Baori Gate is the **Bhagton ki Haveli**. On the external west wall is a locomotive and a steamship. On the wall above dance *gopis* (milkmaids) with the bodies of elephants. Adjacent, women perform the Ginder dance during the festival of Holi.

Above the doorway to the inner courtyard is a very detailed picture of the marriage of Rukmani. Krishna cheated the groom Sisupal of his prospective wife by touching the toran first, thus claiming her for himself. The walls of the salon are reminiscent of marble – the wall is first painted black then decorative incisions are made. The inner chamber upstairs contains the family quarters, also elaborately painted. A room on the west side has a picture of a European man with a cane and pipe and a small dog on his shoulder. Adjacent, a melancholy English woman plays an accordion.

On Dharni Dharka Rd is the **Parsurampura Haveli**, which dates from early in the 20th century and belongs to a merchant from Parsurampura. The paintings are very grand, and almost *too* perfect – the European influence is evident. Themes include both the religious and secular.

In the street behind this haveli is the **Dharni Dharka Haveli**, which dates from 1930. There is an ornate painted carving above the arches and portraits of Gandhi, Nehru in an automobile, and Krishna and Radha on a swing.

A short distance to the south of the fort is the **Chhauchharia Haveli**, with paintings dating from the last decade of the 19th century. Some of the more interesting pictures include those of a hot-air balloon being inflated by several Europeans blowing vigorously through pipes, and a man who on first glance appears to be, well, exposing himself – closer examination reveals that he is holding out his finger! There are very elaborate floral motifs over the enormous doorway and, in the outer court, intricate geometric and floral designs and inlaid mirrors above scalloped archways.

To the south-west of the fort is the **Shankar Lal Haveli**, which is famous for its different representations of cars. Other pictures on its external walls include an English couple sitting stiffly on a bench and a tractor with a tip-tray – a new invention.

A short distance to the north is the **Geevrajka Haveli**, which has very fine paintings on the ceiling of the entrance, including various Hindu deities.

On the right as you enter the town centre from Tahsil Rd is the **Jhunjhunuwala Haveli**, which is an unfortunate example of the lack of will to conserve the havelis. The main courtyard of this building has been destroyed with the construction of six shops. The side wall retains a fine procession frieze – a train, horses, camels and soldiers carrying a palanquin.

The **Anandi Lal Poddar Haveli** (entry is Rs 15), which dates from 1920, is now a secondary school. The paintings of this haveli are some of the few in Nawalgarh which have been restored. A side wall retains the paintings in their deteriorated condition, which are in stark contrast to the paintings across the front facade. In the first courtyard close to the entrance is a tiny picture of Christ.

Ganga Mai Temple Several hundred metres to the south of the Nansa Gate is the Ganga Mai Temple, which, as its name suggests, is dedicated to the goddess Ganga. There is fine mirrorwork around the inner sanctum. The courtyard is surrounded by four aisles formed by five archways, above each of which are floral motifs. There are some good, small paintings above the *mandapa* (courtyard before the inner sanctum). The temple was built by the wealthy Chhauchharia merchants in 1868.

Organised Tours

Ramesh Jangid and his son Rajesh are keen to promote rural tourism, which entails staying with families in small villages in the Shekhawati region. Numbers are kept to a minimum (a maximum of two couples only per host family) and an English-speaking interpreter is provided. They can also organise three-day treks in the Aravalli Range, camel safaris around Rajasthan, and informative guided tours around the painted havelis of Shekhawati, including trips by bicycle.

Costs of treks are from Rs 1250 per person per day for up to two people, Rs 1000 per person for three people, and Rs 850 for four people. Prices for jeep tours to the villages of Shekhawati from Nawalgarh are as follows: three hour trip taking in Dundlod and Parsurampura, Rs 800 for up to four people; five hour trip taking in Mandawa, Dundlod and Fatehpur, Rs 1050 for up to four people; seven to eight hour trip visiting Mandawa, Fatehpur, Ramgarh and Mahansar, Rs 1250. See Places to Stay for Ramesh Jangid's contact details.

The Roop Niwas Palace provides English-speaking guides for walking tours of the painted walls of Nawalgarh for about Rs 150/300 for a half/full day. Horse rides cost Rs 300 for one hour, or Rs 750/1750 for a half/full day. Camel rides are Rs 250/400/800 for one hour/half day/full day.

Places to Stay & Eat

The *Ramesh Jangid's Tourist Pension* (☎ 24060, fax 24061) is near the Maur Hospital – Ramesh is well-known, so if you get lost, just ask one of the locals to point you in the right direction. This family-run guesthouse is within easy walking distance of some of Nawalgarh's best havelis, and you'll have no hassles whatsoever. It's great value for money, with clean singles/doubles with attached bath for Rs 250/280, or Rs 150/180 for the upstairs rooms, which have a private bathroom and open onto a sunny terrace. Hot water is by the bucket (no charge). Pure veg meals are available, including a veg thali for Rs 50.

Apani Dhani (☎ 22239, fax 24061), or Eco Farm, is Ramesh's second place to stay, located near the TV tower, on the west side of the main Jaipur road. This is a delightful place and Ramesh has implemented his various experiments in alternative energy, such as solar water heaters, organic toilets, biogas and solar cookers. Rooms are decorated in traditional style and have thatched roofs and mud plaster. They cost Rs 600/750 for singles/doubles with attached bath. The farm has buffaloes, cows and goats, their manure is used on the vegie garden and to produce biogas for cooking. Fresh vegies from the garden make up the bulk of the pure veg meals; set breakfast/lunch/dinner is Rs 75/125/150.

Nawal Hotel (☎ 22155) is a seedy place right at the bus stand, about 1km from the town centre. It costs Rs 60 for a single with attached bath and there are doubles from Rs 150 with bath. Lunch/dinner is Rs 100. This is not the best place for single women.

Roop Niwas Palace (☎ 22008, fax 23388) is on the northern edge of town, about 1km from the fort. It has comfortable singles/doubles for Rs 950/1150, although the decor is somewhat eclectic. This was the residence of the thakur of Nawalgarh, Nawal Singh (1880-1926). Amenities include a swimming pool and restaurant (the set lunch or dinner is Rs 200). See Organised Tours earlier, for more details about camel and horse excursions.

NORTHERN RAJASTHAN

Getting There & Away

Bus There are buses every 30 minutes between Nawalgarh and Jaipur (express 3½ hrs, Rs 57; deluxe 5 hrs, Rs 69), and several services each day to Delhi (8 hrs, Rs 100). There is also an overnight service to Delhi.

There are two buses during the day and two night buses to Jodhpur (9 hrs, Rs 135).

Buses for destinations in Shekhawati leave every few minutes and share jeeps leave according to demand (Sikar, Rs 11; Jhunjhunu, Rs 15; Fatehpur, Rs 16).

There is a daily deluxe service to Ahmedabad (18 hrs, Rs 200), Chittorgarh (12 hrs, Rs 160) and Udaipur (14 hrs, Rs 160).

Train There are rail connections to several destinations in Shekhawati. The 9734 *Shekhawati Express* leaves Nawalgarh at 10 pm, arriving at Delhi's Sarai Rohilla station at 5.30 am (Rs 117/549 in 2nd/1st class). To Jaipur, the 9733 *Shekhawati Express* leaves Nawalgarh at 6.33 am, reaching Jaipur at 10 am (Rs 40/393). The railway inquiries number is ☎ 22025.

Getting Around

Bicycles can be hired near Nansa Gate. If you're staying at Ramesh Jangid's Tourist Pension, bicycles can also be organised there. The cost is approximately Rs 15 per day.

A share auto-rickshaw from the train or bus station to the main market is Rs 3, and you can wave it down anywhere along this route. To hire an auto-rickshaw or horse-drawn tonga from either the bus or train station to the fort costs about Rs 30.

PARSURAMPURA

This tiny village, 20km south-east of Nawalgarh, has some of the best preserved and oldest paintings in the Shekhawati region. The paintings on the interior of the dome of the **Chhatri of Thakur Sardul Singh** date from the mid-18th century. The very fine and detailed work here is reminiscent of miniature painting. The antiquity of the paintings is evident in the muted, russet colours used. Pictures include those of the thakur and his five sons, graphic battle scenes from the *Ramayana*, and the love story of Dhola Maru, a common theme employed by the painters of Shekhawati. To visit the cenotaph you must obtain the key from the caretaker, Sri Banwari Lal (nicknamed Maharaj), who lives in the Shamji Sharaf Haveli. Maharaj is a Brahmin priest, and it is almost entirely through his efforts that the chhatri is so well maintained. He is also responsible for the pretty flower beds of roses and jasmine which surround the chhatri. He is more than happy to explain the various paintings and a small donation would be welcome – it will be put to good use.

The **Shamji Sharaf Haveli** dates from the end of the 18th century. Pictures include a grandmother having her hair dressed, an Indian woman spinning and an English woman in shiny patent leather shoes carrying a parasol. A frieze shows a celebration, probably of a marriage, and on one side is a frame showing a priest presiding over the ceremony. The opposite wall depicts Europeans in a car. Above the lintel are some very well-preserved portraits, and below, portrayals of Ganesh, Vishnu, Krishna and Radha. Saraswati is riding a peacock in the right-hand corner.

Also in Parsurampura is the small **Gopinathji Mandir**, on the left just before you leave the village on the road to Nawalgarh. The temple was built by Sardul Singh in 1742 and it is believed that the same artist responsible for the paintings on the Chhatri of Sardul Singh executed the fine paintings in the temple. According to local lore, the artist had half completed the work in the temple when the son of Sardul Singh chopped his hands off because he wanted the artist's work to be exclusive to his father's chhatri. Not to be deterred, the valiant artist completed the work with his feet!

Getting There & Away

There are numerous buses throughout the day to Parsurampura from Nawalgarh. The trip can take up to one hour (because of the many stops en route) and costs Rs 6. You'll probably have to fight for a seat (or roof space!), and it's a dusty, corrugated road

Backstreet scene, Jaisalmer.

Vishnu on bed of snakes with Laxmi, Nawalgarh.

Turban wrapping troubles, near Jaisalmer.

View of the Old City or 'Blue City' of Jodhpur, at the edge of the Thar Desert.

Camel trekking in the Sam sand dunes, near Jaisalmer.

View of Jaisalmer town from a bastion of the fort which crowns the 80m high Trikuta hill.

Meherangarh overlooking Jodhpur, with the white marble Jaswant Thada in the foreground.

which crosses a dry riverbed just before the village.

DUNDLOD
☎ 01594

Dundlod is a tiny village lying about 7km north of Nawalgarh. Its small fort was built in 1750 by Keshri Singh, the fifth and youngest son of Sardul Singh. Major additions were made in the early 19th century by his descendant Sheo Singh, who resettled in the region despite attempts on his life by Shyam Singh of Bissau, who murdered his father and brother in an endeavour to claim the region for himself. Members of the wealthy Goenka merchant family also settled at Dundlod, and their prosperity is evident in their richly painted havelis here.

Things to See

The **Dundlod Fort** dates from 1750 and features a blend of the Rajputana and Mughal styles of art and architecture. The *diwan-i-khas*, or private audience hall, has stained-glass windows, fine Louis XIV antiques and an impressive collection of rare books. Above the diwan-i-khas is the *duchatta*, or women's gallery, from where the women in purdah could view the proceedings below. The *zenana*, or women's quarters, features walls of duck-egg blue, and opens onto the reading room of the *thakurani* (noblewoman), which has a hand-carved wooden writing table bearing oriental motifs in the form of dragons. Above the entrance to the ladies' quarters can be seen 10 torans, indicating that 10 daughters from the Singh family of the fort were married.

Only one room retains paintings, which can be seen on the ceiling of a small alcove. Unfortunately, they are irreparably damaged, although Krishna can still be made out.

The beautiful **Chhatri of Ram Dutt Goenka** and the adjacent well were both built by Ram Chandra Goenka in 1888. They lie about five minutes walk to the south-east of the fort. The interior of the dome has floral motifs extending in banners down from its centre. The dome is encircled by a frieze depicting Krishna dancing with

the gopis, interspersed with peacocks and musicians. The dominant colours are blue, red, yellow, turquoise and brown. Paintings around the inner base of the dome show a battle scene from the *Mahabharata*, a marriage celebration and Vishnu reclining on a snake.

The **Tuganram Goenka Haveli** is often locked, but you can see fine mirrorwork above the windows on the upper walls of the courtyard. Finely preserved paintings under the eaves mostly comprise portraits in round frames. The haveli opposite is interesting, as the work has not been completed, and it is possible to see how the artist sketched the drawings before adding colour. Pictures include those of an elephant, camel and rider, and a horse.

In a small square to the right just before the fort entrance is the **Satyanarayan Temple**, which was built by a member of the Goenka family in 1911. On the west wall of the temple is a long frieze showing Europeans on bicycles, in cars, and a long train, above which electricity lines extend. The portraits under the eaves show various nobles engaged in leisure pursuits, such as smelling flowers and reading. One fine mustachioed and turquoise-turbaned fellow has a bird in his hand, and another painting shows a woman admiring herself in a mirror.

A short distance to the south of the temple is a **Goenka Haveli** built by Arjun Dass Goenka in 1875. Above the window arches, mirrors are arranged in florets. Better preserved paintings can be seen on the east wall of the nearby **Jagathia Haveli**. There is a good railway station scene – in one carriage, a man appears to be in a passionate embrace with his wife, but closer inspection reveals his angry expression and that he is in fact beating her. A man hurries along on a bicycle parallel to the train, pursued by a dog.

Organised Tours

The Dundlod Fort (see Places to Stay) can organise horse safaris around the Shekhawati region. It's also possible to hire a camel and an English-speaking guide to visit the havelis of Dundlod (Rs 350 per hour). Jeep safaris (minimum of four people) are also possible for Rs 1200/1800 for a half/full day. You can even learn equestrian skills, including polo, at the Royal Equestrian Polo Centre at the hotel. Lessons are for two or more days, and prices are available on application.

Places to Stay & Eat
Dundlod Fort (☎ 52519; Jaipur ☎/fax 0141-211276), at the fort, is still in the family of Dundlod's founder. It has air-cooled standard rooms for Rs 1195/1350 for singles/doubles. Each room is different, and while not luxurious, they are certainly cosy and comfortable. Breakfast is Rs 150 and lunch/dinner is Rs 250/300.

Getting There & Away
It's possible to walk from Nawalgarh to Dundlod, although it's a hot walk along a busy, dusty road. For just a few rupees, you can catch one of the many local buses that frequently ply between these two towns every day.

MUKUNDGARH
There are some interesting painted havelis to be seen in this town, located about 5km from Dundlod.

Mukundgarh Fort (☎ 01594-52396, fax 52395) has 50 rooms which start at Rs 1195/2500 a single/double. The Maharaja suite costs Rs 5500 and can accommodate up to six people. The set lunch/dinner in the restaurant costs Rs 280/350. There's a pool and camel safaris can be arranged. A two hour trip in a camel cart is Rs 300 per person.

JHUNJHUNU
☎ 01592
Jhunjhunu lies 245km from Delhi and 180km from Jaipur, and is one of the largest towns of Shekhawati. It is currently the district headquarters of the region.

The town was founded by the Kaimkhani nawabs in the middle of the 15th century, and remained under their control until it was taken by the Rajput ruler Sardul Singh in 1730. It was in Jhunjhunu that the British based their Shekhawati Brigade, a troop raised locally in the 1830s to try to halt the activities of *dacoits* (bandits). The dacoits were largely local petty rulers who had decided it was easier to become wealthy by pinching other peoples' money than by earning their own.

Information
The Tourist Reception Centre (☎ 32909) is a little out of the town centre at the Churu bypass, Mandawa Circle. It's open Monday to Friday and every second Saturday from 10 am to 5 pm. They can arrange taxi hire.

Currently, the only government-approved guide in town is the knowledgeable Laxmi Kant Jangid (owner of the Hotel Shiv Shekhawati – see Places to Stay & Eat). His fee is Rs 230/345 (maximum of four people) or Rs 345/460 (five to 15 people) for a half/full day.

Money At the time of writing, no banks in Jhunjhunu changed money, but this may change.

Things to See
On the north-west side of the town is the **Badani Chand Well**. The well is surmounted by four imposing minarets (two minarets generally symbolise the presence of a stepwell). Because water is such a precious commodity in the desert, wells were treated almost like temples, and in fact it is not unusual to see a temple at a well – there is a small temple at this well which is sacred to Hanuman. Wells were often decorated in rich paintings, with one or two pavilions erected nearby at which women could gather and exchange news – the local village well served as an important social centre. As at this well, you will often find a neem tree nearby, the twigs from which are used to clean the teeth.

Unfortunately, the paintings on the minarets at this well have faded. Nearby on its west side is an old inn at which caravans would once have halted.

A few kilometres farther north is the picturesque artificial **Ajit Sagar**, built by Jitmal Khaitan in 1902. The lake, fed by rainwater,

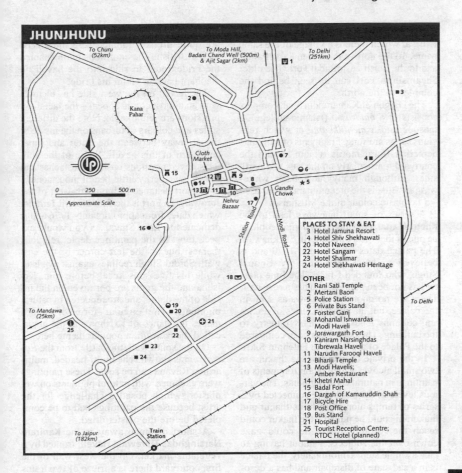

JHUNJHUNU

To Churu (52km)

To Moda Hill, Badani Chand Well (500m) & Ajit Sagar (2km)

To Delhi (251km)

Kana Pahar

Cloth Market

Nehru Bazaar

Gandhi Chowk

To Mandawa (25km)

To Delhi

To Jaipur (182km)

Train Station

0   250   500 m
Approximate Scale

PLACES TO STAY & EAT
3   Hotel Jamuna Resort
4   Hotel Shiv Shekhawati
20 Hotel Naveen
22 Hotel Sangam
23 Hotel Shalimar
24 Hotel Shekhawati Heritage

OTHER
1   Rani Sati Temple
2   Mertani Baori
5   Police Station
6   Private Bus Stand
7   Forster Ganj
8   Mohanlal Ishwardas Modi Haveli
9   Jorawargarh Fort
10 Kaniram Narsinghdas Tibrewala Haveli
11 Narudin Farooqi Haveli
12 Bihariji Temple
13 Modi Havelis; Amber Restaurant
14 Khetri Mahal
15 Badal Fort
16 Dargah of Kamaruddin Shah
17 Bicycle Hire
18 Post Office
19 Bus Stand
21 Hospital
25 Tourist Reception Centre; RTDC Hotel (planned)

NORTHERN RAJASTHAN

runs down from the sides of nearby Moda Pahar *(pahar* means 'hill') and very rarely dries up. There are pavilions on each corner of the lake, some of which retain paintings beneath their domes. Livestock drink from the tank on the north side of the lake.

The **Mertani Baori** is to the north-west of the fort, and is named after the woman who commissioned it – Mertani, the widow of Sardul Singh. It was built in 1783 and has recently been restored. The stepwell is approximately 30m deep, and its sulphuric

waters are said to cure skin diseases. On either side of the well, steps give access to a series of cool rooms in which visitors could rest. Stepwells were often used by visitors who didn't want to carry the rope necessary for normal wells. The steps give access to the water table.

To the south of Kana Pahar is the **Dargah of Kamaruddin Shah**. A ramp leads up to the imposing entrance and there is a very good view from the top down over the town (steps lead to the rooftop from the inside courtyard). To the east is **Kali Pahadi** (Black Hill), at which there is a village of the same name. To the north can be seen **Kana Pahar**, and to the north-east, **Badal Fort**. The older **Shyamsingh Fort** can be seen behind the complex to the north.

The Dargah of Kamaruddin Shah complex consists of a *madrassa* (Islamic college), a mosque and a *mehfilkhana*, at which religious songs are sung. Fragments of paintings depicting floral motifs remain around the courtyard, particularly on the east and north sides, although many have been whitewashed. Blue is the predominant colour used – a favourite colour of the Muslims.

A series of small laneways lead to the **Khetri Mahal**, considered by some people to be one of the finest buildings in Shekhawati. The palace dates from around 1770 and is believed to have been built by Bhopal Singh, who founded Khetri. The lime plaster has not been painted, and has a rosy cast. There are no doors or windows as such in the palace, but an intricate series of arches and columns lend an elegant symmetry to the building. The palace has been compared to the Palace of the Winds at Fatehpur Sikri.

In the private chamber of the thakur are two small alcoves which retain fragments of paintings in natural earth pigments. The various levels of the palace are connected by a series of ramps along which the thakur and thakurani could be pulled – the thakur could reach the rooftop, where he could gaze down over his subjects, without having to take a single step! Unfortunately, the palace is in a sad state of disrepair and has a desolate, forlorn atmosphere. There are good views over the town from the rooftop.

Near the Khetri Mahal are two havelis opposite each other, known as the **Modi Havelis**. The haveli on the east side has a painting of a woman in a blue sari sitting before a gramophone, and a frieze depicts a train, alongside which soldiers race on horses. The spaces between the brackets above show the Krishna legends, and above this are floral arabesques. Part of the facade of the haveli on the east side of the road has been painted over. Still remaining, however,

are numerous portrayals of rabbits which are quite lifelike; rabbits were introduced by the British. The enormous ramp enabled the bridegroom to ride into the haveli on elephant back to claim his bride.

The haveli on the west side has pictures with an almost comic appeal – the facial expressions are remarkable. Note the different styles and colours of turbans on the inside of the archway between the outer and inner courtyard of this haveli. Some of the subjects have enormous bushy moustaches and others have perky little pencil moustaches.

A short distance to the north-west of the Jorawargarh Fort is the fine **Bihariji Temple**, which dates from approximately 1776 and is dedicated to Lord Shiva. As you would expect, most of the paintings depict religious themes, but on the left corner of the east wall, Sardul Singh reclines against a bolster while his five sons kneel before him. Krishna and the gopis are portrayed on the inside of the dome, and are rendered in natural pigments. The circular form of domes makes the dance of Krishna and the gopis, called the *rasalila*, a popular theme here.

On the south wall, the battle from the *Ramayana* is shown. The multi-headed, multi-armed Ravana can be seen. These paintings were executed with natural pigments on wet plaster, which posed a challenge for the artist because the paintings had to be completed before the plaster dried.

A short distance away is the **Kaniram Narsinghdas Tibrewala Haveli**, fronted by a vegetable market. On the west wall of the first courtyard there is a frieze of two trains approaching each other. That on the left is a passenger train and on the right is a goods train whose carriages contain livestock. The artist had probably never actually seen a real train and used his imagination. On the north wall, a man ties his turban while another holds a looking glass in front of him. Close by, a man and woman pass a child between them.

A short distance to the west is the **Narudin Farooqi Haveli**, close to the Noor Mosque. In usual Muslim style, only floral motifs are depicted – there are no animal or human representations – and blue is the dominant colour. Unfortunately, the arches leading to the salons off the first courtyard have been sealed off with concrete.

On the north side of Nehru Bazaar is the **Mohanlal Ishwardas Modi Haveli**, which dates from 1896. There is the inevitable train on the front facade. Above the entrance to the outer courtyard are scenes from the legend of Krishna. In the centre is Krishna stealing the clothes of the gopis, who stand waist deep in water. Krishna is hiding up a tree with the gopis' saris around him. On a smaller, adjacent arch can be seen British imperial figures, including monarchs and judges in robes. On the opposite side are Indian rulers, including maharajas and nawabs.

Around the archway between the inner and outer courtyard are portrait miniatures behind glass. There is also fine mirror and glass tilework. In the second half of the antechamber, Krishna dances with the gopis while angels fly overhead. This is very fine work. In the inner courtyard, the hierarchy of the universe is shown, with deities in the upper frieze, human portraits in the middle band, and animal and floral motifs below.

Close by is **Forster Ganj**, which was the headquarters of the Shekhawati Brigade and the home of Henry Forster. There's a plaque on the gate with an inscription in both English and Hindi.

In the north-east corner of town is the enormous **Rani Sati Temple**. It's fronted by two courtyards, around which 300 rooms offer shelter to pilgrims. This temple apparently receives the second highest number of donations in India and is particularly revered by the wealthy merchant class. The temple is of marble with elaborate silver repoussé work before the inner sanctum.

A tile and mirror mosaic on the ceiling of the mandapa depicts a merchant's wife who committed *sati* (self-immolation for the sake of honour) in 1595, and to whom the temple is dedicated, while Shiva, Ganesh and Durga watch over her. A relief frieze on the north wall shows her story. Her husband is killed by the nawab's army; after battling the soldiers (one of whom has been decapitated),

Rani Sati ascends the funeral pyre; she is consumed by flames while Durga sends her power to withstand the pain. In the next panel Rani commands a chariot driver to place her ashes on a horse, and to build a temple over the spot where the horse halts. The final panel shows the ostentatious temple built in her honour. Rani Sati is the patron goddess of the merchant class, which is believed to hold 60% of the wealth in India and control all the major newspapers.

Painting Classes

For tuition in traditional Shekhawati painting, contact Laxmi Kant Jangid at the Hotel Shiv Shekhawati (see Places to Stay & Eat). Laxmi can organise lessons with a local artist in traditional Shekhawati painting, and offers a 50% discount on accommodation at the Hotel Shiv Shekhawati for anybody who stays more than five days.

Organised Tours

Camel and jeep safaris can be arranged at the Hotel Shiv Shekhawati. For a camel safari, the charge per person is Rs 300/500 for a half/full day. Jeep safaris are Rs 1000 per day (maximum of five people).

Places to Stay & Eat

Hotel Shiv Shekhawati (☎ *32651, fax 32 603)* is 2km from the bus stand in a quiet area on the eastern edge of town. This is a red hot favourite with travellers. Well-kept singles/doubles with attached bath and air-cooling are Rs 300/400. Deluxe air-con rooms are Rs 700/800. There are plans to also open some cheaper rooms with common bath. The set breakfast is Rs 100, veg lunch or dinner is Rs 150, and nonveg is Rs 200. The affable owner, Laxmi Kant Jangid, is a wealth of knowledge on the villages of Shekhawati (see Information earlier).

Hotel Jamuna Resort (☎ *32871, fax 32 603)*, about 1km distant, is also run by Laxmi Kant Jangid and is set in a pleasant garden. Traditionally decorated air-cooled cottages featuring mirrorwork are Rs 700/800. The vibrant 'painted room' is Rs 1500. There's a small swimming pool (open to nonresidents for Rs 50); a pool-side oil massage is Rs 100/hour. The restaurant welcomes nonguests; you can sit indoors or out on the lawn. The set veg/nonveg meal is Rs 150/200. À la carte dining is also available; most dishes are below Rs 40; mixed vegetables are Rs 30 and dhal is Rs 25.

Hotel Sangam (*☎ 32544*), located behind the bus stand, has basic singles with common bath for Rs 85, and singles/doubles with bath are Rs 100/200. The best room costs Rs 399. Only room service meals are available. This is a large, somewhat impersonal hotel; the budget rooms are at the front and could be a bit noisy.

Hotel Naveen (*☎ 32527*), next to the bus stand, has dreary rooms for Rs 60/100 with common bath, or Rs 80/150 with bath. The best rooms cost Rs 400/500.

Hotel Shekhawati Heritage (*☎ 35757, fax 35378*), also in this area, has OK rooms for Rs 300/400 with attached bath. Better air-con rooms are Rs 500/600. Vegetarian meals are available.

Hotel Shalimar (*☎ 34505, fax 35225*) has decent singles/doubles with private bath for Rs 200/500 and air-con rooms for Rs 700/800. There's a veg dining hall (open to nonresidents) with most main dishes for below Rs 50; a special thali is Rs 50, a dosa is Rs 20 and a veg sandwich is Rs 15. An RTDC hotel near the Tourist Reception Centre is planned.

Getting There & Away

Bus There are regular buses between Jhunjhunu and Jaipur (6 hrs, Rs 70). To Churu there are buses every hour from 6 am (1¾ hrs, Rs 13) which travel via Bissau (40 mins, Rs 9.50). There are numerous buses to Mandawa from 6.30 am (1 hr, Rs 6) and Nawalgarh (1 hr, Rs 15).

Buses leave for Delhi every 30 minutes from 5 am (6 hrs, Rs 86). There are also buses to Jodhpur (8 hrs, Rs 148), Ajmer (8 hrs, Rs 121) and Bikaner (5 hrs, Rs 89). The Roadways inquiries number is ☎ 32664.

Train There are several daily passenger trains between Jaipur and Jhunjhunu (Rs 46/184 in 2nd/1st class). The *Shekhawati Express* runs between Jhunjhunu and Delhi (Rs 95/495). It leaves Jhunjhunu at 11 pm and arrives in Delhi at 5.15 am. For inquiries call ☎ 32251.

Getting Around

Auto-Rickshaw For local sightseeing, you'll pay about Rs 25 per hour for an auto-rickshaw. A rickshaw from the train station to the Hotel Shiv Shekhawati costs about Rs 20.

Bicycle Bicycles can be rented at BLB Cycleworks on Station Rd (near Nehru Bazaar). They charge Rs 3/15 per hour/day.

BAGGAR

This small village is located about 15km from Jhunjhunu.

Piramal Haveli (*☎ 01592-22220*) or book at Delhi (*☎ 011-4616145, fax 4621112*) has just eight rooms for Rs 1500/2000 a single/double. Advance bookings are essential. Pure veg meals are available at this atmospheric old haveli.

BISSAU

The small town of Bissau lies 32km to the north-west of Jhunjhunu. Old 1950s round-snouted Tata Mercedes buses ply this route, with turbaned villagers hanging precariously to their rooftops. Bissau was founded in 1746 by the last of Sardul Singh's sons, Keshri Singh. The town prospered under Keshri, but fell into brigandry during the rule of his grandson Shyam Singh. According to local lore, the merchants of Bissau, who had been encouraged to set up in the town by Keshri, promptly packed up and left when Shyam extracted vast sums of money from them. The thakur then resorted to brigandry, embarking on raids with dacoits to neighbouring regions. The British called on the Shekhawati Brigade to restore order in the anarchic town, although by the time the expedition was mounted, Shyam Singh had expired and his heir, Hammir Singh, had driven out the brigands and encouraged the merchants to return. The British were impressed by the town's prosperity and left without a shot being fired.

In October each year, 10 days before the festival of Dussehra, Bissau hosts dramatic performances of the *Ramayana*. The local actors wear costumes and masks made in the town and the performance takes place in the bazaar at twilight.

Things to See
On the facade of the **Chhatri of Hammir Singh**, which is near the bus stand and dates from 1875, can be seen British folk in various fancy carriages, including one in the shape of a lion and another in the form of a hybrid lion-elephant. The chhatri is now a primary school and some of the rooms are used to store fodder. On the external back wall is a portrayal of Dhola Maru, and unusually, the bard who features in the love story is also depicted. On the south wall, a man on a horse dispatches a lion with a sword. The paintings on the four corner pavilions are badly deteriorated.

If you walk north from the bus stand and take the first street to the left, on the right-hand side at the next intersection is the **Haveli of Girdarilal Sigtia**. The paintings on the external walls have been destroyed, but the rooms retain some vibrant paintings in bright oranges, blues, reds and greens. A room in the north-east corner of the haveli shows Shiva, who is unusually depicted with a moustache, with the Ganges flowing from his hair. There is also a woman nursing a tiny child. Note the orange handprints on the outer courtyard wall, signifying the birth of a boy child. The handprints are a peculiarly Shekhawati custom.

On the opposite side of this lane is the **Motiram Jasraj Sigtia Haveli**, which is now a junior school. On the north wall, Krishna has stolen the gopis' clothes. The maidens have been modestly covered by the artist in the coils of snakes, although one reptile can be seen emerging from between a gopi's legs!

Getting There & Away
There are daily buses from Bissau to Jhunjhunu every 30 minutes (40 mins, Rs 10), to Fatehpur (30 mins, Rs 12) and to Mahansar (15 mins, Rs 3).

Getting Around
Bicycles can be hired for Rs 4/12 per hour/day from the shops near the Chhatri of Hammir Singh. They are an excellent way to tour this region, and are particularly good for the 6km trip to Mahansar.

MAHANSAR
A turn-off to the left as you leave Bissau on the Churu road leads 6km to the sleepy little village of Mahansar. This is a dusty place, where donkeys outnumber motorised vehicles. There is not an overabundance of painted havelis, although the wealthy Poddar clan have left a legacy of very fine paintings in those that can be seen. It's peaceful and pristine, and a good place to break a journey.

Mahansar was founded by Nawal Singh in 1768, and the town prospered for several decades until one of the Poddars lost his livelihood when two shiploads of opium sunk without trace.

Things to See
The **Raghunath Temple**, in the town centre, dates from the mid-19th century. It has fine floral arabesques beneath the arches on either side of the courtyard and a very fine facade.

A short distance to the north-east of the Raghunath Temple is the **Sona ki Dukan Haveli**, which, unusually for Shekhawati, incorporates gold leaf in its painting, particularly around the alcoves in the first chamber. The scenes from the *Ramayana* in the southern section of the ceiling in the first chamber are particularly fine and detailed. The lower walls are richly adorned with floral and bird motifs, creating an almost utopian fantasy with butterflies, trees laden with fruit, and flowers. Painted in gold script on panels on the west wall of this chamber are the names of the gods. Carved wooden beams divide the ceiling into three sections: on the north side, the life of Krishna is portrayed. A golden river connects the holy cities of Vrindavan, where Krishna spent his childhood, and Mathura, where he lived as a king. There is a small entry charge.

About 10 minutes walk from the bus stand past the fort on the right-hand side of Ramgarh Rd is the **Sahaj Ram Poddar Chhatri**. Unfortunately, some of the archways have been bricked in, but there are still some well-preserved paintings on the lower walls, and this is a well-proportioned and attractive building.

Places to Stay & Eat
Narayan Niwas Castle (☎ 01595-64322), in the old fort, about 100m north of the bus stand, is the only place to stay in this remote village. It is an authentic Rajasthani castle (without the commercial flavour of many of today's royal hotels – thank goodness!). This creaky castle is run by the down-to-earth thakur of Mahansar and his wife, an elderly couple who have interesting stories about days long gone. Singles/doubles have attached bath and cost Rs 700/900. Breakfast is Rs 85, and lunch and dinner are each Rs 175. Some of the rooms have fine antique furniture and one room is completely covered in paintings. Ask to see several rooms before checking in, as some are better than others (room No 5 is quite atmospheric). The thakur's nephew has some cheaper rooms in a separate portion of the castle.

Getting There & Away
There are regular bus services between Mahansar and Ramgarh and Bissau, with connections at these towns through to Jhunjhunu and Fatehpur.

RAMGARH
Sixteen kilometres south of Churu and 20km north of Fatehpur is Ramgarh, which was founded by a disaffected group from the wealthy Poddar family in 1791. The Poddars defected from nearby Churu after the thakur of that town imposed an extortionate wool levy on the merchants. The town prospered until the late 19th century, but is today a fairly quiet place. It retains a rich legacy of painted buildings.

The town is easy to explore on foot. The bus stand is at the western edge of town. In the northern section, about 600m from the bus stand, there is a concentration of havelis, as well as the main Shani Temple and the Ganga Temple. There's a smaller Shani Temple beyond the Fatehpur Gate, the southern entrance to the town, about 400m from the bus stand via the busy bazaar. There is currently nowhere to stay in Ramgarh.

Things to See
The imposing **Ram Gopal Poddar Chhatri**, just to the north of the bus stand, was built in 1872. The main dome of the chhatri is encompassed by a series of smaller domes. On the west side of the outer rim of the main dome, one of the projecting braces bears a picture of a naked woman stepping into her *lehanga* (skirt), while another woman shields her from the eyes of a man by holding the hem of her own skirt before her. The drum of the main dome is very brightly painted and has well-preserved paintings in blues and reds depicting the battle from the *Ramayana*. The building on the north side of the chhatri was where family members paying homage to their dead ancestor could rest. Unfortunately, the chhatri is in a sorry state – the north-east corner of the building is badly water damaged. To enter the compound, you will need to get the key from the little kiosk to the left of the main gate.

Just a short distance to the north of the Churu Gate, on the east side of the road, is the fine **Ganga Temple** which is now a junior school. The temple was built by one of the Poddar clan in 1845, and is an imposing building with large elephant murals on its facade. The right side of the facade is deteriorating – the foundations are crumbling. The temple is open only for morning and evening *pujas* (prayers). Other paintings depict religious themes, with some of Krishna.

About 20m farther north on the left-hand side is a **Ganesh Temple**. It has a densely painted forecourt and a series of interesting paintings between the brackets under the eaves, mostly featuring birds and religious themes.

If you pass back through the Churu Gate and immediately turn left, a road flanked by antique dealers leads to a second exit through the town wall. Pass through this gate and turn right, and you'll reach the beautiful and tiny **Shani Mandir** (Saturn Temple). The temple was built in 1840, and features some crude paintings on the facade. However, the exterior belies the richly ornate interior, which is completely covered in fantastic mirrorwork. There are some fine murals in the chamber before the inner sanctum, incorporating gold paint, and the overall effect is dazzling. Scenes from the *Mahabharata* are featured, and depictions of Krishna and Radha. To the south (left) of the inner sanctum is a painting on the ceiling featuring the marriage of Shiva and Parvati. Unfortunately, the ceiling in the chamber on the right-hand side of the inner sanctum is badly damaged, apparently by damp.

If you go back to the Churu Gate, and continue past the gate for about 50m then turn left, you'll come to a group of **Poddar havelis**. Popular motifs include soldiers, trains, and an unusual design, peculiar to Ramgarh, of three fish arranged in a circle with their faces touching each other. One haveli has a painting of women carrying water in pitchers on their heads, and there is an interesting portrayal of the Dhola Maru legend on the west wall of another: while Maru fires at the advancing assailants, Dhola nonchalantly smokes a hookah!

There is a second, less well-known, **Shani Mandir** on the south side of town on the left as you approach the post office from the Fatehpur Gate. It also features exquisite mirrorwork, and the chamber fronting the inner sanctum has some fine paintings interspersed with large mirrors on the ceiling and in the antechambers on either side. The floors of these two chambers are painted. The temple is presided over by a friendly *mataji* (female priest) and its plain blue exterior belies the rich work within.

Getting There & Away
There are buses to Nawalgarh (1¼ hrs, Rs 14), Jhunjhunu (1 hr, Rs 12) and Fatehpur (25 mins, Rs 6). Ramgarh is on the narrow-gauge line which runs between Sikar and Churu; daily services connect these towns.

FATEHPUR
☎ 01571
Fatehpur was established in 1451 as a capital for Muslim nawabs, but it was taken by the Shekhawat Rajputs in the 18th century. The relative wealth of the community of merchants here, who counted among their numbers the rich Poddar, Choudhari and Ganeriwala families, is evident in the many vibrantly painted havelis and fine chhatris. Unfortunately, the best of these are generally locked. The town does, however, serve as a good base for visiting nearby villages Mandawa and Lakshmangarh.

Things to See
On the right of the Mandawa road, about 50m east of the main intersection with the Churu-Sikar road, is the badly deteriorating Choudharia Haveli – extreme caution is needed, as the entire edifice looks as if it will soon be a great heap of rubble. Poor drainage has caused water damage and is responsible for the haveli's sorry state. On the eastern wall is an interesting erotic painting. A woman embraces a man with one hand and holds a glass in the other while she is ravished, as a servant stands by. It's possible to take the stairs to the 2nd floor, but be very careful. The front room upstairs overlooking the street is colourfully painted, with fragments of stained glass still in the window spaces and a large carved wooden beam overhead.

Unfortunately, these are practically all that remain of the original architectural embellishments, most of which have been stripped by antique dealers. On the north wall of an upstairs room on the east side of the building, the baby Ganesh takes milk through his trunk from his mother's (Parvati's) breast.

On the western side of Mandawa road, about 50m west of the Churu-Sikar road, and on the left-hand side past the lac bangle vendors, is the **Geori Shankar Haveli**. There are very good mirror mosaics on the ceiling of the antechamber. You'll probably be asked for a donation to enter this haveli.

Nearby on the same road is the **Mahavir Prasad Goenka Haveli**, which is considered

FATEHPUR

To Churu (38km)

To Mandawa (19km)

0   100   200 m

1 Barthia Haveli
2 Barthia Haveli
3 Jagannath Singhania Chhatri
4 Jagannath Singhania Haveli
5 Nand Lal Devra Haveli
6 Chauhan Well
7 Choudharia Haveli
8 Mahavir Prasad Goenka Haveli
9 Geori Shankar Haveli
10 Post Office
11 Baori
12 Private Bus Stand
13 Harikrishnan Das Saraogi Haveli
14 Vishnunath Keria Haveli
15 Bike Hire
16 Roadways Bus Stand
17 TGH Guest House

To Fort

To RTDC's Hotel Haveli (300m), Lakshmangarh (20km) & Sikar (52km)

There is a finely carved lintel with Ganesh sculpted over the centre (Ganesh, the protector of households, is often seen here). Fifty metres south of this haveli is the small **Chauhan Well**, which dates from the early 18th century. There is some uninspiring painting around the windows and a couple of the pavilions, and the minarets retain fragments of geometric and floral designs.

Return to the Nand Lal Devra Haveli, and from there retrace your steps to the main Churu-Sikar road. Cross this and continue along the same road, and after a short distance, on the right-hand side, is the **Jagannath Singhania Haveli.** It is often locked, but has some interesting paintings on the facade, including those of Krishna and Radha framed by four elephants, and above this, some British men with guns.

In the north-west of the town (take the turn to the left off the Churu-Sikar road opposite the large Jagannath Singhania Chhatri) are **two large havelis** which were built by the Barthia family, and are still inhabited by members of this family. The paintings are not exceptional, but are excellently preserved and maintained. These havelis are reminiscent of Victorian-era theatres.

The **Jagannath Singhania Chhatri**, on the east side of the Churu-Sikar road (enter through a gateway behind the chhatri), has very pretty and well-tended gardens. This is an imposing building, although not very comprehensively painted. Paintings, some of which appear to be unfinished, include hunting scenes. There is a small Shiva shrine in the basement of the chhatri at which villagers still pay homage.

Near the private bus stand is a large **baori** which was built by Sheikh Mohammed of Nagaur in 1614. There's a path to the baori from a lane opposite the private bus stand. Unfortunately, the baori is in a shocking state of disrepair. In fact, it's downright dangerous, and you shouldn't approach the edges too closely. It was obviously a feat of some magnitude to dig to this depth, and around the sides are a series of arched galleries, most of which have collapsed. The baori is now used as a rubbish dump. On the south side an

by some to have the very best paintings of Shekhawati, combining a perfect synthesis of colour and design. Unfortunately, it is usually locked.

At the first intersection to the north past the Mandawa road and Churu-Sikar road intersection, if you turn right, on the right-hand side after a short distance is the **Nand Lal Devra Haveli**. The facade retains some paintings, predominantly in tones of red and blue. Above the window frames are silhouettes of various creatures against a red background.

haveli has half fallen into the well, and its courtyard paintings are exposed. Two ornate columns hang poised precariously over the abyss. The baori's minarets still stand as a testament to its obvious former grandeur.

Diagonally opposite the baori, on the south side of the private bus stand, the **Harikrishnan Das Saraogi Haveli** features a colourful facade with iron lacework on the upper verandas and shops at street level. There's a vibrantly coloured outer courtyard. In one picture, a woman appears to be smoking a hookah. The inner courtyard has an interesting juxtaposition: a camel-drawn cart next to a motorcar.

Adjacent to this haveli (to the south) is the **Vishnunath Keria Haveli**. The outer courtyard has interesting pictures on either side of the door to the inner courtyard. Radha and Krishna can be seen in strange gondola-type flying contraptions, one with an animal's head, the other with the front portion of a vintage car, and both featuring angel-type wings. On the north wall of the outer courtyard is a portrait of King George and Queen Victoria with an Indian-inspired backdrop. The paintings in the south-east corner of the inner courtyard have been badly smoked by the kitchen fire. In this courtyard, the sun god Surya can be seen being drawn by horses in a carriage. On the southern external wall, pictures include Queen Victoria, a train, a holy man and Krishna playing a gramophone for Radha's listening enjoyment!

Places to Stay & Eat
RTDC's Hotel Haveli (☎ 20293), about 500m south of the bus stand on the Churu-Sikar road, is the most comfortable place to stay. Ordinary singles/doubles are Rs 300/400 with attached bath and hot water; more luxurious air-con rooms cost Rs 500/600. Beds in the small bed dorm go for Rs 50. There's a dining hall with a good range of dishes including chicken curry (Rs 48) and curd lassi (Rs 13).

TGH Guest House is a possibility, but it's quite primitive. Single/double rooms with *charpoys* (string beds) go for Rs 25/100

(common bath with cold water only). It's right behind the Roadways bus stand.

Getting There & Away
From the private bus stand, on the Churu-Sikar road, buses leave for Jhunjhunu (1 hr, Rs 12), Mandawa (30 mins, Rs 6), Churu (1 hr, Rs 13), Ramgarh (30 mins, Rs 6), Mahansar (50 mins, Rs 10) and for Sikar (2 hrs, Rs 13).

From the Roadways bus stand, which is farther south down this road, buses leave for Jaipur (4 hrs, Rs 65), Delhi (6 hrs, Rs 110) and Bikaner (4 hrs, Rs 72).

Getting Around
Bicycles can be hired (Rs 4/15 per hour/day) from the north side of the Roadways bus stand.

MANDAWA
☎ 01592
The compact and busy little market town of Mandawa, 19km north-east of Fatehpur, was settled in the 18th century and fortified by the dominant merchant families. It has some fine painted havelis and is becoming increasingly popular among travellers, which would account for the alarming number of antique shops cropping up along the main drag.

Information
The State Bank of Bikaner & Jaipur, near the Hotel Castle Mandawa, changes money.

Things to See
To the left of the main Fatehpur-Jhunjhunu road, about 50m before the bus stand, are several havelis belonging to the Goenka family. To the right of the entrance to the **Hanuman Prasad Goenka Haveli** is an unusual composite picture which shows either Lord Indra on an elephant, or Lord Shiva on his bull, depending on which way you look at it. Nearby is the **Goenka Double Haveli** which has two entrance gates and monumental pictures, including elephants and horses, on the facade. The paintings on the haveli to the left are badly deteriorated.

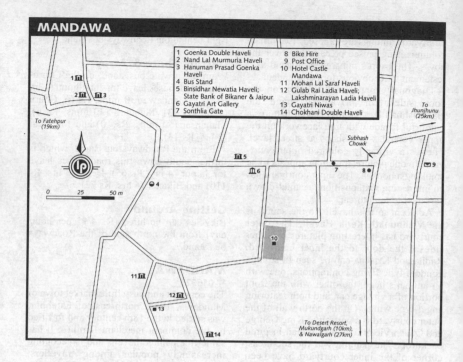

MANDAWA

1 Goenka Double Haveli
2 Nand Lal Murmuria Haveli
3 Hanuman Prasad Goenka Haveli
4 Bus Stand
5 Binsidhar Newatia Haveli; State Bank of Bikaner & Jaipur
6 Gayatri Art Gallery
7 Sonthlia Gate
8 Bike Hire
9 Post Office
10 Hotel Castle Mandawa
11 Mohan Lal Saraf Haveli
12 Gulab Rai Ladia Haveli; Lakshminarayan Ladia Haveli
13 Gayatri Niwas
14 Chokhani Double Haveli

To Fatehpur (19km)

To Jhunjhunu (25km)

Subhash Chowk

0   25   50 m

To Desert Resort, Mukundgarh (10km), & Nawalgarh (27km)

Adjacent is the **Nand Lal Murmuria Haveli**. From the sandy courtyard in front of this haveli, you can get a good view of the southern external wall of the adjacent double haveli: it features a long frieze of a train with a crow flying above the engine and much activity at the railway crossing. The Nand Lal Murmuria Haveli also reflects a strong European influence in its paintings. Nehru is depicted on horseback holding the Indian flag. Above the arches on the south side of the courtyard are two paintings of gondolas on the canals of Venice.

The **Binsidhar Newatia Haveli**, on the north side of the Fatehpur-Jhunjhunu road, is now the premises of the State Bank of Bikaner & Jaipur. The interior paintings have been whitewashed, but there are still some interesting paintings on the external eastern wall (accessible through the bank). These include a European woman in a car driven by

a chauffeur; a man on a bicycle; the Wright brothers evoking much excitement in their aeroplane as women in saris, among others, point with astonishment; a boy on a telephone; and a bird man flying by in a winged device. The paintings date from the 1920s.

Unfortunately, many of the erotic images on the **Gulab Rai Ladia Haveli**, to the southwest of the fort, have been systematically defaced by prudish souls. In the last pair of brackets on the first half of the southern wall a woman can be seen giving birth, attended by maidservants. There is an erotic image in the fifth niche from the end on this wall, but don't draw too much attention to it, or it might suffer the same fate as the other erotic art on this building. There is also something untoward happening in a train carriage in this wall.

About 150m past this haveli to the south is the **Chokhani Double Haveli**. The pictures are not that special, but the building is rather grand. Paintings inside include floral arabesques and peacocks above the archways, as well as the Krishna legends.

Behind the Gulab Rai Ladia Haveli is the **Lakshminarayan Ladia Haveli**. On the west wall is a faded picture of a man enjoying a hookah, and a good procession frieze. Between the wall brackets, gopis emerge from the tentacles of a sea monster upon whose head Krishna dances. Other pictures include that of Rama slaying Ravana.

About 30m farther north (continue along the road at the back of the Lakshminarayan Ladia Haveli) is the **Mohan Lal Saraf Haveli**. On the south wall, a maharaja grooms his bushy moustache. There is fine mirror and mosaic work around the door to the inner courtyard and Surya, the sun god, can be seen over the lintel.

Organised Tours

You can organise camel and horse rides at the Hotel Castle Mandawa (see Places to Stay & Eat). A one hour camel ride is Rs 400, a half/full-day trip is Rs 700/1000. A far cheaper option is the Hotel Heritage Mandawa (see Places to Stay & Eat), which organises camel rides for Rs 100 per person for two hours. Per day, it costs Rs 300 per person, which includes meals and a mattress and blanket – you sleep under the stars. They can also arrange jeep hire for Rs 500 per day (maximum of five people).

Places to Stay & Eat

Hotel Castle Mandawa (☎ 23124, fax 23 171) is one of the most upmarket places to stay in Shekhawati. This large hotel, with a somewhat contrived medieval atmosphere, has tastefully designed single/double rooms ranging from Rs 1300/1600 to Rs 1995/ 3995. Some rooms have more charm than others, so try to look at a few first. Like many hotels that expand over the years, the personal touch has faded. The buffet breakfast/lunch/dinner is Rs 175/300/350.

Desert Resort (☎ 23245) is run by the same people as the Hotel Castle Mandawa and is similarly priced. It is located on the road to Mukundgarh. While it is not as centrally placed, it is in a tranquil setting with pleasant rooms and a swimming pool.

Hotel Heritage Mandawa (☎ 23243), near the Subhash Chowk bus stand, is an old haveli and a great budget choice. It has clean singles/doubles with private bath and constant hot water for Rs 300/400. The set lunch/dinner is Rs 75/100, and consists of soup, three vegetable dishes, dhal, rice, roti and dessert; nonresidents are welcome.

Gayatri Niwas (☎ 23065) is an authentic 142-year-old haveli that has basic but cheap rooms. Singles/doubles with common bath are Rs 100/200 (free bucket hot water). This place can be tough to find – get directions from Kalyan Singh or Madhusudan Khemani at the Gayatri Art Gallery, opposite the State Bank of Bikaner & Jaipur, near the Hotel Castle Mandawa.

Getting There & Away

There are buses to Nawalgarh (1 hr, Rs 8), Fatehpur (30 mins, Rs 6), Bissau (1 hr, Rs 8) and Ramgarh (40 mins, Rs 8). There are also direct buses to Jaipur (4 hrs, Rs 68) and Bikaner (4 hrs, Rs 60). A taxi between Mandawa and Fatehpur costs Rs 150 (one way).

Getting Around

Bikes can be hired from Subhash Chowk, at the eastern end of the Jhunjhunu-Fatehpur road, for about Rs 4/30 per hour/day.

LAKSHMANGARH

The most imposing building in this town, only 20km south of Fatehpur, is its small fortress, which looms over the well-laid out township to its west . The fort was built by Lakshman Singh, the raja of Sikar, in the early 19th century after the prosperous town was besieged by Kan Singh Saledhi. Unlike some other towns of Shekhawati, it is easy to find your way around Lakshmangarh, as it is laid out on a grid pattern, with a main north-south oriented bazaar dissected at intervals by three busy squares, or *chaupars*. The villagers here are unfamiliar with tourist hordes. The children can be a little tiresome – even downright aggressive!

Things to See

About 50m north of the bus stand through the busy bazaar, a wide cobblestone path wends its way up the east side of the **fort**. A sign advises that the fort is private property, but there's a good view from the top of the ramp before the main entrance. From here you can see the layout of the double Char Chowk Haveli, below and to the north-east. Head for this when you descend the ramp.

Beneath the eaves on the northern external wall of the **Char Chowk Haveli** is a picture of a bird standing on an elephant with another elephant in its beak. The large paintings on the facade of the northern face have mostly faded, and the paintings in the outer downstairs courtyard are covered by blue wash. The paintings in the inner courtyard are well preserved. The walls and ceiling of a small upstairs room on the east side of the northern haveli are completely covered with paintings. It has some explicit erotic images, but is very badly illuminated, so although they're well preserved you'll need a flashlight to see them properly.

In the same building, a room in the north-west corner retains floral swirls and motifs on the ceiling with scenes from the Krishna legends interspersed with inlaid mirrors. The black and white rectangular designs on the lower walls create a marbled effect. No one now lives in the haveli, but there may be someone around who will open it for you (for a small fee). The front facade is in very poor condition at the lower levels, with the plaster crumbling and the bricks exposed. The southern haveli is still inhabited.

About 50m east of this haveli is the large **Radhi Murlimanohar Temple**, which dates from 1845. It retains a few paintings beneath the eaves and some sculptures of deities around the external walls. To the south of this temple is the busy bazaar, flanked by a series of shops whose overhanging balconies have three scalloped open arches between two blank arches with lattice friezes. The shops were constructed in the mid-19th century by a branch of the Poddar family known as Ganeriwala, who hailed from the village of Ganeri.

If you turn left at the first intersection south of the temple, on the corner of the first laneway on the left is the **Chetram Sanganeeria Haveli**. The lower paintings on the west wall are badly damaged: the plaster has peeled away and concrete rendering has been applied. Paintings on this wall include a woman in a swing suspended from a tree; a woman spinning; a man dancing on a pole balancing knives; people enjoying a ride on a ferris wheel; a man ploughing fields with oxen; and men sawing timber.

On the north-east corner of the clock tower square, which is about 100m south of the temple via the busy bazaar, is the **Rathi Family Haveli**. On the west wall, a European woman in a smart red frock sews on a treadle machine. The European influence is very much in evidence here, with painted roses and a Grecian column effect. On the south side of this haveli are ostentatious flourishes and the British crown flanked by unicorns. On the east side is depicted a railway station (a painted sign reads 'A Railway Station', in case you weren't sure!), and some blue-eyed British soldiers.

There is a busy set of *chai* (tea) stalls on the west side of the haveli, and this is a good place to sit and admire these extraordinarily over-the-top paintings.

Behind this haveli, a short distance to the east, is the **Shyonarayan Kyal Haveli**, which dates from around 1900. Under the eaves on the east wall, a man and woman engage in a tryst while a maidservant stands by with a glass of wine at the ready. Other pictures include those of a woman admiring herself in a mirror and Europeans being drawn by horses with a tiny coachman at the reins.

Getting There & Away

There are many buses between Lakshmangarh and both Sikar (Rs 7) and Fatehpur (Rs 6), as well as Nawalgarh (Rs 12) and Jhunjhunu (Rs 15).

Getting Around

A bicycle shop just to the south of the Radhi Murlimanohar Temple hires bikes for a nominal price.

CHURU
☎ 01562

Churu is not technically part of Shekhawati, falling within the administrative district of Bikaner. However, it is usually included in a discussion of the painted walls, as it was also a centre of trade and commerce, and many rich merchant families that hailed from here left a legacy of fine painted havelis. About 95km to the south-west of Churu is the small Tal Chhapar Wildlife Sanctuary (described in Around Churu), home to a substantial population of black-bucks and other mammals and birds.

Things to See

You'll need help to find the **Malji ka Kamra**, which is to the north of the bus stand, down a lane on the west side of the main bazaar. It's well worth the effort to find this place: it's an extraordinary edifice covered in pale blue stucco and perched on green pillars like some baroque travesty of a wedding cake. This once grand building is now home to pigeons and rubbish-grazing cows. Statues on the facade include a bored-looking woman in a sari with a handbag and wings, turbaned men and angels. It was built in 1925, but its days of glory are long gone.

A short distance to the north-west (within easy walking distance) is the **Surana Double Haveli**. This five storey edifice with hundreds of windows achieves something of a Georgian effect. On the lower levels of the west wall are fragments of paintings, including processions and peacocks. The haveli is beyond an archway at the end of a narrow laneway.

A farther 100m to the north-west is the **Surajmal Banthia Haveli**, which was built in the 1920s. It is best known for its infamous picture of Christ with a cigar, on the external north wall, rather incongruously juxtaposed between two British ladies. Across the lane to the north is an haveli with what may well be the most bizarre paintings on any of the havelis of Shekhawati – beneath the eaves of the facade is a series of paintings of naked men fondling rabbits!

Places to Stay & Eat

Not many travellers choose to stay in Churu, but if you do find yourself here for a night there is one reasonably decent hotel, although English can be a problem.

Hotel Deluxe (☎ 51114) is directly opposite the private bus stand. It has no-frills double rooms with attached bath and hot water by the bucket for Rs 200. There's a restaurant downstairs which cooks up veg fare at modest prices.

Getting There & Away

The Roadways bus stand is 500m south of the private bus stand. There are regular services to destinations in Shekhawati from the private bus stand, and to Delhi (8 hrs, Rs 108), Bikaner (5 hrs, Rs 76) and Jaipur (5 hrs, Rs 80) from the Roadways stand.

The train station is 100m north of the private bus stand. To Bikaner, the train takes approximately 4½ hours (Rs 52/255 in 2nd/1st class). There are trains to Delhi (7 hrs, Rs 71/347) and to Jaipur (6 hrs, Rs 96/266).

AROUND CHURU
Tal Chhapar Wildlife Sanctuary

This small grassland sanctuary, which lies about 95km south-west of Churu and 210km north-west of Jaipur, covers 70 sq km and has healthy populations of black-buck, as well as chinkara (Indian gazelle) and smaller mammals, such as the desert fox. The sanctuary lies on the migration route of a number of bird species, most notably harriers, which descend here during September. Other birds include various types of eagle (tawny, imperial, short-toed), which migrate here in winter, and the demoiselle crane, which also descends in large numbers in the winter months (early September to late March). Throughout the year there are populations of crested larks, ring and brown doves and skylarks.

It is best to visit the sanctuary between September and March. There is a *forest resthouse* at Chhapar. For more information, contact the Deputy Conservator of Forests (Wildlife), in Jodhpur.

Western Rajasthan

Encompassing a vast area, including the districts of Jodhpur, Jaisalmer, Bikaner and Barmer, this desolate and arid land was believed to have been created by the falling of an arrow fired by Rama, hero of the *Ramayana*. The arrow was destined for the sea god who inhabited the straits between India and Lanka (Sri Lanka). However, when the sea god apologised to Rama for opposing his desire to cross the straits, Rama fired the arrow to the north-west, rendering this region a desolate wasteland.

Western Rajasthan includes the vast Thar Desert, which extends through the adjacent states of Punjab, Haryana, Gujarat and into Pakistan, and is the world's most populous arid zone. It has been the scene of bloody conflicts over the ages, as feudal kings fought both with each other and against external invaders such as the Muslims.

Western Rajasthan has two of the most stunning palace-fort complexes in India at Jodhpur and Jaisalmer. Nothing rivals Meherangarh at Jodhpur for sheer awe-inspiring majesty, while the Jaisalmer fort is romance incarnate, an extraordinary edifice in yellow sandstone which rises from the desert landscape. It is a tribute to the valour of the Bhatti Rajputs, who ruled here for centuries. Enormous rocks can still be seen perched precariously across the top of the battlements; they were intended for the heads of advancing enemies, and those who escaped these missiles would then have to dodge the cauldrons of boiling oil poured from the ramparts.

Bikaner's fort, Junagarh, is only slightly less impressive, and you can lose yourself for hours in the colourful bazaars of its old walled city, which also encompasses two exquisite Jain temples.

Ancient Osiyan, north-west of Jodhpur, also has ancient temples, and from late August/early September to the end of March at nearby Khichan you can see hundreds of graceful demoiselle cranes which descend

morning and evening on the fields surrounding this village to feed on grain distributed by villagers.

HISTORY

The district of Jodhpur was, until comparatively recent times, known as the ancient kingdom of Marwar, the largest kingdom in Rajputana and the third largest of the Indian kingdoms, after Kashmir and Hyderabad.

Little historical evidence remains of the period prior to the 3rd century BC. In 231 BC, Chandragupta Maurya's empire came to power, extending its dominion across northern India from its capital at present-day Patna, in Bihar. The indigenous inhabitants were subjugated by the Aryans during their invasion of northern India between 1500 and 200 BC. In subsequent centuries, the region fell to the Kushanas, the Hunas and the Guhilas. However, it was the Rajput Rathores, who hailed from Kanauj in present-day Uttar Pradesh, who consolidated themselves in this region, ousting the local tribal leaders. From them, historians can

Highlights

- **Exquisite havelis** – marvel at these outdoor works of art
- **Jaisalmer's glorious fort** – it rises from a stark desert landscape
- **Camel safaris** – ride across the dunes and lonely plains around Jaisalmer
- **The mighty Meherangarh** – one of Rajasthan's most impressive forts
- **Karni Mata Temple** – this fascinating temple in Deshnok is a sanctuary for hundreds of holy rats
- **The ancient temples at Osiyan** – with fine devotional sculpture

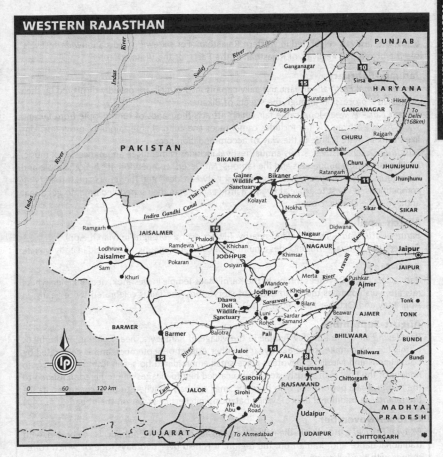

WESTERN RAJASTHAN

more accurately trace the emergence of the state of Marwar. The Rathores originally settled at Pali, south-east of present-day Jodhpur, but in 1381 shifted their capital to Mandore. In 1459 the Rathore leader, Rao Jodha, shifted the capital 9km to the south and founded the city of Jodhpur.

Meanwhile the Muslims were entrenched at Nagaur, after Mohammad Bahlim, the governor of Sind, erected a fort here in 1122 upon subduing the local Hindu chief, Ajayaraja. Subsequently, rule of Nagaur fell variously to Ajayaraja (again), the sultanate of Delhi, the Rathores, an independent local dynasty led by Shams Khan Dandani, the Lodi sultans of Delhi and the Mughals under Akbar. In 1572, Akbar granted it to the chief of Bikaner, Raisimha. In the early 18th century, Nagaur was acquired by the maharaja of Jodhpur.

The desert city of Bikaner was founded by one of the sons of Rao Jodha, founder of Jodhpur, following a schism in the ruling Rathore family.

Festivals of Western Rajasthan

Below are festivals celebrated in western Rajasthan. For statewide and nationwide festivals, see the boxed text Festivals of Rajasthan in the Facts for the Visitor chapter.

January-February

Bikaner Camel Festival – In January, gaily caparisoned camels are proudly displayed by their owners in a procession through the streets of Bikaner.

Nagaur Fair – A week-long cattle fair which attracts thousands of rural people from far and wide. As at Pushkar, the fair includes camel races and cultural entertainment programs. Unlike Pushkar, there is little in the way of accommodation here.

Jaisalmer Desert Festival – This annual festival includes camel races and dances, folk music, traditional ballads, puppeteers and the famous 'Mr Desert' competition. It's become more and more touristy over the years, with tugs-of-war between locals and foreigners and turban tying competitions. It's best to arrive at events a little earlier than their scheduled time, to get a seat and avoid the chaotic crowds.

March-April

Barmer Cattle Fair – This is held at nearby Tilwara over a fortnight in March-April.

Barmer Thar Festival – This includes a number of cultural programs and is held in early March.

April-May

Karni Mata Fair – Devotees throng to the Karni Mata Temple in Deshnok, near Bikaner, where rats are worshipped as the incarnations of storytellers. The fair is celebrated twice yearly, in April-May and October-November.

August-September

Ramdevra Fair – The Ramdev Temple in the village of Ramdevra, near Pokaran, is the focus of this fair, which takes place each year in either August or September, and is celebrated by both Hindus and Muslims. Devotees place small embroidered horses in Ramdev's temple in honour of the holy man's trusty steed, who carried him to villages where he administered to the poor. Female performers, who have 13 small cymbals attached to their costumes, dance the *terahtal* (a traditional dance), while balancing pitchers of water on their heads.

October-November

Marwar Festival – In Jodhpur, the rich cultural legacy of Marwar (Jodhpur) is celebrated, with traditional dance and drama from the region. It is held over two days, one of which corresponds with the full moon.

Kolayat Fair – Near Bikaner, it takes place around the same time as the Pushkar Camel Fair. Devotees take a holy dip in the lake on the full moon.

JODHPUR

• pop 770,000   ☎ 0291

Jodhpur stands at the edge of the Thar Desert and is the largest city in Rajasthan after Jaipur. This bustling desert city is dominated by a massive fort, topping a sheer rocky ridge which rises right in the middle of the town.

The old city of Jodhpur is surrounded by a 10km-long wall, which was built about a century after the city was founded. From the fort, you can clearly see where the old city ends and the new one begins. It's fascinating to wander around the jumble of winding streets in the old city, out of which eight gates lead. Part of the film *Rudyard*

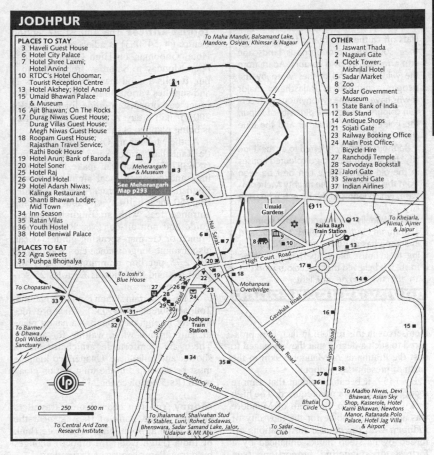

JODHPUR

PLACES TO STAY
3 Haveli Guest House
6 Hotel City Palace
7 Hotel Shree Laxmi;
   Hotel Arvind
10 RTDC's Hotel Ghoomar;
   Tourist Reception Centre
13 Hotel Akshey; Hotel Anand
15 Umaid Bhawan Palace
   & Museum
16 Ajit Bhawan; On The Rocks
17 Durag Niwas Guest House;
   Durag Villas Guest House;
   Megh Niwas Guest House
18 Roopam Guest House;
   Rajasthan Travel Service;
   Rathi Book House
19 Hotel Arun; Bank of Baroda
20 Hotel Soner
25 Hotel Raj
26 Govind Hotel
29 Hotel Adarsh Niwas;
   Kalinga Restaurant
30 Shanti Bhawan Lodge;
   Mid Town
34 Inn Season
35 Ratan Vilas
36 Youth Hostel
38 Hotel Beniwal Palace

PLACES TO EAT
22 Agra Sweets
31 Pushpa Bhojnalya

OTHER
1 Jaswant Thada
2 Nagauri Gate
4 Clock Tower;
   Mishrilal Hotel
5 Sadar Market
8 Zoo
9 Sadar Government
   Museum
11 State Bank of India
12 Bus Stand
14 Antique Shops
21 Sojati Gate
23 Railway Booking Office
24 Main Post Office;
   Bicycle Hire
27 Ranchodji Temple
28 Sarvodaya Bookstall
32 Jalori Gate
33 Siwanchi Gate
37 Indian Airlines

To Maha Mandir, Balsamand Lake,
Mandore, Osiyan, Khimsar & Nagaur

Meherangarh
& Museum

See Meherangarh
Map p293

Umaid
Gardens

Raika Bagh
Train Station

To Khejarla,
Nimaj, Ajmer
& Jaipur

High Court Road

Nai Sarak

To Joshi's
Blue House

To Chopasani

Mohanpura
Overbridge

Gavshala Road

Station Road

Jodhpur
Train
Station

To Barmer
& Dhawa
Doli Wildlife
Sanctuary

Ratanada Road

Airport Road

Residency Road

Bhatia
Circle

To Madho Niwas, Devi
Bhawan, Asian Sky
Shop, Kasserole, Hotel
Karni Bhawan, Newtons
Manor, Ratanada Polo
Palace, Hotel Jag Villa
& Airport

0   250   500 m

To Central Arid Zone
Research Institute

To Jhalamand, Shalivahan Stud
& Stables, Luni, Rohet, Sodawas,
Bhenswara, Sadar Samand Lake, Jalor,
Udaipur & Mt Abu

To Sadar
Club

Kipling's Jungle Book, starring Sam Neill and John Cleese, was shot in Jodhpur and yes, it was from here that those baggy-tight horse-riding trousers, jodhpurs, took their name.

As one of the closest major Indian cities to the border with Pakistan, Jodhpur has a large defence contingent. Don't dive for cover when you hear booming jet fighter planes above – Jodhpur is not under siege; the air force is simply doing its routine training exercise.

History

Founded in 1459 by Rao Jodha, a chief of the Rajput clan known as the Rathores, Jodhpur was the capital of the Rathore kingdom once known as Marwar, the Land of Death. The Rathores were driven from their homeland of Kanauj by Afghans serving Mohammed of Ghori, and fled west to the region around Pali, a short distance to the south of Jodhpur. An expedient marriage alliance between the Rathore Siahaji and the sister of a local prince enabled the Rathores to consolidate

Jodhpur's Got the Blues

Hats off to the Rajasthanis for converting their somewhat monotonous landscape into a mosaic of vivid colours. Apart from the wildly colourful clothes worn by the people, a number of Rajasthan's major towns have become synonymous with certain colours – there's the pink city of Jaipur, the golden city of Jaisalmer and the blue city of Jodhpur.

Jodhpur is fondly referred to as the 'blue city' because of the indigo coloured houses in the old town. These can best be seen from the ramparts of the mighty Meherangarh, which looms high above the buzzing city.

Traditionally, blue signified the home of a Brahmin, but these days anyone and everyone has got into the spirit of colouring their house blue. Apart from looking fresh, it is believed that the colour works as an effective mozzie repellent.

themselves in this region. In fact, they prospered to such a degree that they managed to oust the Pratiharas of Mandore, 9km to the north of present-day Jodhpur.

By 1459, it became evident that a more secure headquarters was required. The high rocky ridge 9km to the south of Mandore was an obvious choice for the new city of Jodhpur, with the natural fortifications afforded by its steep flanks enhanced by a fortress of staggering proportions (see Meherangarh later in this entry).

Orientation

The Tourist Reception Centre, train stations and bus stand are all outside the old city. High Court Rd runs from the Raika Bagh train station, past Umaid Gardens, the RTDC's Hotel Ghoomar and Tourist Reception Centre, beside the city wall towards the main station and the main post office. Trains from the east stop at the Raika Bagh station before the main station – handy if you're staying at a hotel on the eastern side of town.

Information

Tourist Offices The Tourist Reception Centre (☎ 545083) is adjacent to RTDC's Hotel Ghoomar, on High Court Rd. It is open Monday to Saturday from 8 am to 7 pm. It sells a good map of Jodhpur (Rs 2) and supplies various tourist brochures. The office can organise a guide for around Rs 200 for half a day. A smaller tourist office is being planned at the airport.

At the Mohanpura Overbridge is the little Rajasthan Travel Service (RTS) office (☎ 638785), which can make hotel bookings and organise local sightseeing with English, French or German-speaking guides (Rs 750 for a half-day city tour excluding entrance fees with an English-speaking guide and non air-con car; Rs 850 for a French or German-speaking guide). It can also arrange long-distance cars and drivers (Rs 2.75 per km, minimum 300km) and book bus and train tickets for a Rs 25 service fee per person.

At the main train station is an International Tourists Bureau (☎ 439052), which provides help for foreign passengers – a handy place to hang around while waiting for a train. There are comfortable armchairs and a shower and toilet here. Unattended luggage must be deposited in the train station cloak room (Rs 5 per piece for 24 hours).

Money You can change only travellers cheques at the Bank of Baroda, near the Hotel Arun at Sojati Gate. The State Bank of India (High Court Rd branch) changes both travellers cheques and currency.

Post & Communications The main post office is on Station Rd, less than half a kilometre north of the main train station. It's open Monday to Saturday from 10 am to 5 pm and on Sunday from 10 am to 3 pm.

There are scores of telephone booths around town, where you can make local, interstate and international calls.

Internet Resources There is just one place where you can reliably send emails – although more might have opened – the

Asian Sky Shop (☎ 431992) is at J/2/C Subhash Colony, Street No 4, Palace Rd, Ratanada. To get there, go down the lane directly opposite the main gate of the Devi Bhawan guest house, then take the first lane right. From here you'll see the shop's signboard. It is open daily from 10 am to 8 pm, but it's a good idea to ring first to make sure the Internet operator, Lokesh Goyal, is around. Lokesh charges Rs 50 per page for sending/receiving an email.

Bookshops Off Station Rd, opposite the Ranchodji Temple, is the Sarvodaya Bookstall. It has English-language newspapers, magazines, a good range of books on India and a few western novels. It also stocks some good maps of Rajasthan. On the Mohanpura Overbridge is the Rathi Book House, with a more limited selection which includes interesting old novels in English.

Meherangarh

Still run by the maharaja of Jodhpur, Meherangarh, Majestic Fort, is just that. Sprawled across a 125m-high hill, this is perhaps the most formidable fort in Rajasthan. It has been added to over the centuries by reigning Jodhpur maharajas, but the original fort was built in 1459 by Rao Jodha, after whom the city takes its name. A winding road leads up to the entrance from the city, 5km below. The second gate is still scarred by cannonball hits, showing that this was a fort which earned its keep. To the right, just beyond the ticket office, is the **Chhatri of Kiratsingh Sodha**. This cenotaph was built over the site where a soldier fell defending Jodhpur against Jaipurians in 1806.

The gates, of which there are seven, include the **Jayapol** (*pol* means gate) built by Maharaja Man Singh in 1806 following his victory over the armies of Jaipur and Bikaner. This is the main entrance to the fort. The **Fatehpol**, or Victory Gate, at the south-west side of the fort, was erected by Maharaja Ajit Singh to commemorate his defeat of the Mughals.

The final gate into the fort is the **Lohapol**, or Iron Gate. Beside it are 15 handprints, the

sati (self-immolation) marks of Maharaja Man Singh's widows who threw themselves upon his funeral pyre in 1843. The marks still attract devotional attention and are usually covered in red powder (and paper-thin silver during special festivals).

Inside the fort is a series of courtyards and palaces. The **palace apartments** have evocative names like the Moti Mahal, or Pearl Palace, the Sukh Mahal, or Pleasure Palace and the Phool Mahal, or Flower Palace. They now house one of the most fascinating collections of artefacts in Rajasthan, in the **museum**. The exhibits may be rearranged (so not in the sequence described here). Entry to the museum is via the Surajpol. To the right, just beyond the entrance, is a collection of elephant carriages. Some of the howdahs feature exquisite repoussé silverwork, with designs such as rampant lions. These are followed

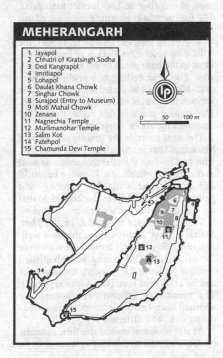

MEHERANGARH

1 Jayapol
2 Chhatri of Kiratsingh Sodha
3 Ded Kangrapol
4 Imritiapol
5 Lohapol
6 Daulat Khana Chowk
7 Singhar Chowk
8 Surajpol (Entry to Museum)
9 Moti Mahal Chowk
10 Zenana
11 Nagnechia Temple
12 Murlimanohar Temple
13 Salim Kot
14 Fatehpol
15 Chamunda Devi Temple

0   50   100 m

by the maharajas' palanquins, including covered palanquins for the ladies in *purdah* (seclusion). In the **armoury**, which has exhibits dating from the 17th to the 19th centuries, is an assortment of deadly weapons, each of which is a remarkable work of art. Note the amazing small cannon in the shape of a wild boar (it resembles a dog).

Beyond the armoury is the **Umaid Mahal**, which has miniatures from all the schools of art which flourished in Rajasthan under the Rajputs. The paintings depict many themes, including those of hunts, festivals, polo matches and, of course, religious themes. Off the north side of this room is a palace which was a place of prayer. It is covered with glass tiles and extraordinary modern Christmas ball-like decorations suspended from the ceiling.

Upstairs is the **Phool Mahal**, in which traditional dances were performed. It was also used as a durbar hall by former maharajas. The fine paintings adorning the walls of this palace were executed by a single artist, and took over 10 years to complete. In fact, the artist died before the work was finished, evident in the bare patch to the left of the hallway. The gold ceiling is embellished with over 80kg of gold plate, and around it the various maharajas of Jodhpur are depicted. The stained glass in this room further accentuates the room's opulence.

The next room is the private chamber of Maharaja Thakhat Singh (reigned 1843-73), who had no less than 30 maharanis as well as numerous concubines. There's a beautiful ceiling adorned with lac painting and painted walls. Nearby in the **Zhanki Mahal** are the cradles of infant princes, including that of the current maharaja. In the **Moti Mahal** are five alcoves along the west wall. The other tiny alcoves around the wall were for oil lamps. The ceiling is embellished with glass tiles and gold paint. An astrologer can be consulted here (see Astrology later). The **zenana**, or women's apartments, are adorned with fine latticework screens, featuring over 150 different designs.

At the southern end of the fort, cannons on the ramparts overlook the sheer drop to the old town beneath. You can clearly hear voices and city sounds carried up by the air currents from the houses far below. Aldous Huxley wrote:

From the bastions of the Jodhpur Fort one hears as the Gods must hear from Olympus – the Gods to whom each separate word uttered in the innumerable peopled world below, comes up distinct and individual to be recorded in the books of omniscience.

The views from these ramparts are nothing less than magical. You can see the many houses painted blue, traditionally to distinguish them as those of Brahmins (see the boxed text Jodhpur's Got the Blues). The **Chamunda Devi Temple**, dedicated to Durga in her wrathful aspect, stands at this end of the fort.

The fort is open daily from 9 am to 1 pm and 2 to 5 pm. There's an elevator which costs Rs 10 one way (free for mobility-impaired visitors). If possible, it's better to walk rather than take the lift, so you see more. To enter the fort costs Rs 10/50 for Indians/foreigners, plus Rs 50/100 for a still/video camera. The fee includes a guided tour of the museum only; for a guided tour of the whole fort, expect to pay Rs 100 (maximum of four people).

The tours operated by the RTDC (see Organised Tours later) only give you an hour at the fort, so if you want to stay here longer (there's plenty to see), get here under your own steam. There is a restaurant at the fort, just before the museum on the right, where you can get a veg thali for Rs 45.

Jaswant Thada

This white marble memorial to Maharaja Jaswant Singh II is about 400m north-east of the fort, just off the fort road. The cenotaph, built in 1899, was followed by the royal crematorium and three later cenotaphs which stand nearby. There is marble *jali* (lattice) work over the windows and carved wooden doors. Some parts of the white marble are translucent. Good views are afforded from the terrace in front of the cenotaph, which is fronted by a little garden of flowering shrubs. Swimming in the Devakund, just a short distance to the west of the cenotaph, is prohibited. Entry to Jaswant Thada is Rs 5/10 for Indians/foreigners.

Clock Tower & Markets

The clock tower is a popular landmark in the bustling old city and a wonderful place to simply ramble around. The vibrant Sadar Market is close to the tower, and narrow alleys lead from here to bazaars selling textiles, silver, handicrafts, aromatic spices (see Shopping later), vegetables and colourful Indian sweets.

Umaid Gardens & Sadar Government Museum

The pleasant Umaid Gardens (free entry) contain the Sadar Government Museum, the zoo (entry Rs 1), and the library. The clean museum has a well-displayed but poorly labelled collection and unfortunately there are no guides to provide explanations. There is the usual collection of sculptures, weapons and moth-eaten stuffed animals, including a number of almost featherless desert birds in two glass cases. The military section includes wooden biplane models. The museum is open daily except Friday from 10 am to 4.30 pm; entry is Rs 3.

Umaid Bhawan Palace

Constructed of marble and pink sandstone, this immense palace is also known as the Chhittar Palace because it uses local Chhittar sandstone. Begun in 1929, it was designed by the president of the British Royal Institute of Architects for Maharaja Umaid Singh, and took 15 years to complete.

Probably the most surprising thing about this grandiose palace is that it was built so close to Independence, after which the maharajas, princely states and the grand extravagances common to this class would soon be a thing of the past. It has been suggested that the palace was built as some sort of royal job creation program.

Maharaja Umaid Singh died in 1947, four years after the palace was completed; the current maharaja, Maharaja Gaj Singh II

(known as Bapji), still lives in part of the building. The rest has been turned into a hotel – and what a hotel! While it lacks the charm of Udaipur's palace hotels, it certainly makes up for it in spacious grandeur (see Places to Stay). There are even recent Hollywood hit movies screened for hotel guests in the palace's home theatre, the Ali Akbar auditorium. The palace (not including the museum) is only open to nonguests if you pay a visiting fee of Rs 330 – it is deducted from any food or drink you might purchase (see Places to Eat for dining options in the palace).

Museum The museum is open to everyone and is well worth a visit. It has the usual assortment of beautifully crafted weapons; an array of stuffed leopards; an enormous banner presented by Queen Victoria to Maharaja Jaswant Singh Bahadur in 1877; human-sized Chinese urns and other fine china; and a fantastic clock collection, including specimens shaped like windmills and lighthouses. Admission is Rs 10/50 for Indians/foreigners (a camera/video charge may soon be introduced).

Astrology

Astrologer Mr Sharma's office (☎ 548992) at Meherangarh (in the Moti Mahal section), is open daily from 9 am to 1 pm and 2 to 5 pm. He charges Rs 100/250 for a 15/30 minute palm reading. Mr Sharma, who has been studying astrology for over 30 years, also offers consultations from the Umaid Bhawan Palace (☎ 433316) each evening from 7 to 9 pm (but the charge is higher here). Don't wear nailpolish if you intend getting a reading, as the nails are used to ascertain your state of health.

Golf

Sadar Club, at Ratanada, has a golf course which has been recently revamped. These brown grounds offer some challenging shots for golfers. Expect to pay Rs 100 for 18 holes, plus Rs 50 for equipment and Rs 20 for a caddie. You have to buy the balls from the club. For details and equipment rental, call the honorary secretary of the club, Rattan Singh, at the Devi Bhawan guest house (☎/fax 434215). This club, popular with the British during the Raj, is about 100 years old. You can still see the damage inflicted on one section of the building, which was bombed during the first war between India and Pakistan!

Organised Tours

The Tourist Reception Centre operates daily tours of **Jodhpur** from 9 am to 1 pm and 2 to 6 pm. These take in all the main sites including the Umaid Bhawan Palace, Meherangarh, Jaswant Thada, and the Mandore Gardens north of Jodhpur. The tours start from the Tourist Reception Centre (see Information earlier) and cost Rs 63 per person (not including entry fees).

To go on a **horse safari**, contact Heggie at Shalivahan Stud & Stables (☎ 740842), Basni Baghela, Pali Rd (12km south of Jodhpur). There are currently 20 horses and all are Marwaris – a local breed characterised by ears that turn inwards. You can stay at Heggie's stud farm, which has four rooms. A comfortable double costs Rs 1000, and a room with a kitchen is Rs 1300. Alternatively, you can pay Rs 4500 per person per day, which includes accommodation, all meals and all horse rides. For short horse rides, you'll pay Rs 400 per person per hour. Bring your own riding hat and boots.

Jodhpur is known for its interesting **village safaris**. You visit villages of the Bishnoi, a people whose belief in the sanctity of the environment and the need to protect trees and animals dates from the 15th century. The owner of the Madho Niwas (☎/fax 434486) conducts informative and reasonably priced safaris – Rs 400 per person for a half-day, including a meal (minimum of two people; advance bookings essential). Other hotels can arrange safaris, including the Ajit Bhawan (☎ 437410) and the Durag Niwas Guest House (☎ 639092). Safaris can also be organised through the Tourist Reception Centre (☎ 545083). Some travellers caution to choose carefully if you book through a travel agent, as some are overpriced and poorly run.

Camel safaris can be arranged through Joshi Cosy Guest House (☎ 612066) and the Govina Hotel (☎ 622758) but we haven't been on one yet. Let us know what they're like.

Places to Stay – Homestays

There are a number of families registered with the Paying Guest House Scheme in Jodhpur. Costs per night range from Rs 90 to Rs 800. Inquire at the Tourist Reception Centre (see Information earlier).

Places to Stay – Budget

Haveli Guest House (☎ 614615, Makrana Mohalla) is one of the best budget options in Jodhpur. It's a down-to-earth place run by a friendly family. Rooms (all doubles) have attached bathrooms and go for Rs 200. You can get *mehndi* (henna) done for Rs 50 per hand or foot and the rooftop veg restaurant sports stunning views of the fort, Jaswant Thada and the blue city. The food is home-cooked and menu items include palak paneer (Rs 35) and dum aloo (Rs 30).

Madho Niwas (Bhenswara House) (☎/fax 434486, New Airport Rd, Ratanada) is run by Dalvir Singh and is a homey place to stay with a quiet lawn area. Singles/doubles with private bathroom and soft mattresses cost Rs 350/400. An air-con room is Rs 750/900. Good meals are available at this establishment; the Marwari-style barbecue chicken with a squeeze of lemon is delicious (must be ordered at least two hours in advance; not available on Monday). Good village safaris are available and they can also arrange a sojourn at *Ravla Bhenswara* (see Around Jodhpur).

Durag Niwas Guest House (☎ 639092, 1 Old Public Park) is another family-run place, with decent double rooms with private bath from Rs 250 to Rs 500. Camel and village safaris are available.

Durag Villas Guest House (☎ 621300), next door, is very good value for money. It offers doubles with bathroom from Rs 150. Meals are available and it can organise village safaris (a half-day jeep safari with lunch is Rs 350 per person).

Megh Niwas Guest House *(☎ 640530, 30 Umed Club Rd)*, nearby, has rooms with bathroom starting at Rs 300/350. It can provide meals; a veg thali is Rs 70.

Roopam Guest House *(☎ 627374, 7 Jagannath Bldg, Mohanpura Overbridge)* is opposite a small pink sandstone Shiva temple. Run by retired Major TS Rathore, it has one room with common bath for Rs 200/250, and three rooms with bath for Rs 400/500. Meals are available with notice.

Hotel Arun *(☎ 620238)*, near Sojati Gate, has OK but not exceptional singles/doubles with common bath for Rs 120/170, and with attached bath for Rs 170/250. There's a vegetarian restaurant here.

Hotel Soner *(☎ 626732, 5 Nai Sarak)*, also in this area, has rooms with common bath for Rs 100/175, and with attached bath for Rs 150/300. Air-con doubles are Rs 450. Meals can be arranged.

Shree Laxmi Hotel *(☎ 547047, 132-133 Nai Sarak)*, is a reasonably good place which has simple rooms, some with balcony, for Rs 150/200 with attached bath (most with Indian-style toilet). There are cheaper rooms with common bath for Rs 100/150. The singles are tiny, but adequate.

Hotel Arvind *(☎ 547159, fax 547423, 135 Nai Sarak)* is slightly better than the Shree Laxmi Hotel. It has singles/doubles with common bath for Rs 90/150, or Rs 165/200 with attached bath. For Rs 200/250 you get a room with a balcony. Most rooms have an Indian-style toilet.

Joshi Cosy Guest House *(☎ 612066, Novechokiya Rd, Brahm Puri, Chuna ki Choki)*, is an atmospheric and unpretentious little place in the old city. This family-run, blue-coloured house is said to be 500 years old (don't expect modern gadgets). Simple singles/doubles with common bath range from Rs 60/90 to Rs 100/150 (free bucket hot water). Go to the rooftop for a splendid view. Camel safaris can be arranged here.

RTDC's Hotel Ghoomar *(☎ 548010, High Court Rd)* has rooms upwards of Rs 300/375, but dorm beds are Rs 50. There's a reasonable nonveg restaurant and a bar (a bottle of beer is Rs 55).

Govind Hotel *(☎ 622758)*, opposite the main post office, is just five minutes walk from the train station – ideal if you've got an early morning train departure. Run by the helpful Jagdish Sadarangani, who will organise a camel safari if you like, this is a very traveller-friendly place. Dorm beds go for Rs 50, small singles with common bath are Rs 60, and singles/doubles with bath attached cost Rs 150/175. Air-con rooms are Rs 475/525. The rooms at the back are the quietest although some have no external window. The rooftop veg restaurant has wonderful views of the palace and fort. In season (winter) you can slurp on a refreshing chikku shake (Rs 20).

Hotel Raj *(☎ 628447)* is in the laneway near the Govind Hotel, but is not as geared up for travellers. Located on the second floor, it has rooms from Rs 125/200 to Rs 200/300 (hot water by the bucket is Rs 4).

Shanti Bhawan Lodge *(☎ 637001, fax 621689)* is in the street which runs directly opposite (ie away from) the main train station. Rooms are spartan and a little scruffy, and the bathrooms could be cleaner. Rates are Rs 70/100 with common bath, or Rs 150 for a double with attached bath (bucket hot water), and Rs 600 for a double with geyser.

Hotel Akshey *(☎ 437327)*, opposite the Raika Bagh train station, has dorm beds for Rs 50, ordinary rooms for Rs 175/225, and better rooms for Rs 400/500. Meals are available. Some travellers have complained about the cleanliness and service here.

Hotel Anand *(☎ 614483)*, next door, charges Rs 200/250 for a single/double with private bath, and Rs 400/500 for an air-con room.

Retiring rooms at the main train station cost Rs 100 for an ordinary double room with attached bath, or Rs 300 for a double with air-con. Meals are available.

Places to Stay – Mid-Range

Devi Bhawan *(☎/fax 434215, 1 Ratanada Area)* is a splendid place to stay and you'll have no hassles here whatsoever. Run by a charming couple, this green oasis has fresh rooms for Rs 700/750 a single/double, and a cottage for Rs 850. There's a good restaurant and the garden would have to be one of the loveliest in Jodhpur.

Ratan Vilas (*☎/fax 614418, Loco Shed Rd, Ratanada*) is another very well-kept family villa set in a pleasant garden. Comfortable doubles cost Rs 600 and meals are available in the homey dining room. The set breakfast/lunch/dinner is Rs 75/125/145. If you're interested in getting authentic jodhpur trousers made, ask the owner's son, Brijraj. Some of the tailors are quite elderly, so allow at least a week for your jodhpurs to be stitched.

Newtons Manor (*☎ 430686, fax 610603, 86 Jawahar Colony, Ratanada*), opposite Green Gate No 8, is also a great choice with a cosy ambience. There are just five doubles: one has a separate bathroom (Rs 895); those with attached bathroom are Rs 995; and a big room with a bathtub is Rs 1100. An extra bed is Rs 150. The rooms are clean, the outdoor area is nice, and there's even a fish tank. Scrumptious home-cooked meals are available; the set lunch/dinner is Rs 180 (veg), or Rs 230 (nonveg).

Hotel Adarsh Niwas (*☎ 627338, fax 627314*) is in the street directly opposite the main train station. Singles/doubles range from Rs 650/850 to Rs 750/1000. The rooms are drab, but handy if you want to be near the train station.

Hotel City Palace (*☎ 431933, fax 639033, 32 Nai Sarak*), near Sojati Gate, is a good choice in this area. Singles/doubles are Rs 790/990 (some rooms are a bit dark). You can eat at *Gossip*, a veg restaurant and bar; a masala dosa is Rs 30 and pizzas are around Rs 40.

Hotel Beniwal Palace (*☎ 616236, fax 638064*), near the Ajit Bhawan, is a nondescript building fronting a main road. Singles/doubles start at Rs 800/950.

Hotel Jag Villa (*☎ 645490, fax 622274*), in the Shikargarh area, is about 5km out of the city centre. It's an option if you want to stay away from the hustle and bustle of the city centre hotels. Deluxe singles/doubles

cost Rs 900/1100 and a suite is Rs 1500. Meals are available.

There are some more upmarket and expensive hotels in this range, which are recommended.

Ajit Bhawan (*☎ 437410, fax 637774, Airport Rd*) has long been a favourite with travellers. It has a series of modern stone cottages arranged around a relaxing garden. These cost Rs 1550/1800. More expensive suites are also on offer. There's a sensational swimming pool (open to nonresidents for Rs 250), meals are available and village safaris can be arranged. The setting of this hotel is delightful, let down only by the somewhat impersonal staff.

Hotel Karni Bhawan (*☎ 432220, fax 433495, Palace Rd*) is a modern place with traditional touches. Set in well-manicured gardens and with a pool, comfortable singles/doubles start at Rs 1175/1425 (the rooms in the new wing have more character than those in the old block). You can eat indoors or under the stars, while listening to live Rajasthani music. It has a country retreat at Sodawas, 90km south of Jodhpur.

Inn Season (*☎/fax 616400*), opposite the PWD office, is another fine choice, with well-kept rooms from Rs 1200 to Rs 1500 for a lovely suite. The restaurant serves Indian and continental food; the set lunch/dinner is Rs 175 (veg), or Rs 200 (nonveg). Check out the funky old German record player with an equally funky collection of classic records, including Louis Armstrong and Ella Fitzgerald.

Places to Stay – Top End

Umaid Bhawan Palace (*☎ 433316, fax 635373*), east of the city centre, is *the* place to stay in Jodhpur if you have a passion for pure luxury. This very elegant palace has an indoor swimming pool, tennis court, billiard room, lush lawns and several restaurants (see Places to Eat). A wing of the palace is still occupied by the current maharaja of Jodhpur and his family. Standard rooms cost US$195/220, and suites range from US$350 to a phenomenal US$990. If possible, pay the king's ransom and opt for a suite, as the cheaper rooms are suitably comfortable, but hardly palatial.

Ratanada Polo Palace (☎ 431910, fax 433118, Residency Rd) is in its own spacious grounds, but is a bit low on character. It has a pool, restaurant and rooms for Rs 1800/2400. The set breakfast/lunch/dinner is Rs 150/300/350.

Taj Hari Mahal Palace should be up and running by the time you read this. For details contact its office in Mumbai (☎ 022-202 5515, fax 284 6683).

Places to Eat

While you're in Jodhpur, try a glass of makhania lassi, a filling saffron-flavoured variety of that most refreshing of drinks.

Mishrilal Hotel, at the clock tower, is nothing fancy in terms of decor, but whips up the best lassis in town. A delicious glass of creamy special makhania lassi is Rs 10. One glass can do you for lunch!

Agra Sweets, opposite Sojati Gate, also sells a jolly good creamy lassi (Rs 10), as well as espresso coffee (Rs 6). It has Jodhpur dessert specialities such as mawa ladoo (Rs 5) and the baklava-like mawa kachori (Rs 9).

Kalinga Restaurant, at the Hotel Adarsh Niwas, near the train station, is a pleasant place to eat (and kill time while waiting for a train). It serves Indian, Chinese and continental dishes; chicken curry is Rs 65. You can get hearty continental breakfasts here including sausage, eggs, toast, juice and coffee for Rs 85. It's open daily from 7 am to 10.30 pm.

Mid Town, nearby, is a bit pricey but not bad. Most mains cost between Rs 40 and Rs 65, and there are Rajasthani specials such as chakki-ka-sagh (wheat sponge cooked in rich gravy – a speciality of Jodhpur) and roti for Rs 55, or bajara-ki-roti pachkuta (bajara wheat roti with local dry vegetables), also for Rs 55. A Gujarati or Rajasthani thali is Rs 60.

Kasserole, not far from the Hotel Karni Bhawan, is the place to go for a Chinese chow down. The Buddhist chef whips up specialities such as shredded lamb in hot garlic sauce (Rs 50), chicken chow mein

(Rs 45) and sweet & sour vegies (Rs 30). This unpretentious restaurant is on the top floor of a private house called Chatterjee Mansion, and is only open for dinner (every night) from 7 to 11 pm.

On the Rocks at the Ajit Bhawan hotel is very popular, especially with the locals and especially at dinnertime (for reservations call ☎ 437410). It serves tasty Indian cuisine; half a tandoori chicken is Rs 85 and a veg biryani is Rs 50. The service can be a tad sluggish, particularly when it's busy. In the same compound, there's an attractive little *bar* – women should be prepared for stares by the predominantly male clientele. There's also an excellent *bakery* with freshly baked muffins, bread, biscuits and cakes (birthday cakes can be made with advance notice).

Umaid Bhawan Palace has four restaurants (open to nonresidents; the visiting fee of Rs 330 is deducted from any food or drink you purchase), including the very grand *Marwar Hall* (however, the buffet here is pretty average).

Overlooking the back lawn and with a view of the fort is *The Pillars*, a pleasant informal Indian and continental eatery recommended for a light bite – a Moroccan burger is Rs 180; the more formal *Risala* specialises in continental cuisine, such as barbecued spare ribs (Rs 150) and caramel custard (Rs 95); and the *Kebab Konner*, a casual open-air restaurant, is especially popular with the locals. It specialises in moderately priced barbecue Indian food (dinner only).

If you're just feeling thirsty, you can have a drop of amber fluid at the *Trophy Bar*.

Pushpa Bhojnalya, a tiny place close to Jalori Gate and about 10 minutes' walk from the train station, serves authentic Rajasthani cuisine such as churma.

The *refreshment room* on the 1st floor of the main train station is surprisingly good. It's a cool, quiet haven, and the food is cheap. The veg/nonveg thali is Rs 16/22. There are also lighter options such as cheese sandwiches (Rs 15) and sweet lassis (Rs 7). This place is open daily from 6 am to 10.30 pm.

Shopping

Jodhpur specialises in antiques, with the greatest concentration of antique shops along the road connecting the Ajit Bhawan with the Umaid Bhawan Palace. These shops are well-known to western antique dealers who come here with wallets stuffed with plastic cards. As a result, you'll be hard pressed to find any bargains. The trade in antique architectural fixtures is contributing towards the desecration of India's cultural heritage and as such is not condoned by Lonely Planet. Most of these warehouse-sized showrooms also deal in antique reproductions, for a growing number of overseas export houses. They're fascinating places to wander around.

Certain restrictions apply to the export of Indian items over 100 years old – see Antiques in the Shopping section of the Facts for the Visitor chapter.

For excellent Indian spices, go to Mohanlal Verhomal (☎/fax 615846), shop 209B at the *sabzi* (vegetable) market, close to the clock tower. For sale is a tantalizing array, including a 'winter tonic' which apparently enhances sexual stamina (Rs 175). There's also a packet of 'spice for bad sneeze' (Rs 175). The owner has a deep passion for spices, and will happily answer any questions you may have about them.

Getting There & Away

Air Indian Airlines (☎ 636757) has an office south of the centre, near the Ajit Bhawan hotel, which is open daily from 10 am to 1.15 pm and 2 to 4.30 pm. It operates several flights each week to Jaipur (US$70), Delhi (US$95), Udaipur (US$55), Jaisalmer (US$60) and Mumbai (US$135). The telephone number of the Jodhpur airport is ☎ 430617.

Bus Rajasthan State Transport Corporation (RSTC) buses leave from the Roadways bus stand (☎ 544686, 544989).

There are a number of private bus companies opposite the train station. Quoted rates for deluxe buses with 2 x 2 (two seat by two seat) pushback seats are:

destination	duration (hrs)	cost (Rs)
Ahmedabad	10	130
Ajmer	4	70
Delhi	12½	160
Jaipur	7	80
Jaisalmer	5	70
Pune	25	400
Udaipur	8	70

The main highway between Jodhpur and Jaisalmer is via Agolai, Dechu and Pokaran, but it's more interesting to go on the less frequently travelled route via Osiyan and Phalodi (for Khichan), which meets the main route at Pokaran.

Train The booking office is on Station Rd, between the train station and Sojati Gate. Demand for tickets is heavy, so come here soon after you arrive. There's a tourist quota and the office is open Monday to Saturday from 8 am to 8 pm, until 1.45 pm on Sunday. At the main train station is an International Tourist Bureau (see Information).

Make sure you find out what the current train times are, as they have a tendency to change. The 2466 *Intercity* Jodhpur-Jaipur leaves at 5.55 am (4½ hrs, Rs 79/252 in 2nd/1st class). To Kota, the 192 *Jodhpur-Kota Passenger* leaves at 7.30 am (13 hrs, Rs 54 – only 2nd class available). The 394 *Jodhpur-Bikaner Passenger* leaves Jodhpur at 2.45 pm (5 hrs, Rs 117/500). There is a train to Delhi (10 hrs, Rs 197/866).

There are two trains to Jaisalmer – one leaves Jodhpur at 8.20 am and arrives in Jaisalmer at 5 pm, and the other leaves Jodhpur at 11.30 pm and arrives in Jaisalmer at 6 am. A ticket costs Rs 104.

Taxi There is a taxi stand to the right as you exit the main train station. A one-way taxi trip to Jaisalmer will cost around Rs 1780, Rs 1700 to Udaipur and Rs 2000 to Jaipur.

Getting Around

To/From the Airport The airport is only 5km from the city centre. It costs about Rs 50 in an auto-rickshaw and Rs 110 in a taxi.

Taxi To hire a taxi for sightseeing in Jodhpur expect to pay around Rs 600 per day. To Mandore a taxi costs Rs 100 including a one hour halt. To Osiyan it is Rs 400 return including a one hour stay there.

Auto-Rickshaw Most journeys in the town area by auto-rickshaw should cost no more than Rs 25.

Bicycle You can hire a bike from several places near the Kalinga Restaurant, not far from the main post office. The usual charge is about Rs 2/15 per hour/day.

AROUND JODHPUR
Jhalamand
Hotel Jhalamand Garh (☎ 0291-740481, fax 741125), 10km south of Jodhpur, is a tranquil 18th-century royal abode with singles/doubles from Rs 1000/1100. It's ideal to be a stones throw away from the tumult of Jodhpur. The set lunch/dinner is Rs 250 and village safaris can be arranged.

Maha Mandir & Balsamand Lake
About 4km north-east of the city is the Maha Mandir (Great Temple). It's built around a 100-pillared Shiva temple but is nothing to write home about. The picturesque Balsamand Lake is 5km farther north.

Balsamand Palace, near the lake, offers comfort in a lush and serene setting not too far away from Jodhpur. Singles/doubles in the former stables go for US$60/75, all with a private terrace area. Suites range from US$125 to US$325 for the presidential suite which has a lake view. There are two restaurants which serve Indian and continental cuisine; the buffet lunch/dinner is US$8/10. Around sunset, hordes of creepy bats swoop into the lake for a sip of water – a fascinating sight that should not be missed. Bookings for this hotel should be made through the Umaid Bhawan Palace in Jodhpur *(☎ 0291-433316, fax 635373)*.

Mandore
Mandore, 9km to the north of Jodhpur, was the capital of Marwar before the foundation of Jodhpur. It was founded in the 6th century, and passed to the Rathore Rajputs in 1381 after a marriage alliance between a princess of the original founders, the Pratiharas, and the Rathore raja, Rao Chandor.

Today the extensive Mandore Gardens with high rock terraces make it a popular attraction. The gardens also contain the chhatris of the Rathore rulers. One of the most imposing is the **Chhatri of Maharaja Dhiraj Ajit Singh**, an enormous edifice with elephant acroteria, *amalaka* (disk-shaped flourishes with fluted edges), a pillared forechamber and fine sculpture. Opposite is the 17th century **Chhatri of Maharaja Dhiraj Jaswant Singh**, an enormous octagonal pavilion with a vast dome and huge pillars. It achieves a remarkable symmetry, with a gallery supported by pillars and sculptures of Krishna and the *gopis* (milkmaids).

At the rear of the complex, to the right, is the **Hall of Heroes**, with 15 figures carved out of a rock wall. The brightly painted figures represent Hindu deities or local Rajput heroes on horseback. The **Shrine of 33 Crore Gods** is painted with figures of deities and spirits (1 crore = 10 million).

There is a small **government museum** in Mandore, open daily except Friday from 10 am to 4.30 pm. There's a small entry fee.

Places to Stay The delightful *Mandore Guest House (☎ 0291-545620, fax 546959)* has good accommodation set in a shady garden. It's great value with singles/doubles with attached bathroom costing Rs 350/500. Meals are prepared for guests and you can even opt to dine with the owner and his family at their house next door.

Getting There & Away There are many buses throughout the day between Jodhpur and Mandore, which is on the main road between Jodhpur and Nagaur. Mandore is also included on the RTDC city tours (see Organised Tours under Jodhpur earlier).

Bishnoi Villages
The Bishnoi are renowned for their conservationist philosophies, and hold all animal

life as sacred, in particular the blackbuck, or Indian antelope, which thrives in large numbers in Bishnoi regions. The Bishnoi cult, established in the late 15th century by Guru Jambhoji, outlines 29 conservation principles (*bishnoi* = 29). The Bishnoi can be considered as early conservationist martyrs – in 1730, a Bishnoi woman, Amritdevi, clung to a tree which had been marked for felling to provide timber for the maharaja. She was killed, as were the 362 other villagers who followed her example by clinging to trees destined for the axe. This collective sacrifice is commemorated each September at **Khejadali** village, where there is a memorial to the victims fronted by a small grove of khejri trees.

At **Guda Bishnoi**, locals are traditionally engaged in animal husbandry; there is a small artificial lake here where migratory birds and mammals such as blackbuck and chinkara can be seen, particularly at dusk, when they feed at the lake. The lake is full only during the monsoon (July and August). There are plans to shift Jodhpur airport here within the next decade.

Salawas is traditionally a centre for weaving *dhurries* (carpets). A beautiful 1.3m x 2m dhurrie can take about one month to complete, depending on the intricacy of the design and the number of colours used, and costs from Rs 2500 to Rs 3000, with all profits going to the artisan. One of these artisans, Roopraj, will happily answer your questions about this craft.

These days, chemical rather than natural dyes are used. Dhurries are usually of cotton, but sometimes camel or goat hair, or silk, is used. After the weaving is completed, the dhurries are sometimes stonewashed to give an antique effect. The dhurrie weavers can arrange post by sea or air. Also in Salawas, several families, mostly of the Muslim community, are engaged in blockprinting. The hand-woven, block-printed cloth is known as *fetia*. A single bed sheet costs around Rs 550, and a double sheet is Rs 650.

At the villages of **Zhalamand**, **Salawas** and **Kakani**, potters can be seen at work using hand-turned wheels. **Guda Mogra** is a tiny desert village where the inhabitants live in thatched huts, and a tour here may include lunch at a family home.

Getting There & Away The Bishnoi villages are strung along and off the Pali road, to the south-east of Jodhpur. Various operators, including the RTDC in Jodhpur, conduct jeep safaris to the villages. A tour is essential to visit this region: some of these villages are tiny, along tracks which can be barely made out in the sand, and which you will be hard pressed to find on any maps. See Organised Tours under Jodhpur.

Sardar Samand Lake

The route to this wildlife centre, 66km south-east of Jodhpur, passes through a number of colourful little villages. Some of the wildlife found in this area include blackbuck, chinkara and birdlife.

Sardar Samand Palace, formerly the maharaja of Jodhpur's summer palace, is now a hotel, with rooms for US$60/75. There's a restaurant and a stylish lakeside swimming pool to enjoy. This place is a world away from the clamour of Jodhpur. Book at the Umaid Bhawan Palace in Jodhpur (☎ 0291-433316, fax 635373).

Rohet

In this village, 40km south of Jodhpur, the former local ruler has converted his 350-year-old manor into a heritage hotel. *Rohet Garh* (☎ 02936-68231) has comfortable air-cooled singles/doubles for Rs 1100/1700, or air-con rooms for Rs 1175/1850. All rooms have a special character of their own. There's a fantastic swimming pool and a relaxing garden to sit back with a good book; you can buy a cookbook (Rs 50) of local Rajasthani recipes. Village safaris and horse rides can be arranged. The place seems to attract travel writers: Bruce Chatwin wrote *The Songlines* here and William Dalrymple began *City of Djinns*.

From Jodhpur, there are local daily buses to Rohet (Rs 11) or you can get a taxi for around Rs 500 one way.

Luni

Fort Chanwa (☎/fax Jodhpur 0291-432460), not too far from Rohet, is another delightful place to stay in the Jodhpur environs. It offers tasteful accommodation in a red sandstone fort dating back to the 19th century. A single/double costs Rs 1550/1800. There's a pool, restaurant (the set lunch/dinner is Rs 250/350) and some interesting walks in the area. Village safaris are available with advance notice.

There is no direct bus from Jodhpur to Luni, but there are rail connections from Jodhpur.

Bhenswara

Bhenswara, which translates to 'the place where buffaloes were kept', is located 130km south of Jodhpur.

Ravla Bhenswara (☎ 02978-22080, reservations ☎/fax Jodhpur 0291-434486) is an unpretentious rural manor which is perfect if you want some respite from travelling. This place is run by a lovely young couple, Shiv Pratap Singh and Uma Kumari, who give this hotel a homey appeal. The quaint rooms start at Rs 800/950 a single/double and each room has a personality of its own. The set lunch/dinner is Rs 175. There's a swimming pool and jeep village safaris can be organised; it costs Rs 400 per person (minimum of two people). A village bullock cart ride is Rs 200 per person (minimum of two people). You can indulge in a traditional Indian massage (Rs 110 for 30 minutes), or get mehndi put on your hands (Rs 50 per hand). Don't miss the early evening parakeet invasion at nearby **Madho Bagh**. The hotel owners can arrange a visit to the nearby **Jalor Fort**. The climb up to the fort takes about 45 minutes (carry water as the ascent can be a hot one).

There are local buses from Jodhpur to Bhenswara for Rs 42.

Dhawa Doli Wildlife Sanctuary

This sanctuary is about 40km south-west of Jodhpur, on the road to Barmer. There is no accommodation here, but it is possible to take a half-day tour from Jodhpur for Rs 700.

Check at the Tourist Reception Centre (☎ 0291-545083) in Jodhpur. Animals and birds which can be seen here include blackbuck, partridges, desert fox and nilgai.

Khejarla

Fort Khejarla (☎ 02930-58311), 85km east of Jodhpur en route to Ajmer, is not as swish as most other fort-hotels in Rajasthan, but it has a certain rustic charm. Singles/doubles at this 400-year-old fort go for Rs 850/950 (hot water is by the bucket). The set breakfast/lunch/dinner is Rs 125/ 200/250.

Village safaris can be arranged, as well as a visit to an old stepwell (ask Dalip Singh about the ghost).

Khimsar

Khimsar Fort (☎ 01585-62345, fax 62228), is about 75km north of Jodhpur. It dates back to 1523, and has been converted into an upmarket hotel. Well-appointed rooms cost US$85/135 a single/double. Amenities include a swimming pool (with a nearby hammock to laze away the day), a good restaurant (the buffet breakfast/lunch is US$ 8/11; dinner is US$12) and pleasant gardens. It is possible to arrange a jeep safari or a horse/camel ride, for US$10 per person for two hours. A massage costs US$7 for 30 minutes.

A local bus from Jodhpur is Rs 29.50. A taxi is about Rs 650 (one way).

Nimaj

Nimaj is about halfway between Jodhpur and Ajmer. As with many forts in Rajasthan, the one in this village has been converted into a hotel. If you just want to have lunch at the hotel, you should ring ahead to let them know when you are coming.

Jagram Durg (☎ 02939-86522) is a modest place which has single/double rooms for Rs 600/900. Breakfast is Rs 100, lunch or dinner is Rs 200.

NAGAUR

Nagaur, 135km north-east of Jodhpur, has the historic **Ahhichatragarh**, an ancient fort which is currently being restored (entry costs Rs 5/15 for Indians/foreigners, plus Rs 25/50 for a camera/video). The fort is protected by massive double walls which encompass a richly painted **palace**. Within the walls of the old city are several **mosques**, including one commissioned by Akbar for a disciple of the Sufi saint Khwaja Muin-ud-din Chishti, who roamed India in the 13th century.

Nagaur also hosts a fair, which is a smaller version of Pushkar's Camel Fair – see the boxed text Festivals of Western Rajasthan at the start of this chapter.

Places to Stay & Eat

Royal Tents are available during the fair for US$175/225 a single/double. These luxurious tents must be booked in advance through the Umaid Bhawan Palace in Jodhpur (☎ *0291-433316, fax 635373)*.

RTDC's Kurjan Nagaur, just outside the town, has good rooms for Rs 250/300 with bath and you can get a decent veg thali (Rs 45) in the dining room. During the fair, tariffs shoot up to US$40/53 – for more details contact the General Manager, Central Reservations (☎ *0141-202586, fax 201045)*, RTDC's Hotel Swagatam Campus, Near Railway Station, Jaipur, 302006, Rajasthan.

Hotel Bhaskar (☎ *01582-22100)*, near the train station, has ordinary singles/doubles with private bath for Rs 100/250; Rs 700 for air-con doubles. Meals are available.

Hotel Mahaveer International (☎ *01 582-43158)* is at Vijai Vallabh Chowk, about 1.5km from the fort. It was in the final stages of construction at the time of writing, but looks like it will be the most upmarket hotel in Nagaur. Singles/doubles with bath are expected to cost Rs 200/300, or Rs 550/650 with air-con. If you do stay here, let us know what you think.

Getting There & Away

Nagaur is on the main route between Jodhpur and Bikaner, and there are numerous buses throughout the day connecting it with these cities. A local bus from Jodhpur costs Rs 43.50 and a taxi (one way) costs Rs 825.

JODHPUR TO JAISALMER (NORTHEN ROUTE)

The most direct route by road to Jaisalmer is via Shergarh, Dechhu and Pokaran; however, there are some interesting places to visit on the lesser travelled northern route via Osiyan and Phalodi, which meets the main route at Pokaran. The exquisite temples at Osiyan, the feeding grounds of the demoiselle cranes at Khichan and the important pilgrimage site of Ramdevra all lie on or just off this route, which numerous buses ply each day.

Osiyan

If you can't make it to Jaisalmer and are desperate to get a taste of the desert, this is a good alternative. The ancient Thar Desert town of Osiyan, 65km north of Jodhpur, was a great trading centre between the 8th and 12th centuries when it was dominated by the Jains, and was known as Upkeshpur. The wealth of Osiyan's medieval inhabitants enabled them to build lavish and beautifully sculpted temples. The stone used to build these temples was extracted from local quarries, and for the most part has withstood the ravages of time. The village of Osiyan is inhabited mostly by Brahmins, as evidenced by the predominance of blue-painted houses.

Temples The temples of Osiyan rival the Hoysala temples of Karnataka and the Sun Temple of Konark in Orissa. About 200m north of the bus stand is the **Sachiya Mata Temple** (Sachiya Mata is the ninth, and last, incarnation of the goddess Durga). In the forechamber before the *mandapa* (chamber before the inner sanctum), and beyond the impressive *torana* (gateway), are sandstone statues of various incarnations of Durga which were excavated by archaeologists and installed here. The main temple is flanked by nine smaller temples, each dedicated to an incarnation of the goddess, and built only in the last decade. Abutting the sides of the main temple is a series of ancient temples contemporary with the Sachiya Mata Temple.

The drum of the mandapa is elaborately carved, featuring 16 sculptures of dancing *apsaras* (maidens) who welcome the goddess to her temple. The mirrorwork seen here is modern. The image of Sachiya Mata enshrined in the inner sanctum is of stone and, according to legend, was recovered from the ground where it was buried by a maharaja. The pillars flanking the sanctum are encircled by lions' heads.

To the right is a small temple to Surya, the sun god, which has a dancing snake motif on the ceiling of the mandapa, and in the centre are Krishna and Radha. On the top left-hand corner of the lintel a sculpture over 1000 years old depicts a woman applying lip rouge with the aid of a mirror.

Outside the main temple (right-hand side), a small temple dedicated to Laxminarayan has some mildly erotic sculptures. In the top left-hand corner of the lintel is a lovely little sculpture of Ganesh with his consort, Chandrika, on his knee. Around the external walls is a series of extraordinary sculptures depicting men and women battling monster-like beasts. There are good views out over Osiyan from the platform adjacent to this small temple. To the southwest can be seen the oldest temple in Osiyan, dedicated to Surya. To the west is the Jain Mahavira Temple. The sandstone temples immediately to the south are dedicated to Harihara (Shiva and Parvati).

On the north side of the small Surya Temple, which flanks the Sachiya Mata Temple, is a very rare statue of Harihara. It is depicted with one breast, and Shiva's vehicle, the Nandi bull, is shown.

To the left of the Sachiya Mata temple are two small temples dedicated to Ganesh and Shiva respectively. The lintels are completely covered in sculptures depicting erotic contortions, particularly notable on the Shiva Temple.

Five minutes walk from the Sachiya Mata Temple is the **Mahavira Temple** (entry costs Rs 5, plus Rs 25/100 for a camera/video), dedicated to the last of the Jain *tirthankars* (prophets). This is a more spacious temple than the Sachiya Mata Temple, with an open-air pavilion-type mandapa supported by carved pillars. As at the Sachiya Mata Temple, the drum of the dome features sculptures of apsaras. There is a beautiful torana before the temple, with very intricate sculptural work.

The image of Mahavira is difficult to make out in the dimly lit inner sanctum. According to legend it is over 2000 years old, and is made of sand and milk and coated in gold. On either side of the mandapa are identical marble statues of Adinath, the first Jain tirthankar. Fortunately, the garish mirrors which can be seen in the Sachiya Mata Temple have been removed from this temple, and you are able to appreciate it in its original state. In the right-hand corner is an ancient frieze which retains fragments of colour.

The four temples on two sides of the main temple are dedicated to eight of the 24 tirthankars. Behind the temple are fragments of sculpture retrieved from the precincts which were thrown down by the Mughals.

Among the other temples in Osiyan are those dedicated to Surya, Shiva and Harihara, but they are in poor condition and are being restored. There is also a badly deteriorating *baori* (stepwell).

Places to Stay & Eat Few travellers choose to stay overnight in Osiyan, which accounts for the lack of accommodation. Brahmin priest, energetic Bhanu Prakash Sharma, has a small *guest house* (☎ 02922-74232), just near the Mahavira Temple. It costs Rs 200 for a room (maximum of five people). It's pretty simple, though, with *charpoys* (Indian string beds) and bucket hot water. A veg lunch or dinner is Rs 80. He can arrange jeep excursions and camel rides, and is also a guide to the temples. To find him, ask any of the village children, who will happily track him down for you.

The Camel Camp in Osiyan offers a range of tented accommodation in a magical location – atop a secluded sand dune overlooking the town. There are double occupancy tents with common bath for Rs 300.

More luxurious tents with attached bath (and shower!) are also available. There's a breezy bar with views of the temples – a great place to lash out on a bottle of bubbly (Indian champagne is Rs 1000 per bottle). Camel safaris, jeep safaris and bird-watching excursions are available with advance notice. The cool and casual owner, Reggie, is here most of the time and is planning to build a pool on a dune! Advance bookings are essential. Contact 'The Safari Club' (☎/fax 0291-437023), High Court Colony, Jodhpur. Let Reggie know when you will be arriving in Osiyan, and he can arrange for a jeep to pick you up from the train station or bus stand.

Getting There & Away Few people travel to Osiyan. Buses to Jodhpur depart every 30 minutes or so, (1½ hrs, Rs 20); and to Phalodi (2 hrs, Rs 16).

There's also a daily train from Jodhpur (1½ hrs, Rs 15/135 in 2nd/1st class). A taxi from Jodhpur will cost about Rs 400 (return).

Phalodi

Phalodi is a fairly nondescript large town lying about midway between Jodhpur and Jaisalmer. The main attraction here is the tiny village of **Khichan**, about 10km east of Phalodi, and a feeding ground during the winter months for the beautiful demoiselle crane (see the boxed text The Demoiselle Cranes of Khichan). Khichan also has some beautiful red sandstone *havelis* (mansions), some around 100 years old and many featuring fine carvings. A series of sand dunes affords a stunning desert panorama. If you want someone to escort you to Khichan, contact Surya Prakash at the Hotel Sunrise.

Places to Stay & Eat The *Hotel Sunrise* (☎ 02925-22257) is directly opposite the Roadways bus stand. It costs Rs 150/200 for a basic but acceptable single/double room with attached bath and bucket hot water. Meals can be arranged with notice.

Getting There & Away Phalodi is about 135km from Jodhpur, 165km from Jaisalmer and 150km from Bikaner. There are

numerous buses from the Roadways bus stand to Jodhpur (3½ hrs, Rs 35/55 for a local/express bus). There are local buses for Bikaner (4½ hrs, Rs 45), an express (3½ hrs, Rs 54); and local buses to Jaisalmer (4½ hrs, Rs 65) and an express (Rs 74) which takes a little less time.

Phalodi is on the broad-gauge line and has rail connections with both Jodhpur (Rs 25/41 for the day/night train) and Jaisalmer (Rs 27/48 for the day/night train).

Getting Around There are daily buses between Phalodi and Khichan (15 mins, Rs 2). An auto-rickshaw will cost Rs 50 (return) to Khichan and a Rs 50 per hour waiting time.

Ramdevra

This tiny, desolate and windswept desert village lies 10km north of Pokaran and, while it's probably not the most salubrious place to stay overnight, it has a very important temple dedicated to a deified local hero Ramdev, who lived in the Middle Ages. Ramdev was born in Tanwar village to a Rajput family and was opposed to all forms of untouchability, believing that all human beings are equal.

Ramdev Mandir The temple itself, with its brightly coloured facade, is not architecturally of great interest, but the devotional activities of the hundreds of pilgrims who pay homage at this shrine certainly are. The temple is full of statues of horses, including two life-sized silver horses featuring fine repoussé work. They commemorate Ramdev's trusty horse, who went with him from village to village as he helped ailing villagers. There are also elaborately caparisoned wooden horses covered with finely embroidered silk cloths. Pilgrims leave tiny models of horses at the temple – hundreds of embroidered horses are here, like the ones for sale all over Rajasthan. The silver image of Ramdev is fronted by a sacred fire at which priests anoint pilgrims' foreheads with *tikkas* (dots) and give *prasad* (sacred food).

You'll probably be assailed by people with receipt books demanding donations, both as you enter the temple complex and within the

The Demoiselle Cranes of Khichan

From the last week of August or the first week of September until the last week of March, over 7000 demoiselle cranes (*Anthropoides virgo*) fly every morning and evening to the fields around Khichan to feed on the grain which has been spread there by villagers.

The demoiselle crane stands about 76cm high and is a brown-grey colour with a black chest and throat. It has a long neck and short beak. The cranes, which are known locally as *kurjas*, appear in traditional Marwari songs, in which women beseech them to bring back messages from their loved ones when the birds return from distant lands. The cranes consume a phenomenal 600kg of grain each day, all of which is funded by donations (donations are very welcome).

The practice of feeding the cranes dates back some 150 years, and the number of cranes is increasing by about 10% to 15% each year. The grain is spread at night, ready for the birds to feed at sunrise (about 6.30 am), and again around 1 pm, in time for the birds' return between about 3 and 5 pm. The sight of these wonderful birds in such large numbers descending on the fields is truly awe-inspiring, and shouldn't be missed if you're in the area. Please keep a distance from the birds and refrain from making a noise, so as not to scare them.

The migration route of the demoiselle cranes has not yet been established, but two theories have been proposed. The International Crane Foundation (ICF) believes the birds originate from Mongolia and fly over China and Tibet to India. Locals believe that the birds originate from central Africa, and fly across central Asia, including Afghanistan, Pakistan and then India.

For more information about the demoiselle cranes and the feeding program at Khichan, write to the International Crane Foundation, PO Box 447, E-11376 Shady Lane Rd, Baraboo, WI 53913-0447, USA (☎ 608-356 9462, fax 356 9465).

---

temple itself, even by men who 'guard' your shoes! A festival is held in Ramdevji's honour at the temples in August/September – see the boxed text Festivals of Western Rajasthan at the beginning of this chapter.

Places to Stay & Eat The *Hotel Poonam Palace* (☎ 02996-37042) has doubles with bath for Rs 120 and a restaurant. English can be a bit of a problem here.

Getting There & Away Most buses between Phalodi and Pokaran pass through Ramdevra. Jeep taxis leave when full along the main street for Pokaran (20 mins, Rs 3). A taxi from Jodhpur costs Rs 1050 one way.

Pokaran

At the junction of the Jaisalmer, Jodhpur and Bikaner roads, 110km from Jaisalmer, is this desert town, site of another fort, although not of the formidable dimensions of the Jodhpur and Jaisalmer forts. The bus stand is on the Jodhpur road at the southern edge of town. The fort is 1.5km to the northeast of the bus stand. The post office is on the left-hand side on the road leading up to the fort. There is nowhere to change money in Pokaran, so take enough rupees.

It was in the Pokaran area, in May 1998, that India detonated five nuclear devices, heightening tension between India and neighbouring Pakistan – rivals since the

Partition in 1947. The crux of contention between the two countries has been the disputed territory of Kashmir, which is claimed by both India and Pakistan. While world leaders vehemently condemned the Indian nuclear tests, hundreds of thousands of Hindu loyalists celebrated Prime Minister Atal Behari Vajpayee's controversial decision. Pakistan swiftly responded to India by detonating its own nuclear devices, igniting global concern about a nuclear arms race in south Asia.

Pokaran Fort & Museum The Pokaran Fort is an evocative place, although it has a rather ramshackle and abandoned atmosphere. The museum is nothing special, with an assortment of weaponry, some brocaded clothes, old wooden printing blocks and various games of former rulers of Pokaran, including dice and dominoes. There is a small shrine to Durga here.

The fort is open daily from 7 am to 7 pm; entry is Rs 20 and Rs 10 for a camera or video. There is no entry charge if you have a meal at the Fort Pokaran hotel.

Places to Stay & Eat A stop at Pokaran breaks the long journey between Jodhpur and Jaisalmer, but accommodation is lacklustre so most travellers stop here for lunch rather than overnight.

RTDC's Motel Godavan (☎ 02994-22275), 3km west of the bus stand, conveniently rents out double rooms with bath for a half/full day for Rs 200/300. There are also more expensive cottages (Rs 250/400 for a half/full day). An Indian lunch or dinner is Rs 135/165 for veg/nonveg. The continental veg/nonveg lunch or dinner is Rs 140/200. This place is a lot better than most other RTDC hotels.

Fort Pokaran (☎ 02994-22274, fax 22279), within the fort itself, offers accommodation not nearly as grand as that offered in some of Rajasthan's other amazing fort-and-palace complexes. It does have a certain faded appeal, but is in need of restoration. Singles/doubles with bath are rather overpriced at Rs 950/1100. Air-con

doubles are Rs 1500. Breakfast is Rs 110, the nonveg lunch or dinner is Rs 225.

Getting There & Away There are regular RSTC buses to Jaisalmer (2½ hrs, Rs 30). There are buses to Bikaner (4½ hrs, Rs 80) and to Jodhpur (4 hrs, Rs 45).

There are daily rail services to Jaisalmer (Rs 15) and Jodhpur (Rs 25).

JAISALMER
• pop 46,500   ☎ 02992

Nothing else in India is remotely similar to Jaisalmer. This enchanting city has been dubbed the 'Golden City' because of the honey colour imparted to its stone ramparts by the setting sun. The vision of Jaisalmer's massive fort thrusting heavenwards out of the barren desertscape is unforgettable, and the magic doesn't diminish as you approach its walls and bastions, and lose yourself in its labyrinthine streets and bazaars. The fort, which resembles a gigantic sandcastle, is home to several thousand people and this is what makes it so special. Although it is showing signs of decay, this desert fort is still like something out of *Tales of the Arabian Nights*.

Today, Jaisalmer is a major tourist tramping ground, with hordes of visitors converging on the town in the cooler winter months. The tourism boom in Jaisalmer has had some adverse effects. The number of hotels in the fort has increased and a major concern is that the poor plumbing and open drains have saturated the foundations, causing subsidence and collapse in buildings. The old open drains were created to take a limited amount of water and waste, and cannot cope with the pressure being placed upon them today. In 1997, the Jaisalmer Conservation Initiative (JCI) was formed to encourage sustainable tourism, as the city relies heavily on tourism revenue. JCI aims to save the fort through restoration, urban planning, and by raising local awareness of the problems facing the fort. Tourists can do their bit by simply showing an interest in conserving Jaisalmer's heritage and encouraging locals to take pride in it. As in other parts of Rajasthan, dispose of rubbish properly and try to encourage hoteliers to do so as well. For more information, contact the Jaisalmer Conservation Initiative, 71 Lodi Estate, New Delhi 110003 (☎ 011-463 1818, fax 461 1290), or the British-registered charity Jaisalmer in Jeopardy (☎/fax 0171-460 8592, after April 2000 ☎/fax 020-7460 8592, email jaisalmer@lineone.net), 20E Redcliffe Gardens, London SW10 9EX.

History

Most historians place the foundation of the city and fort at around 1156, when the Bhatti Rajput ruler Jaisala moved the city from the vulnerable former capital of Lodhruva, 15km to the north-west. Subsequent history has been derived from the tales and songs of the bards. The succession of maharajas of Jaisalmer trace their lineage back to a ruler of the Bhatti Rajput clan, Jaitasimha.

In the 13th century, the emperor of Delhi, Ala-ud-din Khilji, mounted an expedition to Jaisalmer to retrieve treasure which the Bhattis had taken from a caravan train en route to the imperial capital. He laid siege to Jaisalmer fort for nine years. When defeat was imminent, *jauhar* (collective sacrifice) was declared, the women of Jaisalmer committing themselves to the flames while the men donned saffron robes and rode out to certain death. The Rathores of Mallani mounted an unsuccessful raid on Jaisalmer, but were vanquished by Jaitasimha's son Duda. Duda perished in a later attack on the fort led by Ala-ud-din.

Duda's descendants continued to rule over the desert kingdom, and in 1541, Lunakarna of Jaisalmer fought against Humayun when he passed through Jaisalmer en route to Ajmer. The relationship between the Jaisalmer rulers and the Mughal empire was not always hostile, and various marriages were contracted between the two parties to cement their alliance. Later Jaisalmer notables include Sabala Simha, who won the patronage of the Muslim emperor Shah Jahan (reigned 1627-58), when he fought with distinction in a campaign at Peshawar. Although not the legitimate heir to the *gaddi*,

throne, Shah Jahan invested Sabala Simha with the power to rule Jaisalmer and he annexed areas which now fall in the administrative districts of Bikaner and Jodhpur.

The Jaisalmer rulers lined their coffers with illicit gains won through cattle rustling and by more orthodox methods such as imposing levies on the caravans which passed through the kingdom to Delhi. They were renowned both for their valour in battle and their treachery, as they fought to enlarge and secure their territories.

Religion and the fine arts flourished under the rulers of Jaisalmer, and although professing Hinduism, they were tolerant of Jainism, encouraging the construction of the beautiful temples which now grace the old city within the fort walls. Sculptural depictions of both Hindu and Jain deities and holy men stand side by side on the walls of these fine edifices. The visionary rulers commissioned scholars to copy precious sacred manuscripts and books of ancient learning which may otherwise have been lost during Muslim raids.

Jaisalmer's strategic position on the camel train routes between India and Central Asia brought it great wealth. The merchants and townspeople built magnificent houses and mansions, all carved from wood and golden-yellow sandstone. These havelis can be found elsewhere in Rajasthan (notably in Shekhawati), but nowhere are they quite as exquisite as in Jaisalmer. Even the humblest of shops and houses display something of the Rajput love of the decorative arts in its most whimsical form. It's likely to remain that way too, since the city planners are keen to ensure that all new buildings blend in with the old.

The rise of shipping trade and the port of Mumbai (Bombay) saw the decline of Jaisalmer. At Independence, Partition and the cutting of trade routes through to Pakistan seemingly sealed the city's fate, and water shortages could have pronounced the death sentence. However, the 1965 and 1971 Indo-Pakistan wars revealed Jaisalmer's strategic importance, and the Indira Gandhi Canal to the north is restoring life to the desert.

WESTERN RAJASTHAN

JAISALMER

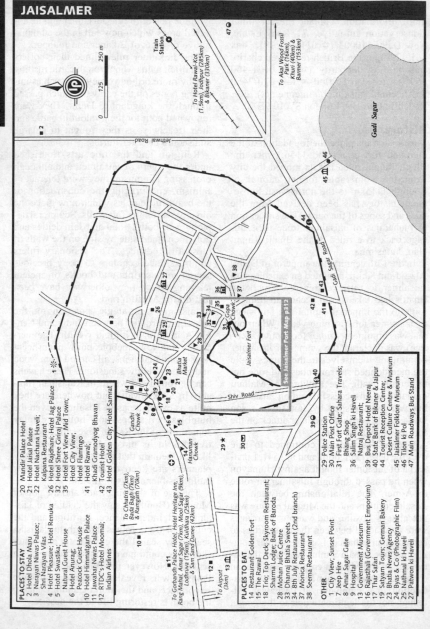

Gadi Sagar

Train Station

Jethwal Road

To Hotel Rawal-Kot
(1.5km), Jodhpur (285km)
& Bikaner (330km)

To Akal Wood Fossil
Park (16km),
Khuri (40km) &
Barmer (153km)

See Jaisalmer Fort Map p312

Jaisalmer Fort

Gopa Chowk

Bhatia Market

Gandhi Chowk

Shiv Road

Hanuman Chowk

Gadi Sagar Road

To Chhatris (7km),
Bada Bagh (7km)
& Ramgarh (70km)

To Gorbandh Palace Hotel, Hotel Heritage Inn,
Rang Mahal, Amar Sagar (7km), Mool Sagar (9km),
Lodhruva (15km), Kuldhara (25km)
& Sam Sand Dunes (42km)

To Airport
(3km)

0   125   250 m

PLACES TO STAY
2 Hotel Dhola Maru
3 Narayan Niwas Palace;
   Shri Narayan Vilas
4 Hotel Pleasure; Hotel Renuka
5 Hotel Swastika;
   Natural Guest House
6 Hotel Anurag;
   Peacock Guest House
10 Hotel Himmatgarh Palace
11 Jawahar Niwas Palace
12 RTDC's Hotel Moomal;
   Indian Airlines
20 Mandir Palace Hotel
21 Hotel Jaisal Palace
22 Hotel Nachana Haveli;
   Kalpana Restaurant
26 Hotel Rajdhani; Hotel Jag Palace
32 Hotel Shree Giriraj Palace
35 Hotel Fort View; Mid Town;
   Hotel City View;
   Hotel Flamingo
41 Hotel Rawal;
   Khadi Gramodyog Bhavan
42 Tourist Hotel
43 Hotel Golden City; Hotel Samrat

PLACES TO EAT
14 Restaurant Golden Fort
15 The Rawal
18 Trio; Top Deck; Skyroom Restaurant;
   Sharma Lodge; Bank of Baroda
28 Mohan Juice Centre
33 Dhanraj Bhatia Sweets
34 8th July Restaurant (2nd branch)
37 Monica Restaurant
38 Seema Restaurant

OTHER
1 City View; Sunset Point
7 Jeep Hire
8 Amar Sagar Gate
9 Hospital
13 Government Museum
16 Rajasthali (Government Emporium)
17 Thar Safari
19 Satyam Tours; German Bakery
23 Bhatia News Agency
24 Byas & Co (Photographic Film)
25 Nathmal ki Haveli
27 Patwon ki Haveli
29 Police Station
30 Main Post Office
31 First Fort Gate; Sahara Travels;
   Bhang Shop
36 Salim Singh ki Haveli
39 Bus Depot; Hotel Neeraj
40 State Bank of Bikaner & Jaipur
44 Tourist Reception Centre;
   Desert Culture Centre & Museum
45 Jaisalmer Folklore Museum
46 Tilon ki Pol
47 Main Roadways Bus Stand

Today, tourism rivals the military base as the pillar of the city's economy. The presence of the Border Security Force hardly impinges at all on the life of the old city and only the occasional sound of war planes in the distance disturbs the tranquillity of this desert gem.

Orientation

Jaisalmer is a fabulous place to explore at leisure. The streets within the old city walls are a tangled maze, but it's small enough not to matter. You simply head off in what seems like the right direction and you'll get somewhere eventually.

The old city was once completely surrounded by an extensive wall, much of which has sadly been torn down in recent years for building material. Some of it remains, however, including the city gates and, inside them, the massive fort which rises above the city and is the essence of Jaisalmer. The fort itself, which is entered via the First Fort Gate, is a warren of narrow, paved streets complete with Jain temples and the old palace of the former ruler.

The main market, Bhatia Market, is directly below the hill, while the banks, the new palace and several other shops and offices are near the Amar Sagar Gate to the west. Continue outside the walled city in this direction and you'll soon come to the turn-off to the RTDC's Hotel Moomal.

Information

Tourist Offices The Tourist Reception Centre (☎ 52406) is on Gadi Sagar Rd, about 2km south-east of the First Fort Gate. It's open daily except Sunday from 10 am to 5 pm and supplies various brochures, including a map of Jaisalmer (Rs 2). There's a smaller tourist information counter at the train station.

Money The Bank of Baroda at Gandhi Chowk changes travellers cheques and issues cash advances on Visa and Master-Card. The State Bank of Bikaner & Jaipur, opposite the Hotel Neeraj, changes travellers cheques and major currencies. In the fort, there's a small money exchange booth just before the Fourth Fort Gate, which changes money (but the rate may not be as good as the banks).

Post & Communication The main post office is on Hanuman Circle Rd, just west of the fort. It is open every day except Sunday from 10 am to 5 pm. Inside the fort is a small post office which only sells stamps; it's open Monday to Saturday from 10 am to 3 pm. There are ample phone booths (both inside and outside the fort), where you can call home.

Internet Resources At the time of writing, there were no places to surf the Net.

Bookshops Day-old newspapers as well as postcards can be bought at the well-stocked Bhatia News Agency, in Bhatia Market. There is an excellent selection of new books (especially novels) here, as well as some second-hand books (in English, French, German, Spanish and several other languages), which can be either bought or swapped.

In the fort, the Students' Book Store, near the 8th July Restaurant, has a reasonable selection of new books (in English, German, French and Spanish) and a 50% refund if you return them.

Film & Photography In Bhatia Market (opposite the Bhatia News Agency) is Byas & Co, where you can buy fresh slide and print film and batteries for still and movie cameras. A pack of Fuji print film (36 shots) costs Rs 90; Rs 210 for slide film. To develop print film they charge Rs 15 for developing, plus Rs 3 per print. It takes one day.

Jaisalmer Fort

Built in 1156 by the Bhatti Rajput ruler Jaisala, and reinforced by later rulers, the fort crowns the 80m-high Trikuta Hill. Over the centuries it was the focus of a number of battles between the Bhattis, the Mughals of Delhi and the Rathores of Jodhpur. This

JAISALMER FORT

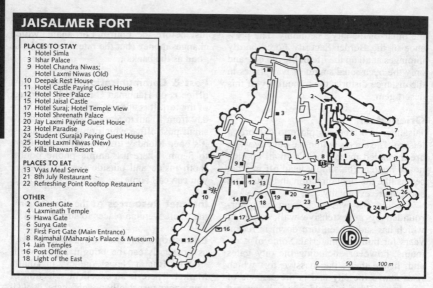

PLACES TO STAY
1 Hotel Simla
3 Ishar Palace
9 Hotel Chandra Niwas;
   Hotel Laxmi Niwas (Old)
10 Deepak Rest House
11 Hotel Castle Paying Guest House
12 Hotel Shree Palace
15 Hotel Jaisal Castle
17 Hotel Suraj; Hotel Temple View
19 Hotel Shreenath Palace
20 Jay Laxmi Paying Guest House
23 Hotel Paradise
24 Student (Suraja) Paying Guest House
25 Hotel Laxmi Niwas (New)
26 Killa Bhawan Resort

PLACES TO EAT
13 Vyas Meal Service
21 8th July Restaurant
22 Refreshing Point Rooftop Restaurant

OTHER
2 Ganesh Gate
4 Laxminath Temple
5 Hawa Gate
6 Surya Gate
7 First Fort Gate (Main Entrance)
8 Rajmahal (Maharaja's Palace & Museum)
14 Jain Temples
16 Post Office
18 Light of the East

0   50   100 m

is one of the planet's only living forts, with about a quarter of the old city's population residing in it. The fort has 99 bastions around its circumference and is protected by three walls. The lower wall is of solid stone blocks which reinforce the loose rubble of which Trikuta Hill is composed. The second wall snakes around the fort, and between this and the third, or inner, wall, the warrior Rajputs hurled boiling oil and water, and massive round missiles on their unwitting enemies below.

Above the fort flies the Jaisalmer standard, featuring a *chhatri*, or umbrella-shaped device, against a red and yellow background. The fort looks especially magical when it is lit up at night.

It's fascinating to wander around this living fort. It's packed with houses, temples, handicraft shops, beauty parlours, and honeycombed with narrow, winding lanes, all of them paved in stone. It's also quiet – vehicles are not allowed up here and even building materials have to be carried up by camel cart. The fort walls provide superb views over the old city and surrounding desert. Strolling around the outer fort ramparts is a popular activity at sunset.

The fort is entered from the First Fort Gate through a forbidding series of massive gates via an enormous stone-paved ramp, which leads to a large courtyard. The former maharaja's seven storey palace fronts onto this. The square was formerly used to review troops, hear petitions and present extravagant entertainment for important visitors.

Jain Temples Within the fort walls are seven beautifully carved Jain temples built between the 12th and 15th centuries, including very fine temples dedicated to Rikhabdev and Sambhavanth. They are all connected by a series of corridors and walkways, and are open daily from 7 am to noon. It is free to enter the complex; Rs 40/70 if you wish to take a camera/video inside. Shoes and all leather items must be removed before entering the temple.

The first temple you come to is that dedicated to **Chandraprabhu**, the eighth tirthankar, or Jain prophet. It was built in 1509 and features fine sculpture in sandstone in the mandapa. Around the inside of the drum are 12 statues of Ganesh, and around the hall which encompasses the inner sanctum are numerous statues of tirthankars. The mandapa is supported by elaborately sculpted pillars which form a series of toranas. No mortar was used in the construction of this temple; blocks of masonry are held together by iron staples. Around the upper gallery are 108 marble images of Parasnath, the 22nd tirthankar. In the inner sanctum is an image of Chandraprabhu. Note that the statue is unclothed. This is typical of Jain statues, and contrasts with those of Hindu deities, which are always elaborately garbed.

A few steps behind this temple is that dedicated to **Parasnath**. Entry is via an enormous and beautifully carved torana culminating in an image of the Jain tirthankar at its apex. However, this temple was not open to non-Jains (check if this is still the case). There is a voluptuous carving of a sinuous dancing woman balancing sets of balls on her raised forearm. The spacious mandapa is supported by fine pillars, and in the drum of the dome the sculptures are painted. They represent dancing figures and musicians, who welcome the gods.

A door on the south side of the temple leads to the small **Shitalnath Temple**, dedicated to the 10th tirthankar. The image of Shitalnath enshrined here is composed of eight precious metals. A door in the north wall leads to the beautiful **Sambhavanth Temple**. In the courtyard before this temple, Jain priests grind sandalwood in mortars for devotional use in the temples. As with the Parasnath Temple, the drum of the dome here has sculpted dancing figures. The statues flanking the wall are of Jaisalmer sandstone, but have been so highly polished they resemble marble. On either side of the inner sanctum, carved Jain saints stand with their heads hooded by cobras.

Steps in the courtyard of this temple lead to the **Gyan Bhandar**, a library founded in 1500 by Acharya Maharaj Jin Bhadra Suri. This small underground vault houses price-

less ancient illustrated manuscripts, some dating from the 11th century. Other exhibits include astrological charts and the Jain version of the Christian's Shroud of Turin: the Shroud of Gindhasuri, a Jain hermit and holy man who died in Ajmer. When his body was placed on the funeral pyre, the shroud was miraculously unsinged. In a small locked cabinet are images of Parasnath made of various precious stones, including emerald, crystal and ivory. The Gyan Bhandar is currently closed to visitors, but there are plans to shift the library outside the temple so it can be visited.

Steps lead from the courtyard before the Sambhavanth Temple to the **Shantinath Temple**, which was built in 1536. Curiously, the image enshrined here, which is made of eight different metals, is oriented to the north, rather than to the east as is customary. The enclosed gallery around this temple is flanked by hundreds of images of saints, some of marble, and some of Jaisalmer sandstone. Steps lead below this temple to the **Kunthunath Temple**, which was also built in 1536.

To the right of the Chandraprabhu Temple is the **Rikhabdev Temple**. There are some fine sculptures around the walls protected by glass cabinets, and the pillars are beautifully sculpted. This temple has a lovely, tranquil atmosphere. On the south side of the inner sanctum, a carving depicts a mother holding a child reaching up for fruit she is holding just out of reach. Behind the sanctum is a depiction of the Hindu goddess Kali, flanked by a Jain sculpture of a woman, unclothed. Here it is possible to compare the elaborately garbed Hindu statue with its unadorned Jain equivalent.

Laxminath Temple This Hindu temple, in the centre of the fort, is simpler than the Jain temples, although there are some interesting paintings in the drum of the dome. Devotees offer grain which is distributed before the temple. There is a repoussé silver architrave around the entrance to the inner sanctum, and a heavily garlanded image enshrined within.

Rajmahal Part of this palace is open to the public, although it's not comparable to the museum housed within the palaces at Meherangarh in Jodhpur. The entrance is to the right just after you pass through the last gate into the fort proper. It's open daily from 8 am to 5 pm, and entry costs Rs 10. A camera/video is Rs 20/50.

On the eastern wall is a sculpted pavilion-type balcony. Here drummers raised the alarm when the fort was under siege. The doorways connecting the rooms of the palace are quite low – not a reflection on the stature of the Rajputs, but to force those walking through to adopt a humble, stooped position, in case the room they were entering contained the maharaja.

A room on the east side of the palace affords fine views out over the entrance ramp to the fort and over the town spread beneath it. From here you can clearly see the numerous round rocks piled on top of the battlements, ready to roll onto advancing enemies. There is a small *diwan-i-am* (public audience hall) with the lower walls lined with porcelain tiles.

The adjacent room is lined with blue and white tiles. Upstairs, in a room close to the maharaja's private chamber on the east side of the palace, is a room which has some exquisitely carved stone panel friezes, which on first glance appear to be carved from wood. A door leads from the maharaja's chamber to the maharanis' chambers. There are very fine paintings in a room off this passage, but unfortunately it and the passage are closed to visitors. The views from the top of the palace are superb.

Havelis

There are several impressive havelis in Jaisalmer which were built by wealthy merchants, and some are in excellent condition.

Patwon ki Haveli This most elaborate and magnificent of all the Jaisalmer havelis stands in a narrow lane. It's divided into six apartments, two owned by the Archaeological Survey of India, two private homes, and two containing craftshops. The havelis were originally built between 1800 and 1860 by five Jain brothers who made their fortunes in trading jewellery and fine brocades. They retain remnants of paintings in vibrant reds and gold, as well as fine mirrorwork. There's a Rs 2 entry fee.

Salim Singh ki Haveli This private haveli was built about 300 years ago and part of it is still occupied. Salim Singh was the prime minister when Jaisalmer was the capital of a princely state, and his mansion has a beautifully arched roof with superb carved brackets in the form of peacocks. The stone elephants before the haveli are traditionally erected before the homes of prime ministers. The mansion is just below the hill and, it is said, once had two additional wooden storeys in an attempt to make it as high as the maharaja's palace, but the maharaja had the upper storeys torn down! Entry costs Rs 15, and it's open daily between 8 am and 6 pm.

Nathmal ki Haveli This late 19th century haveli was also a prime minister's house. The left and right wings of the building were carved by brothers and are very similar, but not identical. Yellow sandstone elephants guard the building, and even the front door is a work of art.

Gadi Sagar

This tank, south of the city walls, was once the water supply, and, befitting its importance in providing precious water to the inhabitants of this arid city, it is surrounded by small temples and shrines. A wide variety of waterfowl flock here in winter. The tank took advantage of a natural declivity which already retained some water, and was built in 1367 by Maharaja Gadsi Singh.

The beautiful yellow sandstone gateway arching across the road down to the tank is the **Tilon ki Pol**, and is said to have been built by a famous prostitute, Tilon. When she offered to pay to have this gateway constructed, the maharaja refused permission on the grounds that he would have to pass under it to go down to the tank, and he felt that this would be beneath his dignity.

While he was away, she built the gate anyway, adding a Krishna temple on top so that the king could not tear it down.

Museums

There are two museums, not far from each other, which house similar items. Next to the Tourist Reception Centre is the **Desert Culture Centre & Museum**, which has textiles, old coins, fossils, traditional Rajasthani musical instruments and a *karal* (opium mixing box), among other things. Its aim is to preserve cultural heritage and conduct research on local history. The museum is open every day from 9 am to 8 pm. Admission is Rs 5/10 for Indians/foreigners, which includes entry to the **Jaisalmer Folklore Museum** – located on the road leading down to the lake (open daily between 8 am and 7 pm). The hill near this museum is a tremendous place to soak up the sunset.

Close to the RTDC's Hotel Moomal is the small **Government Museum**, which is open daily except Friday from 10 am to 4.30 pm. Entry is Rs 3 (Rs 1 for students), free on Monday. Photography is not allowed. This museum has a limited although interesting collection of fossils, some of which date back to the Jurassic era (160 to 180 million years ago!), and other artefacts. Other exhibits include examples of ancient script, coins, religious sculptures (some from the 11th century), puppets and textiles. There is even a stuffed great Indian bustard, the state bird of Rajasthan, which thrives in the Thar Desert but is declining in numbers elsewhere.

Organised Tours

Few travellers visit Jaisalmer without taking a camel safari into the desert. For details, see the boxed text Camel Safaris Around Jaisalmer later in this section.

The Tourist Reception Centre offers a morning and evening city sightseeing tour (Rs 60 per person), and a sunset tour to the Sam sand dunes (Rs 100 per person). On request, the tours to Sam may stop at Kanoi, 5km before the dunes, from where it's possible to get a camel to the dunes in time for sunset (for about Rs 50).

The Hotel Fort View (see Places to Stay) has a travel counter (☎ 50740, ask for Om Vyas) which operates various excursions at very competitive prices. These include a three hour city sightseeing trip (Rs 30 per person), and a full-day trip which also incorporates attractions in the environs of Jaisalmer (Rs 200 per person including lunch). Both these tours require a minimum of four people. It can also arrange camel/jeep safaris to places of interest around Jaisalmer – a trip to Khuri, for instance, costs Rs 400 (maximum of six people), plus Rs 80 for a camel ride at sunset. You leave Jaisalmer at 3 pm and return at around 8 pm. Many other travel agencies in town offer similar excursions.

Places to Stay

Jaisalmer is a tourist hotbed, and many hotels have sprung up to meet the demand. In the past few years, the touting situation had reached such proportions that the district magistrate set up a mobile 'Tourist Protection Force', to keep the touts at a distance. Their aims are laudable – but alas they can only do so much. You may still encounter touts around the train and bus stations, trying to grab the new arrivals. Unfortunately, some of them are less than honest – don't believe *anyone* who offers to take you 'anywhere you like' for just a few rupees, and take with a grain of salt claims that the hotel you want to stay in is 'full', 'closed', 'no good any more' or has suffered some other inglorious fate. They'll only lead you to a succession of hotels, where of course they get commission if you stay. If you still insist on staying where *you* want, you'll be dropped unceremoniously outside the main fort gate, from where you'll have to walk. If you just want a lift into the centre, these people may be of use, but be prepared for the roundabout tour and pressure to stay in a particular place.

To overcome the touting problem, many of the popular budget hotels send a vehicle to meet you with a sign and free transport.

Camel Safaris Around Jaisalmer

The most interesting way to explore the desert is on a camel safari and virtually everyone who comes here goes on one. October to February is the best time.

Competition between safari organisers is cut-throat and standards vary considerably – there are often complaints that promises made were not kept. Touts will hassle you even before you get off the bus; at the budget hotels, rooms can be as little as Rs 20 – provided you take the hotel's safari. Talk to other travellers about who is currently offering good, reliable and honest service, and don't be pressured by agents who say if you don't go on the trip leaving tomorrow there won't be another until next week.

None of the hotels have their own camels, so the hoteliers and the travel agents are just go-betweens, though the hotels often organise the supplies. Don't jump at what appears to be a bargain. Camel drivers are paid around Rs 100 per camel per day, so if you're offered a safari at Rs 140 per day, this leaves only a small margin for food and the agent's profit. You can't possibly expect reasonable meals on these margins, but this is frequently what is promised. Then travellers feel they've been ripped off when the food is not what was offered.

The realistic minimum price for a basic safari is about Rs 350 per person per day. For this you can expect a breakfast of porridge, tea and toast, and a lunch and dinner of rice, dhal and chapatis. Blankets are also supplied. You must bring your own water. Of course, you can pay more for greater levels of comfort – tents, stretcher beds, better food, beer etc.

Several camel safari agents that are not linked to any hotels have been recommended. Sahara Travels (☎ 52609), by the First Fort gate, is run by Mr Bissa, alias Mr Desert. If you think you've seen his face it's because he's the rugged model in the cigarette ads. His basic tours cost Rs 350 a day for two to four days (you get your own camel). Tented safaris start at Rs 500. Other options include Satyam Tours (☎ 50773), at Gandhi Chowk, which also charges Rs 350 per person per night (you may have to share a camel), and nearby Thar Safari (☎/fax 52722), which has safaris from Rs 450 per person per night. Insist that all rubbish is carried back to Jaisalmer, and not left where the wind will carry it across the desert.

However much you decide to spend, make sure you know exactly what is being provided and that it's there before you leave Jaisalmer. And know where they're going to take you. Attempting to get a refund for services not provided is a waste of time.

Most safaris last three to four days to get to the most interesting places and this is a bare minimum. So bring something comfortable to sit on – many travellers come back with very sore legs and backsides! A wide-brimmed hat (or Rajput-style turban), long trousers, toilet paper, sun cream and a personal water bottle (with a strap so you can secure it) are recommended. A long-sleeved shirt is good protection from the sun. It can get very cold at night, so bring your sleeping bag if you have one, even if you're told that lots of blankets will be supplied. Women should consider wearing a sports bra, as the trotting momentum of the camels can cause some discomfort after even just a few hours.

If you're on your own it's worth getting a group of at least four people together before looking for a safari. Organisers will make up groups but four days is a long time to spend with people you might not get on with. Usually each person is assigned their own camel, but check this, as some agencies might try to save money by hiring fewer camels, meaning you'll share your camel with a camel driver or cook, which is not nearly as much fun. The reins are fastened to the camel's nose peg, so the animals are easily steered. At resting points, the camels are completely unsaddled and hobbled. They limp away to graze on nearby shrubs

Camel Safaris Around Jaisalmer

while the cameleers brew sweet chai or prepare food. The whole crew rests in the shade of thorn trees by a tank or well.

The desert is surprisingly well populated and sprinkled with ruins. You often come across tiny fields of millet, girls picking berries or boys herding flocks of sheep or goats. The latter are usually fitted with tinkling neck bells and, in the desert silence, it's music to the ears. Unfortunately the same cannot be said about the notoriously flatulent camels! Camping out at night, huddled around a tiny fire beneath the stars and listening to the camel drivers' yarns can be quite romantic. The drivers will expect a tip or gift at the end of the trip. Please don't neglect to do this.

Take care of your possessions, especially on the return journey. In one scam the drivers suggest you walk to nearby ruins while they keep an eye on your bags. The police station in Jaisalmer receives numerous reports of missing items but seems unwilling to help.

The usual circuit takes in such places as Amar Sagar, Lodhruva, Mool Sagar, Bada Bagh and Sam, as well as various abandoned villages along the way. You can't ride by camel to the Sam sand dunes in a day; in 1½ days you could get a jeep to Sam, stay there overnight, and take a camel from there to either Kuldhara or to Kanoi (catch a jeep back to Jaisalmer). If you're really pressed for time, you could opt for a half-day camel safari (with jeep transfers).

In 2½ days you could travel by camel to Lodhruva, spend the second night at the Sam sand dunes, and return the following day to Jaisalmer by jeep. If you have more time, obviously you can travel at a more leisurely pace through these regions and forgo the jeep component.

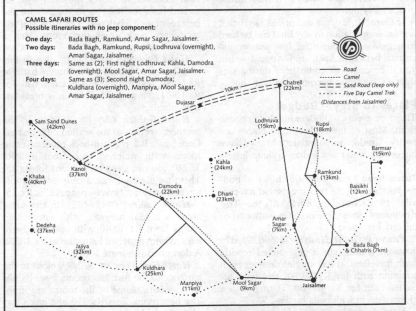

CAMEL SAFARI ROUTES
Possible itineraries with no jeep component:

One day:	Bada Bagh, Ramkund, Amar Sagar, Jaisalmer.
Two days:	Bada Bagh, Ramkund, Rupsi, Lodhruva (overnight), Amar Sagar, Jaisalmer.
Three days:	Same as (2); First night Lodhruva; Kahla, Damodra (overnight), Mool Sagar, Amar Sagar, Jaisalmer.
Four days:	Same as (3); Second night Damodra; Kuldhara (overnight), Manpiya, Mool Sagar, Amar Sagar, Jaisalmer.

Road
Camel
Sand Road (Jeep only)
Five Day Camel Trek
(Distances from Jaisalmer)

Chatrell (22km)
Dujasar
10km
Lodhruva (15km)
Rupsi (18km)
Barmsar (15km)
Sam Sand Dunes (42km)
Kahla (24km)
Ramkund (13km)
Baisikhi (12km)
Kanoi (37km)
Khaba (40km)
Damodra (22km)
Dhani (23km)
Amar Sagar (7km)
Dedeha (37km)
Bada Bagh & Chhatris (7km)
Jajiya (32km)
Kuldhara (25km)
Manpiya (11km)
Mool Sagar (9km)
Jaisalmer

Staying at one of the hotels within the fort itself is the most imaginative choice, but there are equally good hotels outside the fort walls. Motorised traffic is not permitted within the fort at most times, which means you'll have to lug your backpack up the steep ramp and cart it around with you while you check out the options. To overcome this, you could spend the first night in a guesthouse outside the fort walls, and check out the places to stay within the fort for subsequent nights unencumbered by your pack. Many hotels in Jaisalmer have an ungenerous 9 am check-out time.

Unfortunately, quite a few of the cheap hotels are really into the high-pressure selling of camel safaris. Some places can get quite ugly if you book a safari through someone else. Not only will they refuse to hold your baggage, they'll actually evict you from the hotel! Before you check in, make it clear that you will only stay if you don't have to do a safari – if they hassle you, simply move on.

If there's a festival on, prices skyrocket and accommodation of any kind can be hard to get. Many places offer low-season discounts between April and August – but you'd be crazy to come here during this time, as Jaisalmer becomes hellishly hot.

Places to Stay – Budget
There are plenty of budget hotels to choose from. Most of the rock-bottom places are pretty similar in standard. Many have bucket hot water and Indian-style toilets.

Town Area There's a good choice of budget hotels along the two streets that run parallel to each other north of the Trio Restaurant, about five minutes walk east of the city bus stand.

Peacock Guest House (☎ 50039) is a possibility, although it gets mixed reports from travellers. It has singles/doubles with common bath for Rs 30/50, and with attached bath for Rs 80/100. There's also a gloomy dorm with beds for Rs 25.

Hotel Swastika (☎ 52483), opposite the Peacock Guest House, gets better reports and deservedly so. It has decent singles/doubles with common bath for Rs 100/150; with attached bath for Rs 150/220 and Rs 220/250. Beds in the dorm are Rs 60. They even throw in a free cup of *chai* (tea) in the morning. It costs a steep Rs 20 per day to store luggage if you take a camel safari, unless you book through the hotel, when it's free.

Natural Guest House has three rooms with common bath for a low Rs 50/80, and one double with bath for Rs 100. It has a shop next door which sells stuff like biscuits, chocolate, mineral water and toilet paper.

Hotel Anurag (☎ 50276) offers singles/doubles with common bath for a mere Rs 30/40, or Rs 40/50 with attached bath. They also offer a free cup of tea. There are good rooftop views.

Hotel Renuka (☎ 52757), nearby, is a family-run place. Rooms with common bath from Rs 40 to Rs 100, and with attached bath for Rs 100 to Rs 200 for the best room with a balcony. There's a roof terrace here with great fort views, and a rooftop restaurant.

Hotel Pleasure (☎ 52323), also in this area, has good rooms with common bath for Rs 60/80, and rooms with attached bath for Rs 100/120 a single/double. Only breakfast is available.

Hotel Golden City (☎ 51664), in the southern section of the walled city, just off Gadi Sagar Rd, is a laid-back place offering rooms with attached bath from just Rs 35/50. You can sleep on the roof for Rs 15. There's a pleasant, reasonably priced rooftop restaurant; a 'lovely pancake' is Rs 35.

Hotel Samrat (☎ 51498), in the same area, is a real bargain, with very clean rooms from Rs 30/40 with common bath. Rooms with attached bath start at Rs 40/50. A dorm bed is a mere Rs 10.

Hotel Fort View (☎ 52214), close to the entrance to the fort, has rooms from Rs 66/88 with bath (some of the rooms are tiny). The best room costs Rs 350 and has a fort view. Travel bookings can be made here and there's a popular restaurant on the top floor.

Hotel City View (☎ 52804), next door, has tidy rooms with bath from Rs 50/60.

Hotel Flamingo (☎ 52889), also in this area, has rooms with common bath for Rs 30/45, or Rs 75/150 with bath.

Hotel Shree Giriraj Palace (☎ 52268) is a little bit farther west (towards Bhatia Market). This is a cheap and cheerful place with singles/doubles for Rs 50/80 with common bath, or Rs 80/120 with private bath. The best double is Rs 250, although the bathroom could be better for this price. There's a restaurant upstairs that has fort views.

Hotel Rajdhani (☎ 52746), near the Patwon ki Haveli, has small, spartan but clean rooms with common bath for Rs 60/100, and rooms with attached bath for Rs 150/200. There are larger rooms with balcony and air-cooling for Rs 300. Climb right to the top of the hotel for a fabulous fort view.

Hotel Jag Palace (☎ 50438), nearby, has decent rooms with bath for Rs 150/200. Vegetarian meals are available on the roof terrace.

Retiring rooms at the train station are not bad at all. Doubles with private bath are Rs 100 (try to get one of the thatched huts which are set back from the station). No meals are available.

Fort *Hotel Simla* (☎ 53061), in the north corner of the fort, is a wonderful place – you'll have no hassles here whatsoever. Rooms with common bath are Rs 60/100 and Rs 150/200. With attached bath, singles/doubles are Rs 250/350, and a pretty room with an alcove and balcony is Rs 300/450. It's possible to sleep on the roof for Rs 25, which includes a blanket, mattress and great view. There's also a small tent on the roof (Rs 50 a double). The manager, Jora, is a friendly fellow and you even get a free cup of tea.

Deepak Rest House (☎ 52665, fax 52070), in the western part of the fort, is a popular place, although it gets mixed reports about the service. Singles/doubles with common bath go for Rs 40/60, and rooms with attached bath start at Rs 60/80.

The bathrooms in some rooms are not the cleanest. A room with a view costs Rs 150/200. The best rooms are No 8 (Rs 250/300) and No 9 (Rs 300/350). The hotel is actually part of the fort wall, so the views from some rooms are stunning, as are those from the rooftop. Both rooms No 2 (Rs 100/125 with common bath) and No 16 (Rs 150/200 with attached bath) are in old circular bastions. A bed in the tatty dorm is Rs 20. The rooftop veg restaurant has a good range of dishes; veg biryani is Rs 30; french fries are Rs 25.

Hotel Chandra Niwas, nearby, is a splendid place to stay with just a handful of well-maintained double rooms, which range from Rs 70 with common bath to Rs 200 with attached bath. You'll be well taken care of here by the friendly owners. Veg meals are available.

Ishar Palace (☎ 53062) is near the Laxminath Temple. Rooms are spartan but quite clean, and cost Rs 50/80 for singles/doubles with common bath. A room with attached bath is Rs 100, or you might like to sleep on the roof (Rs 15). This was the home of a 19th century prime minister, Ishar Singh, as evidenced by the statues of elephants before the building. Meals can be arranged with advance notice.

Hotel Shree Palace (☎ 52327), near the Jain temples, has just been renovated. There are good views of the temples from the roof. Doubles start at around Rs 150.

Nearby *Hotel Castle Paying Guest House* (☎ 52988) has doubles with common/attached bath for Rs 100/250. Rooms are a little shabby but OK.

Hotel Laxmi Niwas (old) (☎ 52758) has very small rooms with common bath for Rs 50/100 (the common shower is a bit primitive, and the toilet is tiny). The menu is painted on the wall.

Hotel Laxmi Niwas (new) (☎ 52758) is in the south-east corner of the fort. It has only six rooms, ranging from Rs 200/250 with common bath to Rs 225/300 with attached bath. Although the rooms are nothing special, they are well kept.

Hotel Paradise (☎ 52674) is a very popular place with travellers. You'll see it on the far side of the main square from the palace as you come through the last gate into the fort. It's a kind of haveli, with 23 rooms arranged around a leafy courtyard and has excellent views from the roof. Singles/doubles with common bath are Rs 60/150, and doubles with bath cost from Rs 350 to Rs 650. It's possible to sleep on the roof for Rs 30 – a blanket and mattress are provided. Only breakfast is available.

Jay Laxmi Paying Guest House, nearby, has just two double rooms with a primitive attached bath for a very cheap Rs 80. You can get mehndi done here; a small arm 'tattoo' is Rs 20, and one hand is Rs 50. There are facials (around Rs 100), head massages (Rs 50 for 15 minutes) and body massages (Rs 100 for 30 minutes). Its *Geeta Restaurant* serves an extensive selection of veg Indian and continental dishes – a vegetable cheeseburger is Rs 30 and a 'desert thali' is Rs 100.

Hotel Temple View (☎ 52832), near the Jain temples, has small but decent rooms for Rs 60/100 with common bath, or Rs 250 for a double with private bath. The owner, Sunny, is a helpful chap.

Student (Suraja) Paying Guest House (☎ 50617), run by Pappu, has doubles with common/attached bath for Rs 75/400. It's in the south-east corner of the fort.

Places to Stay – Mid-Range
Town Area The charming *Hotel Nachana Haveli* (☎ 52110, fax 52778, Gandhi Chowk) is a 200-year-old haveli that has been converted into a hotel, with rooms set around a courtyard. Comfortable air-cooled rooms are Rs 650/750, and deluxe air-cooled rooms are Rs 950/1150. Meals are available with advance notice.

Hotel Jaisal Palace (☎ 52717, fax 50257), nearby, is a clean and well-run place with single/double/triple rooms from Rs 500/600/900. Go up to the chair swing on the roof terrace to soak up the view. Meals are available.

RTDC's Hotel Moomal (☎ 52392) is west of the walled city and the exterior is more impressive than the interior. In the grounds are air-cooled thatched huts for Rs

750. In the main complex, ordinary (and rather musty) rooms are Rs 450/500, and air-con rooms are Rs 750/900. Beds in the dorm cost Rs 50. There's a restaurant serving veg and nonveg fare.

Mandir Palace Hotel (☎ 52788, fax 51158, Gandhi Chowk), just inside the town walls, is a royal palace in part of which the erstwhile royal family still lives. Frankly it's a little bit run-down, and is not really great value for money. Ordinary rooms cost Rs 850/1350, and deluxe suites are Rs 1250/ 2000.

Hotel Neeraj (☎ 52442, fax 52545) is outside the town walls, south-west of the fort, fronting a busy road. Rooms are unremarkable; a single/double is Rs 700/800, or Rs 1000/1100 with air-con. The set breakfast/lunch/dinner is Rs 100/200/250.

Shri Narayan Vilas (☎ 52283) is inside the town walls, to the north of the fort. It is rather run-down but the rooms are OK. They start from Rs 525/625 a single/double.

Tourist Hotel (☎ 52484), in the southern part of the walled city, has reasonably large and clean doubles with bath for Rs 400. Next door is the slightly cheaper *Hotel Rawal* (☎ 52570), which is a little lacking in atmosphere, but not a bad choice.

Fort *Hotel Shreenath Palace* (☎ 52907), close to the Jain temples, is a family-run establishment in a beautiful old haveli. The rooms reek with atmosphere, with little alcoves and balconies, and some with magnificent sunset views over the temple. Omjee, the owner, claims descent from one of Jaisalmer's past prime ministers. Rooms (all doubles) cost Rs 350 with common bath and free bucket hot water (No 4 is a particularly nice room).

Hotel Suraj (☎ 51623), nearby, is another atmospheric old haveli which features fine sculpture on the facade and good views from the roof. Each room is different, and they all have attached bath with hot shower and start at Rs 300/350. The best rooms cost Rs 550/650. The restaurant serves basic veg fare; the set lunch/dinner is Rs 50/75. It also

continued on page 321

TRADITIONAL DRESS

Although it is not unusual to see Rajasthani women in *saris*, the traditional dress consists of a full, often brightly coloured, ankle-length skirt known as a *lehanga* or *ghaghara*, which is worn with a short blouse called a *choli* or *kanchali*. A looser blouse, a *kurti* or *angarkhi*, is worn over the choli. As well, an *odhni*, (head scarf) of a bold, vibrant fabric, either plain or patterned and often with a fancy border in silver thread, is worn. Sometimes odhnis are also adorned with mirrorwork, beads and shells. If the woman is a widow, the odhni is not brightly coloured. The leather shoes worn by men and women are called *jootis* or *mojdis*. Women's jootis have no heel. Men's jootis curl up at the toes.

For special occasions such as weddings and festivals, women decorate their palms, feet and fingers with intricate henna designs known as *mehndi*. The lehanga, traditionally worn by a bride, is generally a Sanganeri or Jaipur printed fabric, and the odhni is always red.

Everyday wear for men consists of a long shirt with either a short upright collar or no collar, which is known as a *kurta*. It is worn over a *dhoti*, which is simply a long piece of material wrapped around and

SARA-JANE CLELAND

Inset: Traditional Rajasthani fabric. Photo: Chris Mellor.

Top: Vibrant colours bring the desert to life.

Right: Women at Camel Fair, Pushkar.

Far Right: Traditional dancer at festival, Jaipur.

RICHARD I'ANSON

ANDREW LUBRAN

drawn up between the legs. Today Rajasthani men have adopted the *Jodhpuri*, a buttoned coat which is the official judicial dress of Rajasthan's courts. The turban is worn by men of most classes. It can be either plain or vividly coloured, and is tied in various ways according to the class of the wearer. Men also take pride in their moustaches. Rajputs are renowned for their long, bushy moustaches, which are supposed to suggest chivalry. As with turbans, the way the moustache is worn varies from region to region.

Bridegrooms traditionally carry a sword known as a *dalwar*.

Jewellery

Rajasthani women, most notably those in the villages, bedeck themselves in heavy and ornate jewellery, generally of silver, the lavishness and extent of which symbolises the relative affluence of their husbands. Even the poorest families ensure that their daughters are married appropriately adorned in silver ornaments, which form part of their dowries.

RICHARD I'ANSON

SARA-JANE CLELAND

SARA-JANE CLELAND

Top: Women waiting below Amber Palace.

Left: Tribal women, Pushkar.

Far Left: Young village woman wearing chudas.

The ornament worn by women on their forehead is known as a *bor*, *tikka* or *rakhadi*. Ear ornaments have various names, such as *jhela*, *bhujali*, or *bali*. Not just worn for decorative purposes, the manipulation of an earring is believed to restore equilibrium to internal organs. Nose pins and rings are known as *nathdis*, *laonghs* and *bhanvatiyas*, and are sometimes connected to earrings by silver chains.

Necklaces are known as *timania* and *galsadi*, among other names. They may be just a simple thread upon which a small token is hung, a beautiful and elaborate locket, or a heavy and chunky neckpiece of silver.

Bangles, which cover the entire arm, increasing in diameter from the wrist to just below the shoulder, are called *chudas*. Today, poorer women may wear chudas of plastic, while their richer sisters adorn their arms with ivory chudas. A chuda may also consist of a single ornament, often of silver, which covers the entire upper arm. Toe rings, known as *bichiyas*, are only worn by married women. The silver anklets worn by women are called *payal*. Silver ornaments worn on the back of the hand, and connected to four rings, one on each finger, are known as *hathphool*, from *phool*, meaning flower, and *hath*, for hand – literally, hand flower.

Top: Dressed for a festive occasion, Pushkar. Photo: Richard l'Anson.

Right: Preparing chapatis in Salawas village.

Far Right: Brightly coloured plastic jewellery.

MICHELLE COXALL

SARA-JANE CLELAND

MICHELLE COXALL

Rajasthani Turbans

The turbans of Rajasthan are perhaps the most colourful and impressive in the whole of India. Known as a *safa*, *paag* or *pagri*, the turban is a prominent and important part of a Rajput man's dress. It is said that turbans were first worn to protect the head from evil spirits. They were also worn in battle to protect the head against weapons such as swords and axes. A saffron-coloured turban signified chivalry, and was thus often worn by warriors. The exchange of turbans symbolises a bond of friendship and honour. There are a number of instances of wives burning themselves to death along with their husband's turban, the husband having fallen on a battlefield far from home. A male heir will don his deceased father's turban, a symbol of his assumption of duties as the head of the household. To kick or step over another man's turban is considered a big insult.

An average turban is about 9m long, but it can be much longer – up to 20m! It is possible to identify which part of Rajasthan a man comes from and his social class according to the way his turban is tied. Safa-style turbans are favoured by Rajputs, while businessmen prefer the pagri style. Today, not only is it traditional to wear a turban, but it also serves as protection from the harsh desert sun.

The versatile turban has a wide variety of other practical uses. It can be used as a pillow or sheet, a rope to draw water from a well, or as protective headgear in case the wearer falls over or is hit on the head!

Today many young men, particularly in cities such as Jaipur and Jodhpur, are rejecting the turban as a symbol of rural parochialism, although the turban is always worn by the groom at a marriage celebration.

MICHELLE COXALL

MICHELLE COXALL

Top: A Sikh from Alwar displays the *khanda* set in his turban. The khanda is a symbol of Sikhism and is made up of a double edged sword which cleaves truth from lies, a circle which represents the perfection of god, and two *kirpans*, reminding Sikhs of their equal responsibility to spirituality and society.

Left: Turban tying, Salawas village.

Far Left: Porter, Jaipur Train Station.

continued from page 320

has some cheaper rooms (Rs 250/350 a single/double with bath) at its nearby *Gokul Paying Guest House*.

Hotel Jaisal Castle (☎ 52362, fax 52101) is another restored haveli, this one is in the south-west corner of the fort. Its biggest attraction is its position, high on the ramparts overlooking the desert. The cheapest rooms are Rs 500/650, and both veg and nonveg meals are available. This is also one of the only places in the fort where you can get a beer (Rs 80). The only drawback to this hotel, is that the staff can be a bit indifferent at times.

Killa Bhawan Resort (☎ 51204), in the south-east corner of the fort, offers comfortable but somewhat small double rooms with common bath from Rs 1000 to Rs 1250. Only breakfast is available, which is included in the room rate. Although this place is comparatively expensive, it does have character.

Places to Stay – Top End

Rang Mahal (☎ 50907, fax 51305), about 2.5km west of the fort, is a dramatic building with impressive rooms from Rs 1500/1850. The deluxe suites (Rs 3800) are divine and a pool is being planned.

Gorbandh Palace Hotel (☎ 51511, fax 52749), nearby, is another upmarket modern hotel with traditional design elements. Constructed of local sandstone, the friezes around the hotel were sculpted by local artisans. Standard rooms in a fairly nondescript block behind the main building cost Rs 1195/2395 and there's a coffee shop, bar, restaurant, travel desk, and superb pool (open to nonresidents for Rs 200).

Hotel Heritage Inn (☎ 52769, fax 51638), next door, has rooms for Rs 1190/1950. A family suite is Rs 2950.

Jawahar Niwas Palace (☎ 52208, fax 52611), about 1km west of the fort, is a stunning palace, standing rather forlornly in its own sandy grounds. It has been vigorously renovated, and should be ready by now and worth checking out. Rates were expected to be Rs 2495/2995 for a single/ double.

Hotel Himmatgarh Palace (☎ 52002, fax 52005, 1 Ramgarh Rd) has comfortable rooms in the main block for Rs 1195/1950, and air-con cottages for Rs 2395. Breakfast/lunch/dinner is Rs 250/350/400.

Narayan Niwas Palace (☎ 52408, fax 52101) is closer to the fort, and counts among its former guests Britain's Princess Anne. However, these days the rooms get mixed reports from travellers. They cost Rs 1175/1800 a single/double. Suites are Rs 2050. There's a rather gloomy indoor swimming pool. Every evening there is a cultural program including traditional Rajasthani dancing, and nonguests are welcome to attend (Rs 300, including a buffet dinner).

Hotel Dhola Maru (☎ 52863, fax 53124, Jethwai Rd), to the north-east of the walled city, is a few kilometres from the fort entrance. It's a popular choice and although the location is not great, this is compensated for by the comfortable rooms. The design on some of the passage floor tiles can make you downright dizzy – so don't look when you walk! Air-con rooms are Rs 1100/1800, and suites are Rs 2050. There's an extraordinary little bar, which has incorporated tree roots into its décor, and a restaurant. Another good, if slightly inconveniently located, place in this category is the *Hotel Rawal-Kot (☎ 51874, fax 50444)*, located just east of Jaisalmer.

The Oberoi Group is planning to open an upmarket boutique hotel in Jaisalmer (similar to the Raj Vilas in Jaipur). Contact their Delhi corporate office for details on ☎ 011-291 4841, fax 292 9800.

Places to Eat

With so many tourists visiting Jaisalmer, you may find service at some restaurants rather lackadaisical. Nonetheless, there are plenty of places where you can kick back.

Town Area The *Mid Town*, Gopa Chowk, outside the fort, cooks up vegetarian food. A Rajasthani special thali is Rs 40, and most main courses are under Rs 50. The food is OK, but nothing to rave about, and the tables are tightly packed.

Monica Restaurant is a short distance away and gets lots of good reports from travellers. There's an extensive menu with Indian (including Rajasthani), continental and Chinese food. To taste authentic local specialities, try the Rajasthani thali (Rs 70), chicken curry (Rs 50), lasagna (Rs 65) and potato peas curry (Rs 35).

Natraj Restaurant is a few minutes walk down from the Monica and is also a good place to eat. Chicken Mughlai is Rs 50, palak paneer is Rs 35, and a beer will set you back Rs 70. For sweet-tooths, apple pie (Rs 35) and fried ice cream (Rs 30) feature on the dessert list. The open-air top floor has a nice view of the upper part of the Salim Singh ki Haveli next door, and away to the south of town.

Seema Restaurant, opposite the Natraj, has comparable prices and a range of veg and nonveg dishes.

Trio, near the Amar Sagar Gate, is worth a try. This long-running Indian and continental restaurant is pricier than its neighbours, but the food is excellent, and musicians play in the evening. The saagwala mutton (with creamed spinach) for Rs 80 is delicious. There's even mashed potato (Rs 30) – ideal for tender tummies.

Skyroom Restaurant has a somewhat limited menu, but has pretty good fort views. Half a tandoori chicken is Rs 80, a banana pancake is Rs 30 and a bottle of beer is Rs 70.

Kalpana Restaurant, in the same area, is quite frankly nothing special when it comes to the food, but it's a good place to just watch the world go by while sipping on a banana lassi (Rs 14) or snacking on a toasted chicken sandwich (Rs 30).

Top Deck, also in this area, has reasonably priced Indian, Chinese and continental cuisine. Options include chicken wings (Rs 55), egg curry (Rs 20) and sizzlers (Rs 50). Its fruit lassi (Rs 15) is refreshing.

Sharma Lodge (signboard in Hindi) is a very simple eatery located beneath the Top Deck. It has a filling Indian thali for Rs 20.

German Bakery is a small, simple place near Satyam Tours at Gandhi Chowk. Items on offer include croissants (Rs 8), peanut cookies (Rs 8) and various cakes (Rs 20 per slice).

Gorbandh Palace Hotel (see Places to Stay) is open to nonresidents and you can opt for buffet or à la carte dining. The all-you-can-eat buffet costs Rs 250/400/500 for breakfast/lunch/dinner, or you can just have a drink in the dimly lit bar.

Mohan Juice Centre, Bhatia Market, sells an assortment of interesting lassis, such as apple lassi (Rs 10), honey lassi (Rs 11) and even chocolate lassi (Rs 10). A glass of fresh orange juice is Rs 12.

Bhang Shop, outside the First Fort Gate, not far from Sahara Travels, is a government-authorised bhang shop! Lassis are Rs 25 per glass and bhang cookies can be baked with advance notice. Bhang does not agree with everyone – see the boxed text Bhang Lassi Warning under Drinks in the Facts for the Visitor chapter.

Dhanraj Bhatia Sweets, at Sadar Bazaar in Bhatia Market (opposite the 8th July restaurant's second branch outside the fort), has been churning out traditional sweet treats for the past 10 generations. It is renowned in Jaisalmer and beyond, for its local speciality sweets, such as ghotua and panchadhari ladoos (Rs 4.50 each). This simple little shop is worth visiting just to watch the sweetmakers ply their trade.

The Rawal, beside Hanuman Chowk, whips up interesting Indian dishes such as a tandoori thali (Rs 150) which contains tandoori chicken, chicken tikka, vegetable kebab, paneer tikka, butter naan and papadam. There's also an array of continental and Chinese fare and its mixed fruit lassi (Rs 22) is positively divine. There are fine fort views from this rooftop restaurant. Nearby is the *Restaurant Golden Fort* which also has panoramic views, but a more limited menu. Items include egg curry (Rs 30) and paneer tikka (Rs 50).

Fort The *8th July Restaurant*, above the main square in the fort, is certainly centrally located, but the food and service is variable. The menu largely caters to western tastes and is purely vegetarian. Vegemite-deprived Aussies can get the black wonder-spread here (Rs 30 for three slices of toast). Other menu items include cheese pizza (Rs 30), palak paneer (Rs 35) and apple pie (Rs 40). There's another branch outside the fort but it's not as atmospheric.

Refreshing Point Rooftop Restaurant, nearby, is better and so popular that you'll probably have to wait for a table. There's a phenomenal menu offering Indian, continental, Italian, Mexican, Tibetan, Chinese and even Greek cuisine. Moussaka is Rs 40, sizzlers are Rs 65, and enchiladas with rice and salad are Rs 40. It also serves hearty breakfasts. On the premises is a small German bakery selling goodies such as choco banana croissants (Rs 20) and cakes (Rs 20 per slice).

Vyas Meal Service, near the Jain temples, is a brilliant place to eat home-made food. This family-run veg restaurant offers traditional cuisine from Jaisalmer. It does wholesome thalis and also brews a jolly good masala tea. You can buy a packet of this tea for Rs 30 (makes 30 cups).

Shopping

Jaisalmer is famous for embroidery, Rajasthani mirrorwork, rugs, blankets, old stonework and antiques. Watch out for silver items as the metal may be adulterated with bronze.

Tie-dye and other fabrics are made at the Khadi Gramodyog Bhavan (Seemagram), at Dhibba Para, not far from the fort. Items for sale include tie-dye woollen shawls (upwards of Rs 370), cushion covers (upwards of Rs 66) and cotton bed sheets (doubles start at Rs 300).

There's a Rajasthani handicraft emporium, just outside Amar Sagar Gate, which sells all sorts of products, from embroidered cushion covers to wooden ornaments. There's a smaller branch at Gandhi Chowk.

On the laneway leading up to the Jain temples within the fort is an enthralling little shop, Light of the East, which sells crystals and rare mineral specimens, including zeolite, which can fetch up to Rs 5000 depending on the quality. Ask the owner to show you the amazing apophyllite piece which is carefully hidden away in a box. Don't set your heart on it – unfortunately it's not for sale.

Getting There & Away

Air Indian Airlines has flights between Jaisalmer and Jodhpur (US$60), Jaipur (US$110), Mumbai (US$175) and Delhi (US$140). Indian Airlines office (☎ 51912) is in the grounds of RTDC's Hotel Moomal and is open daily from 9.30 am to 1 pm and 2 to 5.30 pm.

Bus The main Roadways bus stand (☎ 51541) is some distance from the centre of town, near the train station. Fortunately, all buses start from a bus depot just behind the Hotel Neeraj, which is more conveniently located.

To Jodhpur there are frequent deluxe buses (5½ hrs, Rs 60). There is one daily deluxe bus which runs direct to Jaipur (13 hrs, Rs 130) and several daily direct deluxe buses which run to Bikaner (7 hrs, Rs 100).

You can book luxury buses through most of the travel agencies. Quoted rates were:

destination	Rs
Ajmer	140
Bikaner	110
Delhi	250
Jaipur	150
Jodhpur	75
Mt Abu	200
Udaipur	150

The trip to Udaipur requires a change of bus at Jodhpur. Others may also require a change en route, so check when making your booking.

Train The reservation office at the train station is open daily from 8 am to 8 pm.

The *IJPJ* leaves Jaisalmer daily at 7.15 am, arriving in Jodhpur at 3.30 pm (Rs 44/ 340 in 2nd/1st class). The *Jodhpur Express* leaves Jaisalmer at 10.30 pm and arrives in

Jodhpur at 5.20 am (Rs 124/568). From Jodhpur you can get rail connections to other destinations (see the Jodhpur section).

Jeep It's possible to hire jeeps from the stand on Gandhi Chowk. To Khuri or the Sam sand dunes expect to pay Rs 300 return with a one hour halt. For Lodhruva, you'll pay Rs 150 return with a one hour stop. To cut the cost, find other people to share with (maximum of five people per jeep).

Getting Around

Auto-Rickshaw Rickshaw drivers can be rapacious in Jaisalmer, so bargain hard. An auto-rickshaw to Gadi Sagar costs about Rs 15 one way from the fort entrance. From the fort to the airport it costs around Rs 30.

Bicycle A good way to get around is by bi·cycle. There are a number of hire places, including one at Gandhi Chowk in the lane opposite the Skyroom Restaurant (Rs 3/15 per hour/day), and one in the carpark area, just outside the main gate of the fort, which charges a steep Rs 5/40 per hour/day.

AROUND JAISALMER

There are fascinating places to see around Jaisalmer, although it soon fades into a barren sand dune desert which stretches across the lonely border into Pakistan.

Due to alleged arms smuggling across the border from Pakistan, most of Rajasthan west of National Highway No 15 is restricted area. Special permission is required from the Collector's office (☎ 02992-52201) in Jaisalmer if you want to go there, and is only issued in exceptional circumstances. Places exempted are Amar Sagar, Bada Bagh, Lodhruva, Kuldhara, Akal, Sam, Ramkund, Khuri and Mool Sagar.

Bada Bagh & Chhatris

About 7km north of Jaisalmer, Bada Bagh is a fertile oasis with a huge old dam. It was built by Maharaja Jai Singh II and completed after his death by his son.

Above the gardens are royal chhatris with beautifully carved ceilings and equestrian statues of former rulers. In recent years some have fallen into disrepair, but they are currently being restored. Entry is Rs 10.

Amar Sagar

This once pleasant formal garden, 7km north-west of Jaisalmer, has now fallen into ruin. The lake here dries up several months into the dry season. According to locals, the stepwells here were built by prostitutes.

Nearby is a finely carved Jain temple. Restoration commenced in the 1970s with craftspeople brought in from Agra in Uttar Pradesh. It is free to enter the temple, but it costs Rs 25/50 for a camera/video.

Lodhruva

Farther out beyond Amar Sagar, 15km north-west of Jaisalmer, are the deserted ruins of Lodhruva which was the ancient capital before the move to Jaisalmer. It was probably founded by the Lodra Rajputs, and passed to the ruler of Devagarh, Bhatti Devaraja, in the 10th century. In 1025, Mahmud of Ghazni lay siege to the town, and it was sacked various times over subsequent decades, prompting Jaisala to shift the capital to a new location, resulting in the foundation of Jaisalmer in 1156.

The **Jain temples**, rebuilt in the late 1970s, are the only reminders of the city's former magnificence. The main temple enshrines an image of Parasnath, the 23rd tirthankar, and is finely wrought in silver and surrounded by fine sculptures. The temple has its own resident cobra, which is said to be 1.5m long and over 400 years old. It lives in a hole on the north side of the main temple. It's supposed to be very auspicious to see the cobra, but probably as close as you'll get is viewing the photograph of it which is separately housed inside the temple.

The small sculptures around the lower course of the inner sanctum are badly damaged, and still bear the scars of Muslim raids. Behind the inner sanctum is a 200-year-old carved Jaisalmer stone slab which bears carvings of the tirthankars' feet in miniature. The ornate rosette in the centre of the drum of the dome over the mandapa was carved from a single piece of stone, and before the temple is a beautiful torana.

The small temple to the right is dedicated to Adinath, the first tirthankar.

There is nowhere to stay in Lodhruva – the *dharamsala* (pilgrims' lodging) beside the temple is for Jains only. There is a cold drink stall opposite the entrance to the temple. It's free to enter the temple (Rs 40/70 for a camera/video). You can hire a guide (Rs 50) at the temple. There are three daily buses from Jaisalmer to Lodhruva (Rs 5).

Mool Sagar

Situated 9km west of Jaisalmer, this is another pleasant but rather neglected, small garden and tank. It belongs to the royal family of Jaisalmer and was originally built as a cool summer retreat. In the lemon grove, there's a small Shiva temple carved from two pieces of sandstone. Admission is Rs 5.

Kuldhara

This small village is located 25km west of Jaisalmer. Around 400 years ago, all the villagers left after a dispute with the prime minister. However, according to legend, they couldn't carry all their gold and silver, so they buried it. Several years ago some westerners arrived at Kuldhara on motorcycles armed with gold detectors and found hundreds of gold and silver coins. However, local villagers became suspicious and called the police, and the treasure hunters were apprehended and divested of their booty! Kuldhara is included on some of the extended camel treks.

Restoration work is being done; there's a Rs 5 entry fee, plus Rs 50 for car entry.

Sam Sand Dunes

A desert national park has been established in the Thar Desert near Sam village. One of the most popular excursions is to the sand dunes on the edge of the park, 42km from Jaisalmer along a very good sealed road (which is maintained by the Indian army).

This is Jaisalmer's nearest real Sahara-like desert. It's best to be here at sunrise or

sunset, and many camel safaris spend a night at the dunes. Just before sunset jeep loads of trippers arrive from Jaisalmer to be chased across the sands by tenacious camel owners offering short rides and young boys selling soft drinks. Yes, this place has become a massive tourist attraction, so don't set your heart on a solitary desert sunset experience. The hordes of people here at sunset turns the place into somewhat of a carnival atmosphere. If you want a less touristy sand dunes experience , Khuri is a much more peaceful and pristine alternative (see following).

Despite the tourist hype, it is still quite a magical place, and it's possible to frame pictures of solitary camels against lonely dunes. The desert dung beetles are fascinating to watch. These industrious little creatures can roll lumps of dung twice their size. It's a heartbreaking sight to see a beetle lose control of a piece of dung it has rolled halfway up a sand dune.

One tragic consequence of the increasing number of visitors to the dunes is the debris and rubbish lying at their base. Visitors are now charged Rs 2 to visit the dunes, money which could be put to good use to clean them up, but is more likely lining the pocket of some local official. If you feel strongly about the rubbish here, a letter to the Chief Tourism Officer, RTDC Tourism, Hotel Swagatam Campus, Near Railway Station, Jaipur 302006, Rajasthan, might have some effect. For further information, contact the Deputy Director, Desert National Park, Jaisalmer (☎ 02992-52489).

Places to Stay & Eat There's really only one place to stay, but most travellers prefer to visit the dunes on a day trip from Jaisalmer anyhow.

RTDC's Hotel Sam Dhani has eight good double rooms with attached bathroom for Rs 300, and dorm beds for Rs 50. There is currently no power, but lanterns are provided. Veg meals are available; a thali is Rs 58. Bookings can be made through the RTDC's Hotel Moomal (☎ *02992-52392*) in Jaisalmer.

Getting There & Away There are three daily buses to Sam (1½ hrs, Rs 15).

Khuri

Khuri is a small village 40km south-west of Jaisalmer, with its own desert sand dunes. It has far less tourist hype (at least for now) than the Sam sand dunes, and is becoming increasingly popular for camel/jeep safaris. It's a peaceful place with houses of mud and straw decorated like the patterns on Persian carpets. There are, thankfully, no craftshop-lined streets or banana pancake restaurants. The attraction out here is the desert solitude and the brilliant star-studded sky at night.

Places to Stay & Eat Places to stay in Khuri are pretty basic with charpoys and bucket hot water. All provide meals and most can arrange camel safaris. Accommodation is limited and you won't get any bargains; basically you're paying for the peace and quiet rather than the facilities, which are minimal.

Khuri Guest House (☎ 02992-75444) is on the left of the main road as you enter the village. It's run by a friendly fellow and has conventional rooms with common bath for a reasonably Rs 75/100. Huts with common bath are Rs 100/125 a single/double, or Rs 300 for a double with private bath. Camel safaris are Rs 300 per person per day.

Mama's Guest House (☎ 02992-9267 5423) is actually clusters of thatched huts. The cheapest costs a rather hefty Rs 350 per night with common bath, which includes meals and free bucket hot water. These cost Rs 200 in the low-season, but would be hellishly hot. The huts are set in a semi-circle around a campfire. There is a group of huts for Rs 450 each, which have a greater number of common bathrooms, and are better thatched, so will be cooler. The top-of-the-range huts are Rs 750, and include an electric fan. There are only two huts in this group, so it's very private. It's also possible to stay in a conventional room (but not nearly so romantic!) for Rs 300 with common bath. Camel safaris in the region range from Rs 350 to Rs 750 per day.

Sodha Guest House (☎ 02992-926 75403) has doubles with common bath for Rs 150. Lunch/dinner is Rs 100 per person and camel excursions can be organised.

Gangaur Guest House (☎ 02992-9267 5464) has huts ranging from Rs 150 to Rs 300. Lunch/dinner is Rs 150.

Getting There & Away There are several buses daily to Khuri from Jaisalmer (2 hrs, Rs 13).

Akal Wood Fossil Park

Three kilometres off the road to Barmer, 16km from Jaisalmer, are the fossilised remains of a 180-million-year-old forest. To the untrained eye it's not very interesting. Entry to the park is Rs 5/20 for Indians/foreigners, plus Rs 10 per vehicle. Guides (Rs 50) are available, although there were none when this author visited. The park is open daily from 8 am to 1 pm and 2 to 5 pm.

BARMER
☎ 02982

Barmer is a centre for woodcarving, carpets, embroidery, block-printing and other handicrafts and its products are famous. The centre for embroidery is Sadar Bazaar; crafts are for sale on Station Rd at more reasonable prices than you'll find elsewhere. Otherwise this desert town, 153km south of Jaisalmer, isn't very interesting, and few travellers make the trek out here. There's no fortress and perhaps the best part is the journey here through peaceful, small villages, their mud-walled houses decorated with geometric designs. Barmer district hosts two major festivals – see the boxed text Festivals of Western Rajasthan earlier.

Places to Stay & Eat

RTDC's Khartal (☎ 22956), out of the town centre, has neat, clean singles/doubles with bath for Rs 225/350. A veg thali is Rs 60.

Hotel Krishna (☎ 20785, Station Rd) has good singles/doubles with common bath for Rs 100/200, or Rs 300 for a double with bath. An air-con double is Rs 700. There's a restaurant.

Kailash Sarover Hotel (☎ 20730, Station Rd), farther away from the station and on the opposite side, has cheaper rooms. These start at Rs 75/100 with common bath; air-cooled rooms with attached bath go for Rs 175/250, and with air-con, geyser and TV they're Rs 400/550. Veg food is available. This place is not quite as impressive as the Hotel Krishna.

Raj Restaurant (Station Rd), between the train station and the Hotel Krishna, has vegetarian dishes at reasonable prices.

Getting There & Away

There are several daily express buses to Jodhpur (4 hrs, Rs 82) from in front of the train station. To Jaisalmer, there are frequent daily express buses (4 hrs, Rs 58). They leave from the main bus stand, which is about 1km north of the train station.

There is a train which goes to Luni (Rs 30), from where you can catch a connecting train to nearby Jodhpur. Barmer should soon be converted to broad gauge, enabling greater rail connections.

AROUND BARMER

About 35km from Barmer, the **Kiradu Temples** feature very fine sculpture. The temples conform to a style of architecture known as Solanki, and the most impressive of the five temples here is the **Someshvara Temple**, which has a multiturreted spire and beautiful sculpture. However, you'll need permission from the District Magistrate (☎ 02992-20003) and superintendent of police (☎ 02992-20005) to visit it, as it's on the border road towards Pakistan.

BIKANER

- **pop 493,000**   ☎ 0151

Bikaner holds a secondary rank amongst the principalities of Rajputana. It is an offset of Marwar, its princes being scions of the house of Jodha, who established themselves by conquest on the northern frontier of the parent state; and its position in the heart of the desert, has contributed to the maintenance of their independence.

Excerpt from Colonel James Tod's *Annals &
Antiquities of Rajasthan*

This desert town in the north of the state was founded in 1488 by Rao Bika, a descendant of Jodha, the founder of Jodhpur. Like many others in Rajasthan, the old city is surrounded by a high crenellated wall and, like Jaisalmer, it was once an important staging post on the great caravan trade routes. The Ganga Canal, built between 1925 and 1927, irrigates a large area of previously arid land around Bikaner.

As the tourist hype in Jaisalmer heightens, Bikaner is becoming more and more appealing to travellers. It's easy to see why – Bikaner has a brilliant fort, camel safaris (see Organised Tours later) and 30km to the south is the extraordinary Karni Mata Temple in Deshnok (see Around Bikaner) where thousands of holy rats are worshipped.

Orientation

The old city is encircled by a 7km long city wall with five entrance gates, constructed in the 18th century. The fort and palace, built of the same reddish-pink sandstone as Jaipur's famous buildings, are outside the city walls.

Information

Tourist Offices The Tourist Reception Centre (☎ 544125), headed by the helpful Mr RS Shekhawat, is in the RTDC's Hotel Dhola Maru compound, about 1km from the city centre on Pooran Singh Circle. The office is open every day except Sunday from 10 am to 5 pm. It has various brochures (including a good map of Bikaner for Rs 2) and a toilet that can be used by tourists.

Money Travellers cheques and currency can be changed at the State Bank of Bikaner & Jaipur (SBBJ), near the Thar Hotel, PBM Hospital Rd. There's another SBBJ branch, known as the public park branch (not far from Junagarh), where you can also change money. At the time of writing, no banks issued cash advances on credit cards.

Post The main post office is near Junagarh and is open daily except Sunday from 10 am to 1 pm and 2 to 4.30 pm.

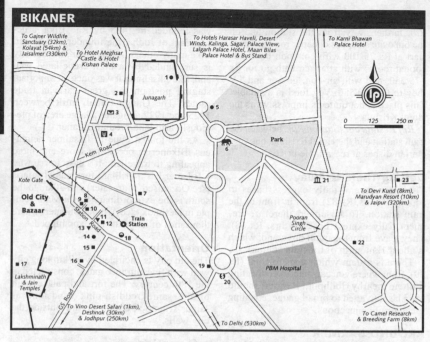

BIKANER

PLACES TO STAY
2 Bhairon Vilas
7 Hotel Jaswant Bhawan
8 Hotel Akashdeep;
   Hotel Amit;
   Delight Guest House
9 Hotel Deluxe & Restaurant
10 Evergreen Hotel
12 Hotel Joshi; Kwality
15 Hotel Shri Shanti Niwas
16 Indre Lodge;

Hotel Marudhar Heritage
17 Hotel Bhanwar Niwas
19 Thar Hotel
22 RTDC's Hotel Dhola Maru;
   Tourist Reception Centre
23 Hotel Padmini Niwas

PLACES TO EAT
11 Chhotu Motu Joshi Sweet
   Shop
13 Amber Restaurant

OTHER
1 Abhivyakti (Urmul Trust Shop)
3 Main Post Office
4 Ratan Behari Temple & Garden
5 Courts
6 Zoo
14 Dau Cycle Shop
18 Taxi Stand; Clock Tower
20 State Bank of Bikaner & Jaipur
21 Ganga Golden Jubilee
   Museum

Internet Resources Only one place had Internet facilities, at 7/C Sadul Ganj, opposite the Moomal Restaurant, not far past the Tourist Reception Centre. It is a private residence, so you will need to ask for Arun Badia (☎ 521545) to organise access. It costs Rs 15 to send an email and Rs 10 to receive one.

Junagarh

Junagarh would have to be one of Rajasthan's most impressive fort complexes. It was constructed between 1588 and 1593 by Raja Rai Singh, a general in the army of the Mughal emperor Akbar, with embellishments in the form of palaces and luxurious suites added by subsequent maharajas. This fort has a 986m-long wall with 37 bastions, a moat and two entrances. The **Surajpol**, or Sun Gate, is the main entrance. The palaces within the fort are on the southern side and make a picturesque ensemble of courtyards, balconies, kiosks, towers and windows. A major feature of the fort and palaces is the superb quality of the stone carving.

Despite the fact that Junagarh doesn't command a hilltop position, as do some of Rajasthan's other grand forts, it is no less imposing and – a credit to its planners and architects – has never been conquered.

The fort is open daily from 10 am to 4.30 pm. Entry is Rs 10/50 for Indians/foreigners, and to take in a camera/video is Rs 30/50. You may be besieged by 'guides' offering their services before you arrive at the ticket counter. Unless you want an individual tour, this is unnecessary, as the ticket price includes a tour with a group and official guide.

The gold-painted ceiling of the beautiful **diwan-i-khas** (private audience hall) was executed in 1631, and the silver gaddi of the maharajas can still be seen here. Before the Anup Mahal (see the next paragraph) is a fine courtyard, paved with Italian tiles. Through the fine lattice screens around the courtyard, the ladies of the zenana could watch the activities below. In the **Phool Mahal**, or Flower Palace, which was built during the reign of Maharaja Gaj Singh, is a marble statue of Surya, the sun god, and around the upper edges of the walls, there are paintings depicting scenes from the *Ramayana*.

The beautiful **Anup Mahal** was commissioned by Maharaja Karan Singh (1631-69). According to local lore, the maharaja was camping at Golkonda, in southern India, in his capacity as a general in the Mughal army, when an artist showed him fine works in gold. The artist told the maharaja that he originally hailed from Jaisalmer, but had migrated to southern India when a famine swept over his homeland. The maharaja was inspired by the proficiency and great beauty of the work he had been shown, and invited the artist to return to Bikaner where he was given royal patronage.

It is the work of this artist and of his students which features in the Karan Mahal and Anup Mahal. Three types of work can be seen here: the *sonakin* style features white plaster decorated with delicate patterns and painted with gold leaf; the *jangali sunthari* style features plaster with a green background depicting floral motifs; and the *manovat* style features a pillar of clay embossed on plaster and the entire work painted with gold leaf.

In the **Badal Mahal**, or Cloud Palace, the walls are painted with blue cloud motifs and there is a statue here of Vishnu and Laxmi. The large pillars were installed with the aid of elephants nearly 400 years ago.

The **Gaj Mandir** was the private chambers of Maharaja Gaj Singh. The maharani's chamber is decorated with mirror tiles and gold painting, and on the ceiling is wooden lac painting. The maharaja's chamber has a beautiful painted wood ceiling featuring florets and geometric motifs, and carved ivory doors.

In the **Hawa Mahal**, or Summer Palace, is an ingenious device which alerted the maharaja to potential enemies: a mirror positioned over the bed enabled Maharaja Dunga Singh to see reflections of those people walking across the courtyard below – or at least this is the purpose of the mirror according to the official fort guides! The ceiling features floral arabesques and scenes of Krishna dancing. The blue tiles were imported from both Europe and China.

The handprints which can be seen close to the **Daulatpol** commemorate the wives of Rajput soldiers lost in battles who committed sati on their husbands' funeral pyres.

Museum This interesting exhibition is housed in several rooms at the fort. In the armoury are enormous bore guns which were used for shooting from the backs of camels, as well as the usual collection of sinister-looking pistols and swords.

In the diwan-i-khas of Ganga Singh are three massive arches, intricately carved, and a throne of sandalwood. Here also can be seen a 56kg suit of armour, including chain mail, and sculptures of Krishna dancing and stealing the clothes of the gopis. Beautiful if deadly weapons, each an exquisite work of art – swords with ivory and crystal handles, some in the shape of lions – can also be seen here. In a separate chamber are the royal vestments of Maharaja Ganga Singh, as well as items from his office including a paperweight and his briefcase. From a gallery it is possible to look down on an old biplane which was presented to Ganga Singh by the British government during WWI. This is one of only two models of this plane in the world.

Jain Temples

Two Jain temples can be found in the southeast end of the walled city. They are closed to visitors daily between noon and 4 pm. The **Bhandasar Jain Temple** is dedicated to the fifth tirthankar, Sumtinath, and the building was commissioned in 1468 by a wealthy Jain merchant, Bhandasa Oswal. It was completed after his death, in 1514.

The interior of the temple is stunning, with, unusually for a Jain temple, a series of vibrant paintings. The pillars bear floral arabesques and stories which depict the lives of the 24 Jain tirthankars. It is said that 40,000kg of ghee was used instead of water in the mortar, which locals insist seeps through the walls on hot days.

There are fine carvings on either side of the inner sanctum, which is also decorated with English tiles. The floor is covered in Italian marble, and the foundation stones were transported from Jaipur. The corners of the inner sanctum have elaborate carvings depicting the 24 tirthankars. The inner sanctum enshrines an image of Sumtinath. The altar is covered in gilt and mirrorwork.

On the 1st floor of the three storey temple are beautiful miniatures of the sentries of the gods. There are fine views out over the city from the 3rd floor, with the desert stretching behind it to the west. Photography is permitted inside the temple.

The second Jain temple here is the **Sandeshwar Temple**. It is smaller than the Bhandasar Temple, and has good carving around the door architraves and columns, and ornately carved painted pillars. Inside the drum of the *shikhara* (spire) are almost ethereal paintings, and the sanctum itself has a marble image of Sandeshwar flanked by smaller marble statues of other Jain tirthankars.

Lakshminath Temple

Behind the Bhandasar Temple, to the right, is the Hindu Lakshminath Temple. It was built during the reign of Rao Lunkaran between 1505 and 1526. Lakshminath was the patron god of the rulers of Bikaner, and during major religious festivals a royal procession led by the maharaja paid homage at the temple. The elaborate edifice was maintained with tributes received from five villages and several shops which were granted to the temple by Maharaja Ganga Singh (1887-1943). Photography at this temple is not permitted.

Lalgarh Palace

This red sandstone palace, 3km north of the city centre, was built by Maharaja Ganga Singh in memory of his father Maharaja Lal Singh. Although it's an imposing building with overhanging balconies and delicate latticework, it's not the most beautiful of Rajasthani royal residences.

The **Shri Sadul Museum** covers the entire 1st floor of the palace. The museum was established in 1976 and is open daily except Wednesday from 10 am to 5 pm. Entry is Rs 5 and photography is not allowed. There is a reasonable collection of artefacts and personal possessions of the Bikaner maharajas, reflecting the privileged lifestyles of these rulers, including (empty!) wine and sherry bottles and a brass vessel known as a *tokna* used to collect revenue which was transported by camel to the Bikaner state treasury. There's even a funky old film projector made in New York in 1921. Other more pedestrian exhibits include Maharaja Karni Singh's golf tees, an electric toothbrush, swimming goggles, and even his earplugs and sneakers! There is also a somewhat disturbing pictorial display of tiger carnage, including a shot of the five tigers shot in three minutes by Maharaja Ganga Singh in 1937.

In front of the palace is a carriage from the maharaja's royal train.

Ganga Golden Jubilee Museum

This interesting museum is on the Jaipur road and is open daily except Friday from 10 am to 4.30 pm. Entry is Rs 3; only still cameras (no videos) are permitted (no charge). Exhibits include terracotta ware from the Gupta period, a range of Rajasthani traditional musical instruments, miniature wooden models of the Gajner and Lalgarh palaces and a miniature of the Royal Bikaner train with the roof folded back to reveal its comfortable amenities. There is a separate exhibition hall with antique carpets and royal vestments.

Other interesting exhibits include decrees issued by the Mughals to the maharajas of Bikaner, including one advising Rai Singh to proceed to Delhi 'without any delay and with utmost expedition and speed, travelling over as great a distance as possible during the day time as well as by night' as 'Emperor Akbar is dying'. It was issued by Crown Prince (who would shortly become Emperor) Jehangir.

There are also some fine oil paintings, including one entitled 'Maharaja Padam Singh avenging ... the death of his brother, Maharaja Mohan Singhji by killing the Emperor's brother-in-law ... He drew his sword, rushed upon his enemy ... and severed him in two with a blow which also left a mark upon the pillar'!

The sculptures include a beautiful and voluptuous image of Devi, and a marble Jain sculpture of Saraswati which dates from the 11th century.

Organised Tours

The Tourist Reception Centre (see Information earlier) can arrange English-speaking guides (Rs 75/250 for two hours/full day).

If you wanted to take a camel safari in Jaisalmer but didn't because it was too much of a scene, Bikaner is an excellent alternative. One good camel safari operator is

Vino Desert Safari (☎ 204445, fax 525150), opposite the Gopeshwar Temple. It's run by the helpful Vinod Bhojak. There are camel treks (minimum of two days) for Rs 400 per person per day, including meals and blankets (you sleep under the stars). More expensive safaris in tented accommodation are also available. English-speaking guides are provided with these safaris and Vinod also speaks some French and German.

Safaris can be tailor-made according to your preferences and some options include a visit to Deshnok (see Around Bikaner) and Bishnoi villages. For more upmarket camel safaris, there's Rajasthan Safaris & Treks (☎ 543738); prices begin at about Rs 1200 per person per day (minimum of six people).

Places to Stay – Homestays

The Tourist Reception Centre at the RTDC's Hotel Dhola Maru (☎ 544125) has a list of families registered with Bikaner's Paying Guest House Scheme. It costs from around Rs 200 to Rs 500 per night.

Places to Stay – Budget

There are numerous budget options, many near the train station. Station Rd is an amazingly busy thoroughfare, so the noise level in any room fronting it can be diabolical – choose carefully. Many places in the rock-bottom bracket have Indian-style toilets.

Hotel Meghsar Castle (☎ 527315, fax 522041, 9 Gajner Rd) is popular with travellers and has clean, spacious singles/doubles with attached bathroom from Rs 250/300 to Rs 500/800. Meals are available; a chicken curry costs Rs 90. *Hotel Kishan Palace (☎ 527762)*, next door, has a budget cottage (which can get traffic noise) for Rs 100/150 with attached bath, and regular rooms with bath from Rs 200/300 to Rs 300/400. Meals are available.

Hotel Desert Winds (☎ 542202), north of the fort, near the Karni Singh Stadium, has singles/doubles with private bath from Rs 200/250 to Rs 400/550. Meals are available.

Evergreen Hotel (☎ 542061) is not a bad choice. Rooms are clean and have a TV.

Singles/doubles with common bath are Rs 80/125; with attached bath Rs 125/175/200 for singles/doubles/triples. All rooms have hot water by the bucket (Rs 5). There's a restaurant downstairs, which serves veg Indian, Chinese and continental food. A veg biryani is Rs 30, cheese pizza is Rs 40, and an almond milkshake is Rs 15.

Hotel Deluxe (☎ 528127), nearby, is not as good – travellers have complained about the cleanliness. Basic singles/doubles with attached bath are Rs 100/130. Veg meals are available.

Hotel Akashdeep (☎ 543745), behind the Hotel Deluxe, has somewhat shabby rooms with bath for Rs 100/150 and free hot water by the bucket. This is not the most welcoming place for lone female travellers.

Delight Guest House (☎ 542313) is in the laneway behind the Hotel Deluxe. Quite frankly, this is a dingy flophouse, but rooms are quite cheap at Rs 55/80 with common bath, and Rs 80/110 with attached bath. Hot water is available in buckets for Rs 4. Only breakfast is available.

Hotel Amit (☎ 544451) is also in this laneway. The impressive looking marble lobby is deceptive – rooms are cramped and tatty. They cost Rs 100/150 with common bath, or Rs 200/300 with attached bath (hot water in buckets). Meals are not available.

Hotel Shri Shanti Niwas (☎ 521925), on the road directly opposite the train station, has basic but clean singles/doubles at Rs 75/125 with bath. Slightly better rooms are Rs 175/250. No meals are served here.

Indre Lodge (☎ 524813) is not far away, down a laneway that leads to the right. Its appeal is that it's quieter than most other hotels in this area. Singles/doubles with attached bath go for Rs 70/150 (hot water is Rs 4 per bucket). Better rooms cost Rs 125/220. No meals are available. The signboard for this hotel is in Hindi, so ask someone to point it out if you can't find it.

Hotel Marudhar Heritage (☎ 522524, fax 201334), nearby, is considerably more luxurious. Rooms with private bath are Rs 225/300, Rs 350/450 with air-cooling, and Rs 750 for an air-con double.

RTDC's Hotel Dhola Maru (☎ 529621) is near Pooran Singh Circle, about 1km from the centre of the city. The rooms are bland: ordinary singles/doubles with bath Rs 175/225; air-cooled deluxe Rs 275/350 and air-con Rs 450/550. There's a restaurant here; a veg/nonveg thali is Rs 55/77.

Retiring rooms at the train station cost Rs 75/115 for rooms with attached bath. Air-con singles/doubles are Rs 150/200, and dorm beds are Rs 35/50 for 12/24 hours.

Places to Stay – Mid-Range

Bhairon Vilas (☎/fax 544751), near Junagarh, opposite the main post office, is the most funky place to stay in Bikaner and is managed by the equally funky Harshvardhan Singh. Quaint doubles range from Rs 500 to Rs 1600 – request a quiet room. Some of the cheaper rooms are quite small, but OK. Meals are available with advance notice in the atmospheric dining room, which is filled with old photos and paraphernalia.

Hotel Harasar Haveli (☎ 209891, fax 525150), near the Karni Singh Stadium, is another fabulous place to stay, with clean singles/doubles for Rs 450/650. The owner, Visvajeet Singh, can organise traditional fire dance performances at his farmhouse in Khara village, 20km from Bikaner (Rs 400 per person, minimum of five people).

Hotel Palace View (☎ 543625, fax 522741, Lalgarh Palace Campus) is the closest hotel to the palace. There are, as you would expect, views of the palace, and this is a peaceful and well-run place. Rooms go for Rs 750/850, and there are also some smaller rooms for Rs 400/500. Breakfast is Rs 100 and lunch or dinner is Rs 200.

Hotel Sagar (☎ 520677) is a large salmon pink building – the first place to the left of the driveway as you approach the palace. Air-cooled rooms cost Rs 950/1100, and there are also overpriced thatched huts (Rs 750/850). A set lunch/dinner in the restaurant costs Rs 225/250.

Hotel Kalinga (☎ 209751), opposite the Hotel Sagar, is OK but not exceptional. Rooms are spartan but reasonabe at Rs 300/400.

Hotel Padmini Niwas (☎ *522794, 148 Sadul Ganj*) has clean singles/doubles from Rs 425/550 to Rs 650/750 with air-con, and is a good place to stay. There's a restaurant and nice lawn area.

Hotel Joshi (☎ *527700, fax 521213, Station Rd*) is close to the train station. It's more salubrious than the budget flophouses farther north, with air-cooled rooms for Rs 300/375, and better air-con rooms for Rs 575/675. The best doubles are Rs 875. There's a veg restaurant. You can pop next door to *Kwality* for ice cream, chocobars (Rs 12), small cups of strawberry ice cream (Rs 6.50) and family packs (Rs 55).

Thar Hotel (☎ *543050, fax 525150, PBM Hospital Rd*) has mundane rooms for Rs 511/660 a single/double. Air-con rooms cost Rs 700/850. There's a nonveg restaurant with menu items such as chicken biryani (Rs 55) and mushroom paneer (Rs 50). Continental and Chinese food is also available.

Hotel Bothra Planet (☎ *544502, fax 544501, Bothra Complex, Alakh Sagar Rd*), opposite the train station, is a modern hotel in a shopping complex. It is new and should be up and running by now. Singles/doubles were expected to start at Rs 500/600.

Hotel Jaswant Bhawan (☎/*fax 521834, Alakh Sagar Rd*) is not far from the train station. Singles/doubles start at Rs 450/500. If you stay here, drop us a postcard to let us know how it was.

Marudyan Resort (☎ *86945, fax 544107, Jaipur Rd*), 10km out of Bikaner, has modern cottage-style accommodation for Rs 950/1150 a single/double.

Places to Stay – Top End

Hotel Bhanwar Niwas (Rampuri Haveli) (☎ *201043, fax 200880, Jail Rd*) is the most atmospheric place. It's in the old city near the *kotwali* (police station). If you turn left at the Kote Gate, this road will take you straight to the haveli, about 500m distant. The hotel is close to a community of kite-makers, who can be seen practising their craft. It's a beautiful pink sandstone building, with rooms set around a courtyard.

There are 17 rooms which cost Rs 1999/2900 a single/double, and all rooms are different. The set breakfast/lunch/dinner is Rs 150/250/275.

The haveli was completed in 1927 for Seth Bhanwarlal Rampura, heir to a textile and real estate fortune. In the foyer is a stunning 1927 blue Buick with a silver horn in the shape of a dragon, and an immaculate 1942 Indian Ambassador.

Lalgarh Palace Hotel (☎ *540201, fax 522253*), 3km north of the city centre, is set in its own pleasant grounds, and has well-appointed singles/doubles for US$85/135. There's a resident masseur (Rs 150 for 30 minutes) and a consultation with the astrologer, including casting your horoscope, is Rs 600. Residents have exclusive use of the indoor swimming pool, billiard room and croquet facilities. The hotel can organise a three hour camel safari for Rs 500 per person (minimum of four people). In the same compound is the smaller *Maan Bilas Palace Hotel* (☎ *524711*); it can also be booked through the Karni Bhawan Palace Hotel. It has nine rooms for Rs 1195/1675.

Karni Bhawan Palace Hotel (☎ *524701, fax 522408, Gandhi Colony*) is about 800m east of the Lalgarh Palace Hotel. This was briefly the residence of Maharaja Karni Singh, and although it's a rather ugly building, it's comfortable and well-run. Art Deco style singles/doubles cost Rs 1195/2395 and huge suites are Rs 3500. There's a good restaurant; the buffet lunch/dinner is Rs 350/400. It can arrange a visit to stunning Gajner Palace Hotel (see Around Bikaner).

Places to Eat

Bikaner is noted for the spicy snacks known as namkin, sold in the shops along Station Rd, among other places.

Deluxe Restaurant, at the hotel of the same name on Station Rd, features limited but cheap veg South Indian and Chinese cuisine. All dishes are under Rs 30.

Amber Restaurant is opposite the Hotel Joshi and is popular for its vegetarian food. Most dishes are under Rs 40, and there are some continental creations such as baked macaroni (Rs 36). South Indian snacks are available between 8 am and 7 pm, and there is a variety of Indian sweets including delicious gulab jamuns (Rs 18).

Hotel Bhanwar Niwas (see Places to Stay) welcomes nonguests to its vegetarian dining hall (advance notice is essential). The set breakfast/lunch/dinner is Rs 150/250/275. You can have a drink before dinner in the courtyard.

Lalgarh Palace Hotel (see Places to Stay) is also open to nonguests and has a buffet breakfast/lunch/dinner for US$7/10/ 11. A la carte dining is also possible, or you may just prefer to sip on a beer (Rs 100 a bottle) in the bar, with stuffed beasts peering down at you. Snacks, such as vegetable pakora (Rs 100), are available.

Chhotu Motu Joshi Sweet Shop, on Station Rd, is the town's most loved Indian sweet shop. It is a very busy place, selling a range of sweets including the milk-based rasmalai and kesar cham cham, the latter is a sausage-shaped sticky confection of milk, sugar and saffron which, when bitten, oozes a sweet sugar syrup. Fresh samosas are available out the front in the mornings.

Entertainment

Bikaner is known for its traditional fire dances, performed by members of a religious sect called the Naths. The Tourist Reception Centre (see Information earlier) can arrange fire dance performances with at least two days advance notice. Prices are available on application. The owner of the Hotel Harasar Haveli can also organise fire dances (see Places to Stay). There were plans to hold an annual fire dance festival at a village near Bikaner – contact the Tourist Reception Centre in order to get the latest developments.

Shopping

On the right-hand side immediately as you enter the fort is a small craftshop called Abhivyakti, run by the Urmul Trust. Items sold here are of high quality and made by people from surrounding villages. Proceeds go directly to health and education projects in these villages. You can browse here without the usual constant hassles to buy.

If you are part of a guided group going to the fort, your guide might try to steer you away from this shop to a place where he receives commission. It's worth insisting that you be given five minutes at least to wander through the shop. *Pattus*, lovely handloom shawls, cost from Rs 293 to Rs 1248. Cushion covers are from Rs 59 to Rs 390, and the traditional folding chairs known as *pidas* cost Rs 840 for a single seat and Rs 1200 for a double seat. *Jootis* (traditional Rajasthani shoes) are Rs 210 and sandals are similarly priced. There are also hand-printed cotton garments, puppets, cotton birds and more. The shop is open daily from 9 am to 6 pm. For more information on the good work of the Urmul Trust, see the Volunteer Work section in the Facts for the Visitor chapter.

Go to Usta St in the old city to see them making *usta* (camel leather) products.

Getting There & Away

Bus The bus stand is north of the city centre, almost opposite the road leading to the Lalgarh Palace Hotel (if your bus is coming from the south and you want to be dropped off in the town centre, ask the driver.

There are frequent express buses to:

destination	duration (hrs)	cost (Rs)
Ahmedabad	10	249
Ajmer	7	105
Barmer	11	177
Delhi	11	184
Jaipur	7	137
Jaisalmer	7½	133
Jhunjhunu	5½	90
Jodhpur	5½	101
Kota	9	186
Udaipur	12	213

For Roadways inquiries ring ☎ 523800.

Train Bikaner has rail connections to several destinations, including Jaipur, Churu, Jodhpur and Delhi – the Tourist Reception

Centre has a useful chart with details about timings and costs. The railways inquiry number is ☎ 131.

Getting Around

Auto-Rickshaw An auto-rickshaw from the train station to the palace should cost about Rs 20, but you'll probably be asked for more.

Bicycle Bicycles can be hired at the Dau Cycle Shop, opposite the police station on Station Rd (Rs 2/10 per hour/day).

AROUND BIKANER
Devi Kund

Eight kilometres east of Bikaner, this is the site of the royal chhatris of many of the Bika dynasty rulers. The white marble chhatri of Maharaja Surat Singh is among the most imposing.

Camel Research & Breeding Farm

This government-managed station, 8km from Bikaner, is probably unique in Asia. There are about 230 camels at the Bikaner Camel Research and Breeding Farm, and three different breeds are reared here. The British army had a camel corps drawn from Bikaner during WWI. As this is essentially a research centre and not a tourist site, there's frankly not a great deal to see here and it's not really worth the bother, unless perhaps you missed seeing the camels at Jaisalmer. There are sometimes baby camels, which makes the trip more worthwhile (see the boxed text Get to Know your Camel).

The farm is open Monday to Friday and every second Saturday from 3 to 5 pm (free entry). Cameras are theoretically prohibited, but this doesn't seem to be policed.

For the round trip including a half-hour wait at the camel farm, you'll pay around Rs 60 for an auto-rickshaw, or Rs 120 for a taxi.

Gajner Wildlife Sanctuary

The lake and forested hills of this reserve, 32km from Bikaner on the Jaisalmer road,

---

Get to Know your Camel

The camels reared at the Bikaner Camel Research & Breeding Farm are of three breeds: the long-haired camels with hair in their ears are local camels from the Bikaner district. They are renowned for their strength. The light-coloured camels are from the Jaisalmer district, and are renowned for their speed – up to 22km/h! The dark-coloured camels are from Gujarat, and the females are renowned for the quantity of milk they produce: up to 7 or 8L at each milking. The milk tastes a little salty and is reputedly good for the liver. If you have a cup of chai in a small desert village, you're quite possibly drinking camel milk. The stout of heart might even like to try fresh, warm camel milk at the farm. The camels on the farm are crossbred so, in theory, camels should be the strongest, fastest and best milk-producing camels you'll find just about anywhere! Breeding season is from around November to March, and at this time the male camels froth disconcertingly at the mouth.

This is also a stud farm: locals bring their female camels here to be serviced free of charge. Female camels give birth every two to three years depending on their age and health, following a long (13 month) gestation period. A male camel can inseminate up to three cows per day.

Adult camels consume about 20kg of fodder in summer, and drink 70L of water per day. In winter, they drink about 40L per day. In winter, a camel can work up to one month without food or water, and in summer, up to one week.

---

are inhabited by wildfowl, hare, wild boar, desert foxes and a number of deer and antelope including blackbuck and bluebull. Imperial sand grouse migrate here in winter. There are no authorised guides at the sanctuary and, apart from the Gajner Palace Hotel, no accommodation or infrastructure for visitors. The reserve is only accessible by Gajner Palace Hotel vehicles (which can be hired by nonguests). The charge is Rs 1000 per jeep (maximum six people).

Places to Stay & Eat *Gajner Palace Hotel (☎ 01534-55065, fax 55060)* booked through the Karni Bhawan Palace Hotel *(☎ 0151-524701, fax 522408 in Bikaner)* is the erstwhile royal winter palace and is ideally situated on the banks of a lake. It's an impressive building made of red sandstone and is set in serene, lush surroundings – ideal for some serious rest and relaxation. Standard rooms are Rs 1195/2395 (the Gulab Niwas garden rooms are best). Old-fashioned suites (all with a lake view) are in the main palace and cost Rs 3500 – these rooms are not particularly flash, but have a certain antiquated charm. Some of the rugs in the main palace were woven by prisoners of the Bikaner jail. There's an indoor restaurant, or you can eat outdoors as you watch the birds bobbing on the calm lake; the buffet lunch/dinner is Rs 350/400. A boat ride on the lake costs Rs 50 per person (minimum four people).

If you're not staying at the hotel, you'll have to pay Rs 100 per person to visit, which includes a soft drink, tea or coffee. No extra charge is levied if you are taking a safari or having a meal at the palace (advance bookings recommended).

Getting There & Away There are frequent daily buses to Gajner village, located about 1km away from the hotel. A return taxi from Bikaner should cost around Rs 250, including 40 minutes waiting time.

Kolayat
This small temple town set around a lake, 22km south of Gajner, is often referred to as a mini-Pushkar. It lacks the vibrant character of Pushkar, but is far less touristy. There's a *mela* (fair) here around the same time as the Pushkar Camel Fair in November (minus the camels and cattle, but with plenty of sadhus). The main temple at Kolayat is the Kapil Muni Temple (closed between 3 and 5 pm).

There are frequent daily buses from Bikaner to Kolayat (1½ hrs, Rs 20).

Deshnok
A visit to the fascinating temple of Karni Mata, an incarnation of Durga, at this village 30km south of Bikaner along the Jodhpur road, is not for the squeamish. Here the holy rodents are considered to be incarnations of storytellers, and run riot over the temple complex.

Karni Mata, who lived in the 14th century, asked the god of death, Yama, to restore to life the son of a grieving storyteller. When Yama refused, Karni Mata reincarnated all dead storytellers as rats, in order to deprive Yama of human souls, which were later incarnated as human beings.

The temple is an important place of pilgrimage, with pilgrims being disgorged every few minutes from buses. Once at the village, they buy prasaad in the form of sugar balls to feed to the rats. The pilgrims are anointed with a tikka in the form of ash from a holy fire in the inner sanctum, while the objects of their devotion run over their toes (sorry, no shoes permitted!). Before the temple is a beautiful marble facade with solid silver doors donated by Maharaja Ganga Singh. Across the doorway to the inner sanctum are repoussé silver doors – one panel shows the goddess with her holy charges at her feet. An image of the goddess is enshrined in the inner sanctum. There are special holes around the side of the temple courtyard to facilitate the rats' movements, and a wire grille has been placed over the courtyard to prevent birds of prey and other predators consuming the holy rodents.

The rats are known as *kabas*, and it is considered highly auspicious to have one run across your feet – you'll probably find you'll be inadvertently graced in this manner whether you want it or not! White kabas are quite rare, although there are one or two at the temple, and sighting one augers well for your spiritual progress. Frankly, the holy charges here are a rather moth-eaten assortment, who engage in decidedly unholy behaviour as they fight each other to get the best position around the enormous bowls of milk which are constantly replenished by the temple priests.

There is a special festival at this temple, but dates vary according to the Hindu lunar calendar – ask at the Tourist Reception Centre (☎ 0151-544125) in Bikaner, and also see the boxed text Festivals of Western Rajasthan at the beginning of this chapter.

The temple is open daily from 6 am to 9.30 pm. It costs Rs 20/50 to bring in a camera/video.

Places to Stay The *Shri Karni Yatri Niwas* is the only place to stay in Deshnok,

but you are much better off staying in Bikaner and visiting Deshnok on a day trip. Dusty doubles in this poorly maintained place are Rs 150 with bath. The service provided is minimal and there are no meals available.

Getting There & Away Buses from the bus stand in Bikaner depart daily every hour for Deshnok (40 mins, Rs 12). A return trip by taxi or by auto-rickshaw should cost about Rs 250/150. This should include a 30 minute halt at Deshnok, but you will need to make sure you specify this before setting off.

Agra

• **pop 1,118,800**   ☎ **0562**

Although in the state of Uttar Pradesh, Agra with its stunning Taj Mahal can be visited en route to or from Rajasthan.

In the 16th and 17th centuries, Agra was the capital of India under the Mughals, and its superb monuments date from this era. They include a magnificent fort and the building which many people come to India solely to see – the Taj Mahal.

Badal Singh is credited with building a fort on the site of the present Agra Fort in 1475. Sikander Lodi made his capital on the opposite bank of the Yamuna in 1501. Agra became the Mughal capital after Babur defeated the last Lodi sultan in 1526 at Panipat, 80km north of Delhi. It reached its glorious peak between the mid-16th and mid-17th centuries under the reigns of Ak-bar, Jehangir and Shah Jahan when the fort, Taj Mahal and Agra's major tombs were built. In 1638 Shah Jahan built a new city in Delhi, and Aurangzeb moved the capital there 10 years later.

In 1761 Agra fell to the Jats, who looted its monuments, including the Taj Mahal. It was taken by the Marathas in 1770, before the British wrested control in 1803. There was heavy fighting around the fort during the Uprising of 1857, and after the British regained control, they shifted the administration of the North Western Provinces to Allahabad. Agra has since developed as an industrial centre.

Agra is worth more than a flying visit, particularly if you intend to see the nearby deserted city of Fatehpur Sikri.

Orientation

Agra is on the western bank of the Yamuna River, 204km south of Delhi. The old part of the city and main marketplace (Kinari Bazaar) are north-west of the fort. The spacious British-built cantonment is south, and the main road running through it is called The Mall. The commercial centre of the cantonment is Sadar Bazaar.

Highlights

• **The Taj Mahal** – one of the world's most beautiful architectural feats

• **The Agra Fort** – a huge complex, great to explore

• **Itimad-ud-daulah** – an impressive piece of Mughal architecture

• **Fatehpur Sikri** – a deserted city, testimony to the wealth and power of the Mughal emperors

---

The labourers and artisans who toiled on the Taj set up home immediately south of the mausoleum. This area full of congested alleyways is known as Taj Ganj and today it contains most of Agra's budget hotels. The 'tourist class' hotels are predominantly in the area south of here.

Agra's main train station, Agra Cantonment (abbreviated as Agra Cantt), is west of Sadar Bazaar. The city's major bus stand, Idgah, is nearby. Agra's airport is 7km west of the city.

Information

The Government of India tourist office (☎ 363959), 191 The Mall, is open weekdays from 9 am to 5.30 pm, 9 am to 1 pm Saturday. It has an informative brochure on Fatehpur Sikri. There's a helpful UP tourist office (☎ 360517) at 64 Taj Rd, open daily (except Sunday and the 2nd Saturday in the month) from 10 am to 5 pm. The tourist information counter (☎ 368598) is at Agra Cantonment train station and is open daily from 8 am to 8 pm.

The State Bank of India branch south of Taj Ganj and the Andhra Bank in Sadar Bazaar (next to the Hotel Pawan) are the best banks to change money. You'll find slightly lower rates at Clarity Financial Services, but

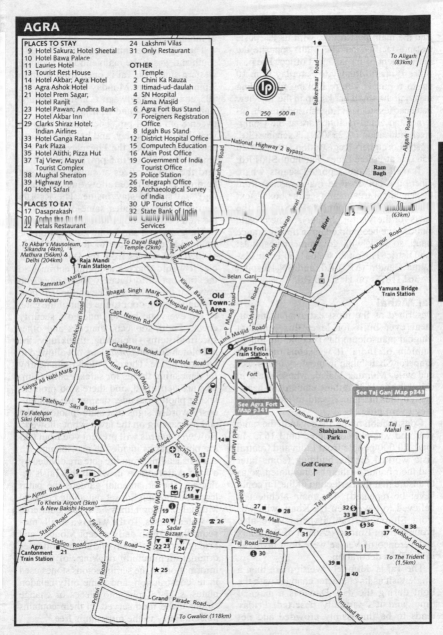

AGRA

PLACES TO STAY
- 9 Hotel Sakura; Hotel Sheetal
- 10 Hotel Bawa Palace
- 11 Lauries Hotel
- 13 Tourist Rest House
- 14 Hotel Akbar; Agra Hotel
- 18 Agra Ashok Hotel
- 21 Hotel Prem Sagar;
  Hotel Ranjit
- 23 Hotel Pawan; Andhra Bank
- 27 Hotel Akbar Inn
- 29 Clarks Shiraz Hotel;
  Indian Airlines
- 33 Hotel Ganga Ratan
- 34 Park Plaza
- 35 Hotel Atithi; Pizza Hut
- 37 Taj View; Mayur
  Tourist Complex
- 38 Mughal Sheraton
- 39 Highway Inn
- 40 Hotel Safari

PLACES TO EAT
- 17 Dasaprakash
- 19 Zorba the Buddha
- 22 Petals Restaurant

- 24 Lakshmi Vilas
- 31 Only Restaurant

OTHER
- 1 Temple
- 2 Chini Ka Rauza
- 3 Itimad-ud-daulah
- 4 SN Hospital
- 5 Jama Masjid
- 6 Agra Fort Bus Stand
- 7 Foreigners Registration
  Office
- 8 Idgah Bus Stand
- 12 District Hospital Office
- 15 Computech Education
- 16 Main Post Office
- 19 Government of India
  Tourist Office
- 25 Police Station
- 26 Telegraph Office
- 28 Archaeological Survey
  of India
- 30 UP Tourist Office
- 32 State Bank of India
- 36 Enlay Financial
  Services

To Aligarh
(83km)

To Akbar's Mausoleum,
Sikandra (4km),
Mathura (56km) &
Delhi (204km)

To Bharatpur

To Dayal Bagh
Temple (2km)

Raja Mandi
Train Station

Ramratan Marg

Panchkuhan Road

Saiyad Ali Nabi Marg

Fatehpur
Sikri Road

To Fatehpur
Sikri (40km)

Ajmer Road

Station Road

To Kheria Airport (3km)
& New Bakshi House

Agra
Cantonment
Train Station

Station Road

Prithvi Taj Road

Grand Parade Road

To Gwalior (118km)

Fatehpur Sikri Road

Mahatma Gandhi (MG) Rd

Sadar
Bazaar

Gwalior Road

Namner Road

Kachahari Road

Mahatma Gandhi (MG) Rd

Old
Town
Area

Bhagat Singh Marg

Capt Naresh Rd

Ghalibpura Road

Mantola Road

Hospital Road

Kinari Bazaar

Jama Masjid Road

Jama P Mandi Road

Chhata Road

Chillinti Rd

Nehru Rd

Belan Ganj

National Highway 2 Bypass

Karbala Road

Pandit Kalicharan Marg

Yamuna River

Balkeshwar Road

Aligarh Road

Ram
Bagh

To Mainpuri
(63km)

Kanpur Road

Yamuna Bridge
Train Station

Agra Fort
Train Station

Fort

See Agra Fort
Map p341

Yamuna Kinara Road

Shahjahan
Park

Golf Course

The Mall

Gough Road

Taj Road

Field Marshal Cariappa Road

Shamshabad Rd

Taj Road

Fatehbad Road

See Taj Ganj Map p343

Taj
Mahal

To The Trident
(1.5km)

0   250   500 m

AGRA

it's quick and open daily 9 am to 9 pm. You'll find the main post office, with its lax poste restante facility, on The Mall, opposite the Government of India tourist office. The post office is open Monday to Saturday from 10 am to 6 pm. If you're looking for reading material, the small bookshop in the Taj View hotel carries stock in English and French. Internet and email facilities are at the Computech Education (☎ 253059), Kachahari Rd.

The Foreigners Registration Office (☎ 26 9563) is at Police Lines, Fatehpur Sikri Rd.

Travellers have reported scams where diners are poisoned to make money from their medical treatment (see the boxed text Diahhorea With Your Meal, Sir? in the Facts for the Visitor chapter). Some private clinics have been mixed up in this insurance fraud, so stick with government hospitals: the District Hospital (☎ 363139) is on Mahatma Gandhi (MG) Rd, and SN Hospital (☎ 361318) is on Hospital Rd.

Taj Mahal

Described as the most extravagant monument ever built for love, this poignant Mughal mausoleum has become the tourist emblem of India. It was constructed by Emperor Shah Jahan in memory of his second wife, Mumtaz Mahal, whose death in childbirth in 1631 left the emperor so heartbroken that his hair is said to have turned grey overnight.

Construction of the Taj began in the same year and was not completed until 1653. In total, 20,000 people from India and Central Asia worked on the building (some later had their hands or thumbs amputated, so as to ensure that the perfection of the Taj could never be repeated). The main architect is believed to have been Isa Khan, who was from Shiraz in Iran. Experts were also brought from Europe – Austin of Bordeaux and Veroneo of Venice were both involved in the Taj's decoration.

The Taj is definitely worth more than a single visit as its character changes with the light during the day. Dawn is a magical time, and it's virtually deserted. Friday tends to be impossibly crowded and not conducive to appreciating this most serene of monuments.

There are three entrances to the Taj (east, south and west); the main entrance is on the western side. The Taj is open from 6 am to 7 pm daily except Monday. Entry costs Rs 105 at sunrise (between 6 and 8 am) and sunset (between 4 and 7 pm), and Rs 15 between 8 am and 4 pm. There's no charge to visit the Taj on Friday, and between 1 April and 30 September the cheaper period extends from 7.30 am to 5 pm. If you can't afford the higher prices at sunset, enter just before the price hike (allow time for queuing) and simply stay inside. The Rs 105 sunrise ticket includes same-day entry to the Red Fort and other attractions

The grand red sandstone **gateway** on the south side of the interior forecourt is inscribed with verses from the Quran in Arabic. It would make a stunning entrance to the Taj, but unfortunately these days you only exit through here. The entrance is now through a small door to the right of the gate, where everyone has to undergo a security check. Food, tobacco, matches and other specified items (including, thankfully, the red blotch-forming *paan*) are not allowed to be taken inside. There's a cloakroom nearby for depositing things for safekeeping. Cameras are permitted, and there's no problem taking photos outside, despite the ambiguously-worded signs that state 'photography and trespassing on the lawn is not allowed'. However, guards will prevent you from taking photographs inside the mausoleum.

Paths leading from the gate are divided by a long **watercourse** in which the Taj is reflected. The ornamental gardens the paths lead you through are set out along classical Mughal *charbagh* lines – a square quartered by watercourses. To the west is a small **museum** that's open daily except Monday and Friday between 10 am and 5 pm. It houses original architectural drawings of the Taj, information on the semiprecious stones used in its construction, and some nifty celadon plates, said to split into pieces or change colour if the food served on them contains poison. Entry to the museum is free.

The Taj Mahal itself stands on a raised marble platform on the northern edge of the ornamental gardens. Tall, purely decorative white **minarets** grace each corner of the platform – as the Taj Mahal is not a mosque, nobody is called to prayer from them. Twin red sandstone buildings frame it; the one on the western side is a mosque, the identical one on the eastern side is for symmetry. It cannot be used as a mosque, as it faces the wrong direction.

The central Taj structure has four small domes surrounding the bulbous central dome. The **tombs** of Mumtaz Mahal and Shah Jahan are in a basement. Above them in the main chamber are false tombs, a common practice in mausoleums of this type. Light is admitted into the central chamber by finely cut marble screens. The echo in this high domed chamber is superb, and there is always someone there to demonstrate it.

Ironically, the perfect symmetry of the Taj is disrupted only by the tomb of the man who built it. When Shah Jahan died in 1666, Aurangzeb placed his casket next to that of Mumtaz Mahal. His presence, which was never intended, unbalances the mausoleum's interior.

Although the Taj is amazingly graceful from almost any angle, it's the close-up detail which is really astounding. Semiprecious stones are inlaid into the marble in beautiful patterns using a process known as *pietra dura*. As many as 43 different gems were used for Mumtaz's tomb alone.

Agra Fort

Construction of the massive red sandstone Agra Fort on the bank of the Yamuna River was begun by Emperor Akbar in 1565, and additions were made up until the rule of his grandson, Shah Jahan.

The auricular fort's colossal double walls rise over 20m in height and measure 2.5km in circumference. They are encircled by a fetid moat and contain a maze of buildings which form a small city within a city. Unfortunately, not all buildings are open to visitors, including the white marble Moti Masjid (Pearl Mosque), regarded by some

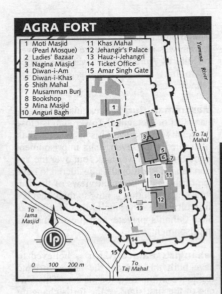

AGRA FORT

1	Moti Masjid (Pearl Mosque)	11	Khas Mahal
2	Ladies' Bazaar	12	Jehangir's Palace
3	Nagina Masjid	13	Hauz-i-Jehangri
4	Diwan-i-Am	14	Ticket Office
5	Diwan-i-Khas	15	Amar Singh Gate
6	Shish Mahal		
7	Musamman Burj		
8	Bookshop		
9	Mina Masjid		
10	Anguri Bagh		

AGRA

as the most beautiful mosque in India. The Amar Singh Gate to the south is the sole entry point. It's open from 6 am to 5.30 pm daily; admission is Rs 15, except on Friday when there's no charge.

Diwan-i-Am The Hall of Public Audiences was built by Shah Jahan and replaced an earlier wooden structure. His predecessors had a part in the hall's construction, but the throne room, with its typical inlaid marble work, indisputably bears Shah Jahan's influence. This is where the emperor met officials and listened to petitioners. Beside the diwan-i-am is the small **Nagina Masjid** or Gem Mosque. A door leads from here into the **Ladies' Bazaar**, where female merchants came to sell goods to the ladies of the Mughal court. No males were allowed to enter the bazaar except Akbar, though according to one apocryphal story he still enjoyed visiting in female disguise.

Diwan-i-Khas The Hall of Private Audiences was also built by Shah Jahan, between 1636 and 1637. It is where the

AGRA

emperor received important dignitaries or foreign ambassadors. The famous Peacock Throne was kept here before being moved to Delhi by Aurangzeb. It was later carted off to Iran and its remains are now in Tehran.

Musamman Burj The exquisite Musamman Burj or Octagonal Tower stands close to the diwan-i-khas. This is where Shah Jahan died after seven years imprisonment in the fort. The tower looks out over the Yamuna and is traditionally considered to have one of the most poignant views of the Taj, but Agra's pollution is now so thick that it's difficult to see. The small Mina Masjid was Shah Jahan's private mosque during his imprisonment.

Jehangir's Palace Akbar is believed to have built this palace, the largest private residence in the fort, for his son. This was one of the first signs of the fort's changing emphasis from military to luxurious living quarters. The palace also displays an interesting blend of Hindu and Central Asian architectural styles – a contrast to the unique Mughal style used by Shah Jahan.

Jama Masjid

Across the train tracks from the Delhi Gate of Agra Fort is the Jama Masjid, built by Shah Jahan in 1648. An inscription over the main gate indicates that it was built in the name of Jahanara, Shah Jahan's favourite daughter, who was eventually imprisoned with Shah Jahan by Aurangzeb.

Itimad-ud-Daulah

On the opposite bank of the Yamuna, north of the fort, is the exquisite Itimad-ud-daulah – the tomb of Mirza Ghiyas Beg. This Persian gentleman was Jehangir's *wazir*, or chief minister, and his beautiful daughter Nur Jahan later married the emperor. Nur Jahan constructed the tomb from 1622-28 in a style similar to the tomb she built for Jehangir near Lahore in Pakistan.

Interestingly, many of its design elements foreshadow the Taj, construction of which started only a few years later. The Itimad-ud-daulah was the first Mughal structure totally built from marble and the first to make extensive use of pietra dura, the marble inlay work which is so characteristic of the Taj. Though small and squat compared to its more famous cousin (it's known as the 'baby Taj'), its human scale is attractive. Extremely fine marble latticework passages admit light to the interior, and the beautifully patterned surface of the tomb is superb. The Itimad-ud-daulah is open from around 6 am to 6 pm daily; admission is Rs 12 except on Friday when it's free.

Akbar's Mausoleum

The sandstone and marble tomb of Akbar, the greatest of the Mughal emperors, lies in the centre of a peaceful garden grazed by deer at Sikandra, 4km north-west of Agra. Akbar started its construction himself, blending Islamic, Hindu, Buddhist, Jain and Christian motifs and styles, much like the syncretic religious philosophy he developed called Deen Ilahi.

When Akbar died, the mausoleum was completed by his son, Jehangir, but he significantly modified the original plans. This accounts for its somewhat cluttered architectural lines. The mausoleum is open from sunrise to sunset every day; entry is Rs 12, except on Friday when it is free; Rs 25 for a video.

Other Attractions

The alleyways of **Kinari Bazaar**, or old marketplace, start near the Jama Masjid. There are several distinct areas of the old marketplace whose names are relics of the Mughal period, although they don't always bear relation to the goods that are sold there today.

The **Loha Mandi** (Iron Market) and **Sabji Mandi** (Vegetable Market) are still operational, but the **Nai ki Mandi** (Barber's Market) is now famous for textiles.

Something entirely different is for sale in the **Malka Bazaar**, where women beckon to passing men from upstairs balconies.

Swimming

The following hotels allow nonguests to use their pools for a fee: Agra Ashok Hotel (Rs 150), Lauries Hotel (Rs 150) Hotel Atithi (Rs 250), and the Clarks Shiraz Hotel (Rs 300). Ashok has the best pool.

Organised Tours

Guided tours depart from the Government of India tourist office at 9.30 am and proceed to Agra Cantonment train station to pick up passengers arriving from Delhi on the *Taj Express*, which pulls in at 9.47 am. The tours include the Taj Mahal, Agra Fort and a rather hasty visit to Fatehpur Sikri. They finish at 6 pm so day trippers can catch the *Taj Express* returning to Delhi at 6.35 pm. Buy tickets (Rs 175) from the tourist information counter at the train station (you can board the bus at the Government of India tourist office before buying).

Places to Stay – Budget

Agra's paying guest house scheme enables you to stay with local families for between Rs 200 and Rs 500. Contact the tourist information counter at the train station when you arrive.

Unless stated otherwise, rooms mentioned have attached bathroom.

Taj Ganj Area The *Hotel Host* (☎ 331 010), not far from the Taj's western gate, has comfortable carpeted rooms with air-cooling and hot water. Singles/doubles are a bargain at Rs 80/100; doubles for Rs 150 have a TV.

Close by, *Hotel Sidhartha* (☎ 331238) is a clean, friendly, spacious place built motel-style around a garden courtyard. Singles/doubles with bucket hot water cost Rs 100, or Rs 175/250 with hot water on tap.

Hotel Kamal (☎ 330126, email siit@ del2.vsnl.net.in) has helpful staff and OK singles/doubles for Rs 120/200. It has a prime view of the Taj from the sitting area on the roof and gets positive reviews from travellers.

Hotel Shahjahan (☎ 331159) in the heart of Taj Ganj has dorm beds for Rs 30, and

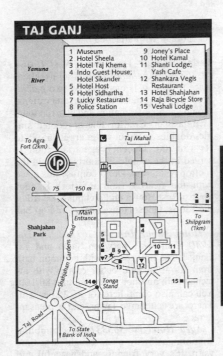

TAJ GANJ

1 Museum
2 Hotel Sheela
3 Hotel Taj Khema
4 Indo Guest House;
   Hotel Sikander
5 Hotel Host
6 Hotel Sidhartha
7 Lucky Restaurant
8 Police Station
9 Joney's Place
10 Hotel Kamal
11 Shanti Lodge;
   Yash Cafe
12 Shankara Vegis
   Restaurant
13 Hotel Shahjahan
14 Raja Bicycle Store
15 Veshali Lodge

reasonable rooms with hot water cost from Rs 50/100.

Indo Guest House, near the Taj's southern gate, is clean, basic and family-run. Rooms with hot water are Rs 60/80 or Rs 100/120. Next door is the *Hotel Sikander* (☎ 330279), which is similar in price and standard.

Hotel Sheela (☎ 331194), near the Taj's eastern gate, is surrounded by a large garden and has singles/doubles with hot water for Rs 120/150 to Rs 200/250. The cheaper rooms are excellent value, so it's often full.

South of Taj Ganj The *Hotel Safari* (☎ 360110, Shamsabad Rd) is popular and good value. Air-cooled singles/doubles with hot water cost Rs 120/175.

Highway Inn (☎ 332758) nearby is popular with overlanders for its camping facilities which cost Rs 30 per person. Rooms

AGRA

are OK at Rs 75/150 with common bath and Rs 150/250 with attached bath.

Sadar Bazaar The *Tourist Rest House* (☎ *363961, Kachahari Rd)* is an excellent place to stay. It is managed by two benign brothers who make train/air reservations, provide good information and also run tours to Rajasthan. Comfortable air-cooled singles/doubles with hot water are Rs 65/85 to Rs 150/200. Decent vegetarian food is served in the candle-lit courtyard or in the rooftop restaurant. Don't confuse this place with the nearby (and inferior) Kapoor Tourist Rest House on Fatehpur Sikri Rd or the Tourist Guest House near Agra Fort bus stand.

Hotel Akbar Inn (☎ *363212, 21 The Mall)* is midway between Sadar and Taj Ganj. It has tiny rooms with common bath from Rs 40/60 and better rooms with attached bath and hot water from Rs 80/100. You can also camp here for Rs 25 per tent. There are extensive lawns and a pleasant terrace.

Agra Hotel (☎ *363331)* is a rambling crumbling, dowdy place caught in a time warp. It's very friendly and peaceful and has a good range of rooms which start from Rs 150/200.

Hotel Pawan (☎*/fax 262442)*, also known as Hotel Jaiwal, is on the main drag of Sadar Bazaar close to shops and restaurants. Air-cooled rooms with hot water cost between Rs 200/300 and Rs 300/400.

West of Sadar Bazaar Places here are convenient for transport options.

Two good choices are 200m from the Idgah bus stand, on the Ajmer Rd: *Hotel Sakura* (☎ *369793)* and next-door *Hotel Sheetal* (☎ *369420)*. Private buses to Rajasthan depart from outside. Both have friendly staff. The rooms vary so ask to see several. Singles/doubles start at Rs 125/150 in Sakura and Rs 100/125 in Sheetal.

The retiring rooms at *Agra Cantonment station* are reasonable, with dorm beds for Rs 50, doubles for Rs 200 and air-con doubles for Rs 400.

Places to Stay – Mid-Range

The Mayur Tourist Complex (☎ *332302, fax 332907, Fatehbad Rd)* has pleasant cottage-style rooms arranged around a lawn with a swimming pool, but beware of mosquitoes. Air-cooled singles/doubles will cost you Rs 800/950.

Hotel Atithi (☎ *330879, fax 330878, Fatehbad Rd)* has good-sized air-con rooms from Rs 1050/1270, plus a swimming pool and restaurants. Rates are usually negotiable. Across the road, *Hotel Ganga Ratan* (☎ *330329)* is a little less grand, but the rooms from Rs 900/1020 are almost as good.

Lauries Hotel (☎ *364536, MG Rd)* is an established hotel where Queen Elizabeth II's party stayed in 1961. Any regal pretensions have long since faded, though it retains spacious arcaded corridors and extensive grounds. Large rooms cost Rs 650/800. You can also camp for Rs 50.

New Bakshi House (☎ *302176, fax 301448, 5 Laxman Nagar)* is between the train station and the airport. It's effectively a private home, with comfortable, nonstandard doubles from Rs 750 to Rs 1250, some with air-con. However, it's a bit pricey, especially as they add a 'service tax' of 10% to 17.5%.

Places to Stay – Top End

All the top-end hotels are air-conditioned and have pools. All are on Fatehbad Rd except for Agra Ashok and Clarks Shiraz Hotel.

Agra Ashok Hotel (☎ *361223, fax 361620, 6B The Mall)* is a well-managed, pleasant place to stay despite being part of the ITDC chain. Room rates are Rs 1500/2500.

The Trident (☎ *331818, fax 331827)* is a low-rise Mughal-style hotel with a garden and restaurant. Singles/doubles are excellent value at Rs 1195/2350 in summer, but from October to April prices soar to an impossible Rs 3550/3750.

Park Plaza (☎ *331870, fax 330408)* is a squeaky-clean hotel offering good rooms for US$45/75.

Clarks Shiraz Hotel (☎ 361421, fax 361428, email clarkraz@nda.vsnl.net.in) is a long-standing Agra landmark. Rooms go for US$45/90.

Taj View (☎ 331841, fax 331860), part of the Taj Group of hotels, has rooms with a distant view of the Taj Mahal for US$115/130; rooms without views are US$105/120.

Mughal Sheraton (☎ 331701, fax 331730) is Agra's top hotel. It boasts all the usual luxuries (but no lift) and has standard rooms from US$130/140, or US$175/200 with a medium-range view of the Taj Mahal.

Places to Eat

Taj Ganj Area There are scores of makeshift eateries, many of them on rooftops or terraces. Beer can be 'arranged' in most places. For quality Mughlai cuisine, you'll need to dip into the luxury hotels – and deep into your wallet.

Try the local speciality, ultra-sweet candied pumpkin called *peitha*.

Joney's Place is tiny but it's long-running, serving great western breakfasts and good Indian and Israeli food. It is justly famous for its banana lassis.

Shankara Vegis Restaurant has rooftop dining. It tries its hand at Indian veg, Chinese, spaghetti and western breakfasts. Meals cost roughly Rs 30 to Rs 55. There are plenty of games available if you run out of conversation.

Lucky Restaurant has the usual have-a-go-at-everything menu but it's one of the more convivial places to hang out. There's an open-sided ground floor area, and tables on the roof, with views of the Taj.

Yash Cafe has a wide menu and an enjoyable atmosphere, aided by western music, games, and comfy chairs.

Elsewhere The *Dasaprakash*, in the Meher Cinema complex behind the Agra Ashok Hotel, serves tasty and highly regarded South Indian food in the Rs 45 to Rs 100 range.

Zorba the Buddha in Sadar Bazaar is a spotlessly clean, nonsmoking, Osho-run vegetarian restaurant. Excellent main dishes cost around Rs 70 to Rs 80. It can be hard to get a table in the evening. The restaurant is closed each May and June.

Lakshmi Vilas (Taj Rd) is a cheap South Indian veg restaurant nearby, recommended for its 23 varieties of *dosa* (lentil pancakes) from Rs 20.

Petals Restaurant (19A Taj Rd) is a comfortable restaurant serving Indian, Chinese and continental food. Prices start at Rs 45/85 for veg/nonveg.

For those craving western familiarity there's a *Pizza Hut* on Fatehbad Rd, next to Hotel Atithi, but it's rather pricey.

Only Restaurant, at the Taj Ganj end of The Mall, is highly rated by locals. Unfortunately the food (from Rs 55) is pretty bland, but at least there's live Indian music in the evening.

For top-end dining, try the restaurants in *Clarks Shiraz Hotel* and at the *Mughal Sheraton*.

Shopping

Agra is well known for leather goods, jewellery, *dhurrie* (rug) weaving and marble items inlaid with coloured stones, similar to the pietra dura work on the Taj. Sadar Bazaar and the area south of Taj Ganj are full of emporiums, but prices are more expensive than in the bazaars of the old part of the city. The best jewellery shops are around Pratapur, also in the old part, though you can pick up precious stones cheaper in Jaipur.

About 1km along the road running from the eastern gate of the Taj is Shilpgram, a crafts village and open-air emporium. Prices are on the high side, but the quality and range is good.

Do not let rickshaw-wallahs persuade you to visit shops on the way to your destination – you'll pay inflated prices to cover their commission.

Getting There & Away

Air The Indian Airlines office (☎ 360948) is at the Clarks Shiraz Hotel. It's open daily from 10 am to 1.15 pm and 2 to 5 pm. The Agra-Delhi fare is US$50.

Bus Most buses leave from the Idgah bus stand. Buses to Delhi (5 hrs, Rs 70), Jaipur (6 hrs, Rs 93) and Mathura (1½ hrs, Rs 21) depart hourly. Buses to Fatehpur Sikri (1½ hrs, Rs 13) leave every 30 minutes. Rajasthan government buses depart from a small booth outside Hotel Sheetal, close to the Idgah bus stand. Buses leave here every hour for Jaipur (6 hrs, Rs 112 deluxe), but you should book these one day in advance.

Train Agra's train connections to cities in Rajasthan have been disrupted by Rajasthan's conversion from metre gauge to broad gauge. Currently, the only direct train to Jodhpur (via Jaipur) is the *Marudhar Express*, leaving Agra Fort station at 4.40 am and taking 14 hours.

Agra Cantonment station is on the main Delhi to Mumbai (Bombay) line. The fastest train to Delhi is the daily air-con *Shatabdi Express* (2 hrs, Rs 370 in chair car class). It leaves New Delhi at 6.15 am and departs from Agra for the return trip at 8.18 pm, making it ideal for day tripping.

A much cheaper alternative is the daily *Taj Express* (2½ hrs, Rs 53/258 in 2nd/1st class). It leaves Delhi's Nizamuddin station at 7.15 am and departs from Agra for the return trip at 6.35 pm. Take care at New Delhi station; miscreants are aware that this is a popular tourist route and work overtime at parting unwary visitors from their valuables.

Getting Around

To/From the Airport Agra's Kheria airport is 7km from the centre of town and 3km west of Idgah bus stand. From Taj Ganj, taxis charge around Rs 75 and auto-rickshaws Rs 40.

Taxi & Auto-Rickshaw Tempos (large three-wheelers) operate on set routes: from the Agra Fort bus stand to Taj Ganj it's just Rs 2. Taxis and auto-rickshaws are unmetered so be prepared to haggle.

Prepaid transport is available from Agra Cantonment train station to Taj Ganj (Rs 38/82 by rickshaw/taxi), to Sadar Bazaar (Rs 17/35) and to the Taj Mahal and back with an hour's waiting time (Rs 65/125). A prepaid rickshaw for local sightseeing costs Rs 250 for a full day or Rs 135 for four hours; taxis cost Rs 400 for a full day locally, or Rs 550 if you also want to go to Fatehpur Sikri.

Cycle-Rickshaw From Taj Ganj to Sadar Bazaar is less than Rs 15, and to Agra Cantonment it is less than Rs 20, which is the most you should pay to get anywhere in Agra.

Bicycle Raja Bicycle Store, near the Taj Ganj tonga and rickshaw stand, hires bicycles for Rs 5 per hour, Rs 15 for half a day and Rs 30 for a full day; a new bike will cost Rs 10/25/50. Some hotels can arrange bike hire.

AROUND AGRA
Fatehpur Sikri
- pop 29,280   ☎ 05619

Between 1571 and 1585, during the reign of Emperor Akbar, the capital of the Mughal Empire was situated here, 40km west of Agra. Then, as suddenly and dramatically as this new city had been built, it was abandoned, mainly due, it is thought, to difficulties with the water supply. Today it's a perfectly preserved example of a Mughal city at the height of the empire's splendour.

Legend says that Akbar was without a male heir and made a pilgrimage to this spot to see the saint Shaikh Salim Chishti. The saint foretold the birth of Akbar's son, the future emperor Jehangir, and in gratitude Akbar named his son Salim. Furthermore, Akbar transferred his capital to Sikri and built a new and splendid city.

Spending the night at Fatehpur Sikri enables you to watch the impressive sunset over the ruins. The best viewpoint is from the top of the city walls, a 2km walk to the south.

Orientation & Information The deserted city lies along the top of a ridge, 40km west of Agra. The village, with its bus stand and train station, is at the bottom of the ridge's southern face. A Rs 4.50 fee per car is payable at Agra Gate, the eastern entrance to the village.

The historic enclosure is open from 6 am to 5.30 pm; entry is Rs 5, free on Friday; Rs 25 for a video. There's no entry fee to visit the Jama Masjid and the tomb of Shaikh Salim Chishti as they are outside the city enclosure. The function and even the names of many buildings remain contentious so you may find it useful to hire a guide. Licensed guides cost around Rs 50 and loiter near the ticket office; unlicensed guides solicit tourists at the Buland Darwaza.

Places to Stay & Eat *The Maurya Rest House* (☎ *882348*), near the Buland Darwaza, is the most pleasant of the budget hotels in the village. There are basic singles/doubles with common bath for Rs 50/70, or Rs 90/120 with attached bath. Another budget option is the *Goverdhan Tourist Complex* (☎ *882648*). The *Gulistan Tourist Complex* (☎ *882490*) is more upmarket, with rooms from Rs 400/450.

Fatehpur Sikri's speciality is *khataie*, the biscuits you'll see piled high in the bazaar.

Getting There & Away Tour buses only stop for an hour or so at Fatehpur Sikri, so if you want to spend longer (which is recommended) it's worth catching a bus from Agra's Idgah bus terminal (1½ hrs, Rs 13). There are also four trains a day from Agra Fort (1 hr, Rs 8).

You can spend a day in Fatehpur Sikri and continue on to Bharatpur in the evening. Buses depart from Fatehpur Sikri's bus stand every hour until 4.30 pm (Rs 10).

Don't encourage the villagers along the Agra road who force dancing bears to stop the passing traffic.

AGRA

Delhi

• pop 9.4 million   ☎ 011

Most visitors to Rajasthan fly into Delhi, a major international gateway. Delhi is the capital of India, north India's industrial hub and the country's third-largest city. Despite its intense air pollution and persistent touts, Delhi has plenty of interesting things to see and a fascinating history.

There have been at least eight cities around the modern Delhi, beginning with Indraprastha, which featured in the epic *Mahabharata* over 3000 years ago.

Old Delhi was the capital of Muslim India between the 17th and 19th centuries. New Delhi was built as the imperial capital of India by the British. They announced their intention to shift the capital from Calcutta in 1911, and New Delhi was finally inaugurated in 1931. Following Independence in 1947, Delhi became the capital of the new republic of India.

For a much more in-depth guide to the city, get a copy of Lonely Planet's *Delhi*.

ORIENTATION

Delhi is a relatively easy city to find your way around although it is very spread out. The section of interest to visitors is on the west bank of the Yamuna River and is divided basically into two parts – the tightly packed streets of Old Delhi and the spacious, planned areas of New Delhi.

Old Delhi is the 17th century walled city of Shahjahanabad, with city gates, narrow alleys, constant traffic jams, terrible air pollution, the enormous Red Fort and Jama Masjid, temples, mosques, bazaars and the famous street known as Chandni Chowk. Here you will find the Delhi train station and, a little further north, the main interstate bus station near Kashmiri Gate.

Near New Delhi train station is the crowded market area of Paharganj. This has become the budget travellers' hang-out – it has many good budget hotels, cafes and restaurants.

Highlights

• **Red Fort** – wander at leisure around Delhi's massive Mughal-era fort

• **Qutab Minar** – a magnificent tower built to proclaim the arrival of Islam in India

• **Jama Masjid** – the largest mosque in India built by Shah Jahan, of Taj Mahal fame

• **Connaught Place** – the thriving heart of New Delhi

• **Humayun's Tomb** – a fine example of early Mughal architecture

New Delhi is a planned city of wide, tree-lined streets, parks and fountains.

The hub of New Delhi is the great circle of Connaught Place and the streets that radiate from it. Here are most of the airline offices, banks, travel agencies, various state tourist offices and the national one, more budget accommodation and several of the big hotels. The Regal Cinema, south of the circle, and the Plaza Cinema, at the north, are two important landmarks, useful for telling taxi drivers where you want to go.

Janpath, running off Connaught Place to the south, has the Government of India tourist office, the Student Travel Information Centre in the Imperial Hotel and a number of other useful addresses.

South of the New Delhi government areas are Delhi's more expensive residential areas. The Indira Gandhi international airport is to the south-west of the city, and about halfway between the airport and Connaught Place is Chanakyapuri, the diplomatic enclave.

The 250 page *Eicher City Map* (Rs 270) includes 174 area maps, and is a good reference if you are venturing further into the

Delhi environs. It's available at most larger bookstores and modern service stations.

INFORMATION

Tourist Offices The Government of India tourist office (☎ 332 0008) at 88 Janpath is open Monday to Friday 9 am to 6 pm and Saturday 9 am to 2 pm. It has a good give-away map of the city.

In the arrivals hall at the international airport terminal there is a tourist counter (☎ 569 1171) open around the clock.

Delhi Tourism (☎ 331 3637), N Block, Connaught Place, is open weekdays from 7 am to 9 pm. It also has counters at New Delhi, Old Delhi, and Nizamuddin train stations, as well as at the Interstate bus station at Kashmiri Gate.

There are several listings guides available from news stands – *Delhi City Guide* and *Delhi Diary* among them. *First City* (Rs 30) is a monthly magazine that has good listings and reviews of cultural events and restaurants. The online information service at www.delhigate.com is very useful.

Most of the state governments have information centres in Delhi – the Rajasthan tourist information centre is at Bikaner House on Pandara Rd (☎ 338 3837, fax 338 2823).

Money The Central Bank has a 24 hour branch at the Ashok Hotel in Chanakyapuri, but it doesn't accept all currencies. There is a fast and convenient money changing office in Paharaganj's Main Bazaar near the Camran Lodge, open until 9 pm weekdays.

Many of the large international banks now have ATMs (open 24 hours).

American Express (☎ 332 5221, fax 371 5352) is in A Block, Connaught Place. You don't have to have Amex cheques to change money here. It's open every day from 9 am to 7 pm. For lost or stolen cheques, contact their 24 hour number (☎ 614 5920) as soon as possible.

Post & Communications There is a small post office in A Block at Connaught Place but the main post office is on the roundabout on Baba Kharak Singh Marg, 500m south-west of Connaught Place. Poste restante mail can be collected nearby from the Foreign Post Office on Market Rd (Bhai Vir Singh Marg). The poste restante office is around the back and up the stairs (open weekdays from 9 am to 5 pm). Make sure your correspondents specify 'New Delhi', so your letters don't end up at the Old Delhi post office.

There are plenty of private STD/ISD call offices around the city and a growing number offer email access.

Internet/email cafes include the Calculus Cyber Centre on Connaught Place in the Regal Cinema building, and the Internet office at the British Council on Kasturba Gandhi Marg. In Paharganj there's the E-Mail Centre near the Hotel Vishal. All charge Rs 100 per hour.

Foreign Embassies Delhi has most of the country's foreign missions – see the Facts for the Visitor chapter at the beginning of this book.

Visa Extensions Applications can be lodged at the Foreigners' Regional Registration Office (FRRO) in Delhi – see Visas & Documents in the Facts for the Visitor chapter.

Travel Agencies In the Imperial Hotel, the Student Travel Information Centre (☎ 332 7582) is used by many travellers and is the place to renew or obtain student cards.

Agencies include: Cozy Travels (☎ 331 2873), BMC House, 1N Connaught Place; Y Tours & Travel (☎ 371 1662) at the YMCA; and Tan's Travel (☎ 332 1490), 72 Janpath.

In Paharganj are Aa Bee Travels (☎ 752 0117) based at Hare Rama Guest House; Hotel Namaskar (☎ 752 1234); and the travel agency at the Hotel Ajanta (☎ 752 0925), Arakashan Rd.

For upmarket travel arrangements try: Cox & Kings (☎ 332 0067); Sita World Travels (☎ 331 1133); and Travel Corporation of India (☎ 331 5834).

DELHI

DELHI

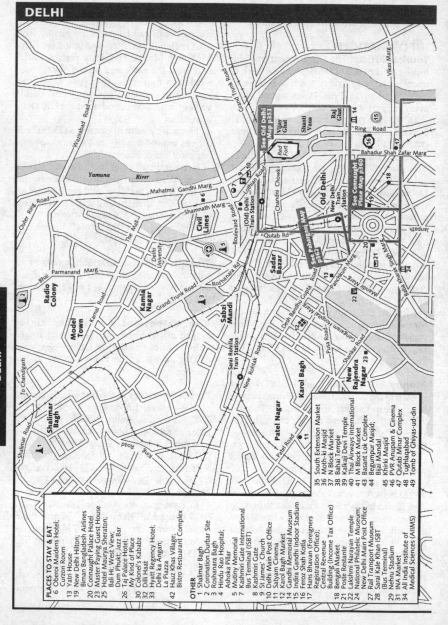

See Old Delhi Map p353

See Connaught Place Map p360

See Paharganj Map p362

PLACES TO STAY & EAT
6 Oberoi Maidens Hotel;
  Curzon Room
13 Yatri House
19 New Delhi Hilton;
  Biman Bangladesh Airlines
20 Connaught Palace Hotel
23 Master Paying Guest House
25 Hotel Maurya Sheraton;
  Bali Hi; West View;
  Dum Phukt; Jazz Bar
26 Taj Palace Hotel;
  My Kind of Place
30 Colonel's Kababz
32 Dilli Haat
33 Hyatt Regency Hotel;
  La Piazza
42 Hauz Khas Village;
  Delhi ka Angan;
  Bistro Restuarant Complex

OTHER
1 Shalimar Bagh
2 Coronation Durbar Site
3 Roshanara Bagh
4 Hindu Rao Hospital;
  Ashoka Pillar
5 Mutiny Memorial
7 Kashmiri Gate International
  Bus Terminal (ISBT)
8 Kashmiri Gate
9 St James' Church
10 Delhi Main Post Office
11 Karol Bagh Market
12 Gandhi Memorial Museum
14 Indira Gandhi Indoor Stadium
16 Feroz Shah Kotla
17 Hans Bhavan (Foreigners'
  Registration Office);
  Central Revenue
  Building (Income Tax Office)
18 Bengali Market
21 Poste Restante
22 Lakshmi Narayan Temple
24 National Philatelic Museum;
  New Delhi Main Post Office
27 Rail Transport Museum
28 Sarai Kale Khan ISBT
  (Bus Terminal)
29 Nehru Stadium
31 NIA Market
34 All India Institute of
  Medical Sciences (AIIMS)
35 South Extension Market
36 Moth-ki Masjid
37 N Block Market
38 Bahai Temple
39 Kalkaji Devi Temple
40 Thai Airways International
41 M Block Market
43 Basant Lok Complex
44 Begumpur Masjid;
  Bijai Mandal
45 Khirki Masjid
46 PVR Anupam & Cinema
47 Qutab Minar Complex
48 Tughlaqabad
49 Tomb of Ghiyas-ud-din

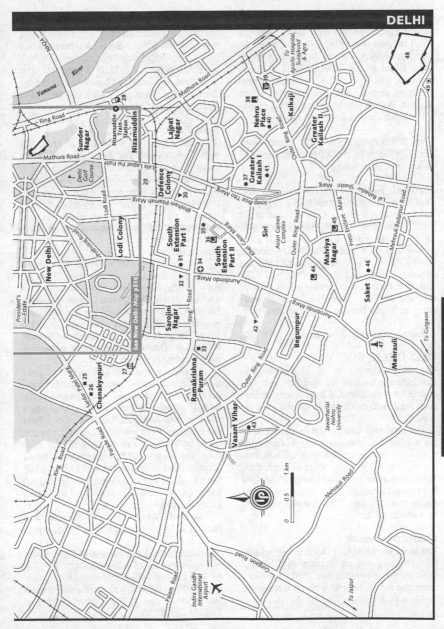

DELHI

See New Delhi Map p356

Bookshops Good bookshops around Connaught Place include: New Book Depot at 18 B Block; Piccadilly Book Store, 64 Shankar Market; Oxford Book Shop opposite N Block on the Outer Circle; and Bookworm at 29B Radial Rd No 4. Also worth checking out is The Bookshop at Khan Market. Prabhu Book Service in Hauz Khas Village has second-hand and rare books.

Film & Photography Delhi Photo Company, 78 Janpath, processes both print and slide film competently.

Medical Services Reliable places are: East West Medical Centre (☎ 462 3738, 469 9229), near the Delhi Golf Course at 38 Golf Links Rd; Apollo Hospital (☎ 692 5858), Sarita Vihar, Mathura Rd; Dr Ram Manohar Lohia Hospital (☎ 336 5525), Baba Kharak Singh Marg; and All India Institute of Medical Sciences (☎ 656 1123), Ansari Nagar. Embassies have lists of doctors and dentists. There's a 24 hour pharmacy at Super Bazaar in Connaught Place.

Emergency Ambulance number is ☎ 102.

OLD DELHI

The old walled city of Shahjahanabad stands to the west of the Red Fort and was at one time surrounded by a sturdy defensive wall, only fragments of which now exist.

The **Kashmiri Gate**, at the northern end of the walled city, was the scene of desperate fighting when the British retook Delhi during the 1857 Uprising. West of here, near Sabzi Mandi, is the British-erected **Mutiny Memorial** to the soldiers who lost their lives during the Uprising. Near the monument is an **Ashoka pillar**.

Chandni Chowk

The main street of Old Delhi is the colourful shopping bazaar known as Chandni Chowk. At the east (Red Fort) end is a Digambara Jain temple with an interesting bird hospital; entry is free but donations are gratefully accepted.

Next to the *kotwali* (old police station) is the Sunehri Masjid. In 1739, Nadir Shah, who carried off the Peacock Throne when he sacked Delhi, stood on this roof to watch his soldiers massacre Delhi's residents. The west end of Chandni Chowk is marked by the Fatehpuri Mosque, which was erected in 1650 by one of Shah Jahan's wives.

Red Fort

The red sandstone walls of Lal Qila, the Red Fort, extend for 2km. Emperor Shah Jahan started construction in 1638 and it was completed in 1648. He never completely moved here from Agra, as he was deposed and imprisoned by his son Aurangzeb, the first and last great Mughal emperor to rule from here. Entry is Rs 2 (free on Friday) from the kiosk opposite the main gate.

You enter the fort through the **Lahore Gate**, so named because it faces Lahore, now in Pakistan, and find yourself in a vaulted arcade, the **Chatta Chowk** (Covered Bazaar), which once sold the quality items required by the royal household – silks, jewellery and gold. This leads to the **Naubat Khana**, or Drum House, where musicians used to play for the emperor.

The elegant **diwan-i-am**, or hall of public audiences, was where the emperor heard complaints or disputes. The **diwan-i-khas**, or hall of private audiences, built of white marble, was the luxurious chamber where the emperor held private meetings. Centrepiece of the hall was the magnificent Peacock Throne but the Persian emperor, Nadir Shah, carted it off to Iran in 1739. In 1760 the Marathas removed the silver ceiling, so today the hall is a pale shadow of its former glorious self.

The **Moti Masjid**, or Pearl Mosque, was built in 1659 by Aurangzeb for his own personal use.

Each evening a **sound-and-light show** recreates events of India's history. English sessions are at 7.30 pm November to January, 8.30 pm February to April and September-October, and at 9 pm May to August. Tickets are Rs 20.

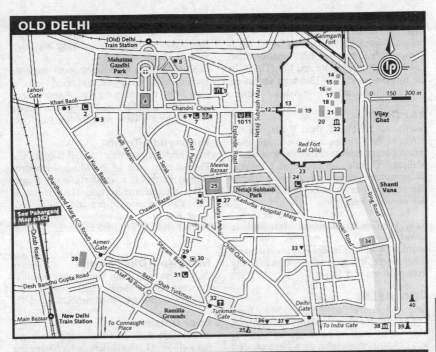

OLD DELHI

PLACES TO STAY

3	Bharat Hotel; Star Guest House
26	Hotel New City Palace
27	Hotel Bombay Orient; Karim's
35	Tourist Camp

PLACES TO EAT

6	Ghantewala
33	Moti Mahal Restaurant
36	Hotel Broadway
37	Hotel President (Tandoor)

OTHER

1	Gadodia Market
2	Fatehpuri Masjid
4	Town Hall
5	Delhi Public Library
7	Sunehri Masjid
8	Sisganj Gurdwara
9	Begum Samru's Palace
10	Gauri Shankar Temple
11	Digambara Jain Temple; Bird Hospital
12	Lahore Gate; Ticket Kiosk
13	Chatta Chowk
14	Shahi Burj
15	Hammams
16	Moti Masjid
17	Diwan-i-Khas
18	Khas Mahal
19	Naubat Khana
20	Diwan-i-Am
21	Rang Mahal
22	Mumtaz Mahal & Museum
23	Delhi Gate
24	Sunehri Masjid
25	Jama Masjid
28	Madrasah of Ghazi-ud-din
29	Bishan Swaroup Haveli
30	Sultan Raziya's Tomb
31	Kalan Masjid
32	Holy Trinity Church; Tomb of Hazrat Shah Turkman
34	Zinat-ul Masjid
38	Gandhi Memorial Museum
39	Gandhi Memorial
40	Raj Ghat

Jama Masjid

The great mosque of Old Delhi is both the largest in India and the final architectural extravagance of Shah Jahan, who also built the Taj Mahal and Delhi's Red Fort. Begun in 1644, it was not completed until 1658. The general public can enter by either the north or south gate (Rs 10).

FEROZ SHAH KOTLA

Built by Feroz Shah Tughlaq in 1354, the ruins of Ferozabad, fifth city of Delhi, are at Feroz Shah Kotla, just off Bahadur Shah Zafar Marg between Old and New Delhi. In the fortress-palace is a 13m-high sandstone Ashoka pillar inscribed with Ashoka's edicts.

RAJ GHAT

North-east of Feroz Shah Kotla, on the banks of the Yamuna, a simple square platform of black marble marks the spot where Mahatma Gandhi was cremated following his assassination in 1948. A commemorative ceremony takes place each Friday, the day he was killed.

The Raj Ghat area is now a beautiful park. The Gandhi Memorial Museum here is well worth a visit. A macabre relic is the pistol with which Gandhi was assassinated. Entry is free; it's open daily except Monday from 9.30 am to 5.30 pm.

NEW DELHI

Only a short stroll down Sansad Marg from **Connaught Place** is the **Jantar Mantar**, an observatory built by Maharaja Jai Singh II in 1725. It is dominated by a huge sundial known as the Prince of Dials.

The immensely broad **Rajpath**, or Kingsway, is a feature of architect Lutyens' New Delhi. The Republic Day parade is held here every 26 January, attracting millions of people.

The 42m-high **India Gate** is at the eastern end of the Rajpath. The official residence of the President of India, **Rashtrapati Bhavan**, stands at its west end. Completed in 1929, it is an interesting blend of Mughal and western architecture. Prior to Independence this was the viceroy's residence. He had 418 gardeners, 50 of them employed to chase away birds!

Sansad Bhavan, the Indian parliament building, stands almost hidden at the end of Sansad Marg, just north of Rajpath.

Purana Qila

Just south-east of India Gate and north of Humayun's Tomb is the old fort, Purana Qila.

This is the supposed site of Indraprastha, the original city of Delhi. The Afghan ruler, Sher Shah, completed the fort during his reign from 1538-45.

There's a small archaeological museum just inside the main gate, and good views of New Delhi from atop the gate. A sound-and-light show is underway. Timings and tickets (Rs 25) are available from the tourist office.

Humayun's Tomb

Built mid-16th century by Haji Begum, the Persian-born wife of the Mughal emperor Humayun, this is a wonderful early example of Mughal architecture. Haji Begum is buried in the tomb of red-and-white sandstone and black-and-yellow marble. Entry is Rs 5 (Rs 25 for video cameras); free on Friday.

Nizam-ud-Din's Shrine

Across the road from Humayun's tomb is the shrine of the Muslim Sufi saint, Nizam-ud-din Chishti, who died in 1325 aged 92.

Lodi Gardens

About 3km west of Humayun's tomb are the well-kept Lodi Gardens, which have the tombs of the Sayyid (15th century) and Lodi (15th to 16th century) rulers. The Bara Gumbad Mosque is a fine example of its type of plaster decoration.

Safdarjang's Tomb

Beside the small Safdarjang airport, this tomb was built in 1753-54 by the nawab of Avadh for his father, Safdarjang, and is one of the last examples of Mughal architecture before the great empire collapsed. Entry is Rs 0.50; free on Friday.

Hauz Khas Village

Midway between Safdarjang's tomb and the Qutab Minar, this area was once the reservoir for the second city of Delhi – Siri. Sights include Feroz Shah's tomb (1398) and the remains of an ancient college. Hauz Khaus is now one of the more chic suburbs in the city. The Moth ki Masjid, to the east of Hauz Khas, is the finest mosque in the Lodi style.

Qutab Minar Complex

These buildings, 15km south of Delhi, date from the onset of Muslim rule in India and are fine examples of early-Afghan architecture. The complex is open from sunrise to sunset; entry is Rs 2. The **Qutab Minar** is a soaring tower of victory that was started in 1193, immediately after the defeat of the last Hindu kingdom in Delhi.

At the foot of the Qutab Minar stands the **Quwwat-ul-Islam Masjid** (Might of Islam Mosque), the first mosque built in India. Qutab-ud-din began construction on it in 1193, but it has had a number of additions and extensions over the centuries.

The 7m-high **Iron Pillar** stands in the courtyard of the mosque and has been there since long before the mosque's construction. A Sanskrit inscription indicates that it was erected outside a Vishnu temple, and was raised in memory of the Gupta King Chandragupta Vikramaditya, who ruled from 375 to 413.

MUSEUMS & GALLERIES

The **National Museum** is on Janpath just south of Rajpath. It has exhibits dating back to the Mauryan period (2nd to 3rd century BC); from South India's Vijayanagar period (14th to 16th centuries); miniature and mural paintings; and costumes of India's Adivasis (tribal peoples). It's open Tuesday to Sunday from 10 am to 5 pm, with free guided tours at 10.30 and 11.30 am, noon and 2 pm. Admission is Rs 0.50.

The **National Gallery of Modern Art** is near India Gate. It has excellent works by Indian and colonial artists. It's open Tuesday to Sunday from 10 am to 5 pm. Entry is free.

The **Crafts Museum** is in the Aditi Pavilion at Pragati Maidan Exhibition Grounds, Mathura Rd. It has a collection of traditional Indian crafts in textiles, metal, wood and ceramics. Open Tuesday to Sunday from 9.30 am to 4.30 pm. Admission is free.

ORGANISED TOURS

The ITDC, under the name Ashok Travels & Tours (☎ 332 5035), L Block, Connaught Place, near Nirula's Hotel, has half-day (Rs 100 to Rs 125) and full-day (Rs 200) tours. You can also book at the tourist office on Janpath (see Information earlier) or at major hotels. Delhi Tourism (☎ 331 3637), N Block, Middle Circle, Connaught Place, has similar tours.

PLACES TO STAY

If Delhi is your first stop in India, it's very wise to make an advance accommodation booking. Good hotels can fill up fast, leaving you prey to hotel touts who earn their commissions by getting you into the rip-off joints.

Places to Stay – Budget

Many travellers head for Paharganj near New Delhi train station – midway between Old Delhi and New Delhi.

The alternative area is around Janpath at the southern side of Connaught Place in New Delhi, but there's less choice.

Camping The *Tourist Camp* (☎ 327 2898) is in Old Delhi, near Delhi Gate on Jawaharlal Nehru Marg, 2km from Connaught Place. It's Rs 50 with your own tent; basic rooms with shared bathroom are Rs 125/200; air-cooled doubles are Rs 250 (Rs 390 with bathroom).

Connaught Place & Janpath Area The *Ringo Guest House* (☎ 331 0605, 17 Scindia House), down a small side street near the tourist office, has dorm beds for Rs 90, singles/doubles with common bath for Rs 125/250 and doubles with private bath for Rs 350. The rooms are very small but it's clean enough.

Not far away is the *Sunny Guest House* (☎ 331 2909, 152 Scindia House) with similar prices and standards.

Paharganj Area The following five places are all on Main Bazaar:

Hotel Gold Regency (☎ 354 0101, fax 354 0202) has large clean doubles from Rs 700 to Rs 900. It has a good restaurant and a noisy disco.

DELHI

NEW DELHI

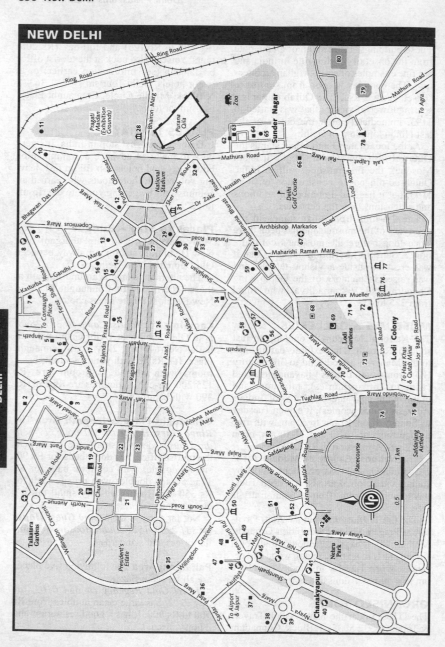

NEW DELHI

PLACES TO STAY

2	YWCA Blue Triangle Family Hostel
4	Ashok Yatri Niwas ITDCl
5	ITDC Hotel Janpath; Air Lanka
6	ITDC Hotel Kanishka; Kanishka Shopping Plaza; Jammu & Kashmir Tourist Office; Kerala Tourist Office
17	Hotel Le Meridien; Le Belvedere; Golden Phoenix; CJ's
34	Taj Mahal Hotel; House of Ming; Captains Cabin; Haveli; Longchamp
36	Diplomat Hotel
37	Vishwa Yuvak Kendra
43	Ashok Hotel; Iran Air; Kazakhstan Airlines
48	Youth Hostel (Bishwa Yuvak Kendra)
55	Claridges Hotel; Dhaba; Jade Garden; Pickwicks; Corbetts
61	Ambassador Hotel; Das-aprakash; Larry's China
62	Maharani Guest House
63	Kailash Inn; La Sagrita Tourist Home
64	Jukaso Inn
66	Oberoi Hotel

OTHER

1	Dr Ram Manohar Lohia Hospital
3	Indian Airlines
7	Max Mueller Bhavan
8	Nepalese Embassy
9	Rabindra Bhavan (Sangeet Natak Akademi; Lalit Kala Akademi; Shahitya Akademi)
10	Supreme Court
11	Appu Ghar
12	Patiala House
13	Baroda House
14	Hyderabad House
15	Andhra Pradesh Tourist Office
16	Andaman & Nicobar Islands Tourist Office
18	Sansad Bhavan (Parliament House)
19	Gurdwara Rakab Ganj
20	Cathedral Church of the Redemption
21	Rashtrapati Bhavan
22	Secretariat (North Block)
23	Secretariat (South Block)
24	Vijay Chowk
25	Indira Gandhi National Centre for the Arts
26	National Museum; Archeological Survey of India
27	India Gate
28	Crafts Museum
29	Children's Park
30	Bikaner House (Rajasthan Tourist Office & Deluxe Buses to Jaipur)
31	National Gallery of Modern Art
32	Sher Shah's Gate; Khairul Manzil Masjid
33	Pandara Market (Ichiban; Pindi; Chicken Inn)
35	Dandi March Sculpture
38	New Sikkim House (Sikkim Tourist Office)
39	US Embassy
40	French Embassy
41	Australian Embassy
42	Santushti Shopping Centre (Basil & Thyme)
44	UK Embassy
45	Norwegian Embassy
46	Sri Lankan High Commission; Mizoram Tourist Office
47	Mizoram Tourist Office
49	Nehru Planetarium
50	Nehru Museum
51	Tripura Tourist Office
52	Arunachal Pradesh Tourist Office
53	Indira Gandhi Memorial Museum
54	Gandhi Smriti
56	Danish Embassy
57	Israeli Embassy
58	Brazilian Embassy
59	Lok Nayak Bhavan (Ministry of Home Affairs)
60	Khan Market (The Bookshop; Bahri Sons; China Garden; Chian Fare)
65	Sunder Nagar Market
67	East West Medical Centre
68	Sikander Lodi's Tomb
69	Bara Gumbad Masjid
70	Goa Tourist Office
71	India International Centre
72	World Wide Fund for Nature India
73	Mohammed Shah's Tomb
74	Safdarjang's Tomb
75	Indian Airlines (24 Hours)
76	Indian Habitat Centre; Habitat World
77	Tibet House
78	Nizam-ud-din's Shrine
79	Isa Khan's Tomb
80	Humayun's Tomb

DELHI

Ajay Guest House (☎ 354 3125) has clean rooms with bath from Rs 160/ 210. It has a pleasant rooftop and a German bakery in the foyer.

Hare Rama Guest House (☎ 352 9273), opposite, is popular with Israeli travellers. It has rooms from Rs 120/210 without/with bath. The restaurant is open 24 hours.

Hare Krishna Guest House (☎ 753 3017) has nice, clean doubles from Rs 190. There's a rooftop restaurant.

Anoop Hotel (☎ 352 9366) is good value, with rooms with bath for Rs 180/250. There's a rooftop terrace and snack bar. Checkout is 24 hours.

Just north of New Delhi train station, past the Desh Bandhu Gupta Rd flyover, on Arakashan Rd are two good hotels: *Hotel Ajanta (☎ 752 0925)*, at No 36, charges Rs 745/845 for deluxe/air-con doubles and has a restaurant, email centre and travel agency; *Hotel Tourist Lodge (☎ 732990),* at No 26, has air-cooled/air-con doubles for Rs 450/ 650, and deluxe rooms with chintzy honeymoon suite furnishings for Rs 700.

Airport The *Retiring Rooms* at the airport are at both the domestic *(Terminal I, ☎ 329 5126)* and the international *(Terminal II, ☎ 545 2011)* airports. You can use them if you have a confirmed departure within 24 hours of arrival. Dorm beds cost Rs 80.

Places to Stay – Mid-Range
There's a luxury tax of 10% on rooms over Rs 500, and some places also levy a service charge of 5% to 10%.

The Ys The Ys are popular so book ahead. The *YMCA Tourist Hotel (☎ 336 1915, fax 374 6032, Jai Singh Rd)*, near the Jantar Mantar, is open 24 hours. It has rooms from Rs 500/950 without/with bath. Breakfast is included, and there's a pool.

The *YWCA International Guest House (☎ 336 1517, fax 334 1763, 10 Sansad Marg)* has singles/doubles with bath for Rs 550/ 850, including breakfast. It's near Connaught Place and has a good restaurant and travel agency.

YWCA Blue Triangle Family Hostel (☎ 336 0133, fax 336 0202, Ashoka Rd) is just off Sansad Marg. Rates, including breakfast, start at Rs 550/850 for clean rooms with private bath.

Connaught Place & Janpath Area The *Hotel 55 (☎ 332 1244, fax 332 0769, 55 H Block, Connaught Place)* has comfortable rooms with balcony for Rs 1000/1500.

Hotel Central Court (☎ 331 5013, N Block) has rooms from Rs 800/1150.

Other Areas There are two excellent private guesthouses to the west of Connaught Place: *Master Paying Guest House (☎ 574 1089 & 578 8914, R-500 New Rajendra Nagar)*, a homey and friendly place with lovely doubles for Rs 350 to Rs 750; and *Yatri House (☎ 752 5563, 3/4 Rani Jhansi Rd)*, with clean rooms from Rs 900.

Places to Stay – Top End
Expect to add taxes of at least 20% to the tariffs.

Hotel Marina (☎ 332 4658, fax 332 8609, G Block, Connaught Place) has rooms for Rs 2600/3200, including breakfast.

Claridges Hotel (☎ 301 0211, fax 301 0625, 12 Aurangzeb Rd) is a comfortable, older place, with four good restaurants, a swimming pool and a health club. Rooms start at US$175.

Imperial Hotel (☎ 332 5332, fax 332 4542, Janpath) is a pleasant old-fashioned hotel with a pool and a big garden. Rooms are from US$200.

Near the airport is the *Radisson Hotel Delhi (☎ 613 7373)*, just 3km from the international terminal. Singles/doubles start at US$350/450.

Centaur Hotel (☎ 565 2223, fax 565 2256), with rooms for US$150/170, is on Gurgaon Rd, 2km from the international terminal and 5km from the domestic terminal.

Hotel Maurya Sheraton (☎ 611 2233, fax 615 5555), on Sardar Patel Marg, is a 500-room hotel (from US$400) with two excellent restaurants, a solar-heated swimming pool (the only one in Delhi) and disco.

PLACES TO EAT
Delhi has an excellent array of places to eat – from cheap dhabas with dishes for less than Rs 15 to swanky restaurants where a meal for two can top Rs 3500.

Janpath & Connaught Place
Nirula's (L Block, Outer Circle) does a wide variety of snacks, both Indian and western and is open from 10 am to midnight. Above it is a sit-down restaurant called *Pot Pourri*, and the *Chinese Room*, with meals for two in the Rs 400 region. Downstairs there's the congenial British-style pub Pegasus.

Sona Rupa Restaurant (Janpath) does good north and south Indian veg food (excellent dosas). It's good value at around Rs 80 per person.

Don't Pass Me By, in the same lane as the Ringo and Sunny guesthouses, is both popular and cheap. It caters to international tastes and is great for breakfast. There are other cheap eateries along the lane.

Vega, at the Hotel Alka, specialises in veg food cooked Delhi style (in pure ghee but without onion and garlic).

Paharganj Area

Main Bazaar in Paharganj has a handful of cheap restaurants that cater to foreign travellers.

German Bakery, in the foyer of the Hotel Ajay, does sandwiches, snacks and a wide range of sugar-laden cakes for about Rs 25 per piece.

Metropolis Restaurant in the hotel of the same name just past Rajguru Rd, is a good place to eat, either in the ground floor restaurant or on the rooftop. Most main dishes are around Rs 175.

Old Delhi

There are many places to eat in Old Delhi at the west end of Chandni Chowk. *Ghantewala*, near the Siganj Gurdwara, is reputed to have some of the best Indian sweets in Delhi.

Tandoor, at the Hotel President on Asaf Ali Rd near the Tourist Camp, is excellent. It has the usual two-waiters-per-diner service and a sitar playing pleasantly in the background.

Chor Bizaare is close by in the Hotel Broadway. The food is good but pricey; Rs 800 for two.

Moti Mahal Restaurant, around the corner on Netaji Subhash Marg in Daryaganj, has been going for 50 years and is still noted for its tandoori dishes.

ENTERTAINMENT

First City magazine tells you what's going on in town. Major dance and live music venues include *Habitat World* (☎ 469 1920, *Lodhi Rd*) at the India Habitat Centre, the nearby *India International Centre* (☎ 461 9431), *Kamani Auditorium* (☎ 338 8084, *Copernicus Marg*) and the *Triveni Chamber Theatre* (205 Tansen Marg) at Triveni Kala Sangam, close to Rabindra Bhavan.

There are a number of cinemas around Connaught Place, showing Hindi mass appeal movies; seats range from Rs 25 to Rs 50. *Habitat World* has a cinema showing Indian documentaries and art house films.

El Rodeo, a bar-restaurant on Connaught Place, has a cover charge of Rs 200 after 7.30 pm if you only want to drink and not eat. Draught beer is Rs 80.

Jazz Bar at the Maurya Sheraton is very good, with live jazz each evening, but drinks are expensive – over Rs 200!

CJ's is a nightclub at Hotel Le Meridien. Entry is Rs 500 per couple.

SHOPPING

Good buys include silk products, precious stones, leather and woodwork. The Central Cottage Industries Emporium is on Janpath. Here you will find items from across India. Along Baba Kharak Singh Marg, two streets from Janpath, are a number of state emporiums. Each sells handicrafts from their state.

There are scores of shops around Connaught Place and Janpath. By the Imperial Hotel are a number of stalls and small shops run by Tibetan refugees and rapacious Kashmiris selling carpets, jewellery and many (often instant) antiques.

In Old Delhi, Chandni Chowk is the famous shopping street. Here you will find carpets and jewellery of all descriptions. Perfumes are made in the narrow street, Cariba Kalan.

Main Bazaar in Paharganj has an interesting variety of perfumes, oils, soaps and incense at two places (both signposted), one near the Hotel Vivek and another near the Camran Lodge. Monday is the official weekly holiday for the shops in Main Bazaar but you'll find many shops are open seven days a week.

GETTING THERE & AWAY

Delhi is a major international gateway to India; for details on arriving from overseas see the Getting There & Away chapter at the beginning of this book.

Delhi is a major centre for domestic travel, with extensive bus, rail and air connections.

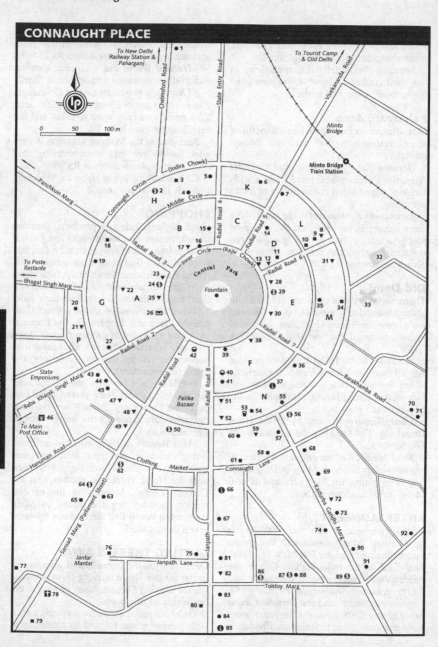

CONNAUGHT PLACE

To New Delhi
Railway Station &
Paharganj

To Tourist Camp
& Old Delhi

Chelmsford Road

State Entry Road

Vivekananda Road

Minto
Bridge

Minto Bridge
Train Station

Panchkuin Marg

Connaught Circus

(Indira Chowk)

Middle Circle

Radial Road 3

Radial Road 4

Radial Road 5

Inner Circle — (Rajiv Chowk)

Radial Road 6

Central Park

Fountain

To Poste
Restante

Bhagat Singh Marg

Radial Road 2

Radial Road 1

Radial Road 8

Radial Road 7

State
Emporiums

Baba Kharak Singh Marg

Palika
Bazaar

Barakhamba Road

To Main
Post Office

Hanuman Road

Clothing   Market

Connaught Lane

Kasturba Gandhi Marg

Sansad Marg (Parliament Street)

Jantar
Mantar

Janpath

Janpath Lane

Tolstoy Marg

CONNAUGHT PLACE

PLACES TO STAY
3 Hotel 55
6 York Hotel
9 Nirula's Hotel
10 Jukaso Inn Down Town
11 Hotel Palace Heights
18 Hotel Marina
20 Hotel Alka; Vega
34 Hotel Blue
54 Hotel Central Court
58 Sunny Guest House
61 Ringo Guest House;
   Don't Pass Me By Café;
   Don't Pass Me By Travels
65 Park Hotel; Las Meninas;
   Someplace Else
76 Mr SC Jain's Guest House
77 YMCA Tourist Hotel;
   Y Tours & Travels
79 YWCA International Guest
   House; VINstring Holidays
80 Imperial Hotel; Spice Route;
   Tavern Restaurant; Garden
   Party; Thomas Cook;
   Student Travel
   Information Centre

PLACES TO EAT
8 Nirula's Restaurants;
   Pegasus
12 Embassy
13 Pizza Express
17 Cafe 100; Zen Restaurant;
21 McDonald's
22 Fa Yian
23 Wenger's
25 El Rodeo
28 Kovil Pizza Hut
30 United Coffee House
31 Domino's Pizza
38 The Host
47 Gaylord
48 El Arab Restaurants;
   The Cellar

49 Kwality Restaurant;
   People Tree
51 Nirula's (Branch)
52 Wimpy
59 Croissants Etc
72 Parikrama; Tarom
73 Air Canada
82 Sona Rupa Restaurant; Royal
   Nepal Airlines Corporation
   (RNAC)

OTHER
1 Railway Booking Office
2 ANZ Grindlays Bank
4 Cox & Kings
5 Plaza Cinema
7 English Book Depot
14 Odeon Cinema
15 Bookworm
16 New Book Depot
19 Gulf Air Jet Airways
24 American Express;
   Gulf Air; Singapore Airlines;
   Jet Airways
26 Post Office
27 Malaysia Airlines; Royal
   Jordanian
29 ANZ Grindlays Bank
32 Shankar Market
   (Piccadilly Book Store)
33 Super Bazaar
35 Singapore Airlines (SIA)
36 Aeroflot
37 Delhi Tourism
39 Sita World Travels
40 EATS Airport Bus
41 Indian Airlines
42 Prepaid Auto-Rickshaw Kiosk
43 Khadi Gramodyog Bhavan
44 Calculus Cyber Centre
45 Regal Cinema
46 Hanuman Mandir
50 Citibank; Air India
53 Blues Bar

55 Travel Corporation
   of India
56 Hongkong & Shanghai
   Bank
57 Air France
60 Oxford Book Shop
62 Bank of Baroda
63 British Airways; Swissair
64 Standard Chartered Bank;
   Allahabad Bank
66 Government of India
   Tourist Office;
   Delhi Photo Company
67 Tan's Travel
68 PIA
69 American Center
70 Emirates;
   Wheels Rent-a-Car
71 Kuwait Airways; Saudia
74 British Council
75 Map Sales Office
78 Free Church
81 Lufthansa Airlines
83 Central Cottage Industries
   Emporium
84 Japan Airlines
85 Chandralok Building
   (Haryana, Himachal Pradesh
   & Uttar Pradesh Tourist
   Offices; Delta Airlines; Druk
   Air; Japan Airlines;
   Lufthansa Airlines)
86 Deutsche Bank;
   Cathay Pacific Airlines
87 Deutsche Bank
88 Jagson Airlines
89 Credit Lyonnaise
90 Asian Airlines;
   Ethiopian Airlines
91 United; Sahara India;
   Scandinavian Airlines (SAS)
92 KLM; Northwest Airlines;
   El Al Israel Airline;
   Uzbekistan Airways

DELHI

Air

The domestic terminals (Terminals IA & IB of the Indira Gandhi international airport) are 15km from the centre, and the international terminal (Terminal II) is a further 5km. There's a free IAAI bus between the two terminals, or you can use the EATS service (see the Getting Around section, later in this chapter).

There's a 24 hour State Bank of India and Thomas Cook foreign exchange counters in the arrivals hall, after you go through customs and immigration.

Several airlines require you to have the baggage you're checking in X-rayed and sealed, so do this at the machines just inside the departure hall before you queue to check in. Nearly all tickets have the departure tax

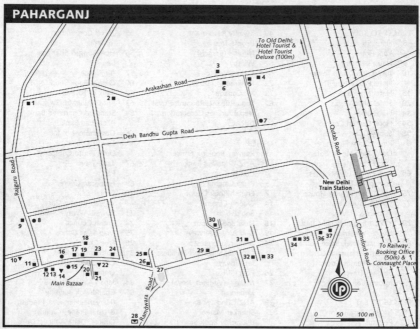

PAHARGANJ

PLACES TO STAY
1   Hotel Diplomat Inn
2   Hotel Shiva Continental
3   Hotel Soma
4   Hotel Ajanta
5   Hotel Syal
6   Tourist Inn; Swad Restaurant
9   Hotel Kelson
11 Metropolis Tourist Home;
    Metropolis Restuarant
12 Hotel Star View
13 Hotel Satyam
17 Hotel Vishal; Lords Café;
    Hare Krishna Guest House
18 Major's Den
19 Anoop Hotel
20 Ajay Guest House; German
    Bakery
21 Hare Rama Guest House; Aa
    Bee Travels
23 Ankush Guest House
24 Hotel Vivek
25 Hotel Navrang
26 Hotel Payal
29 Camran Lodge; Money
    Changer
30 Hotel Namaskar; Smyle Inn
31 Hotel Bright Guest House
32 Hotel Star Palace
33 Hotel Down Town
34 Kiran Guest House
35 Kailash Guest House
36 Traveller Guest House Inn
37 Hotel Gold Regency

PLACES TO EAT
10 Malhotra Restaurant
14 Khosla Cafe
22 Diamond Cafe

OTHER
7   Shiela Cinema
8   Imperial Cinema
15 Book Exchange;
    Bicycle Hire
16 E-Mail Centre
27 Vegetable Market
28 Paharganj Post Office

included in the price; if not you must pay at the State Bank counter in the departures hall, also before check-in.

Indian Airlines has a number of offices. The Malhotra Building office (☎ 331 0517), F Block, Connaught Place, is probably the most convenient, though busy at most times. It's open daily except Saturday from 10 am to 5 pm.

There is another office in the PTI Building (☎ 371 9168), Sansad Marg. It's open daily except Sunday from 10 am to 5 pm. At Safdarjang airport on Aurobindo Marg there's a 24 hour office (☎ 141). This is a quick place for booking. For pre-recorded flight departure information, ring ☎ 142.

Note that if you have an onward connection to another city in India, it may be with Air India, the country's international carrier, rather than the domestic carrier, Indian Airlines. If so, you must check in at the international terminal (Terminal II) rather than the domestic terminal.

Other Domestic Airlines As well as the offices listed below, private airlines have offices at the airport's domestic terminal.

Archana Airways
 (☎ 684 2001) 41A Friends Colony East, Mathura Rd
Jagson Airlines
 (☎ 372 1593) 12E Vandana Bldg, 11 Tolstoy Marg
Jet Airways
 (☎ 685 3700) Jetair House, 13 Community Centre, Yusuf Sarai
Sahara India
 (☎ 332 6851) Ambadeep Bldg, Kasturba Gandhi Marg

International Airlines International airlines include the following:

Air Canada
 (☎ 372 0014) Hindustan Times House, Kasturba Gandhi Marg
Air France
 (☎ 331 2853) 7 Atma Ram Mansion, Connaught Place
Air India
 (☎ 331 1225) Jeevan Bharati Bldg, Connaught Place
Air Lanka
 (☎ 332 6843) Hotel Janpath
Biman Bangladesh Airlines
 (☎ 335 4401) World Trade Centre, Babar Rd, Connaught Place
British Airways
 (☎ 332 7428) DLF Bldg, Sansad Marg

Delta Airlines
 (☎ 332 5222) Chandralok Bldg, Janpath
Druk Air (Bhutan)
 (☎ 331 0990) Chandralok Bldg, 36 Janpath
El Al
 (☎ 335 7965) Prakash Deep Bldg, 7 Tolstoy Marg
Emirates
 (☎ 332 4665) Kanchenjunga Bldg, 18 Barakhamba Rd
Gulf Air
 (☎ 332 7814) G-12, Connaught Place
KLM-Royal Dutch Airlines
 (☎ 372 1141) Prakash Deep Bldg, 7 Tolstoy Marg
Lufthansa Airlines
 (☎ 332 3310) 56 Janpath
Malaysia Airlines
 (☎ 332 1300) G33, Connaught Place
Northwest
 (☎ 372 1141) Prakash Deep Bldg, 7 Tolstoy Marg
Pakistan International Airlines (PIA)
 (☎ 331 3161) Kailash Bldg, Kasturba Gandhi Marg
Royal Jordanian Airlines
 (☎ 332 0635) G-56 Connaught Place
Royal Nepal Airlines Corporation
 (☎ 332 1164) 44 Janpath
Singapore Airlines (SIA)
 (☎ 332 0145) G11, Connaught Place
Swissair
 (☎ 332 5511) DLF Bldg, Sansad Marg
United Airlines
 (☎ 335 3377) Amba Deep Bldg, Kasturba Gandhi Marg

Bus

The main bus station is the Interstate bus terminal (ISBT) at Kashmiri Gate, north of the (Old) Delhi train station. It has 24 hour left-luggage facilities, a State Bank of India branch, post office, pharmacy, and restaurant. City buses depart from here to locations all around Delhi.

A number of state government bus companies operate from here, including Rajasthan Roadways (☎ 296 1246), central block. There are fast and frequent bus services to Jaipur (5½ hrs, Rs 84).

Deluxe buses for Jaipur leave from Bikaner House, Pandara Rd (5 hrs, Rs 150 and Rs 270 for better but less frequent air-con service).

From the Sarai Kale Khan ISBT, close to Nizamuddin train station, there are frequent departures for Agra (5 hrs, Rs 75 to Rs 100 depending on class).

Train

The best place to make bookings is the special foreign tourist booking office upstairs in New Delhi train station, open Monday to Saturday from 7.30 am to 5 pm. This is the place to go if you want a tourist-quota allocation, are the holder of an Indrail Pass or want to buy an Indrail Pass. Tickets must be paid with rupees backed up by a bank exchange certificate, or in US dollars and pounds sterling with any change given in rupees.

The main ticket office is on Chelmsford Rd, between New Delhi train station and Connaught Place. Take a number as you enter the building, and wait at the allotted window.

It's best to arrive first thing in the morning, or when it reopens after lunch. The office is open Monday to Saturday from 7.45 am to 9 pm. On Sunday it's open until 1.50 pm only.

There are two main stations – Delhi train station in Old Delhi, and New Delhi train station at Paharganj. If you're departing from the Old Delhi station allow up to an hour to wind your way through the traffic snarls. Between the Old and New Delhi stations you can take the No 6 bus.

There's also the Nizamuddin train station south of the New Delhi area. It's worth getting off here if you are staying south of Connaught Place.

Some trains to Jaipur, Jodhpur and Udaipur operate out of Sarai Rohilla station – it's about 3.5km north-west of Connaught Place on Guru Govind Singh Marg. The exception is the *Shatabdi Express* to Jaipur, which operates from New Delhi station. For details about trains to Agra, see Getting There & Away in the Agra chapter.

GETTING AROUND

Delhi is large, congested, and the buses get hopelessly crowded. The alternative is a taxi, an auto-rickshaw, or for the truly brave, a bicycle.

To/From the Airport

The Ex-Servicemen's Air Link Transport Service (EATS; ☎ 331 6530) has a regular bus service between the airport (both terminals) and Connaught Place (Rs 30 plus Rs 5 per large piece of luggage). They will drop you off at major hotels en route and at the entrance to New Delhi train station for Paharganj. In Connaught Place the service leaves from near the Indian Airlines office, between 4 am and 11.30 pm.

When leaving the international terminal, the counter for the EATS bus is just to the right as you exit the building. This is probably the best, although not the quickest, way into the city if you arrive late at night (see the warning about pre-paid taxis that follows).

Just outside the terminal is the Delhi Traffic Police Pre-Paid Taxi Booth where you'll get the lowest prices (Rs 170 to Paharganj). You'll be given a voucher to present at the booth just outside the airport building.

If you're heading into the centre late at night, most budget hotels are locked from around midnight until at least 6 am, so unless you have arranged a late arrival, your options are limited. If you take a taxi from the airport late at night, before getting into the vehicle make an obvious point of noting down the registration number, and try to find a companion in a similar predicament. A number of travellers have been taken to a hotel, told it's full, then taken on to another hotel (often in Karol Bagh) and intimidated into staying there at vastly inflated prices (up to US$150). If this is your first trip to India it may be best to wait in the terminal building until daylight when there is much less risk of getting led astray.

At the domestic terminal, the taxi booking desk is just inside the terminal and charges Rs 170 to Paharganj, plus Rs 5 per bag.

Bus

Avoid buses during the rush hours. Whenever possible try to board (and leave) at a starting or finishing point, such as the Regal and Plaza cinemas in Connaught Place. There are some seats reserved for women on the left-hand side of the bus. The White

Line and Green Line buses are slightly more expensive and thus a little less crowded. Private buses and minibuses also run on these routes.

Taxi & Auto-Rickshaw

All taxis and auto-rickshaws are metered but the meters are invariably out of date, 'not working' or the drivers simply refuse to use them.

If you're near Connaught Place pick up an auto-rickshaw from the pre-paid booth near Palika Bazaar. Otherwise, negotiate a price before you set out. At the end of a metered journey you will have to pay according to a perversely complicated scale of revised charges. There are fare charts printed in *Delhi City Guide* (Rs 15, available from newsagents). If you have one, pay what you think is the right price and leave it at that.

A trip from Connaught Place to the Red Fort should cost around Rs 60 by taxi or Rs 30 by auto-rickshaw. From Connaught Place to Paharganj is Rs 15. From Connaught Place to Humayun's Tomb about Rs 30 is fair for an auto-rickshaw. From 11 pm to 5 am there is a 20% surcharge for auto-rickshaws and 25% in taxis.

To hire a taxi for eight hours should cost around Rs 450, though the driver will expect a tip of around Rs 100.

Cycle-Rickshaw

Cycle-rickshaws are banned from the Connaught Place area and New Delhi itself, but they can be handy for travelling between the northern edge of Connaught Place and Paharganj, and around Old Delhi.

Motorcycle

The range of machines available for hire when you get to Rajasthan is rather limited, so you may wish to make your motorcycle arrangements in Delhi.

If you are in the market for a new Enfield motorcycle, Karol Bagh is the place to look. Try Essaar on Jhandi Walan Extension and Nanna Motors at 112 Press Road.

For second-hand bikes and parts, try Madaan Motors at 1770/53 Naiwala Gali, Harkisan Das Road, or try Chawla Motorcycles, next door.

Mumbai (Bombay)

Although Delhi is closer to Jaipur, the capital of Rajasthan, some people fly into Mumbai, which is the main international gateway to India.

Mumbai is an exhilarating city fuelled by entrepreneurial energy, determination and dreams. It's the economic powerhouse of the nation.

To many visitors, Mumbai is the glamour of Bollywood cinema, cricket on the *maidans* on weekends, *bhelpuri* (a delicious puffed bread snack stuffed with vegetables) on the beach at Chowpatty and red double-decker buses. It is also the infamous red-light district of Kamathipura, Asia's largest slums, communalist politics and powerful underworld dons.

For a more in-depth guide to the city, get hold of Lonely Planet's *Mumbai*.

Orientation

Mumbai is an island connected by bridges to the mainland. The principal part of the city is concentrated at the southern claw-shaped end of the island known as south Mumbai. The southernmost peninsula is Colaba where most travellers gravitate since it has a decent range of hotels and restaurants.

Directly north of Colaba is the congested commercial area known as Fort. On the northern and western fringes of this area are most of the city's impressive colonial buildings, including Victoria Terminus (VT) and the main post office. It's bordered on the west by a series of maidans – interconnected grass areas. Beyond the maidans is Churchgate train station and the poorly planned modern high-rise business centre of Nariman Point. Marine Drive sweeps around Back Bay, connecting Nariman Point with Chowpatty Beach and the classy residential peninsula of Malabar Hill.

South Mumbai ends around Crawford Market. North of here, and in complete con-

Highlights

- **Elephanta Island** – stand in awe before the triple-headed Shiva sculpture
- **Bazaars** – lose yourself in the bustling bazaars of Bhuleshwar and Kalbadevi
- **Juhu Beach** – get into the carnival spirit on a weekend afternoon

trast, are the congested central bazaars of Kalbadevi. The island's eastern seaboard is dominated by the city's docks, which are off limits. Farther north, across Mahim Creek, on what was once the separate island of Salsette, are the suburbs of Greater Mumbai and the international and domestic airports. The satellite city of New Bombay is taking shape on the mainland east of Mumbai.

Information

Tourist Offices The efficient Government of India tourist office (☎ 203 3144, fax 201 4496) at 123 Maharshi Karve Rd, opposite Churchgate train station, is open weekdays from 8.30 am to 6 pm, and on Saturday to 2 pm. It operates a tourist hotline (☎ 1913), a 24 hour booth (☎ 832 5331) at the international airport, and a counter (☎ 614 9200) at the domestic airport.

The practical Tours Division & Reservation Office of the Maharashtra Tourism Development Corporation (MTDC; ☎ 202 6713, fax 285 2182) at CDO Hutments, Madame Cama Rd, Nariman Point, makes bookings for city tours and MTDC hotels.

Money American Express (☎ 204 8291) in the Regal Cinema Bldg, Shivaji Marg, Colaba, handles foreign exchange transactions and provides cash advances on American Express credit cards Monday to Saturday

What's in a Name?

The city of Bombay officially became Mumbai in January 1996. Many locals are clearly in favour of the name change – it had been part of the democratically elected Shiv Sena's agenda for decades. They believe the new name reclaims the city's heritage and signifies its emergence from a colonial past. Others see the change as an assertion of Maratha identity (Mumbai is the Maratha name) that is inappropriate in a city built and inhabited by people from all over India.

Supporters of 'Mumbai' believe that the city's name came from the goddess Mumba, worshipped by the original Koli inhabitants at the Mumbadevi Temple which stood on the present site of Victoria Terminus. When the Portuguese arrived they called the harbour Bombaim. This may have stemmed from 'buan bahia', meaning 'good bay' in Portuguese, or (much more likely) is a corruption of the original Koli name. When the islands were donated to the British, they anglicised Bombaim into Bombay.

from 9.30 am to 6.30 pm. Thomas Cook (☎ 204 8556) at 324 Dr D Naoroji Rd, Fort, also provides speedy foreign exchange. It's open weekdays from 9.30 am to 7 pm, and until 6.30 pm on Saturday.

ANZ Grindlays Bank (☎ 267 0162) at 90 Mahatma Gandhi (MG) Rd, Fort, offers cash advances on Visa and MasterCard. Bobcards (☎ 202 0630) on the 1st floor, Bank of Baroda, Colaba Causeway, provides a similar service but charges a 1% commission.

Citibank (☎ 823 2484) at 293 Dr D Naoroji Rd, Fort, has 24 hour ATMs, one of which is linked to international banking networks. There are 24 hour foreign exchange bureaus at both Mumbai airports.

Post & Communications The main post office is near VT. It's open from 10 am to 8 pm Monday to Saturday. The parcel post office is in a separate building behind the main post office, accessible from a driveway off P D'Mello Rd. It's open Monday to Saturday from 11 am to 4 pm (closed 1 to 1.30 pm). There's a post office in Colaba on Henry Rd.

The international telecommunications centre run by the carrier VSNL (☎ 262 4020, fax 262 4027) is on Bhaurao Patil Marg in Fort. It's most useful for Home Direct, collect call and call-back services. It's open from 8 am to 8 pm daily.

The British Council Library (☎ 282 3560) at Mittal Tower A Wing, 1st floor, Barrister Rajni Patel Marg, Nariman Point, offers Internet use (Rs 50 for 30 minutes).

Travel Agencies Transway International (☎ 262 6066, email transkam.etn@smt. sprintrpg.ems.vsnl.net.in), on the 2nd floor of Pantaky House, 8 Maruti Cross Lane, off Maruti St, Fort, can provide advice on bus and rail travel but does not issue tickets for either. Avoid the decoy Transunique agency on the same floor.

Space Travels (☎ 266 3258) at Nanabhay Mansion, Sir P Mehta Rd, and Thomas Cook (see the Money section) are reliable. Magnum Leisure Holidays (☎ 283 8628) at 10 Henry Rd is handy for those in Colaba.

Bookshops The best bookshop is Crossword (☎ 492 0253), 1st floor, 22 Bhulabhai Desai Rd, Breach Candy. There's also the Strand Book Stall (☎ 266 1994), just off Sir P Mehta Rd, Fort, and the Nalanda Bookshop in the Taj Mahal Hotel, Colaba.

Visa Extensions Applications can be lodged at the Foreigners' Registration Office in Mumbai – see Visas & Documents in the Facts for the Visitor chapter.

Medical Services The Breach Candy Hospital (☎ 363 2657) is at 60 Bhulabhai Desai Rd, Breach Candy. The Apollo Pharmacy (☎ 284 2683), 18 K Dubash Marg, Fort, is a central 24 hour chemist.

Emergency Call ☎ 102 for an ambulance.

MUMBAI

MUMBAI

Reay Road

P D'Mello Road

Nandlal Jani Road

To Eastern
Express
Highway

Patanwala Marg

Dr Babasaheb Ambedkar Marg

Victoria Gardens

Byculla
Train Station

Byculla

Victoria Road

Motishah Road

S Balwant Singh Road

Jijibhoy Road

Jail Road

Babula Tank Road

Merchant Rd.

Ali Road

Metherali Road

Mohammed Ali Road

Abdul Rahman Street

Sheikh Memon St.

Kalbadevi Rd

Kalbadevi

Girgaum

Clare Road

Clerk Road

Bapurao Jagtap Marg

Maulana Azad Road

Maulana Azad Road

Dhabu St

To Juhu, Airports &
Western Express
Highway

Mahalaxmi
Train Station

Sane Guruji Marg

Arthur Road

Morland Road

Pupraji Road

Suklaji
Street

Dr Boman Behram Marg

Dr Anandrao Nair Road

Kamathipura

Grant Rd (Maulana Shaukatali Rd)

Grant Rd

N Desai Road

Vithalbhai Patel Road

Patel Road

Jaganath Shankar Shet Rd

Charni Road
Train Station

Mahalaxmi
Racecourse

Entrance

Keshavro Khade Marg

Lala Lajpatrai Marg

Mumbai Central
Train Station

Falkland Road

Grant Road
Train Station

Dr Bhadkam Road

Girgaum Road

Cumballa
Hill

Tardeo Road

Tardeo Road

To Worli &
Nehru Centre
(100m)

S K Bardewala Marg

Peddar Road (Dr G Deshmukh Marg)

Bhulabhai Desai Road (Warden Road)

Kemp's
Corner

Fly-over

Rama Bai

Pandita

A Krani Marg

Chowpatty Seaface

Chowpatty
Beach

Kamala
Nehru
Park

Hanging
Gardens

Arabian
Sea

Jagmohandas Marg (Lakshminbhai Marg)

Nepean Sea Road

Bal Gangadhar Kher Marg

Walkeshwar Rd

Malabar
Hill

0   250   500 m

PLACES TO STAY
15 Hotel Kemp's Corner;
    Shalimar Hotel
23 Hotel Sapna
40 West End Hotel
42 Bentley Hotel
47 Ambassador & Chateau
    Windsor hotels
51 Sea Green &
    Sea Green South hotels
56 Ritz Hotel; Samrat Restaurant
57 Marine Plaza
61 Oberoi & Oberoi Towers
67 Fariyas Hotel
73 Hotel President

PLACES TO EAT
16 China Garden
22 Cafe Naaz
27 New Kulfi Centre
28 Cafe Ideal & Cream Centre
30 Bhelpuri Stalls
48 Purohit
50 The Pizzeria
66 Kailash Parbat

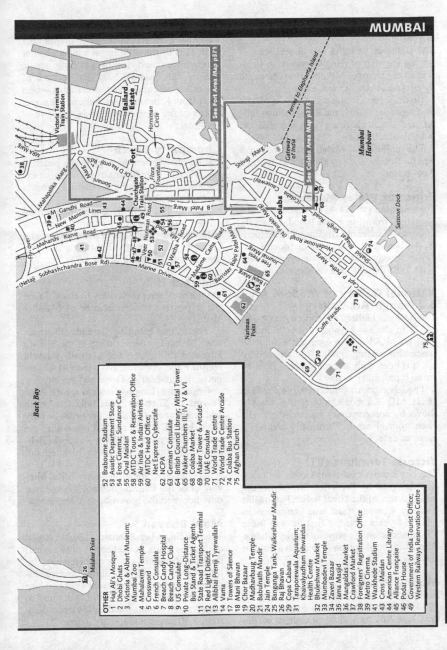

MUMBAI

OTHER
1 Haji Ali's Mosque
2 Dhobi Ghats
3 Victoria & Albert Museum;
   Mumbai Zoo
4 Mahalaxmi Temple
5 Crossword
6 French Consulate
7 Breach Candy Hospital
8 Breach Candy Club
9 US Consulate
10 Private Long-Distance
   Bus Stand & Ticket Agents
11 State Road Transport Terminal
12 Red Light District
13 Allibhai Premji Tyrewallah
14 Vama
17 Towers of Silence
18 Mani Bhavan
19 Chor Bazaar
20 Madhavbaug Temple
21 Babulnath Mandir
24 Jain Temple
25 Banganga Tank; Walkhleshwar Mandir
26 Raj Bhavan
29 Copa Cabana
31 Taraporewala Aquarium;
   Khavalyadham Ishwardas
   Health Centre
32 Bhuleshwar Market
33 Mumbadevi Temple
34 Zaveri Bazaar
35 Jama Masjid
36 Mangaldas Market
37 Crawford Market
38 Foreigners' Registration Office
39 Metro Cinema
41 Wankhede Stadium
43 Cross Maidan
44 American Centre Library
45 Alliance Française
46 Podar House
49 Government of India Tourist Office;
   Western Railways Reservation Centre

52 Brabourne Stadium
53 Asiatic Department Store
54 Eros Cinema; Sundance Cafe
55 Oval Maidan
58 MTDC Tours & Reservation Office
59 Air India & Indian Airlines
60 MTDC Head Office;
   Net Express Cybercafe
62 NCPA
63 German Consulate
64 British Council Library; Mittal Tower
65 Maker Chambers III, IV, V & VI
68 Colaba Market
69 Maker Tower & Arcade
70 UAE Consulate
71 World Trade Centre
72 World Trade Centre Arcade
74 Colaba Bus Station
75 Afghan Church

Gateway of India & Taj Mahal Hotel

The **Gateway of India** was conceived following the visit of King George V in 1911. It is on the shore of Mumbai Harbour at the tip of Apollo Bunder in Colaba.

Boats depart from the Gateway's wharfs for Elephanta Island, and touts, balloon sellers and snake charmers give the area the hubbub of a bazaar.

The majestic **Taj Mahal Hotel** overlooks Apollo Bunder and has good views from its Apollo Bar.

Prince of Wales Museum

This museum (☎ 284 4519) has impressive sculptures from Elephanta Island, terracotta figurines, Gandharan Buddhas and weaponry. It is between Colaba and Fort; open Tuesday to Sunday from 10.15 am to 6 pm. Entry is Rs 5; Rs 30/200 for a camera/video.

National Gallery of Modern Art & Jehangir Art Gallery

The National Gallery of Modern Art (☎ 285 2457) in the Sir Cowasji Jehangir Public Hall on MG Rd is a dramatic exhibition space showcasing quality Indian modern art. It is open daily except Monday from 11 am to 6 pm; entry is free.

The Jehangir Art Gallery (☎ 284 3989) at 161B MG Rd hosts interesting weekly shows by contemporary Indian artists. It's open from 11 am to 7 pm daily and has a pleasant cafe. Entry is free.

Victoria Terminus (VT)

The city's most exuberant Gothic building was designed by Frederick Stevens as the headquarters of the Great Indian Peninsular Railway Company and was completed in 1887, 34 years after the first train in India left this site on its way to nearby Thana. Don't wait until you have to catch a train to see it.

Marine Drive

Built on land reclaimed from Back Bay in 1920, Marine Drive (Netaji Subhashchandra Bose Rd) runs along the shore of the Arabian Sea from Nariman Point past Chowpatty Beach to the foot of Malabar Hill. This is one of Mumbai's most popular promenades and sunset-watching spots, dubbed the Queen's Necklace because of the dramatic curve of its streetlights – best seen from Kamala Nehru Park or the upper floors of the Ambassador and Oberoi Towers hotels.

Chowpatty Beach

Eating bhelpuri on the edge of the beach at night is an essential part of the Mumbai experience; so is getting a head rub from a *malish-wallah* (Rs 10).

During the **Ganesh Chaturthi Festival** (August to September) enormous crowds gather to watch images of the elephant god Ganesh being paraded through the city streets and immersed in the sea.

Malabar Hill

On the northern promontory of Back Bay is the expensive residential area of Malabar Hill.

The formal **Hanging Gardens** (Pherozeshah Mehta Gardens) on top of the hill are a reasonable place for a stroll. **Kamala Nehru Park,** opposite, has views of Chowpatty Beach, Marine Drive and the city.

Beside the Hanging Gardens are the Parsi **Towers of Silence**. Parsis hold fire, earth and water sacred so do not cremate or bury their dead. Corpses are laid out within the towers to be picked clean by vultures. Elaborate precautions are taken to keep out sightseers.

At the end of the promontory is **Raj Bhavan**, once the British governor's house and now home to the governor of Maharashtra.

Mani Bhavan

The building where Mahatma Gandhi stayed during his visits to Bombay is now a small museum. Gandhi's simple room remains untouched and there is a library and photographic exhibits of Gandhi's life. Mani Bhavan (☎ 380 5864) is at 19 Laburnum Rd, near August Kranti Maidan. It's open daily from 9.30 am to 6 pm; entry is free.

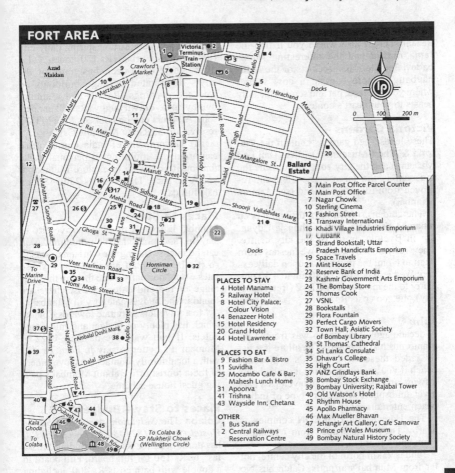

FORT AREA

3 Main Post Office Parcel Counter
6 Main Post Office
7 Nagar Chowk
10 Sterling Cinema
12 Fashion Street
13 Transway International
16 Khadi Village Industries Emporium
17 Citibank
18 Strand Bookstall; Uttar
   Pradesh Handicrafts Emporium
19 Space Travels
21 Mint House
22 Reserve Bank of India
23 Kashmir Government Arts Emporium
24 The Bombay Store
26 Thomas Cook
27 VSNL
28 Bookstalls
29 Flora Fountain
30 Perfect Cargo Movers
32 Town Hall; Asiatic Society
   of Bombay Library
33 St Thomas' Cathedral
34 Sri Lanka Consulate
35 Dhavar's College
36 High Court
37 ANZ Grindlays Bank
38 Bombay Stock Exchange
39 Bombay University; Rajabai Tower
40 Old Watson's Hotel
42 Rhythm House
45 Apollo Pharmacy
46 Max Mueller Bhavan
47 Jehangir Art Gallery; Cafe Samovar
48 Prince of Wales Museum
49 Bombay Natural History Society

PLACES TO STAY
4 Hotel Manama
5 Railway Hotel
8 Hotel City Palace;
   Colour Vision
14 Benazeer Hotel
15 Hotel Residency
20 Grand Hotel
44 Hotel Lawrence

PLACES TO EAT
9 Fashion Bar & Bistro
11 Suvidha
25 Mocambo Cafe & Bar;
   Mahesh Lunch Home
31 Apoorva
41 Trishna
43 Wayside Inn; Chetana

OTHER
1 Bus Stand
2 Central Railways
   Reservation Centre

Haji Ali's Mosque

At the end of a long causeway poking into the Arabian Sea is a whitewashed fairy-tale mosque containing the tomb of the Muslim saint Haji Ali. The mosque becomes an island at high tide, but is accessible at other times via a causeway.

Crawford Market

This colourful market (officially called Mahatma Phule Market) is the last outpost of British Bombay before the tumult of the central bazaars begins. It sells some of the best fruit and vegetables in the country. The animal market at the rear sells everything from sausage dogs to cockatoos, most kept in cruelly small cages. The fish market is just across MRA Marg.

Kalbadevi & Bhuleshwar

No visit to Mumbai is complete without a foray into the bazaars of Kalbadevi and Bhuleshwar, north of Crawford Market. Highlights are **Mangaldas Market, Zaveri**

Bazaar, **Bhuleshwar Market** and **Chor Bazaar**. This is also where you'll find the **Jama Masjid** and the interesting **Mumbadevi Temple**. The precincts of the **Madhavbaug Temple** contain a cow shelter where you can feed, pat and scratch the holy beasts to your heart's content.

Victoria Gardens

These landscaped gardens contain the **Victoria & Albert Museum** (Dr Bhau Daji Lad Museum) and the city **zoo**. Just outside the museum is the large stone elephant removed from Elephanta Island (see Around Mumbai).

The gardens, which have officially been renamed Veermata Jijabai Bhonsle Udyan, are in Byculla, north of the city centre. They're open daily except Wednesday from 9 am to 6 pm; the museum is open daily except Wednesday from 10.30 am to 4.30 pm. Entry to the museum costs Rs 2 (free Thursday); the zoo costs Rs 4.

Juhu

A decade ago, Juhu Beach was fronted by glamorous luxury hotels. The allure is a little jaded these days, but it's a pleasant beach if you're not expecting a sunbathe or a swim, and on weekends it develops a carnival atmosphere with every type of Indian beach entertainment.

The Hare Krishna **ISKCON** complex is nearby. The temple is open from 7.15 am to 1 pm and 4 to 9 pm.

Juhu is 25km north of the city centre, not far from Mumbai's airports. Catch bus No 231 from Santa Cruz train station or an auto-rickshaw from Vile Parle train station.

Swimming

Mumbai is hot and sticky but if you are not staying at a luxury hotel your choice for somewhere to swim is limited to a tiny pool at the Fariyas Hotel in Colaba (Rs 330) or a huge pool at the Breach Candy Club (☎ 367 4381) on the shoreline at Bhulabhai Desai Rd; a day ticket costs Rs 200 on weekdays, Rs 300 on Saturday and Rs 500 on Sunday.

Organised Tours

The MTDC operates uninspiring daily city (Rs 75) and suburban (Rs 130) tours. It also offers short open-deck bus tours of the city's illuminated heritage buildings on weekend evenings (Rs 50) and a similar tour by horse-drawn buggy (Rs 500 per person). All tours can be booked at the MTDC reservation office on Madame Cama Rd.

The Government of India tourist office can arrange a multilingual personal guide for you if you wish to explore Mumbai at your own pace. They cost Rs 230/345 for a half/full day.

Places to Stay

Mumbai is India's most expensive city to stay in, and pressure for accommodation can be intense during the Christmas season so it's best to plan ahead. Hotels whose rates would normally place them in the mid-range or top-end category elsewhere are found in the budget category in Mumbai.

Most travellers gravitate towards Colaba, which has plenty of budget and mid-range hotels. If you want the daytime buzz of Mumbai it's better to stay in Fort. To stay with a local family, contact the Government of India tourist office about Mumbai's paying guest house scheme.

Places to Stay – Budget

Colaba The *Salvation Army Red Shield Hostel* (☎ 284 1824, 30 Mereweather Rd) has dorm beds for Rs 100 including breakfast, or Rs 150 for full board. Full board in a double with bath costs Rs 400, including tax. Checkout is an ungenerous 9 am. Lockers are available.

Hotel Prosser's (☎ 284 1715, 2 Henry Rd), close to the harbour, has adequate singles/doubles with common bath for Rs 300/350, and more spacious rooms for Rs 450/500, including tax.

Bentley's Hotel (☎ 288 2890, email bentleyshotel@hotmail.com, 17 Oliver Rd) is a friendly hotel with rooms from Rs 650, including breakfast and tax.

Hotel Whalley's (☎ 282 1802, 41 Mereweather Rd) has singles/doubles from Rs

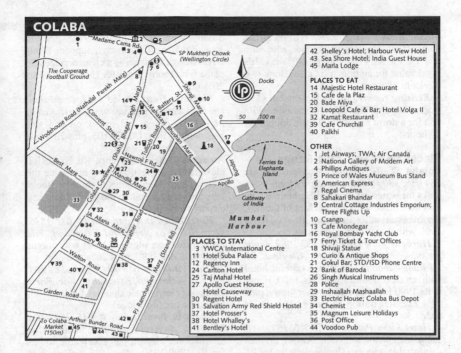

COLABA

PLACES TO STAY
- 3 YWCA International Centre
- 11 Hotel Suba Palace
- 12 Regency Inn
- 24 Carlton Hotel
- 25 Taj Mahal Hotel
- 27 Apollo Guest House; Hotel Causeway
- 30 Regent Hotel
- 31 Salvation Army Red Shield Hostel
- 37 Hotel Prosser's
- 38 Hotel Whalley's
- 41 Bentley's Hotel
- 42 Shelley's Hotel; Harbour View Hotel
- 43 Sea Shore Hotel; India Guest House
- 45 Marla Lodge

PLACES TO EAT
- 14 Majestic Hotel Restaurant
- 15 Cafe de la Plaz
- 20 Bade Miya
- 23 Leopold Cafe & Bar; Hotel Volga II
- 32 Kamat Restaurant
- 39 Cafe Churchill
- 40 Palkhi

OTHER
- 1 Jet Airways; TWA; Air Canada
- 2 National Gallery of Modern Art
- 4 Phillips Antiques
- 5 Prince of Wales Museum Bus Stand
- 6 American Express
- 7 Regal Cinema
- 8 Sahakari Bhandar
- 9 Central Cottage Industries Emporium; Three Flights Up
- 10 Csango
- 13 Cafe Mondegar
- 16 Royal Bombay Yacht Club
- 17 Ferry Ticket & Tour Offices
- 18 Shivaji Statue
- 19 Curio & Antique Shops
- 21 Gokul Bar; STD/ISD Phone Centre
- 22 Bank of Baroda
- 26 Singh Musical Instruments
- 28 Police
- 29 Inshaallah Mashaallah
- 33 Electric House; Colaba Bus Depot
- 34 Chemist
- 35 Magnum Leisure Holidays
- 36 Post Office
- 44 Voodoo Pub

500/650 with common bath to Rs 750/1100 with air-con and bath (tax and breakfast included).

Fort Area The *Hotel Lawrence* (☎ 928 43618, 3rd floor, Rope Walk Lane) has clean, plain singles/doubles/triples with common bath for Rs 300/400/600, including taxes. Book three weeks in advance.

Hotel Residency (☎ 262 5525, fax 261 9164, 26 Rustom Sidhwa Marg) is a comfortable option in the heart of Fort. It has spotless air-con singles/doubles with bath and TV from Rs 990/1090.

Hotel City Palace (☎ 261 5515, fax 267 6897, 121 City Terrace, W Hirachand Marg) has compact, clean singles/doubles/triples with bath and TV for Rs 700/850/1050, plus 4% tax. A few air-con broom closets with common bath go for Rs 450/650.

Retiring rooms (1st floor, Victoria Terminus) cost Rs 180 for a dorm bed and Rs 600 for a double for 24 hours.

Domestic Airport *Shangri-La* (☎ 612 8983, Nanda Patkar Rd, Vile Parle East) has no-frills doubles with bath and TV for Rs 350, including tax. It's a 10 minute walk from the terminal.

Hotel Aircraft International (☎ 612 1419, fax 618 2942, 179 Dayaldas Rd, off Western Express Highway, Vile Parle East) has air-con singles/doubles with bath and TV for Rs 850/950, plus 4% tax.

Elsewhere The Bentley Hotel (☎ 281 5244, Krishna Mahal, 3rd floor, Cnr of Marine Drive and D Rd) is the only budget hotel on Back Bay. It offers no-frills B&B in a variety of box-like singles/doubles with common bath for Rs 430/550, plus 4% tax.

MUMBAI

Hotel Kemp's Corner (☎ *363 4646, 131 August Kranti Marg, Kemp's Corner)* has compact air-con singles/doubles with bath and TV for Rs 975/1100, plus 9% tax. It's good value for an upmarket area. Book two weeks in advance.

Retiring rooms (3rd floor, Mumbai Central) at Mumbai Central train station cost Rs 180 for a dorm and Rs 600 for a double for 24 hours.

Places to Stay – Mid-Range
Colaba *Shelleys Hotel* (☎ *284 0229, fax 284 0385, 30 PJ Ramchandani Marg)* overlooks the waters of Mumbai Harbour. It's an excellent place with a slight hint of the Raj. Doubles start at Rs 1415 and shoot up to Rs 1900 with water views; includes tax.

Harbour View Hotel (☎ *282 1089, email parkview@bom3.vsnl.net.in, 4th floor, 25 PJ Ramchandani Marg)* is a tasteful hotel with spotless doubles from Rs 1500, rising to Rs 1990 for rooms with water views, plus 14% tax. Its rooftop restaurant is a major plus.

Hotel Suba Palace (☎ *202 0636, email subapalace@hotmail.com, Battery St)* has comfortable, modern singles/doubles for Rs 1195/1800, plus 14% tax. It gets positive reviews from travellers.

Fort Area The *Grand Hotel* (☎ *261 8211, email grandh@bom3.vsnl.net.in, 17 Shri Shiv Sagar Ramgulam Rd, Ballard Estate)* has clean, spacious singles/doubles with dowdy furniture for Rs 1980/2392, including tax (no fridge).

West End Hotel (☎ *203 9121, email west.hotel@gems.vsnl.net.in, 45 New Marine Lines)* has huge, spotless, old-fashioned singles/doubles/triples for Rs 2160/2394/3591, including tax (no fridge).

Marine Drive *Sea Green Hotel* (☎ *282 2294, fax 283 6158, 145 Marine Drive)* and the *Sea Green South Hotel* (☎ *282 1613, fax 283 6303, 145A Marine Drive)* are identical hotels offering spacious but spartan rooms for Rs 1250/1550, plus 14% tax. Ask for a sea view.

Chowpatty & Kemp's Corner The *Hotel Sapna* (☎ *367 0041, fax 361 9115, Pandita Ramabai Marg, Chowpatty)*, opposite Bharatiya Vidhya Bhavan, is a clean serviceable place with rooms from Rs 1395/1645, plus 20% tax.

Shalimar Hotel (☎ *363 1311, email shalimar@giasbm01.vsnl.net.in, August Kranti Marg)* has decent but pricey air-con singles/doubles from US$70/105, plus 20% tax.

Airports Hotels on Nehru Rd Extension close to the domestic airport are twice the price of equivalent rooms in the city. Bookings are recommended; most offer courtesy airport pick-up.

Hotel Bawa International (☎ *611 3636, fax 610 7096, Nehru Rd Extension, Vile Parle East)* is a pleasant hotel with rooms from Rs 3300/3800, plus 20% tax.

Hotel Atithi (☎ *618 7941, fax 611 1998, 77 A-B Nehru Rd Extension, Vile Parle East)* has clean, basic doubles for Rs 2495, including tax (no fridge).

Kumaria Presidency (☎ *835 2601, fax 837 3850, Anderhi-Kurla Rd)*, facing Sahar international airport, has acceptable rooms for Rs 1700/1950, plus 10% tax; not bad value for the area.

Juhu Beach The *Juhu Hotel* (☎ *618 4012, fax 619 2578, Juhu Tara Rd)* is a small single-storey beachfront hotel with rooms for Rs 1150/1800, plus 4% tax (no fridge).

ISKCON (☎ *620 6860, fax 620 5214, Hare Krishna Land)* has good value fan-cooled singles/doubles with bath for Rs 960/1150; air-con costs Rs 1050/1440, plus 4% tax (no TV, no fridge). Bookings recommended.

Places to Stay – Top End
Colaba The *Taj Mahal Hotel* (☎ *202 3366, fax 287 2711, Apollo Bunder)*, next to the Gateway of India, is one of the best hotels in the country. Singles/doubles in the superb old wing cost from US$295/325, rising to US$325/365 with a harbour view, plus 20% tax. Rooms in the modern wing are 20% cheaper.

Fariyas Hotel (☎ 204 2911, email fariyas@bom3.vsnl.net.in, 25 Justice De-vshanker V Vijas Marg) is a comfortable, modern four star establishment offering quality rooms from US$125. It has a tiny pool, a restaurant and popular bar.

Marine Drive *The Oberoi (☎ 202 5757, email reservations@oberoi-mumbai.com, Marine Drive, Nariman Point)* is a modern, service-oriented, luxury business hotel overlooking the Arabian Sea. It offers singles/doubles for US$325/355, rising to US$360/380 with a sea view, plus 20% tax.

Marine Plaza (☎ 285 1212, fax 282 8585, 29 Marine Drive, Nariman Point) is a modern boutique five-star hotel with Art Deco flourishes. It has stylish rooms from US$230 with sea views, plus 20% tax.

Airports The *Leela Kempinski (☎ 836 3636, email leela.bom@leela.sprintrpg.ems .vsnl.net.in)* is opposite Sahar international airport, Andheri. Comfortable singles/doubles start at US$315/340, plus 20% tax.

The Orchid (☎ 610 0707, email info@ orchidhotel.com, off Nehru Rd Extension, Vile Parle East) is a stylish five-star hotel next to the domestic airport. It's the first certified eco-friendly hotel in Asia and deserves all the support it can get. Excellent rooms start at US$225, plus 20% tax.

Juhu Beach The *Holiday Inn (☎ 620 4444, email reserve@holidayinn.sprintsmx.ems .vsnl.net.in, Balraj Sahani Marg)* has a beachfront location, a decent pool and a relaxing ambience. Fine rooms cost from US$220, plus 20% tax.

Places to Eat
Mumbai has the best selection of restaurants in India. Ring ☎ 888 8888 (24 hours) for information about them.

Colaba *Leopold Cafe & Bar (☎ 202 0131, cnr Colaba Causeway and Nawroji F Rd)* is a Mumbai institution dating back to 1871.

Bade Miya (☎ 284 1649, Tulloch Rd) is an evening street stall with a citywide rep-

utation. It serves excellent kababs, *tikkas* (marinated meats) and *rotis* (tandoor-baked bread) for around Rs 30.

Kailash Parbat, (☎ 287 4823, 5 Sheela Mahal, 1st Pasta Lane) is a Mumbai legend thanks to its inexpensive Sindhi-influenced pure veg snacks (Rs 15) and its mouthwatering sweets (around Rs 17 each).

Palkhi (☎ 284 0053, 15 Walton Rd) specialises in Mughlai and north Indian cuisine, including a succulent assortment of kababs (Rs 150). It's very swanky and makes a great alternative to dining in an upmarket hotel.

Tanjore (☎ 202 3366, Apollo Bunder) offers a select menu of *khad* cuisine (cooked and served in mud pots). Indian music and dance performances accompany dinner. Dress smartly.

Fort *Wayside Inn (☎ 284 4324, 38 K Dubash Marg)* is a comfortable historic spot to hang out in central Mumbai. It serves nostalgic Raj fare; meals cost around Rs 70. It's open daily except Sunday from 9 am to 7 pm.

Mahesh Lunch Home (☎ 287 0938, 8B Cawasji Patel St) is the place to try Mangalorean seafood. It's renowned for its ladyfish, pomfret (Rs 70) and crabs (Rs 170).

Apoorva Restaurant & Bar (☎ 287 0335, Noble Chambers, SA Brelvi Rd) is also a seafood specialist well known for its crabs and prawn *gassis*. Dishes start at Rs 45 and rise to Rs 250.

Churchgate *Purohit (☎ 204 9231, Veer Nariman Rd)* looks new but has been serving vegetarian food at Churchgate for over 60 years. It knows a thing or two about Gujarati *thalis* for Rs 120.

Samrat Restaurant (☎ 282 0942, Prem Court, J Tata Rd) is an upmarket pure veg restaurant dishing up quality Gujarati thalis (Rs 95).

Chowpatty Beach & Malabar Hill The *stalls* on Chowpatty Beach in the evening are atmospheric spots to snack on bhelpuri, *panipuri* (bhelpuris immersed in spicy water) and ice cream.

MUMBAI

Cafe Ideal (☎ 363 0943, Fulchand Niwas, Chowpatty Seaface) is a bustling Irani-style cafe with a CD jukebox. Most dishes cost around Rs 35; beer is more popular at Rs 60.

New Kulfi Centre (cnr of Chowpatty Seaface and Sardar V Patel Rd) makes some of the most delicious *kulfi* (a frozen sweet) in Mumbai.

Cream Centre (☎ 369 2025, Chowpatty Seaface) is an iconic vegetarian snack bar and ice cream parlour that's been on the Chowpatty must-do list for over 40 years.

Entertainment

The Thursday edition of *Mid-Day* incorporates *The List*, a weekly guide to Mumbai entertainment. Newspapers have information on mainstream events and film screenings.

Bars & Nightclubs The *Cafe Mondegar (☎ 202 0591, Metro House, 5A Colaba Causeway)* is a cramped cafe-bar with a CD jukebox that's popular with travellers. It's open daily from 8 am.

Fashion Bar (☎ 207 7270, 1st floor, Dhiraj Chambers Annex, 16 Marzaban Rd, Fort) is the hippest spot in town. There's a cover charge of Rs 200 per person (Rs 300 on Friday and Saturday) which is redeemable at the bar. It's open daily from 7 pm; couples only.

Cinemas Check out a Bollywood blockbuster at *Eros (☎ 282 2335)* opposite Churchgate train station or *Metro (MG Rd)*. You'll need to reserve tickets, especially on weekends; tickets go on sale two days in advance.

Performing Arts The *NCPA (☎ 283 3737)*, at the tip of Nariman Point, is the hub of Mumbai's music, theatre and dance scene. In any given week, it might host Marathi theatre, dance troupes from Bihar, ensembles from Europe, and Indian classical music. It contains the Tata Theatre (which occasionally has English-language plays) and the Experimental Theatre.

Shopping

Mumbai is India's great marketplace. Every Sunday from November to January

K Dubash Marg hosts the Kala Ghoda Fair – a celebration of arts and crafts with performing arts, and food and handicraft stalls.

The main areas of the dense bazaars north of Fort are Crawford Market (fruit & veg), Mangaldas Market (silk and cloth), Zaveri Bazaar (jewellery), Bhuleshwar Market (fruit & veg) and Chor Bazaar (thieves' market).

Specialist streets worth checking out in Kalbadevi include Shamsheth Lane, two streets north of the Jama Masjid, for lace and Dhabu St in Chor Bazaar for leather goods. Mutton St in Chor Bazaar specialises in antiques, ingenious reproductions and miscellaneous junk.

There are handicrafts in the labyrinthine World Trade Centre Arcade near Cuffe Parade; and on Sir P Mehta Rd, Fort.

You can save a small fortune at 'Fashion Street', the stalls lining MG Rd between Cross and Azad maidans. Shops along Colaba Causeway sell cheap, decent western-style clothes. For pieces by Indian designers try the boutiques at Kemp's Corner, between the flyover and the junction with Nepean Sea Rd. Ready-made traditional Indian clothing can be picked up at the Khadi Village Industries Emporium (☎ 207 3280) at 286 Dr D Naoroji Rd, Fort.

Getting There & Away

Air The international terminal (Sahar) is about 4km from the domestic terminal (Santa Cruz). They are 30km and 26km respectively north of Nariman Point in downtown Mumbai.

Facilities in Sahar's arrival hall include a duty-free shop, several foreign exchange counters offering acceptable rates, a Government of India tourist office (☎ 832 5331), a hotel reservation counter (☎ 615 5239, email yez.patel@usa.net) and a pre-paid taxi booth – all open 24 hours. There's a left-luggage shed in the car park, about 200m left of the arrivals hall exit.

Mumbai's Santa Cruz domestic airport has two terminals, a couple of minutes' walk apart. Terminal A handles Indian Airlines flights, while terminal B caters for Jet Airways, Sahara and Gujarat Airways flights.

Both terminals have foreign exchange bureaus, ticketing counters and a restaurant-bar. The 24 hour left-luggage facility is midway between the two terminals. Flights on domestic sectors of Air India routes depart from the international airport.

There are flights to more than 30 Indian cities, including Jaipur, Jodhpur, Jaisalmer and Udaipur.

Domestic Airlines Addresses of domestic carriers that service Mumbai include:

Gujarat Airways
    (☎ 617 7063) Santa Cruz airport
Indian Airlines
    (☎ 202 3031) Air India Bldg, Nariman Point
Jet Airways
    (☎ 838 6111) Amarchand Mansion, Madame Cama Rd
Sahara India
    (☎ 283 5671) 7 Tulsiani Chambers, Free Press Journal Marg, Nariman Point

International Airlines Most international airline offices are in or close to Nariman Point. These include:

Air Canada
    (☎ 202 1111) Amarchand Mansion, Madame Cama Rd
Air France
    (☎ 202 5021) 1st floor, Maker Chambers VI, J Bajaj Marg, Nariman Point
Air India
    (☎ 282 5994) Air India Bldg, Nariman Point
Air Lanka
    (☎ 282 3288) 12D Raheja Centre, ground floor, Free Press Journal Marg, Nariman Point
Air New Zealand
    (☎ 284 2681) Podar House, 10 Marine Drive
Alitalia
    (☎ 204 5023) Industrial Insurance Bldg, Veer Nariman Rd, Churchgate
Biman Bangladesh Airlines
    (☎ 282 4659) 199 J Tata Rd, Churchgate
British Airways
    (☎ 282 0888) Valcan Insurance Bldg, 202B Veer Nariman Rd, Churchgate
Cathay Pacific Airways
    (☎ 202 9112) Taj Mahal Hotel, Apollo Bunder, Colaba
Druk Air (Bhutan)
    (☎ 287 4936) ground floor, 2 Raheja Centre, Free Press Journal Marg, Nariman Point

Emirates
    (☎ 287 1645) ground floor, Mittal Chambers, Nariman Point
Gulf Air
    (☎ 202 1626) ground floor, Maker Chambers V, J Bajaj Marg, Nariman Point
Kenya Airways
    (☎ 282 0064) 199 J Tata Rd, Churchgate
KLM
    (☎ 283 3338) Khaitan Bhavan, 198 J Tata Rd, Churchgate
Malaysia Airlines
    (☎ 218 1431) GSA Stic Travels & Tours, 6 Maker Arcade, Cuffe Parade
Pakistan International Airlines (PIA)
    (☎ 202 1373) 4th floor, B Wing, Mittal Towers, Free Press Journal Marg, Nariman Point
Qantas
    (☎ 202 9297) 4th floor, 42 Sakhar Bhavan, Nariman Point
Royal Nepal Airlines (Corporation)
    (☎ 283 6197) 2nd floor, Maker Chambers V, J Bajaj Marg, Nariman Point
TWA
    (☎ 282 3080) Amarchand Mansion, Madame Cama Rd
United Airlines
    (☎ 204 7027) Podar House, 10 Marine Drive

Bus Private long-distance buses depart for all points from Dr Anadrao Nair Rd, near Mumbai Central train station.

Long-distance buses run by state governments depart from the state road transport terminal close to Mumbai Central train station. Booking office (☎ 307 4272; inquiries only) is on the 1st floor, and open from 8 am to 8 pm daily.

Train Two train systems operate out of Mumbai. Central Railways has services to the east and south, plus a few to the north. It operates from Victoria Terminus (VT), also known as Chhatrapati Shivaji Terminus (CST). The reservation centre at VT is open Monday to Saturday from 8 am to 8 pm, and until 2 pm on Sunday. Tourist-quota tickets (which can be fully booked several weeks in advance during the high season) and Indrail passes can be bought at counter No 7 Monday to Saturday from 9 am to 1 pm and 1.30 to 4 pm.

The other train system is Western Railways, which has services to the north from

MUMBAI

Mumbai Central (MC) train station (still usually called Bombay Central). Book for Western Railways trains at the reservation centre opposite Churchgate train station. It's open Monday to Saturday from 8 am to 8 pm, and until 2 pm on Sunday. Tourist-quota tickets are issued only 24 hours before train departures; they're sold from a desk on the 1st floor on weekdays from 9.30 am to 4.30 pm, and until 2 pm Saturday.

Getting Around
To/From the International Airport
There's a pre-paid taxi booth at the international airport with set fares to various city destinations. It's Rs 242 to Colaba, Fort and Marine Drive during the day and Rs 282 between midnight and 5 am; it's an extra Rs 5 per bag. The journey takes about an hour at night and 1½ to two hours during the day.

Don't try to catch an auto-rickshaw from the airport to the city. They're prohibited from entering downtown Mumbai and will drop you a few kilometres down the road at Mahim Creek.

Bus No 13 shuttles between the international airport and VT every 20 minutes between 8 am and 8.45 pm daily (1½ to 2 hrs, Rs 12). Heading to the airport, board the bus at Dr D Naoroji Rd, outside the Bombay Municipal Corporation building. Allow plenty of time for the inevitable delays and cancellations.

Minibuses outside the arrival hall offer free shuttle services to the airports and Juhu hotels. There's also a free Air India shuttle between the international and domestic airports.

A taxi from the city centre to the international airport costs around Rs 200 on the meter, plus extra for baggage; taxi drivers in Colaba always ask for Rs 300. It costs about 30% more between midnight and 5 am.

To/From the Domestic Airport
Taxis and auto-rickshaws queue up outside both domestic terminals. There's no pre-paid taxi counter so make sure that drivers use the meter. A taxi takes between one and 1½ hours to reach the city centre and costs

around Rs 180, plus extra for any baggage. Auto-rickshaws are not allowed into the city centre.

Bus No 2 stops on nearby Nehru Rd, opposite the junction to Nanda Patkar Rd, and terminates at the Prince of Wales Museum (Rs 9.50). It stops on the highway opposite the airport when heading out of the city.

Another alternative is to catch an auto-rickshaw to Vile Parle train station (Rs 10), and catch a suburban train between Vile Parle and Churchgate or VT (45 mins, Rs 5). Don't attempt this during rush hour. Note that Santa Cruz train station is not the closest station to Santa Cruz airport. Most airport and Juhu hotels offer free airport pick-up.

Bus Fares around south Mumbai cost less than Rs 5 so have some small change available. Route numbers and destinations on the front of buses are written in Marathi, and English signs are on the side. All buses depart from Colaba Causeway and pass Flora Fountain.

Train There are only three main lines, making it easy to navigate. The most useful ones operate from Churchgate heading north to stations like Charni Rd (for Chowpatty Beach), Mumbai Central, Vile Parle (Santa Cruz airport), Andheri (Sahar international) and Borivali (Sanjay Gandhi National Park).

A couple of other suburban lines operate from VT. Trains begin operating just after 4 am and run until almost 1 am.

Taxi & Auto-Rickshaw Mumbai has a huge fleet of metered black-and-yellow taxis. Auto-rickshaws are confined to the suburbs north of Mahim Creek.

Taxi meters are out of date, so the fare is calculated using a conversion chart which all drivers carry – ask to see it at the end of the journey. It's about 25% more expensive between midnight and 6 am.

Cool Cabs (☎ 613 1111) operates correctly metered, blue, air-con taxis. They're about 33% more expensive than regular cabs and can be booked by telephone.

Motorcycle Should you wish to motor cycle around Rajasthan, you will find the range of machines available for hire or to purchase is far better in Mumbai. Allibhai Premji Tyrewallah (☎ 309 9313, email premjis@bom3.vsnl.net.in) at 205 Lamington Rd, Opera House, is the place for motorcycles. Hire bikes cost between Rs 1500 and Rs 2000 per week, depending on the model. It's possible to buy a bike and pre-arrange to sell it back to the store after a specific period. The buy-back price after three months on a secondhand Enfield is around Rs 18,000 less than the original price.

Note that Mumbai is no place to learn how to ride a motorcycle.

AROUND MUMBAI
Elephanta Island

The rock-cut temples on Elephanta Island, 9km north-east of the Gateway of India, are Mumbai's major tourist attraction. Little is known of their origins, but are thought to have been created between 450 and 750 AD.

The caves are open daily except Monday from 9 am to 5.30 pm. It costs Rs 5 to enter; Rs 25 to take in your video. A free English-language guide service is offered to travellers with deluxe launch tickets. Tours depart every hour on the half hour from the ticket booth. If you prefer to explore independently, pick up Pramod Chandra's *A Guide to the Elephanta Caves* (Rs 40) from the stalls lining the stairway. The best time to visit Elephanta is during the week. The tree-top terrace of the MTDC's *Chalukya Restaurant & Beer Bar (☎ 284 8323)* at the top of the stairway is a fine spot to sit back and take in the expansive views of Mumbai Harbour.

Getting There & Away Launches head to Elephanta Island from the Gateway of India. Small economy boats cost Rs 50 return and more spacious deluxe launches, Rs 70 return. Tickets are sold by touts at the Gateway and booths nearby. Economy boats leave from the wharf near the ticket booths; deluxe launches moor next to the Gateway.

Boats depart every half hour from around 9 am to 2.30 pm Tuesday to Sunday. The voyage takes an hour.

MUMBAI

Language

Hindi is the predominant language of Rajasthan (over 90% of the population speak it). It's by far the most useful language with which to communicate across the state.

Rajasthani is the collective name for the various dialects spoken in Rajasthan. There are five main dialects – Marwari, Mewari, Dhundhari, Mewati and Hadoti, with Marwari the most common.

English is widely spoken in the hospitality industry, and at popular tourist attractions. English-speaking guides are available in towns and cities such as Jaipur, Udaipur, Jodhpur, Bikaner and Jaisalmer. In some places it's also possible to hire Spanish, German and French-speaking guides.

In rural areas, little if any English is spoken. Attempts at a few Hindi phrases will greatly enhance your enjoyment of travelling through these more remote regions.

One word which you'll probably hear frequently during your travels in Rajasthan is *padharo* (Please come/You're welcome). The small hole-in-the-wall eateries, which are known elsewhere in India as *dhabas*, are often referred to as *bhojnalyas* in Rajasthan. Beware of *acha*, the all-purpose word for 'OK'. It can also mean 'OK, I understand what you mean, but it isn't OK'.

HINDI

For a more in-depth guide to Hindi, get a copy of Lonely Planet's *Hindi & Urdu phrasebook*, which has sections on grammar and pronunciation, and a comprehensive list of words and phrases tailored to meet the needs of the traveller.

Basics

Hello/Goodbye.	*namaste*
Excuse me.	*maaf kijiyeh*
Please.	*meharbani seh*
Thank you.	*shukriya*
Yes/No.	*haan/nahin*
How are you?	*aap kaiseh hain?*
Very well, thank you.	*bahut acha, shukriya*

What's your name?	*aap ka shubh naam kya hai?*
My name is …	*meraa naam … hai*
Do you speak English?	*kya aap angrezi aatee hai?*
I don't understand.	*meri samajh mei nahin aaya*
What time is it?	*kitneh bajeh hain?*

Where is the ...?	*... kahan hai?*
bus stop	*bas staap*
hotel	*hotal*
station	*steshan*

How far is ...?	*... kitni duur hai?*
How do I get to (Jaipur)?	*(jaipur) mai wahan kaiseh jaun?*
What street is this?	*ye kaun gali ... hai?*
When will the next bus leave?	*agli bas kab jaaegi?*
Which bus goes to ...?	*... kaun sii bas jaati hai?*

Do you have any rooms available?	*koi kamra khaali hai?*
How much is it per night?	*ek raat ke kitneh paise lagein-ge?*
Does it have a bathroom?	*saath meh baathroom hai?*

Food & Shopping

I/We'd like some food.	*khaana chaahiyeh*
Do you have drinking water?	*piineh kaa paani hai?*
Please show me the menu.	*mujheh minu dikhaiyeh*
I only eat vegetarian food.	*main shakahaari huun*
The bill please.	*bill de dijiyeh*
How much?	*kitneh paiseh/hai?*
This is expensive.	*yeh bahut mehnga hai*

fruit	*phal*
vegetables	*sabzi*
sugar	*chini*
rice	*chaaval*

water	*paani*
tea	*chai*
coffee	*kaafi*
milk	*dudh*
chemist/pharmacy	*davai kii dukaan*
market	*baazaar/markit*
shop	*dukaan*

Health

Where's the ...?	*... kahaan hai?*
doctor	*doktar*
dentist	*daanton kaa doktar*
hospital	*haspataal*
My stomach is upset.	*meraa peit kharaab hai*
It hurts here.	*yahaan dard hai*
I'm allergic to penicillin.	*mujhe penicilin se elargii hai*
medicine	*dava-ee*
pregnant	*garbhvatii*
prescription	*priskripshan*

Numbers

Whereas English speakers count in tens, hundreds, thousands, millions and billions, the Hindi numbering system counts in tens, hundreds, thousands, hundred thousands, ten millions. A hundred thousand is a *lakh,* and 10 million is a *crore.*

These two words are almost always used in place of their English equivalent. Thus you will see 10 *lakh* rather than one million and one crore rather than 10 million. Furthermore, the numerals are generally written that way too – thus three hundred thousand appears as 3,00,000 not 300,000, and ten million, five hundred thousand would appear numerically as 1,05,00,000

(one *crore*, five *lakh*) not 10,500,000. If you say something costs five *crore* or is worth 10 *lakh*, it always means 'of rupees'. Many of Rajasthan's younger generation refer to rupees as 'bucks'.

1	*ek*
2	*do*
3	*teen*
4	*char*
5	*panch*
6	*chhe*
7	*saat*
8	*aath*
9	*nau*
10	*das*
11	*gyaranh*
12	*baranh*
13	*teranh*
14	*chodanh*
15	*pandranh*
16	*solanh*
17	*staranh*
18	*aatharanh*
19	*unnis*
20	*bis*
21	*ikkis*
30	*tis*
40	*chalis*
50	*panchas*
60	*saath*
70	*sattar*
80	*assi*
90	*nabbe*
100	*so*
200	*do so*
1000	*ek hazaar*
100,000	*lakh*
ten million	*crore*

Glossary

adgaliya – veranda of village hut

agarbathi – incense

Agnikula – 'Fire Born', name of the mythological race of four Rajput clans who were manifested from a sacred fire on Mt Abu; one of the three principal races from which Rajputs claim descent

ahimsa – non-violence and reverence for all life

andhi – a dust storm in the Thar Desert

angrezi – foreigner

apsara – celestial maiden

Aryan – Sanskrit word for noble; refers to those who migrated from Persia and settled in northern India

ashram – spiritual community or retreat

auto-rickshaw – a noisy three-wheel device with a motorbike engine; seats for two passengers behind the driver

Ayurveda – Indian herbal medicine

azan – Muslim call to prayer

bagh – garden

baithak – salon in a *haveli* where merchants met their clients

baksheesh – tip, bribe or donation

bandh – general strike

bandhani – popular form of tie-dye

Banjaras – nomad tribe, believed to be the ancestors of Europe's gypsies

banyan – Indian fig tree

baori – well; particularly a stepwell with landings and galleries

baraat – marriage party

bazaar – market area (or market town)

betel – nut of the betel tree; chewed as a stimulant and digestive

bhang – dried leaves and flowering shoots of the marijuana plant

Bhils – a tribal people of southern Rajasthan

bhojanalya – basic restaurant or snack bar; known elsewhere in India as a *dhaba*

Bhopa – Bhil priest; also traditional storytellers of Rajasthan

bhuut – ghost

bichiya – toe ring

bidi (beedi) – small, hand-rolled cigarette; really just a rolled-up leaf

bindi – forehead mark

Bishnoi – a nomadic tribe, known for their reverence for the environment

bo tree – *Ficus religiosa*, under which the Buddha attained enlightenment

bohara – village moneylender

bor – forehead ornament; also known as a *tika* or *rakhadi*

Brahma – source of all existence and worshipped as the Creator in the Hindu triad. Brahma is depicted with four heads (a fifth was burnt by Shiva's central eye when he spoke disrespectfully). His vehicle is a swan or goose

Brahmin – member of the priest caste, the highest Hindu caste

Buddha – Awakened One; originator of Buddhism, who lived in the 5th century BC; regarded by Hindus as the ninth reincarnation of Vishnu

bund – embankment or dyke

bunti – wooden block used in block-printing fabric

cantonment – administrative and military area of a Raj-era town

caste – Hindu's hereditary station in life

chai – tea

chajeras – masons employed by Marwari businessmen of Shekhawati to build their havelis

chakki – handmill used to grind grain

champlevé – method of *meenakari* enamelling

chapati – unleavened Indian bread; also known as *roti*

chappals – sandals

charpoy – Indian rope bed

chaupar – town square formed by the intersection of major roads

chhan – see *dogla*

chhapa – wooden block, also known as a *bunti*, used to block-print fabric

383

chhatri – cenotaph (literally 'umbrella')

chiteras – painters of the *havelis* in Shekhawati

choli – cropped blouse worn by Indian women

chowk – a town square, intersection or marketplace

chowkidar – caretaker

chudas – bangles worn by Rajasthani women

chureil – evil spirit. Also known as a *dakin*

crore – 10 million

curd – milk set with acid or rennet

cycle-rickshaw – three-wheeler bicycle with two passengers behind the rider

dacoit – bandit

dakin – evil spirit

dalwar – sword

dargah – shrine or place of burial of a Muslim saint

darwaza – gateway or door

Devi – *Shiva's* wife

dhaba – hole-in-the-wall restaurant or snack bar. Boxed lunches delivered to office workers

dhal – lentil soup

dhobi ghat – where clothes are washed

dhobi-wallah – person who washes clothes

dhoti – length of fabric worn by men which is drawn up between the legs

dhurrie – cotton rug

Digambara – sky-clad; a Jain sect whose monks may show their disdain for worldly goods by going naked

diwan-i-am – public audience hall in a palace

diwan-i-khas – private audience hall

dogla – building adjacent to a village dwelling in which livestock and grain are kept. Also known as a *chhan*

dosa – paper-thin pancakes made from lentil flour (curried vegetables wrapped inside a dosa make it a *masala dosa*)

dowry – money and goods paid by a bride's parents to their son-in-law's family; it's illegal but no arranged marriage can be made without it

dupatta – scarf worn by Punjabi women

durbar – royal court, or maharajas meeting hall; also used to describe a government

Durga – the Inaccessible; a form of Shiva's wife, Parvati, a beautiful but fierce woman riding a tiger; major goddess of the Shakti cult. (Shakti is the creative/reproductive energy of the gods which often manifests in their spouses.)

gaddi – throne of a Hindu prince

Ganesh – god of good fortune. Elephant-headed son of Shiva and Parvati and probably the most popular god in the Hindu pantheon. Also known as Ganapati, his vehicle is a rat-like creature. In his four hands he holds a water lily, a club, a shell and a discus

ganja – dried flowering tips of marijuana plant; highly potent

gaon – village

garh – fort

Garuda – man-bird vehicle of Vishnu

geyser – hot water heater

ghaghara – very full skirt also known as a *lehanga*

ghat – steps or landing on a river, range of hills, or road up hills

ghazal – Urdu songs derived from poetry; sad love themes

ghee – clarified butter

ghoomer – dance performed by women during festivals and weddings

godown – warehouse

Gogaji – deified 11th century folk hero, believed to cure snakebite

goondas – ruffians or toughs

gopis – milkmaids. *Krishna* was very fond of them

gram panchayat – government at the village level

gufa – cave

Gujjars – people traditionally engaged in animal husbandry

gur – sweetmeat made from unrefined sugar

gurdwara – Sikh temple

guru – teacher or holy person

halwa – cereal or lentils fried and cooked in a sugar syrup

Hanuman – Hindu monkey god
hathi – elephant
hathphool – ornament worn on the back of the hand by Rajasthani women
haveli – traditional mansion with interior courtyards
hijra – eunuch
hookah – water pipe
howdah – seat for carrying people on an elephant's back

IMFL – Indian made foreign liquor; beer or spirits produced in India
Induvansa – Race of the Moon (Lunar Race); one of the three principal races from which Rajputs claim descent

jaggery – sweetener like brown sugar made from kitul palm sap
jagirdari – feudal system of serfdom imposed on the peasants of Rajasthan
Jagirdars – feudal lords of Rajasthan
jajman – patron of folk entertainers
jali – stone or wood tracery used in windows
Jats – traditionally, people engaged in agriculture; these days, Jats play a strong role in administration and politics
jauhar – ritual mass suicide by immolation, used by Rajput women after military defeat to avoid dishonour
jhonpa – village hut with mud walls and thatched roof
jogi – priest
jootis – (also known as *mojdis*) traditional leather shoes of Rajasthan; men's jootis often have curled-up toes
Julaha – weaver caste

kaarkhana – embroidery workshop; established during the Mughal era
kabas – the holy rats believed to be the incarnations of storytellers at Karni Mata Temple at Deshnok
Kalbelias – a nomadic tribal group associated with snake charming
Kali – the Black; a terrible form of Devi
karma – Hindu-Buddhist principle of retributive justice for past deeds
Karni Mata – incarnation of Devi worshipped in her temple at Deshnok

kashida – embroidery on *jootis*
kathputli – puppeteer; also known as a *putli-wallah*
khadi – homespun cloth; Mahatma Gandhi encouraged people to spin khadi rather than buy English cloth
kheis – shawl. Also known as a *pattu*
kopi – camel-hide water bottle
kot – fort
kotwali – police station
Krishna – Vishnu's eighth incarnation, often blue; a popular Hindu deity, he revealed the *Bhagavad Gita* to Arjuna
Kshatriya – caste of soldiers and governors, second in the caste hierarchy. Rajputs claim lineage to the Kshatriyas
kuldevi – clan goddess. Every family pays homage to a clan goddess
kulfi – pistachio-flavoured sweet similar to ice cream
kund – lake or tank
kundan – type of jewellery featuring enamelwork *(meenakari)* on one side and precious stones on the other
kurta – long cotton shirt with either short collar or no collar

lakh – 100,000
Lakshmi – *Vishnu's* consort; Hindu goddess of wealth
lassi – yoghurt and iced-water drink
lehanga – see *ghaghara*
lingam – phallic symbol; symbol of Shiva
loharia – form of *bandhani* tie-dye which gives a ripple effect
lungi – like a sarong

madrassa – Islamic college
Mahabharata – Vedic epic poem of the Bharata dynasty; describes the battle between the Pandavas and the Kauravas
mahal – house or palace
maharaj kumar – son of a maharaja; prince
maharaja, maharana, maharao, maharawal – great king
maharani – wife of a princely ruler or a ruler in her own right
Mahavir – the 24th and last *tirthankar* (Jain teacher, or prophet)

mahout – elephant rider/master
mandana – folk paintings in red chalk on village dwellings
mandapa – chamber before the inner sanctum of a temple
mandir – temple
mantra – sacred word or syllable used by Buddhists and Hindus to aid concentration; metric psalms of praise found in the *Vedas*
Maratha – warlike central Indians who controlled much of India at times and fought against the Mughals and Rajputs
marg – major road
masjid – mosque
Marwar – kingdom of the Rathore dynasty which ruled from Mandore, and later from Jodhpur
masuria – finely woven cloth of silk and cotton produced in Kaithoon
mataji – female priest. Also a respectful form of address to a mother or older woman
meenakari – type of enamelwork used on ornaments and jewellery
mehfilkhana – Islamic building in which religious songs are sung
mehndi – intricate henna designs applied by women to their hands and feet
mela – a fair
Mewar – kingdom of the Sisodia dynasty; ruled Udaipur and Chittorgarh
Moghul – another spelling for Mughal
mojdis – see *jootis*
moksha – release from cycle of birth and death
monsoon – rainy season; June to October
moosal – pestle
mosar – death feast
Mughal – Muslim dynasty of Indian emperors from Babur to Aurangzeb (16th-18th centuries)

namaz – Muslim prayers
Nandi – bull, vehicle of Shiva
nathdi – nose ornament. Also known as a *laongh* and a *bhanvatiya*
nautch girls – dancing girls; a nautch is a dance
nawab – Muslim ruling prince or powerful landowner
nilgai – antelope

niwas – house, building
NRI – non-resident Indian

odhni – headscarf
okhli – mortar; bowl for grinding grain with a pestle *(moosal)*
Om – sacred invocation that represents the essence of the divine principle

paag – turban. Also called *pagri* and *safa*
paan – chewable preparation made from betel leaves, nuts and lime
Pabuji – deified folk hero; particularly revered by the nomadic Bhopas
pagri – see *paag*
pahar – hill
panchayat sammiti – local government representing several villages
panghat-poojan – ceremony performed at a village well following the birth of a child
Parvate – another form of Devi
pattu – shawl. Also known as a *kheis*
payal – anklet worn by Rajasthani women
PCO – public call office
phad – painted scroll used in Bhopa performances to illustrate legends concerned with the life of Pabuji
pichwai – religious paintings on homespun cloth, generally of events from the life of Krishna, which are hung behind the image of Sri Nathji at Nathdwara
pida – low folding chair featuring decorative woodcarving, traditionally made in Shekhawati and Bikaner
pitar – soul of a dead man
pitari – soul of a woman who has died before her husband
pol – gate
prasaad – sacred food offered to the gods
puja – literally 'respect'; offering or prayer
purdah – seclusion; wives of Rajputs were kept in purdah and seen by no man other than their husband
puri – flat pieces of dough that puff up when deep fried
putli-wallah – puppeteer; also known as a *kathputli*

Rabaris – nomadic tribe from Jodhpur area
raga – any conventional pattern of melody

and rhythm that forms the basis for free composition

raj – rule or sovereignty

raja – king

Rajput – 'Sons of Princes'; Hindu warrior caste, rulers of western India

Rama – seventh incarnation of Vishnu. His life story is the central theme of the *Ramayana*

Ramdev – deified folk hero, who, along with his horse, is worshipped in a temple at Ramdevra, near Pokaran

rani – wife of a king

ras gullas – balls of sweet cream cheese flavoured with rose water

rawal – nobleman

reet – bride price; opposite of dowry

road – railway town which serves as a communication point to a larger town off the line, eg Mt Abu and Abu Road

RTDC – Rajasthan Tourism Development Corporation

sabzi – vegetables

sadar – main

sadhu – ascetic, holy person, one who is trying to achieve enlightenment; usually addressed as 'swamiji' or 'babaji'

safa – see *paag*

sagar – lake, reservoir

sahib – title applied to any gentleman

sal – gallery in a palace

sambar – deer

Sanganeri print – block-printed fabric of Sanganer village, near Jaipur

sapera – snake charmer; traditionally associated with the Kalbelias tribe

sarangi – stringed folk instrument

sati – suicide by immolation; banned more than a century ago, sati is still occasionally performed

Scheduled Tribes – government classification for tribal groups of Rajasthan. The tribes are grouped with the lowest casteless class, the Dalits

shikhar – hunting expedition

shikhara – temple spire

Shiva (Siva) – the Destroyer; also the Creator, in which form he is worshipped as a *ʾm* (phallic symbol)

Sikh – member of the monotheistic religion Sikhism which separated from Hinduism in the 16th century; it has a military tradition. Sikh men can be recognised by their beards and turbans

singh – literally 'lion'; a surname adopted by Rajputs and Sikhs

sitar – Indian stringed instrument

sonf – aniseed seeds; come complimentary with the bill after a meal and used as a digestive

Sufi – Muslim mystic

Surya – the sun; a major deity in the *Vedas*

Suryavansa – Race of the Sun (Solar Race); one of the three principal races from which Rajputs claim descent

tabla – pair of drums

Tejaji – deified folk hero believed to cure snakebite

tempo – noisy three-wheel public transport; bigger than an auto-rickshaw

thakur – nobleman

thali – all-you-can-eat meal; actually the plate on which the meal is served

tika – a mark devout Hindus put on their foreheads with *tika* powder

tirthankars – the group of the 24 great Jain teachers

tokna – large vessel in which the maharajas' treasurers collected taxes

tonga – two wheeled passenger vehicle drawn by horse or pony

toran – shield-shaped device above a lintel which a bridegroom pierces with his sword before claiming his bride

torana – elaborately sculpted gateway before temples

tripolia – triple gateway

Vaisya – the caste comprising tradespeople and farmers; the third caste in the hierarchy

Varuna – supreme Vedic god; Aryan god of water

Vedas – the Hindu sacred books; a collection of hymns composed during the second millennium BC and divided into four books: *Rig-Veda*, *Yajur-Veda*, *Sama-Veda* and *Atharva-Veda*

Vishnu – the third in the Hindu trinity of gods with Brahma and Shiva. The Preserver and Restorer, who has nine *avataars* (incarnations): the fish Matsya; the tortoise Kurma; the wild boar Naraha; the man-lion Narasimha; the dwarf Vamana; the Brahmin Parashu-Rama; Rama; Krishna; the Buddha

wallah – literally 'man', thus taxi-wallah, Delhi-wallah

yagna – self-mortification; holy offering

zenana – women's quarters

zila parishad – government at district level

Acknowledgments

THANKS

Many thanks to the travellers who used the last edition and wrote to us with helpful hints, useful advice and interesting anecdotes:

Aloma Treister, Anna Kwiecinska, Anne Marie Ligtenberg, Basil Anand D'Souza, Bill O'Toole, Bruce Cone, Bruno Liechter, E Wheeler, Graham Lupp, Heinz Gunther Fischer, Joshy Wedgwood, Katherine Grech, Louise M Byrnes, Lynne Muir, Marie-Louise Neill, Rosy Fernandes, Nathalie De Sutter, Nynne Carl, Philippa Matherson, Ramesh C Jangid, Suzanne Roberts, T S Rathore, Victoria Knighton

LONELY PLANET

Phrasebooks

Lonely Planet phrasebooks are packed with essential words and phrases to help travellers communicate with the locals. With colour tabs for quick reference, an extensive vocabulary and use of script, these handy pocket-sized language guides cover day-to-day travel situations.

- handy pocket-sized books
- easy to understand Pronunciation chapter
- clear & comprehensive Grammar chapter
- romanisation alongside script to allow ease of pronunciation
- script throughout so users can point to phrases for every situation
- full of cultural information and tips for the traveller

'...vital for a real DIY spirit and attitude in language learning'
– Backpacker

'the phrasebooks have good cultural backgrounders and offer solid advice for challenging situations in remote locations'
– San Francisco Examiner

Arabic (Egyptian) • Arabic (Moroccan) • Australian *(Australian English, Aboriginal and Torres Strait languages)* • Baltic States *(Estonian, Latvian, Lithuanian)* • Bengali • Brazilian • British • Burmese • Cantonese • Central Asia • Central Europe *(Czech, French, German, Hungarian, Italian, Slovak)* • Eastern Europe *(Bulgarian, Czech, Hungarian, Polish, Romanian, Slovak)* • Ethiopian (Amharic) • Fijian • French • German • Greek • Hill Tribes • Hindi/Urdu • Indonesian • Italian • Japanese • Korean • Lao • Latin American Spanish • Malay • Mandarin • Mediterranean Europe *(Albanian, Croatian, Greek, Italian, Macedonian, Maltese, Serbian, Slovene)* • Mongolian • Nepali • Papua New Guinea • Pilipino (Tagalog) • Quechua • Russian • Scandinavian Europe *(Danish, Finnish, Icelandic, Norwegian, Swedish)* • South-East Asia *(Burmese, Indonesian, Khmer, Lao, Malay, Tagalog Pilipino, Thai, Vietnamese)* • South Pacific Languages • Spanish (Castilian) *(also includes Catalan, Galician and Basque)* • Sri Lanka • Swahili • Thai • Tibetan • Turkish • Ukrainian • USA *(US English, Vernacular, Native American languages, Hawaiian)* • Vietnamese • Western Europe *(Basque, Catalan, Dutch, French, German, Greek, Irish)*

LONELY PLANET

Lonely Planet Journeys

JOURNEYS is a unique collection of travel writing – published by the company that understands travel better than anyone else. It is a series for anyone who has ever experienced – or dreamed of – the magical moment when they encountered a strange culture or saw a place for the first time. They are tales to read while you're planning a trip, while you're on the road or while you're in an armchair in front of a fire.

These outstanding titles explore our planet through the eyes of a diverse group of international writers. JOURNEYS books catch the spirit of a place, illuminate a culture, recount a crazy adventure or introduce a fascinating way of life. They always entertain, and always enrich the experience of travel.

IN RAJASTHAN
Royina Grewal
As she writes of her travels through Rajasthan, Indian writer Royina Grewal takes us behind the exotic facade of this fabled destination: here is an insider's perceptive account of India's most colourful state, conveying the excitement and challenges of a region in transition.

SHOPPING FOR BUDDHAS
Jeff Greenwald
In his obsessive search for the perfect Buddha statue in the backstreets of Kathmandu, Jeff Greenwald discovers more than he bargained for ... and his souvenir-hunting turns into an ironic metaphor for the clash between spiritual riches and material greed. Politics, religion and serious shopping collide in this witty account of an enlightening visit to Nepal.

BRIEF ENCOUNTERS
Stories of Love, Sex & Travel
edited by Michelle de Kretser
Love affairs on the road, passionate holiday flings, disastrous pick-ups, erotic encounters ... In this seductive collection of stories, 22 authors from around the world write about travel romances. A tourist in Peru falls for her handsome guide; a writer explores the ambiguities of his relationship with a Japanese woman; a beautiful young man on a train proposes marriage ... Combining fiction and reportage, *Brief Encounters* is must-have reading – for everyone who has dreamt of escape with that perfect stranger.

Includes stories by Pico Iyer, Mary Morris, Emily Perkins, Mona Simpson, Lisa St Aubin de Terán, Paul Theroux and Sara Wheeler.

LONELY PLANET

Guides by Region

L onely Planet is known worldwide for publishing practical, reliable and no-nonsense travel information in our guides and on our Web site. The Lonely Planet list covers just about every accessible part of the world. Currently there are nine series: travel guides, shoestring guides, walking guides, city guides, phrasebooks, audio packs, travel atlases, diving and snorkeling guides and travel literature.

AFRICA Africa – the South • Africa on a shoestring • Arabic (Egyptian) phrasebook • Arabic (Moroccan) phrasebook • Cairo • Cape Town • Central Africa • East Africa • Egypt • Egypt travel atlas • Ethiopian (Amharic) phrasebook • The Gambia & Senegal • Kenya • Kenya travel atlas • Malawi, Mozambique & Zambia • Morocco • North Africa • South Africa, Lesotho & Swaziland • South Africa, Lesotho & Swaziland travel atlas • Swahili phrasebook • Tanzania, Zanzibar & Pemba • Trekking in East Africa • Tunisia • West Africa • Zimbabwe, Botswana & Namibia • Zimbabwe, Botswana & Namibia travel atlas
Travel Literature: The Rainbird: A Central African Journey • Songs to an African Sunset: A Zimbabwean Story • Mali Blues: Traveling to an African Beat

AUSTRALIA & THE PACIFIC Australia • Australian phrasebook • Bushwalking in Australia • Bushwalking in Papua New Guinea • Fiji • Fijian phrasebook • Islands of Australia's Great Barrier Reef • Melbourne • Micronesia • New Caledonia • New South Wales & the ACT • New Zealand • Northern Territory • Outback Australia • Papua New Guinea • Papua New Guinea (Pidgin) phrasebook • Queensland • Rarotonga & the Cook Islands • Samoa • Solomon Islands • South Australia • South Pacific Languages phrasebook • Sydney • Tahiti & French Polynesia • Tasmania • Tonga • Tramping in New Zealand • Vanuatu • Victoria • Western Australia
Travel Literature: Islands in the Clouds • Sean & David's Long Drive

CENTRAL AMERICA & THE CARIBBEAN Bahamas and Turks & Caicos • Barcelona • Bermuda • Central America on a shoestring • Costa Rica • Cuba • Dominican Republic & Haiti • Eastern Caribbean • Guatemala, Belize & Yucatán: La Ruta Maya • Jamaica • Mexico • Mexico City • Panama
Travel Literature: Green Dreams: Travels in Central America

EUROPE Amsterdam • Andalucía • Austria • Baltic States phrasebook • Barcelona • Berlin • Britain • British phrasebook • Canary Islands • Central Europe • Central Europe phrasebook • Corsica • Croatia • Czech & Slovak Republics • Denmark • Dublin • Eastern Europe • Eastern Europe phrasebook • Edinburgh • Estonia, Latvia & Lithuania • Europe • Finland • France • French phrasebook • Germany • German phrasebook • Greece • Greek phrasebook • Hungary • Iceland, Greenland & the Faroe Islands • Ireland • Italian phrasebook • Italy • Lisbon • London • Mediterranean Europe • Mediterranean Europe phrasebook • Norway • Paris • Poland • Portugal • Portugal travel atlas • Prague • Provence & the Côte d'Azur • Romania & Moldova • Rome • Russia, Ukraine & Belarus • Russian phrasebook • Scandinavian & Baltic Europe • Scandinavian Europe phrasebook • Scotland • Slovenia • Spain • Spanish phrasebook • St Petersburg • Switzerland • Trekking in Spain • Ukrainian phrasebook • Vienna • Walking in Britain • Walking in Italy • Walking in Ireland • Walking in Switzerland • Western Europe • Western Europe phrasebook
Travel Literature: The Olive Grove: Travels in Greece

INDIAN SUBCONTINENT Bangladesh • Bengali phrasebook • Bhutan • Delhi • Goa • Hindi/Urdu phrasebook • India • India & Bangladesh travel atlas • Indian Himalaya • Karakoram Highway • Nepal • Nepali phrasebook • Pakistan • Rajasthan • South India • Sri Lanka • Sri Lanka phrasebook • Trekking in the Indian Himalaya • Trekking in the Karakoram & Hindukush • Trekking in the Nepal Himalaya
Travel Literature: In Rajasthan • Shopping for Buddhas

LONELY PLANET

Mail Order

Lonely Planet products are distributed worldwide. They are also available by mail order from Lonely Planet, so if you have difficulty finding a title please write to us. North and South American residents should write to 150 Linden St, Oakland, CA 94607, USA; European and African residents should write to 10a Spring Place, London NW5 3BH, UK; and residents of other countries to PO Box 617, Hawthorn, Victoria 3122, Australia.

ISLANDS OF THE INDIAN OCEAN Madagascar & Comoros • Maldives • Mauritius, Réunion & Seychelles

MIDDLE EAST & CENTRAL ASIA Arab Gulf States • Central Asia • Central Asia phrasebook • Iran • Israel & the Palestinian Territories • Israel & the Palestinian Territories travel atlas • Istanbul • Jerusalem • Jordan & Syria • Jordan, Syria & Lebanon travel atlas • Lebanon • Middle East on a shoestring • Turkey • Turkish phrasebook • Turkey travel atlas • Yemen
Travel Literature: The Gates of Damascus • Kingdom of the Film Stars: Journey into Jordan

NORTH AMERICA Alaska • Backpacking in Alaska • Baja California • California & Nevada • Canada • Chicago • Florida • Hawaii • Honolulu • Los Angeles • Louisiana • Miami • New England USA • New Orleans • New York City • New York, New Jersey & Pennsylvania • Pacific Northwest USA • Puerto Rico • Rocky Mountain States • San Francisco • Seattle • Southwest USA • Texas • USA • USA phrasebook • Vancouver • Washington, DC & the Capital Region
Travel Literature: Drive Thru America

NORTH-EAST ASIA Beijing • Cantonese phrasebook • China • Hong Kong • Hong Kong, Macau & Guangzhou • Japan • Japanese phrasebook • Japanese audio pack • Korea • Korean phrasebook • Kyoto • Mandarin phrasebook • Mongolia • Mongolian phrasebook • North-East Asia on a shoestring • Seoul • South-West China • Taiwan • Tibet • Tibetan phrasebook • Tokyo
Travel Literature: Lost Japan

SOUTH AMERICA Argentina, Uruguay & Paraguay • Bolivia • Brazil • Brazilian phrasebook • Buenos Aires • Chile & Easter Island • Chile & Easter Island travel atlas • Colombia • Ecuador & the Galapagos Islands • Latin American Spanish phrasebook • Peru • Quechua phrasebook • Rio de Janeiro • South America on a shoestring • Trekking in the Patagonian Andes • Venezuela
Travel Literature: Full Circle: A South American Journey

SOUTH-EAST ASIA Bali & Lombok • Bangkok • Burmese phrasebook • Cambodia • Hanoi • Hill Tribes phrasebook • Ho Chi Minh City • Indonesia • Indonesia's Eastern Islands • Indonesian phrasebook • Indonesian audio pack • Jakarta • Java • Laos • Lao phrasebook • Laos travel atlas • Malay phrasebook • Malaysia, Singapore & Brunei • Myanmar (Burma) • Philippines • Pilipino (Tagalog) phrasebook • Singapore • South-East Asia on a shoestring • South-East Asia phrasebook • Thailand • Thailand's Islands & Beaches • Thailand travel atlas • Thai phrasebook • Thai audio pack • Vietnam • Vietnamese phrasebook • Vietnam travel atlas

ALSO AVAILABLE: Antarctica • Brief Encounters: Stories of Love, Sex & Travel • Chasing Rickshaws • Not the Only Planet: Travel Stories from Science Fiction • Travel with Children • Traveller's Tales

LONELY PLANET

Lonely Planet Travel Atlases

L onely Planet has long been famous for the number and quality of its guidebook maps. Now we've gone one step further and produced a handy companion series: Lonely Planet travel atlases – maps of a country produced in book form.

Unlike other maps, which look good but lead travellers astray, our travel atlases have been researched on the road by Lonely Planet's experienced team of writers. All details are carefully checked to ensure the atlas corresponds with the equivalent Lonely Planet guidebook.

- full-colour throughout
- maps researched and checked by Lonely Planet authors
- place names correspond with Lonely Planet guidebooks
- no confusing spelling differences
- legend and travelling information in English, French, German, Japanese and Spanish
- size: 230 x 160 mm

Available now: Chile & Easter Island ● Egypt ● India & Bangladesh ● Israel & the Palestinian Territories ● Jordan, Syria & Lebanon ● Kenya ● Laos ● Portugal ● South Africa, Lesotho & Swaziland ● Thailand ● Turkey ● Vietnam ● Zimbabwe, Botswana & Namibia

---

Lonely Planet TV Series & Videos

L onely Planet travel guides have been brought to life on television screens around the world. Like our guides, the programs are based on the joy of independent travel, and look honestly at some of the most exciting, picturesque and frustrating places in the world. Each show is presented by one of three travellers from Australia, England or the USA and combines an innovative mixture of video, Super-8 film, atmospheric soundscapes and original music.

Videos of each episode – containing additional footage not shown on television – are available from good book and video shops, but the availability of individual videos varies with regional screening schedules.

Video destinations include: Alaska ● American Rockies ● Australia – The South-East ● Baja California & the Copper Canyon ● Brazil ● Central Asia ● Chile & Easter Island ● Corsica, Sicily & Sardinia – The Mediterranean Islands ● East Africa (Tanzania & Zanzibar) ● Ecuador & the Galapagos Islands ● Greenland & Iceland ● Indonesia ● Israel & the Sinai Desert ● Jamaica ● Japan ● La Ruta Maya ● Morocco ● New York ● North India ● Pacific Islands (Fiji, Solomon Islands & Vanuatu) ● South India ● South West China ● Turkey ● Vietnam ● West Africa ● Zimbabwe, Botswana & Namibia

The Lonely Planet TV series is produced by: Pilot Productions
The Old Studio
18 Middle Row
London W10 5AT, UK

LONELY PLANET

FREE Lonely Planet Newsletters

We love hearing from you and think you'd like to hear from us.

Planet Talk

Our FREE quarterly printed newsletter is full of tips from travellers and anecdotes from Lonely Planet guidebook authors. Every issue is packed with up-to-date travel news and advice, and includes:

- a postcard from Lonely Planet co-founder Tony Wheeler
- a swag of mail from travellers
- a look at life on the road through the eyes of a Lonely Planet author
- topical health advice
- prizes for the best travel yarn
- news about forthcoming Lonely Planet events
- a complete list of Lonely Planet books and other titles

To join our mailing list, residents of the UK, Europe and Africa can email us at go@lonelyplanet.co.uk; residents of North and South America can email us at info@lonelyplanet.com; the rest of the world can email us at talk2us@lonelyplanet.com.au, or contact any Lonely Planet office.

Comet

Our FREE monthly email newsletter brings you all the latest travel news, features, interviews, competitions, destination ideas, travellers' tips & tales, Q&As, raging debates and related links. Find out what's new on the Lonely Planet Web site and which books are about to hit the shelves.

Subscribe from your desktop: www.lonelyplanet.com/comet

Index

Text

A

Abhaneri 66, 173
Abu Road 262
accommodation 109-11
  geysers 111
  homestay/paying guest
    house scheme 110
  palaces, forts & castles 110
  railway retiring rooms 110
  taxes & service charges 111
  tourist bungalows 109
Achalgarh 261
acrobats 43
activities 103-6
Adhai-din-ka-Jhonpra 192
Agra 338-46, **339**
  Agra Fort 341-2, **341**
  getting there & away 345-6
  places to stay 343-4
  Taj Ganj **343**
  Taj Mahal 340
Ahhichatragarh 303
air travel 119-25
  departure tax 121
  domestic 128-9, 131
  international 119-25
  ticket centres 121-4
Ajmer 190-6, **191**
Akal Wood Fossil Park 18,
  326
Akbar 15, 289
Akbar's Palace 192-3
Alwar 185-8, **186**
Amar Sagar 324
Amber 169-71
Ana Sagar 192
Anjaneshwar Mahadev 250
Aravalli Range 18
arts 36-54
astrology 107, 156, 295
Aurangzeb 15, 142
auto-rickshaw 139

B

Bada Bagh 324
Badnor 196-7

Bold indicates maps.

Baggar 278
Bagru 172
Bairat 172
Bala Qila 268
Bala Quila 185-8
Balaji 173
Balsamand Lake 301
Bambora 251
Baneshwar 253
Barmer 326-7
Baroli 224
Bera 251
Bhainsrodgarh 224
Bharatpur 177, **178**
Bhatti people 14
Bhenswara 303
Bhil people 15, 36
Bhinasar Gochar Andolan 23
Bijaipur 229-30
Bijolia 230
Bikaner 327-35, **328**
  getting there & away 334
  places to stay 331-4
birds 27-9
  peacock 27
Bishnoi people 22, 24
Bishnoi villages 301-2
Bissau 278-9
boating 106
books 81-4
  health guides 89
Brahma Kumaris Spiritual
  University 255
British 16
Bundi 215-19
bus travel 129, 131
business hours 102

C

camel
  Pushkar Camel Fair 199
  safaris 103
  safari routes **317**
  Research & Breeding Farm
    335
car travel 129-30, 135-7
  rental 135-6
  road safety 136-7
carpets 52
CD-ROMs 84

Central Arid Zone Research
  Institute 21-3
Chambal River 18
charities 107-9
Chauhan dynasty 13
children 100
Chittorgarh (Chittor) 14, 226-9,
  227
  Fort 226-8
Churu 287
climate 19-20
conservation 21-2
  endangered species 28-9
  Jaisalmer Conservation
    Initiative 308
  organisations 23, 28
  Ranthambhore Foundation
    204
courses 107, 156
  meditation 156
  music & dance 156
  painting & pottery 156
cranes 27
  demoiselle 27
  Siberian 27, 180
cricket 115
culture 54-61
  caste system 59
  etiquette 60-1
  traditional beliefs 57-9
  village life 60
  women in society 59-60
customs 75
cycling 106, 137, 139

D

Dalhanpur 225
dance 37-42
Dargah 192
Darrah Wildlife Sanctuary 31,
  223
Deeg 184-5
Delhi 348-65, **350**
  Connaught Place **360**
  getting there & away 359-
    64
  New Delhi 354-5, **356**
  Old Delhi 352-3, **353**
  Paharganj **362**
  places to stay 355-8

Deogarh 250
Desert National Park &
    Sanctuary 32
desertification 20-2
Deshnok 336-7
Devi Kund 335
Dhamotar 252
Dhariyawad 252
Dhawa Doli Wildlife Sanctuary
    32, 303
Dholpur 210
Dilwara Temples 257
disabled travellers 99-100, 120
    RADAR 99
documents 73
dowry 56
drinks 111-15
drugs 102
Dundlod 273
    organised tours 273
Dungarpur 252

E

Eastern Plains 19
Eastern Rajasthan 174-210,
    175
    festivals 176
    history 174-7
ecology 20-2
economy 33-5
education 35
Eklingji 247
electricity 86
Elephanta Island 379
embassies 73-5
endangered species see conser-
    vation
entertainment 115
environment see ecology &
    conservation

F

Fateh Sagar 236
Fatehpur 281-3, **282**
Fatehpur Sikri 346-7
fauna 23-9
fax services 81
festivals 102-3
    festival calendar 103
films 84
flora 22-3
food 90, 112-13

G

Gadi Sagar 314
Gagron Fort 225
Gajner Wildlife Sanctuary 32,
    335-6
Galiakot 253
Galta 153
Gandhi, Mahatma 16
Ganga Golden Jubilee Museum
    331
Gaumukh Temple 261
gay travellers 99
geography 17-19
geology 17-19
Ghanerao 250
golf 106, 156, 295
government 32
Guda Bishnoi 302
Guda Mogra 302

H

Hadoti Plateau 19
Haldighati 247
handicrafts 34-5
    Rajasthan Small Industries
        Corporation 34
havelis 265-6, 268-71, 274-7
Hawa Mahal 152-3
health 87-98
    dengue fever 95
    diarrhoea 92-3
    environmental hazards 91-2
    food 90
    health guides 89
    hepatitis 93-4
    HIV & AIDS 94
    immunisations 87-9
    malaria 95
    water 90-1
Help in Suffering 108
Hinduism 61-4
    Hindu lunar months 103
history 13-17
hitching 138
Holi 101
holidays see festivals
horse riding 106

I

Independence 16-17, 144
Indira Gandhi canal 22
insurance, travel 72
internet resources 81
itineraries 67-8
ivory carving 54

J

Jagat 230-1
Jagniwas Island 235
Jaigarh 171
Jainism 64-5
Jaipur 142-69, **146**
    City Palace 150-1
    getting there & away 165-9
    Jantar Mantar 151-2
    New City 154-5
    Old City (Pink City) 149-53
    organised tours 157
    places to eat 162-3
    places to stay 157-62
Jaisalmer 67, 308-24, **310**
    getting there & away 323
    havelis 314
    Jain Temples 312-14
    Jaisalmer Conservation
        Initiative 308
    Jaisalmer Fort 311-14, **312**
    Laxminath Temple 313
    places to eat 321-2
    places to stay 315-21
Jaisamand Lake 251
Jaisamand Wildlife Sanctuary
    31, 251
Jai Singh II 142-4
Jal Mahal 171
Jantar Mantar 151-2
Jaswant Thada 294-5
jewellery 52-3
Jhalamand 301
Jhalawar 224-5
Jhalrapatan 225
Jhunjhunu 274-8, **275**
    havelis 274-7
Jodhpur 290-301, **291**
    getting there & away 300
    Meherangarh 293-4, **293**
    organised tours 296
    places to eat 299
    places to stay 296-9
Junagarh 328-30

K

Kachhwaha dynasty 13, 143,
    169
Kakani 302
Kankroli 248
Karauli 173
Karna Ram Bheel 42
Keoladeo Ghana National Park
    23, 27, 31, 179-84
Kesroli 188
Khejadali village 302

Khichan 32, 306
Khimsar 303
Khuri 326
Kiradu Temples 327
Kishangarh 196
Kolayat 336
Kota 220-3, **221**
Kuldhara 325
Kumbhalgarh 248
    Wildlife Sanctuary 249

L

Lake Palace 235
Lake Pichola 233-5
Lakshmangarh 285-6
Lalgarh Palace 330
land travel see overland travel
laundry 86
leatherwork 54
legal matters 102
Les Amis du Shekhawati 108
lesbian travellers 99
literature 43-4
Lodhruva 324
Lohagarh 178-9
Luni 303
Luni River 18

M

Maha Mandir 301
Mahansar 279-80
malaria 88-9, 95
Man Singh II 17
Mandalgarh 230
Mandawa 283-5
Mandore 301
Marathas 16
Marusthali see Thar Desert
Meherangarh 293-4, **293**
Menal 230
Mewar, kingdom of 14
Mina people 36
money 75-9
    banknotes 75
    bargaining 78
    encashment certificates 77
    exchange rates 76
    tipping (baksheesh) 78
Mool Sagar 325
Mother Teresa Home 108
motorcycle travel 129-30, 137
    organised tours 137
Mt Abu 253-61, **254, 256**
Mt Abu Wildlife Sanctuary 31,
    261
Mughals 14

Mukundgarh 274
Mumbai 366-79, **368**
    Colaba **373**
    Fort area **371**
    getting there & away 376-8
    places to stay 372-5
music 41

N

Nagaur 303-4
Nagda 247
Nagri 230
Nahargarh 153
Nakki Lake 255
Narlai 250
Nathdwara 248
National Chambal Wildlife
    Sanctuary 31, 223
national parks and sanctuaries
    29-32
    organisations 30
Nawalgarh 268-72, **269**
    organised tours 271
Neemrana 188
newspapers & magazines 84-5
Nimaj 303
Northern Rajasthan 263-87, **264**
    festivals 265
    getting around 268
    getting there & away 268
    havelis 265-6
    history 263-5
    responsible tourism 266-8

O

organised tours 127, 157, 271,
    273, 296, 315
    bicycle 137
    international companies 128
    motorcycle 137
    RTDC & other tours 140-1
    safaris 296, 316, **317**, 331
Osiyan 304-6
    temples 304-6
overland travel 125-7

P

Pachewar 196
painting 44-6
    cloth 46
    domestic 46
    miniature 44-5
    portrait & courtly 45-6
Palace on Wheels 140
Parsurampura 272

Phalodi 306
photography 85-6
    etiquette 60, 86
    planning 68-70
Pokaran 307-8
politics 32
    history 16-17
pollution 21
polo 106, 115-16, 164
population 35
postal services 79-81
pottery 50
public holidays see festivals
puppetry 43
purdah 56-7
Pushkar 66, 197-203, **198**
    Camel Fair 199

R

radio 85
Rajputs 13-16
Rajsamand Lake 248
Ramdevra 306
Ramgarh 172, 280-1
Ranakpur 249
Ranthambhore Fort 14, 207
Ranthambhore National Park
    23, 29, 204, **205**
    Ranthambhore Foundation
        204
Rathore dynasty 13, 289
religion 61-5
responsible tourism 70, 266-8
Rishabdeo 251
Rohet 302
Royal Gaitor 153

S

safaris
    camel 103, **317**
    horse 106
    wildlife 206
safety 98-9, 100-2
    road safety 136-7
Salawas 302
Sam sand dunes 67, 325-6
Samode 172
Sanganer 66, 171
Sardar Samand Lake 302
Sariska Tiger Reserve & Na-
    tional Park 30, 189
sati 57, 309
Sawai Madhopur 204, **205**
sculpture 46-50
sea travel 127
senior travellers 100

Shekhawati see Northern
  Rajasthan
Shilpgram 237
shopping 116-18
Siliserh 188
Sisodia dynasty 13
Sisodia Rani Palace 153
Sitamata Wildlife Sanctuary 31,
  252
society & conduct see culture
Sorsan grasslands 223
SOS Worldwide 108
Southern Rajasthan 211-62, **212**
  festivals 214
  history 213-15
sport 115
stonework see sculpture
Suraj Mahl's Palace 184
swimming 106

T

Taj Mahal 340-1
Tal Chhapar Wildlife Sanctuary
  31, 287
Taragarh 192, 217
Tarun Bharat Sangh 23
taxi 138
telephone services 80-1
tempo 139
tennis 106, 115, 157
ten-pin bowling 106

textiles 50-2
  appliqué & embroidery 52
  print 51
  tie-dye 51
Thar Desert 18, 288, 290, 325-6
tigers 24, 29, 189, 204
time 86
toilets 86-7
Tonk 203-4
tourist offices 70-1
train travel 129, 132-5
  Palace on Wheels 140
  reservations 133
  sleepers 134
  timetables 132
trekking 106
tribal people 36
TV 85

U

Ubeshwar Vikas Mandal 23
Udaipur 230-47, **232**
  Ahar Museum 237
  City Palace complex 235-6
  Durbar Hall 239
  Fateh Sagar 236-7
  getting there & away 246
  Lake Pichola 233
  Monsoon Palace 237-8
  places to stay 238-43
  Shilpgram 237

Umaid Bhawan Palace
  295
Urmul Trust 109

V

video 85-6
  etiquette 86
Vidyadharji ka Bagh 153
Vindhyas 18
visas 71-3
  extensions 72

W

water 90-1, 114
weights & measures 86
Western Rajasthan 288-337,
  289
  festivals 290
  history 288
women travellers 98-9
  health 96-7
woodwork 53-4
work, volunteer 107-9

Y

yoga 107

Z

Zhalamand 302

Boxed Text

Air Fares 166
Air Travel Glossary 122-3
Art of Haggling, The 78
Banknotes 75
Bhang Lassi Warning 115
Camel Fair 199
Camel Safaris around Jaisalmer
  316-7
Conservation Organisations 23
Cult of Conservation 24
Death by Fire of Roop Kanwar
  58
Demoiselle Cranes of Khichan
  307
Dhobi-Wallahs 87
Diarrhoea with your Meal, Sir?
  101
Durbar Hall 239
Everyday Health 88
Female Infanticide 55

Festivals, Eastern Rajasthan 176
Festivals, Jaipur District 144
Festivals, Northern Rajasthan 265
Festivals of Rajasthan 104-5
Festivals, Southern Rajasthan 214
Festivals, Western Rajasthan 290
Get to Know your Camel 335
Indian Rail Fares in Rupees 133
Indira Gandhi Canal Project 22
Jaipur Train Services 168
Jodhpur's Got the Blues 292
Karna the Dacoit 42
Legend of Dhola Maru 267
Mayo College 193
Medical Kit Check List 89
Mewar's Most Honoured
  Mother 213
Mumal & Mahendra 44
Nutrition 90
Palace on Wheels 140

Patrons & Performers 41
Polo 116
Pushkar Passports 200
Rajasthani Cuisine 112-113
Ranthambhore Revival 204
Reconfirmation 119
Regional Festival Calendar 103
RSTC Bus Services from Jaipur
  167
Siberian Cranes 180
Sons of the Sun 15
Stalked, Slaughtered and
  Stuffed 28
Tie the Knot with an Exotic
  Twist 234
Tie-Dye 150
Tribal People of Rajasthan 36-7
Warning 100, 117, 120
What's in a Name? 367
Wildlife Conservation Organi-
  sations & Resources 30

MAP LEGEND

BOUNDARIES

—··—·—··—··.............International
—··—·—·—·...........................State
— — — — — ....Disputed

HYDROGRAPHY

...........................Coastline
.....................River, Creek
.....................................Lake
..........Intermittent Lake
..........................Salt Lake
....Canal
⊚ —→·...............Spring, Rapids
—+⊱—⊱·.........................Waterfalls
....................................Swamp

ROUTES & TRANSPORT

.........................Freeway
.........................Highway
.....................Major Road
.......................Minor Road
══════Unsealed Road
.........................City Freeway
.........................City Highway
.........................City Road
.................City Street, Lane

⇒)═══:...................Pedestrian Mall
⇒)═══:...........................Tunnel
├─├─├─●─┼....Train Route & Station
═·─·─Ⓜ·─....Metro & Station
——————————.Tramway
╫─╫─╫─╫─╫─ .. Cable Car or Chairlift
— — — — — — ....Walking Track
·············.......... Walking Tour
— — — — — —........Ferry Route

AREA FEATURES

.......................Building
✿ ....Park, Gardens
⊹ + ⊹ × ⊹
⊥ ⊥ ⊻ ⊻ ....Cemetery

.......................Market
.................Beach, Desert
.................Urban Area

MAP SYMBOLS

❂ **CAPITAL**...........National Capital
◉ **CAPITAL** ....State Capital
● **CITY** ....City
● **Town** ....Town
• **Village** ....Village

○ ....Point of Interest
■ ....Place to Stay
⚠ ....Camping Ground
▼ ....·Place to Eat
🍺 ....Pub or Bar
✈ ✝ ....Airport, Airfield
∿ .....Ancient or City Wall
∴ ....Archaeological Site

❸ ....Bank
▣ ....Buddhist (Therevada)
☗ ....Castle or Fort
⌒ ....Cave
▯ ⛪ ....Church
∿∿∿ ...... Cliff or Escarpment
◯ ....Embassy
⊞ ....Hindu Temple
✛ ....Hospital
※ ....Lookout
⚱ ....Monument
◖ ....Mosque
▲ ....Mountain or Hill
血 ....Museum

🍄 ....National Park
🅿 ....Parking
)(.............................Pass
🅑 ....Petrol Station
★ ....Police Station
✉ ....Post Office
❖ ....Shopping Centre
🆅 ....Sikh Temple
🏛 .Stately Home or Haveli
☎ ....Telephone
❶ ......Tourist Information
▣ ....Tomb
⊖ ....Transport
🐘 ....Zoo

Note: not all symbols displayed above appear in this book

LONELY PLANET OFFICES

Australia
PO Box 617, Hawthorn, Victoria 3122
☎ 03 9819 1877 fax 03 9819 6459
email: talk2us@lonelyplanet.com.au

USA
150 Linden St, Oakland, CA 94607
☎ 510 893 8555 TOLL FREE: 800 275 5555
fax 510 893 8572
email: info@lonelyplanet.com

UK
10a Spring Place, London NW5 3BH
☎ 020 7428 4800 fax 020 7428 4828
email: go@lonelyplanet.co.uk

France
1 rue du Dahomey, 75011 Paris
☎ 01 55 25 33 00 fax 01 55 25 33 01
email: bip@lonelyplanet.fr
minitel: 3615 lonelyplanet *(1,29 F TTC/min)*

World Wide Web: www.lonelyplanet.com *or* AOL keyword: lp
Lonely Planet Images: lpi@lonelyplanet.com.au